OR
1175
.L432
1935

W9-ANV-834

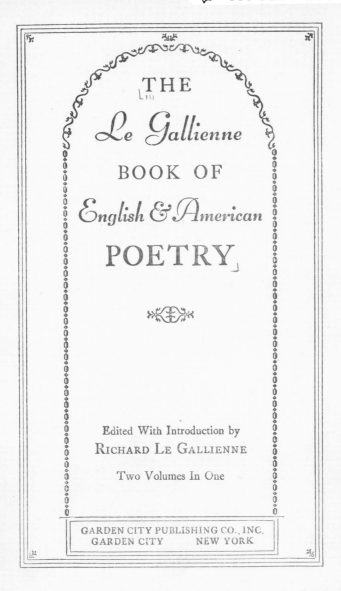

THE
Le Gallienne
BOOK OF
English & American
POETRY

Edited With Introduction by
RICHARD LE GALLIENNE

Two Volumes In One

GARDEN CITY PUBLISHING CO., INC.
GARDEN CITY   NEW YORK

Salem Academy and College
Gramley Library
Winston-Salem, N.C. 27108

THE LE GALLIENNE BOOK OF ENGLISH VERSE

Copyright, 1922, by
BONI & LIVERIGHT, INC.

THE LE GALLIENNE BOOK OF AMERICAN VERSE

Copyright, 1925, by
BONI & LIVERIGHT, INC.

THE LE GALLIENNE BOOK OF ENGLISH AND AMERICAN POETRY

Reissued, 1935, by
GARDEN CITY PUBLISHING COMPANY, INC.

Printed in the United States of America

THE LE GALLIENNE BOOK OF
ENGLISH AND AMERICAN
POETRY

March 2, 1936 Salem Book Store 1.20

SALEM COLLEGE
LIBRARY
Winston-Salem, N. C.

17306

VOLUME I

ACKNOWLEDGMENTS

The Editor and the Publisher wish to acknowledge the kindness of the following Publishers who have permitted the use of many selections from their lists in this Anthology:

To the John Lane Co., for permission to use poems by John Davidson, William Watson, Ernest Dowson, Francis Thompson, A. E. Housman, A. C. Benson, Victor Plarr, Rosamund Marriott-Watson, Arthur Symons, Lionel Johnson, Lascelles Abercrombie, W. M. Letts, Laurence Hope, Stephen Phillips and Rupert Brooke.

To G. P. Putnam's Sons, for the use of "In Flanders Field," by Colonel John Macrae, and poems by Norman Gale.

To Brentano's, for poems by Francis Ledwidge.

To Houghton, Mifflin Co., for poem by John Drinkwater.

To Henry Holt and Co., for poems by Walter de la Mare.

To B. W. Huebsch, Inc., for poems by D. H. Lawrence and James Joyce.

To E. P. Dutton and Co., for poems by Siegfried Sassoon.

To Alfred A. Knopf, Inc., for poems by Robert Graves.

To Small, Maynard and Co., for poems by Bliss Carman.

To Mitchell Kennerley for poems by Richard Middleton.

To L. C. Page and Co., for poems by C. G. D. Roberts.

To F. A. Stokes Co., for poems by Alfred Noyes and Robert Nichols.

To The Macmillan Co., for poems by W. B. Yeats, W. W. Gibson, Ralph Hodgson and James Stephens.

And to Mr. Curtis Brown for his courtesy in obtaining the consent of John Masefield for inclusion in this volume.

VOLUME II

ACKNOWLEDGMENTS

I wish to make grateful acknowledgment to the many publishers who have granted me permission to include in this Anthology the poems I have selected to represent the course of American poetry—so specifically my acknowledgment is due to

D. Appleton & Co. for the privilege of including "De Big Bethel Church" by Joel Chandler Harris.

Barse & Hopkins for the use of "The Song of the Soldier-Born," selected from the poems of Robert W. Service.

The Bobbs-Merrill Co. for "A Life Lesson," "Bereaved," and "A Parting Guest" by James Whitcomb Riley.

W. B. Conkey Company for "Solitude," written by Ella Wheeler Wilcox.

Dodd, Mead & Company for "Discovered" and "Compensation" by Paul Laurence Dunbar; Robert Munger's "The Derelict," taken from his volume, "The Land of Lost Music."

George H. Doran Company for their kind permission to include "To a Photographer" from "Songs of a Workaday World" by Berton Braley; the following selections from poems by Joyce Kilmer: "Trees" and "Old Poets" from the volume "Trees and Other Poems," as well as "Ballade of My Lady's Beauty," "Wealth," and "Dave Lilly"; "To a Post-Office Inkwell" by Christopher Morley, and taken from his book entitled "Rocking Horse"; "Peregrine" and "Let No Charitable Hope" by Elinor Wylie, included in the volume "Black Armour"; "When Amaryllis Bowls" and "Magic" from "The Middle Twenties" by John Farrar.

Doubleday, Page & Co. for the use of five selections from the poems of Don Marquis and "The Rich Man" from the volume "Tobogganing on Parnassus" by Franklin P. Adams.

Duffield & Co. for granting the use of "The Frozen Grail" by Elsa Barker.

E. P. Dutton & Co. for "A Chant of Love for England" written by Helen Gray Cone.

Forbes Publishing Co. for "If I Should Die Tonight" by Ben King.

Harcourt, Brace & Co. for reprint permission on "The Mother" and "Mia Carlotta" from the volume "Carmina"

ACKNOWLEDGMENTS

by T. A. Daly; two selections, "Landscapes" and "Caliban in the Coal Mines," from Louis Untermeyer's book entitled "Challenge."

Harper & Brothers for permitting the reprinting of "Out of the Old House, Nancy" from "Farm Ballads" by Will Carleton; one selection from the poetry of Guy Wetmore Carryl; for "Elaine" and "Lament" from "Second April," copyright 1921, and "Afternoon on a Hill" from "Renascence," copyright 1917, by Edna St. Vincent Millay.

Harr Wagner Publishing Co. for five poems from the work of Joaquin Miller. (Publishers of the Complete Works of Joaquin Miller.)

Henry Holt & Company for the use of "The Factories" from the volume "Factories" and "Remembrance: Greek Folk-Song" by Margaret Widdemer; Lew Sarett's "Leave Me To My Own" from "Box of God"; an extract from "Death-Chant of the Centaurs" included in the volume "Heavens and Earth" by Stephen Vincent Benét; "After Apple-Picking," "The Road Not Taken," and "Birches," selected from the poems of Robert Frost; Carl Sandburg's "Chicago," "At A Window," and "Joy."

Houghton Mifflin Company for permission to reprint one selection from the work of William Dean Howells; "Tears of the Poplars" and "The Quiet Pilgrim" by Edith M. Thomas; two poems by Richard Watson Gilder; "The Monk in the Kitchen" and "Grieve Not, Ladies" by Anna Hempstead Branch; "Robinson Crusoe's Story" written by Charles Edward Carryl; "Tryste Noël" and "Of Joan's Youth" by Louise Imogen Guiney; by William Vaughn Moody: "In New York" and "At Assisi" from "Song-Flower and Poppy," and "Heart's Wild-Flower"; "Anticipation" and "A Gift" by Amy Lowell; Grace Fallow Norton's "O Sleep"; poems from the volume "Preludes and Symphonies" by John Gould Fletcher; "Jim Bludso" written by John Hay; "Waiting" by John Burroughs; Edmund Clarence Stedman's "Pan in Wall Street"; "Heredity" by Thomas Bailey Aldrich; "The Singing Man" written by Josephine Preston Peabody; Edward Rowland Sill's "The Fool's Prayer"; "To a Rose" by Frank Dempster Sherman; "Radiant Loss" and "Debt" written by Jessie Rittenhouse.

B. W. Huebsch for the use of "Sinfonia Domestica" by Jean Starr Untermeyer; a selection from "The Ghetto" by Lola Ridge.

Mitchell Kennerley for the right to include "To A Tawny Thrush" and "At the Aquarium" by Max Eastman; Arthur Davison Ficke's poems, "To an Old Friend," from "Sonnets of a Portrait-Painter," and "The Three Sis-

ACKNOWLEDGMENTS

ters"; "Be in Me as the Eternal Moods" and "Piccadilly" by Ezra Pound.

Alfred A. Knopf for the reprint of "Dirge" and "The Lonely Death" from the writings of Adelaide Crapsey; "The Mystic" from "Grenstone Poems" and an extract from "The New World" which he published for Witter Bynner; selected poems from the work of James Oppenheim; "Old Manuscript" from Alfred Kreymborg's volume "Mushroom"; Ezra Pound's "Ortus" and "The Ballad of the Goodly Fere"; "Completion" and "Parting After A Quarrel" from "Body and Raiment" by Eunice Tietjens.

Little, Brown & Co. for selections from the poetry of Emily Dickinson; "Poppies in the Wheat" and "Habeas Corpus" by Helen Hunt Jackson; three poems by Louise Chandler Moulton.

The Macmillan Company for permission to reproduce from "The Congo" by Nicholas Vachel Lindsay, also "General William Booth Enters into Heaven," "The Eagle That Is Forgotten," and "The Flower of Mending"; "April Theology" from "The Quest" by John G. Neihardt; Louis V. Ledoux's "Hymn to Demeter," taken from "The Story of Eleusis"; "Before Dawn in the Woods" from "Bluestone" by Marguerite Wilkinson; three selected poems from the work of Sara Teasdale: "The Flight" and "The Debt" from "Love Songs," as well as "The Answer" from "Rivers to the Sea"; Padraic Colum's "River-Mates" and "The Sea Bird to the Wave" from "Wild Earth"; Charles L. O'Donnell's "Forgiveness" and "The Poet's Bread"; "The Sky-Goer" and "North Star" by Zona Gale.

Moffat, Yard & Co. for the use of "Song" by Haniel Long, taken from his volume entitled "Poems."

Thomas B. Mosher for his permission to use "Evoe" from the volume "The Flower from the Ashes" by Edith M. Thomas; three poems selected from the work of Lizette Woodworth Reese; "Sometimes" and "From the Hills" by Thomas S. Jones, Jr.

The New York Evening Sun for permission to include "Old Garrets" and "The Puddle" by Moris Abel Beer.

Oxford University Press and to Mr. Houston Mifflin for permission to include three selected poems by Lloyd Mifflin.

Poetry (Chicago) for permission to use "Sweetgrass Range" written by Edwin Ford Piper.

G. P. Putnam's Sons for "The Four Winds" taken from Sara Teasdale's volume entitled "Helen of Troy."

Grant Richards, Ltd. (London), for granting permission to

ACKNOWLEDGMENTS

reprint selections from "The Interpretations" written by Zoë Akins.

Charles Scribner's Sons for reprint in this volume of "Luke Havergal," "Miniver Cheevy," and "The Master," by Edwin Arlington Robinson; an extract from "The Divine Phantasy" published by them for John Hall Wheelock; three Sidney Lanier poems: "The Marshes of Glynn," "The Song of the Chattahoochee," and "Evening Song"; Eugene Field's "The Lyttel Boy," "Wynken, Blynken and Nod," and "Little Boy Blue"; "An Angler's Wish" by Henry van Dyke; two selected poems by Henry Cuyler Bunner: "Behold the Deeds" and "A Pitcher of Mignonette"; "I Have a Rendezvous With Death" by Alan Seeger; "Geese" and "The Mon-Goos" from "Child's Natural History" written by Oliver Herford.

Thomas Seltzer for permission to reprint "Candle Light" and "To a Certain Lady" by John Cowper Powys.

Small, Maynard & Company for the use of several selections from the poems of John Banister Tabb; "The Rain-Crow" written by Madison Cawein.

Acknowledgments are also due to these authors who have kindly allowed their work to be included:

Morris Abel Beer, "Old Garrets" and "The Puddle."
Wm. Rose Benét, "The Falconer of God."
Maxwell Bodenheim, "Old Jew," "To a Friend," "Advice to a Buttercup."
Alice Brown, "Cloistered" and "West-Country Lover."
Gelett Burgess, "Purple Cow."
Richard Burton, "City of the Dead."
Willa Sibert Cather, "The Palatine."
Robert W. Chambers, "The Recruit."
Arthur Colton, "To Faustine."
Padraic Colum, "River-Mates" and "The Sea Bird to the Wave" from "Wild Earth."
Olive Tilford Dargan, four selections from "The Cycle's Rim."
Mary Carolyn Davies, "The Day Before April" and "Cloistered."
Maurice Francis Egan, "Maurice de Guérin."
Theodosia Garrison, "Stains."
Hermann Hagedorn, "Departure."
Maurice Hanline, "A Song of Pierrot."
Robert Underwood Johnson, "The Wistful Days."
Harry Kemp, "Prithee, Strive Not" and "The Conquerors."
Louis V. Ledoux, "Hymn to Demeter" from "The Story of Eleusis."

ACKNOWLEDGMENTS

Nicholas Vachel Lindsay, selections from "The Congo" and other poems.

Percy Mackaye, "The Automobile" and "France."

Edwin Markham, "The Man with the Hoe," "Lincoln, the Man of the People," and "A Look into the Gulf."

Edgar Lee Masters, selections from "New Spoon River Anthology" and other poems.

Ada Foster Murray, "The Shadowed Star," "Her Dwelling Place," "The One Who Stayed," and "When You Came."

John G. Neihardt, "April Theology" from "The Quest."

Rose O'Neill, "Faun-Taken" and "Love-Ending."

Walter Adolphe Roberts, "Villanelle of the Living Pan."

George Santayana, "As in the Midst of Battle" and "What Riches Have You?"

Clinton Scollard, "As I Came Down from Lebanon."

Vincent Starrett, "Dancer" and "Villon Strolls at Midnight."

George Sterling, "Omnia Exeunt in Mysterium," "The Black Vulture," and "A Legend of the Dove."

Arthur Stringer, "You Bid Me to Sleep."

Sara Teasdale, one poem from "Helen of Troy," two from "Love Songs," and one from "Rivers to the Sea."

Ridgely Torrence, "The Singers in a Cloud" and "Evensong."

Charles Hanson Towne, "Baboon" and "Of One Self-Slain."

George Sylvester Viereck, "The Candle and the Flame."

John Hall Wheelock, "Pitiless Beauty."

George E. Woodberry, "At Gibraltar."

And to

Louis Loveman for kind permission to use "April Rain" by his brother, the late Robert Loveman.

THE MODERN BOOK OF ENGLISH VERSE

CONTENTS

CONTENTS

CONTENTS

CONTENTS

CONTENTS

CONTENTS

CONTENTS

CONTENTS

CONTENTS

CONTENTS

CONTENTS

CONTENTS

CONTENTS

CONTENTS

CONTENTS

CONTENTS

CONTENTS

CONTENTS

PUBLISHER'S NOTE

As this edition of the LE GALLIENNE BOOK OF ENGLISH AND AMERICAN
POETRY *contains two complete books of verse in one volume, the table
of contents and the introduction to* THE MODERN BOOK OF AMERICAN
VERSE *will be found with that book which follows immediately page 566
of the first section comprising* THE MODERN BOOK OF ENGLISH VERSE.

THE MODERN BOOK OF ENGLISH VERSE

INTRODUCTION

The aim of this collection of English poetry is simple. It is merely to bring together as much of the best of that poetry as it is possible to include in one companionable volume, so much of the best of it, indeed, that little will be left outside these covers. What that best is grows less and less a matter of individual judgment. Editorial appraisers of this great inheritance have from time to time inspected it anew, and have here and there made trifling corrections in former estimates. Once or twice even they have done more. A poet previously undervalued has occasionally thus come into his own—as Arthur O'Shaugnessy, for example, owing to Palgrave's large inclusions of him in the second series of his "Golden Treasury." Once in our time, indeed, a poet all but utterly forgotten has been rescued from the poppy of oblivion, and set upon a high lyric throne. Such was the service Dr. A. H. Bullen did for Thomas Campion, whose lyrics now sweeten so many pages of our anthologies. But you will look for his name in vain in perhaps the best general anthology of English literature so far made—that of Robert Chambers, a "cyclopædia," which, in the main, eminently illustrates the old truth that all good taste and judgment and scholarship in the arts are not confined to fashionable living critics and editors.

To do such service to the lovers of English poetry

has seldom been the fortunate opportunity of the anthologist. In the main, there has been little left for him but to confirm the judgment of his predecessors—for the best of the most voluminous poets soon gets itself sifted out. There is not likely, for instance, to be much disagreement in a jury of poetry-lovers as to the immortal and the perishable parts of Wordsworth, or of Shelley or of Byron. More than is the case, perhaps, with any other English poets, the "collected works" of these poets contain a larger proportion of inert matter, banks of sand in which the most industrious placer miners will seek in vain for any appreciable glitter of gold. Occasionally some perverse solitary of scholarship will arise to contest the general judgment in cases of this kind, and proclaim his preference for those productions of the poet which the rest of the world finds unreadable. For all that, Byron's epitaph on "The Excursion" will remain the last word on that poem; as Carlyle's epigram on "Sordello" will be recognized as generally just, if somewhat rough justice, to that poem, which an occasional glory will hardly save from forgetfulness. In the same way, no critical trumpets of resurrection can raise Byron's dramas from the grave; nor the most loyal enthusiasm for Shelley support any of us in a re-reading of his "Revolt of Islam." The same applies—alas! to have to say it—to Scott's "Lady of the Lake," and his other ballad-epics; and what remains of poor Southey save that one sad sonnet of his lonely broken mind? To that his pyramidal productivity is now pathetically sifted down. Yet that is something, and that the general judgment has rescued "My Days

Among the Dead Are Past" from so vast a mound of
forgotten words shows how difficult it is for the most
secluded good thing to escape recognition.

There is an anthology of English lyrics, made but
a short time ago by a critic whose love for and knowledge of literature are alike deep, in which he would
seem to have been guided by that crochetty preference
for the less known poems of the various poets represented to which I have referred. The effect, therefore, of the volume is very curious. While, undoubt-
edly, in a few cases, forgotten or less remembered
pieces are thus serviceably brought back to mind, those
other pieces immortally associated with the names of
their writers are hauntingly absent. So, by the
way, a very learned and famous lady omitted Gray's
"Elegy," of deliberate intent, from another anthology
conceived in a similar spirit of editorial caprice. Had
the other editor to whom I am referring but allowed
his critical idiosyncrasy to carry him a step or two
further, he might have added to the curiosities of literature a volume which might well have borne the title
of "The Worst Poems by the Best Poets." As it is,
his anthology, for the most part, whimsically gathers
together the second and third best of the poets he un-
doubtedly knows and loves: possibly a service to their
memory, but a questionable service to that general
reader for whom the volume appears to have been designed.

That everyone is supposed to know Milton's
"Lycidas" can hardly be considered a reason for omit-
ting it from a representative collection of English
poetry. Otherwise, the originality of an anthology
would have to be based on its omissions, as, indeed,

that might be said to be the only basis for singularity
left to the present-day anthologist. Of that opportunity I have not in the present collection availed myself, but, on the contrary, being of the opinion that
Time is the most trustworthy of all anthologists, the
severest critic and the weightiest authority on what
is best worth preserving out of all the works of man,
including those works we call "poetical," I have been
content, in the main, to accept his judgments and
adopt his selections. I believe that what has been
oftenest read in the past will continue to be oftenest
read in the future, and, though this may be an unfash-
ionable opinion at the moment, I may perhaps point to
the recent renewal of enthusiasm for Greek poetry as
something in favour of my quaint point of view.
Therefore, the reader will probably not find much in
this volume that he has not known and loved before,
though, it is, doubtless, impossible but that the editor's
life-long reading of poetry has not in some degree
swayed his choice among beautiful things so often
chosen before, and has, therefore, given to this collection a certain tinge of personal preference. His
chief solicitude has been, however, rather than that the
reader should find novelties in this collection, that he
should not miss too many of the old perfections, or
sigh the lack of many a thing he sought.

One of the most distinguished of English lyric
poets, who happily continues to escape Westminster
Abbey, wrote of Tennyson's poetry as being "rich
with sweets from every Muse's hive." The phrase
is not only true of "The Mantuan of our age and
clime," but it might with even fuller aptness be applied to English poetry as a whole, from Chaucer till

our own time. Perhaps no poetry has borrowed more
from the poetry of other races, and yet the poetry of
no other race seems so distinctive as that of England.
Never was there such an example of literary alchemy.
How much that English poetry which seems most
English owes in its origin to France and Italy is
known to every young student of literature. Even
those most cherished "wood-notes wild" of Elizabeth's day are surprisingly indebted to England's
"sweet enemy France." The debt of English lyricism
to Ronsard and his school has perhaps not been sufficiently acknowledged, while English indebtedness to
Italy has perhaps been over-emphasized. But, all indebtedness whatsoever acknowledged, the curious fact
remains that the final result is something that has
not been borrowed, something that immensely, so to
say, over-pays the loan—or theft. Whatever, for example, Elizabethan lyricism may have owed to Ronsard and his "Pléiade," however much those "sweet
influences of Pleiades" may have originally aerified
and heightened the English lyric art, the music of
England's "Nest of Singing Birds" has a quality
peculiarly its own. What is it that is in "Under the
Greenwood Tree" that has never been found in the
poetry of any other land? It seems as though there
had been a peculiar divine sap in the original tree of
English song, which, whatever the alien grafts made
upon it, gave to the blossom a beauty at once starrier
and yet more earth-sweet, as though star-light and
the breath of hawthorn in English country lanes had
become blended together in words. Even in such remains of Anglo-Saxon poetry as we possess, remote

as the uncouth language makes them, we feel the presence already of this native sweetness exhaling from
strength—the sweetness hived in the hearts of strong
men.   However great the mere formal or themal
influences of France and Italy upon English poetry
may have been, they seem to have been those chiefly
of fashion or manner.   The spirit of English poetry
has been entirely different from theirs, and perhaps
that spirit is nearest of all to that of the great Latin
poets, with their large accent, their noble gravity of
mood, and such sweetness as in Catullus reminds one
of the robust sweetness of Shakespeare.   In its pre-
eminent genius for the elegy, English poetry is also
akin to the Latin.   The greatest poems in English are
elegies, or spiritual, philosophic meditations, elegiac
in their mood.   But these also are pierced with that
curious English sweetness which is like the music of
the spheres combined with the smell of apples.   Yes!
earth-sweetness, spiritual intensity, elegiac meditative-
ness are the main qualities of English poetry, and
perhaps in English nature-poetry we find them combined in their highest expression.   "The poetry of
earth is never dead," and English earth, and the Eng-
lishman's love of it, his mystic passion for it, indeed,
and "reading" of it, have played no little part, it is
evident, in the making of English song.

But, better than characterising it, analyzing it, or
accounting for it, is merely and simply to enjoy it—
and a greater or more lasting treasure of enjoyment
is not to be found than in this book of English poetry.
It is the greatest spiritual inheritance of Englishmen,
the greatest gift of England to the world.   Whatever

its special qualities, English poetry has also the infinite variety and freshness of nature itself. Mr. Kipling, in a phrase worth a multitude of critical volumes, has said:

> There are nine and sixty ways
> Of inditing tribal lays,
> And every blessed one of them is right.

Yes! and you will find them all in English poetry, find examples of them all in this book.

It remains only for me to make one or two acknowledgments. My indebtedness to Robert Chambers' "Cyclopædia of English Literature" is recorded above; and no one could compile a collection of English poetry, since their appearance, without being under great obligations to Sir Arthur Quiller-Couch for "The Oxford Book of Verse," and to Mr. Burton E. Stevenson for that glorious Leviathan of poetry, "The Home Book of Verse." Other anthologies and collections too numerous to mention have assisted me, particularly Dr. George Saintsbury's "Seventeenth Century Lyrics," and, of course, our old familiar friend and classic in this kind, Palgrave's "Golden Treasury."

I wish also to acknowledge the various, generous assistance given me by my friend, Edwin Justus Mayer.

RICHARD LE GALLIENNE.

THE MODERN BOOK OF ENGLISH VERSE

KING CNUT (1017-1035)

MERRILY sang the monkes in Ely
When Cnut the King rowed by;
And hear ye the monkes' song.
Row, knightes, near the land.

ANONYMOUS (1250)

Summer Is I-Comen In

SUMMER is i-comen in,
Loud sing cuckoo;
Groweth seed and bloweth mead,
And springeth the wood anew.
Sing cuckoo!
Ewe bleateth after lamb,
Loweth after calfe cow,
Bullock sterteth,
Bucke verteth,
Merrie sing cuckoo!
Cuckoo, cuckoo;
Well thou singest, cuckoo!
Nor cease thou never now.

LAYAMON (12th or 13th century)

King Arthur

WHEN that Arthur was King
Hearken now a marvelous thing;
He was liberal
To each man alive,
Knight with the best,
Wond'rously keen.
He was to the young for father,
To the old for comforter,
And with the unwise
Wonderfully stern.
Wrong was to him exceeding loathsome
And the right ever dear.

1

GEOFFREY CHAUCER (1328-1400)

Some Characters from "The Canterbury Tales"

A knight ther was, and that a worthy man,
    That fro the time that he first began
To riden, he loved chevalrie,
Trouthe and honour, fredom and curtesie.
Ful worthy was he in his lordes werre;
And, thereto, hadde he ridden, none more ferre,
As wel in Cristendom as in Hethenesse,
And ever honoured for his worthinesse . . .
Though that he was worthy he was wise;
And of his past, as meke as is a mayde:
He never yet no vilainie ne sayde,
In all his lif, unto no manere wight,
He was a veray parfit gentil knight. . . .
With him, ther was his sone, a young Squier,
A lover, and a lusty bacdeler;

With lockes crull as they were laide in presse.
Of twenty yere of age he was, I gesse.
Of his stature he was of even lengthe;
And wonderly deliver, and grete of strengthe,
And he hadde be, sometime, in chevachie
In Flaunders, in Artois, and in Picardie,
And borne him wel, as of so titel space,
In hope to standen in his ladies' grace.

Embrouded was he, as it were a mede
All full of freshe flowres, white and rede.
Singing he was, or floyting all the day:
He was as freshe as is the moneth of May.
Short was his goune, with sleves long and wide.
Wel coude he sitte on hors, and fayre ride,
He coude songes make, and wel endite;
Juste and eke dance; and well pourtraie and write:
So hote he loved, that by nightestale
He slep no more than doth the nightingale:
Curteis he was, lowly and servisable;
And carf before his fader at the table.

    .   .   .   .   .

Ther was also a Nonne, a Prioresse,
That of hire smiling was full simple and coy;
Hire gretest othe n'as but by Saint Eloy;
And she was cleped Madame Eglentine.
Ful wel she sange the service devine,
Entuned in hire nose ful swetely;

And Frenche she spake ful fayre and fetisly,
After the scole of Stratford atte Bowe,
For Frenche of Paris was to hire unknowe.
At mete was she wele ytaughte withalle;
She lette no morsel from her lippes falle,
Ne wette hire fingres in hire sauce depe. .
Wel coude she carie a morsel, and wel kepe,
Thatte no drope ne fell upon hire brest.
In curtesie was sette full moche hire lest.
Hire over-lippe wiped she so clene,
That in hire cuppe was no ferthing sene
Of grese, whan she dronken hadde hire draught.
Ful semely after hire mete she raught.
And sickerly she was of grete disport,
And ful plesant, and amiable of port,
And peined hire to contrefeten chere
Of court, and ben estatlich of manere,
And to ben holden digne of reverence . . .
Ful semely hire wimple ypinched was;
Hire nose tretis; hire eyen grey as glas;
Hire mouth ful smale, and thereto soft and red;
But sikerly she hadde a fayre forehed.
It was almost a spaune brode I trowe;
For hardily she was not undergrowe.
Full fetise was hire cloke, as I was ware.
Of smale corall about hire arm she bare
A pair of bedes, gauded all with grene;
And thereon heng a broche of gild ful shene,
On whiche was first ywritten a crowned A,
And after, *Amor vincit omnia.*

A clerk ther was of Oxenforde also,
That unto logike hadde long ygo.
As lene was his hors as is a rake,
And he was not right fat I undertake;
But looked holwe, and thereto soberly.
Ful thredbare was his overest courtepy,
For he hadde geten him yet no benefice,
He was nought worldly to have an office.
For him was lever han, at his beddes hed,
Twenty bokes clothed in black and red,
Of Aristotle and his philosophie,
Than robes riche, or fidel, or sautrie;
But all be that he was a philosophre,
Yet hadde he but litel gold in cofre;
But all that he might of his frendes hente,
On bokes and on lerning he it spente;
And besily gan for the soules praie

Of hem that gave him wherwith to scolaie.
Of studie toke he most care and hede.
Not a word spake he more than was nede;
And that was said in forme and reverence,
And short and quike, and full of high sentence:
Souning in moral vertue was his speche;
And gladly wolde he lerne, and gladly teche.

From "The Dream"

AND right anon as I the day espied,
No longer would I in my bed abide,
I went forth myself alone and boldely,
And held the way down by a brook side,
Till I came to a land of white and green,
So fair a one had I never in been.
The ground was green y-powdered with daisy,
The flowers and the groves alike high,
All green and white was nothing else seen.

The Complaint to His Empty Purse

TO you, my purse, and to none other wight
Complain I, for ye be my lady dear!
I am so sorrow, now that ye be light;
For certës, but ye make me heavy cheer,
Me were as lief be laid upon my bier;
For which unto your mercy thus I cry:
Be heavy again, or elles might I die!

Now voucheth safe this day, or it be night,
That I of you the blissful sound may hear,
Or see your colour like the sun bright
That of yellowness had never a peer.
Ye be my life, ye be my hertës stere,
Queen of comfort and of good company:
Be heavy again, or elles might I die!

Now purse, that be to me my life's light,
And saviour, as down in this world here,
Out of this toune help me through your might,
Since that ye wole not be my treasurer;
For I am shaved as nigh as any frere.
But yet I pray unto your courtesy
Be heavy again, or elles might I die!

O Conqueror of Brutë's Albion
Which that by line and free electiön
Be very king, this song to you I send;
And ye, that mighten all our harm amend,
Have mind upon my supplication!

Merciles Beaute

(A Triple Roundel)

I. CAPTIVITY

YOUR eyen two wol slee me sodenly,
  I may the beautè of hem not sustene,
So woundeth hit through-out my herte kene.
And but your word wol helen hastily
My hertes wounde, whyl that hit is grene,
  Your eyen two wol slee me sodenly,
  I may the beautè of hem not sustene.

Upon my trouthe I sey yow feithfully,
That ye ben of my lyf and deeth the quene;
For with my deeth the trouthe shal be sene.
  Your eyen two wol slee me sodenly,
  I may the beautè of hem not sustene,
  So woundeth hit through-out my herte kene.

2. REJECTION

So hath your beautè fro your herte chaced
Pitee, that me ne availeth not to pleyne;
For Daunger halt your mercy in his cheyne.

Giltles my deeth thus han ye me purchaced;
I sey yow sooth, me nedeth not to feyne;
  So hath your beautè fro your herte chaced
  Pitee, that me ne availeth not to pleyne.
Allas! that nature hath in yow compassed
So great beautè, that no man may atteyne
To mercy, though he sterve for the peyne.
  So hath your beautè fro your herte chaced
  Pitee, that me ne availeth not to pleyne;
  For Daunger halt your mercy in his cheyne.

halt] holdeth.

3. ESCAPE

Sin I fro Love escaped am so fat,
I never thenk to ben in his prison lene;
Sin I am free, I counte him not a bene.
He may answere and seye this or that
I do no fors, I speke right as I mene,
Sin I fro Love escaped am so fat,
I never thenk to ben in his prison lene.

Love hath my name y-strike out of his sclat
And he is strike out of my bokes clene
For ever-mo; ther is non other mene.
Sin I fro Love escaped am so fat,
I never thenk to ben in his prison lene;
Sin I am free, I counte him not a bene.

Written on His Deathbed

FLY from the press, and dwell with sothfastness;
  Suffice unto thy good, though it be small;
For hoard hath hate, and climbing fickleness,
Press hath envy, and weal is blent o'er all;
Savour no more than thee beloven shall;
Rede well thyself, that other folk can'st rede,
And truth thee shall deliver 'tis no drede.

Pain thee not each crooked to redress,
In trust of her that turneth as a ball;
Great rest standeth in little business;
Beware also to spurn against a nalle;
Strive not as doth a crocké with a wall;
Deemeth thyself that deemest other's deed,
And truth thee shall deliver 'tis no drede.
That thee is sent receive in buxomness;
The wrestling of this world asketh a fall;
Here is no home, here is but wilderness;
Forth, pilgrim, forth, O beast out of thy stall;
Look up on high, and thank thy God of all;
Waiveth thy lust and let thy ghost thee lead,
And truth thee shall deliver 'tis no drede.

JAMES I OF SCOTLAND (1395-1437)

From "The King's Quhair"

BEWAILING in my chamber, thus alone,
    Despairing of all joy and remedy,
For-tired of my thought, and woe-begone,
And to the window gan I walk in by
To see the world and folk that went forebye,
As, for the time, though I of mirthis food
Might have no more, to look it did me good.

Now was there made, fast by the town's wall,
A garden fair; and in the corners set
Ane arbour green, with wandis long and small
Railed about, and so with trees set
Was all this place, and hawthorn hedges knet,
That lyf was none walking there forbye,
That might within scarce any might espy

So thick the boughis and the leavis green
Beshaded all the alleys that there were,
And mids of every arbour might be seen
The sharpe greene sweete juniper,
Growing so fair with branches here and there,
That it seemed to a lyf without,
The boughis spread the arbour all about.

And on the smalle greene twistis sat,
The little sweete nightingale, and sung
So loud and clear, the hymnis consecrat
Of love's use, now soft, now loud among,
That all the gardens and the wallis rung
Right of their song . . .

. . . Cast I down mine eyes again,
Where as I saw, walking under the tower,
Full secretly, new comen here to plain,
The fairest or the freshest younge flower
That ever I saw, methought, before that hour,
For which sudden abate, anon astart,
The blood of all my body to my heart.

And though I stood abasit tho a lite,
No wonder was; for why? my wittis all
Were so overcome with pleasure and delight,
Only through letting of my eyen fall,
That suddenly my heart became her thrall,

For ever of free will,—for of menace
There was no token in her sweete face.

And in my head I drew right hastily,
And eftesoons I leant it out again,
And saw her walk that very womanly,
With no wight mo', but only women twain.
Then gan I study in myself, and sayn,
"Ah, sweet! are ye a worldly creature,
Or heavenly thing in likeness of nature?"

WILLIAM DUNBAR (1460-1521)

O reverend Chaucer! rose of rhetoris all,
    As in our tongue ane flower imperial,
That raise in Britain ever, who reads right,
Thou bears of makaris the triumph riall,
Thy fresh enamelled terms celicall:
This matter could illumined have full bright.
Was thou not of our English all the light,
Surmounting every tongue terrestrial,
As far as Mayis morrow does midnight.

STEPHEN HAWES (——1523)

His Epitaph

O mortal folk, you may behold and see
    How I lie here, sometime a mighty knight
The end of joy and all prosperitee
Is death at last, thorough his course and might:
After the day there cometh the dark night,
    For though the daye be never so long,
    At last the bells ringeth to evensong.

JOHN SKELTON (1460-1529)

To Mistress Margery Wentworth

MERRY Margaret,
    As midsummer flower,
Gentle as falcon,
Or hawk of the tower;
With solace and gladness,
Much mirth and no madness,
All good and no badness;
So joyously,

So maidenly,
So womanly,
Her demeaning,
In everything,
Far, far passing
That I can indite,
Or suffice to write,
Of merry Margaret,
As midsummer flower,
Gentle as falcon,
Or hawk of the tower;
As patient and as still,
And as full of goodwill,
As fair Isiphil,
Coliander,
Sweet Pomander,
Good Cassander;
Stedfast of thought,
Well made, well wrought,
Far may be sought,
Ere you can find
So courteous, so kind,
As merry Margaret,
This midsummer flower,
Gentle as falcon,
Or hawk of the tower.

SIR THOMAS WYATT (1503-1542)

My Lute, Awake

MY lute, awake, perform the last
    Labour that thou and I shall waste,
And end that I have now begun,
And, when this song is sung and past,
My lute, be still, for I have done!

As to be heard where ear is none,
As lead to grave in marble stone,
My song may pierce her heart as soon:
Should we, then, sigh or sing or moan?
No, no, my lute, for I have done!

The rocks do not so cruelly
Repulse the waves continually,
As she my suit and affection:
So that I am past remedy:
Whereby my lute and I have done!

Proud of the spoil that thou hast got
Of simple hearts thorough Love's shot,
By whom unkind thou hast them won,
Think not he hath his bow forgot,
Although my lute and I have done!

Vengeance shall fall on thy disdain,
That mak'st but game of earnest pain,
Trow not alone under the sun
Unquit to cause thy lover's plain,
Although my lute and I have done.

Now cease, my lute, this is the last
Labour that thou and I shall waste,
And ended is that we begun:
Now is this song both sung and past—
My lute, be still, for I have done.

HENRY HOWARD, EARL OF SURREY (1517-1547)
Summer Is Come

THE soote season, that bud and bloom forth brings,
　With green hath clad the hill, and eke the vale.
The nightingale with feathers new she sings;
The turtle to her mate hath told her tale.
Summer is come, for every spray now springs,
The hart hath hung his old head on the pale;
The buck in brake his winter coat he slings;
The fishes flit with new repaired scale;
The adder all her slough away she slings;
The swift swallow pursueth the flies smale;
The busy bee her honey now she mings;
Winter is worn that was the flowers' bale.
　And thus I see among these pleasant things
　Each care decays, and yet my sorrow springs!

RICHARD EDWARDES (1523-1566)
Amantium Iræ

IN going to my naked bed, as one that would have slept,
　I heard a wife sing to her child, that long before had wept.
She sighed sore, and sang full sweet, to bring the babe to rest,
That would not cease, but cried still, in sucking at her breast.
She was full weary of her watch, and grieved with her child;
She rocked it, and rated it, until on her it smiled;

Then did she say: "Now have I found the proverb true to
    prove,
The falling out of faithful friends renewing is of love."

Then took I paper, pen, and ink, this proverb for to write,
In register for to remain of such a worthy wight.
As she proceeded thus in song unto her little brat,
Much matter uttered she of weight in place whereas she sat;
And proved plain, there was no beast, nor creature bearing
    life,
Could well be known to live in love without discord and
    strife:
Then kissed she her little babe, and sware by God above,
"The falling out of faithful friends renewing is of love."

"I marvel much, pardie," quoth she, "for to behold the rout,
To see man, woman, boy and beast, to toss the world about;
Some kneel, some crouch, some beck, some check, and some
    can smoothly smile,
And some embrace others in arms, and there think many a
    wile.
Some stand aloof at cap and knee, some humble, and some
    stout,
Yet are they never friends indeed until they once fall out."
Thus ended she her song, and said, before she did remove:
"The falling out of faithful friends renewing is of love."

QUEEN ELIZABETH (1533-1603)

The Doubt

THE doubt of future foes
    Exiles my present joy,
And wit me warns to shun such snares
    As threatens mine annoy.

For fastened now doth flow,
    And subject faith doth ebb,
Which would not be if reason ruled,
    Or wisdom weaved the web.

But clouds of toys untried
    Do cloak aspiring minds,
Which turn to rain of late repent,
    By course of changèd winds.

The top of hope supposed
    The root of truth will be,

Salem Academy and College
Gramley Library
Winston-Salem, N.C. 27108

SALEM COLLEGE
LIBRARY
Winston-Salem, N. C.

And fruitless all their graffèd guiles,
  As shortly ye shall see.

Then dazzled eyes with pride,
Which great ambition blinds,
Shall be unsealed by worthy wights,
Whose foresight falsehood finds.

The daughter of debate
That eke discord doth sow,
Shall reap no gain where former rule
Hath taught still peace to grow.

No foreign banished wight
Shall anchor in this port;
Our realm it brooks no stranger's force;
Let them elsewhere resort.

Our rusty sword with rest
Shall first his edge employ,
To pall their tops that seek such change
And gape for future joy.

JOHN STILL, BISHOP OF BATH AND WELLS
(1543-1608)

Jolly Good Ale and Old

From "Gammer Gurton's Needle"

I cannot eat but little meat,
  My stomach is not good;
But sure I think that I can drink
  With him that wears a hood.
Though I go bare, take ye no care,
  I nothing am a-cold;
I stuff my skin so full within
  Of jolly good ale and old.
    Back and side go bare, go bare;
    Both foot and hand go cold;
    But, belly, God send thee good ale enough,
    Whether it be new or old.

I love no roast but a nut-brown toast,
  And a crab laid in the fire;
A little bread shall do me stead;
  Much bread I not desire.

No frost nor snow, no wind, I trow,
  Can hurt me if I wold;
I am so wrapped and thoroughly lapped
  Of jolly good ale and old.

And Tib, my wife, that as her life
  Loveth well good ale to seek,
Full oft drinks she till ye may see
  The tears run down her cheek:
Then doth she trowl to me the bowl
  Even as a maltworm should,
And saith, "Sweetheart, I took my part
  Of this jolly good ale and old."

Now let them drink till they nod and wink,
  Even as good fellows should do;
They shall not miss to have the bliss
  Good ale doth bring men to;
And all poor souls that have scoured bowls
  Or have them lustily trolled,
God save the lives of them and their wives,
  Whether they be young or old.
    Back and side go bare, go bare;
    Both foot and hand go cold;
    But, belly, God send thee good ale enough,
    Whether it be new or old.

NICOLAS BRETON (1545?-1626?)
A Cradle Song

COME little babe, come silly soul,
  Thy father's shame, thy mother's grief,
Born as I doubt to all our dole,
And to thyself unhappy chief:
  Sing lullaby, and lap it warm,
  Poor soul that thinks no creature harm.

Thou little think'st and less dost know
The cause of this thy mother's moan;
Thou want'st the wit to wail her woe,
And I myself am all alone:
  Why dost thou weep? why dost thou wail?
  And know'st not yet what thou dost ail.

Come, little wretch—ah, silly heart!
Mine only joy, what can I more?
If there be any wrong thy smart,

That may the destinies implore:
'Twas I, 1 say, against my will,
I wail the time, but be thou still.

And dost thou smile? O, thy sweet face!
Would God Himself He might thee see!—
No doubt thou wouldst soon purchase grace,
I know right well, for thee and me:
  But come to mother, babe, and play,
  For father false is fled away.

Sweet boy, if it by fortune chance
Thy father home again to send,
If death do strike me with his lance,
Yet may'st thou me to him commend:
  If any ask thy mother's name,
  Tell how by love she purchased blame.

Then will his gentle heart soon yield:
I know him of a noble mind:
Although a lion in the field,
A lamb in town thou shalt him find:
  Ask blessing, babe, be not afraid,
  His sugared words hath me betrayed.

Then may'st thou joy and be right glad;
Although in woe I seem to moan,
Thy father is no rascal lad,
A noble youth of blood and bone:
  His glancing looks, if he once smile,
  Right honest women may beguile.

Come, little boy, and rock asleep;
Sing lullaby and be thou still;
I, that can do naught else but weep,
Will sit by thee and wail my fill:
  God bless my babe, and lullaby
  From this thy father's quality.

SIR WALTER RALEIGH (1552?-1618)

The Faerie Queen

(To Spenser)

METHOUGHT I saw the grave where Laura lay,
  Within that temple where the vestal flame
Was wont to burn: and, passing by that way

To see that buried dust of living flame,
Whose tomb fair love and fairer Virtue kept,
All suddenly I saw the Faerie Queen,
At whose approach the soul of Petrarch wept;
And from henceforth those graces were not seen,
For they this Queen attended; in whose stead
Oblivion laid him down on Laura's hearse.
Hereat the hardest stones were seen to bleed,
And groans of buried ghosts the heavens did pierce:
Where Homer's spright did tremble all for grief,
And curse the access of that celestial thief.

His Pilgrimage

GIVE me my scallop-shell of quiet,
My staff of faith to walk upon,
My scrip of joy, immortal diet,
My bottle of salvation,
My gown of glory, hope's true gage;
And thus I'll take my pilgrimage.

Blood must be my body's balmer,
No other balm will there be given;
Whilst my soul, like quiet palmer,
Traveleth towards the land of Heaven;
Over the silver mountains
Where spring the nectar fountains:
There will I kiss
The bowl of bliss,
And drink mine everlasting fill
Upon every milken hill,
My soul will be a-dry before;
But after, it will thirst no more.

Then by that happy, blissful day,
More peaceful pilgrims I shall see,
That have cast off their rags of clay,
And walk appareled fresh like me.
I'll take them first
To quench their thirst,
And taste of nectar's suckets
At those clear wells
Where sweetness dwells
Drawn up by saints in crystal buckets.
And when our bottles and all we
Are filled with immortality,
Then the blessèd paths we'll travel,
Strowed with rubies thick as gravel;—
Ceilings of diamonds, sapphire floors,

High walls of coral, and pearly bowers.
From thence to Heaven's bribeless hall,
Where no corrupted voices brawl;
No conscience molten into gold,
No forged accuser bought or sold,
No cause deferred, no vain-spent journey,
For there Christ is the King's Attorney,
Who pleads for all without degrees,
And He hath angels, but no fees.
And when the grand twelve-million jury
Of our sins, with direful fury,
Against our souls black verdicts give,
Christ pleads His death, and then we live.

Be Thou my speaker, taintless pleader,
Unblotted lawyer, true proceeder!
Thou giv'st salvation even for alms;
Not with a bribèd lawyer's palms.
And this is mine eternal plea
To Him that made heaven, earth, and sea,
That, since my flesh must die so soon,
And want a head to dine next noon,
Just at the stroke, when my veins start and spread,
Set on my soul an everlasting head!
Then am I ready, like a palmer, fit
To tread those blest paths which before I writ.

O death and judgment, heaven and hell,
Who oft doth think, must needs die well.

The Conclusion

EVEN such is Time, that takes in trust
  Our youth, our joys, our all we have,
And pays us but with earth and dust;
  Who in the dark and silent grave,
When we have wandered all our ways,
Shuts up the story of our days;
But from this earth, this grave, this dust,
My God will raise me up, I trust.

BALLADS—ANONYMOUS
Thomas the Rhymer

TRUE Thomas lay on Huntlie bank;
  A ferlie he spied wi' his e'e;
And there he saw a lady bright,
  Come riding down by the Eildon Tree.

Her skirt was o' the grass-green silk,
  Her mantle o' the velvet fine;
At ilka tett o' her horse's mane
  Hung fifty siller bells and nine.

True Thomas he pu'd aff his cap,
  And louted low down on his knee:
"Hail to thee, Mary, Queen of Heaven!
  For thy peer on earth could never be."

"O no, O no, Thomas!" she said,
  "That name does not belang to me;
I'm but the Queen o' fair Elfland,
  That am hither come to visit thee.

"Harp and carp, Thomas!" she said,
  "Harp and carp along wi' me;
And if ye dare to kiss my lips,
  Sure of your body I will be."

"Betide me weal, betide me woe,
  That weird shall never daunten me."
Syne he has kissed her rosy lips,
  All underneath the Eildon Tree.

"Now, ye maun go wi' me," she said;
  "True Thomas, ye maun go wi' me;
And ye maun serve me seven years,
  Through weal or woe as may chance be."

She's mounted on her milk-white steed;
  She's ta'en true Thomas up behind;
And aye, whene'er her bridle rang,
  The steed gaed swifter than the wind.

O they rade on, and farther on,
  The steed gaed swifter than the wind;
Until they reached a desert wide,
  And living land was left behind.

"Light down, light down now, true Thomas,
  And lean your head upon my knee;
Abide ye there a little space,
  And I will show you ferlies three.

"O see ye not yon narrow road,
  So thick beset wi' thorns and briers?
That is the Path of Righteousness,
  Though after it but few inquires.

"And see ye not yon braid, braid road,
    That lies across the lily leven?
That is the Path of Wickedness,
    Though some call it the Road to Heaven.

"And see yet not yon bonny road,
    That winds about the fernie brae?
That is the Road to fair Elfland,
    Where thou and I this night maun gae.

"But, Thomas, ye sall haud your tongue,
    Whatever ye may hear or see;
For speak ye word in Elfyn-land,
    Ye'll ne'er win back to your ain countrie."

O they rade on, and farther on,
    And they waded rivers abune the knee;
And they saw neither sun nor moon,
    But they heard the roaring of the sea.

It was mirk, mirk night, there was nae starlight,
    They waded through red blude to the knee;
For a' the blude that's shed on earth
    Rins through the springs o' that countrie.

Syne they came to a garden green,
    And she pu'd an apple frae a tree:
"Take this for thy wages, true Thomas;
    It will give thee tongue that can never lee."

"My tongue is mine ain," true Thomas, he said;
    "A gudely gift ye wad gie to me!
I neither dought to buy nor sell,
    At fair or tryst where I might be.

"I dought neither speak to prince or peer,
    Nor ask of grace from fair lady!"
"Now haud thy peace!" the lady said,
    "For as I say, so must it be."

He has gotten a coat of the even cloth,
    And a pair o' shoon of the velvet green;
And till seven years were gane and past,
    True Thomas on earth was never seen.

Helen of Kirconnell

I wish I were where Helen lies,
　Night and day on me she cries;
O that I were where Helen lies,
　On fair Kirconnell lea!

Curst be the heart that thought the thought,
And curst the hand that fired the shot,
When in my arms burd Helen dropt,
　And died to succour me!

O think na ye my heart was sair,
When my Love dropp'd and spak nae mair!
There did she swoon wi' meikle care,
　On fair Kirconnell lea.

As I went down the water side,
None but my foe to be my guide,
None but my foe to be my guide,
　On fair Kirconnell lea;

I lighted down my sword to draw,
I hackèd him in pieces sma',
I hackèd him in pieces sma',
　For her sake that died for me.

O Helen fair, beyond compare!
I'll mak a garland o' thy hair,
Shall bind my heart for evermair,
　Until the day I die!

O that I were where Helen lies!
Night and day on me she cries;
Out of my bed she bids me rise,
　Says, "Haste, and come to me!"

O Helen fair! O Helen chaste!
If I were with thee, I'd be blest,
Where thou lits low and taks thy rest,
　On fair Kirconnell lea.

I wish my grave were growing green,
A winding-sheet drawn owre my e'en,
And I in Helen's arms lying,
　On fair Kirconnell lea.

I wish I were where Helen lies!
Night and day on me she cries;
And I am weary of the skies,
    For her sake that died for me.

Waly, Waly

O waly, waly, up the bank,
    And waly, waly, doun the brae,
And waly, waly, yon burn-side,
    Where I and my Love wont to gae!
I lean'd my back unto an aik,
    I thocht it was a trustie tree;
But first it bow'd and syne it brak—
    Sae my true love did lichtlie me.

O waly, waly, gin love be bonnie
    A little time while it is new!
But when 'tis auld it waxeth cauld,
    And fades awa' like morning dew.
O wherefore should I busk my heid,
    Or wherefore should I kame my hair?
For my true Love has me forsook,
    And says he'll never lo'e me mair.

Now Arthur's Seat sall be my bed,
    The sheets sall ne'er be 'filed by me;
Saint Anton's well sall be my drink;
    Since my true Love has forsaken me.
Marti'mas wind, when wilt thou blaw,
    And shake the green leaves aff the tree?
O gentle Death, when wilt thou come?
    For of my life I am wearie.

'Tis not the frost, that freezes fell,
    Nor blawing snaw's inclemencie,
'Tis not sic cauld that makes me cry;
    But my Love's heart grown cauld to me.
When we cam in by Glasgow toun,
    We were a comely sicht to see;
My Love was clad in the black velvèt,
    And I mysel in cramasie.

But had I wist, before I kist,
    That love had been sae ill to win,
I had lock'd my heart in a case o' gowd,
    And pinn'd it wi' a siller pin.
And O! if my young babe were born,
    And set upon the nurse's knee;
And I mysel were dead and gane,
    And the green grass growing over me!

Barbara Allen's Cruelty

IN Scarlet town, where I was born,
    There was a fair maid dwellin',
Made every youth cry *Well-a-way!*
    Her name was Barbara Allen.

All in the merry month of May,
    When green buds they were swellin',
Young Jemmy Grove on his death-bed lay,
    For love of Barbara Allen.

He sent his man in to her then,
    To the town where she was dwellin',
"O haste and come to my master dear,
    "If your name be Barbara Allen."

So slowly, slowly rase she up,
    And slowly she came nigh him,
And when she drew the curtain by—
    'Young man, I think you're dyin'.'

"O it's I am sick and very very sick,
    And it's all for Barbara Allen."
"O the better for me ye'se never be,
    Tho' your heart's blood were a-spillin'!"

"O dinna ye mind, young man," says she,
    "When the red wine ye were fillin',
That ye made the healths go round and round,
    And slighted Barbara Allen?"

He turn'd his face unto the wall,
    And death was with him dealin':
"Adieu, adieu, my dear friends all,
    And be kind to Barbara Allen!"

As she was walking o'er the fields,
    She heard the dead-bell knellin';
And every jow the dead-bell gave
    Cried 'Woe to Barbara Allen."

"O mother, mother, make my bed,
  O make it saft and narrow:
My love has died for me to-day,
  I'll die for him to-morrow.

"Farewell," she said, "ye virgins all,
  And shun the fault I fell in:
Henceforth take warning by the fall
  Of cruel Barbara Allen."

Phillada Flouts Me

O what a plague is love!
  How shall I bear it?
She will inconstant prove,
  I greatly fear it.
She so torments my mind
  That my strength faileth,
And wavers with the wind
  As a ship saileth.
Please her the best I may,
  She loves still to gainsay;
Alack and well-a-day!
  Phillada flouts me.

At the fair yesterday
  She did pass by me;
She look'd another way
  And would not spy me:
I woo'd her for to dine,
  But could not get her;
Will had her to the wine—
  He might entreat her.
With Daniel she did dance,
On me she look'd askance:
O thrice unhappy chance!
  Phillada flouts me.

Fair maid, be not so coy,
  Do not disdain me!
I am my mother's joy:
  Sweet, entertain me!
She'll give me, when she dies,
  All that is fitting:
Her poultry and her bees,
  And her goose sitting,

A pair of mattrass beds,
And a bag full of shreds;
And yet, for all this guedes,
  Phillada flouts me!

She hath a clout of mine
  Wrought with blue coventry,
Which she keeps for a sign
  Of my fidelity:
But i' faith, if she flinch
  She shall not wear it;
To Tib, my t'other wench,
  I mean to bear it.
And yet it grieves my heart
So soon from her to part:
Death strike me with his dart!
  Phillada flouts me.

Thou shalt eat crudded cream
  All the year lasting,
And drink the crystal stream
  Pleasant in tasting;
Whig and whey whilst thou lust,
  And bramble-berries,
Pie-lid and pastry-crust,
  Pears, plums, and cherries.
Thy raiment shall be thin,
Made of a weevil's skin—
Yet all's not worth a pin!
  Phillada flouts me.

In the last month of May
  I made her posies;
I heard her often say
  That she loved roses.
Cowslips and gillyflowers
  And the white lily
I brought to deck the bowers
  For my sweet Philly.
But she did all disdain,
And threw them back again;
Therefore 'tis flat and plain
  Phillada flouts me.

Fair maiden, have a care,
  And in time take me;
I can have those as fair
  If you forsake me:
For Doll the dairy-maid
  Laugh'd at me lately,

And wanton Winifred
   Favours me greatly.
One throws milk on my clothes,
T'other plays with my nose;
What wanting signs are those?
   Phillada flouts me.

I cannot work nor sleep
   At all in season:
Love wounds my heart so deep
   Without all reason.
I 'gin to pine away
   In my love's shadow,
Like as a fat beast may,
   Penn'd in a meadow.
I shall be dead, I fear,
Within this thousand year:
And all for that my dear
   Phillada flouts me.

Clerk Saunders

CLERK Saunders and may Margaret
   Walk'd owre yon garden green;
And deep and heavy was the love
   That fell thir twa between.

"A bed, a bed," Clerk Saunders said,
   "A bed for you and me!"
"Fye na, fye na," said may Margaret,
   "Till anes we married be!"

"Then I'll take the sword frae my scabbard
   And slowly lift the pin;
And you may swear, and save your aith,
   Ye ne'er let Clerk Saunders in.

"Take you a napkin in your hand,
   And tie up baith your bonnie e'en,
And you may swear, and save your aith,
   Ye saw me na since late yestreen."

It was about the midnight hour,
   When they asleep were laid,
When in and came her seven brothers,
   Wi' torches burning red:

When in and came her seven brothers,
  Wi' torches burning bright:
They said, "We hae but one sister,
  And behold her lying with a knight!"

Then out and spake the first o' them,
  "I bear the sword shall gar him die."
And out and spake the second o' them,
  "His father has nae mair but he."

And out and spake the third o' them,
  "I wot that they are lovers dear."
And out and spake the fourth o' them,
  "They hae been in love this mony a year."

Then out and spake the fifth o' them,
  "It were great sin true love to twain."
And out and spake the sixth o' them,
  "It were shame to slay a sleeping man."

Then up and gat the seventh o' them,
  And never a word spake he;
But he has striped his bright brown brand
  Out through Clerk Saunders' fair bodye.

Clerk Saunders he started, and Margaret she turn'd
  Into his arms as asleep she lay;
And sad and silent was the night
  That was atween thir twae.

And they lay still and sleepit sound
  Until the day began to daw';
And kindly she to him did say,
  "It is time, true love, you were awa'."

But he lay still, and sleepit sound,
  Albeit the sun began to sheen;
She look'd atween her and the wa',
  And dull and drowsie were his e'en.

Then in and came her father dear;
  Said, "Let a' your mourning be;
I'll carry the dead corse to the clay,
  And I'll come back and comfort thee."

"Comfort weel your seven sons,
  For comforted I will never be:

striped] thrust.

I ween 'twas neither knave nor loon
  Was in the bower last night wi' me."

The clinking bell gaed through the town,
  To carry the dead corse to the clay;
And Clerk Saunders stood at may Margaret's window,
  I wot, an hour before the day.

"Are ye sleeping, Marg'ret?" he says,
  "Or are ye waking presentlie?
Give me my faith and troth again,
  I wot, true love, I gied to thee."

'Your faith and troth ye sall never get,
  Nor our, true love sall never twin,
Until ye come within my bower,
  And kiss me cheik and chin."

"My mouth it is full cold, Marg'ret;
  It has the smell, now, of the ground;
And if I kiss thy comely mouth,
  Thy days of life will not be lang.

"O cocks are crowing a merry midnight;
  I wot the wild fowls are boding day;
Give me my faith and troth again,
  And let me fare me on my way."

"Thy faith and troth thou sallna get,
  And our true love sall never twin,
Until ye tell what comes o' women,
  I wot, who die in strong traivelling?"

"Their beds are made in the heavens high,
  Down at the foot of our good Lord's knee,
Weel set about wi' gillyflowers;
  I wot, sweet company for to see.

"O cocks are crowing a merry midnight;
  I wot the wild fowls are boding day;
The psalms of heaven will soon be sung,
  And I, ere now, will be miss'd away."

Then she has taken a crystal wand,
  And she has stroken her troth thereon;
She has given it him out at the shot-window,
  Wi' mony a sad sigh and heavy groan.

twin] break in two.

"I thank ye, Marg'ret; I thank ye, Marg'ret;
  And ay I thank ye heartilie;
Gin ever the dead come for the quick,
  Be sure, Marg'ret, I'll come for thee."

It's hosen and shoon, and gown alone,
  She climb'd the wall, and follow'd him,
Until she came to the green forest,
  And there she lost the sight o' him.

"Is there ony room at your head, Saunders?
  Is there ony room at your feet?
Or ony room at your side, Saunders,
  Where fain, fain, I wad sleep?"

"There's nae room at my head, Marg'ret,
  There's nae room at my feet;
My bed it is fu' lowly now,
  Amang the hungry worms I sleep.

"Cauld mould is my covering now,
  But and my winding-sheet;
The dew it falls nae sooner down
  Than my resting-place is weet.

"But plait a wand o' bonny birk,
  And lay it on my breast;
And shed a tear upon my grave,
  And wish my saul gude rest."

Then up and crew the red, red cock,
  And up and crew the gray:
"'Tis time, 'tis time, my dear Marg'ret,
  That you were going away.

"And fair Marg'ret, and rare Marg'ret,
  And Marg'ret o' veritie,
Gin e'er ye love another man,
  Ne'er love him as ye did me."

The Twa Corbies

AS I was walking all alane
  I heard twa corbies making a mane:

The tane unto the tither did say,
"Whar sall we gang and dine the day?"

corbies] ravens.

"—In behint yon auld fail dyke
I wot there lies a new-slain knight;
And naebody kens that he lies there
But his hawk, his hound, and his lady fair.

"His hound is to the hunting gane,
His hawk to fetch the wild-fowl hame,
His lady's ta'en anither mate,
So we may mak our dinner sweet.

"Ye'll sit on his white hause-bane,
And I'll pike out his bonny blue e'en:
Wi' ae lock o' his gowden hair
We'll theek our nest when it grows bare.

"Mony a one for him maks mane,
But nane sall ken whar he is gane:
O'er his white banes, when they are bare,
The wind sall blaw for evermair."

Binnorie

THERE were twa sisters sat in a bour;
Binnorie, O Binnorie!
There cam a knight to be their wooer,
By the bonnie milldams o' Binnorie.

He courted the eldest with glove and ring,
But he lo'ed the youngest abune a' thing.

The eldest she was vexèd sair,
And sair envied her sister fair.

Upon a morning fair and clear,
She cried upon her sister dear:

"O sister, sister, tak my hand,
And let's go down to the river-strand."

She's ta'en her by the lily hand,
And led her down to the river-strand.

The youngest stood upon a stane,
The eldest cam and push'd her in.

"O sister, sister, reach your hand!
And ye sall be heir o' half my land:

"O sister, reach me but your glove!
And sweet William sall be your love."

Sometimes she sank, sometimes she swam,
Until she cam to the miller's dam.

Out then cam the miller's son,
And saw the fair maid soummin' in.

"O father, father, draw your dam!
There's either a mermaid or a milk-white swan."

The miller hasted and drew his dam,
And there he found a drown'd womàn.

You couldna see her middle sma',
Her gowden girdle was sae braw.

You couldna see her lily feet,
Her gowden fringes were sae deep.

All amang her yellow hair
A string o' pearls was twisted rare.

You couldna see her fingers sma',
Wi' diamond rings they were cover'd a'.

And by there cam a harper fine,
That harpit to the king at dine.

And when he look'd that lady on,
He sigh'd and made a heavy moan.

He's made a harp of her breast-bane,
Whose sound wad melt a heart of stane.

He's ta'en three locks o' her yellow hair,
And wi' them strung his harp sae rare.

He went into her father's hall,
And there was the court assembled all.

He laid his harp upon a stane,
And straight it began to play by lane.

"O yonder sits my father, the King,
And yonder sits my mother, the Queen;

"And yonder stands my brother Hugh,
And by him my William, sweet and true."

soummin'] swimming.

But the last tune that the harp play'd then—
Binnorie, O Binnorie!
Was, "Woe to my sister, false Helèn!"
By the bonnie milldams o' Binnorie.

Sir Patrick Spens

I. THE SAILING

THE king sits in Dunfermline town
  Drinking the blude-red wine;
"O whare will I get a skeely skipper
  To sail this new ship o' mine?"

O up and spak an eldern knight,
  Sat at the king's right knee;
"Sir Patrick Spens is the best sailor
  That ever sail'd the sea."

Our king has written a braid letter,
  And seal'd it with his hand,
And sent it to Sir Patrick Spens,
  Was walking on the strand.

"To Noroway, to Noroway,
  To Noroway o'er the faem;
The king's daughter o' Noroway   -
  'Tis thou must bring her hame."

The first word that Sir Patrick read
  So loud, loud laugh'd he;
The neist word that Sir Patrick read
  The tear blinded his e'e.

"O wha is this has done this deed
  And tauld the king o' me,
To send us out, at this time o' year,
  To sail upon the sea?

"Be it wind, be it weet, be it hail, be it sleet,
  Our ship must sail the faem;
The king's daughter o' Noroway,
  'Tis we must fetch her hame."

They hoysed their sails on Monenday morn
  Wi' a' the speed they may;
They hae landed in Noroway
  Upon a Wodensday.

skeely] skilful.

II. THE RETURN

"Mak ready, mak ready, my merry men a'!
  Our gude ship sails the morn."
"Now ever alack, my master dear,
  I fear a deadly storm.

"I saw the new moon late yestreen
  Wi' the auld moon in her arm;
And if we gang to sea, master,
  I fear we'll come to harm."

They hadna sail'd a league, a league,
  A league but barely three,
When the lift grew dark, and the wind blew loud,
  And gurly grew the sea.

The ankers brak, and the topmast lap,
  It was sic a deadly storm:
And the waves cam owre the broken ship
  Till a' her sides were torn.

"Go fetch a web o' the silken claith,
  Another o' the twine,
And wap them into our ship's side,
  And let nae the sea come in."

They fetch'd a web o' the silken claith,
  Another o' the swine,
And they wrapp'd them round that gude ship's side,
  But still the sea came in.

O laith, laith were our gude Scots lords
  To wet their cork-heel'd shoon;
But lang or a' the play was play'd
  They wat their hats aboon.

And mony was the feather bed
  That flatter'd on the faem;
And mony was the gude lord's son
  That never mair cam hame.

And lang, lang may the maidens sit
  Wi' their gowd kames in their hair,
Before they see Sir Patrick Spens
  Come sailing to the strand!

lift] sky.   lap] sprang.   flatter'd] tossed afloat.
  kames] combs.

And lang, lang mad the maidens sit
  Wi' their gowd kames in their hair,
A-waiting for their ain dear loves!
  For them they'll see nae mair.

Half-owre, half-owre to Aberdour,
  'Tis fifty fathoms deep;
And there lies gude Sir Patrick Spens,
  Wi' the Scots lords at his feet!

Chevy-Chase

GOD prosper long our noble king,
  Our lives and safeties all;
A woful hunting once there did
  In Chevy-Chase befall.

To drive the deer with hound and horn
  Earl Percy took his way;
The child may rue that is unborn
  The hunting of that day.

The stout Earl of Northumberland
  A vow to God did make,
His pleasure in the Scottish woods
  Three summer days to take;

The chiefest harts in Chevy-Chase
  To kill and bear away.
These tidings to Earl Douglas came,
  In Scotland where he lay;

Who sent Earl Percy present word
  He would prevent his sport.
The English earl, not fearing that,
  Did to the woods resort,

With fifteen hundred bowmen bold,
  All chosen men of might,
Who knew full well in time of need
  To aim their shafts aright.

The gallant greyhounds swiftly ran
  To chase the fallow dear;
On Monday they began to hunt,
  When daylight did appear;

And long before high noon they had
  A hundred fat bucks slain;
Then, having dined, the drovers went
  To rouse the deer again.

The bowmen mustered on the hills,
  Well able to endure;
And all their rear, with special care,
  That day was guarded sure.

The hounds ran swiftly through the woods
  The nimble deer to take,
That with their cries the hills and dales
  An echo shrill did make.

Lord Percy to the quarry went,
  To view the slaughtered deer;
Quoth he, "Earl Douglas promisèd
  This day to meet me here;

"But if I thought he would not come,
  No longer would I stay;"
With that, a brave young gentleman
  Thus to the earl did say:—

"Lo, yonder doth Earl Douglas come,—
  His men in armor bright;
Full twenty hundred Scottish spears
  All marching in our sight;

"All men of pleasant Teviotdale,
  Fast by the river Tweed;"
"Then cease your sports," Earl Percy said,
  "And take your bows with speed;

"And now with me, my countrymen,
  Your courage forth advance;
For never was there champion yet,
  In Scotland or in France,

"That ever did on horseback come,
  But if my hap it were,
I durst encounter man for man,
  With him to break a spear."

Earl Douglas on his milk-white steed,
  Most like a baron bold,
Rode foremost of his company,
  Whose armor shone like gold.

"Show me," said he, "whose men you be,
  That hunt so boldly here,
That, without my consent, do chase
  And kill my fallow-deer."

The first man that did answer make,
  Was noble Percy, he—
Who said, "We list not to declare,
  Nor show whose men we be:

"Yet will we spend our dearest blood
  Thy chiefest harts to slay."
Then Douglas swore a solemn oath,
  And thus in rage did say:—

"Ere thus I will out-bravèd be,
  One of us two shall die;
I know thee well, an earl thou art,—
  Lord Percy, so am I.

"But trust me, Percy, pity it were,
  And great offense, to kill
Any of these our guiltless men,
  For they have done no ill.

"Let you and I the battle try,
  And set our men aside."
"Accursed be he," Earl Percy said,
  "By whom this is denied."

Then stepped a gallant squire forth,
  Witherington was his name,
Who said, "I would not have it told
  To Henry, our king, for shame,

"That e'er my captain fought on foot,
  And I stood looking on.
You two be earls," said Witherington,
  "And I a squire alone;

"I'll do the best that do I may,
  While I have power to stand;
While I have power to wield my sword,
  I'll fight with heart and hand."

Our English archers bent their bows,—
  Their hearts were good and true;
At the first flight of arrows sent,
  Full fourscore Scots they slew.

Yet stays Earl Douglas on the bent,
  As chieftain stout and good;
As valiant captain, all unmoved,
  The shock he firmly stood.

His host he parted had in three,
  As leader ware and tried;
And soon his spearmen on their foes
  Bore down on every side.

Throughout the English archery
  They dealt full many a wound;
But still our valiant Englishmen
  All firmly kept their ground.

And throwing straight their bows away,
  They grasped their swords so bright;
And now sharp blows, a heavy shower,
  On shields and helmets light.

They closed full fast on every side,
  No slackness there was found;
And many a gallant gentleman
  Lay gasping on the ground.

In truth, it was a grief to see
  How each one chose his spear,
And how the blood out of their breasts
  Did gush like water clear.

At last these two stout earls did meet;
  Like captains of great might,
Like lions wode, they laid on lode,
  And made a cruel fight.

They fought until they both did sweat,
  With swords of tempered steel,
Until the blood, like drops of rain,
  They trickling down did feel.

"Yield thee, Lord Percy," Douglas said,
  "In faith I will thee bring
Where thou shalt high advancèd be
  By James, our Scottish king.

"Thy ransom I will freely give.
  And this report of thee,—
Thou art the most courageous knight
  That ever I did see."

"No, Douglas," saith Earl **Percy** then,
"Thy proffer I do scorn;
I will not yield to any Scot
That ever yet was born."

With that there came an arrow keen
Out of an English bow,
Which struck Earl Douglas to the heart,—
A deep and deadly blow;

Who never spake more words than these:
"Fight on, my merry men all;
For why, my life is at an end;
Lord Percy sees my fall."

Then leaving life, Earl Percy took
The dead man by the hand;
And said, "Earl Douglas, for thy life
Would I had lost my hand.

"In truth, my very heart doth bleed
With sorrow for thy sake;
For sure a more redoubted knight
Mischance did never take."

A knight amongst the Scots there was
Who saw Earl Douglas die,
Who straight in wrath did vow revenge
Upon the Earl Percy.

Sir Hugh Muntgomery was he called,
Who, with a spear full bright,
Well-mounted on a gallant steed,
Ran fiercely through the fight;

And past the English archers all,
Without a dread or fear;
And through Earl Percy's body then
He thrust his hateful spear.

With such vehement force and might
He did his body gore,
The staff ran through the other side
A large cloth-yard and more.

So thus did both these nobles die,
Whose courage none could stain.
An English archer then perceived
The noble earl was slain;

He had a bow bent in his hand,
  Made of a trusty tree:
An arrow of a cloth-yard long
  To the hard head drew he.

Against Sir Hugh Mountgomery
  So right the shaft he set,
The gray goose-wing that was thereon
  In his heart's blood was wet.

This fight did last from break of day
  Till setting of the sun;
For when they rung the evening-bell
  The battle scarce was done.

With stout Earl Percy there were slain
  Sir John of Egerton,
Sir Robert Ratcliff, and Sir John,
  Sir James, that bold baròn.

And with Sir George and stout Sir James,
  Both Knights of good account,
Good Sir Ralph Raby there was slain,
  Whose prowess did surmount.

For Witherington my heart is woe
  That ever he slain should be,
For when his legs were hewn in two,
  He knelt and fought on his knee.

And with Earl Douglas there were slain
  Sir Hugh Mountgomery,
Sir Charles Murray, that from the field
  One foot would never flee;

Sir Charles Murray of Ratcliff, too,—
  His sister's son was he;
Sir David Lamb, so well esteemed,
  But saved he could not be.

And the Lord Maxwell in like case
  Did with Earl Douglas die:
Of twenty hundred Scottish spears,
  Scarce fifty-five did fly.

Of fifteen hundred Englishmen,
  Went home but fifty-three;
The rest in Chevy-Chase were slain,
  Under the greenwood tree.

Next day did many widows come,
  Their husbands to bewail;
They washed their wounds in brinish tears,
  But all would not prevail.

Their bodies, bathed in purple blood,
  They bore with them away;
They kissed them dead a thousand times,
  Ere they were clad in clay.

The news was brought to Edinburgh,
  Where Scotland's king did reign,
That brave Earl Douglas suddenly
  Was with an arrow slain:

"O heavy news," King James did say;
  "Scotland can witness be
I have not any captain more
  Of such account as he."

Like tidings to King Henry came
  Within as short a space,
That Percy of Northumberland
  Was slain in Chevy-Chase:

"Now God be with him," said our King,
  "Since 'twill no better be;
I trust I have within my realm
  Five hundred as good as he.

"Yet shall not Scots or Scotland say
  But I will vengeance take;
I'll be revengèd on them all
  For brave Earl Percy's sake."

This vow full well the king performed
  After at Humbledown;
In one day fifty knights were slain
  With lords of high renown;

And of the rest, of small account,
  Did many hundreds die:
Thus endeth the hunting of Chevy-Chase,
  Made by the Earl Percy.

God save the king, and bless this land,
  With plenty, joy, and peace;
And grant, henceforth, that foul debate
  'Twixt noblemen may cease.

EDMUND SPENSER (1552-1599)

Epithalamion

YE learnèd sisters, which have oftentimes
  Been to me aiding, others to adorn,
Whom ye thought worthy of your graceful rhymes,
That even the greatest did not greatly scorn
To hear their names sung in your simple lays,
But joyèd in their praise;
And when ye list your own mishaps to mourn,
Which death, or love, or fortune's wreck did raise,
Your string could soon to sadder tenor turn,
And teach the woods and waters to lament
Your doleful dreariment:
Now lay those sorrowful complaints aside;
And, having all your heads with garlands crowned,
Help me mine own love's praises to resound;
Nor let the same of any be envide:
So Orpheus did for his own bride!
So I unto myself alone will sing;
The woods shall to me answer, and my echo ring.

Early, before the world's light-giving lamp
His golden beam upon the hills doth spread,
Having dispersed the night's uncheerful damp,
Do ye awake; and, with fresh lusty-hed,
Go to the bower of my belovèd love,
My truest turtle dove;
Bid her awake; for Hymen is awake,
And long since ready forth his mask to move,
With his bright Tead that flames with many a flake,
And many a bachelor to wait on him,
In their fresh garments trim.
Bid her awake therefore, and soon her dight,
For lo! the wishèd day is come at last,
That shall, for all the pains and sorrows past,
Pay to her usury of long delight:
And, whilst she doth her dight,
Do ye to her of joy and solace sing,
That all the woods may answer, and your echo ring.

Bring with you all the Nymphs that you can hear,
Both of the rivers and the forests green,
And of the sea that neighbors to her near,
All with gay garlands goodly well beseen.
And let them also with them bring in hand
Another gay garland,
For my fair love, of lilies and of roses,

Bound true love wise with a blue silk riband;
And let them make great store of bridal posies,
And let them eke bring store of other flowers,
To deck the bridal bowers.
And let the ground whereas her foot should wrong,
For fear the stones her tender foot should wrong,
Be strewed with fragrant flowers all along,
And diapered like the discolored mead;
Which done, do at her chamber door await,
For she will waken straight;
The whiles do ye this song unto her sing,
The woods shall to you answer, and your echo ring.

Ye Nymphs of Mulla, which with careful heed
The silver scaly trouts do tend full well,
And greedy pikes which use therein to feed
(Those trouts and pikes all others do excel);
And ye likewise, which keep the rushy lake,
Where none do fishes take;
Bind up the locks the which hang scattered light,
And in his waters, which your mirror make,
Behold your faces as the crystal bright,
That when you come whereas my love doth lie,
No blemish she may spy.
And eke, ye lightfoot maids, which keep the deer,
That on the hoary mountain used to tower;
And the wild wolves, which seek them to devour,
With your steel darts do chase from coming near;
Be also present here,
To help to deck her, and to help to sing,
That all the woods may answer, and your echo ring.

Wake, now, my love, awake! for it is time;
The rosy morn long since left Tithon's bed,
All ready to her silver coach to climb;
And Phœbus 'gins to show his glorious head.
Hark, how the cheerful birds do chant their lays
And carol of love's praise.
The merry lark her matins sings aloft;
The thrush replies; the mavis descant plays;
The ouzel shrills; the ruddock warbles soft;
So goodly all agree, with sweet consent,
To this day's merriment.
Ah! my dear love, why do ye sleep thus long,
When meeter were that ye should now awake,
To await the coming of your joyous mate,
And hearken to the birds' love-learnèd song,
The dewy leaves among!
For they of joy and pleasance to you sing,
That all the woods them answer, and their echo ring.

My love is now awake out of her dreams,
And her fair eyes, like stars that dimmèd were
With darksome cloud, now show their goodly beams
More bright than Hesperus his head doth rear.
Come now, ye damsels, daughters of delight,
Help quickly her to dight:
But first come, ye fair hours, which were begot
In Jove's sweet paradise of Day and Night;
Which do the seasons of the year allot,
And all that ever in this world is fair,
Do make and still repair:
And ye three handmaids of the Cyprian queen,
The which do still adorn her beauty's pride,
Help to adorn my beautifulest bride;
And as ye her array, still throw between
Some graces to be seen,
And, as ye use to Venus, to her sing,
The whiles the woods shall answer, and your echo ring.

Now is my love all ready forth to come:
Let all the virgins therefore well await:
And ye fresh boys, that tend upon her groom,
Prepare yourselves; for he is coming straight;
Set all your things in seemly good array,
Fit for so joyful day:
The joyfulest day that ever sun did see.
Fair Sun! show forth thy favorable ray,
And let thy life-full heat not fervent be,
For fear of burning her sunshiny face,
Her beauty to disgrace.
O fairest Phœbus! father of the Muse!
If ever I did honor thee aright,
Or sing the thing that might thy mind delight,
Do not thy servant's simple boon refuse;
But let this day, let this one day, be mine;
Let all the rest be thine.
Then I thy sovereign praises loud will sing,
That all the woods shall answer, and their echo ring.

Hark! how the Minstrels 'gin to shrill aloud
Their merry music that resounds from far,
The pipe, the tabor, and the trembling croud,
That well agree withouten breach or jar.
But, most of all, the Damsels do delight
When they their timbrels smite,
And thereunto do dance and carol sweet,
That all the senses they do ravish quite;
The whiles the boys run up and down the street,
Crying aloud with strong confusèd noise,

As if it were one voice,
Hymen, iö Hymen, Hymen, they do shout;
That even to the heavens their shouting shrill
Doth reach, and all the firmament doth fill;
To which the people standing all about,
As in approvance, do thereto applaud,
And loud advance her laud;
And evermore they Hymen, Hymen sing,
That all the woods them answer, and their echo ring.

Lo! where she comes along with portly pace,
Like Phœbe, from her chamber of the East,
Arising forth to run her mighty race,
Clad all in white, that seems a virgin best.
So well it her beseems, that ye would ween
Some angel she had been.
Her long loose yellow locks like golden wire,
Sprinkled with pearl, and pearling flowers atween,
Do like a golden mantle her attire;
And, being crownèd with a garland green,
Seem like some maiden queen.
Her modest eyes, abashèd to behold
So many gazers as on her do stare,
Upon the lowly ground affixèd are;
Nor dare lift up her countenance too bold,
But blush to hear her praises sung so loud,
So far from being proud.
Nathless do ye still loud her praises sing,
That all the woods may answer, and your echo ring.

Tell me, ye merchants' daughters, did ye see
So fair a creature in your town before;
So sweet, so lovely, and so mild as she,
Adorned with beauty's grace and virtue's store?
Her goodly eyes like sapphires shining bright,
Her forehead ivory white,
Her cheeks like apples which the sun hath ruddied,
Her lips like cherries charming men to bite,
Her breast like to a bowl of cream uncrudded,
Her paps like lilies budded,
Her snowy neck like to a marble tower;
And all her body like a palace fair,
Ascending up, with many a stately stair,
To honor's seat and chastity's sweet bower.
Why stand ye still, ye virgins, in amaze,
Upon her so to gaze,
Whiles ye forget your former lay to sing,
To which the woods did answer, and your echo ring?

But if ye saw that which no eyes can see,
The inward beauty of her lively spright,
Garnished with heavenly gifts of high degree,
Much more then would ye wonder at that sight,
And stand astonished like to those which read
Medusa's mazeful head.
There dwells sweet love, and constant chastity,
Unspotted faith, and comely womanhood,
Regard of honor, and mild modesty;
There virtue reigns as queen in royal throne,
And giveth laws alone,
The which the base affections do obey,
And yield their services unto her will;
Nor thought of thing uncomely ever may .
Thereto approach to tempt her mind to ill.
Had ye once seen these her celestial treasures,
And unrevealèd pleasures,
Then would ye wonder, and her praises sing,
That all the woods should answer, and your echo ring.

Open the temple gates unto my love,
Open them wide that she may enter in,
And all the posts adorn as doth behove,
And all the pillars deck with garlands trim,
For to receive this Saint with honor due,
That cometh in to you.
With trembling steps, and humble reverence,
She cometh in, before the Almighty's view;
Of her ye virgins learn obedience,
When so ye come into those holy places,
To humble your proud faces:
Bring her up to the high altar, that she may
The sacred ceremonies there partake,
The which do endless matrimony make;
And let the roaring organs loudly play
The praises of the Lord in lively notes;
The whiles, with hollow throats,
The Choristers the joyous Anthems sing,
That all the woods may answer, and their echo ring.

Behold, whiles she before the altar stands,
Hearing the holy priest that to her speaks,
And blesseth her with his two happy hands,
How the red roses flush up in her cheeks,
And the pure snow, with goodly vermill stain
Like crimson dyed in grain:
That even the Angels, which continually
About the sacred altar do remain,
Forget their service and about her fly,

Oft peeping in her face, that seems more fair,
The more they on it stare.
But her sad eyes, still fastened on the ground,
Are governèd with goodly modesty,
That suffers not one look to glance awry,
Which may let in a little thought unsound.
Why blush ye, love, to give to me your hand,
The pledge of all our band?
Sing, ye sweet Angels, Alleluja sing,
That all the woods may answer, and your echo ring.

Now all is done: bring home the bride again;
Bring home the triumph of our victory:
Bring home with you the glory of her gain;
With joyance bring her and with jollity.
Never had man more joyful day than this,
Whom heaven would heap with bliss.
Make feast therefore now all this live-long day;
This day for ever to me holy is.
Pour out the wine without restraint or stay,
Pour not by cups, but by the belly full,
Pour out to all that will,
And sprinkle all the posts and walls with wine,
That they may sweat, and drunken be withal.
Crown ye God Bacchus with a coronal,
And Hymen also crown with wreaths of vine;
And let the Graces dance unto the rest,
For they can do it best:
The whiles the maidens do their carol sing,
To which the woods shall answer, and their echo ring.

Ring ye the bells, ye young men of the town,
And leave your wonted labors for this day:
This day is holy; do ye write it down,
That ye for ever it remember may.
This day the sun is in his chiefest height,
With Barnaby the bright,
From whence declining daily by degrees,
He somewhat loseth of his heat and light,
When once the Crab behind his back he sees.
But for this time it ill ordainèd was,
To choose the longest day in all the year,
And shortest night, when longest fitter were:
Yet never day so long, but late would pass.
Ring ye the bells, to make it wear away,
And bonfires make all day;
And dance about them, and about them sing,
That all the woods may answer, and your echo ring.

Ah! when will this long weary day have end,
And lend me leave to come unto my love?
How slowly do the hours their numbers spend?
How slowly does sad Time his feathers move?
Haste thee, O fairest Planet, to thy home,
Within the Western foam:
Thy tirèd steeds long since have need of rest.
Long though it be, at last I see it gloom,
And the bright evening-star with golden crest
Appear out of the East.
Fair child of beauty! glorious lamp of love!
That all the host of heaven in ranks dost lead,
And guidest lovers through the night's sad dread,
How cheerfully thou lookest from above,
And seems to laugh atween thy twinkling light,
As joying in the sight
Of these glad many, which for joy do sing,
That all the woods them answer, and their echo ring!

Now, cease, ye damsels, your delights fore-past;
Enough is it that all the day was yours:
Now day is done, and night is nighing fast,
Now bring the bride into the bridal bowers.
The night is come, now soon her disarray,
And in her bed her lay;
Lay her in lilies and in violets,
And silken curtains over her display,
And odored sheets, and Arras coverlets.
Behold how goodly my fair love does lie,
In proud humility!
Like unto Maia, when as Jove her took
In Tempe, lying on the flowery grass,
'Twixt sleep and wake, after she weary was,
With bathing in the Acidalian brook.
Now it is night, ye damsels may be gone,
And leave my love alone,
And leave likewise your former lay to sing:
The woods no more shall answer, nor your echo ring.

Now welcome, night! thou night so long expected,
That long day's labor dost at last defray,
And all my cares, which cruel Love collected,
Hast summed in one, and cancellèd for aye:
Spread thy broad wing over my love and me,
That no man may us see;
And in thy sable mantle us enwrap,
From fear of peril and foul horror free.
Let no false treason seek us to entrap,
Nor any dread disquiet once annoy
The safety of our joy;

But let the night be calm, and quietsome,
Without tempestuous storms or sad affray:
Like as when Jove with fair Alcmena lay,
When he begot the great Tirynthian groom:
Or like as when he with thyself did lie
And begot Majesty.
And let the maids and young men cease to sing;
Nor let the woods them answer, nor their echo ring.

Let no lamenting cries, nor doleful tears,
Be heard all night within, nor yet without:
Nor let false whispers, breeding hidden fears,
Break gentle sleep with misconceivèd doubt.
Let no deluding dreams, nor dreadful sights,
Make sudden sad affrights;
Nor let house-fires, nor lightning's helpless harms,
Nor let the Puck, nor other evil sprites,
Nor let mischievous witches with their charms,
Nor let hobgoblins, names whose sense we see not,
Fray us with things that be not:
Let not the screech-owl nor the stork be heard,
Nor the night raven, that still deadly yells;
Nor damnèd ghosts, called up with mighty spells,
Nor grizzly vultures, make us once afraid:
Nor let the unpleasant choir of frogs still croaking
Make us to wish their choking.
Let none of these their dreary accents sing;
Nor let the woods them answer, nor their echo ring.

But let still Silence true night-watches keep,
That sacred Peace may in assurance reign,
And timely Sleep, when it is time to sleep,
May pour his limbs forth on your pleasant plain;
The whiles an hundred little wingèd loves,
Like divers-feathered doves,
Shall fly and flutter round about your bed,
And in the secret dark, that none reproves,
Their pretty stealths shall work, and snares shall spread
To filch away sweet snatches of delight,
Concealed through covert night.
Ye sons of Venus, play your sports at will!
For greedy pleasure, careless of your toys,
Thinks more upon her paradise of joys,
Then what ye do, albeit good or ill.
All night therefore attend your merry play,
For it will soon be day:
Now none doth hinder you, that say or sing;
Nor will the woods now answer, nor your echo ring.

Who is the same, which at my window peeps?
Or whose is that fair face that shines so bright?
Is it not Cynthia, she that never sleeps,
But walks about high heaven all the night?
O! fairest goddess, do thou not envy
My love with me to spy:
For thou likewise didst love, though now unthought,
And for a fleece of wool, which privily
The Latmian shepherd once unto thee brought,
His pleasures with thee wrought.
Therefore to us be favorable now;
And since of women's labors thou hast charge,
And generation goodly dost enlarge,
Incline thy will to effect our wishful vow,
And the chaste womb inform with timely seed,
That may our comfort breed:
Till which we cease our hopeful hap to sing;
Nor let the woods us answer, nor our echo ring.

And thou, great Juno! which with awful might
The laws of wedlock still dost patronize,
And the religion of the faith first plight
With sacred rites hast taught to solemnize;
And eke for comfort often callèd art
Of women in their smart;
Eternally bind thou this lovely band,
And all thy blessings unto us impart.
And thou, glad Genius! in whose gentle hand
The bridal bower and genial bed remain,
Without blemish or stain;
And the sweet pleasures of their love's delight
With secret aid dost succor and supply,
Till they bring forth the fruitful progeny;
Send us the timely fruit of this same night.
And thou, fair Hebe! and thou, Hymen free!
Grant that it may so be.
Till which we cease your further praise to sing;
Nor any woods shall answer, nor your echo ring.

And ye high heavens, the temple of the gods,
In which a thousand torches flaming bright
Do burn, that to us wretched earthly clods
In dreadful darkness lend desirèd light:
And all ye powers which in the same remain,
More than we men can feign,
Pour out your blessing on us plenteously,
And happy influence upon us rain,
That we may raise a large posterity,
Which from the earth, which they may long possess

With lasting happiness,
Up to your haughty palaces may mount;
And, for the guerdon of their glorious merit,
May heavenly tabernacles there inherit,
Of blessèd Saints for to increase the count.
So let us rest, sweet love, in hope of this,
And cease till then our timely joys to sing:
The woods no more us answer, nor our echo ring!

Song! made in lieu of many ornaments,
With which my love should duly have been decked,
Which cutting off through hasty accidents,
Ye would not stay your due time to expect,
But promised both to recompense;
Be unto her a goodly ornament,
And for short time an endless monument.

Prothalamion

CALME was the day, and through the trembling ayre
Sweete-breathing Zephyrus did softly play
A gentle spirit, that lightly did delay
Hot Titans beames, which then did glyster fayre;
When I, (whom sullein care,
Through discontent of my long fruitlesse stay
In Princes Court, and expectation vayne
Of idle hopes, which still doe fly away,
Like empty shaddowes, did afflict my brayne,)
Walkt forth to ease my payne
Along the shoare of silver streaming Themmes;
Whose rutty Bancke, the which his River hemmes,
Was paynted all with variable flowers,
And all the meades adorned with daintie gemmes
Fit to decke maydens bowres,
And crowne their Paramours
Against the Brydale day, which is not long:
Sweete Themmes! runne softly, till I end my Song.

There, in a Meadow, by the Rivers side,
A Flocke of Nymphes I chauncèd to espy, — nymphs
All lovely Daughters of the Flood thereby,
With goodly greenish locks, all loose untyde,
As each had bene a Bryde;
And each one had a little wicker basket,
Made of fine twigs, entraylèd curiously,
In which they gathered flowers to fill their flasket,
And with fine Fingers cropt full feateously
The tender stalkes on hye.

Of every sort, which in that Meadow grew,
They gathered some; the Violet, pallid blew,
The little Dazie, that at evening closes,
The virgin Lillie, and the Primrose trew,
With store of vermeil Roses,
To decke their Bridegromes posies
Against the Brydale day, which was not long:
   Sweete Themmes! runne softly, till I end my Song.

With that I saw two Swannes of goodly hewe
Come softly swimming downe along the Lee;
Two fairer Birds I yet did never see;
The snow, which doth the top of Pindus strew,
Did never whiter shew;
Nor Jove himselfe, when he a Swan would be,   *Leda*
For love of Leda, whiter did appeare;
Yet Leda was (they say) as white as he,
Yet not so white as these, nor nothing neare;
So purely white they were,
That even the gentle streame, the which them bare,
Seem'd foule to them, and bad his billowes spare
To wet their silken feathers, least they might
Soyle their fayre plumes with water not so fayre,
And marre their beauties bright,
That shone as heavens light,
Against their Brydale day, which was not long:
   Sweete Themmes! runne softly, till I end my Song.

Eftsoones the Nymphes, which now had Flowers their fill,
Ran all in haste to see that silver brood,
As they came floating on the Christal Flood;
Whom when they sawe, they stood amazèd still,
Their wondring eyes to fill;
Them seem'd they never saw a sight so fayre,
Of Fowles, so lovely, that they sure did deeme
Them heavenly borne, or to be that same payre
Which through the Skie draw Venus silver Teeme;
For sure they did not seeme
To be begot of any earthly Seede,
But rather Angels, or of Angels breede;
Yet were they bred of Somers-heat, they say,
In sweetest Season, when each Flower and weede
The earth did fresh aray;
So fresh they seem'd as day,
Even as their Brydale day, which was not long:
   Sweete Themmes! runne softly, till I end my Song.

Then forth they all out of their baskets drew
Great store of Flowers, the honour of the field,
That to the sense did fragrant odours yield.

All which upon those goodly Birds they threw
And all the Waves did strew,
That like old Peneus Waters they did seeme,
When downe along by pleasant Tempes shore,
Scattred with Flowres, through Thessaly they streeme,
That they appeare, through Lillies plenteous store,
Like a Brydes Chamber flore.
Two of those Nymphes, meane while, two Garlands bound
Of freshest Flowres which in that Mead they found,
The which presenting all in trim Array,
Their snowie Foreheads therewithall they crown'd,
Whil'st one did sing this Lay,
Prepar'd against that Day,
Against their Brydale day, which was not long:
  Sweete Themmes! runne softly, till I end my Song.

"Ye gentle Birdes! the worlds faire ornament,
And heavens glorie, whom this happie hower
Doth leade unto your lovers blisfull bower,
Joy may you have, and gentle hearts content
Of your loves couplement;
And let faire Venus, that is Queene of love,
With her heart-quelling Sonne upon you smile,
Whose smile, they say, hath vertue to remove
All Loves dislike, and friendships faultie guile
For ever to assoile.
Let endlesse Peace your steadfast hearts accord,
And blessèd Plentie wait upon your bord;
And let your bed with pleasures chast abound,
That fruitfull issue may to you afford,
Which may your foes confound,
And make your joyes redound
Upon your Brydale day, which is not long:
  Sweete Themmes! runne softlie, till I end my Song."

So ended she; and all the rest around
To her redoubled that her undersong,
Which said their brydale daye should not be long:
And gentle Eccho from the neighbor ground
Their accents did resound.
So forth those joyous Birdes did passe along,
Adowne the Lee, that to them murmurde low,
As he would speake, but that he lackt a tong,
Yet did by signes his glad affection show,
Making his streame run slow.
And all the foule which in his flood did dwell
Gan flock about these twaine, that did excell
The rest, so far as Cynthia doth shend
The lesser starres. So they, enrangèd well,
Did on those two attend.

And their best service lend
Against their wedding day, which was not long:
   Sweete Themmes! runne softly, till I end my Song.

At length they all to mery London came,
To mery London, my most kyndly Nurse,
That to me gave this Life's first native source,
Though from another place I take my name,
An house an auncient fame:
There when they came, whereas those bricky towres
The which on Themmes brode agèd backe doe ryde,
Where now the studious Lawyers have their bowers,
There whylome wont the Templer Knights to byde,
Till they decayd through pride:
Next whereunto there standes a stately place,
Where oft I gaynèd giftes and goodly grace
Of that great Lord, which therein wont to dwell,
Whose want too well now feeles my freendles case;
But ah! here fits not well
Olde woes, but joyes, to tell
Against the Brydale daye, which is not long:
   Sweete Themmes! runne softly, till I end my Song.

Yet therein now doth lodge a noble Peer,
Great Englands glory, and the Worlds wide wonder,
Whose dreadfull name late through all Spaine did thunder,
And Hercules two pillors standing neere
Did make to quake and feare:
Faire branch of Honor, flower of Chevalrie!
That fillest England with thy triumphes fame,
Joy have thou of thy noble victorie,
And endless happinesse of thine owne name
That promiseth the same;
That through thy prowesse, and victorious armes,
Thy country may be freed from forraine harmes;
And great Elisaes glorious name may ring
Through al the world, fil'd with thy wide Alarmes,
Which some brave muse may sing
To ages following,
Upon the Brydale day, which is not long:
   Sweete Themmes! runne softly, till I end my Song.

From those high Towers this noble Lord issuing,
Like Radiant Hesper, when his golden hayre
In th' Ocean billowes he hath bathèd fayre,
Descended to the Rivers open vewing,
With a great traine ensuing.
Above the rest were goodly to bee seene
Two gentle Knights of lovely face and feature,
Beseeming well the bower of anie Queene,

With gifts of wit, and ornaments of nature,
Fit for so goodly stature,
That like the twins of Jove they seem'd in sight,
Which decke the Bauldricke of the Heavens bright;
They two, forth pacing to the River's side,
Received those two faire Brides, their Loves delight;
Which, at th' appointed tyde,
Each one did make his Bryde
Against their Brydale day, which is not long:
    Sweete Themmes! runne softly, till I end my Song.

Sonnets

FRESH Spring, the herald of love's mighty king
    In whose coat-armour richly are displayed
All sorts of flowers the which on earth do spring,
In goodly colors gloriously arrayed;
Go to my love where she is careless laid
Yet in her winter's bower not well awake;
Tell her the joyous time will not be stayed
Unless she do him by the forelock take;
Bid her, therefore, herself soon ready make
To wait on Love among his lovely crew;
Where every one that misseth then her make
Shall be by him amerced with pennance due.
Make haste, therefore, sweet Love, while it is prime,
For none can call again the passèd time.

Oft when my spirit doth spread her bolder wings,
In mind to mount up to the purest sky,
It down is weighed with thought of earthly things,
And clogged with burden of mortality;
Where when that sovereign beauty it doth spy,
Resembling heaven's glory in her light,
Drawn with sweet pleasure's bait it back doth fly,
And unto heaven forgets her former flight.
There my frail fancy, fed with full delight,
Doth bathe in bliss, and mantleth most at ease;
Me thinks of other heaven but how it might
Her heart's desire with most contentment please.
Heart need not wish none other happiness
But here on earth to have such heaven's bliss.

One day I wrote her name upon the strand;
But come the waves and washèd it away:
Again I wrote it with a second hand,
But come the tide and made my pains his prey.
Vain man! said she, that dost in vain assay

A mortal thing to immortalize;
For I myself shall like to this decay,
And eke my name be wipèd out likewise.
Not so, quoth I; let base things devise
To die in dust, but you shall live by fame:
My verse your virtues rare shall eternize,
And in the heavens write your glorious name,—
Where, whereas death shall all the world subdue,
Our love shall live, and later life renew.

JOHN LYLY (1553-1606)

Cupid and Campaspe

CUPID and my Campaspe played
    At cards for kisses; Cupid paid:
He stakes his quiver, bow, and arrows,
His mother's doves, and team of sparrows;
Loses them too; then down he throws
The coral of his lip, the rose
Growing on's cheek (but none knows how);
With these, the crystal of his brow,
And then the dimple on his chin;
All these did my Campaspe win:
And last he set her both his eyes—
She won, and Cupid blind did rise.
    O Love! has she done this to thee?
    What shall, alas! become of me?

The Fairy Frolic

BY the moon we sport and play,
    With the night begins our day:
As we frisk the dew doth fall:
Trip it, little urchins all!
Lightly as the little bee,
Two by two, and three by three:
And about go we, and about go we!

SIR PHILIP SIDNEY (1554-1586)

Sonnets from "Astrophel and Stella"

LOVING in truth, and fain in verse my love to show,
    That She, dear She! might take some pleasure of my pain;
Pleasure might cause her read, reading might make her know,
Knowledge might pity win, and pity grace obtain:

I sought fit words to paint the blackest face of woe,
Studying inventions fine, her wits to entertain;
Oft turning others' leaves, to see if thence would flow
Some fresh and fruitful showers upon my sunburnt brain:
But words came halting forth, wanting Invention's stay.
Invention, Nature's child, fled step-dame Study's blows;
And others' feet still seemed but strangers in my way.
Thus, great with child to speak, and helpless in my throes,
  Biting my truant pen, beating myself for spite:
  "Fool!" said my Muse to me, "look in thy heart, and write!"

With how sad steps, O Moon, thou climb'st the skies!
How silently, and with how wan a face!
What! may it be that even in heavenly place
That busy archer his sharp arrows tries?
Sure, if that long-with-love-acquainted eyes
Can judge of love, thou feel'st a lover's case;
I read it in thy looks. Thy languished grace
To me, that feel the like, thy state descries.
Then, even of fellowship, O Moon, tell me,
Is constant love deemed there but want of wit?
Are beauties there as proud as here they be?
Do they above love to be loved, and yet
  Those lovers scorn whom that love doth possess?
  Do they call virtue there, ungratefulness?

Come Sleep! O Sleep, the certain knot of peace,
The baiting-place of wit, the balm of woe,
The poor man's wealth, the prisoner's release,
The indifferent judge between the high and low!
With shield of proof, shield me from out the press
Of those fierce darts Despair at me doth throw:
O make in me those civil wars to cease!
I will good tribute pay if thou do so.
Take thou of me, smooth pillows, sweetest bed,
A chamber deaf to noise and blind to light,
A rosy garland, and a weary head:
And if these things, as being thine in right,
Move not thy heavy grace, thou shalt in me
Livelier than elsewhere, Stella's image see.

Thou blind man's mark, thou fool's self-chosen snare,
Fond fancy's scum, and dregs of scattered thought:
Band of all evils; cradles of causeless care;
Thou web of will, whose end is never wrought:
Desire! Desire! I have too dearly bought,
With price of mangled mind, thy worthless ware;
Too long, too long, asleep thou hast me brought,
Who should my mind to higher things prepare.

But yet in vain thou hast my ruin sought;
In vain thou mad'st me to vain things aspire;
In vain thou kindlest all thy smoky fire;
For Virtue hath this better lesson taught,—
Within myself to seek my only hire,
Desiring nought but how to kill Desire.

Leave me, O Love, which reachest but to dust;
And thou, my mind, aspire to higher things;
Grow rich in that which never taketh rust;
Whatever fades, but fading pleasure brings.
Draw in thy beams, and humble all thy might
To that sweet yoke where lasting freedoms be;
Which breaks the clouds, and opens forth the light
That doth both shine, and give us sight to see.
O take fast hold; let that light be thy guide
In this small course which birth draws out to death,
And think how ill becometh him to slide,
Who seeketh heaven, and comes of heavenly breath.
Then farewell, world; thy uttermost I see:
Eternal Love, maintain thy life in me!

Song from "Astrophel and Stella"

O NELY Joy, now here you are,
    Fit to heare and ease my care,
Let my whispering voyce obtaine
Sweete reward for sharpest paine;
Take me to thee, and thee to me:
"No, no, no, no, my Deare, let be."

Night hath clos'd all in her cloke,
Twinkling starres love-thoughts provoke,
Danger hence, good care doth keepe,
Jealouzie itself doth sleepe;
Take me to thee, and thee to me:
"No, no, no, no, my Deare, let be."

Better place no wit can find,
Cupid's yoke to loose or binde;
These sweet flowers on fine bed too,
Us in their best language woo;
Take me to thee, and thee to me:
"No, no, no, no, my Deare, let be."

This small light the moone bestowes
Serves thy beames but to disclose;
So to raise my hap more hie,

Feare not else none can us spie;
Take me to thee, and thee to me:
"No, no, no, no, my Deare, let be."

That you heard was but a mouse,
Dumbe sleepe holdeth all the house:
Yet asleepe, me thinkes they say,
Yong folkes take time while you may;
Take me to thee, and thee to me:
"No, no, no, no, my Deare, let be."

Niggard time threats, if we misse
This large offer of our blisse,
Long stay, ere he graunt the same:
Sweet, then, while ech thing doth frame,
Take me to thee, and thee to me:
"No, no, no, no, my Deare, let be."

Your faire mother is a-bed,
Candles out and curtaines spread;
She thinkes you do letters write;
Write, but let me first endite;
Take me to thee, and thee to me:
"No, no, no, no, my Deare, let be."

Sweet, alas, why strive you thus?
Concord better fitteth us;
Leave to Mars the force of hands
Your power in your beautie stands;
Take thee to me, and me to thee:
"No, no, no, no, my Deare, let be."

Wo to me, and do you sweare
Me to hate? but I forbeare;
Cursèd be my destinies all,
That brought me so high to fall;
Soone with my death I will please thee:
"No, no, no, no, my Deare, let be."

From the "Arcadia"

MY true-love hath my heart, and I have his,
    By just exchange one for the other given:
I hold his dear, and mine he cannot miss;
    There never was a better bargain driven:
His heart in me keeps him and me in one,
    My heart in him his thoughts and senses guides:

He loves my heart, for once it was his own,
  I cherish his, because in me it bides.
His heart his wound receivèd from my sight;
  My heart was wounded from his wounded heart;
For as from me, on him his hurt did light,
  So still me thought in me his heart did smart:
Both equal hurt, in this change sought our bliss,
My true love hath my heart, and I have his.

A Dirge

RING out your bells, let mourning shews be spread;
  For Love is dead:
    All Love is dead, infected
With plague of deep disdain:
    Worth, as nought worth, rejected,
And Faith fair scorn doth gain.
    From so ungrateful fancy,
    From such a female frenzy,
    From them that use men thus,
    Good Lord, deliver us!

Weep, neighbors, weep; do you not hear it said
That Love is dead?
    His death-bed, peacock's folly:
His winding-sheet is shame;
    His will, false-seeming wholly;
His sole executor, blame.
    From so ungrateful fancy,
    From such a female frenzy,
    From them that use men thus,
    Good Lord, deliver us!

Let Dirge be sung, and Treutals rightly read,
For Love is dead;
    Sir Wrong his tomb ordaineth
My mistress marble-heart,
    Which epitaph containeth,
"Her eyes were once his dart."
    From so ungrateful fancy,
    From such a female frenzy,
    From that that use men thus,
    Good Lord, deliver us!

Alas, I lie: rage hath this error bred;
Love is not dead;

Love is not dead, but sleepeth
In her unmatchèd mind,
    Where she his counsel keepeth,
Till due desert she find.
    Therefore from so vile fancy,
    To call such wit a frenzy,
    Who Love can temper thus,
    Good Lord, deliver us!

THOMAS LODGE (1556-1625)

Rosalind's Madrigal, from "Rosalind"

LOVE in my bosom like a bee
        Doth suck his sweet:
Now with his wings he plays with me,
        Now with his feet.
Within mine eyes he makes his nest,
His bed amidst my tender breast;
My kisses are his daily feast,
And yet he robs me of my rest:
        Ah! wanton, will ye?

And if I sleep, then percheth he
        With pretty flight,
And makes his pillow of my knee
        The livelong night.
Strike I my lute, he tunes the string;
He music plays if so I sing;
He lends me every lovely thing,
Yet cruel he my heart doth sting:
        Whist, wanton, still ye!

Else I with roses every day
        Will whip you hence,
And bind you, when you long to play,
        For your offence.
I'll shut mine eyes to keep you in;
I'll make you fast it for your sin;
I'll count your power not worth a pin.
—Alas! what hereby shall I win
        If he gainsay me?

What if I beat the wanton boy
        With many a rod?
He will repay me with annoy,
        Because a god.

Then sit thou safely on my knee;
Then let thy bower my bosom be;
Lurk in mine eyes, I like of thee;
O Cupid, so thou pity me,
     Spare not, but play thee!

GEORGE PEELE (1558?-1597?)

A Farewell to Arms

(*To Queen Elizabeth*)

HIS golden locks Time hath to silver turned:
  O Time too swift, O swiftness never ceasing!
His youth 'gainst time and age hath ever spurned,
  But spurned in vain; youth waneth by increasing:
Beauty, strength, youth, are flowers but fading seen;
Duty, faith, love, are roots, and ever green.

His helmet now shall make a hive for bees;
  And lovers' sonnets turned to holy psalms,
A man-at-arms must now serve on his knees,
  And feed on prayers, which are Age his alms:
But though from court to cottage he depart,
His Saint is sure of his unspotted heart.

And when he saddest sits in homely cell,
  He'll teach his swains this carol for a song,—
"Blest be the hearts that wish my sovereign well,
  Curst be the souls that think her any wrong."
Goddess, allow this aged man his right
To be your beadsman now that was your knight.

From "The Love of King David and Fair Bethsabe"

DAVID. Bright Bethsabe shall wash in David's bower,
  In water mixed with purest almost flower,
And bathe her beauty in the milk of kids;
Bright Bethsabe gives earth to my desires,
Verdure to earth, and to that verdure flowers,
To flowers sweet odors, and to odors wings,
That carries pleasures to the hearts of kings.
    *   *   *   *   *   *
Now comes my lover tripping like the roe,
And brings my longings tangled in her hair.
To 'joy her love I'll build a kingly bower.

Seated in hearing of a hundred streams,
That, for their homage to her sovereign joys,
Shall, as the serpents fold into their nests,
In oblique turnings wind the nimble waves
About the circles of her curious walks,
And with their murmur summon easeful sleep,
To lay his golden sceptre on his brows.

ROBERT GREENE (1560?-1592)

Sephestia's Lullaby

WEEP not, my wanton, smile upon my knee:
　　When thou art old there's grief enough for thee.
　　Mother's wag, pretty boy,
　　Father's sorrow, father's joy;
　　When thy father first did see
　　Such a boy by him and me,
　　He was glad, I was woe;
　　Fortune changèd made him so,
　　When he left his pretty boy,
　　Last his sorrow, first his joy.

Weep not, my wanton, smile upon my knee;
When thou art old there's grief enough for thee.
　　Streaming tears that never stint,
　　Like pearl-drops from a flint,
　　Fell by course from his eyes,
　　That one another's place supplies;
　　Thus he grieved in every part,
　　Tears of blood fell from his heart,
　　When he left his pretty boy,
　　Father's sorrow, father's joy.

Weep not, my wanton, smile upon my knee;
When thou art old there's grief enough for thee.
　　The wanton smiled, father wept,
　　Mother cried, baby leapt;
　　More he crowed, more we cried,
　　Nature could not sorrow hide:
　　He must go, he must kiss
　　Child and mother, baby bliss,
　　For he left his pretty boy,
　　Father's sorrow, father's joy.
Weep not, my wanton, smile upon my knee;
When thou art old there's grief enough for thee.

SAMUEL DANIEL (1562-1619)

From "To Delia"

WHEN men shall find thy flower, thy glory pass,
  And thou, with careful brow, sitting alone,
Receivèd hast this message from thy glass,
That tells the truth, and says that *All is gone;*
Fresh shalt thou see in me the wounds thou madest,
Though spent thy flame, in me the heat remaining:
I that have loved thee thus before thou fadest,
My faith shall wax, when thou art in thy waning!
The world shall find this miracle in me,
That fire can burn when all the matter's spent:
Then what my faith hath been, thyself shalt see,
And that thou wast unkind, thou may'st repent!
  Thou may'st repent that thou hast scorned my tears,
  When Winter snows upon thy golden hairs.

Care-charmer Sleep, son of the sable Night,
Brother to Death, in silent darkness born:
Relieve my languish, and restore the light;
With dark forgetting of my care, return!
And let the day be time enough to mourn
The shipwreck of my ill-adventured youth:
Let waking eyes suffice to wail their scorn,
Without the torment of the night's untruth.
Cease, dreams, the images of day-desires,
To model forth the passions of the morrow;
Never let rising sun approve you liars,
To add more grief to aggravate my sorrow.
  Still let me sleep, embracing clouds in vain;
  And never wake to feel the day's disdain.

HENRY CONSTABLE (1562-1613)

MY Lady's presence makes the Roses red,
  Because to see her lips they blush for shame.
The Lily's leaves, for envy, pale became;
And her white hands in them this envy bred.
The Marigold the leaves abroad doth spread,
Because the sun's and her power is the same.
The Violet of purple color came,
Dyed in the blood she made my heart to shed.

In brief, all flowers from her their virtue take;
From her sweet breath their sweet smells do proceed;
The living heat, which her eye-beams do make,
Warmeth the ground, and quickeneth the seed.
The rain, wherewith she watereth these flowers,
Falls from mine eyes, which she dissolves in showers.

MICHAEL DRAYTON (1563-1631)

Agincourt (*October* 25, 1415)

FAIR stood the wind for France
  When we our sails advance,
Nor now to prove our chance
  Longer will tarry;
But putting to the main,
At Caux, the mouth of Seine,
With all his martial train
  Landed King Harry.

And taking many a fort,
Furnished in warlike sort,
Marcheth towards Agincourt
  In happy hour;
Skirmishing day by day
With those that stopped his way,
Where the French general lay
  With all his power.

Which, in his height of pride,
King Henry to deride,
His ransom to provide
  Unto him sending;
Which he neglects the while
As from a nation vile,
Yet with an angry smile
  Their fall portending.

And turning to his men,
Quoth our brave Henry then,
"Though they to one be ten
  Be not amazèd:
Yet have we well begun:
Battles so bravely won
Have ever to the sun
  By fame been raisèd.

"And for myself (quoth he)
This my full rest shall be:
England ne'er mourn for me
  Nor more esteem me:
Victor I will remain
Or on this earth lie slain,
Never shall she sustain
  Loss to redeem me.

"Poitiers and Cressy tell,
When most their pride did swell,
Under our swords they fell:
    No less our skill is
Than when our grandsire great
Claiming the regal seat,
By many a warlike feat
    Lopped the French lilies."

The Duke of York so dread
The eager vanguard led;
With the main Henry sped
    Among his henchmen.
Excester had the rear,
A braver man not there;
O Lord, how hot they were
    On the false Frenchmen!

They now to fight are gone,
Armor on armor shone,
Drum now to drum did groan,
    To hear was wonder;
That with the cries they make
The very earth did shake:
Trumpet to trumpet spake,
    Thunder to thunder.

Well it thine age became,
O noble Erpingham,
Which didst the signal aim
    To our hid forces!
When from a meadow by,
Like a storm suddenly
The English archery
    Struck the French horses.

With Spanish yew so strong,
Arrows a cloth-yard long
That like to serpents stung,
    Piercing the weather;
None from his fellow starts,
But playing manly parts,
And like true English hearts
    Stuck close together.

When down their bows they threw,
And forth their bilbos drew,
And on the French they flew,
    Not one was tardy;

Arms were from shoulders sent,
Scalps to the teeth were rent,
Down the French peasants went—
    Our men were hardy.

This while our noble king,
His broadsword brandishing,
Down the French host did ding
    As to o'erwhelm it;
And many a deep wound lent,
His arms with blood besprent,
And many a cruel dent
    Bruisèd his helmet.

Gloster, that duke so good,
Next of the royal blood,
For famous England stood
    With his brave brother;
Clarence, in steel so bright,
Though but a maiden knight.
Yet in that furious fight
    Scarce such another.

Warwick in blood did wade,
Oxford the foe invade,
And cruel slaughter made
    Still as they ran up;
Suffolk his axe did ply,
Beaumont and Willoughby
Bare them right doughtily,
    Ferrers and Fanhope.

Upon Saint Crispin's Day
Fought was this noble fray,
Which fame did not delay
    To England to carry.
O when shall English men
With such acts fill a pen?
Or England breed again
    Such a King Harry?

The Parting

SINCE there's no help, come, let us kiss and part!
  Nay, I have done. You get no more of me!
And I am glad, yea, glad with all my heart,
That thus so cleanly I myself can free.
Shake hands for ever! Cancel all our vows!
And when we meet at any time again.

Be it not seen in either of our brows
That we one jot of former love retain.
Now at the last gasp of Love's latest breath,
When, his pulse failing, Passion speechless lies,
When Faith is kneeling by his bed of death,
And Innocence is closing up his eyes:
   Now, if thou wouldst, when all have given him over,
   From death to life thou might'st him yet recover!

CHRISTOPHER MARLOWE (1564-1593)

From "The Life and Death of Dr. Faustus"

WAS this the face that launch'd a thousand ships
   And burn'd the topless towers of Ilium?
Sweet Helen, make me immortal with a kiss!
Her lips suck forth my soul—see where it flies.
Come, Helen, come give me my soul again;
Here will I dwell, for heaven is in these lips,
And all is dross that is not Helena.
O thou art fairer than the evening air,
Clad in the beauty of a thousand stars!

Chorus on the Death of Faustus

CUT is the branch that might have grown full straight,
   And burnèd is Apollo's laurel bough
That sometime grew within this learned man:
Faustus is gone!

The Passionate Shepherd to His Love

COME live with me and be my Love,
   And we will all the pleasures prove
That hills and valleys, dales and fields,
Or woods or steepy mountain yields.

And we will sit upon the rocks,
And see the shepherds feed their flocks
By shallow rivers, to whose falls
Melodious birds sing madrigals.

And I will make thee beds of roses
And a thousand fragrant posies;
A cap of flowers, and a kirtle
Embroidered all with leaves of myrtle.

A gown made of the finest wool
Which from our pretty lambs we pull;
Fair-linèd slippers for the cold,
With buckles of the purest gold.

A belt of straw and ivy-buds
With coral clasps and amber studs:
And if these pleasures may thee move,
Come live with me and be my Love.

The shepherd swains shall dance and sing
For thy delight each May morning:
If these delights thy mind may move,
Then live with me and be my Love.

WALTER RALEIGH (1552?-1618)

The Nymph's Reply to the Passionate Shepherd

IF all the world and love were young,
  And truth in every shepherd's tongue,
These pretty pleasures might me move
To live with thee, and be thy Love.

But Time drives flocks from field to fold;
When rivers rage and rocks grow cold;
And Philomel becometh dumb;
The rest complains of cares to come.

The flowers do fade, and wanton fields
To wayward Winter reckoning yields:
A honey tongue, a heart of gall,
Is fancy's spring, but sorrow's fall.

Thy gowns, thy shoes, thy beds of roses,
Thy cap, thy kirtle, and thy posies,
Soon break, soon wither,—soon forgotten
In folly ripe, in reason rotten.

Thy belt of straw and ivy-buds,
Thy coral clasps and amber studs,—
All these in me no means can move
To come to thee and be thy Love.

But could youth last, and love still breed,
Had joys no date, nor age no need,
Then these delights my mind might move
To live with thee and be thy Love.

WILLIAM SHAKESPEARE (1564-1616)

Song from "The Two Gentlemen of Verona"

WHO is Silvia? What is she?
    That all our swains commend her?
Holy, fair, and wise is she;
    The heaven such grace did lend her,
That she might admirèd be.

Is she kind as she is fair?
    For beauty lives with kindness:
Love doth to her eyes repair,
    To help him of his blindness;
And, being helped, inhabits there.

Then to Silvia let us sing,
    That Silvia is excelling;
She excels each mortal thing
    Upon the dull earth dwelling:
To her let us garlands bring.

Songs from "Love's Labour Lost"

I

WHEN daisies pied, and violets blue,
    And lady-smocks all silver-white,
And cuckoo-buds of yellow hue,
    Do paint the meadows with delight,
The cuckoo then, on every tree,
Mocks married men; for thus sings he,
            Cuckoo;
Cuckoo, cuckoo,—O word of fear,
Unpleasing to a married ear!

When shepherds pipe on oaten straws,
    And merry larks are ploughmen's clocks,
When turtles tread, and rooks, and daws,
    And maidens bleach their summer smocks,
The cuckoo then, on every tree,
Mocks married men; for thus sings he,
            Cuckoo;

Cuckoo, cuckoo,—O word of fear,
Unpleasing to a married ear!

II

When icicles hang by the wall,
  And Dick the shepherd blows his nail,
And Tom bears logs into the hall,
  And milk comes frozen home in pail,
When blood is nipped, and ways be foul,
Then nightly sings the staring owl,
      Tu-who;
Tu-whit, tu-who,—a merry note,
While greasy Joan doth keel the pot.

When all aloud the wind doth blow,
  And coughing drowns the parson's saw,
And birds sit brooding in the snow,
  And Marian's nose looks red and raw,
When roasted crabs hiss in the bowl,
Then nightly sings the staring owl,
      Tu-who;
Tu-whit, tu-who,—a merry note,
While greasy Joan doth keel the pot.

Songs from "A Midsummer-Night's Dream"

I

OVER hill, over dale,
    Through bush, through brier,
Over park, over pale,
  Through flood, through fire,
    I do wander everywhere,
    Swifter than the moonè's sphere;
    And I serve the fairy queen,
    To dew her orbs upon the green:
    The cowslips tall her pensioners be;
    In their gold coats spots you see;
    Those be rubies, fairy favors,
    In those freckles live their savors:
I must go seek some dew-drops here,
And hang a pearl in every cowslip's ear.

II

You spotted snakes with double tongue,
  Thorny hedgehogs, be not seen;
Newts and blind-worms, do no wrong;
  Come not near our fairy queen

Philomel, with melody,
    Sing in our sweet lullaby;
Lulla, lulla, lullaby; lulla, lulla, lullaby!
    Never harm,
    Nor spell nor charm,
    Come our lovely lady nigh;
    So, good night, with lullaby.

Weaving spiders, come not here;
    Hence, you long-legged spinners, hence!
Beetles black, approach not near;
    Worm nor snail, do no offence.

Philomel, with melody,
    Sing in our sweet lullaby;
Lulla, lulla, lullaby; lulla, lulla, lullaby!
    Never harm,
    Nor spell nor charm,
    Come our lovely lady nigh;
    So, good night, with lullaby.

Songs from "As You Like It"

I

UNDER the greenwood tree,
    Who loves to lie with me,
And turn his merry note
Unto the sweet bird's throat,
Come hither, come hither, come hither:
    Here shall he see
    No enemy
But winter and rough weather.

Who doth ambition shun,
And loves to live i' the sun,
Seeking the food he eats,
And pleased with what he gets,
Come hither, come hither, come hither:
    Here shall he see
    No enemy
But winter and rough weather.

II

Blow, blow, thou winter wind,
Thou art not so unkind
    As man's ingratitude;

Thy tooth is not so keen,
Because thou art not seen,
   Although thy breath be rude.
Heigh-ho! sing heigh-ho! unto the green holly;
Most friendship is feigning, most loving mere folly:
   Then, heigh-ho, the holly!
   This life is most jolly!

Freeze, freeze, thou bitter sky,
Thou dost not bite so nigh
   As benefits forgot:
Though thou the waters warp,
Thy sting is not so sharp
   As friend remembered not.
Heigh-ho! sing heigh-ho! unto the green holly;
Most friendship is feigning, most loving mere folly:
   Then, heigh-ho, the holly!
   This life is most jolly!

III

It was a lover and his lass,
   With a hey, and a ho, and a hey nonino,
That o'er the green corn-field did pass,
   In the spring time, the only pretty ring time,
When birds do sing, hey ding a ding, ding;
Sweet lovers love the spring.

Between the acres of the rye,
   With a hey, and a ho, and a hey nonino,
These pretty country folks would lie,
   In the spring time, the only pretty ring time,
When birds do sing, hey ding a ding, ding;
Sweet lovers love the spring.

This carol they began that hour,
   With a hey, and a ho, and a hey nonino,
How that life was but a flower
   In the spring time, the only pretty ring time,
When birds do sing, hey ding a ding, ding;
Sweet lovers love the spring.

And, therefore, take the present time
   With a hey, and a ho, and a hey nonino,
For love is crownèd with the prime
   In the spring time, the only pretty ring time,
When birds do sing, hey ding a ding, ding;
Sweet lovers love the spring.

Song from "Much Ado About Nothing"

SIGH no more, ladies, sigh no more,
   Men were deceivers ever:
One foot in sea, and one on shore;
   To one thing constant never.
     Then sigh not so,
     But let them go,
   And be you blithe and bonny,
Converting all your sounds of woe
   Into Hey nonny, nonny.

Sing no more ditties, sing no moe
   Of dumps so dull and heavy;
The fraud of men was ever so,
   Since summer first was leavy.
     Then sigh not so,
     But let them go,
   And be you blithe and bonny,
Converting all your sounds of woe
   Into Hey nonny, nonny.

Song from "Hamlet"

HOW should I your true love know
   From another one?
By his cockle hat and staff,
   And his sandal shoon.

He is dead and gone, lady,
   He is dead and gone;
At his head a grass-green turf,
   At his heels a stone.

White his shroud as the mountain snow,
   Larded all with sweet flowers,
Which bewept to the grave did go
   With true-love showers.

Song from "Twelfth Night"

O mistress mine, where are you roaming?
   O stay and hear; your true Love's coming,
That can sing both high and low:
Trip no further, pretty Sweeting;
Journeys end in lovers meeting,
   Every wise man's son doth know.

What is love? 'tis not hereafter;
Present mirth hath present laughter;
  What's to come is still unsure:
In delay there lies no plenty:
Then come kiss me, sweet-and-twenty,
  Youth's a stuff will not endure.

Songs from "Measure for Measure" *

I

TAKE, O take those lips away,
      That so sweetly were forsworn;
And those eyes, the break of day,
    Lights that do mislead the morn:
But my kisses bring again, bring again;
Sealed of love, but sealed in vain, sealed in vain.

II

Hide, O hide those hills of snow,
  Which thy frozen bosom bears,
On whose tops the pinks that grow
  Are of those April wears!
But first set my poor heart free,
Bound in those icy chains by thee.

Songs from "Cymbeline"

I

HARK, hark! the lark at heaven's gate sings,
    And Phœbus 'gins arise,
His steeds to water at those springs
  On chaliced flowers that lies;
And winking Mary-buds begin
  To ope their golden eyes:
With everything that pretty bin,
  My lady sweet, arise:
    Arise, arise.

II

Fear no more the heat o' the sun
  Nor the furious winter's rages;

* Second stanza from "The Bloody Brother."
                    John Fletcher (1570-1625)

Thou thy worldly task hast done,
   Home art gone and ta'en thy wages:
Golden lads and girls all must,
As chimney-sweepers, come to dust.

Fear no more the frown o' the great,
   Thou art past the tyrant's stroke;
Care no more to clothe and eat;
   To thee the reed is as the oak:
The scepter, learning, physic, must
All follow this, and come to dust.

Fear no more the lightning-flash
   Nor the all-dreaded thunder-stone;
Fear not slander, censure rash;
   Thou hast finished joy and moan:
All lovers young, all lovers must
Consign to thee, and come to dust.

Song from "The Winter's Tale"

WHEN daffodils begin to peer,
   With heigh! the doxy, over the dale,
Why, then comes in the sweet o' the year;
   For the red blood reigns in the winter's pale.

The white sheet bleaching on the hedge,
   With heigh! the sweet birds, O how they sing!
Doth set my pugging tooth on edge;
   For a quart of ale is a dish for a king.

The lark, that tirra-lirra chants,
   With heigh! with heigh! the thrush and the jay,
Are summer songs for me and my aunts,
   While we lie tumbling in the hay.

Songs from "The Tempest"

I

COME unto these yellow sands,
   And then take hands:
Court'sied when you have, and kissed,—
   The wild waves whist.—
Foot it featly here and there:
And. sweet sprites, the burthen bear.
    Hark, hark!
     Bow, wow,
    The watch-dogs bark:
     Bow, wow.

Hark, hark! I hear
The strain of strutting chanticleer
Cry, Cock-a-diddle-dow!

II

Where the bee sucks, there suck I:
    In a cowslip's bell I lie;
There I couch when owls do cry.
On the bat's back I do fly
After summer merrily:
    Merrily, merrily, shall I live now,
    Under the blossom that hangs on the bough.

III

Full fathom five thy father lies:
    Of his bones are coral made;
Those are pearls that were his eyes:
    Nothing of him that doth fade,

But doth suffer a sea-change
Into something rich and strange.
Sea-nymphs hourly ring his knell:
    Hark! now I hear them,—
    Ding, dong, Bell.

From "The Passionate Pilgrim"

CRABBÈD Age and Youth
    Cannot live together:
Youth is full of pleasance,
Age is full of care;
Youth like summer morn,
Age like winter weather;
Youth like summer brave,
Age like winter bare.
Youth is full of sport,
Age's health is short;
Youth is nimble, Age is lame;
Youth is hot and bold,
Age is weak and cold;
Youth is wild, and Age is tame.
Age, I do abhor thee:
Youth, I do adore thee;
O, my Love, my Love is young!
Age, I do defy thee:
O, sweet shepherd, hie thee!
For methinks thou stay'st too long.

From the "Sonnets"

XXIX

WHEN, in disgrace with fortune and men's eyes,
    I all alone beweep my outcast state,
And trouble deaf heaven with my bootless cries,
And look upon myself, and curse my fate,
Wishing me like to one more rich in hope,
Featured like him, like him with friends possessed,
Desiring this man's art and that man's scope,
With what I most enjoy contented least;
Yet in these thoughts myself almost despising,
Haply I think on thee: and then my state,
Like to the lark at break of day arising
From sullen earth, sings hymns at heaven's gate:
    For thy sweet love remembered such wealth brings
    That then I scorn to change my state with kings.

XXX

When to the sessions of sweet silent thought
I summon up remembrance of things past,
I sigh the lack of many a thing I sought,
And with old woes new wail my dear time's waste:
Then can I drown an eye, unused to flow,
For precious friends hid in death's dateless night,
And weep afresh love's long-since cancelled woe,
And moan the expense of many a vanished sight:
Then can I grieve at grievances foregone,
And heavily from woe to woe tell o'er
The sad account of fore-bemoanèd moan,
Which I new pay as if not paid before:
    But if the while I think on thee, dear friend,
    All losses are restored, and sorrows end.

XXXIII

Full many a glorious morning have I seen
Flatter the mountain-tops with sovereign eye,
Kissing with golden face the meadows green,
Gilding pale streams with heavenly alchemy.
Anon permit the basest clouds to ride
With ugly rack on his celestial face,
And from the forlorn world his visage hide,
Stealing unseen to west with this disgrace:
Even so my sun one early morn did shine
With all-triumphant splendor on my brow;
But out, alack! he was but one hour mine,

The region cloud hath masked him from me now.
Yet him for this my love no whit disdaineth;
Suns of the world may stain when heaven's sun staineth.

LV

Not marble, nor the gilded monuments
Of princes, shall outlive this powerful rhyme;
But you shall shine more bright in these contents
Than unswept stone, besmear'd with sluttish time.
When wasteful war shall statues overturn,
And broils root out the work of masonry,
Nor Mars his sword nor war's quick fire shall burn
The living record of your memory.
'Gainst death and all-oblivious enmity
Shall you pace forth; your praise shall still find room
Even in the eyes of all posterity
That wear this world out to the ending doom.
So, till the judgment that yourself arise,
You live in this, and dwell in lovers' eyes.

LX

Like as the waves make towards the pebbled shore,
So do our minutes hasten to their end;
Each changing place with that which goes before,
In sequent toil all forwards do contend.
Nativity, once in the main of light,
Crawls to maturity, wherewith being crowned,
Crooked eclipses 'gainst his glory fight,
And Time that gave doth now his gift confound.
Time doth transfix the flourish set on youth,
And delves the parallels in beauty's brow;
Feeds on the rarities of nature's truth,
And nothing stands but for his scythe to mow:
And yet, to times in hope, my verse shall stand
Praising thy worth, despite his cruel hand.

LXXIII

That time of year thou may'st in me behold
When yellow leaves, or none, or few, do hang
Upon those boughs which shake against the cold,
Bare ruined choirs, where late the sweet birds sang.
In me thou see'st the twilight of such day
As after sunset fadeth in the west,
Which by and by black night doth take away,
Death's second self, that seals up all in rest.

In me thou see'st the glowing of such fire
That on the ashes of his youth doth lie,
As the death-bed whereon it must expire,
Consumed with that which it was nourished by.
　This thou perceiv'st, which makes thy love more
　　strong
　To love that well which thou must leave ere long.

CIV

To me, fair friend, you never can be old;
For as you were when first your eye I eyed,
Such seems your beauty still.　Three Winters cold
Have from the forests shook three Summers' pride;
Three beauteous Springs to yellow Autumn turned
In process of the seasons have I seen,
Three April perfumes in three hot Junes burned,
Since first I saw you fresh, which yet are green.
Ah! yet doth beauty, like a dial-hand,
Steal from his figure, and no pace perceived;
So your sweet hue, which methinks still doth stand,
Hath motion, and mine eye may be deceived:
　For fear of which, hear this, thou age unbred:
　Ere you were born was beauty's Summer dead.

CVI

When in the chronicle of wasted time
I see descriptions of the fairest wights,
And beauty making beautiful old rhyme
In praise of ladies dead, and lovely knights;
Then in the blazon of sweet beauty's best
Of hand, of foot, of lip, of eye, of brow,
I see their antique pen would have expressed
Even such a beauty as you master now.
So all their praises are but prophecies
Of this our time, all. you prefiguring;
And, for they looked but with divining eyes,
They had not skill enough your worth to sing:
　For we, which now behold these present days,
　Have eyes to wonder, but lack tongues to praise.

CXVI

Let me not to the marriage of true minds
Admit impediments.　Love is not love
Which alters when it alteration finds,
Or bends with the remover to remove:
O, no! it is an ever-fixèd mark
That looks on tempests, and is never shaken;

It is the star to every wandering bark,
Whose worth's unknown, although his height be taken.
Love's not Time's fool, though rosy lips and cheeks
Within his bending sickle's compass come;
Love alters not with his brief hours and weeks,
But bears it out even to the edge of doom:
  If this be error, and upon me proved,
  I never writ, nor no man ever loved.

CXLVI

Poor soul, the centre of my sinful earth—
My sinful earth these rebel powers array—
Why dost thou pine within and suffer dearth,
Painting thy outward walls so costly gay?
Why so large cost, having so short a lease,
Dost thou upon thy fading mansion spend?
Shall worms, inheritors of this excess,
Eat up thy charge? Is this thy body's end?
Then, soul, live thou upon thy servant's loss,
And let that pine to aggravate thy store;
Buy terms divine in selling hours of dross;
Within be fed, without be rich no more:
  So shalt thou feed on Death, that feeds on men;
  And Death once dead, there's no more dying then.

From "The Merchant of Venice"

I

THE quality of mercy is not strain'd;
  It droppeth as the gentle rain from heaven
Upon the place beneath. It is twice blessed;
It blesseth him that gives, and him that takes.
'Tis mightiest in the mightiest; it becomes
The thronèd monarch better than his crown:
His sceptre shows the force of temporal pow'r,
The attribute to awe and majesty,
Wherein doth sit the dread and fear of kings.
But mercy is above this sceptred sway;
It is enthroned in the hearts of kings;
It is an attribute to God himself;
And earthly power doth then show likest God's
When mercy seasons justice. Therefore, Jew,
Though justice be thy plea, consider this—

That, in the course of justice, none of us
Should see salvation: we do pray for mercy;
And that same prayer doth teach us all to render
The deeds of mercy.

II

How sweet the moonlight sleeps upon this bank!
Here will we sit, and let the sounds of music
Creep in our ears; soft stillness and the night
Become the touches of sweet harmony.
Sit, Jessica; look how the floor of heaven
Is thick inlaid with patines of bright gold;
There's not the smallest orb which thou behold'st,
But in his motion like an angel sings,
Still quiring to the young-eyed cherubins;
Such harmony is in immortal souls;
But whilst this muddy vesture of decay
Doth grossly close it in, we cannot hear it. . . .
        . . . Therefore, the poet
Did feign that Orpheus drew trees, stones, and floods;
Since nought so stockish, hard, and full of rage,
But music for the time doth change his nature.
The man that hath no music in himself,
Nor is not mov'd with concord of sweet sounds,
Is fit for treasons, stratagems, and spoils;
The motions of his spirit are dull as night,
And his affections dark as Erebus:
Let no such man be trusted.

From "Romeo and Juliet"

O then, I see queen Mab hath been with you.
    She is the fairies' midwife, and she comes
In shape no bigger than an agate-stone
On the fore-finger of an alderman,
Drawn with a team of little atomies,
Athwart men's noses as they lie asleep:
Her wagon-spokes made of long spinners' legs;
The cover, of the wings of grasshoppers;
Her traces, of the smallest spider's web;
Her collars, of the moonshine's wat'ry beams;
Her whip, of cricket's bone; the lash, of film;
Her wagoner, a small grey-coated gnat,
Not half so big as a round little worm,
Prick'd from the lazy finger of a maid:
Her chariot is an empty hazel-nut,
Made by the joiner squirrel, or old grub,
Time out of mind the fairies' coach-makers.
And in this state she gallops night by night,
Through lovers' brains, and then they dream of love;
O'er courtiers' knees, that dream on courtsies straight;
O'er lawyers' fingers, who straight dream on fees;

O'er ladies' lips, who straight on kisses dream,
Which oft the angry Mab with blisters plagues,
Because their breaths with sweetmeats tainted are.
Sometimes she gallops o'er a courtier's nose,
And then dreams he of smelling out a suit:
And sometimes comes she with a tithe-pig's tail,
Tickling a parson's nose as a' lies asleep,
Then dreams he of another benefice!
Sometimes she driveth o'er a soldier's neck,
And then dreams he of cutting foreign throats,
Of breaches, ambuscadoes, Spanish blades,
Of healths five fathom deep; and then anon
Drums in his ear, at which he starts and wakes;
And, being thus frighted, swears a prayer or two,
And sleeps again. This is that very Mab
That plats the manes of horses in the night;
And bakes the elf-locks in foul sluttish hairs,
Which once untangled, much misfortune bodes.

From "Henry V"

O for a Muse of fire, that would ascend
The brightest heaven of invention,
A kingdom for a stage, princes to act
And monarchs to behold the swelling scene!
Then should the warlike Harry, like himself,
Assume the port of Mars; and at his heels,
Leash'd in like hounds, should famine, sword and fire
Crouch for employment.

From "As You Like It"

ALL the world's a stage,
And all the men and women merely players;
They have their exits and their entrances,
And one man in his time plays many parts,
His acts being seven ages. At first, the infant,
Mewling and puking in his nurse's arms:
Then the whining school-boy, with his satchel
And shining morning face, creeping like snail
Unwillingly to school. And then the lover,
Sighing like furnace, with a woful ballad
Made to his mistress' eye-brow. Then, a soldier,
Full of strange oaths, and bearded like the pard,
Jealous in honor, sudden and quick in quarrel;
Seeking the bubble reputation
Even in the cannon's mouth. And then, the justice,

In fair round belly, with good capon lined,
With eyes severe, and beard of formal cut,
Full of wise saws and modern instances;
And so he plays his part. The sixth age shifts
Into the lean and slipper'd pantaloon,
With spectacles on nose, and pouch on side;
His youthful hose well sav'd, a world too wide
For his shrunk shank; and his big manly voice,
Turning again towards childish treble, pipes
And whistles in his sound. Last scene of all,
That ends this strange eventful history,
Is second childishness, and mere oblivion:
Sans teeth, sans eyes, sans taste, sans everything.

From "Hamlet"

TO be, or not to be, that is the question—
    Whether 'tis nobler in the mind to suffer
The slings and arrows of outrageous fortune,
Or to take arms against a sea of troubles,
And, by opposing, end them. To die—to sleep——
No more; and by a sleep to say we end
The heart-ache, and the thousand natural shocks
That flesh is heir to!—'tis a consummation
Devoutly to be wish'd. To die—to sleep——
To sleep!—perchance to dream!—ay, there's the rub;
For in that sleep of death what dreams may come,
When we have shuffled off this mortal coil,
Must give us pause—there's the respect
That makes calamity of so long life:
For who would bear the whips and scorns of time,
The oppressor's wrong, the proud man's contumely,
The pangs of despised love, the law's delay,
The insolence of office, and the spurns
That patient merit of th' unworthy takes,
When he himself might his quietus make
With a bare bodkin! Who would fardels bear,
To groan and sweat under a weary life,
But that the dread of something after death
(That undiscover'd country from whose bourn
No traveller returns) puzzles the will,
And makes us rather bear those ills we have,
Than fly to others that we know not of?
Thus conscience does make cowards of us all;
And thus the native hue of resolution
Is sicklied o'er with the pale cast of thought,
And enterprises of great pith and moment,
With this regard, their currents turn awry,
And lose the name of action.

From "Measure for Measure"

AY, but to die, and go we know not where;
    To lie in cold obstruction, and to rot;
This sensible warm motion to become
A kneaded clod; and the delighted spirit
To bathe in fiery floods, or to reside
In thrilling regions of thick-ribbed ice;
To be imprison'd in the viewless winds,
And blown with restless violence round about
The pendant world; or to be worse than worst
Of those, that lawless and incertain thoughts
Imagine howling: 'tis too horrible!
The weariest and most loathed worldly life,
That age, ache, penury, and imprisonment,
Can lay on nature, is a paradise
To what we fear of death.

From "Antony and Cleopatra"

THE barge she sat in, like a burnish'd throne,
    Burn'd on the water: the poop was beaten gold;
Purple the sails, and so perfumed that
The winds were love-sick with them; the oars were silver,
Which to the tune of flutes kept stroke and made
The water which they beat to follow faster,
As amorous of their strokes. For her own person,
It beggar'd all description: she did lie
In her pavilion, cloth-of-gold of tissue,
O'er-picturing that Venus where we see
The fancy outwork nature: on each side her
Stood pretty dimpled boys, like smiling Cupids,
With divers-color'd fans, whose wind did seem
To glow the delicate cheeks which they did cool,
And what they undid did.

From "The Winter's Tale"

                        . . . O Proserpina,
For the flowers now, that frighted thou let'st fall
From Dis's wagon! daffodils,
That come before the swallow dares, and take
The winds of March with beauty; violets dim,
But sweeter than the lids of Juno's eyes
On Cytherea's breath; pale primroses

That die unmarried, ere they can behold
Bright Phœbus in his strength, a malady
Most incident to maids; bold oxlips and
The crown-imperial; lilies of all kinds,
The flower-de-luce being one!

From "The Tempest"

OUR revels now are ended: these our actors,
  As I foretold you, were all spirits, and
Are melted into air, into thin air;
And, like the baseless fabric of this vision,
The cloud-capt towers, the gorgeous palaces,
The solemn temples, the great globe itself,
Yea, all which it inherit, shall dissolve;
And, like this insubstantial pageant faded,
Leave not a rack behind! We are such stuff
As dreams are made on, and our little life
Is rounded with a sleep.

THOMAS CAMPION (1567-1620)

Follow Your Saint

FOLLOW your saint, follow with accents sweet!
  Haste you, sad notes, fall at her flying feet!
There, wrapped in cloud of sorrow, pity move,
And tell the ravisher of my soul I perish for her love:
But, if she scorns my never-ceasing pain,
Then burst with sighing in her sight and ne'er return again.

All that I sang still to her praise did tend,
Still she was first, still she my songs did end;
Yet she my love and music both doth fly,
The music that her echo is and beauty's sympathy:
Then let my notes pursue her scornful flight!
It shall suffice that they were breathed and died for her delight.

Vobiscum est Iope

WHEN thou must home to shades of underground,
  And there arrived a new admired guest,
The beauteous spirits do engirt thee round,
White Iope, blithe Helen, and the rest,
To hear the stories of thy finished love
From that smooth tongue whose music hell can move;

Then wilt thou speak of banqueting delights,
Of masques and revels which sweet youth did make,
Of tourneys and great challenges of knights,
And all these triumphs for thy beauty's sake:
When thou hast told these honors done to thee,
Then tell, O tell, how thou didst murder me!

Cherry-Ripe

THERE is a garden in her face
    Where roses and white lilies blow;
A heavenly paradise is that place,
    Wherein all pleasant fruits do flow:
      There cherries grow which none may buy
      Till "Cherry-ripe" themselves do cry.

Those cherries fairly do enclose
    Of orient pearl a double row,
Which when her lovely laughter shows,
    They look like rose-buds filled with snow;
      Yet them nor peer nor prince can buy
      Till "Cherry-ripe" themselves do cry.

Her eyes like angels watch them still:
    Her brows like bended bows do stand,
Threatening with piercing frowns to kill
    All that attempt with eye or hand
      Those sacred cherries to come nigh,
      Till "Cherry-ripe" themselves do cry.

Winter Nights

NOW winter nights enlarge
    The number of their hours,
And clouds their storms discharge
Upon the airy towers.
Let now the chimneys blaze,
And cups o'erflow with wine;
Let well-tuned words amaze
With harmony divine.
Now yellow waxen lights
Shall wait on honey love,
While youthful revels, masques, and courtly sights
Sleep's leaden spells remove.
This time doth well dispense

With lovers' long discourse;
Much speech hath some defence
Though beauty no remorse.
All do not all things well;
Some measures comely tread,
Some knotted riddles tell,
Some poems smoothly read.
The summer hath his joys
And winter his delights;
Though love and all his pleasures are but toys,
They shorten tedious nights.

Amarillis

I care not for these ladies,
  That must be wooed and prayed:
Give me kind Amarillis,
The wanton countrymaid.
Nature art disdaineth,
Her beauty is her own.
Her when we court and kiss,
She cries, Forsooth, let go!
But when we come where comfort is,
She never will say No.

If I love Amarillis,
She gives me fruit and flowers:
But if we love these ladies,
We must give golden showers.
Give them gold, that sell love,
Give me the Nut-brown lass,
Who, when we court and kiss,
She cries, Forsooth, let go:
But when we come where comfort is,
She never will say No.

These ladies must have pillows,
And beds by strangers wrought;
Give me a bower of willows,
Of moss and leaves unbought,
And fresh Amarillis,
With milk and honey fed;
Who, when we court and kiss,
She cries, Forsooth, let go:
But when we come where comfort is,
She never will say No!

SIR HENRY WOTTON (1568-1639)

Elizabeth of Bohemia

YOU meaner beauties of the night,
  That poorly satisfy our eyes
More by your number than your light,
  You common people of the skies;
  What are you when the moon shall rise?

You curious chanters of the wood,
  That warble forth Dame Nature's lays,
Thinking your passions understood
  By your weak accents; what's your praise
When Philomel her voice shall raise?

You violets that first appear,
  By your pure purple mantles known
Like the proud virgins of the year,
  As if the spring were all your own;
  What are you when the rose is blown?

So, when my mistress shall be seen
  In form and beauty of her mind,
By virtue first, then choice, a Queen,
  Tell me, if she were not designed
  Th' eclipse and glory of her kind.

The Character of a Happy Life

HOW happy is he born and taught
  That serveth not another's will;
Whose armor is his honest thought,
  And simple truth his utmost skill!

Whose passions not his masters are;
  Whose soul is still prepared for death,
Not tied unto the world by care
  Of public fame or private breath;

Who envies none that chance doth raise,
  Nor vice; who never understood
How deepest wounds are given by praise;
  Nor rules of state, but rules of good;

Who hath his life from rumors freed;
  Whose conscience is his strong retreat;

Whose state can neither flatterers feed,
  Nor ruin make oppressors great;

Who God doth late and early pray
  More of His grace than gifts to lend;
And entertains the harmless day
  With a well-chosen book or friend;

—This man is freed from servile bands
  Of hope to rise, or fear to fall:
Lord of himself, though not of lands,
  And having nothing, yet hath all.

THOMAS DEKKER (1570-1641)

The Happy Heart, from "Patient Grissell"

ART thou poor, yet hast thou golden slumbers?
          O sweet content!
Art thou rich, yet is thy mind perplexèd
          O punishment!
Dost thou laugh to see how fools are vexèd
To add to golden numbers, golden numbers?
O sweet content! O sweet, O sweet content!
  Work apace, apace, apace, apace;
  Honest labor bears a lovely face;
Then hey nonny nonny, hey nonny nonny!
Canst drink the waters of the crispèd spring?
          O sweet content!
Swimm'st thou in wealth, yet sink'st in thine own tears?
          O punishment!
Then he that patiently want's burden bears
No burden bears, but is a king, a king!
O sweet content! O sweet, O sweet content!
  Work apace, apace, apace, apace;
  Honest labor bears a lovely face;
Then hey nonny nonny, hey nonny nonny!

From "The Honest Whore"

PATIENCE! why, 'tis the soul of peace:
    Of all the virtues, 'tis nearest kin to heaven:
It makes men look like gods. The best of men
That e'er wore earth about him was a sufferer,
A soft, meek, patient, humble, tranquil spirit:
The first true gentleman that ever breath'd.

The Old and Young Courtier

AN old song made by an aged old pate,
   Of an old worshipful gentleman, who had a great estate,
That kept a brave old house at a bountiful rate,
And an old porter to relieve the poor at his gate;
      Like an old courtier of the queen's,
      And the queen's old courtier.

With an old lady, whose anger one word assuages;
They every quarter paid their old servants their wages,
And never knew what belonged to coachmen, footmen, nor
      pages,
But kept twenty old fellows with blue coats and badges;
      Like an old courtier . . .

With an old study filled full of learned old books;
With an old reverend chaplain—you might know him by his
      looks;
With an old buttery hatch worn quite off the hooks;
And an old kitchen, that maintained half-a-dozen old cooks;
      Like an old courtier . . .

With an old hall, hung about with pikes, guns, and bows,
With old swords and bucklers, that had borne many shrewd
      blows;
And an old frieze coat, to cover his worship's trunk hose;
A cup of old sherry, to comfort his copper nose;
      Like an old courtier . . .

With a good old fashion, when Christmas was come,
To call in all his old neighbors with bagpipe and drum,
With good cheer enough to furnish every old room,
And old liquor able to make a cat speak, and man dumb;
      Like an old courtier . . .

With an old falconer, huntsmen, and a kennel of hounds,
That never hawked, nor hunted, but in his own grounds;
Who, like a wise man, kept himself within his own bounds,
And when he died, gave every child a thousand good pounds;
      Like an old courtier of the queen's,
      And the queen's old courtier.

                    (*Attributed to Dekker.*)

BEN JONSON (1573-1637)

From "Cynthia's Revels"

QUEEN and huntress, chaste and fair,
 Now the sun is laid to sleep,
Seated in thy silver chair,
State in wonted manner keep:
  Hesperus entreats thy light,
  Goddess excellently bright.

Earth, let not thy envious shade
Dare itself to interpose;
Cynthia's shining orb was made
Heaven to clear, when day did close:
  Bless us then with wishèd sight,
  Goddess excellently bright.

Lay thy bow of pearl apart,
And thy crystal-shining quiver;
Give unto the flying hart
Space to breathe, how short soever:
  Thou that mak'st a day of night,
  Goddess excellently bright.

From "The Forest"

DRINK to me only with thine eyes,
 And I will pledge with mine;
Or leave a kiss but in the cup
 And I'll not look for wine.
The thirst that from the soul doth rise
 Doth ask a drink divine;
But might I of Jove's nectar sup,
 I would not change for thine.

I sent thee late a rosy wreath,
 Not so much honoring thee
As giving it a hope that there
 It could not withered be;
But thou thereon didst only breathe,
 And sent'st it back to me;
Since when it grows, and smells, I swear,
 Not of itself but thee!

Simplex Munditiis

STILL to be neat, still to be drest,
  As you were going to a feast;
Still to be powdered, still perfumed:
Lady, it is to be presumed,
Though art's hid causes are not found,
All is not sweet, all is not sound.

Give me a look, give me a face,
That makes simplicity a grace;
Robes loosely flowing, hair as free:
Such sweet neglect more taketh me
Than all the adulteries of art;
They strike mine eyes, but not my heart.

From "Love's Chariot"

HAVE you seen but a bright lily grow
  Before rude hands have touched it?
Have you marked but the fall of the snow
  Before the soil hath smutched it?
Have you felt the wool of the beaver,
        Or swan's down ever?
Or have smelt o' the bud of the brier,
        Or the nard in the fire?
Or have tasted the bag of the bee?
O so white, O so soft, O so sweet is she!

From "An Ode to Sir Lucius Cary and Sir H. Morrison"

IT is not growing like a tree
    In bulk, doth make man better be;
Or standing long an oak, three hundred year,
To fall a log at last, dry, bald, and sear:
    A lily of a day
    Is fairer far in May,
Although it fall and die that night,—
It was the plant and flower of Light.
In small proportions we just beauties see,
And in short measures life may perfect be.

From an Epithalamium

UP, youths and virgins, up and praise
  The god, whose nights outshine his days;
Hymen, whose hallow'd rites

Could never boast of brighter lights;
    Whose hands pass liberty.
Two of your troop, that with the moon were free,
    Are now waged to his war.
        And what they are,
    If you'll perfection see,
        Yourselves must be.
Shine, Hesperus, shine forth, thou wishèd star.

What joy, what honors can compare
    With holy nuptials, when they arc
    Made out of equal parts
Of years, of states, of hands, of hearts!
    When in the happy choice

The spouse and spoused have foremost voice!
    Such, glad of Hymen's war,
        Live what they are,
    And long perfection see;
        And such ours be.
Shine, Hesperus, shine forth, thou wishèd star.

On the Portrait of Shakespeare Prefixed to the First Folio Edition, 1623

THIS figure, that thou here seest put,
    It was for gentle Shakespeare cut;
Wherein the Graver had a strife
With Nature to outdo the life:
O, could he but have drawn his wit
As well in brass, as he hath hit
His face; the Print would then surpass
All that was ever writ in brass.
But since he cannot, Reader, look
Not at his picture, but his book.

To the Memory of My Beloved Master William Shakespeare, and What He Hath Left Us
[1564-1616]

TO draw no envy, Shakespeare, on thy name,
    Am I thus ample to thy book and fame;
While I confess thy writings to be such
As neither Man, nor Muse, can praise too much.
'Tis true, and all men's suffrage. But these ways
Were not the paths I meant unto thy praise;
For silliest ignorance on these may light,
Which, when it sounds at best, but echoes right;

Or blind affection, which doth ne'er advance
The truth, but gropes, and urgeth all by chance;
Or crafty malice might pretend this praise,
And think to ruin, where it seemed to raise.
These are, as some infamous bawd or whore
Should praise a matron. What could hurt her more?
But thou art proof against them, and, indeed,
Above the ill fortune of them, or the need.
I therefore will begin: Soul of the age!
The applause, delight, the wonder of our stage!
My Shakespeare, rise! I will not lodge thee by
Chaucer, or Spenser, or bid Beaumont lie
A little further, to make thee a room:
Thou art a monument without a tomb,
And art alive still while thy book doth live
And we have wits to read and praise to give.
That I not mix thee so, my brain excuses,
I mean with great, but disproportioned Muses;
For if I thought my judgment were of years,
I should commit thee surely with thy peers,
And tell how far thou didst our Lyly outshine,
Or sporting Kyd, or Marlowe's mighty line,
And though thou hadst small Latin and less Greek,
From thence to honor thee, I would not seek
For names; but call forth thundering Æschylus,
Euripides, and Sophocles to us;
Pacuvius, Accius, him of Cordova dead,
To life again, to hear thy buskin tread,
And shake a stage; or, when thy socks were on,
Leave thee alone for the comparison
Of all that insolent Greece or haughty Rome
Sent forth, or since did from their ashes come.
Triumph, my Britain, thou hast one to show
To whom all scenes of Europe homage owe.
He was not for an age, but for all time!
And all the Muses still were in their prime,
When, like Apollo, he came forth to warm
Our ears, or like a Mercury to charm!
Nature herself was proud of his designs
And joyed to wear the dressing of his lines!
Which were so richly spun, and woven so fit,
As, since, she will vouchsafe no other wit,
The merry Greek, tart Aristophanes,   ,
Neat Terence, witty Plautus, now not please;
But antiquated and deserted lie,
As they were not of Nature's family.
Yet must I not give Nature all; thy Art
My gentle Shakespeare, must enjoy a part.
For though the poet's matter nature be,
His art doth give the fashion; and, that he

Who casts to write a living line, must sweat,
(Such as thine are) and strike the second heat
Upon the Muses' anvil; turn the same
(And himself with it) that he thinks to frame,
Or, for the laurel, he may gain a scorn;
For a good poet's made, as well as born.
And such wert thou! Look how the father's face
Lives in his issue, even so the race
Of Shakespeare's mind and manners brightly shines
In his well-turnèd, and true-filèd lines;
In each of which he seems to shake a lance,
As brandished at the eyes of ignorance.
Sweet Swan of Avon! what a sight it were
To see thee in our waters yet appear,
And make those flights upon the banks of Thames,
That so did take Eliza, and our James!
But stay, I see thee in the hemisphere
Advanced, and made a constellation there!
Shine forth, thou Star of Poets, and with rage
Or influence, chide or cheer the drooping stage,
Which, since thy flight from hence, hath mourned
    like night,
And despairs day, but for thy volume's light.

JOHN DONNE (1573-1631)

The Good Morrow

I wonder, by my troth, what thou and I
    Did till we loved! Were we not weaned till then,
But sucked on country pleasures childishly?
    Or snorted we in the Seven Sleepers' den?
'Twas so; but thus all pleasures fancies be.
If ever any beauty I did see,
Which I desired and got,—'twas but a dream of thee.

And, now, good morrow to our waking souls,
    Which watch not one another out of fear;
For Love all love of other sights controls,
    And makes one little room an everywhere.
Let sea-discoverers to new worlds be gone;
Let maps to other worlds our world have shown;
Let us possess one world; each hath one, and is one.

My face in thine eye, thine in mine appears,
    And true plain hearts do in the faces rest.
Where can we find two fitter hemispheres,
    Without sharp North, without declining West?
Whatever dies was not mixed equally;
If our two loves be one, or thou and I
Love so alike that none do slacken, none can die.

Absence

That Time and Absence proves
Rather helps than hurts to loves.

ABSENCE, hear thou my protestation
    Against thy strength,
    Distance and length:
Do what thou canst for alteration,
    For hearts of truest mettle
    Absence doth join and Time doth settle.

Who loves a mistress of such quality,
    His mind hath found
    Affection's ground
Beyond time, place, and all mortality.
    To hearts that cannot vary
    Absence is present, Time doth tarry.

My senses want their outward motion
    Which now within
    Reason doth win,
Redoubled by her secret notion:
    Like rich men that take their pleasure
    In hiding more than handling treasure.

By Absence this good means I gain,
    That I can catch her
    Where none can watch her,
In some close corner of my brain:
    There I embrace and kiss her,
    And so enjoy her and none miss her.

The Dream

DEAR love, for nothing less than thee
    Would I have broke this happy dream,
        It was a theme
For reason, much too strong for fantasy.
Therefore thou waked'st me wisely; yet
My dream thou brok'st not, but continued'st it.
Thou art so true that thoughts of thee suffice
To make dreams truths and fables histories;
Enter these arms, for since thou thought'st it best
Not to dream all my dream, let's act the rest. . . .
                Abridged.

A Valediction Forbidding Mourning

AS virtuous men pass mildly away,
   And whisper to their souls to go:
Whilst some of their sad friends do say,
The breath goes now—and some say, no;

So let us melt, and make no noise,
No tear-floods, nor sigh-tempests move;
'Twere profanation of our joys
To tell the laity our love.

Moving of th' earth brings harms and fears,
Men reckon what it did, and meant;
But trepidation of the spheres,
Though greater far, is innocent.

Dull, sublunary lovers' love—
Whose soul is sense—cannot admit
Absence, because it doth remove
Those things which alimented it.

But we're by love so much refined,
That ourselves know not what it is;
Inter-assurèd of the mind,
Careless eyes, lips, and hands to miss.

Our two souls, therefore, (which are one)
Though I must go, endure not yet
A breach, but an expansion,
Like gold to airy thinness beat.

If they be two, they are two so
As stiff thin compasses are two;
Thy soul, the fix'd foot, makes no show
To move, but doth, if th' other do.

And though it in the centre sit,
Yet when the other far doth roam,
It leans, and hearkens after it,
And grows erect as that comes home.

Such wilt thou be to me, who must,
Like th' other foot, obliquely run;
Thy firmness makes my circles just,
And makes me end where I begun.

The Funeral

WHOEVER comes to shroud me, do not harm
     Nor question much
That subtle wreath of hair about mine arm;
The mystery, the sign you must not touch,
     For 'tis my outward soul.
Viceroy to that which, unto heav'n being gone,
     Will leave this to control
And keep these limbs, her provinces, from dissolution.

For if the sinewy thread my brain lets fall
     Through every part
Can tie those parts, and make me one of all;
Those hairs, which upward grew, and strength and art
     Have from a better brain,
Can better do't: except she meant that I
     By this should know my pain,
As prisoners then are manacled, when they're condemned
     to die.

Whate'er she meant by't, bury it with me,
     For since I am
Love's martyr, it might breed idolatry
If into other hands these reliques came.
     As 'twas humility
'T afford to it all that a soul can do,
     So 'tis some bravery
That, since you would have none of me, I bury some of you.

Song

GO and catch a falling star,
     Get with child a mandrake root,
Tell me where all past years are,
     Or who cleft the Devil's foot;
Teach me to hear mermaid's singing,
Or to keep off envy's stinging.
          And find
          What wind
Serves to advance an honest mind.

If thou be'st born to strange sights,
     Things invisible go see,
Ride ten thousand days and nights
     Till Age snow white hairs on thee;
Thou, when thou return'st, wilt tell me
All strange wonders that befell thee,
          And swear
          No where
Lives a woman true and fair.

If thou find'st one, let me know;
   Such a pilgrimage were sweet.
Yet do not; I would not go,
   Though at next door we might meet.
Though she were true when you met her,
And last till you write your letter,
     Yet she
     Will be
False, ere I come, to two or three.

From "Epithalamion"

THE sunbeams in the east are spread:
   Leave, leave, fair bride, your solitary bed!
No more shall you return to it alone,
It nurseth sadness; and your body's print
Like to a grave the yielding down doth dint.
   You and your other you meet there anon:
   Put forth, put forth that warm balm-breathing thigh,
Which, when next time you in these sheets will smother,
   There it must meet another,
     Which never was, but must be oft more nigh.
Come glad from thence, go gladder than you came:
To-day put on perfection, and a woman's name.

Daughters of London, you which be
Our golden mines and furnished treasury:
   You which are angels, yet still bring with you
Thousands of angels on your marriage days;
Help with your presence, and devise to praise
   These rites, which also unto you grow due.
Conceitedly dress her; and be assigned
By you fit place for every flower and jewel;
   Make her for love fit fuel,
     As gay as Flora and as rich as Inde:
So may she fair and rich, in nothing lame
To-day put on perfection, and a woman's name. . . .

RICHARD BARNFIELD (1574-1627)

Philomel

AS it fell upon a day
   In the merry month of May,
Sitting in a pleasant shade
Which a grove of myrtles made,
Beasts did leap and birds did sing,
Trees did grow and plants did spring;

Everything did banish moan
Save the Nightingale alone:
She, poor bird, as all forlorn
Leaned her breast up-till a thorn,
And there sung the doleful'st ditty,
That to hear it was great pity.
Fie, fie, fie! now would she cry;
Tereu, Tereu! by and by;
That to hear her so complain
Scarce I could from tears refrain;
For her griefs so lively shown
Made me think upon mine own.
Ah! thought I, thou mourn'st in vain,
None takes pity on thy pain:
Senseless trees they cannot hear thee,
Ruthless beasts they will not cheer thee:
King Pandion he is dead,
All thy friends are lapped in lead;
All thy fellow birds do sing
Careless of thy sorrowing:
Even so, poor bird, like thee,
None alive will pity me.

JOHN FLETCHER (1579-1625)

Love's Emblems, from "Valentinian"

NOW the lusty spring is seen;
  Golden yellow, gaudy blue,
  Daintily invite the view:
Everywhere on every green
Roses blushing as they blow,
  And enticing men to pull,
Lilies whiter than the snow,
  Woodbines of sweet honey full:
    All love's emblems, and all cry,
    "Ladies, if not plucked, we die."

Yet the lusty spring hath stayed;
  Blushing red and purest white
  Daintily to love invite
Every woman, every maid:
Cherries kissing as they grow,
  And inviting men to taste,
Apples even ripe below,
  Winding gently to the waist:
    All love's emblems, and all cry,
    "Ladies, if not plucked, we die."

Melancholy, from "The Nice Valor"

HENCE, all you vain delights,
　　As short as are the nights,
　　Wherein you spend your folly:
There's naught in this life sweet
If man were wise to see't,
　　But only melancholy,
　　O sweetest Melancholy!
Welcome, folded arms, and fixèd eyes,
A sigh that piercing mortifies,
A look that's fastened to the ground,
A tongue chained up without a sound!

Fountain-heads and pathless groves,
Places which pale passion loves!
Moonlight walks, when all the fowls
Are warmly housed save bats and owls!
　　A midnight bell, a parting groan!
　　These are the sounds we feed upon;
　　Then stretch our bones in a still gloomy valley;
　　Nothing so dainty sweet as lovely melancholy.

God Læus

GOD Læus, ever young,
　　Ever honor'd, ever sung,
Stain'd with blood of lusty grapes,
In a thousand lusty shapes
Dance upon the mazer's brim,
In the crimson liquor swim:
From thy plenteous hand divine
Let a river run with wine:
　　God of youth, let this day here
　　Enter neither care nor fear.

JOHN WEBSTER (1580?-1625?)

A Dirge, from "The White Devil"

CALL for the robin-redbreast and the wren,
　　Since o'er shady groves they hover,
And with leaves and flowers do cover
The friendless bodies of unburied men.

Call unto his funeral dole
The ant, the field-mouse, and the mole,
To rear him hillocks that shall keep him warm,
And (when gray tombs are robbed) sustain no harm;
But keep the wolf far thence, that's foe to men,
For with his nails he'll dig them up again.

Vanitas Vanitatum

ALL the flowers of the spring
    Meet to perfume our burying;
These have but their growing prime,
And man does flourish but his time:
Survey our progress from our birth—
We are set, we grow, we turn to earth.
Courts adieu, and all delights,
All bewitching appetites!
Sweetest breath and clearest eye
Like perfumes go out and die;
And consequently this is done
As shadows wait upon the sun.
Vain the ambition of kings
Who seek by trophies and dead things
To leave a living name behind,
And weave but nets to catch the wind

RICHARD CORBET (1582-1635)

Farewell to the Fairies

FAREWELL, rewards and fairies!
    Good housewives now may say,
For now foul sluts in dairies
    Do fare as well as they.
And though they sweep their hearts no less
    Than maids were wont to do,
Yet who of late, for cleanliness,
    Finds sixpence in her shoe?

Lament, lament, old abbeys,
    The fairies' lost command!
They did but change priests' babies,
    But some have changed your land;
And all your children sprung from thence,
    Are now grown Puritanes;
Who live as changelings ever since,
    For love of your demains.

At morning and at evening both
  You merry were and glad;
So little care of sleep or sloth
  These pretty ladies had;
When Tom came home from labor,
  Or Ciss to milking rose,
Then merrily merrily went their tabor
  And nimbly went their toes.

Witness those rings and roundelays
  Of theirs, which yet remain,
Were footed in Queen Mary's days
  On many a grassy plain;
But since of late, Elizabeth,
  And later, James came in,
They never danced on any heath
  As when the time hath been.

By which we note the fairies
  Were of the old profession;
Their songs were *Ave-Maries,*
  Their dances were procession.
But now, alas! they all are dead,
  Or gone beyond the seas;
Or farther for religion fled;
  Or else they take their ease.

A tell-tale in their company
  They never could endure;
And whoso kept not secretly
  Their mirth, was punished sure;
It was a just and Christian deed
  To pinch such black and blue:
Oh, how the Commonwealth doth need
  Such justices as you!

WILLIAM BASSE (1583-1653)

RENOWNED Spenser, lie a thought more nigh
  To learnèd Chaucer, and rare Beaumont lie
A little nearer Spenser, to make room
For Shakespeare in your threefold, fourfold Tomb.
To lodge all four in one bed make a shift
Until Doomsday, for hardly will a fifth
Betwixt this day and that by Fate be slain
For whom your curtains may be drawn again.
If your precedency in death doth bar
A fourth place in your sacred sepulchre,
Under this carvèd marble of thine own,

Sleep, rare Tragedian, Shakespeare, sleep alone,
Thy unmolested peace, unshared Cave,
Possess as Lord, not Tenant, of thy Grave,
That unto us and others it may be
Honor hereafter to be laid by thee.

WILLIAM DRUMMOND, OF HAWTHORNDEN
(1585-1649)

Invocation

PHŒBUS, arise,
   And paint the sable skies
With azure, white and red:
Rouse Memnon's mother from her Tithon's bed,
That she thy càreer may with roses spread:
The nightingales thy coming each where sing,
Make an eternal Spring!
Give life to this dark world which lieth dead;
Spread forth thy golden hair
In larger locks than thou wast wont before,
And, emperor-like, decore
With diadem of pearl thy temples fair:
Chase hence the ugly night,
Which serves but to make dear thy glorious light.

This is that happy morn,
That day, long-wishèd day,
Of all my life so dark,
(If cruel stars have not my ruin sworn,
And fates not hope betray,)
Which, only white, deserves
A diamond for ever should it mark.
This is the morn should bring unto this grove
My Love, to hear and recompense my love.
Fair king, who all preserves,
But show thy blushing beams,
And thou two sweeter eyes
Shalt see, than those which by Peneus' streams
Did once thy heart surprise.
Nay, suns, which shine as clear
As thou, when two thou didst to Rome appear.
Now, Flora, deck thyself in fairest guise:
If that ye, winds, would hear
A voice surpassing far Amphion's lyre,
Your stormy chiding stay;
Let Zephyr only breathe,
And with her tresses play,
Kissing sometimes these purple ports of death.

—The winds all silent are,
And Phœbus in his chair
Ensaffroning sea and air,
Makes vanish every star:
Night like a drunkard reels
Beyond the hills, to shun his flaming wheels:
The fields with flowers are decked in every hue,
The clouds bespangle with bright gold their blue:
Here is the pleasant place,
And everything save her, who all should grace.

Sonnet

I KNOW that all the moon decays,
  And what by mortals in this world is brought
In Time's great periods, shall return to nought;
The fairest states have fatal nights and days.
I know that all the Muse's heavenly lays
With toil of sprite which are so dearly bought,
As idle sounds, of few or none are sought,
That there is nothing lighter than vain praise.
I know frail beauty like the purple flower,
To which one morn oft birth and death affords,
That love a jarring is of mind's accords,
Where sense and will bring under Reason's power:
Know what I list, all this cannot me move,
But that alas! I both must write and love.

FRANCIS BEAUMONT (1586-1615)

From Letter to Ben Jonson

METHINKS the little wit I had is lost
  Since I saw you; for wit is like a rest
Set up at tennis, which men do the best,
With the best gamesters: what things have we seen
Done at the Mermaid; heard words that have been
So nimble, and so full of subtle flame,
As if that every one from whence they came
Had meant to put his whole soul in a jest,
And had resolved to live a fool the rest
Of his dull life: then when there had been thrown
Wit able enough to justify the town
For three days past; wit that might warrant be
For the whole city to talk foolishly
Till that were cancelled; and when that was gone,
We left an air behind us, which alone
Was able to make the next two companies
Right witty; though but downright fools were wise.

BEAUMONT AND FLETCHER

Aspatia's Song

L AY a garland on my hearse
    Of the dismal yew;
Maidens, willow branches bear;
    Say, I died true.

My love was false, but I was firm
    From my hour of birth.
Upon my buried body lie
    Lightly, gentle earth!

THOMAS CAREW (1587-1639)

Song

A SK me no more where Jove bestows,
    When June is past, the fading rose;
For in your beauty's orient deep
These flowers, as in their causes, sleep.

Ask me no more whither do stray
The golden atoms of the day;
For in pure love heaven did prepare
Those powders to enrich your hair.

Ask me no more whither doth haste
The nightingale when May is past;
For in your sweet dividing throat
She winters and keeps warm her note.

Ask me no more where those stars 'light
That downwards fall in dead of night;
For in your eyes they sit, and there
Fixèd become as in their sphere.

Ask me no more if east or west
The Phœnix builds her spicy nest;
For unto you at last she flies,
And in your fragrant bosom dies.

Epitaph

T HE Lady Mary Villiers lies
    Under this stone: with weeping eyes
The parents that first gave her breath,
And their sad friends, laid her in earth.

If any of them, reader, were
Known unto thee, shed a tear:
Or if thyself possess a gem,
As dear to thee as this to them;
Though a stranger to this place,
Bewail in theirs thine own hard case;
For thou perhaps at thy return
Mayst find thy darling in an urn.

GEORGE WITHER (1588-1667)

The Lover's Resolution

SHALL I, wasting in despair,
    Die because a woman's fair?
Or make pale my cheeks with care
'Cause another's rosy are?
Be she fairer than the day,
Or the flowery meads in May,
    If she thinks not well of me,
    What care I how fair she be?

Shall my silly heart be pined
'Cause I see a woman kind?
Or a well disposèd nature
Joinèd with a lovely feature?
Be she meeker, kinder, than
Turtle-dove or pelican,
    If she be not so to me,
    What care I how good she be?

Shall a woman's virtues move
Me to perish for her love?
Or her well-deservings known
Make me quite forget my own?
Be she with that goodness blest
Which may merit name of Best,
    If she be not such to me,
    What care I how good she be?

'Cause her fortune seems too high,
Shall I play the fool and die?
She that bears a noble mind,
If not outward helps she find,
Thinks what with them he would do
That without them dares her woo;
    And unless that mind I see,
    What care I how great she be?

Great, or good, or kind, or fair,
I will ne'er the more despair;
If she love me, this believe,
I will die ere she shall grieve;
If she slight me when I woo,
I can scorn and let her go;
    For if she be not for me,
    What care I for whom she be?

WILLIAM BROWNE (1591-1643?)

Epitaph of the Countess Dowager of Pembroke

UNDERNEATH this sable hearse
    Lies the subject of all verse:
Sidney's sister, Pembroke's mother:
Death, ere thou hast slain another,
Fair, and learned, and good as she,
Time shall throw a dart at thee.

Marble piles let no man raise
To her name: in after days,
Some kind woman born as she,
Reading this, like Niobe
Shall turn marble, and become
Both her mourner and her tomb.

FRANCIS QUARLES (1592-1644)

The Vanity of the World

FALSE world, thou ly'st: thou canst not lend
    The least delight:
Thy favors cannot gain a friend,
    They are so slight:
Thy morning pleasures make an end
    To please at night:
Poor are the wants that thou supply'st,
And yet thou vaunt'st, and yet thou vy'st
With heaven; fond earth, thou boast'st; false world, thou
    ly'st.

Thy babbling tongue tells golden tales
    Of endless treasure;
Thy bounty offers easy sales
    Of lasting pleasure;

Thou ask'st the conscience what she ails,
      And swear'st to ease her:
There's none can want where thou supply'st:
There's none can give when thou deny'st.
Alas! fond world, thou boast'st; false world, thou ly'st.

What well advised ear regards
      What earth can say?
Thy words are gold, but thy rewards
      Are painted clay:
Thy cunning can but pack the cards,
      Thou canst not play:
Thy game at weakest, still thou vy'st;
If seen, and then revy'd, deny'st:
Thou art not what thou seem'st; false world, thou ly'st.

Thy tinsel bosom seems a mint
      Of new-coin'd treasure;
A paradise, that has no stint,
      No change, no measure;
A painted cask, but nothing in't,
      Nor wealth, nor pleasure:
Vain earth! that falsely thou comply'st
With man; vain man! that thou rely'st
On earth; vain man, thou dot'st; vain earth, thou ly'st.

What mean dull souls, in this high measure,
      To haberdash
In earth's base wares, whose greatest treasure
      Is dross and trash?
The height of whose enchanting pleasure
      Is but a flash?
Are these the goods that thou supply'st
Us mortals with? Are these the high'st?
Can these bring cordial peace? false world, thou ly'st.

GEORGE HERBERT (1593-1633)

Virtue

SWEET day, so cool, so calm, so bright—
    The bridal of the earth and sky;
The dew shall weep thy fall to-night;
      For thou must die.

Sweet rose, whose hue angry and brave
Bids the rash gazer wipe his eye,
Thy root is ever in its grave,
      And thou must die.

Sweet spring, full of sweet days and roses,
A box where sweets compacted lie,
My music shows ye have your closes,
        And all must die.

Only a sweet and virtuous soul,
Like seasoned timber, never gives;
But though the whole world turn to coal,
        Then chiefly lives.

Easter

I got me flowers to strew Thy way,
   I got me boughs off many a tree;
But Thou wast up by break of day
And brought'st Thy sweets along with Thee.

The sun arising in the east,
Though he give light, and the east perfume,
If they should offer to contest
With Thy arising, they presume.

Can there be any day but this,
Though many suns to shine endeavor?
We count three hundred, but we miss:
There is but one, and that one ever.

ROBERT HERRICK (1594-1674)

His Theme

I sing of brooks, of blossoms, birds, and bowers,
   Of April, May, of June, and July flowers;
I sing of May-poles, hock-carts, wassails, wakes,
Of bridegrooms, brides, and of their bridal cakes.
I write of Youth, of Love, and have access
By these, to sing of cleanly wantonness;
I sing of dews, of rains, and, piece by piece,
Of balm, of oil, of spice, and ambergris;
I sing of times trans-shifting; and I write
How roses first came red, and lilies white;
I write of groves, of twilights, and I sing
The court of Mab, and of the Fairy King.
I write of Hell; I sing and ever shall,
Of Heaven, and hope to have it after all.

To Meadows

YE have been fresh and green,
    Ye have been fill'd with flowers;
And ye the walks have been
    Where maids have spent their hours.

You have beheld how they
    With wicker arks did come
To kiss and bear away
    The richer cowslips home.

Ye've heard them sweetly sing,
    And seen them in a round;
Each virgin, like a spring,
    With honeysuckles crowned.

But now, we see none here,
    Whose silv'ry feet did tread,
And with dishevelled hair
    Adorned this smoother mead.

Like unthrifts, having spent
    Your stock, and needy grown,
Ye're left here to lament
    Your poor estates, alone.

Whenas in Silks My Julia Goes

WHENAS in silks my Julia goes,
    Then, then, methinks, how sweetly flows
That liquefaction of her clothes.
Next, when I cast mine eyes, and see
That brave vibration each way free;
Oh, how that glittering taketh me!

The Night-Piece, to Julia

HER eyes the glow-worm lend thee,
    The shooting stars attend thee;
        And the elves also,
        Whose little cyes glow,
Like the sparks of fire, befriend thee.

No Will-o'-th'-Wisp mislight thee,
Nor snake or slow-worm bite thee;
        But on, on, thy way,
        Not making a stay,
Since ghost there's none to affright thee.

Let not the dark thee cumber;
What though the moon does slumber?
    The stars of the night
    Will lend thee their light,
Like tapers clear, without number.

Then, Julia, let me woo thee,
Thus, thus to come unto me;
    And when I shall meet
    Thy silv'ry feet,
My soul I'll pour into thee.

Corinna's Going A-Maying

GET up, get up for shame, the blooming morn
Upon her wings presents the god unshorn.
    See how Aurora throws her fair
    Fresh-quilted colors through the air:
    Get up, sweet slug-a-bed, and see
    The dew bespangling herb and tree.
Each flower has wept, and bowed toward the east,
Above an hour since: yet you not dressed;
    Nay! not so much as out of bed;
    When all the birds have matins said
    And sung their thankful hymns: 'tis sin,
    Nay, profanation, to keep in,
Whereas a thousand virgins on this day
Spring, sooner than the lark, to fetch in May.

Rise and put on your foliage, and be seen
To come forth, like the spring-time, fresh and green,
    And sweet as Flora. Take no care
    For jewels for your gown or hair:
    Fear not; the leaves will strew
    Gems in abundance upon you:
Besides, the childhood of the day has kept,
Against you come, some orient pearls unwept;
    Come, and receive them while the light
    Hangs on the dew-locks of the night,
    And Titan on the eastern hill
    Retires himself, or else stands still
Till you come forth. Wash, dress, be brief in praying:
Few beads are best, when once we go a-Maying.

Come, my Corinna, come; and, coming, mark
How each field turns a street, each street a park
    Made green and trimmed with trees; see how
    Devotion gives each house a bough
    Or branch: each porch, each door, ere this,
    An ark, a tabernacle is,

Made up of white-thorn, neatly interwove;
As if here were those cooler shades of love.
   Can such delights be in the street
   And open fields, and we not see't?
   Come, we'll abroad; and let's obey
   The proclamation made for May:
And sin no more, as we have done, by staying;
But, my Corinna, come, let's go a-Maying.

There's not a budding boy or girl, this day,
But is got up, and gone to bring in May.
   A deal of youth, ere this, is come
   Back, and with white-thorn laden home.
   Some have despatched their cakes and cream
   Before that we have left to dream:
And some have wept, and wooed and plighted troth,
And chose their priest, ere we can cast off sloth:
   Many a green gown has been given;
   Many a kiss, both odd and even:
   Many a glance, too, has been sent
   From out the eye, love's firmament;
Many a jest told of the keys betraying
This night, and locks picked, yet we're not a-Maying.

Come, let us go, while we are in our prime,
And take the harmless folly of the time.
   We shall grow old apace, and die
   Before we know our liberty.
   Our life is short, and our days run
   As fast away as does the sun;
And, as a vapor or a drop of rain,
Once lost, can ne'er be found again:
   So when or you or I are made
   A fable, song, or fleeting shade,
   All love, all liking, all delight
   Lies drowned with us in endless night.
Then while time serves, and we are but decaying,
Come, my Corinna, come, let's go a-Maying.

To the Virgins, to Make Much of Time

GATHER ye rosebuds while ye may,
   Old Time is still a-flying:
And this same flower that smiles to-day
   To-morrow will be dying.

The glorious land of heaven, the sun,
   The higher he's a-getting,
The sooner will his race be run,
   And nearer he's to setting.

SALEM COLLEGE
LIBRARY
Winston-Salem, N. C.

That age is best which is the first,
　When youth and blood are warmer;
But being spent, the worse, and worst
　Times still succeed the former.

Then be not coy, but use your time,
　And while ye may, go marry:
For having lost but once your prime,
　You may for ever tarry.

Delight in Disorder

A sweet disorder in the dress
　Kindles in clothes a wantonness:
A lawn about the shoulders thrown
Into a fine distraction:
An erring lace, which here and there
Enthrals the crimson stomacher:
A cuff neglectful, and thereby
Ribbons to flow confusedly:
A winning wave, deserving note,
In the tempestuous petticoat:
A careless shoe-string, in whose tie
I see a wild civility:
Do more bewitch me than when art
Is too precise in every part.

To Daffodils

FAIR Daffodils, we weep to see
　You haste away so soon;
As yet the early-rising sun
　Has not attained his noon.
　　　　Stay, stay,
　Until the hasting day
　　　　Has run
　But to the even-song;
And, having prayed together, we
　Will go with you along.

We have short time to stay as you,
　We have as short a spring;
As quick a growth to meet decay,
　As you, or any thing.
　　　　We die
　As your hours do, and dry
　　　　Away,
　Like to the summer's rain;
Or as the pearls of morning's dew,
　Ne'er to be found again.

To Anthea, Who May Command Him Anything

BID me to live, and I will live
    Thy Protestant to be;
Or bid me love, and I will give
    A loving heart to thee.

A heart as soft, a heart as kind,
    A heart as sound and free
As in the whole world thou canst find,
    That heart I'll give to thee.

Bid that heart stay, and it will stay
    To honor thy decree;
Or bid it languish quite away,
    And 't shall do so for thee.

Bid me to weep, and I will weep,
    While I have eyes to see;
And having none, yet will I keep
    A heart to weep for thee.

Bid me despair, and I'll despair,
    Under that cypress tree;
Or bid me die, and I will dare
    E'en death, to die for thee.

Thou art my life, my love, my heart,
    The very eyes of me;
And hast command of every part,
    To live and die for thee.

To Ben Jonson

AH, Ben!
    Say how, or when
Shall we thy guests
    Meet at those lyric feasts,
    Made at the Sun,
The Dog, the Triple Tun?
Where we such clusters had,
As made us nobly wild, not mad;
    And yet each verse of thine
Out-did the meat, out-did the frolic wine.
                     Abridged.

A Thanksgiving to God for His House

L ORD, Thou hast given me a cell
    Wherein to dwell;
A little house, whose humble roof
    Is weather-proof;
Under the spars of which I lie
    Both soft and dry;
Where Thou, my chamber for to ward,
    Hast set a guard
Of harmless thoughts, to watch and keep
    Me, while I sleep.
Low is my porch, as is my fate;
    Both void of state;
And yet the threshold of my door
    Is worn by the poor,
Who thither come, and freely get
    Good words, or meat.
Like as my parlor, so my hall
    And kitchen's small;
A little buttery, and therein
    A little bin,
Which keeps my little loaf of bread
    Unchipped, unflead;
Some brittle sticks of thorn or briar
    Make me a fire,
Close by whose living coal I sit,
    And glow like it.
Lord, I confess too, when I dine,
    The pulse is Thine,
And all those other bits that be
    There placed by Thee:
The worts, the purslain, and the mess
    Of water-cress;
Which of Thy kindness Thou hast sent;
    And my content
Makes those, and my belovèd beet,
    To be more sweet.
'Tis Thou that crown'st my glittering hearth
    With guiltless mirth,
And giv'st me wassail bowls to drink,
    Spiced to the brink.
Lord, 'tis Thy plenty-dropping hand
    That soils my land,
And giv'st me, for my bushel sown,
    Twice ten for one;

Thou mak'st my teeming hen to lay
    Her egg each day;
Besides, my healthful ewes to bear
    Me twins each year;
The while the conduits of my kine
    Run cream, for wine:
All these, and better, Thou dost send
    Me, to this end,—
That I should render, for my part,
    A thankful heart;
Which, fired with incense, I resign,
    As wholly Thine;
—But the acceptance, that must be,
    My Christ, by Thee.

JAMES SHIRLEY (1596-1666)

Death the Conqueror

THE glories of our blood and state
    Are shadows, not substantial things;
There is no armor against fate;
    Death lays his icy hand on kings:
      Sceptre and Crown
      Must tumble down,
And in the dust be equal made
With the poor crooked scythe and spade.

Some men with swords may reap the field,
    And plant fresh laurels where they kill:
But their strong nerves at last must yield;
    They tame but one another still:
      Early or late
      They stoop to fate,
And must give up their murmuring breath
When they, pale captives, creep to death.

The garlands wither on your brow;
    Then boast no more your mighty deeds;
Upon Death's purple altar now
    See where the victor-victim bleeds:
      Your heads must come
      To the cold tomb;
Only the actions of the just
Smell sweet, and blossom in their dust.

THOMAS RANDOLPH (1605-1635)

An Ode to Master Anthony Stafford to Hasten Him into the Country

COME, spur away,
    I have no patience for a longer stay,
        But must go down
And leave the chargeable noise of this great town:
        I will the country see,
        Where old simplicity,
            Though hid in gray,
            Doth look more gay
    Than foppery in plush and scarlet clad.
        Farewell, you city wits, that are
            Almost at civil war—
'Tis time that I grow wise, when all the world grows mad.

        More of my days
    I will not spend to gain an idiot's praise;
        Or to make sport
For some slight Puisne of the Inns of Court.
        Then, worthy Stafford, say,
        How shall we spend the day?
            With what delights
            Shorten the nights?
    When from this tumult we are got secure,
        Where mirth with all her freedom goes,
            Yet shall no finger lose;
Where every word is thought, and every thought is pure?

        There from the tree
    We'll cherries pluck, and pick the strawberry;
        And every day
Go see the wholesome country girls make hay,
        Whose brown hath lovelier grace
        Than any painted face
            That I do know
            Hyde Park can show:
    Where I had rather gain a kiss than meet
        (Though some of them in greater state
            Might court my love with plate)
The beauties of the Cheap, and wives of Lombard Street.

        But think upon
    Some other pleasures: these to me are none.

Why do I prate
Of women, that are things against my fate!
I never mean to wed
    That torture to my bed:
      My Muse is she
      My love shall be.
Let clowns get wealth and heirs: when I am gone
  And that great bugbear, grisly Death,
    Shall take this idle breath,
If I a poem leave, that poem is my son.

    Of this no more!
We'll rather taste the bright Pomona's store.
    No fruit shall 'scape
Our palates, from the damson to the grape.
Then, full, we'll seek a shade,
    And hear what music's made;
      How Philomel
      Her tale doth tell,
And how the other birds do fill the choir;
  The thrush and blackbird lend their throats,
    Warbling melodious notes;
We will all sports enjoy which others but desire.

    Ours is the sky,
Where at what fowl we please our hawk shall fly:
    Nor will we spare
To hunt the crafty fox or timorous hare;
    But let our hounds run loose
     In any ground they'll choose;
      The buck shall fall,
      The stag, and all.
Our pleasures must from their own warrants be,
    For to my Muse, if not to me,
      I'm sure all game is free:
Heaven, earth, are all but parts of her great royalty.

    And when we mean
To taste of Bacchus' blessings now and then,
    And drink by stealth
A cup or two to noble Barkley's health,
    I'll take my pipe and try
    The Phrygian melody;
      Which he that hears,
      Lets through his ears
A madness to distemper all the brain:
    Then I another pipe will take
     And Doric music make,
To civilize with graver notes our wits again.

SIR WILLIAM DAVENANT (1606-1668)

Morning Song

THE lark now leaves his watery nest,
   And climbing shakes his dewy wings,
He takes your window for the east,
   And to implore your light, he sings;
Awake, awake, the morn will never rise,
Till she can dress her beauty at your eyes.

The merchant bows unto the seaman's star,
   The ploughman from the sun his season takes;
But still the lover wonders what they are,
   Who look for day before his mistress wakes;
Awake, awake, break through your veils of lawn!
Then draw your curtains and begin the dawn.

EDMUND WALLER (1606-1687)

"Go, Lovely Rose"

GO, lovely Rose—
   Tell her that wastes her time and me,
   That now she knows,
When I resemble her to thee,
How sweet and fair she seems to be.

   Tell her that's young,
And shuns to have her graces spied,
   That hadst thou sprung
In deserts, where no men abide,
Thou must have uncommended died.

   Small is the worth
Of beauty from the light retired:
   Bid her come forth,
Suffer herself to be desired,
And not blush so to be admired.

   Then die—that she
The common fate of all things rare
   May read in thee;
How small a part of time they share
That are so wondrous sweet and fair!

On a Girdle

THAT which her slender waist confined
   Shall now my joyful temples bind;
No monarch but would give his crown
His arms might do what this has done.

It was my Heaven's extremest sphere,
The pale which held that lovely deer:
My joy, my grief, my hope, my love,
Did all within this circle move.

A narrow compass! and yet there
Dwelt all that's good, and all that's fair!
Give me but what this ribbon bound,
Take all the rest the sun goes round!

Old Age and Death

THE seas are quiet when the winds give o'er;
   So calm are we when passions are no more.
For then we know how vain it was to boast
Of fleeting things, too certain to be lost.
Clouds of affection from our younger eyes
Conceal that emptiness which age descries.

The soul's dark cottage, battered and decayed,
Lets in new light through chinks that time has made:
Stronger by weakness, wiser men become,
As they draw near to their eternal home.
Leaving the old, both worlds at once they view,
That stand upon the threshold of the new.

JOHN MILTON (1608-1674)

Song from "Arcades"

O'ER the smooth enamell'd green,
   Where no print of step hath been,
      Follow me as I sing,
      And touch the warbled string,
Under the shady roof
Of branching elm star-proof.
      Follow me,
I will bring you where she sits,
Clad in splendor as befits
      Her deity.
Such a rural Queen
All Arcadia hath not seen.

From "Comus"

THE star that bids the shepherd fold,
  Now the top of heaven doth hold;
And the gilded car of day
His glowing axle doth allay
In the steep Atlantic stream;
And the slope sun his upward beam
Shoots against the dusky pole,
Pacing toward the other goal
Of his chamber in the east.
Meanwhile welcome Joy, and Feast,
Midnight Shout and Revelry,
Tipsy Dance and Jollity.
Braid your locks with rosy twine,
Dropping odors, dropping wine.
Rigor now is gone to bed,
And Advice with scrupulous head,
Strict Age, and sour Severity,
With their grave saws in slumber lie.
We that are of purer fire
Imitate the starry quire,
Who in their nightly watchful spheres
Lead in swift round the months and years.
The sounds and seas, with all their finny drove,
Now to the moon in wavering morrice move;
And on the tawny sands and shelves
Trip the pert fairies and the dapper elves.
By dimpled brook, and fountain brim,
The wood-nymphs deck'd with daisies trim,
Their merry wakes and pastimes keep;
What hath night to do with sleep?
Night hath better sweets to prove,
Venus now wakes, and wakens Love.
Come let us our rites begin,
'Tis only day-light that makes sin,
Which these dun shades will ne'er report.
Hail Goddess of nocturnal sport,
Dark-veil'd Cotytto, t'whom the secret flame
Of midnight torches burns; mysterious dame,
That ne'er art call'd, but when the dragon womb
Of Stygian darkness spets her thickest gloom,
And makes one blot of all the air;
Stay thy cloudy ebon chair,
Wherein thou rid'st with Hecat, and befriend
Us thy vow'd priests, till utmost end
Of all thy dues be done, and none left out,
Ere the babbling eastern scout,

The nice morn, on the Indian steep
From her cabin'd loophole peep,
And to the tell-tale sun descry
Our conceal'd solemnity.
Come, knit hands, and beat the ground
In a light fantastic round.

       *   *   *   *   *   *

To the ocean now I fly,
And those happy climes that lie
Where day never shuts his eye,
Up in the broad fields of the sky:
There I suck the liquid air
All amidst the gardens fair
Of Hesperus, and his daughters three
That sing about the golden tree:
Along the crispèd shades and bowers
Revels the spruce and jocund Spring,
The Graces, and the rosy-bosom'd Hours,
Thither all their bounties bring;
There eternal Summer dwells,
And west-winds, with musky wing,
About the cedarn alleys fling
Nard and cassia's balmy smells.
Iris there with humid bow
Waters the odorous banks, that blow
Flowers of more mingled hue
That her purfled scarf can show,
And drenches with Elysian dew
(List mortals, if your ears be true)
Beds of hyacinth and roses,
Where young Adonis oft reposes,
Waxing well of his deep wound
In slumber soft, and on the ground
Sadly sits th' Assyrian queen;
But far above in spangled sheen
Celestial Cupid her famed son advanced,
Holds his dear Psyche sweet intranced,
After her wand'ring labors long,
Till free consent the Gods among
Make her his eternal bride,
And from her fair unspotted side
Two blissful twins are to be born,
Youth and Joy; so Jove hath sworn.
But now my task is smoothly done,
I can fly, or I can run
Quickly to the green earth's end,
Where the bow'd welkin slow doth bend,
And from thence can soar as soon
To the corners of the moon.

Mortals, that would follow me,
Love Virtue, she alone is free,
She can teach ye how to climb
Higher than the sphery chime:
Or, if Virtue feeble were,
Heav'n itself would stoop to her.

L'Allegro

HENCE loathèd Melancholy,
  Of Cerberus and blackest Midnight born,
In Stygian Cave forlorn
  'Mongst horrid shapes, and shrieks, and sights unholy!
Find out some uncouth cell,
  Where brooding Darkness spreads his jealous wings,
And the night-Raven sings;
  There, under Ebon shades, and low-browed Rocks,
As ragged as thy Locks,
  In dark Cimmerian desert ever dwell.
But come, thou Goddess fair and free,
In Heaven yclept Euphrosyne,
And by men, heart-easing Mirth,
Whom lovely Venus, at a birth,
With two sister Graces more,
To Ivy-crownèd Bacchus bore;
Or whether (as some Sager sing)
The Frolic Wind that breathes the Spring,
Zephir with Aurora playing,
As he met her once a-Maying,
There, on Beds of Violets blue,
And fresh-blown Roses washed in dew,
Filled her with thee, a daughter fair,
So buxom, blithe, and debonair.
  Haste thee, Nymph, and bring with thee
Jest and youthful Jollity,
Quips and Cranks, and wanton Wiles,
Nods, and Becks, and Wreathèd Smiles,
Such as hang on Hebe's cheek,
And love to live in dimple sleek;
Sport that wrinkled Care derides,
And Laughter holding both his sides.
Come, and trip it as ye go
On the light fantastic toe,
And in thy right hand lead with thee,
The Mountain Nymph, sweet Liberty;
And if I give thee honor due,
Mirth, admit me of thy crew
To live with her, and live with thee,

In unreprovèd pleasures free;
To hear the Lark begin his flight,
And, singing, startle the dull night,
From his watch-tower in the skies,
Till the dappled dawn doth rise;
Then to come in spite of sorrow,
And at my window bid good-morrow,
Through the Sweet-Briar, or the Vine,
Or the twisted Eglantine.
While the Cock, with lively din,
Scatters the rear of darkness thin,
And to the stack, or the Barn-door,
Stoutly struts his Dames before,
Oft listening how the Hounds and horn
Clearly rouse the slumbering morn,
From the side of some Hoar Hill,
Through the high wood echoing shrill.
Some time walking not unseen
By Hedge-row Elms, on Hillocks green,
Right against the Eastern gate,
Where the great Sun begins his state,
Robed in flames, and Amber light,
The clouds in thousand Liveries dight.
While the Plowman, near at hand,
Whistles o'er the Furrowed Land,
And the Milkmaid singeth blithe,
And the Mower whets his scythe,
And every Shepherd tells his tale
Under the Hawthorn in the dale.
Straight mine eye hath caught new pleasures
Whilst the Landscape round it measures,
Russet Lawns, and Fallows Gray,
Where the nibbling flocks do stray,
Mountains on whose barren breast
The laboring clouds do often rest:
Meadows trim with Daisies pied,
Shallow Brooks, and Rivers wide.
Towers, and Battlements it sees
Bosomed high in tufted Trees,
Where perhaps some beauty lies,
The Cynosure of neighboring eyes.
Hard by a Cottage chimney smokes,
From betwixt two aged Oaks,
Where Corydon and Thyrsis met,
Are at their savory dinner set
Of Herbs, and other Country Messes,
Which the neat-handed Phillis dresses;
And then in haste her Bower she leaves,
With Thestylis to bind the Sheaves;

Or, if the earlier season lead,
To the tanned Haycock in the Mead.
Sometimes with secure delight
The upland Hamlets will invite,
When the merry Bells ring round,
And the jocund rebecks sound
To many a youth, and many a maid,
Dancing in the Chequered shade;
And young and old come forth to play
On a Sunshine Holyday,
Till the live-long day-light fail;
Then to the Spicy Nut-brown Ale,
With stories told of many a feat,
How Faery Mab the junkets eat.
She was pinched, and pulled she said;
And he, by Friar's Lantern led,
Tells how the drudging Goblin sweat,
To earn his Cream-bowl duly set,
When in one night, ere glimpse of morn,
His shadowy Flail hath threshed the Corn
That ten day-laborers could not end,
Then lies him down, the lubber fiend,
And stretched out all the Chimney's length,
Basks at the fire his hairy strength;
And Crop-full out of doors he flings,
Ere the first Cock his Matin rings.
Thus done the Tales, to bed they creep,
By whispering Winds soon lulled asleep.
    Towered Cities please us then,
And the busy hum of men,
Where throngs of Knights and Barons bold,
In weeds of Peace high triumphs hold,
With store of Ladies, whose bright eyes
Rain influence, and judge the prize
Of Wit, or Arms, while both contend
To win her Grace, whom all commend.
There let Hymen oft appear
In Saffron robe, with Taper clear,
And pomp, and feast, and revelry,
With mask, and antique Pageantry,
Such sights as youthful Poets dream
On Summer eves by haunted stream.
Then to the well-trod stage anon,
If Jonson's learnèd Sock be on,
Or sweetest Shakespeare, Fancy's child,
Warble his native Wood-notes wild;
And ever, against eating Cares,
Lap me in soft Lydian Airs,
Married to immortal verse

Such as the meeting soul may pierce
In notes, with many a winding bout
Of linkèd sweetness long drawn out,
With wanton heed, and giddy cunning,
The melting voice through mazes running;
Untwisting all the chains that tie
The hidden soul of harmony;
That Orpheus' self may heave his head
From golden slumber on a bed
Of heaped Elysian flowers, and hear
Such strains as would have won the ear
Of Pluto, to have quite set free
His half-regained Eurydice.
These delights, if thou canst give,
Mirth, with thee I mean to live.

Il Penseroso

Hence vain deluding Joys,
        The brood of Folly without father bred!
How little you bestead,
        Or fill the fixèd mind with all your toys;
Dwell in some idle brain,
        And fancies fond with gaudy shapes possess,
As thick and numberless
        As the gay motes that people the sun-beams,
Or likest hovering dreams
        The fickle Pensioners of Morpheus' train.
But hail, thou Goddess, sage and holy,
Hail, divinest Melancholy!
Whose Saintly visage is too bright
To hit the Sense of human sight;
And therefore to our weaker view,
O'er-laid with black, staid Wisdom's hue.
Black, but such as in esteem,
Prince Memnon's sister might beseem,
Or that Starred Ethiope Queen that strove
To set her beauty's praise above
The Sea Nymphs, and their powers offended.
Yet thou art higher far descended:
Thee bright-haired Vesta long of yore,
To solitary Saturn bore;
His daughter she (in Saturn's reign,
Such mixture was not held a stain).
Oft in glimmering Bowers, and glades
He met her, and in secret shades
Of woody Ida's inmost grove,

Whilst yet there was no fear of Jove.
Come, pensive Nun, devout and pure,
Sober, steadfast, and demure,
All in a robe of darkest grain,
Flowing with majestic train,
And sable stole of Cypress Lawn,
Over thy decent shoulders drawn.
Come, but keep thy wonted state,
With even step, and musing gait,
And looks commercing with the skies,
Thy rapt soul sitting in thine eyes:
There, held in holy passion still,
Forget thy self to Marble, till
With a sad Leaden downward cast,
Thou fix them on the earth as fast.
And join with thee calm Peace, and Quiet,
Spare Fast, that oft with gods doth diet,
And hears the Muses in a ring,
Aye round about Jove's Altar sing.
And add to these retirèd Leisure,
That in trim Gardens takes his pleasure;
But first, and chiefest, with thee bring,
Him that yon soars on golden wing,
Guiding the fiery-wheelèd throne,
The Cherub Contemplation,
And the mute Silence hist along,
'Less Philomel will deign a Song,
In her sweetest, saddest plight,
Smoothing the rugged brow of Night,
While Cynthia checks her Dragon yoke,
Gently o'er th' accustomed Oak;
Sweet Bird, that shunn'st the noise of folly,
Most musical, most melancholy!
Thee, Chauntress, oft the Woods among,
I woo to hear thy even-song;
And missing thee, I walk unseen
On the dry smooth-shaven Green,
To behold the wandering Moon,
Riding near her highest noon,
Like one that had been led astray
Through the Heaven's wide pathless way;
And oft, as if her head she bowed,
Stooping through a fleecy cloud.
Oft on a Plat of rising ground,
I hear the far-off Curfew sound,
Over some wide-watered shore,
Swinging slow with sullen roar;
Or if the Air will not permit,
Some still removèd place will fit,

Where glowing Embers through the room
Teach light to counterfeit a gloom,
Far from all resort of mirth,
Save the Cricket on the hearth,
Or the Bellman's drowsy charm,
To bless the doors from nightly harm:
Or let my Lamp, at midnight hour,
Be seen in some high lonely Tower,
Where I may oft out-watch the Bear,
With thrice great Hermes, or unsphere
The spirit of Plato to unfold
What Worlds, or what vast Regions hold
The immortal mind that hath forsook
Her mansion in this fleshly nook:
And of those Dæmons that are found
In fire, air, flood, or under ground,
Whose power hath a true consent
With Planet, or with Element.
Some time let Gorgeous Tragedy
In Sceptered Pall come sweeping by,
Presenting Thebes, or Pelops' line,
Or the tale of Troy divine,
Or what (though rare) of later age,
Ennoblèd hath the Buskined stage.
But, O sad Virgin, that thy power
Might raise Musæus from his bower,
Or bid the soul of Orpheus sing
Such notes as, warbled to the string,
Drew Iron tears down Pluto's cheek,
And made Hell grant what Love did seek.
Or call up him that left half told
The story of Cambuscan bold,
Of Camball, and of Algarsife,
And who had Canace to wife,
That owned the virtuous Ring and Glass,
And of the wondrous Horse of Brass,
On which the Tartar King did ride;
And if aught else great Bards beside,
In sage and solemn tunes have sung,
Of Tourneys and of Trophies hung;
Of Forests, and enchantments drear,
Where more is meant than meets the ear.
Thus, Night, oft see me in thy pale career,
Till civil-suited Morn appear,
Not tricked and frounced as she was wont,
With the Attic Boy to hunt,
But Kerchiefed in a comely Cloud,
While rocking Winds are Piping loud,
Or ushered with a shower still,

When the gust hath blown his fill,
Ending on the rustling Leaves,
With minute-drops from off the Eaves.
And when the Sun begins to fling
His flaring beams, me, Goddess, bring
To archèd walks of twilight groves,
And shadows brown, that Sylvan loves,
Of Pine, or monumental Oak,
Where the rude Ax with heavèd stroke,
Was never heard the Nymphs to daunt,
Or fright them from their hallowed haunt.
There in close covert by some Brook,
Where no profaner eye may look,
Hide me from Day's garish eye,
While the Bee with Honied thigh,
That at her flowery work doth sing,
And the Waters murmuring
With such consort as they keep,
Entice the dewy-feathered Sleep;
And let some strange mysterious dream,
Wave at his Wings, in Airy stream
Of lively portraiture displayed,
Softly on my eye-lids laid.
And as I wake, sweet music breathe
Above, about, or underneath,
Sent by some Spirit to mortals good,
Or th' unseen Genius of the Wood.
   But let my due feet never fail,
To walk the studious Cloister's pale,
And love the high embowèd Roof,
With antique Pillars massy proof.
And storied Windows richly dight,
Casting a dim religious light.
There let the pealing Organ blow,
To the full voiced choir below,
In Service high, and Anthems clear,
As may with sweetness, through mine ear,
Dissolve me into ecstasies,
And bring all Heaven before mine eyes.
And may at last my weary age
Find out the peaceful hermitage,
The Hairy Gown and Mossy Cell,
Where I may sit and rightly spell
Of every Star that Heaven doth shew,
And every Herb that sips the dew;
Till old experience do attain
To something like Prophetic strain.
These pleasures, Melancholy, give,
And I with thee will choose to live.

Lycidas

*(A Lament for a Friend Drowned in His Passage from
Chester on the Irish Seas, 1637)*

YET once more, O ye Laurels, and once more
   Ye Myrtles brown, with Ivy never sere,
I come to pluck your Berries harsh and crude,
And with forced fingers rude,
Shatter your leaves before the mellowing year.
Bitter constraint, and sad occasion dear,
Compels me to disturb your season due:
For Lycidas is dead, dead ere his prime,
Young Lycidas, and hath not left his peer:
Who would not sing for Lycidas? he knew
Himself to sing, and build the lofty rhyme.
He must not float upon his watery bier
Unwept, and welter to the parching wind,
Without the meed of some melodious tear.
  Begin, then, Sisters of the sacred well,
That from beneath the seat of Jove doth spring;
Begin, and somewhat loudly sweep the string.
Hence with denial vain, and coy excuse,
So may some gentle Muse
With lucky words favor *my* destined Urn,
And as he passes turn,
And bid fair peace be to my sable shroud.
For we were nursed upon the self-same hill,
Fed the same flock, by fountain, shade, and rill;
Together both, ere the high Lawns appeared
Under the opening eye-lids of the Morn,
We drove a-field, and both together heard
What time the Gray-fly winds her sultry horn,
Battening our flocks with the fresh dews of night,
Oft till the Star that rose, at Evening, bright
Toward Heaven's descent had sloped his westering wheel.
Meanwhile the Rural ditties were not mute,
Tempered to the Oaten Flute;
Rough Satyrs danced, and Fauns with cloven heel,
From the glad sound would not be absent long,
And old Damætas loved to hear our song.
  But O the heavy change, now thou art gone,
Now thou art gone, and never must return!
Thee, Shepherd, thee the Woods, and desert Caves,
With wild Thyme and the gadding Vine o'ergrown,
And all their echoes mourn.
The Willows, and the Hazel Copses green,
Shall now no more be seen,
Fanning their joyous Leaves to thy soft lays.
As killing as the Canker to the Rose,

Or Taint-worm to the weanling Herds that graze,
Or Frost to Flowers, that their gay wardrobe wear,
When first the White-thorn blows;
Such, Lycidas, thy loss to Shepherd's ear.
　Where were ye, Nymphs, when the remorseless deep
Closed o'er the head of your loved Lycidas?
For neither were ye playing on the steep,
Where your old Bards, the famous Druids, lie,
Nor on the shaggy top of Mona high,
Nor yet where Deva spreads her wizard stream:
Aye me, I fondly dream!
Had ye been there—for what could that have done?
What could the Muse herself that Orpheus bore,
The Muse herself, for her enchanting son
Whom Universal nature did lament,
When, by the rout that made the hideous roar,
His gory visage down the stream was sent,
Down the swift Hebrus to the Lesbian shore?
　Alas! What boots it with uncessant care
To tend the homely slighted Shepherd's trade,
And strictly meditate the thankless Muse,
Were it not better done, as others use,
To sport with Amaryllis in the shade,
Or with the tangles of Neæra's hair?
Fame is the spur that the clear spirit doth raise
(That last infirmity of Noble mind)
To scorn delights, and live laborious days;
But the fair Guerdon when we hope to find,
And think to burst out into sudden blaze,
Comes the blind Fury with the abhorrèd shears,
And slits the thin-spun life. "But not the praise,"
Phœbus replied, and touched my trembling ears;
"Fame is no plant that grows on mortal soil,
Nor in the glistering foil
Set off to the world, nor in broad rumor lies,
But lives and spreads aloft by those pure eyes,
And perfect witness of all-judging Jove;
As he pronounces lastly on each deed,
Of so much fame in Heaven expect thy meed."
　O fountain Arethuse, and thou honored flood,
Smooth-sliding Mincius, crowned with vocal reeds,
That strain I heard was of a higher mood:
But now my Oat proceeds,
And listens to the Herald of the Sea
That came in Neptune's plea.
He asked the Waves, and asked the Felon winds,
What hard mishap hath doomed this gentle swain?
And questioned every gust of rugged wings
That blows from off each beakèd Promontory.

They knew not of his story,
And sage Hippotades their answer brings,
That not a blast was from his dungeon strayed,
The Air was calm, and on the level brine,
Sleek Panope with all her sisters played.
It was that fatal and perfidious Bark
Built in the eclipse, and rigged with curses dark,
That sunk so low that sacred head of thine.
  Next Camus, reverend Sire, went footing slow,
His Mantle hairy, and his Bonnet sedge,
Inwrought with figures dim, and on the edge
Like to that sanguine flower inscribed with woe.
"Ah, who hath reft," (quoth he) "my dearest pledge?"
Last come, and last did go,
The Pilot of the Galilean Lake.
Two massy Keys he bore of metals twain,
(The Golden opes, the Iron shuts amain).
He shook his Mitered locks, and stern bespake,
"How well could I have spared for thee, young swain,
Enow of such as, for their bellies' sake,
Creep and intrude, and climb into the fold!
Of other care they little reckoning make,
Than how to scramble at the shearers' feast,
And shove away the worthy bidden guest.
Blind mouths! that scarce themselves know how to hold
A Sheep-hook, or have learned aught else the least
That to the faithful Herdman's art belongs!
What recks it them? What need they? They are sped;
And when they list, their lean and flashy songs
Grate on their scrannel Pipes of wretched straw,
The hungry Sheep look up, and are not fed,
But swoln with wind, and the rank mist they draw,
Rot inwardly, and foul contagion spread:
Besides what the grim Wolf with privy paw
Daily devours apace, and nothing said.
But that two-handed engine at the door,
Stands ready to smite once, and smite no more."
  Return Alpheus, the dread voice is past,
That shrunk thy streams; return, Sicilian Muse,
And call the Vales, and bid them hither cast
Their Bells, and Flowerets of a thousand hues.
Ye valleys low, where the mild whispers use,
Of shades and wanton winds, and gushing brooks,
On whose fresh lap the swart Star sparely looks,
Throw hither all your quaint enameled eyes,
That on the green turf suck the honied showers,
And purple all the ground with vernal flowers.
Bring the rathe Primrose that forsaken dies,
The tufted Crow-toe, and pale Jessamine,
The white Pink, and the Pansy freaked with jet,

The glowing Violet,
The Musk-rose, and the well-attired Woodbine,
With Cowslips wan that hang the pensive head,
And every flower that sad embroidery wears:
Bid Amaranthus all his beauty shed,
And Daffadillies fill their cups with tears,
To strew the Laureate Hearse where Lycid lies.
For so to interpose a little ease,
Let our frail thoughts dally with false surmise.
Ay me! Whilst thee the shores, and sounding Seas
Wash far away, where e'er thy bones are hurled,
Whether beyond the stormy Hebrides,
Where thou perhaps under the whelming tide
Visit'st the bottom of the monstrous world;
Or whether thou, to our moist vows denied,
Sleep'st by the fable of Bellerus old,
Where the great vision of the guarded Mount
Looks toward Namancos and Bayona's hold;
Look homeward, Angel, now, and melt with ruth:
And, O ye Dolphins, waft the hapless youth.
   Weep no more, woful Shepherds, weep no more,
For Lycidas your sorrow is not dead,
Sunk though he be beneath the watery floor.
So sinks the day-star in the Ocean bed,
And yet anon repairs his drooping head,
And tricks his beams, and with new-spangled Ore,
Flames in the forehead of the morning sky:
So Lycidas sunk low, but mounted high,
Through the dear might of Him that walked the waves
Where, other groves and other streams along,
With Nectar pure his oozy Locks he laves,
And hears the unexpressive nuptial Song,
In the blest Kingdoms meek of joy and love.
There entertain him all the Saints above,
In solemn troops, and sweet Societies,
That sing, and singing in their glory move,
And wipe the tears for ever from his eyes.
Now, Lycidas, the Shepherds weep no more;
Henceforth thou art the Genius of the shore,
In thy large recompense, and shalt be good
To all that wander in that perilous flood.
   Thus sang the uncouth Swain to the Oaks and rills,
While the still morn went out with Sandals gray,
He touched the tender stops of various Quills,
With eager thought warbling his Doric lay:
And now the Sun had stretched out all the hills,
And now was dropt into the Western bay;
At last he rose, and twitched his Mantle blue:
To-morrow to fresh Woods, and Pastures new.

An Epitaph on the Admirable Dramatic Poet, W. Shakespeare

WHAT needs my Shakespeare for his honored bones
    The labor of an age in pilèd stones?
Or that his hallowed relics should be hid
Under a stary-pointing pyramid?
Dear son of memory, great heir of fame,
What need'st thou such weak witness of thy name?
Thou in our wonder and astonishment
Hast built thyself a livelong monument.
For whilst, to the shame of slow-endeavoring art,
Thy easy numbers flow, and that each heart
Hath from the leaves of thy unvalued book
Those Delphic lines with deep impression took,
Then thou, our fancy of itself bereaving,
Dost make *us* marble with too much conceiving;
And so sepùlchered in such pomp dost lie,
That kings for such a tomb would wish to die.

To the Nightingale

O nightingale that on yon bloomy spray
    Warblest at eve, when all the woods are still,
    Thou with fresh hope the lover's heart dost fill,
    While the jolly hours lead on propitious May.
Thy liquid notes that close the eye of day,
    First heard before the shallow cuckoo's bill,
    Portend success in love. O, if Jove's will
    Have linked that amorous power to thy soft lay,
Now timely sing, ere the rude bird of hate
    Foretell my hopeless doom, in some grove nigh;
    As thou from year to year hast sung too late
For my relief, yet hadst no reason why.
    Whether the Muse or Love call thee his mate,
    Both them I serve, and of their train am I.

How Soon Hath Time

HOW soon hath Time, the subtle thief of youth,
    Stolen on his wing my three-and-twentieth year!
My hasting days fly on with full career,
    But my late spring no bud or blossom shew'th.
Perhaps my semblance might deceive the truth
    That I to manhood am arrived so near;
    And inward ripeness doth much less appear,
    That some more timely-happy spirits endu'th.

Yet, be it less or more, or soon or slow,
  It shall be still in strictest measure even
  To that same lot, however mean or high,
Toward which Time leads me, and the will of Heaven,
  All is, if I have grace to use it so,
  As ever in my great Task-Master's eye.

On His Blindness

WHEN I consider how my light is spent
  Ere half my days in this dark world and wide,
And that one talent, which is death to hide,
Lodged with me useless, though my soul more bent
To serve therewith my Maker, and present
My true account, lest He returning chide;
"Doth God exact day-labor, light denied?"
I fondly ask. But Patience, to prevent
That murmur, soon replies, "God doth not need
Either man's work or his own gifts; who best
Bear his mild yoke, they serve him best; his state
Is kingly; thousands at his bidding speed,
And post o'er land and ocean without rest;
They also serve who only stand and wait."

On His Deceased Wife

METHOUGHT I saw my late espousèd Saint
  Brought to me like Alcestis from the grave,
Whom Jove's great Son to her glad Husband gave,
Rescu'd from death by force though pale and faint.
Mine as whom washt from spot of child-bed taint,
Purification in the old Law did save,
And such, as yet once more I trust to have
Full sight of her in Heaven without restraint,
Came vested all in white, pure as her mind:
Her face was veil'd, yet to my fancied sight,
Love, sweetness, goodness, in her person shin'd
So clear, as in no face with more delight.
But O as to embrace me she enclin'd
I wak'd, she fled, and day brought back my night.

On the Late Massacre in Piedmont

AVENGE, O Lord, thy slaughtered saints, whose bones
  Lie scattered on the Alpine mountains cold;
Even them who kept thy truth so pure of old,
When all our fathers worshipped stocks and stones,

Forget not: in thy book record their groans
Who were thy sheep, and in their ancient fold
Slain by the bloody Piedmontese, that rolled
Mother with infant down the rocks.   Their moans
The vales redoubled to the hills, and they
To heaven.   Their martyred blood and ashes sow
O'er all the Italian fields, where still doth sway
A hundredfold, who, having learnt thy way,
Early may fly the Babylonian woe.

SIR JOHN SUCKLING (1608-1641)

A Ballad upon a Wedding

I tell thee, Dick, where I have been,
    Oh, things without compare!
Where I the rarest things have seen;
Such sights again cannot be found
In any place on English ground,
    Be it at wake or fair.

At Charing Cross, hard by the way
Where we (thou know'st) do sell our hay,
    There is a house with stairs;
And there did I see coming down
Such folk as are not in our town,
    Forty at least, in pairs.

At Course-a-Park, without all doubt,
He should have first been taken out
    By all the maids i' the town:
Though lusty Roger there had been,
Or little George upon the green,
    Or Vincent of the Crown.

Amongst the rest, one pest'lent fine,
(His beard no bigger, though, than thine)
    Walk'd on before the rest:
Our landlord looks like nothing to him:
The king, God bless him, 'twould undo him,
    Should he go still so drest.

But wot you what? The youth was going
To make an end of all his wooing;
    The parson for him staid:
Yet by his leave, for all his haste,
He did not so much wish all past,
    Perchance, as did the maid.

The maid, and thereby hangs a tale,
For such a maid no whitsum-ale
    Could ever yet produce:
No grape that's kindly ripe could be
So round, so plump, so soft as she,
    Nor half so full of juice.

Her finger was so small, the ring
Would not stay on which they did bring;
    It was too wide a peck:
And, to say truth (for out it must)
It look'd like the great collar (just)
    About our young colt's neck.

Her feet beneath her petticoat,
Like little mice, stole in and out,
    As if they fear'd the light:
But oh! she dances such a way!
No sun upon an Easter-day
    Is half so fine a sight.

He would have kissed her once or twice,
But she would not, she was so nice,
    She would not do't in sight,
And then she looked as who should say:
I will do what I list to-day,
    And you shall do't at night.

Her cheeks so rare a white was on,
No daisy makes comparison;
    Who sees them is undone;
For streaks of red were mingled there,
Such as are on a Cath'rine pear,
    The side that's next the sun.

Her lips were red; and one was thin,
Compar'd to that was next her chin,
    Some bee had stung it newly;
But, Dick, her eyes so guard her face,
I durst no more upon them gaze,
    Than on the sun in July.

Her mouth so small, when she does speak,
Thou'dst swear her teeth her words did break,
    That they might passage get:
But she so handled still the matter,
They came as good as ours, or better,
    And are not spent a whit.

If wishing should be any sin,
The parson himself had guilty been
    (She look'd that day so purely):

And did the youth so oft the feat
At night, as some did in conceit,
    It would have spoiled him surely.

Passion, oh me! how I run on!
There's that that would be thought upon.
    I trow, besides the bride:
The bus'ness of the kitchen's great,
For it is fit that men should eat,
    Nor was it there denied.

Just in the nick, the cook knock'd thrice,
And all the waiters in a trice
    His summons did obey;
Each serving-man, with dish in hand,
March'd boldly up, like our train'd band,
    Presented, and away.

When all the meat was on the table,
What man of knife, or teeth, was able
    To stay to be intreated?
And this the very reason was,
Before the parson could say grace,
    The company was seated.

Now hats fly off, and youths carouse;
Healths first go round, and then the house,
    The bride's came thick and thick;
And when 'twas nam'd another's health,
Perhaps he made it her's by stealth,
    And who could help it, Dick?

O' th' sudden up they rise and dance;
Then sit again, and sigh, and glance:
    Then dance again, and kiss.
Thus sev'ral ways the time did pass,
Till ev'ry woman wish'd her place,
    And ev'ry man wish'd his.

By this time all were stol'n aside
To counsel and undress the bride:
    But that he must not know:
But yet 'twas thought he guess'd her mind,
And did not mean to stay behind
    Above an hour or so.

When in he came (Dick), there she lay
Like new-fall'n snow melting away
    ('Twas time, I trow, to part);

Kisses were now the only stay,
Which soon she gave, as who should say,
   God b' w' ye, with all my heart.

But, just as Heaven would have, to cross it,
In came the bridesmaids with the posset:
   The bridegroom ate in spite;
For had he left the women to't,
It would have cost two hours to do't,
   Which were too much that night.

At length the candle's out, and now
All that they had not done they do.
   What that is, who can tell?
But I believe it was no more
Than thou and I have done before
   With Bridget and with Nell.

Song

WHY so pale and wan, fond lover?
   Prithee, why so pale?
Will, when looking well can't move her,
   Looking ill prevail?
   Prithee, why so pale?

Why so dull and mute, young sinner?
   Prithee, why so mute?
Will, when speaking well can't win her,
   Saying nothing do't?
   Prithee, why so mute?

Quit, quit, for shame, this will not move:
   This cannot take her.
If of herself she will not love,
   Nothing can make her:
   The devil take her!

RICHARD CRASHAW (1613-1650)

Wishes to His Supposed Mistress

WHOE'ER she be,
   That not impossible She
That shall command my heart and me:

Where'er she lie,
Locked up from mortal eye
In shady leaves of destiny:

Till that ripe birth
Of studied Fate stand forth,
And teach her fair steps tread our earth:

Till that divine
Idea take a shrine
Of crystal flesh, through which to shine:

Meet you her, my Wishes,
Bespeak her to my blisses,
And be ye called my absent kisses.

I wish her Beauty
That owes not all its duty
To gaudy tire, or glistering shoe-tie:

Something more than
Taffeta or tissue can,
Or rampant feather, or rich fan.

More than the spoil
Of shop, or silkworm's toil,
Or a bought blush, or a set smile.

A Face that's best
By its own beauty dressed,
And can alone commend the rest.

A Face, made up
Out of no other shop
Than what Nature's white hand sets ope.

A Cheek, where youth
And blood, with pen of truth,
Write what their reader sweetly ru'th.

A Cheek, where grows
More than a morning rose,
Which to no box its being owes.

Lips, where all day
A lover's kiss may play,
Yet carry nothing thence away.

Looks, that oppress
Their richest tires, but dress
Themselves in simple nakedness.

Eyes, that displace
The neighbor diamond, and outface
That sunshine by their own sweet grace.

Tresses, that wear
Jewels but to declare
How much themselves more precious are:

Whose native ray
Can tame the wanton day
Of gems that in their bright shades play.

Each ruby there,
Or pearl that dare appear,
Be its own blush, be its own tear.

A well-tamed Heart,
For whose more noble smart
Love may be long choosing a dart.

Eyes, that bestow
Full quivers on Love's bow,
Yet play less arrows than they owe.

Smiles, that can warm
The blood, yet teach a charm,
That chastity shall take no harm.

Blushes, that bin
The burnish of no sin,
Nor flames of aught too hot within.

Joys, that confess
Virtue their mistress,
And have no other head to dress.

Fears, fond and slight
As the coy bride's, when night,
First does the longing lover right.

Days that need borrow
No part of their good-morrow
From a fore-spent night of sorrow.

Days that, in spite
Of darkness, by the light
Of a clear mind, are day all night.

Nights, sweet as they,
Made short by lovers' play,
Yet long by the absence of the day.

Life, that dares send
A challenge to his end,
And when it comes, say, "Welcome, friend!"

Sydneian showers
Of sweet discourse, whose powers
Can crown old Winter's head with flowers.

Soft silken hours,
Open suns, shady bowers;
'Bove all, nothing within that lowers.

Whate'er delight
Can make Day's forehead bright,
Or give down to the wings of Night

In her whole frame
Have Nature all the name;
Art and Ornament, the shame!

Her flattery,
Picture and Poesy:
Her counsel her own virtue be.

I wish her store
Of worth may leave her poor
Of wishes; and I wish—no more.

Now, if Time knows
That Her, whose radiant brows
Weave them a garland of my vows;

Her, whose just bays
My future hopes can raise,
A trophy to her present praise;

Her, that dares be
What these lines wish to see;
I seek no further, it is She.

'Tis She, and here,
Lo! I unclothe and clear
My Wishes' cloudy character.

May she enjoy it
Whose merit dare apply it,
But modesty dares still deny it!

Such worth as this is
Shall fix my flying Wishes,
And determine them to kisses.

Let her full glory,
My fancies, fly before ye;
Be ye my fictions—but her Story!

Hymn to the Name of Jesus

I sing the Name which none can say,
   But touch'd with an interior ray;
The name of our new peace; our good;
Our bliss, and supernatural blood;
The name of all our lives and loves:
Hearken and help, ye holy doves!
The high-born brood of day; you bright
Candidates of blissful light,
The heirs elect of love; whose names belong
Unto the everlasting life of song;
All ye wise souls, who in the wealthy breast
Of his unbounded Name build your warm nest.

     *   *   *   *   *   *

Oh, fill our senses, and take from us
All force of so profane a fallacy,
To think aught sweet but that which smells of thee.
Fair flow'ry name! in none but thee,
And thy nectareal fragrancy,
     Hourly there meets
An universal synod of all sweets;
By whom it is defined thus—
       That no perfume
       For ever shall presume
To pass for odoriferous,
But such alone whose sacred pedigree
Can prove itself some kin, sweet name! to thee.

RICHARD LOVELACE (1618-1658)

To Althea, from Prison

WHEN Love with unconfinèd wings
     Hovers within my gates,
And my divine Althea brings
   To whisper at the grates;
When I lie tangled in her hair
   And fettered to her eye,
The birds that wanton in the air
   Know no such liberty.

When flowing cups run swiftly round
   With no allaying Thames,
Our careless heads with roses bound,
   Our hearts with loyal flames;
When thirsty grief in wine we steep,
   When healths and draughts go free—

Fishes that tipple in the deep
　　Know no such liberty.

When, like committed linnets, I
　　With shriller throat shall sing
The sweetness, mercy, majesty,
　　And glories of my King;
When I shall voice aloud how good
　　He is, how great should be,
Enlargèd winds, that curl the flood,
　　Know no such liberty.

Stone walls do not a prison make,
　　Nor iron bars a cage;
Minds innocent and quiet take
　　That for an hermitage;
If I have freedom in my love
　　And in my soul am free,
Angels alone, that soar above,
　　Enjoy such liberty.

To Lucasta, Going to the Wars

TELL me not, Sweet, I am unkind,
　　　That from the nunnery
Of thy chaste breast and quiet mind
　　To war and arms I fly.

True, a new mistress now I chase,
　　The first foe in the field;
And with a stronger faith embrace
　　A sword, a horse, a shield.

Yet this inconstancy is such
　　As thou too shalt adore;
I could not love thee, Dear, so much,
　　Loved I not Honor more.

ABRAHAM COWLEY (1618-1667)

The Wish

WELL then, I now do plainly see
　　This busy world and I shall ne'er agree;
The very honey of all earthly joy
Does, of all meats, the soonest cloy:
　　And they, methinks, deserve my pity
Who for it can endure the stings,
The crowd, and buzz, and murmurings
　　Of this great hive, the city!

Ah, yet, ere I descend to the grave,
May I a small house and large garden have;
And a few friends, and many books, both true,
Both wise, and both delightful too!
    And since Love ne'er will from me flee,—
A mistress moderately fair,
And good as guardian-angels are,
    Only beloved, and loving me!

O fountains! when in you shall I
Myself eased of unpeaceful thoughts espy?
O fields! O woods! when, when shall I be made
The happy tenant of your shade?
    Here's the spring-head of pleasure's flood!
Here's wealthy Nature's treasury,
Where all the riches lie, that she
    Has coined and stamped for good.

Pride and ambition here
Only in far-fetched metaphors appear;
Here naught but winds can hurtful murmurs scatter,
And naught but echo flatter.
    The gods, when they descended, hither
From heaven did always choose their way;
And therefore we may boldly say
    That 'tis the way to thither.

How happy here should I
And one dear She live, and embracing die!
She who is all the world, and can exclude
In deserts solitude.
    I should have then this only fear:
Lest men, when they my pleasures see,
Should hither throng to live like me,
    And so make a city here.

Drinking

(After Anacreon)

THE thirsty earth soaks up the rain,
    And drinks, and gapes for drink again;
The plants suck in the earth, and are,
With constant drinking, fresh and fair;
The sea itself (which one would think
Should have but little need of drink),
Drinks twice ten thousand rivers up,
So filled that they o'erflow the cup.
The busy sun (and one would guess
By's drunken fiery face no less),

Drinks up the sea, and, when he's done,
The moon and stars drink up the sun:
They drink and dance by their own light;
They drink and revel all the night.
Nothing in nature's sober found,
But an eternal "health" goes round.
Fill up the bowl then, fill it high—
Fill all the glasses there; for why
Should every creature drink but I?
Why, men of morals, tell me why?

ANDREW MARVELL (1621-1678)

An Horatian Ode upon Cromwell's Return from Ireland

(1650)

THE forward youth that would appear
    Must now forsake his Muses dear,
    Nor in the shadows sing
    His numbers languishing.

'Tis time to leave the books in dust,
And oil the unused armor's rust,
    Removing from the wall
    The corselet of the hall.

So restless Cromwell could not cease
In the inglorious arts of peace,
    But through adventurous war
    Urged his active star;

And, like the three-forked lightning, first
Breaking the clouds where it was nursed,
    Did through his own side
    His fiery way divide;

For 'tis all one to courage high,
The emulous, or enemy,
    And with such, to enclose
    Is more than to oppose;—

Then burning through the air he went,
And palaces and temples rent;
    And Cæsar's head at last
    Did through his laurels blast.

'Tis madness to resist or blame
The face of angry Heaven's flame;
   And if we would speak true,
   Much to the man is due,

Who, from his private gardens, where
He lived reservèd and austere
   (As if his highest plot
   To plant the bergamot),

Could by industrious valor climb
To ruin the great work of time,
   And cast the Kingdoms old
   Into another mould;

Though Justice against Fate complain,
And plead the ancient rights in vain—
   But those do hold or break
   As men are strong or weak—

Nature, that hateth emptiness,
Allows of penetration less,
   And therefore must make room
   Where greater spirits come.

What field of all the civil war
Where his were not the deepest scar?
   And Hampton shows what part
   He had of wiser art;

Where, twining subtle fears with hope,
He wove a net of such a scope
   That Charles himself might chase
   To Caresbrooke's narrow case;

That thence the Royal actor borne
The tragic scaffold might adorn:
   While round the armèd bands
   Did clap their bloody hands.

He nothing common did or mean
Upon that memorable scene,
   But with his keener eye
   The axe's edge did try;

Nor called the gods, with vulgar spite,
To vindicate his helpless right;
   But bowed his comely head
   Down, as upon a bed.

This was that memorable hour
Which first assured the forcèd power:
    So when they did design
    The Capitol's first line,

A Bleeding Head, where they begun,
Did fright the architects to run;
    And yet in that the State
    Foresaw its happy fate!

And now the Irish are ashamed
To see themselves in one year tamed;
    So much one man can do
    That does both act and know.

They can affirm his praises best,
And have, though overcome, confessed
    How good he is, how just
    And fit for highest trust.

Nor yet grown stiffer with command,
But still in the republic's hand—
    How fit he is to sway
    That can so well obey!

He to the Commons' feet presents
A Kingdom for his first year's rents,
    And, what he may, forbears
    His fame, to make it theirs:

And has his sword and spoils ungirt
To lay them at the public's skirt.
    So when the falcon high
    Falls heavy from the sky,

She, having killed, no more doth search
But on the next green bough to perch;
    Where, when he first does lure,
    The falconer has her sure.

What may not then our Isle presume,
While victory his crest does plume?
    What may not others fear,
    If thus he crowns each year?

As Cæsar, he, ere long, to Gaul,
To Italy an Hannibal,
    And to all States not free
    Shall Climacteric be.

The Pict no shelter now shall find
Within his parti-colored mind,
But, from this valor, sad,
Shrink underneath the plaid.

Happy, if in the tufted brake
The English hunter him mistake,
Nor lay his hounds in near
The Caledonian deer.

But thou, the war's and fortune's son,
March indefatigably on,
And for the last effect,
Still keep the sword erect:

Besides the force it has to fright
The spirits of the shady night;
The same arts that did gain
A power, must it maintain.

The Garden

HOW vainly men themselves amaze
To win the palm, the oak, or bays,
And their incessant labors see
Crowned from some single herb or tree,
Whose short and narrow-vergèd shade
Does prudently their toils upbraid;
While all the flowers and trees do close
To weave the garlands of repose!

Fair Quiet, have I found thee here,
And Innocence, thy sister dear?
Mistaken long, I sought you then
In busy companies of men:
Your sacred plants, if here below
Only among the plants will grow;
Society is all but rude
To this delicious solitude.

No white nor red was ever seen
So amorous as this lovely green.
Fond lovers, cruel as their flame,
Cut in these trees their mistress' name:
Little, alas! they know or heed
How far these beauties hers exceed!
Fair trees! where'er your barks I wound,
No name shall but your own be found.
When we have run our passions' heat,
Love hither makes his best retreat:

The gods, that mortal beauty chase,
Still in a tree did end their race;
Apollo hunted Daphne so
Only that she might laurel grow;
And Pan did after Syrinx speed,
Not as a nymph, but for a reed.

What wondrous life is this I lead!
Ripe apples drop about my head;
The luscious clusters of the vine
Upon my mouth do crush their wine;
The nectarine and curious peach
Into my hands themselves do reach;
Stumbling on melons, as I pass,
Ensnared with flowers, I fall on grass.

Meanwhile the mind, from pleasure less,
Withdraws into its happiness;
The mind, that ocean where each kind
Does straight its own resemblance find;
Yet it creates, transcending these,
Far other worlds, and other seas;
Annihilating all that's made
To a green thought in a green shade.

Here at the fountain's sliding foot,
Or at some fruit-tree's mossy root,
Casting the body's vest aside,
My soul into the boughs does glide;
There, like a bird, it sits and sings,
Then whets and combs its silver wings,
And, till prepared for longer flight,
Waves in its plumes the various light.

Such was that happy Garden-state
While man there walked without a mate:
After a place so pure and sweet,
What other help could yet be meet!
But 'twas beyond a mortal's share
To wander solitary there:
Two paradises 'twere in one,
To live in Paradise alone.

How well the skilful gardener drew
Of flowers and herbs this dial new!
Where, from above, the milder sun
Does through a fragrant zodiac run:
And, as it works, the industrious bee
Computes its time as well as we.
How could such sweet and wholesome hours
Be reckoned, but with herbs and flowers!

HENRY VAUGHAN (1622-1695)

The Retreat

HAPPY those early days, when I
    Shined in my Angel-infancy!
Before I understood this place
Appointed for my second race,
Or taught my soul to fancy aught
But a white, celestial thought;
When yet I had not walked above
A mile or two from my first Love,
And looking back, at that short space,
Could see a glimpse of His bright face;
When on some gilded cloud or flower
My gazing soul would dwell an hour,
And in those weaker glories spy
Some shadows of eternity;
Before I taught my tongue to wound
My Conscience with a sinful sound,
Or had the black art to dispense
A several sin to every sense;
But felt through all this fleshly dress
Bright shoots of everlastingness.

O how I long to travel back,
And tread again that ancient track!
That I might once more reach that plain
Where first I left my glorious train;
From whence the enlightened spirit sees
That shady City of Palm-trees.
But ah! my soul with too much stay
Is drunk, and staggers in the way!
Some men a forward motion love,
But I by backward steps would move;
And, when this dust falls to the urn,
In that state I came, return.

Friends Departed

THEY are all gone into the world of light!
    And I alone sit lingering here;
Their very memory is fair and bright,
    And my sad thoughts doth clear.

It glows and glitters in my cloudy breast,
    Like stars upon some gloomy grove,
Or those faint beams in which this hill is dressed
    After the sun's remove.

I see them walking in an air of glory,
　　Whose light doth trample on my days:
My days, which are at best but dull and hoary,
　　Mere glimmering and decays.

O holy Hope! and high Humility,
　　High as the heavens above!
These are your walks, and you have showed them me,
　　To kindle my cold love.

Dear, beauteous Death! the jewel of the Just!
　　Shining nowhere, but in the dark;
What mysteries do lie beyond thy dust,
　　Could man outlook that mark!

He that hath found some fledged bird's nest may know.
　　At first sight, if the bird be flown;
But what fair dell or grove he sings in now,
　　That is to him unknown.

And yet, as Angels in some brighter dreams
　　Call to the soul, when man doth sleep,
So some strange thoughts transcend our wonted themes,
　　And into glory peep.

If a star were confined into a tomb,
　　Her captive flames must needs burn there;
But when the hand that locked her up gives room,
　　She'll shine through all the sphere.

O Father of eternal life, and all
　　Created glories under Thee!
Resume Thy spirit from this world of thrall
　　Into true liberty.

Either disperse these mists, which blot and fill
　　My perspective still as they pass:
Or else remove me hence unto that hill,
　　Where I shall need no glass.

JOHN BUNYAN (1628-1688)
Shepherd Boy's Song

HE that is down needs fear no fall,
　　He that is low, no pride;
He that is humble ever shall
　　Have God to be his guide. . . .

(Abridged.)

JOHN DRYDEN (1631-1700)

Under the Portrait of Milton

In Tonson's Folio Edition of Paradise Lost, 1688

THREE Poets, in three distant ages born,
　Greece, Italy, and England did adorn.
The first in loftiness of thought surpassed;
The next in majesty; in both the last.
The force of Nature could no further go:
To make a third she joined the former two.

From "Alexander's Feast"

I

'TWAS at the royal feast for Persia won
　By Philip's warlike son—
Aloft in awful state
The godlike hero sate
On his imperial throne;
His valiant peers were placed around,
Their brows with roses and with myrtles bound,
(So should desert in arms be crowned);
The lovely Thais by his side
Sate like a blooming Eastern bride
In flower of youth and beauty's pride:—
Happy, happy, happy pair!
None but the brave
None but the brave
None but the brave deserves the fair!

II

Timotheus, placed on high
Amid the tuneful choir,
With flying fingers touched the lyre:
The trembling notes ascend the sky
And heavenly joys inspire.
The song began from Jove
Who left his blissful seats above—
Such is the power of mighty love!
A dragon's fiery form belied the god;
Sublime on radiant spires he rode
When he to fair Olympia pressed,
And while he sought her snowy breast,
Then round her slender waist he curled,
And stamped an image of himself, a sovereign of the
　world.

—The listening crowd admire the lofty sound!
A present deity! they shout around:
A present deity! the vaulted roofs rebound:
With ravished ears
The monarch hears,
Assumes the god,
Affects to nod
And seems to shake the spheres. . . .

Abridged.

Song

FAREWELL, ungrateful traitor!
  Farewell, my perjured swain!
Let never injured creature
  Believe a man again.
The pleasure of possessing
Surpasses all expressing,
But 'tis too short a blessing,
  And love too long a pain.

'Tis easy to deceive us,
  In pity of your pain;
But when we love, you leave us,
  To rail at you in vain.
Before we have descried it,
There is no bliss beside it,
But she, that once has tried it,
  Will never love again.

The passion you pretended,
  Was only to obtain:
But when the charm is ended,
  The charmer you disdain.
Your love by ours we measure,
Till we have lost our treasure;
But dying is a pleasure,
  When living is a pain.

Ah, How Sweet It Is to Love!

AH, how sweet it is to love!
  Ah, how gay is young Desire!
And what pleasing pains we prove
  When we first approach Love's fire!
Pains of love be sweeter far
Than all other pleasures are.

Sighs which are from lovers blown
  Do but gently heave the heart:
Ev'n the tears they shed alone
  Cure, like trickling balm, their smart.
Lovers, when they lose their breath,
Bleed away in easy death.

Love and Time with reverence use,
  Treat them like a parting friend;
Nor the golden gifts refuse
  Which in youth sincere they send:
For each year their price is more,
And they less simple than before.

Love, like spring-tides full and high,
  Swells in every youthful vein;
But each tide does less supply,
  Till they quite shrink in again:
If a flow in age appear,
'Tis but rain, and runs not clear.

CHARLES SACKVILLE, EARL OF DORSET (1638-1706)

Written at Sea, in the First Dutch War (1665), *the Night Before an Engagement*

TO all you ladies now at land
    We men at sea indite;
But first would have you understand
    How hard it is to write:
The Muses now, and Neptune too,
We must implore to write to you—
    With a fa, la, la, la, la.

For though the Muses should prove kind,
    And fill our empty brain,
Yet if rough Neptune rouse the wind
    To wave the azure main,
Our paper, pen, and ink, and we,
Roll up and down our ships at sea—
    With a fa, la, la, la, la.

Then if we write not by each post,
    Think not we are unkind;
Nor yet conclude our ships are lost
    By Dutchmen or by wind:
Our tears we'll send a speedier way,
The tide shall bring them twice a day—
    With a fa, la, la, la, la.

The King with wonder and surprise
  Will swear the seas grow bold,
Because the tides will higher rise
  Than e'er they did of old:
But let them know it is our tears
Bring floods of grief to Whitehall stairs—
    With a fa, la, la, la, la.

Should foggy Opdam chance to know
  Our sad and dismal story,
The Dutch would scorn so weak a foe,
  And quit their fort at Goree:
For what resistance can they find
From men who've left their hearts behind?—
    With a fa, la, la, la, la.

Let wind and weather do its worst,
  Be you to us but kind;
Let Dutchmen vapor, Spaniards curse,
  No sorrow we shall find:
'Tis then no matter how things go,
Or who's our friend, or who's our foe—
    With a fa, la, la, la, la.

To pass our tedious hours away
  We throw a merry main,
Or else at serious ombre play:
  But why should we in vain
Each other's ruin thus pursue?
We were undone when we left you—
    With a fa, la, la, la, la.

But now our fears tempestuous grow
  And cast our hopes away;
Whilst you, regardless of our woe,
  Sit careless at a play:
Perhaps permit some happier man
To kiss your hand, or flirt your fan—
    With a fa, la, la, la, la.

When any mournful tune you hear,
  That dies in every note
As if it sighed with each man's care
  For being so remote,
Think then how often love we've made
To you, when all those tunes were played—
    With a fa, la, la, la, la.

In justice you cannot refuse
　To think of our distress,
When we for hopes of honor lose
　Our certain happiness:
All those designs are but to prove
Ourselves more worthy of your love—
　　With a fa, la, la, la, la.

And now we've told you all our loves,
　And likewise all our fears,
In hopes this declaration moves
　Some pity for our tears:
Let's hear of no inconstancy—
We have too much of that at sea—
　　With a fa, la, la, la, la.

JOHN WILMOT, EARL OF ROCHESTER (1647-1680)

On Charles II

HERE lies our Sovereign Lord the King,
　Whose word no man relies on,
Who never said a foolish thing,
Nor ever did a wise one.

To His Mistress

WHY dost thou shade thy lovely face? O, why
　Does that eclipsing hand of thine deny
The sunshine of the Sun's enlivening eye?

Without thy light, what light remains in me?
Thou art my life: my way, my light's in thee;
I live, I move, and by thy beams I see.

Thou art my life: if thou but turn away,
My life's a thousand deaths. Thou art my way:
Without thee, Love, I travel not, but stray.

My light thou art: without thy glorious sight,
My eyes are darkened with eternal night.
My Love, thou art my way, my life, my light.

Thou art my way: I wander if thou fly.
Thou art my light: if hid, how blind am I!
Thou art my life: if thou withdraw'st, I die.

My eyes are dark and blind, I cannot see:
To whom, or whither should my darkness flee,
But to that light? and who's that light but thee?

If I have lost my path, dear lover, say,
Shall I still wander in a doubtful way?
Love, shall a lamb of Israel's sheep-fold stray?

My path is lost, my wandering steps do stray,
I cannot go, nor can I safely stay:
Whom should I seek, but thee, my path, my way?

And yet thou turn'st thy face away, and fly'st me!
And yet I sue for grace, and thou deny'st me!
Speak, art thou angry, love, or only try'st me? . . .

Thou art the pilgrim's path, the blind man's eye,
The dead man's life: on thee my hopes rely:
If I but them remove, I surely die.

Dissolve thy sunbeams, close thy wings, and stay!
See, see how I am blind, and dead, and stray,
O thou that art my life, my light, my way!

Then work thy will! If passion bid me flee
My reason shall obey, my wings shall be
Stretched out no farther than from me to thee.

MATTHEW PRIOR (1664-1721)

Chloe

WHAT I speak, my fair Chloe, and what I write, shews
    The difference there is betwixt nature and art;
I court others in verse, but I love thee in prose;
    And they have my whimsies, but thou hast my heart.

The god of us verse-men—you know, child—the Sun,
    How after his journey he sets up his rest;
If at morning o'er earth 'tis his fancy to run,
    At night he reclines on his Thetis's breast.

So when I am wearied with wandering all day,
    To thee, my delight, in the evening I come;
No matter what beauties I saw in my way,
    They were but my visits, but thou art my home.

Epitaph on Himself

NOBLES and heralds, by your leave,
  Here lies what once was Matthew Prior,
The son of Adam and of Eve;
  Can Bourbon or Nassau claim higher?

WILLIAM CONGREVE (1670-1729)

From "The Mourning Bride"

MUSIC hath charms to soothe a savage beast,
  To soften rocks, or bend a knotted oak.
I've read that things inanimate have moved,
And, as with living souls, have been informed,
By magic numbers and persuasive sound.

JOSEPH ADDISON (1672-1719)

"The Spacious Firmament on High"

THE spacious firmament on high,
  With all the blue ethereal sky,
And spangled heavens, a shining frame,
Their great Original proclaim.
The unwearied Sun, from day to day,
Does his Creator's power display;
And publishes to every land
The work of an Almighty hand.

Soon as the evening shades prevail,
The Moon takes up the wondrous tale;
And nightly to the listening Earth
Repeats the story of her birth:
Whilst all the stars that round her burn,
And all the planets in their turn,
Confirm the tidings as they roll
And spread the truth from pole to pole.

What though, in solemn silence, all
Move round the dark terrestrial ball?
What though nor real voice nor sound
Amidst their radiant orbs be found?
In Reason's ear they all rejoice,
And utter forth a glorious voice;
For ever singing as they shine,
"The Hand that made us is divine."

ISAAC WATTS (1674-1748)
"O God! Our Help in Ages Past"

O GOD! our help in ages past,
  Our hope for years to come,
Our shelter from the stormy blast,
  And our eternal home!

Under the shadow of Thy Throne
  Thy saints have dwelt secure;
Sufficient is Thine arm alone,
  And our defense is sure.

Before the hills in order stood,
  Or earth received her fame,
From everlasting Thou art God,
  To endless years the same.

A thousand ages in Thy sight
  Are like an evening gone;
Short as the watch that ends the night
  Before the rising sun.

Time, like an ever-rolling stream,
  Bears all its sons away;
They fly, forgotten, as a dream
  Dies at the opening day.

O God! our help in ages past,
  Our hope for years to come,
Be Thou our guide when troubles last,
  And our eternal home!

WILLIAM OLDYS (1687-1761)

On a Fly Drinking Out of His Cup

BUSY, curious, thirsty fly!
  Drink with me and drink as I:
Freely welcome to my cup,
Couldst thou sip and sip it up:
Make the most of life you may,
Life is short and wears away.

Both alike are mine and thine,
Hastening quick to their decline:
Thine's a summer, mine's no more,
Though repeated to threescore.
Threescore summers, when they're gone,
Will appear as short as one!

ALEXANDER POPE (1688-1744)

From "Satires"

SHUT, shut the door, good John! fatigued I said,
Tie up the knocker; say I'm sick, I'm dead.
The dog-star rages! nay, 'tis past a doubt,
All bedlam or Parnassus is let out:
Fire in each eye, and papers in each hand,
They rave, recite, and madden round the land.
What walls can guard me, or what shades can hide?
They pierce my thickets, through my grot they glide.
By land, by water, they renew the charge;
They stop the chariot, and they board the barge.
No place is sacred, not the church is free,
Ev'n Sunday shines no Sabbath day to me;
Then from the mint walks forth the man of rhyme,
Happy to catch me just at dinner time.
Is there a parson, much bemused in beer,
A maudlin poetess, a rhyming peer,
A clerk, foredoomed his father's soul to cross,
Who pens a stanza, when he should engross? . . .
All fly to Twit'nam and in humble strain
Apply to me, to keep them mad or vain.
Arthur, whose giddy son neglects the laws,
Imputes to me and my damned works the cause:
Poor Cornus sees his frantic wife elope,
And curses wit, and poetry, and Pope. . . .
    Why did I write? what sin to me unknown
Dipped me in ink; my parents', or my own?
As yet a child, nor yet a fool to fame,
I lisped in numbers, for the numbers came.
I left no calling for this idle trade,
No duty broke, no father disobeyed:
The muse but served to ease some friend, not wife;
To help me through this long disease, my life. . . .

From the "Essay on Man"

OH Happiness! our being's end and aim,
Good, Pleasure, Ease, Content, whate'er thy name;
That something still which prompts the eternal sigh,
For which we bear to live, or dare to die,
Which, still so near us, yet beyond us lies,
O'erlooked, seen double, by the fool, and wise! . . .
Ask of the learned the way! the learned are blind;
This bids to serve, and that to shun mankind;
Some place the bliss in action, some in ease;

Those call it pleasure, and contentment these;
Some sunk to beasts, find pleasure end in pain;
Some swelled to gods, confess even virtue vain;
Or indolent, to each extreme they fall,
To trust in everything, or doubt of all.

From "The Rape of the Lock"

AND now, unveiled, the toilet stands displayed,
  Each silver vase in mystic order laid:
First, robed in white, the nymph intent adores,
With head uncovered, the cosmetic powers.
A heavenly image in the glass appears,
To that she bends, to that her eye she rears;
The inferior priestess, at her altar's side,
Trembling begins the sacred rites of pride.
Unnumbered treasures ope at once, and here
The various offerings of the world appear;
From each she nicely culls with curious toil,
And decks the goddess with the glittering spoil.
This casket India's glowing gems unlocks,
And all Arabia breathes from yonder box:
The tortoise here and elephant unite,
Transformed to combs, the speckled and the white.
Here files of pins extend their shining rows,
Puffs, powders, patches, bibles, billet-doux.
Now awful beauty puts on all its arms;
The fair each moment rises in her charms.
Repairs her smiles, awakens every grace,
And calls forth all the wonders of her face;
Sees by degrees a purer blush arise,
And keener lightnings quicken in her eyes.
The busy sylphs surround their darling care,
These set the head, and those divide the hair;
Some fold the sleeve, whilst others plait the gown,
And Betty's praised for labors not her own.

The Dying Christian to His Soul

VITAL spark of heav'nly flame!
  Quit, O quit this mortal frame:
Trembling, hoping, ling'ring, flying,
  O the pain, the bliss of dying!
Cease, fond Nature, cease thy strife,
And let me languish into life.

Hark! they whisper; angels say,
Sister Spirit, come away!
What is this absorbs me quite?
Steals my senses, shuts my sight,
Drowns my spirits, draws my breath?
Tell me, my soul, can this be death?

The world recedes; it disappears!
Heav'n opens on my eyes! my ears
With sounds seraphic ring!
Lend, lend your wings! I mount! I fly!
O Grave! where is thy victory?
O Death! where is thy sting?

JAMES THOMSON (1700-1748)

From "The Castle of Indolence"

A pleasing land of drowsy-head it was,
Of dreams that wave before the half-shut eye:
And of gay castles in the clouds that pass,
For ever flushing round a summer sky:
There eke the soft delights, that witchingly
Distil a wanton sweetness through the breast,
And the calm pleasures, always hovered nigh;
But whate'er smacked of noyance or unrest
Was far, far off expelled from this delicious nest. . . .

Behold! ye pilgrims of this earth, behold!
See all but man with unearned pleasure gay:
See her bright robes the butterfly unfold,
Broke from her wintry tomb in prime of May!
What youthful bride can equal her array?
Who can with her for easy pleasure vie?
From mead to mead with gentle wing to stray,
From flower to flower on balmy gales to fly,
Is all she has to do beneath the radiant sky. . . .

Come, ye who still the cumbrous load of life
Push hard up hill; but as the furthest steep
You trust to gain, and put an end to strife,
Down thunders back the stone with mighty sweep,
And hurls your labors to the valleys deep,
For ever vain; come, and, withouten fee,
I, in oblivion will your sorrows steep,
Your cares, your toils, will steep you in a sea
Of full delight: Oh come, ye weary wights, to me!

Rule, Britannia

(*From "Alfred"*)

WHEN Britain first, at Heaven's command,
    Arose from out the azure main,
This was the charter of the land,
    And guardian angels sung the strain:
      Rule, Britannia, rule the waves,
      Britons never will be slaves.

The nations not so blest as thee
    Must, in their turns, to tyrants fall,
Whilst thou shalt flourish, great and free,
    The dread and envy of them all.

Still more majestic shalt thou rise,
    More dreadful from each foreign stroke;
As the loud blast that tears the skies
    Serves but to root thy native oak.

Thee haughty tyrants ne'er shall tame;
    All their attempts to bend thee down
Will but arouse thy generous flame,
    But work their woe, and thy renown.

To thee belongs the rural reign;
    Thy cities shall with commerce shine;
All thine shall be the subject main,
    And every shore it circles, thine.

The Muses, still with Freedom found,
    Shall to thy happy coast repair:
Blest Isle, with matchless beauty crowned,
    And manly hearts to guard the fair.
      Rule, Britannia, etc.

HENRY CAREY (1693?-1743)

Sally in Our Alley

OF all the girls that are so smart
    There's none like pretty Sally;
She is the darling of my heart,
    And she lives in our alley.
There is no lady in the land
    Is half so sweet as Sally;
She is the darling of my heart,
    And she lives in our alley.

Her father he makes cabbage-nets,
    And through the streets does cry 'em;

Her mother she sells laces long
  To such as please to buy 'em;
But sure such folks could ne'er beget
  So sweet a girl as Sally!
She is the darling of my heart,
  And she lives in our alley.

When she is by, I leave my work,
  I love her so sincerely;
My master comes like any Turk,
  And bangs me most severely:
But let him bang his bellyful,
  I'll bear it all for Sally;
She is the darling of my heart,
  And she lives in our alley.

Of all the days that's in the week
  I dearly love but one day—
And that's the day that comes betwixt
  A Saturday and Monday;
For then I'm dressed all in my best
  To walk abroad with Sally;
She is the darling of my heart,
  And she lives in our alley.

My master carries me to church,
  And often am I blamèd
Because I leave him in the lurch
  As soon as text is namèd;
I leave the church in sermon-time
  And slink away to Sally;
She is the darling of my heart,
  And she lives in our alley.

When Christmas comes about again,
  O, then I shall have money;
I'll hoard it up, and box it all,
  I'll give it to my honey:
I would it were ten thousand pound,
  I'd give it all to Sally;
She is the darling of my heart,
  And she lives in our alley.

My master and the neighbors all
  Make game of me and Sally,
And, but for her, I'd better be
  A slave and row a galley;
But when my seven long years are out,
  O, then I'll marry Sally;
O, then we'll wed, and then we'll bed—
  But not in our alley!

SAMUEL JOHNSON (1709-1784)

One-and-Twenty

LONG-EXPECTED One-and-twenty,
    Ling'ring year, at length is flown:
Pride and pleasure, pomp and plenty,
    Great *** ****, are now your own.

Loosen'd from the minor's tether,
    Free to mortgage or to sell,
Wild as wind and light as feather,
    Bid the sons of thrift farewell.

Call the Betsies, Kates, and Jennies,
    All the names that banish care;
Lavish of your grandsire's guineas,
    Show the spirit of an heir.

All that prey on vice and folly
    Joy to see their quarry fly:
There's the gamester, light and jolly,
    There's the lender, grave and sly.

Wealth, my lad, was made to wander,
    Let it wander as it will;
Call the jockey, call the pander,
    Bid them come and take their fill.

When the bonny blade carouses,
    Pockets full, and spirits high—
What are acres? what are houses?
    Only dirt, or wet or dry.

Should the guardian friend or mother
    Tell the woes of wilful waste,
Scorn their counsel, scorn their pother;—
    You can hang or drown at last!

WILLIAM SHENSTONE (1714-1763)

Written at an Inn at Henley

TO thee, fair freedom! I retire
    From flattery, cards, and dice, and din;
Nor art thou found in mansions higher
    Than the low cot, or humble inn.

'Tis here with boundless power I reign;
  And every health which I begin,
Converts dull port to bright champagne;
  Such freedom crowns it, at an inn.

I fly from pomp, I fly from plate!
  I fly from falsehood's specious grin!
Freedom I love, and form I hate,
  And choose my lodgings at an inn.

Here, waiter! take my sordid ore,
  Which lackeys else might hope to win;
It buys, what courts have not in store;
  It buys me freedom at an inn.

Whoe'er has traveled life's dull round,
  Where'er his stages may have been,
May sigh to think he still has found
  The warmest welcome, at an inn.

THOMAS GRAY (1716-1771)

Elegy Written in a Country Churchyard

THE curfew tolls the knell of parting day,
  The lowing herd winds slowly o'er the lea,
The plowman homeward plods his weary way,
  And leaves the world to darkness and to me.

Now fades the glimmering landscape on the sight,
  And all the air a solemn stillness holds,
Save where the beetle wheels his droning flight,
  And drowsy tinklings lull the distant folds:

Save that from yonder ivy-mantled tower
  The moping owl does to the moon complain
Of such as, wandering near her secret bower,
  Molest her ancient solitary reign.

Beneath those rugged elms, that yew-tree's shade,
  Where heaves the turf in many a moldering heap,
Each in his narrow cell for ever laid,
  The rude forefathers of the hamlet sleep.

The breezy call of incense-breathing morn,
  The swallow twittering from the straw-built shed,
The cock's shrill clarion, or the echoing horn,
  No more shall rouse them from their lowly bed.

For them no more the blazing hearth shall burn,
 Or busy housewife ply her evening care:
No children run to lisp their sire's return,
 Or climb his knees the envied kiss to share.

Oft did the harvest to their sickle yield,
 Their furrow oft the stubborn glebe has broke:
How jocund did they drive their team afield!
 How bowed the woods beneath their sturdy stroke!

Let not Ambition mock their useful toil,
 Their homely joys, and destiny obscure;
Nor Grandeur hear with a disdainful smile
 The short and simple annals of the poor.

The boast of heraldry, the pomp of power,
 And all that beauty, all that wealth e'er gave,
Await alike the inevitable hour:
 The paths of glory lead but to the grave.

Nor you, ye proud, impute to these the fault
 If Memory o'er their tomb no trophies raise,
Where through the long-drawn aisle and fretted vault
 The pealing anthem swells the note of praise.

Can storied urn or animated bust
 Back to its mansion call the fleeting breath?
Can Honor's voice provoke the silent dust,
 Or Flattery soothe the dull cold ear of death?

Perhaps in this neglected spot is laid
 Some heart once pregnant with celestial fire;
Hands, that the rod of empire might have swayed,
 Or waked to ecstasy the living lyre.

But Knowledge to their eyes her ample page
 Rich with the spoils of time did ne'er unroll;
Chill Penury repressed their noble rage,
 And froze the genial current of the soul.

Full many a gem of purest ray serene
 The dark unfathomed caves of ocean bear:
Full many a flower is born to blush unseen,
 And waste its sweetness on the desert air.

Some village Hampden that, with dauntless breast,
 The little tyrant of his fields withstood,
Some mute inglorious Milton here may rest,
 Some Cromwell guiltless of his country's blood.

The applause of listening senates to command,
　The threats of pain and ruin to despise,
To scatter plenty o'er a smiling land,
　And read their history in a nation's eyes,

Their lot forbade: nor circumscribed alone
　Their growing virtues, but their crimes confined;
Forbade to wade through slaughter to a throne,
　And shut the gates of mercy on mankind;

The struggling pangs of conscious truth to hide,
　To quench the blushes of ingenuous shame,
Or heap the shrine of Luxury and Pride
　With incense kindled at the Muse's flame.

Far from the madding crowd's ignoble strife,
　Their sober wishes never learned to stray;
Along the cool, sequestered vale of life
　They kept the noiseless tenor of their way.

Yet even these bones from insult to protect
　Some frail memorial still erected nigh,
With uncouth rhymes and shapeless sculpture decked,
　Implores the passing tribute of a sigh.

Their name, their years, spelt by the unlettered Muse,
　The place of fame and elegy supply:
And many a holy text around she strews,
　That teach the rustic moralist to die.

For who, to dumb Forgetfulness a prey,
　This pleasing anxious being e'er resigned,
Left the warm precincts of the cheerful day,
　Nor cast one longing, lingering look behind?

On some fond breast the parting soul relies,
　Some pious drops the closing eye requires;
E'en from the tomb the voice of Nature cries,
　E'en in our ashes live their wonted fires.

For thee, who, mindful of the unhonored dead,
　Dost in these lines their artless tale relate;
If chance, by lonely contemplation led,
　Some kindred spirit shall inquire thy fate,—

Haply some hoary-headed swain may say,
　"Oft have we seen him at the peep of dawn
Brushing with hasty steps the dews away
　To meet the sun upon the upland lawn.

"There at the foot of yonder nodding beech
   That wreathes its old fantastic roots so high,
His listless length at noontide would he stretch,
   And pore upon the brook that babbles by.

"Hard by yon wood, now smiling as in scorn,
   Muttering his wayward fancies he would rove,
Now drooping, woeful-wan, like one forlorn,
   Or crazed with care, or crossed in hopeless love.

"One morn I missed him on the 'customed hill,
   Along the heath, and near his favorite tree;
Another came; nor yet beside the rill,
   Nor up the lawn, nor at the wood was he:

"The next, with dirges due in sad array,
   Slow through the church-way path we saw him borne.
Approach and read (for thou canst read) the lay
   Graved on the stone beneath yon aged thorn."

THE EPITAPH

HERE rests his head upon the lap of Earth
   A Youth, to Fortune and to Fame unknown.
Fair Science frowned not on his humble birth,
   And Melancholy marked him for her own.

Large was his bounty, and his soul sincere,
   Heaven did a recompense as largely send:
He gave to Misery (all he had) a tear,
   He gained from Heaven ('twas all he wished) a friend.

No farther seek his merits to disclose,
   Or draw his frailties from their dread abode,
(There they alike in trembling hope repose,)
   The bosom of his Father and his God.

From "The Progress of Poetry," a Pindaric Ode

FAR from the sun and summer gale,
   In thy green lap was Nature's darling laid,
What time, where lucid Avon stray'd,
   To Him the mighty mother did unveil
Her awful face: the dauntless child
Stretch'd forth his little arms, and smiled.
This pencil take (she said), whose colours clear
Richly paint the vernal year:
Thine too these golden keys, immortal boy!
This can unlock the gates of joy;
Of horror that, and thrilling fears.
Or ope the sacred source of sympathetic tears.

Nor second he, that rode sublime
Upon the seraph-wings of Ecstasy,
The secrets of th' abyss to spy.
    He pass'd the flaming bounds of place and time:
The living Throne, the sapphire-blaze,
Where Angels tremble while they gaze,
He saw; but blasted with excess of light,
Closed his eyes in endless night.
Behold, where Dryden's less presumptuous car,
Wide o'er the fields of glory bear
Two coursers of ethereal race,
With necks in thunder clothed, and long-resounding pace.

Hark, his hands the lyre explore!
Bright-eyed Fancy hovering o'er
    Scatters from her pictured urn
    Thoughts that breathe, and words that burn.
But ah! 'tis heard no more——
    O Lyre divine! what daring Spirit
    Wakes thee now? Tho' he inherit
Nor the pride, nor ample pinion,
    That the Theban eagle bear
Sailing with supreme dominion
    Thro' the azure deep of air:
Yet oft before his infant eyes would run
    Such forms as glitter in the Muse's ray,
With orient hues, unborrow'd of the Sun:
    Yet shall he mount, and keep his distant way
Beyond the limits of a vulgar fate,
Beneath the Good how far—but far above the Great.

WILLIAM COLLINS (1721-1759)

Fidele's Dirge

TO fair Fidele's grassy tomb
    Soft maids and village hinds shall bring
Each opening sweet, of earliest bloom,
    And rifle all the breathing spring.

No wailing ghost shall dare appear
    To vex with shrieks this quiet grove,
But shepherd lads assemble here,
    And melting virgins own their love.

No withered witch shall here be seen,
    No goblins lead their nightly crew;
The female fays shall haunt the green,
    And dress thy grave with pearly dew;

The redbreast oft, at evening hours,
  Shall kindly lend his little aid,
With hoary moss, and gathered flowers,
  To deck the ground where thou art laid.

When howling winds, and beating rain,
  In tempests shake the sylvan cell,
Or midst the chase, on every plain,
  The tender thought on thee shall dwell.

Each lonely scene shall thee restore,
  For thee the tear be duly shed;
Beloved till life can charm no more;
  And mourned till Pity's self be dead.

"How Sleep the Brave"

OW sleep the brave, who sink to rest
  By all their country's wishes blest!
When Spring, with dewy fingers cold,
Returns to deck their hallowed mould,
She there shall dress a sweeter sod
Than Fancy's feet have ever trod.

By fairy hands their knell is rung;
By forms unseen their dirge is sung;
There Honor comes, a pilgrim gray,
To bless the turf that wraps their clay;
And Freedom shall awhile repair
To dwell, a weeping hermit, there!

Ode to Evening

IF aught of oaten stop, or pastoral song,
  May hope, chaste Eve, to soothe thy modest ear,
    Like thy own solemn springs,
    Thy springs and dying gales;

O Nymph reserved, while now the bright-haired sun
Sits in yon western tent, whose cloudy skirts,
    With brede ethereal wove,
    O'erhang his wavy bed:

Now air is hushed, save where the weak-eyed bat
With short shrill shriek flits by on leathern wing,
    Or where the beetle winds
    His small but sullen horn.

As oft he rises, 'midst the twilight path
Against the pilgrim borne in heedless hum:
    Now teach me, maid composed,
    To breathe some softened strain,

Whose numbers, stealing through thy darkening vale,
May not unseemly with its stillness suit,
    As, musing slow, I hail
    Thy genial loved return!

For when thy folding-star arising shows
His paly circlet, at his warning lamp
    The fragrant Hours, and Elves
    Who slept in buds the day,

And many a Nymph who wreathes her brows with sedge,
And sheds the freshening dew, and, lovelier still,
    The pensive Pleasures sweet,
    Prepare thy shadowy car:

Then lead, calm votaress, where some sheety lake
Cheers the lone heath, or some time-hallowed pile,
    Or upland fallows gray
    Reflect its last cool gleam.

Or, if chill blustering winds, or driving rain,
Prevent my willing feet, be mine the hut
    That, from the mountain's side,
    Views wilds and swelling floods,

And hamlets brown, and dim-discovered spires,
And hears their simple bell, and marks o'er all
    Thy dewy fingers draw
    The gradual dusky veil.

While Spring shall pour his showers, as of the wont,
And bathe thy breathing tresses, meekest Eve!
    While Summer loves to sport
    Beneath thy lingering light;

While sallow Autumn fills thy lap with leaves,
Or Winter, yelling through the troublous air,
    Affrights thy shrinking train,
    And rudely rends thy robes:

So long, regardful of thy quiet rule,
Shall Fancy, Friendship, Science, smiling Peace,
    Thy gentlest influence own,
    And hymn thy favorite name!

CHRISTOPHER SMART (1722-1771)

From "Song to David"

SWEET is the dew that falls betimes,
  And drops upon the leafy limes;
    Sweet, Hermon's fragrant air:
Sweet is the lily's silver bell,
And sweet the wakeful tapers' smell
    That watch for early prayer.

Sweet the young nurse, with love intense,
Which smiles o'er sleeping innocence;
    Sweet, when the lost arrive:
Sweet the musician's ardor beats,
While his vague mind's in quest of sweets,
    The choicest flowers to hive.

Strong is the horse upon his speed;
Strong in pursuit the rapid glede,
    Which makes at once his game:
Strong the tall ostrich on the ground;
Strong through the turbulent profound
    Shoots Xiphias to his aim.

Strong is the lion—like a coal
His eyeball,—like a bastion's mole
    His chest against the foes:
Strong the gier-eagle on his sail;
Strong against tide the enormous whale
    Emerges as he goes.

But stronger still, in earth and air,
And in the sea, the man of prayer,
    And far beneath the tide:
And in the seat to fate assigned,
Where ask is have, where seek is find,
    Where knock is open wide.

OLIVER GOLDSMITH (1728-1774)

From "The Deserted Village"

SWEET Auburn! loveliest village of the plain,
  Where health and plenty cheered the labouring swain,
Where smiling spring its earliest visit paid,
And parting summer's lingering blooms, delayed:

Dear lovely bowers of innocence and ease,
Seats of my youth, when every sport could please:
How often have I loitered o'er thy green,
Where humble happiness endeared each scene!
How often have I paused on every charm,
The sheltered cot, the cultivated farm,
The never-failing brook, the busy mill,
The decent church that topped the neighboring hill,
The hawthorn-bush, with seats beneath the shade,
For talking age and whispering lovers made!

 Ill fares the land, to hastening ills a prey,
Where wealth accumulates, and men decay:
Princes and lords may flourish, or may fade;
A breath can make them, as a breath has made;
But a bold peasantry, their country's pride,
When once destroyed, can never be supplied.

 Near yonder copse, where once the garden smiled,
And still where many a garden-flower grows wild;
There, where a few torn shrubs the place disclose,
The village preacher's modest mansion rose.
A man he was to all the country dear,
And passing rich with forty pounds a year;
Remote from towns he ran his godly race,
Nor e'er had changed, nor wished to change, his place;
Unskillful he to fawn, or seek for power,
By doctrines fashioned to the varying hour;
Far other aims his heart had learned to prize,
More skilled to raise the wretched than to rise.
His house was known to all the vagrant train.
He chid their wanderings, but relieved their pain;
The long-remembered beggar was his guest,
Whose beard descending swept his aged breast;
The ruined spendthrift, now no longer proud,
Claimed kindred there, and had his claims allowed;
The broken soldier, kindly bade to stay,
Sate by his fire, and talked the night away;
Wept o'er his wounds, or, tales of sorrow done,
Shouldered his crutch, and showed how fields were won.
Pleased with his guests, the good man learned to glow,
And quite forgot their vices in their woe;
Careless their merits or their faults to scan,
His pity gave ere charity began.

 Beside yon straggling fence that skirts the way,
With blossomed furze unprofitably gay,
There, in his noisy mansion, skilled to rule;
The village master taught his little school;

A man severe he was, and stern to view;
I knew him well, and every truant knew:
Well had the boding tremblers learned to trace
The day's disasters in his morning face;
Full well they laughed, with counterfeited glee,
At all his jokes, for many a joke had he;
Full well the busy whisper, circling round,
Conveyed the dismal tidings when he frowned;
Yet he was kind, or, if severe in aught,
The love he bore to learning was in fault.
The village all declared how much he knew;
'Twas certain he could write, and cipher too;
Lands he could measure, terms and tides presage,
And e'en the story ran that he could gauge;
In arguing, too, the parson owned his skill,
For, e'en though vanquished, he could argue still,
While words of learnèd length and thundering sound
Amazed the gazing rustics ranged around;
And still they gazed, and still the wonder grew
That one small head could carry all he knew.

But past is all his fame. The very spot
Where many a time he triumphed, is forgot.—
Near yonder thorn, that lifts its head on high,
Where once the sign-post caught the passing eye,
Low lies that house where nut-brown draughts inspired,
Where graybeard mirth and smiling toil retired,
Where village statesmen talked with looks profound,
And news much older than their ale went round.
Imagination fondly stoops to trace
The parlor splendors of that festive place,—
The whitewashed wall; the nicely sanded floor;
The varnished clock that ticked behind the door;
The chest, contrived a double debt to pay,
A bed by night, a chest of drawers by day;
The pictures placed for ornaments and use;
The twelve good rules; the royal game of goose;
The hearth, except when winter chilled the day,
With aspen boughs and flowers and fennel gay;
While broken tea-cups wisely kept for show,
Ranged o'er the chimney, glistened in a row.

Vain, transitory splendors! could not all
Reprieve the tottering mansion from its fall?
Obscure it sinks, nor shall it more impart
An hour's importance to the poor man's heart;
Thither no more the peasant shall repair
To sweet oblivion of his daily care;
No more the farmer's news, the barber's tale,

No more the woodman's ballad shall prevail;
No more the smith his dusky brow shall clear,
Relax his ponderous strength, and lean to hear;
The host himself no longer shall be found
Careful to see the mantling bliss go round;
Nor the coy maid, half willing to be pressed,
Shall kiss the cup to pass it to the rest.

Yes! let the rich deride, the proud disdain,
These simple blessings of the lowly train;
To me more dear, congenial to my heart
One native charm, than all the glow of art.

Woman

WHEN lovely woman stoops to folly
    And finds too late that men betray,
What charm can soothe her melancholy?
    What art can wash her tears away?

The only art her guilt to cover,
    To hide her shame from ev'ry eye,
To give repentance to her lover,
    And wring his bosom is—to die.

WILLIAM COWPER (1731-1800)

To Mary Unwin

MARY! I want a lyre with other strings,
    Such aid from Heaven as some have feigned they
      drew.
An eloquence scarce given to mortals, new
And undebased by praise of meaner things;
That, ere through age or woe I shed my wings,
I may record thy worth with honor due,
In verse as musical as thou art true,
And that immortalizes whom it sings:
But thou hast little need. There is a Book
By seraphs writ with beams of heavenly light,
On which the eyes of God not rarely look,
A chronicle of actions just and bright:
    There all thy deeds, my faithful Mary, shine;
    And, since thou own'st that praise, I spare thee mine.

From "The Task"; Book III, "The Garden"

I WAS a stricken deer that left the herd
   Long since; with many an arrow deep infixed
My panting side was charged, when I withdrew
To seek a tranquil death in distant shades.
There was I found by One who had Himself
Been hurt by the archers. In his side He bore,
And in His hands and feet, the cruel scars.
With gentle force soliciting the darts,
He drew them forth, and healed and bade me live.
Since then, with few associates, in remote
And silent woods I wander, far from those
My former partners of the peopled scene;
With few associates, and not wishing more.
Here much I ruminate, as much I may,
With other views of men and manners now
Than once, and others of a life to come.
I see that all are wanderers, gone astray
Each in his own delusions; they are lost
In chase of fancied happiness, still wooed
And never won. Dream after dream ensues,
And still they dream that they shall still succeed
And still are disappointed. Rings the world
With the vain stir. I sum up half mankind
And add two-thirds of the remaining half,
And find the total of their hopes and fears
Dreams, empty dreams.

From "The Task"

NOW stir the fire, and close the shutters fast,
   Let fall the curtains, wheel the sofa round,
And while the bubbling and loud-hissing urn
Throws up a steamy column, and the cups,
That cheer but not inebriate, wait on each,
So let us welcome peaceful evening in.

A Comparison. Addressed to a Young Lady

SWEET stream, that winds through yonder glade,
   Apt emblem of a virtuous maid!
Silent and chaste she steals along,
Far from the world's gay, busy throng,
With gentle, yet prevailing force,
Intent upon her destined course;
Graceful and useful all she does,
Blessing and blessed where'er she goes;
Pure-bosomed as that watery glass,
And heaven reflected in her face!

Boadicea. An Ode

WHEN the British Warrior Queen,
  Bleeding from the Roman rods,
Sought, with an indignant mien,
  Counsel of her country's gods,

Sage beneath a spreading oak
  Sat the druid, hoary chief,
Every burning word he spoke
  Full of rage and full of grief:

Princess! if our aged eyes
  Weep upon thy matchless wrongs,
'Tis because resentment ties
  All the terrors of our tongues.

"Rome shall perish,—write that word
  In the blood that she has spilt;
Perish hopeless and abhorred,
  Deep in ruin as in guilt.

"Rome, for empire far renowned,
  Tramples on a thousand states,
Soon her pride shall kiss the ground,—
  Hark! the Gaul is at her gates.

"Other Romans shall arise,
  Heedless of a soldier's name,
Sounds, not arms, shall win the prize,
  Harmony the path to fame.

"Then the progeny that springs
  From the forests of our land,
Armed with thunder, clad with wings,
  Shall a wider world command.

"Regions Cæsar never knew
  Thy posterity shall sway,
Where his eagles never flew,
  None invincible as they."

Such the bards prophetic words,
  Pregnant with celestial fire,
Bending as he swept the chords
  Of his sweet but awful lyre.

She, with all a monarch's pride,
  Felt them in her bosom glow,

Rushed to battle, fought and died,
  Dying, hurled them at the foe.

"Ruffians, pitiless as proud,
  Heaven awards the vengeance due;
Empire is on us bestowed,
  Shame and ruin wait for you!"

On the Loss of the "Royal George"

TOLL for the brave!
    The brave that are no more!
All sunk beneath the wave,
  Fast by their native shore!

Eight hundred of the brave
  Whose courage was well-tried,
Had made the vessel heel,
  And laid her on her side.

A land-breeze shook the shrouds,
  And she was overset;
Down went the "Royal George"
  With all her crew complete.

Toll for the brave!
  Brave Kempenfelt is gone;
His last sea-fight is fought;
  His work of glory done.

It was not in the battle;
  No tempest gave the shock;
She sprang no fatal leak;
  She ran upon no rock.

His sword was in its sheath;
  His fingers held the pen,
When Kempenfelt went down
  With twice four hundred men.

Weigh the vessel up,
  Once dreaded by our foes!
And mingle with our cup
  The tears that England owes.

Her timbers yet are sound,
  And she may float again
Full charged with England's thunder,
  And plough the distant main.

But Kempenfelt is gone,
His victories are o'er,
And he and his eight hundred
Shall plough the waves no more.

ANNA LETITIA BARBAULD (1743-1825)

Life

LIFE! I know not what thou art,
But know that thou and I must part;
And when, or how, or where we met,
I own to me's a secret yet.
But this I know, when thou art fled,
Where'er they lay these limbs, this head,
No clod so valueless shall be
As all that then remains of me.

O whither, whither dost thou fly?
Where bend unseen thy trackless course?
And in this strange divorce,
Ah, tell where I must seek this compound I?
To the vast ocean of empyreal flame
From whence thy essence came
Dost thou thy flight pursue, when freed
From matter's base encumbering weed?
Or dost thou, hid from sight,
Wait, like some spell-bound knight,
Through blank oblivious years the appointed hour
To break thy trance and reassume thy power?
Yet canst thou without thought or feeling be?
O say, what art thou, when no more thou'rt thee?

Life! we have been long together,
Through pleasant and through cloudy weather;
'Tis hard to part when friends are dear;
Perhaps 'twill cost a sigh, a tear;—
Then steal away, give little warning,
Choose thine own time;
Say not Good-night, but in some brighter clime
Bid me Good-morning!

SIR WILLIAM JONES (1746-1794)

The State

WHAT constitutes a State?
Not high rais'd battlement or labor'd mound,
Thick wall or moated gate;

Not cities proud with spies and turrets crown'd;
   Not bays and broad arm'd ports,
Where, laughing at the storm, rich navies ride,
   Not starr'd and spangled courts,
Where low-brow'd baseness wafts perfume to pride,
   No:—MEN, high-minded MEN,
With pow'rs as far above dull brutes endued
   In forest, brake, or den,
As beasts excel cold rocks and brambles rude;
   Men, who their *duties* know,
But know their *rights,* and knowing, dare maintain,
   Prevent the long-aim'd blow,
And crush the tyrant while they rend the chain:
   These constitute a State,
And sov'reign Law, that State's collected will,
   O'er thrones and globes elate
Sits Empress, crowning good, repressing ill;
   Smit by her sacred frown
The fiend, Discretion, like a vapor sinks,
   And e'en th' all-dazzling Crown
Hides his faint rays, and at her bidding shrinks.
   Such *was* this heav'n-lov'd isle,
Than Lesbos fairer and the Cretan shore!
   No more shall freedom smile?
Shall Britons languish, and be Men no more?
   Since all must life resign,
Those sweet rewards, which decorate the brave,
   'Tis folly to decline,
And steal inglorious to the silent grave.

JOHN LOGAN (1748-1788)

To the Cuckoo

HAIL, beauteous stranger of the grove!
   Thou messenger of Spring!
Now Heaven repairs thy rural seat,
   And woods thy welcome ring.

What time the daisy decks the green,
   Thy certain voice we hear:
Hast thou a star to guide thy path,
   Or mark the rolling year?

Delightful visitant! with thee
   I hail the time of flowers
And hear the sound of music sweet
   From birds among the bowers.

The school-boy, wandering through the wood
  To pull the primrose gay,
Starts, the new voice of Spring to hear,
  And imitates thy lay.

What time the pea puts on the bloom,
  Thou fli'st thy vocal vale,
An annual guest in other lands,
  Another Spring to hail.

Sweet bird! thy bower is ever green,
  Thy sky is ever clear;
Thou hast no sorrow in thy song,
  No Winter in thy year!

O could I fly, I'd fly with thee!
  We'd make, with joyful wing,
Our annual visit o'er the globe,
  Companions of the Spring.

THOMAS CHATTERTON (1752-1770)
Minstrel's Song in "Ella"

OH! sing unto my roundelay;
    Oh! drop the briny tear with me;
Dance no more at holiday,
  Like a running river be;
    My love is dead,
    Gone to his death-bed,
    All under the willow-tree.

Black his hair as the winter night,
  White his neck as summer snow,
Ruddy his face as the morning light,
  Cold he lies in the grave below:
    My love is dead,
    Gone to his death-bed,
    All under the willow-tree.

Sweet his tongue as throstle's note,
  Quick in dance as thought was he;
Deft his tabor, cudgel stout;
  Oh! he lies by the willow-tree.
    My love is dead,
    Gone to his death-bed,
    All under the willow-tree.

Hark! the raven flaps his wing,
  In the briered dell below;

Hark! the death-owl loud doth sing,
  To the nightmares as they go.
    My love is dead,
    Gone to his death-bed,
    All under the willow-tree.

See! the white moon shines on high;
  Whiter is my true-love's shroud;
Whiter than the morning sky,
  Whiter than the evening cloud.
    My love is dead,
    Gone to his death-bed,
    All under the willow-tree.

Here, upon my true-love's grave,
  Shall the garish flowers be laid,
Nor one holy saint to save
  All the sorrows of a maid.
    My love is dead,
    Gone to his death-bed,
    All under the willow-tree.

With my hands I'll bind the briers,
  Round his holy corse to gre;
Elfin-fairy, light your fires,
  Here my body still shall be.
    My love is dead,
    Gone to his death-bed,
    All under the willow-tree.

Come with acorn cup and thorn,
  Drain my heart's blood all away;
Life and all its good I scorn,
  Dance by night, and feast by day.
    My love is dead,
    Gone to his death-bed,
    All under the willow-tree.

Water-witches, crowned with reytes,
  Bear me to your deadly tide.
I die—I come—my true-love waits.
  Thus the damsel spake, and died.

GEORGE CRABBE (1754-1832)
The Parish Workhouse from "The Village"

THEIRS is yon house that holds the village poor,
  Whose walls of mud scarce bear the broken door;
There, where the putrid vapors flagging, play,
And the dull wheel hums doleful through the day;

There children dwell who know no parents' care;
Parents, who know no children's love, dwell there;
Heart-broken matrons on their joyless bed,
Forsaken wives and mothers never wed,
Dejected widows with unheeded tears,
And crippled age with more than childhood fears;
The lame, the blind, and, far the happiest they!
The moping idiot and the madman gay. . . .
    Say ye, oppressed by some fantastic woes,
Some jarring nerve that baffles your repose;
Who press the downy couch, while slaves advance
With timid eye, to read the distant glance;
Who with sad prayers the weary doctor tease,
To name the nameless ever-new disease;
Who with mock patience dire complaints endure,
Which real pain and that alone can cure;
How would ye bear in real pain to lie,
Despised, neglected, left alone to die?
How would ye bear to draw your latest breath
Where all that's wretched pave the way for death?

"Age, with Stealing Steps . . ."

(From "Tales of the Hall")

SIX years had passed, and forty ere the six,
    When time began to play his usual tricks;
The locks once comely in a virgin's sight,
Locks of pure brown, displayed the encroaching white;
The blood, once fervid, now to cool began,
And Time's strong pressure to subdue the man.
I rode or walked as I was wont before.
But now the bounding spirit was no more;
A moderate pace would now my body heat;
A walk of moderate length distress my feet.
I showed my stranger guest those hills sublime,
But said, "The view is poor; we need not climb."
At a friend's mansion I began to dread
The cold neat parlour and the gay glazed bed:
At home I felt a more decided taste,
And must have all things in my order placed.
I ceased to hunt; my horses pleased me less—
My dinner more; I learned to play at chess.
I took my dog and gun, but saw the brute
Was disappointed that I did not shoot.
My morning walks I now could bear to lose,
And blessed the shower that gave me not to choose:
In fact, I felt a languor stealing on;

The active arm, the agile hand, were gone;
Small daily actions into habits grew,
And new dislike to forms and fashions new.
I loved my trees in order to dispose;
I numbered peaches, looked how stocks arose;
Told the same story oft—in short, began to prose.

WILLIAM BLAKE (1757-1827)
Reeds of Innocence

PIPING down the valleys wild,
    Piping songs of pleasant glee,
On a cloud I saw a child,
    And he laughing said to me:—

"Pipe a song about a Lamb!"
    So I piped with merry cheer.
"Piper, pipe that song again."
    So I piped: he wept to hear.

"Drop thy pipe, thy happy pipe;
    Sing thy songs of happy cheer!"
So I sang the same again,
    While he wept with joy to hear.

"Piper, sit thee down and write
    In a book, that all may read."
So he vanished from my sight;
    And I plucked a hollow reed,

And I made a rural pen,
    And I stained the water clear,
And I wrote my happy songs
    Every child may joy to hear.

Infant Joy

I have no name;
    I am but two days old."
What shall I call thee?
"I happy am,
Joy is my name."
Sweet joy befall thee!

Pretty joy!
Sweet joy, but two days old.
Sweet joy I call thee;
Thou dost smile,
I sing the while;
Sweet joy befall thee!

My Silks and Fine Array

MY silks and fine array,
    My smiles and languished air;
By love are driven away.
    And mournful lean Despair
Brings me yew to deck my grave:
Such end true lovers have.

His face is fair as heaven
    When springing buds unfold;
Oh, why to him was't given,
    Whose heart is wintry cold?
His breast is Love's all-worshipped tomb
Where all love's pilgrims come.

Bring me an axe and spade,
    Bring me a winding sheet;
When I my grave have made,
    Let winds and tempests beat:
Then down I'll lie, as cold as clay,
True love doth pass away.

The Tiger

TIGER, tiger, burning bright
    In the forests of the night,
What immortal hand or eye
Could frame thy fearful symmetry?

In what distant deeps or skies
Burnt the fire of thine eyes?
On what wings dare he aspire?
What the hand dare seize the fire?

And what shoulder, and what art,
Could twist the sinews of thy heart?
And when thy heart began to beat,
What dread hand? and what dread feet?

What the hammer? what the chain?
In what furnace was thy brain?
What the anvil? what dread grasp
Dare its deadly terrors clasp?

When the stars threw down their spears,
And water'd heaven with their tears,
Did he smile his work to see?
Did he who made the lamb make thee?

Tiger, tiger, burning bright
In the forests of the night,
What immortal hand or eye
Dare frame thy fearful symmetry?

The Voice of the Bard

HEAR the voice of the Bard,
    Who present, past, and future, sees;
Whose ears have heard
The Holy Word
That walk'd among the ancient trees;

Calling the lapsèd soul,
And weeping in the evening dew;
That might control
The starry pole,
And fallen, fallen light renew!

"O Earth, O Earth, return!
Arise from out the dewy grass!
Night is worn,
And the morn
Rises from the slumbrous mass.

"Turn away no more;
Why wilt thou turn away?
The starry floor,
The watery shore,
Is given thee till the break of day."

Ah, Sunflower

AH, Sunflower, weary of time,
    Who countest the steps of the sun,
Seeking after that sweet golden clime
Where the traveller's journey is done—

Where the youth pined away with desire,
And the pale virgin, shrouded in snow,
Arise from their graves, and aspire
Where my sunflower wishes to go!

Milton

AND did those feet in ancient time
    Walk upon England's mountains green?
And was the holy Lamb of God
    On England's pleasant pastures seen?

And did the Countenance Divine
   Shine forth upon our clouded hills?
And was Jerusalem builded here
   Among these dark Satanic mills?

Bring me my bow of burning gold!
   Bring me my arrows of desire!
Bring me my spear! O clouds, unfold!
   Bring me my chariot of fire!

I will not cease from mental fight,
   Nor shall my sword sleep in my hand,
Till we have built Jerusalem
   In England's green and pleasant land.

A Poison Tree

I was angry with my friend:
   I told my wrath, my wrath did end.
I was angry with my foe:
I told it not, my wrath did grow.

And I watered it in fears,
Night and morning with my tears;
And I sunnèd it with smiles
And with soft deceitful wiles.

And it grew both day and night,
Till it bore an apple bright;
And my foe beheld it shine,
And he knew that it was mine,

And into my garden stole
When the night had veiled the pole;
In the morning glad I see
My foe outstretched beneath the tree.

The Garden of Love

I went to the Garden of Love,
   And I saw what I never had seen:
A chapel was built in the midst,
Where I used to play on the green.

And the gates of this chapel were shut,
And "Thou shalt not" writ over the door;
So I turned to the Garden of Love
That so many sweet flowers bore;

And I saw it was filled with graves,
And tomb-stones where flowers should be:
And Priests in black gowns were walking their
    rounds,
And binding with briars my joys and desires.

From "The Grey Monk"

BUT vain the Sword and vain the Bow,
    They never can work War's overthrow.
The Hermit's prayer and the Widow's Tear
Alone can free the World from fear.

For a Tear is an Intellectual Thing,
And a Sigh is the Sword of an Angel King,
And the bitter groan of the Martyr's woe
Is an arrow from the Almightie's bow.

ROBERT BURNS (1759-1796)

Bonnie Doon

YE banks and braes o' bonnie Doon,
    How can ye bloom sae fair!
How can ye chant, ye little birds,
    And I sae fu' o' care!

Thou'll break my heart, thou bonnie bird
    That sings upon the bough;
Thou minds me o' the happy days
    When my fause Luve was true.

Thou'll break my heart, thou bonnie bird
    That sings beside thy mate;
For sae I sat, and sae I sang,
    And wist na o' my fate.

Aft hae I roved by bonnie Doon
    To see the woodbine twine,
And ilka bird sang o' its love;
    And sae did I o' mine.

Wi' lightsome heart I pu'd a rose,
    Frae aff its thorny tree:
And my fause luver staw the rose,
    But left the thorn wi' me.

"Comin' Through the Rye"

COMIN' through the Rye, poor body,
    Comin' through the Rye,
She draiglet a' her petticoatie,
    Comin' through the Rye.

        Oh Jenny's a' wat poor body,
            Jenny's seldom dry;
            She draiglet a' her petticoatie,
                Comin' through the Rye.

Gin a body meet a body,
    Comin' through the Rye,
Gin a body kiss a body,
    Need a body cry?

Gin a body meet a body
    Comin' through the glen,
Gin a body kiss a body,
    Need the warld ken?

"Green Grow the Rashes, O!"

THERE'S naught but care on every han',
    In every hour that passes, O!
What signifies the life o' man,
An' 'twere na for the lasses, O?

        Green grow the rashes, O!
        Green grow the rashes, O!
        The sweetest hours that e'er I spend,
        Are spent amang the lasses, O!

The warl'ly race may riches chase,
An' riches still may fly them, O!
An' though at last they catch them fast,
Their hearts can ne'er enjoy them, O!

Gie me a canny hour at e'en;
My arms about my dearie, O!
An' warl'ly cares, an' warl'ly men,
May a' gae tapsalteerie, O!

For you sae douce, ye sneer at this;
Ye'er naught but senseless asses, O!
The wisest man the warl' e'er saw
He dearly loved the lasses, O!

Auld Nature swears the lovely dears
Her noblest work she classes, O!
Her 'prentice han' she tried on man,
An' then she made the lasses, O!

"Ae Fond Kiss"

AE fond kiss, and then we sever;
    Ae fareweel, alas, for ever!
Deep in heart-wrung tears I'll pledge thee,
Warring sighs and groans I'll wage thee!

Who shall say that Fortune grieves him
While the star of Hope she leaves him?
Me, nae cheerfu' twinkle lights me,
Dark despair around benights me.

I'll ne'er blame my partial fancy;
Naething could resist my Nancy;
But to see her was to love her,
Love but her, and love for ever.

Had we never loved sae kindly,
Had we never loved sae blindly,
Never met, or never parted,
We had ne'er been broken-hearted.

Fare thee weel, thou first and fairest!
Fare thee weel, thou best and dearest!
Thine be ilka joy and treasure,
Peace, enjoyment, love, and pleasure!

Ae fond kiss, and then we sever!
Ae fareweel, alas, for ever!
Deep in heart-wrung tears I'll pledge thee,
Warring sighs and groans I'll wage thee!

My Bonnie Mary

GO fetch to me a pint o' wine,
    And fill it in a silver tassie,
That I may drink, before I go,
    A service to my bonnie lassie.
The boat rocks at the pier o' Leith,
    Fu' loud the wind blaws frae the **ferry,**
The ship rides by the Berwick-law,
    And I maun leave my bonnie Mary.

The trumpets sound, the banners fly,
  The glittering spears are rankèd ready;
The shouts o' war are heard afar,
  The battle closes thick and bloody;
But it's no the roar o' sea or shore
  Wad mak me langer wish to tarry;
Nor shout o' war that's heard afar—
  It's leaving thee, my bonnie Mary!

A Red, Red Rose

O my luve's like a red, red rose
    That's newly sprung in June;
O, my luve's like the melodie
  That's sweetly played in tune.

As fair thou art, my bonnie lass,
  So deep in luve am I;
And I will luve thee still, my dear,
  Till a' the seas gang dry.

Till a' the seas gang dry, my dear,
  And the rocks melt wi' the sun;
I will luve thee still, my dear,
  While the sands o' life shall run.

And fare thee weel, my only luve!
  And fare thee weel a while!
And I will come again, my luve,
  Though it were ten thousand mile.

Jean

OF a' the airts the wind can blaw
    I dearly like the west,
For there the bonnie lassie lives,
  The lassie I lo'e best:
There's wild woods grow, and rivers row,
  And monie a hill between;
But day and night my fancy's flight
  Is ever wi' my Jean.

I see her in the dewy flowers,
  I see her sweet and fair:
I hear her in the tunefu' birds,
  I hear her charm the air:
There's not a bonnie flower that springs
  By fountain, shaw, or green,
There's not a bonnie bird that sings
  But minds me o' my Jean.

Auld Lang Syne

SHOULD auld acquaintance be forgot,
  And never brought to min'?
Should auld acquaintance be forgot,
  And days o' lang syne?

      For auld lang syne, my dear,
        For auld lang syne,
      We'll tak a cup o' kindness yet
        For auld lang syne.

We twa hae rin about the braes,
  And pu'd the gowans fine;
But we've wandered monie a weary fit
  Sin' auld lang syne.

We twa hae paidl't i' in the burn,
  Frae mornin' sun till dine;
But seas between us braid hae roared
  Sin' auld lang syne.

And here's a hand, my trusty fiere,
  And gie's a hand o' thine;
And we'll tak a right guid willie-waught
  For auld lang syne.

And surely ye'll be your pint-stowp,
  And surely I'll be mine,
And we'll tak a cup o' kindness yet
  For auld lang syne!

Bruce to His Men at Bannockburn

SCOTS, wha hae wi' Wallace bled,
  Scots, wham Bruce hae aften led;
Welcome to your gory bed,
  Or to victory!

Now's the day, and now's the hour:
See the front o' battle lour:
See approach proud Edward's power,—
  Chains and slavery!

Wha will be a traitor knave?
Wha can fill a coward's grave?
Wha sae base as be a slave?
  Let him turn and flee!

Wha for Scotland's king and law
Freedom's sword will strongly draw,
Freeman stand, or freeman fa',
    Let him follow me!

By oppression's woes and pains!
By your sons in servile chains,
We will drain our dearest veins,
    But they shall be free!

Lay the proud usurpers low!
Tyrants fall in every foe!
Liberty's in every blow!—
    Let us do or dee!

John Anderson

JOHN Anderson my jo, John,
    When we were first acquent
Your locks were like the raven,
Your bonnie brow was brent;
But now your brow is bald, John,
Your locks are like the snow;
But blessings on your frosty pow,
    John Anderson my jo.

John Anderson my jo, John,
We clamb the hill thegither,
And mony a canty day, John,
We've had wi' ane anither:
Now we maun totter down, John,
But hand in hand we'll go,
And sleep thegither at the foot,
    John Anderson my jo.

Highland Mary

YE banks and braes and streams around
    The castle o' Montgomery,
Green be your woods, and fair your flowers,
    Your waters never drumlie!
There simmer first unfauld her robes,
    And there the langest tarry;
For there I took the last fareweel
    O' my sweet Highland Mary.

How sweetly bloomed the gay green birk,
  How rich the hawthorn's blossom,
As underneath their fragrant shade
  I clasped her to my bosom!
The golden hours on angel's wings
  Flew o'er me and my dearie;
For dear to me as light and life
  Was my sweet Highland Mary.

Wi' mony a vow and locked embrace
  Our parting was fu' tender;
And, pledging aft to meet again,
  We tore oursels asunder;
But, O! fell Death's untimely frost,
  That nipped my flower sae early!
Now green's the sod, and cauld's the clay,
  That wraps my Highland Mary!

O pale, pale now, those rosy lips,
  I aft hae kissed sae fondly!
And closed for aye the sparkling glance
  That dwelt on me sae kindly;
And moldering now in silent dust
  That heart that lo'ed me dearly!
But still within my bosom's core
  Shall live my Highland Mary.

To Mary in Heaven

THOU lingering star, with lessening ray,
  Thou lov'st to greet the early morn,
Again thou usher'st in the day
  My Mary from my soul was torn.
O Mary! dear departed shade!
  Where is thy place of blissful rest?
See'st thou thy lover lowly laid?
  Hear'st thou the groans that rend his breast?

That sacred hour can I forget,
  Can I forget the hallowed grove,
Where by the winding Ayr we met,
  To live one day of parting love!
Eternity will not efface
  Those records dear of transports past;
Thy image at our last embrace,—
  Ah! little thought we 'twas our last!

Ayr, gurgling, kissed his pebbled shore,
  O'erhung with wild woods, thickening green;

The fragrant birch, and hawthorn hoar,
  Twined amorous round the raptured scene;
The flowers sprang wanton to be pressed,
  The birds sang love on every spray,—
Till soon, too soon, the glowing west
  Proclaimed the speed of wingèd day.

Still o'er these scenes my memory wakes,
  And fondly broods with miser care!
Time but the impression stronger makes,
  As streams their channels deeper wear.
My Mary! dear departed shade!
  Where is thy place of blissful rest?
See'st thou thy lover lowly laid?
  Hear'st thou the groans that rend his breast?

JAMES HOGG (1770-1835)

A Boy's Song

WHERE the pools are bright and deep,
    Where the gray trout lies asleep,
Up the river and over the lea,
That's the way for Billy and me.

Where the blackbird sings the latest,
Where the hawthorn blooms the sweetest,
Where the nestlings chirp and flee,
That's the way for Billy and me.

Where the mowers mow the cleanest,
Where the hay lies thick and greenest,
There to track the homeward bee,
That's the way for Billy and me.

Where the hazel bank is steepest,
Where the shadow falls the deepest,
Where the clustering nuts fall free,
That's the way for Billy and me.

Why the boys should drive away
Little sweet maidens from the play,
Or love to banter and fight so well,
That's the thing I never could tell.

But this I know, I love to play
Through the meadow, among the hay;
Up the water and over the lea,
That's the way for Billy and me.

WILLIAM WORDSWORTH (1770-1850)

Lucy

I

STRANGE fits of passion I have known:
    And I will dare to tell,
But in the lover's ear alone,
    What once to me befell.

When she I loved was strong and gay,
    And like a rose in June,
I to her cottage bent my way,
    Beneath the evening moon.

Upon the moon I fixed my eye,
    All over the wide lea;
My horse trudged on—and we drew nigh
    Those paths so dear to me.

And now we reached the orchard plot;
    And as we climbed the hill,
Towards the roof of Lucy's cot
    The moon descended still.

In one of those sweet dreams I slept,
    Kind nature's gentlest boon!
And all the while my eyes I kept
    On the descending moon.

My horse moved on; hoof after hoof
    He raised, and never stopped:
When down behind the cottage roof,
    At once, the bright moon dropped.

What fond and wayward thoughts will slide
    Into a lover's head!—
"Oh, mercy!" to myself I cried,
    "If Lucy should be dead!"

II

She dwelt among the untrodden ways
    Beside the springs of Dove,
A Maid whom there were none to praise
    And very few to love:

A violet by a mossy stone
  Half hidden from the eye!
Fair as a star, when only one
  Is shining in the sky.

She lived unknown, and few could know
  When Lucy ceased to be;
But she is in her grave, and oh,
  The difference to me!

IV

Three years she grew in sun and shower;
Then Nature said, "A lovelier flower
  On earth was never sown;
This child I to myself will take;
She shall be mine, and I will make
  A lady of my own.

"Myself will to my darling be
Both law and impulse: and with me
  The girl, in rock and plain,
In earth and heaven, in glade and bower,
Shall feel an overseeing power
  To kindle or restrain.

"She shall be sportive as the fawn
That wild with glee across the lawn
  Or up the mountain springs;
And hers shall be the breathing balm,
And hers the silence and the calm
  Of mute insensate things.

"The floating clouds their state shall lend
To her; for her the willow bend;
  Nor shall she fail to see
Even in the motions of the storm
Grace that shall mold the maiden's form
  By silent sympathy.

"The stars of midnight shall be dear
To her; and she shall lean her ear
  In many a secret place
Where rivulets dance their wayward round,
And beauty born of murmuring sound
  Shall pass into her face.

"And vital feelings of delight
Shall rear her form to stately height,
  Her virgin bosom swell;
Such thoughts to Lucy I will give
While she and I together live
  Here in this happy dell."

Thus Nature spake—The work was done—
How soon my Lucy's race was run!
  She died, and left to me
This heath, this calm and quiet scene;
The memory of what has been,
  And never more will be.

v

A slumber did my spirit seal;
  I had no human fears:
She seemed a thing that could not feel
  The touch of earthly years.

No motion has she now, or force;
  She neither hears nor sees;
Rolled round in earth's diurnal course,
  With rocks, and stones, and trees.

The Solitary Reaper

BEHOLD her, single in the field,
  Yon solitary Highland Lass!
Reaping and singing by herself;
Stop here, or gently pass!
Alone she cuts and binds the grain,
And sings a melancholy strain;
O listen! for the Vale profound
Is overflowing with the sound.

No Nightingale did ever chaunt
More welcome notes to weary bands
Of Travellers in some shady haunt,
Among Arabian sands:
A voice so thrilling ne'er was heard
In spring-time from the Cuckoo-bird,
Breaking the silence of the seas
Among the farthest Hebrides.

Will no one tell me what she sings?
Perhaps the plaintive numbers flow

For old, unhappy, far-off things,
And battles long ago:
Or is it some more humble lay,
Familiar matter of to-day?
Some natural sorrow, loss, or pain,
That has been, and may be again!

Whate'er the theme, the Maiden sang
As if her song could have no ending;
I saw her singing at her work,
And o'er the sickle bending:—
I listened, motionless and still;
And, as I mounted up the hill,
The music in my heart I bore,
Long after it was heard no more.

Perfect Woman

SHE was a phantom of delight
    When first she gleamed upon my sight;
A lovely apparition, sent
To be a moment's ornament;
Her eyes as stars of twilight fair;
Like twilight's, too, her dusky hair;
But all things else about her drawn
From May-time and the cheerful dawn;
A dancing shape, an image gay,
To haunt, to startle, and waylay.

I saw her upon nearer view,
A Spirit, yet a Woman too!
Her household motions light and free,
And steps of virgin liberty;
A countenance in which did meet
Sweet records, promises as sweet;
A creature not too bright or good
For human nature's daily food;
For transient sorrows, simple wiles,
Praise, blame, love, kisses, tears, and smiles.

And now I see with eye serene
The very pulse of the machine ;
A being breathing thoughtful breath,
A traveller between life and death;
The reason firm, the temperate will,
Endurance, foresight, strength, and skill;
A perfect Woman, nobly planned,
To warn, to comfort, and command;
And yet a Spirit still and bright
With something of angelic light.

The Rainbow

MY heart leaps up when I behold
  A rainbow in the sky:
So was it when my life began;
So is it now I am a man;
So be it when I shall grow old,
    Or let me die!
The Child is father of the Man;
And I could wish my days to be
Bound each to each by natural piety.

To the Cuckoo

O blithe new-comer! I have heard,
  I hear thee and rejoice.
O Cuckoo! shall I call thee bird,
  Or but a wandering voice?

While I am lying on the grass,
  Thy two-fold shout I hear,
From hill to hill it seems to pass,
  At once far off and near.

Though babbling only, to the vale,
  Of sunshine and of flowers,
Thou bringest unto me a tale
  Of visionary hours.

Thrice welcome, darling of the Spring!
  Even yet thou art to me
No bird, but an invisible thing,
  A voice, a mystery;

The same whom in my school-boy days
  I listened to; that Cry
Which made me look a thousand ways,
  In bush, and tree, and sky.

To seek thee did I often rove
  Through woods and on the green;
And thou wert still a hope, a love;
  Still longed for, never seen.

And I can listen to thee yet;
  Can lie upon the plain
And listen, till I do beget
  That golden time again.

O blessèd Bird! the earth we pace
   Again appears to be
An unsubstantial, faery place;
   That is fit home for Thee!

"I Wandered Lonely as a Cloud"

I wandered lonely as a cloud
   That floats on high o'er vales and hills,
When all at once I saw a cloud,
A host of golden daffodils;
Beside the lake, beneath the trees,
Fluttering and dancing in the breeze.

Continuous as the stars that shine
And twinkle on the milky way,
They stretched in never-ending line
Along the margin of a bay:
Ten thousand saw I at a glance,
Tossing their heads in sprightly dance.

The waves beside them danced; but they
Out-did the sparkling waves in glee:
A poet could not but be gay,
In such a jocund company:
I gazed—and gazed—but little thought
What wealth the show to me had brought:

For oft, when on my couch I lie
In vacant or in pensive mood,
They flash upon that inward eye
Which is the bliss of solitude;
And then my heart with pleasure fills,
And dances with the daffodils.

Sonnets

Scorn Not the Sonnet

SCORN not the sonnet; critic, you have frowned,
   Mindless of its just honors;—with this key
Shakespeare unlocked his heart; the melody
Of this small lute gave ease to Petrarch's wound;
A thousand times this pipe did Tasso sound;
Camöens soothed with it an exile's grief;
The sonnet glittered a gay myrtle leaf
Amid the cypress with which Dante crowned

His visionary brow: a glow-worm lamp,
It cheered mild Spenser, called from faery-land
To struggle through dark ways; and when a damp
Fell round the path of Milton, in his hand
The thing became a trumpet, whence he blew
Soul-animating strains—alas, too few!

The Sonnet-Prison

NUNS fret not at their convent's narrow room;
  And hermits are contented with their cells;
And students with their pensive citadels:
Maids at the wheel, the weaver at his loom,
Sit blithe and happy; bees that soar for bloom,
High as the highest peak of Furness Fells,
Will murmur by the hour in foxglove bells:
In truth, the prison, unto which we doom
Ourselves, no prison is: and hence to me,
In sundry moods, 'twas pastime to be bound
Within the sonnet's scanty plot of ground
Pleased if some souls (for such there needs must be)
Who have felt the weight of too much liberty,
Should find brief solace there, as I have found.

Sunset and Sea

IT is a beauteous evening, calm and free;
  The holy time is quiet as a nun
Breathless with adoration; the broad sun
Is sinking down in its tranquillity;
The gentleness of heaven is on the sea:
Listen! the mighty Being is awake,
And doth with His eternal motion make
A sound like thunder—everlastingly.
Dear child! dear girl! that walkest with me here,
If thou appear'st untouched by solemn thought,
Thy nature is not therefore less divine:
Thou liest in Abraham's bosom all the year;
And worshipp'st at the temple's inner shrine,
God being with thee when we know it not.

The World Is Too Much With Us

THE world is too much with us; late and soon,
  Getting and spending, we lay waste our powers:
Little we see in Nature that is ours;
We have given our hearts away, a sordid boon!

This sea that bares her bosom to the moon,
The winds that will be howling at all hours,
And are up-gathered now like sleeping flowers;
For this, for everything, we are out of tune;
It moves us not.—Great God! I'd rather be
A Pagan suckled in a creed outworn;
So might I, standing on this pleasant lea,
Have glimpses that would make me less forlorn;
Have sight of Proteus rising from the sea;
Or hear old Triton blow his wreathèd horn.

Composed upon Westminster Bridge, September 3, 1802

E ARTH has not anything to show more fair:
Dull would he be of soul who could pass by
A sight so touching in its majesty:
This City now doth, like a garment, wear
The beauty of the morning; silent, bare,
Ships, towers, domes, theaters, and temples lie
Open unto the fields, and to the sky;
All bright and glittering in the smokeless air.
Never did sun more beautifully steep
In his first splendor, valley, rock, or hill;
Ne'er saw I, never felt, a calm so deep!
The river glideth at his own sweet will:
Dear God! the very houses seem asleep;
And all that mighty heart is lying still!

England, 1802

I

O friend! I know not which way I must look
For comfort, being, as I am, oppressed,
To think that now our life is only dressed
For show; mean handy-work of craftsman, cook,
Or groom!—We must run glittering like a brook
In the open sunshine, or we are unblest:
The wealthiest man among us is the best:
No grandeur now in nature or in book
Delights us. Rapine, avarice, expense,
This is idolatry; and these we adore:
Plain living and high thinking are no more:
The homely beauty of the good old cause
Is gone; our peace, our fearful innocence,
And pure religion breathing household laws.

II

Milton! thou shouldst be living at this hour:
  England hath need of thee: she is a fen
  Of stagnant waters: altar, sword, and pen,
Fireside, the heroic wealth of hall and bower,
Have forfeited their ancient English dower
  Of inward happiness. We are selfish men;
  Oh! raise us up, return to us again,
And give us manners, virtue, freedom, power.
Thy soul was like a Star, and dwelt apart;
  Thou hadst a voice whose sound was like the sea:
  Pure as the naked heavens, majestic, free,
  So didst thou travel on life's common way,
In cheerful godliness; and yet thy heart
  The lowliest duties on herself did lay.

Abridged.

Ode on the Intimations of Immortality from Recollections of Early Childhood

I

THERE was a time when meadow, grove, and stream,
  The earth, and every common sight,
      To me did seem
      Apparelled in celestial light,
The glory and the freshness of a dream.
It is not now as it hath been of yore;—
      Turn wheresoe'er I may,
        By night or day,
The things which I have seen I now can see no more.

II

      The Rainbow comes and goes,
      And lovely is the Rose;
      The Moon doth with delight
Look round her when the heavens are bare;
      Waters on a starry night
      Are beautiful and fair;
  The sunshine is a glorious birth;
  But yet I know, where'er I go,
That there hath passed away a glory from the earth.

III

Now, while the Birds thus sing a joyous song,
      And while the young Lambs bound
        As to the tabor's sound,
To me alone there came a thought of grief:
A timely utterance gave that thought relief,
        And I again am strong.

The Cataracts blow their trumpets from the steep:
No more shall grief of mine the season wrong;
I hear the Echoes through the mountains throng,
The Winds come to me from the fields of sleep,
      And all the earth is gay;
        Land and Sea
      Give themselves up to jollity,
        And with the heart of May
      Doth every Beast keep holiday;—
          Thou Child of Joy,
Shout round me, let me hear thy shouts, thou happy Shep-
    herd boy!

IV

Ye blessèd Creatures, I have heard the call
      Ye to each other make; I see
The heavens laugh with you in your jubilee;
      My heart is at your festival,
      My head hath its coronal,
The fulness of your bliss, I feel—I feel it all.
      O evil day! if I were sullen
      While Earth herself is adorning
      This sweet May morning,
      And the Children are culling
        On every side,
      In a thousand valleys far and wide,
      Fresh flowers; while the sun shines warm,
And the Babe leaps up on his Mother's arm:—
      I hear, I hear, with joy I hear!
      —But there's a Tree, of many, one,
A single Field which I have looked upon,
Both of them speak of something that is gone:
      The Pansy at my feet
      Doth the same tale repeat:
Whither is fled the visionary gleam?
Where is it now, the glory and the dream?

V

Our birth is but a sleep and a forgetting:
The Soul that rises with us, our life's Star,
      Hath had elsewhere its setting,
      And cometh from afar:
      Not in entire forgetfulness,
      And not in utter nakedness,
But trailing clouds of glory do we come
      From God, who is our home:
Heaven lies about us in our infancy!
Shades of the prison-house begin to close
      Upon the growing Boy,

But he beholds the light, and whence it flows,
    He sees it in his joy;
The Youth, who daily farther from the East
    Must travel, still is Nature's Priest,
      And by the vision spendid
      Is on his way attended;
At length the Man perceives it die away,
And fade into the light of common day.

VI

Earth fills her lap with pleasures of her own;
Yearnings she hath in her own natural kind,
And even with something of a Mother's mind,
      And no unworthy aim,
    The homely Nurse doth all she can,
To make her Foster-child, her Inmate Man,
      Forget the glories he hath known,
And that imperial palace whence he came.

VII

Behold the Child among his new-born blisses,
A six years' darling of a pigmy size!
See, where 'mid work of his own hand he lies,
Fretted by sallies of his Mother's kisses,
With light upon him from his Father's eyes!
See, at his feet, some little plan or chart,
Some fragment from his dream of human life,
Shaped by himself with newly-learnèd art;
    A wedding or a festival,
    A mourning or a funeral;
      And this hath now his heart,
    And unto this he frames his song:
      Then will he fit his tongue
To dialogues of business, love, or strife:
      But it will not be long
      Ere this be thrown aside,
      And with new joy and pride
The little Actor cons another part;
Filling from time to time his "humorous stage"
With all the Persons, down to palsied Age,
That Life brings with her in her equipage;
    As if his whole vocation
    Were endless imitation.

VIII

Thou, whose exterior semblance doth belie
    Thy Soul's immensity;
Thou best Philosopher, who yet dost keep
Thy heritage, thou Eye among the blind,
That, deaf and silent, read'st the eternal deep,

Haunted for ever by the eternal mind,—
    Mighty Prophet! Seer blest!
    On whom those truths do rest,
Which we are toiling all our lives to find,
In darkness lost, the darkness of the grave:
Thou, over whom thy Immortality
Broods like the Day, a master o'er a Slave,
A Presence which is not to be put by;
Thou little Child, yet glorious in the might
Of heaven-born freedom on thy being's height,
Why with such earnest pains dost thou provoke
The years to bring the inevitable yoke,
Thus blindly with thy blessedness at strife?
Full soon thy Soul shall have her earthly freight,
And custom lie upon thee with a weight
Heavy as frost, and deep almost as life!

IX

    O joy! that in our embers
    Is something that doth live,
    That nature yet remembers
    What was so fugitive!
The thought of our past years in me doth breed
Perpetual benediction: not indeed
For that which is most worthy to be blest—
Delight and liberty, the simple creed
Of Childhood, whether busy or at rest,
With new-fledged hope still fluttering in his breast:—
    Not for these I raise
    The song of thanks and praise;
But for those obstinate questionings
    Of sense and outward things,
    Fallings from us, vanishings;
  Blank misgivings of a Creature
Moving about in worlds not realized,
High instincts before which our mortal Nature
Did tremble like a guilty thing surprised:
    But for those first affections,
    Those shadowy recollections,
    Which, be they what they may,
Are yet the fountain-light of all our day,
Are yet a master-light of all our seeing;
    Uphold us, cherish, and have power to make
Our noisy years seem moments in the being
Of the eternal Silence: truths that wake,
    To perish never,
Which neither listlessness, nor mad endeavor,
    Nor Man nor Boy,

Nor all that is at enmity with joy,
Can utterly abolish or destroy!
    Hence, in a season of calm weather,
      Though inland far we be,
Our Souls have sight of that immortal sea
      Which brought us hither,
      Can in a moment travel thither
And see the children sport upon the shore,
And hear the mighty waters rolling evermore.

x

Then sing, ye Birds, sing, sing a joyous song!
      And let the young Lambs bound
      As to the tabor's sound!
      We in thought will join your throng,
      Ye that pipe and ye that play,
      Ye that through your hearts to-day
      Feel the gladness of the May!
What though the radiance which was once so bright
Be now for ever taken from my sight,
    Though nothing can bring back the hour
Of splendor in the grass, of glory in the flower;
      We will grieve not, rather find
      Strength in what remains behind;
      In the primal sympathy
      Which having been must ever be;
      In the soothing thoughts that spring
      Out of human suffering;
      In the faith that looks through death,
In years that bring the philosophic mind.

xi

And O, ye Fountains, Meadows, Hills, and Groves,
Forebode not any severing of our loves!
Yet in my heart of hearts I feel your might;
I only have relinquished one delight
To live beneath your more habitual sway.
I love the Brooks, which down their channels fret,
Even more than when I tripped lightly as they:
The innocent brightness of a new-born Day
      Is lovely yet;
The Clouds that gather round the setting sun
Do take a sober colouring from an eye
That hath kept watch o'er man's mortality;
Another race hath been, and other palms are won.
Thanks to the human heart by which we live,
Thanks to its tenderness, its joys, and fears,
To me the meanest flower that blows can give
Thoughts that do often lie too deep for tears.

From "Lines Composed a Few Miles Above Tintern Abbey"

              . . . that blessed mood,
In which the burthen of the mystery,
In which the heavy and the weary weight
Of all this unintelligible world,
Is lightened :—that serene and blessed mood,
In which the affections gently lead us on,—
Until, the breath of this corporeal frame,
And even the motion of our human blood
Almost suspended, we are laid asleep
In body, and become a living soul:
While with an eye made quiet by the power
Of harmony, and the deep power of joy,
We see into the life of things. . . .
                . . . For nature
(The coarser pleasures of my boyish days,
And their glad animal movements all gone by)
To me was all in all.—I cannot paint
What then I was. The sounding cataract
Haunted me like a passion: the tall rock,
The mountain, and the deep and gloomy wood,
Their colors and their forms, were then to me
An appetite: a feeling and a love,
That had no need of a remoter charm,
By thought supplied, or any interest
Unborrowed from the eye.—That time is past,
And all its aching joys are now no more,
And all its dizzy raptures. Not for this
Faint I, nor mourn nor murmur; other gifts
Have followed, for such loss, I would believe,
Abundant recompense. For I have learned
To look on nature, not as in the hour
Of thoughtless youth; but hearing oftentimes
The still, sad music of humanity,
Nor harsh nor grating, though of ample power
To chasten and subdue. And I have felt
A presence that disturbs me with the joy
Of elevated thoughts; a sense sublime
Of something far more deeply interfused,
Whose dwelling is the light of setting suns,
And the round ocean, and the living air,
And the blue sky, and in the mind of man:
A motion and a spirit, that impels
All thinking things, all objects of all thought,
And rolls through all things.

Ode to Duty

STERN Daughter of the Voice of God!
  O Duty! if that name thou love,
Who art a light to guide, a rod
To check the erring and reprove;
Thou, who art victory and law
When empty terrors overawe;
From vain temptations dost set free;
And calm'st the weary strife of frail humanity!

There are who ask not if thine eye
Be on them; who, in love and truth,
Where no misgiving is, rely
Upon the genial sense of youth:
Glad Hearts! without reproach or blot,
Who do thy work, and know it not:
O, if through confidence misplaced
They fail, thy saving arms, dread Power! around them cast.

Serene will be our days and bright,
And happy will our nature be,
When love is an unerring light,
And joy its own security.
And they a blissful course may hold
Even now, who, not unwisely bold,
Live in the spirit of this creed;
Yet seek thy firm support, according to their need.

I, loving freedom, and untried;
No sport of every random gust,
Yet being to myself a guide,
Too blindly have reposed my trust:
And oft, when in my heart was heard
Thy timely mandate, I deferred
The task, in smoother walks to stray;
But thee I now would serve more strictly, if I may.

Through no disturbance of my soul,
Or strong compunction in me wrought,
I supplicate for thy control;
But in the quietness of thought:
Me this unchartered freedom tires;
I feel the weight of chance-desires;
My hopes no more must change their name,
I long for a repose that ever is the same.

Stern Lawgiver! yet thou dost wear
The Godhead's most benignant grace;

SALEM COLLEGE
LIBRARY
Winston-Salem, N. C.

Nor know we anything so fair
As is the smile upon thy face:
Flowers laugh before thee on their beds,
And fragrance in thy footing treads;
Thou dost preserve the stars from wrong;
And the most ancient heavens, through Thee, are fresh and
    strong.

To humbler functions, awful Power!
I call thee: I myself commend
Unto thy guidance from this hour;
O, let my weakness have an end!
Give unto me, made lowly wise,
The spirit of self-sacrifice;
The confidence of reason give;
And in the light of truth thy Bondman let me live!

SIR WALTER SCOTT (1771-1832)

Hunting Song

WAKEN, lords and ladies gay,
    On the mountain dawns the day;
All the jolly chase is here,
With hawk and horse and hunting-spear!
Hounds are in their couples yelling,
Hawks are whistling, horns are knelling.
Merrily, merrily, mingle they,
"Waken, lords and ladies gay."

Waken, lords and ladies gay,
The mist has left the mountain gray,
Springlets in the dawn are steaming,
Diamonds on the brake are gleaming,
And foresters have busy been
To track the buck in thicket green;
Now we come to chant our lay,
"Waken, lords and ladies gay."

Waken, lords and ladies gay,
To the greenwood haste away;
We can show you where he lies,
Fleet of foot and tall of size;
We can show the marks he made
When 'gainst the oak his antlers frayed;
You shall see him brought to bay;
Waken, lords and ladies gay.

Louder, louder chant the lay,
Waken, lords and ladies gay!
Tell them youth, and mirth, and glee
Run a course as well as we;
Time, stern huntsman! who can balk,
Stanch as hound and fleet as hawk?
Think of this, and rise with day,
Gentle lords and ladies gay!

Lucy Ashton's Song

LOOK not thou on beauty's charming;
    Sit thou still when kings are arming;
Taste not when the wine-cup glistens;
Speak not when the people listens;
Stop thine ear against the singer;
From the red gold keep thy finger;
Vacant hand and heart and eye,
Easy live and quiet die.

Sound, Sound the Clarion

Sound, sound the clarion, fill the fife
    To all the sensual world proclaim,
One crowded hour of glorious life
    Is worth an age without a name.

Proud Maisie

PROUD Maisie is in the wood,
    Walking so early;
Sweet Robin sits on the bush,
    Singing so rarely.

"Tell me, thou bonny bird,
    When shall I marry me?"
"When six braw gentlemen
    Kirkward shall carry ye."

"Who makes the bridal bed,
    Birdie, say truly?"
"The gray-headed sexton
    That delves the grave duly.

"The glow-worm o'er grave and stone
    Shall light thee steady;
The owl from the steeple sing
    Welcome, proud lady!"

From "The Lay of the Last Minstrel"

B REATHES there a man with soul so dead,
  Who never to himself hath said,
    This is my own, my native land!
Whose heart hath ne'er within him burned,
As home his footsteps he hath turned
    From wandering on a foreign strand?
If such there breathe, go mark him well:
For him no minstrel raptures swell;
High though his titles, proud his name,
Boundless his wealth as wish can claim;
Despite those titles, power, and pelf,
The wretch, concentred all in self,
Living, shall forfeit fair renown,
And, doubly dying, shall go down
To the vile dust, from whence he sprung,
Unwept, unhonored, and unsung.

O Caledonia! stern and wild,
Meet nurse for a poetic child!
Land of brown heath and shaggy wood,
Land of the mountain and the flood,
Land of my sires! what mortal hand
Can e'er untie the filial band
That knits me to thy rugged strand!

SAMUEL TAYLOR COLERIDGE (1772-1834)

The Rime of the Ancient Mariner

PART I

I T is an ancient Mariner,
  And he stoppeth one of three.
"By thy long gray beard and glittering eye,
Now wherefore stopp'st thou me?

"The Bridegroom's doors are opened wide,
And I am next of kin;
The guests are met, the feast is set:
May'st hear the merry din."

He holds him with his skinny hand,
"There was a ship," quoth he.
"Hold off! unhand me, gray-beard loon!"
Eftsoons his hand dropped he.

He holds him with his glittering eye—
The Wedding-Guest stood still,
And listens like a three years' child:
The Mariner hath his will.

The Wedding-Guest sat on a stone:
He cannot choose but hear;
And thus spake on that ancient man,
The bright-eyed Mariner.

"The ship was cheered, the harbor cleared,
Merrily did we drop
Below the kirk, below the hill,
Below the lighthouse top.

"The Sun came up upon the left,
Out of the sea came he!
And he shone bright, and on the right
Went down into the sea.

"Higher and higher every day,
Till over the mast at noon——"
The Wedding-Guest here beat his breast,
For he heard the loud bassoon.

The bride hath paced into the hall,
Red as a rose is she;
Nodding their heads before her goes
The merry minstrelsy.

The Wedding-Guest he beat his breast,
Yet he cannot choose but hear;
And thus spake on that ancient man,
The bright-eyed Mariner.

"And now the Storm-blast came, and he
Was tyrannous and strong:
He struck with his o'ertaking wings,
And chased us south along.

"With sloping masts and dipping prow,
As who pursued with yell and blow
Still treads the shadow of his foe,
And forward bends his head,
The ship drove fast, loud roared the blast,
And southward aye we fled.

"And now there came both mist and snow,
And it grew wondrous cold:

And ice, mast-high, came floating by,
As green as emerald.

"And through the drifts the snowy clifts
Did send a dismal sheen:
Nor shapes of men, nor beasts we ken—
The ice was all between.

"The ice was here, the ice was there,
The ice was all around:
It cracked and growled, and roared and howled,
Like noises in a swound!

"At length did cross an Albatross,
Through the fog it came;
As if it had been a Christian soul,
We hailed it in God's name.

"It ate the food it ne'er had eat,
And round and round it flew.
The ice did split with a thunder-fit;
The helmsman steered us through!

"And a good south wind sprung up behind;
The Albatross did follow,
And every day, for food or play,
Came to the mariners' hollo!

"In mist or cloud, on mast or shroud,
It perched for vespers nine;
Whiles all the night, through fog-smoke white,
Glimmered the white moonshine."

"God save thee, ancient Mariner,
From the fiends, that plague thee thus!—
Why look'st thou so?" "With my crossbow
I shot the Albatross.

PART II

"The Sun now rose upon the right:
Out of the sea came he,
Still hid in mist, and on the left
Went down into the sea.

"And the good south wind still blew behind,
But no sweet bird did follow,
Nor any day for food or play
Came to the mariners' hollo!

"And I had done a hellish thing,
And it would work 'em woe:
For all averred I had killed the bird
That made the breeze to blow.
Ah wretch! said they, the bird to slay,
That made the breeze to blow!

"Nor dim nor red, like God's own head,
The glorious Sun uprist:
Then all averred I had killed the bird
That brought the fog and mist.
'Twas right, said they, such birds to slay,
That bring the fog and mist.

"The fair breeze blew, the white foam flew,
The furrow followed free;
We were the first that ever burst
Into that silent sea.

"Down dropped the breeze, the sails dropped
     down,
'Twas sad as sad could be;
And we did speak only to break
The silence of the sea!

"All in a hot and copper sky,
The bloody Sun, at noon,
Right up above the mast did stand,
No bigger than the Moon.

"Day after day, day after day,
We stuck, nor breath nor motion;
As idle as a painted ship
Upon a painted ocean.

"Water, water, everywhere,
And all the boards did shrink;
Water, water, everywhere,
Nor any drop to drink.

"The very deep did rot: O Christ!
That ever this should be!
Yea, slimy things did crawl with legs
Upon the slimy sea.

"About, about, in reel and rout
The death-fires danced at night;
The water, like a witch's oils,
Burnt green, and blue, and white.

"And some in dreams assurèd were
Of the Spirit that plagued us so;
Nine fathom deep he had followed us
From the land of mist and snow.

"And every tongue, through utter drought,
Was withered at the root;
We could not speak, no more than if
We had been choked with soot.

"Ah! well-a-day! what evil looks
Had I from old and young!
Instead of the cross, the Albatross
About my neck was hung.

PART III

"There passed a weary time. Each throat
Was parched, and glazed each eye.
A weary time! a weary time!
How glazed each weary eye!
When looking westward, I beheld
A something in the sky.

"At first it seemed a little speck,
And then it seemed a mist;
It moved and moved, and took at last
A certain shape, I wist.

"A speck, a mist, a shape, I wist!
And still it neared and neared:
As if it dodged a water-sprite,
It plunged, and tacked, and veered.

"With throats unslaked, with black lips baked,
We could nor laugh nor wail;
Through utter drought all dumb we stood!
I bit my arm, I sucked the blood,
And cried, A sail! a sail!

"With throats unslaked, with black lips baked,
Agape they heard me call:
Gramercy! they for joy did grin,
And all at once their breath drew in,
As they were drinking all.

"See! see! (I cried) she tacks no more
Hither to work us weal—
Without a breeze, without a tide,
She steadies with upright keel!

"The western wave was all aflame,
The day was wellnigh done!
Almost upon the western wave
Rested the broad, bright Sun;
When that strange shape drove suddenly
Betwixt us and the Sun.

"And straight the Sun was flecked with bars
(Heaven's Mother send us grace!),
As if through a dungeon-grate he peered
With broad and burning face.

"Alas! (thought I, and my heart beat loud)
How fast she nears and nears!
Are those her sails that glance in the Sun,
Like restless gossameres?

"Are those her ribs through which the Sun
Did peer, as through a grate?
And is that Woman all her crew?
Is that a Death? and are there two?
Is Death that Woman's mate?

"Her lips were red, her looks were free,
Her locks were yellow as gold:
Her skin was as white as leprosy,
The Nightmare Life-in-Death was she,
Who thicks man's blood with cold.

"The naked hulk alongside came,
And the twain were casting dice;
'The game is done! I've won! I've won!'
Quoth she, and whistles thrice.

"The Sun's rim dips; the stars rush out
At one stride comes the dark;
With far-heard whisper, o'er the sea,
Off shot the specter-bark.

"We listened and looked sideways up!
Fear at my heart, as at a cup,
My life-blood seemed to sip!
The stars were dim, and thick the night,
The steersman's face by his lamp gleamed white;
From the sails the dew did drip—
Till clomb above the eastern bar
The hornèd Moon, with one bright star
Within the nether tip.

"One after one, by the star-dogged Moon,
Too quick for groan or sigh,
Each turned his face with a ghastly pang,
And cursed me with his eye.

"Four times fifty living men
(And I heard nor sigh nor groan),
With heavy thump, a lifeless lump,
They dropped down one by one.

"The souls did from their bodies fly—
They fled to bliss or woe!
And every soul, it passed me by
Like the whizz of my crossbow!"

PART IV

"I fear thee, ancient Mariner!
I fear thy skinny hand!
And thou art long, and lank, and brown,
As is the ribbed sea-sand.

"I fear thee and thy glittering eye,
And thy skinny hand so brown."—
"Fear not, fear not, thou Wedding-Guest!
This body dropped not down.

"Alone, alone, all, all alone,
Alone on a wide, wide sea!
And never a saint took pity on
My soul in agony.

"The many men, so beautiful!
And they all dead did lie:
And a thousand thousand slimy things
Lived on; and so did I.

"I looked upon the rotting sea,
And drew my eyes away;
I looked upon the rotting deck,
And there the dead men lay.

"I looked to heaven, and tried to pray;
But or ever a prayer had gushed,
A wicked whisper came, and made
My heart as dry as dust.

"I closed my lids, and kept them close,
And the balls like pulses beat;

For the sky and the sea, and the sea and the sky,
Lay like a load on my weary eye,
And the dead were at my feet.

"The cold sweat melted from their limbs,
Nor rot nor reek did they:
The look with which they looked on me
Had never passed away.

"An orphan's curse would drag to hell
A spirit from on high;
But oh! more horrible than that
Is a curse in a dead man's eye!
Seven days, seven nights, I saw that curse,
And yet I could not die.

"The moving Moon went up the sky,
And nowhere did abide;
Softly she was going up,
And a star or two beside—

"Her beams bemocked the sultry main,
Like April hoar-frost spread;
But where the ship's huge shadow lay,
The charmèd water burnt alway
A still and awful red.

"Beyond the shadow of the ship,
I watched the water-snakes:
They moved in tracks of shining white,
And when they reared, the elfish light
Fell off in hoary flakes.

"Within the shadow of the ship
I watched their rich attire:
Blue, glossy green, and velvet black,
They coiled and swam; and every track
Was a flash of golden fire.

"O happy living things! no tongue
Their beauty might declare:
A spring of love gushed from my heart,
And I blessed them unaware:
Sure my kind saint took pity on me,
And I blessed them unaware.

"The selfsame moment I could pray;
And from my neck so free
The Albatross fell off, and sank
Like lead into the sea.

PART V

"O sleep! it is a gentle thing,
Beloved from pole to pole!
To Mary Queen the praise be given!
She sent the gentle sleep from Heaven,
That slid into my soul.

"The silly buckets on the deck,
That had so long remained,
I dreamt that they were filled with dew;
And when I awoke, it rained.

"My lips were wet, my throat was cold,
My garments all were dank;
Sure I had drunken in my dreams,
And still my body drank.

"I moved, and could not feel my limbs:
I was so light—almost
I thought that I had died in sleep,
And was a blessed ghost.

"And soon I heard a roaring wind:
It did not come anear;
But with its sound it shook the sails,
That were so thin and sere.

"The upper air burst into life;
And a hundred fire-flags sheen;
To and fro they were hurried about;
And to and fro, and in and out,
The wan stars danced between.

"And the coming wind did roar more loud,
And the sails did sigh like sedge;
And the rain poured down from one black cloud;
The Moon was at its edge.

"The thick black cloud was cleft, and still
The Moon was at its side;
Like waters shot from some high crag,
The lightning fell with never a jag,
A river steep and wide.

"The loud wind never reached the ship,
Yet now the ship moved on!
Beneath the lightning and the Moon
The dead men gave a groan.

"They groaned, they stirred, they all uprose,
Nor spake, nor moved their eyes;
It had been strange, even in a dream,
To have seen those dead men rise.

"The helmsman steered, the ship moved on;
Yet never a breeze up-blew;
The mariners all 'gan work the ropes,
Where they were wont to do;
They raised their limbs like lifeless tools—
We were a ghastly crew.

"The body of my brother's son
Stood by me, knee to knee:
The body and I pulled at one rope,
But he said naught to me."

"I fear thee, ancient Mariner!"
"Be calm, thou Wedding-Guest:
'Twas not those souls that fled in pain,
Which to their corses came again,
But a troop of spirits blest:

"For when it dawned—they dropped their arms,
And clustered round the mast;
Sweet sounds rose slowly through their mouths.
And from their bodies passed.

"Around, around, flew each sweet sound,
Then darted to the Sun;
Slowly the sounds came back again,
Now mixed, now one by one.

"Sometimes a-dropping from the sky
I heard the skylark sing;
Sometimes all little birds that are,
How they seemed to fill the sea and air
With their sweet jargoning!

"And now 'twas like all instruments,
Now like a lonely flute;
And now it is an angel's song,
That makes the Heavens be mute.

"It ceased: yet still the sails made on
A pleasant noise till noon,
A noise like of a hidden brook
In the leafy month of June,
That to the sleeping woods all night
Singeth a quiet tune.

"Till noon we quietly sailed on,
Yet never a breeze did breathe:
Slowly and smoothly went the ship,
Moved onward from beneath.

"Under the keel nine fathom deep,
From the land of mist and snow,
The Spirit slid: and it was he
That made the ship to go.
The sails at noon left off their tune,
And the ship stood still also.

"The Sun, right up above the mast,
Had fixed her to the ocean:
But in a minute she 'gan stir,
With a short uneasy motion—
Backwards and forwards half her length
With a short uneasy motion.

"Then like a pawing horse let go,
She made a sudden bound:
It flung the blood into my head,
And I fell down in a swound.

"How long in that same fit I lay,
I have not to declare;
But ere my living life returned,
I heard, and in my soul discerned
Two voices in the air.

"'Is it he?' quoth one, 'is this the man?
By Him who died on cross,
With his cruel bow he laid full low
The harmless Albatross.

"'The Spirit who bideth by himself
In the land of mist and snow,
He loved the bird that loved the man
Who shot him with his bow.'

"The other was a softer voice,
As soft as honey-dew:
Quoth he, 'The man hath penance done,
And penance more will do.'

PART VI

First Voice:
"'But tell me, tell me! speak again,
What makes that ship drive on so fast?

Thy soft response renewing—
What is the Ocean doing?'

Second Voice:
" 'Still as a slave before his lord,
The Ocean hath no blast;
His great bright eye most silently
Up to the Moon is cast—

" 'If he may know which way to go;
For she guides him smooth or grim.
See, brother, see! how graciously
She looketh down on him.'

First Voice:
" 'But why drives on that ship so fast,
Without or wave or wind?'

Second Voice:
" 'The air is cut away before,
And closes from behind.

" 'Fly, brother, fly! more high, more high!
Or we shall be belated:
For slow and slow that ship will go;
When the Mariner's trance is abated.'

"I woke, and we were sailing on
As in a gentle weather:
'Twas night, calm night, the Moon was high;
The dead men stood together.

"All stood together on the deck,
For a charnel-dungeon fitter:
All fixed on me their stony eyes,
That in the Moon did glitter.

"The pang, the curse, with which they died,
Had never passed away:
I could not draw my eyes from theirs,
Nor turn them up to pray.

"And now this spell was snapped: once more
I viewed the ocean green,
And looked far forth, yet little saw
Of what had else been seen—

"Like one that on a lonesome road
Doth walk in fear and dread,

And having once turned round, walks on,
And turns no more his head;
Because he knows a frightful fiend
Doth close behind him tread.

"But soon there breathed a wind on me,
Nor sound nor motion made:
Its path was not upon the sea,
In ripple or in shade.

"It raised my hair, it fanned my cheek
Like a meadow-gale of spring—
It mingled strangely with my fears,
Yet it felt like a welcoming.

"Swiftly, swiftly flew the ship,
Yet she sailed softly too:
Sweetly, sweetly blew the breeze—
On me alone it blew.

"O dream of joy! is this indeed
The lighthouse top I see
Is this the hill? is this the kirk?
Is this mine own countree?

"We drifted o'er the harbor-bar,
And I with sobs did pray—
O let me be awake, my God!
Or let me sleep alway.

"The harbor-bay was clear as glass,
So smoothly it was strewn!
And on the bay the moonlight lay,
And the shadow of the Moon.

"The rock shone bright, the kirk no less,
That stands above the rock:
The moonlight steeped in silentness
The steady weathercock.

"And the bay was white with silent light
Till rising from the same,
Full many shapes, that shadows were,
In crimson colors came.

"A little distance from the prow
Those crimson shadows were;
I turned my eyes upon the deck—
O Christ! what saw I there!

"Each corse lay flat, lifeless and flat,
And, by the holy rood!
A man all light, a seraph-man,
On every corse there stood.

"This seraph-band, each waved his hand:
It was a heavenly sight!
They stood as signals to the land,
Each one a lovely light;

"This seraph-band, each waved his hand,
No voice did they impart—
No voice; but O, the silence sank
Like music on my heart.

"But soon I heard the dash of oars,
I heard the Pilot's cheer;
My head was turned perforce away,
And I saw a boat appear.

"The Pilot and the Pilot's boy,
I heard them coming fast:
Dear Lord in Heaven! it was a joy
The dead men could not blast.

"I saw a third—I heard his voice:
It is the Hermit good!
He singeth loud his godly hymns
That he makes in the wood.
He'll shrieve my soul, he'll wash away
The Albatross's blood.

PART VII

"This Hermit good lives in that wood
Which slopes down to the sea.
How loudly his sweet voice he rears!
He loves to talk with marineres
That come from a far countree.

"He kneels at morn, and noon, and eve—
He hath a cushion plump:
It is the moss that wholly hides
The rotted old oak-stump.

"The skiff-boat neared: I heard them talk,
'Why, this is strange, I trow!
Where are those lights so many and fair,
That signal made but now?'

" 'Strange, by my faith!' the Hermit said—
'And they answered not our cheer!
The planks look warped! and see those sails,
How thin they are and sere!
I never saw aught like to them,
Unless perchance it were

" 'Brown skeletons of leaves that lag
My forest-brook along;
When the ivy-tod is heavy with snow,
And the owlet whoops to the wolf below,
That eats the she-wolf's young.'

" 'Dear Lord! it hath a fiendish look—
(The Pilot made reply)
I am a-feared.'—'Push on, push on!'
Said the Hermit cheerily.

"The boat came closer to the ship,
But I nor spake nor stirred;
The boat came close beneath the ship,
And straight a sound was heard.

"Under the water it rumbled on,
Still louder and more dread:
It reached the ship, it split the bay;
The ship went down like lead.

"Stunned by that loud and dreadful sound,
Which sky and ocean smote,
Like one that hath been seven days drowned
My body lay afloat;
But swift as dreams, myself I found
Within the Pilot's boat.

"Upon the whirl, where sank the ship,
The boat spun round and round;
And all was still, save that the hill
Was telling of the sound.

"I moved my lips—the Pilot shrieked
And fell down in a fit;
The holy Hermit raised his eyes,
And prayed where he did sit.

"I took the oars: the Pilot's boy,
Who now doth crazy go,
Laughed loud and iong, and all the while
His eyes went to and fro.

'Ha! ha!' quoth he, 'full plain I see
The Devil knows how to row.'

"And now, all in my own countree,
I stood on the firm land!
The Hermit stepped forth from the boat,
And scarcely he could stand.

" 'O shrieve me, shrieve me, holy man!'
The Hermit crossed his brow,
'Say quick,' quoth he, 'I bid thee say—
What manner of man art thou?'

"Forthwith this frame of mine was wrenched
With a woful agony,
Which forced me to begin my tale;
And then it left me free.

"Since then, at an uncertain hour,
That agony returns:
And till my ghastly tale is told,
This heart within me burns.

"I pass, like night, from land to land;
I have strange power of speech;
That moment that his face I see,
I know the man that must hear me:
To him my tale I teach.

"What loud uproar bursts from that door!
The wedding-guests are there:
But in the garden-bower the bride
And bride-maids singing are:
And hark, the little vesper bell,
Which biddeth me to prayer!

"O Wedding-Guest! this soul hath been
Alone on a wide, wide sea:
So lonely 'twas, that God Himself
Scarce seemèd there to be.

"O sweeter than the marriage-feast,
'Tis sweeter far to me,
To walk together to the kirk
With a goodly company!—

"To walk together to the kirk,
And all together pray,
While each to his great Father bends,
Old men, and babes, and loving friends,
And youths and maidens gay!

"Farewell, farewell! but this I tell
To thee, thou Wedding-Guest!
He prayeth well, who loveth well
Both man and bird and beast.

"He prayeth best, who loveth best
All things both great and small;
For the dear God, who loveth us,
He made and loveth all."

The Mariner, whose eye is bright,
Whose beard with age is hoar,
Is gone: and now the Wedding-Guest
Turned from the bridegroom's door.

He went like one that hatl. been stunned,
And is of sense forlorn:
A sadder and a wiser man
He rose the morrow morn.

Kubla Khan

IN Xanadu did Kubla Khan
A stately pleasure-dome decree:
Where Alph, the sacred river, ran
Through caverns measureless to man
   Down to a sunless sea.
So twice five miles of fertile ground
With walls and towers were girdled round:
And there were gardens bright with sinuous rills,
Where blossomed many an incense-bearing tree;
And here were forests ancient as the hills,
Enfolding sunny spots of greenery.

But O! that deep romantic chasm which slanted
Down the green hill athwart a cedarn cover!
A savage place! as holy and enchanted
As e'er beneath a waning moon was haunted
By woman wailing for her demon-lover!
And from this chasm, with ceaseless turmoil seething,
As if this Earth in fast thick pants were breathing,
A mighty fountain momently was forced,
Amid whose swift half-intermitted burst
Huge fragments vaulted like rebounding hail,
Or chaffy grain beneath the thresher's flail:
And 'mid these dancing rocks at once and ever
It flung up momently the sacred river.

Five miles meandering with a mazy motion
Through wood and dale the sacred river ran,
Then reached the caverns measureless to man,
And sank in tumult to a lifeless ocean:
And 'mid this tumult Kubla heard from far
Ancestral voices prophesying war!

    The shadow of the dome of pleasure
    Floated midway on the waves;
    Where was heard the mingled measure
    From the fountain and the caves.
It was a miracle of rare device,
A sunny pleasure-dome with caves of ice!

    A damsel with a dulcimer
    In a vision once I saw:
    It was an Abyssinian maid,
    And on her dulcimer she played,
    Singing of Mount Abora.
    Could I revive within me
    Her symphony and song,
    To such a deep delight 'twould win me
That with music loud and long,
I would build that dome in air,
That sunny dome! those caves of ice!
And all who heard should see them there,
And all should cry, Beware! Beware!
His flashing eyes, his floating hair!
Weave a circle round him thrice,
And close your eyes with holy dread,
For he on honey-dew hath fed,
And drunk the milk of Paradise.

The Knight's Tomb

WHERE is the grave of Sir Arthur O'Kellyn?
    Where may the grave of that good man be?—
By the side of a spring, on the breast of Helvellyn,
Under the twigs of a young birch tree!
The oak that in summer was sweet to hear,
And rustled its leaves in the fall of the year,
And whistled and roar'd in the winter alone,
Is gone,—and the birch in its stead is grown.—
The Knight's bones are dust,
And his good sword rust;—
His soul is with the saints, I trust.

Work Without Hope

A LL Nature seems at work. Slugs leave their lair—
 The bees are stirring—birds are on the wing—
And Winter slumbering in the open air,
Wears on his smiling face a dream of Spring!
And I the while, the sole unbusy thing,
Nor honey make, nor pair, nor build, nor sing.

Yet well I ken the banks where amaranths blew,
Have traced the fount whence streams of nectar flow.
Bloom, O ye amaranths! bloom for whom ye may,
For me ye bloom not! Glide, rich streams, away!

With lips unbrightened, wreathless brow, I stroll:
And would you learn the spells that drowse my soul?
Work without Hope draws nectar in a sieve,
And Hope without an object cannot live.

Love

A LL thoughts, all passions, all delights,
 Whatever stirs this mortal frame,
All are but ministers of Love,
 And feed his sacred flame.

Oft in my waking dreams do I
Live o'er again that happy hour,
When midway on the mount I lay,
 Beside the ruined tower.

The moonshine, stealing o'er the scene,
Had blended with the lights of eve;
And she was there, my hope, my joy,
 My own dear Genevieve!

She leaned against the armèd man,
The statue of the armèd Knight;
She stood and listened to my lay,
 Amid the lingering light.

Few sorrows hath she of her own,
My hope! my joy! my Genevieve!
She loves me best whene'er I sing
 The songs that make her grieve.

I played a soft and doleful air;
I sang an old and moving story—

An old rude song, that suited well
   That ruin wild and hoary.

She listened with a fitting blush,
With downcast eyes, and modest grace;
For well she knew I could not choose
   But gaze upon her face.

I told her of the Knight that wore
Upon his shield a burning brand;
And that for ten long years he wooed
   The Lady of the Land.

I told her how he pined; and ah!
The deep, the low, the pleading tone
With which I sang another's love,
   Interpreted my own.

She listened with a fitting blush,
With downcast eyes, and modest grace;
And she forgave me, that I gazed
   Too fondly on her face!

But when I told the cruel scorn
That crazed that bold and lovely Knight,
And that he crossed the mountain-woods,
   Nor rested day nor night;

That sometimes from the savage den,
And sometimes from the darksome shade,
And sometimes starting up at once
   In green and sunny glade—

There came and looked him in the face
An angel beautiful and bright;
And that he knew it was a Fiend,
   This miserable Knight!

And that, unknowing what he did,
He leaped amid a murderous band,
And saved from outrage worse than death
   The Lady of the Land;—
And how she wept and clasped his knees;
And how she tended him in vain—
And ever strove to expiate
   The scorn that crazed his brain;—
And that she nursed him in a cave;
And how his madness went away,
When on the yellow forest-leaves
   A dying man he lay;—

His dying words—but when I reached
That tenderest strain of all the ditty,
My faltering voice and pausing harp
    Disturbed her soul with pity!
All impulses of soul and sense
Had thrilled my guileless Genevieve;
The music and the doleful tale,
    The rich and balmy eve;

And hopes, and fears that kindle hope,
An undistinguishable throng,
And gentle wishes long subdued,
    Subdued and cherished long!

She wept with pity and delight,
She blushed with love and virgin-shame;
And like the murmur of a dream,
    I heard her breathe my name.

Her bosom heaved—she stepped aside,
As conscious of my look she stepped—
Then suddenly, with timorous eye
    She fled to me and wept.

She half enclosed me with her arms,
She pressed me with a meek embrace;
And bending back her head, looked up,
    And gazed upon my face.

'Twas partly love, and partly fear,
And partly 'twas a bashful art,
That I might rather feel, than see,
    The swelling of her heart.

I calmed her fears, and she was calm,
And told her love with virgin pride;
And so I won my Genevieve,
    My bright and beauteous Bride.

From "Christabel"

ALAS! they had been friends in youth;
    But whispering tongues can poison truth;
And constancy lives in realms above;
And life is thorny; and youth is vain:
And to be wroth with one we love,
Doth work like madness in the brain.
And thus it chanced, as I divine,
With Roland and Sir Leoline.

Each spake words of high disdain
And insult to his heart's best brother:
They parted—ne'er to meet again!
But never either found another
To free the hollow heart from paining—
They stood aloof, the scars remaining,
Like cliffs which had been rent asunder;
A dreary sea now flows between.
But neither heat, nor frost, nor thunder,
Shall wholly do away, I we'en,
The marks of that which once hath been.

Epitaph on Himself

STOP, Christian passerby! Stop, child of God!
   And read with gentle breast. Beneath this sod
A poet lies, or that which once seemed he—
Oh! lift one thought in prayer for S. T. C.!
That he, who many a year, with toil of breath,
Found death in life, may here find life in death!
Mercy for praise—to be forgiven for fame,
He asked and hoped through Christ—do thou the same.

ROBERT SOUTHEY (1774-1843)

"My Days Among the Dead Are Passed"

MY days among the Dead are passed,
      Around me I behold,
Where'er these casual eyes are cast,
   The mighty minds of old:
My never-failing friends are they,
With whom I converse day by day.

With them I take delight in weal,
   And seek relief in woe;
And while I understand and feel
   How much to them I owe,
My cheeks have often been bedewed
With tears of thoughtful gratitude.

My thoughts are with the Dead; with them
   I live in long-past years,
Their virtues love, their faults condemn,
   Partake their hopes and fears;
And from their lessons seek and find
Instruction with an humble mind.

My hopes are with the Dead; anon
  My place with them will be,
And I with them shall travel on
  Through all Futurity;
Yet leaving here a name, I trust,
That will not perish in the dust.

WALTER SAVAGE LANDOR (1775-1864)

Rose Aylmer

AH, what avails the sceptered race!
    Ah, what the form divine!
What every virtue, every grace!
  Rose Aylmer, all were thine.

Rose Aylmer, whom these wakeful eyes
    May weep, but never see,
A night of memories and sighs
    I consecrate to thee.

Dirce

STAND close around, ye Stygian set,
    With Dirce in one boat conveyed!
Or Charon, seeing, may forget
    That he is old and she a shade.

To Robert Browning

THERE is delight in singing, tho' none hear
  Beside the singer; and there is delight
In praising, tho' the praiser sit alone
And see the prais'd far off him, far above.
Shakespeare is not our poet, but the world's,
Therefore on him no speech! and brief for thee,
Browning! Since Chaucer was alive and hale,
No man hath walkt along our roads with step
So active, so inquiring eye, or tongue
So varied in discourse. But warmer climes
Give brighter plumage, stronger wing: the breeze
Of Alpine heights thou playest with, borne on
Beyond Sorrento and Amalfi, where
The Siren waits thee, singing song for song.

How Many Voices Gaily Sing

HOW many voices gaily sing,
  "O happy morn, O happy spring
Of life!" Meanwhile there comes o'er me
A softer voice from Memory,
And says, "If loves and hopes have flown
With years, think, too, what griefs are gone!"

Why, Why Repine?

WHY, why repine, my pensive friend,
    At pleasures slipt away?
Some the stern Fates will never lend,
    And all refuse to stay.

I see the rainbow in the sky,
    The dew upon the grass,
I see them and I ask not why
    They glimmer or they pass.

With folded arms I linger not
    To call them back; 'twere vain;
In this, or in some other spot,
    I know they'll shine again.

I Strove with None

I strove with none, for none was worth my strife;
    Nature I loved, and, next to nature, art;
I warm'd both hands before the fire of life;
    It sinks, and I am ready to depart.

CHARLES LAMB (1775-1834)

The Old Familiar Faces

I have had playmates, I have had companions,
  In my days of childhood, in my joyful schooldays,—
All, all are gone, the old familiar faces.

I have been laughing, I have been carousing,
Drinking late, sitting late, with my bosom cronies,—
All, all are gone, the old familiar faces.

I loved a Love once, fairest among women:
Closed are her doors on me, I must not see her,—
All, all are gone, the old familiar faces.

I have a friend, a kinder friend has no man:
Like an ingrate, I left my friend abruptly;
Left him, to muse on the old familiar faces.

Ghost-like, I paced round the haunts of my childhood.
Earth seemed a desert I was bound to traverse,
Seeking to find the old familiar faces.

Friend of my bosom, thou more than a brother,
Why wert not thou born in my father's dwelling?
So might we talk of the old familiar faces—

How some they have died, and some they have left me,
And some are taken from me; all are departed,—
All, all are gone, the old familiar faces.

Hester

WHEN maidens such as Hester die,
   Their place ye may not well supply,
Though ye among a thousand try,
   With vain endeavor.
A month or more hath she been dead,
Yet cannot I by force be led
To think upon the wormy bed,
   And her together.

A springy motion in her gait,
A rising step, did indicate
Of pride and joy no common rate,
   That flushed her spirit:
I know not by what name beside
I shall it call; if 'twas not pride,
It was a joy to that allied,
   She did inherit.

Her parents held the Quaker rule,
Which doth the human feeling cool;
But she was trained in Nature's school;
   Nature had blessed her.
A waking eye, a prying mind,
A heart that stirs, is hard to bind;
A hawk's keen sight ye cannot blind,—
   Ye could not Hester.

My sprightly neighbor, gone before
To that unknown and silent shore,
Shall we not meet as heretofore,
    Some summer morning,
When from thy cheerful eyes a ray
Hath struck a bliss upon the day,—
A bliss that would not go away,—
    A sweet forewarning?

THOMAS CAMPBELL (1777-1844)
"Ye Mariners of England"

YE Mariners of England
    That guard our native seas!
Whose flag has braved, a thousand years,
    The battle and the breeze!
Your glorious standard launch again
    To match another foe;
And sweep through the deep,
    While the stormy winds do blow!
While the battle rages loud and long,
    And the stormy winds do blow.

The spirits of your fathers
    Shall start from every wave!—
For the deck it was their field of fame,
    And Ocean was their grave:
Where Blake and mighty Nelson fell
    Your manly hearts shall glow,
As ye sweep through the deep,
    While the stormy winds do blow!
While the battle rages loud and long,
    And the stormy winds do blow.

Britannia needs no bulwarks,
    No towers along the steep;
Her march is o'er the mountain-waves,
    Her home is on the deep.
With thunders from her native oak
    She quells the floods below,
As they roar on the shore,
    When the stormy winds do blow!
When the battle rages loud and long,
    And the stormy winds do blow.

The meteor flag of England
    Shall yet terrific burn;
Till danger's troubled night depart
    And the star of peace return.

Then, then, ye ocean-warriors!
  Our song and feast shall flow
To the fame of your name,
  When the storm has ceased to blow!
When the fiery fight is heard no more,
  And the storm has ceased to blow.

THOMAS MOORE (1779-1852)

"The Young May Moon"

THE young May moon is beaming, love,
  The glow-worm's lamp is gleaming, love;
    How sweet to rove
    Through Morna's grove,
When the drowsy world is dreaming, love!

Then awake!—till rise of sun, my dear,
'Tis never too late for delight, my dear;
    And the best of all ways
    To lengthen our days
Is to steal a few hours from the night, my dear!

Now all the world is sleeping, love,
But the Sage, his star-watch keeping, love,
    And I, whose star
    More glorious far
Is the eye from that casement peeping, love.

Then awake!—till rise of sun, my dear,
The Sage's glass we'll shun, my dear,
    Or in watching the flight
    Of bodies of light
He might happen to take thee for one, my dear!

Tara

THE harp that once through Tara's halls
  The soul of music shed,
Now hangs as mute on Tara's walls
  As if that soul were fled.
So sleeps the pride of former days,
  So glory's thrill is o'er,
And hearts that once beat high for praise
  Now feel that pulse no more.

No more to chiefs and ladies bright
  The harp of Tara swells;
The chord alone that breaks at night
  Its tale of ruin tells.

Thus Freedom now so seldom wakes,—
  The only throb she gives
Is when some heart indignant breaks
  To show that still she lives.

At the Mid Hour of Night

AT the mid hour of night, when stars are weeping, I fly
  To the lone vale we loved, when life shone warm in
    thine eye;
And I think oft, if spirits can steal from the regions of air
To revisit past scenes of delight, thou wilt come to me
    there,
And tell me our love is remember'd even in the sky.

Then I sing the wild song it once was rapture to hear,
When our voices commingling breathed like one on the ear;
  And as Echo far off through the vale my sad orison rolls,
  I think, O my love! 'tis thy voice from the Kingdom of
    of Souls
Faintly answering still the notes that once were so dear.

" 'Tis the Last Rose of Summer"

'TIS the last rose of summer,
    Left blooming alone;
  All her lovely companions
    Are faded and gone;
  No flower of her kindred,
    No rose-bud is nigh,
  To reflect back her blushes,
    Or give sigh for sigh.

  I'll not leave thee, thou lone one!
    To pine on the stem;
  Since the lovely are sleeping,
    Go, sleep thou with them.
  Thus kindly I scatter
    Thy leaves o'er the bed
  Where thy mates of the garden
    Lie scentless and dead.

  So soon may *I* follow,
    When friendships decay,
  And from Love's shining circle
    The gems drop away.
  When true hearts lie withered,
    And fond ones are flown,
  O who would inhabit
    This bleak world alone?

EDWARD THURLOW (LORD THURLOW)

(1781-1829)

May

MAY! queen of blossoms,
    And fulfilling flowers,
With what pretty music
    Shall we charm the hours?
Wilt thou have pipe and reed,
Blown in the open mead?
Or to the lute give heed
    In the green bowers?

Thou hast no need of us,
    Or pipe or wire,
Thou hast the golden bee
    Ripen'd with fire;
And many thousand more
Songsters, that thee adore
Filling earth's grassy floor
    With new desire.

Thou hast thy might herds,
    Tame and free-livers;
Doubt not, thy music too
    In the deep rivers;
And the whole plumy flight
Warbling the day and night—
Up at the gates of light,
    See, the lark quivers!

LEIGH HUNT (1784-1859)

Jenny Kiss'd Me

JENNY kiss'd me when we met,
    Jumping from the chair she sat in;
Time, you thief! who love to get
    Sweets into your list, put that in.
Say I'm weary, say I'm sad;
    Say that health and wealth have miss'd me;
Say I'm growing old, but add—
                    Jenny kiss'd me!

To the Grasshopper and the Cricket

GREEN little vaulter in the sunny grass,
　　Catching your heart up at the feel of June,
Sole voice that's heard amidst the lazy noon,
When even the bees lag at the summoning brass;
And you, warm little housekeeper, who class
　　With those who think the candles come too soon,
　　Loving the fire, and with your tricksome tune
Nick the glad silent moments as they pass;
Oh, sweet and tiny cousins, that belong,
　　One to the fields, the other to the hearth,
Both have your sunshine; both, though small, are strong
　　At your clear hearts; and both were sent on earth
To sing in thoughtful ears this natural song—
　　Indoors and out, summer and winter, mirth.

Abou Ben Adhem

ABOU Ben Adhem—may his tribe increase!—
　　Awoke one night from a deep dream of peace,
And saw, within the moonlight in his room,
Making it rich and like a lily in bloom,
An angel writing in a book of gold.
Exceeding peace had made Ben Adhem bold,
And to the presence in the room he said:
"What writest thou?" The vision raised its head,
And with a look made of all sweet accord,
Answered: "The names of those who love the Lord."
"And is mine one?" said Abou. "Nay, not so,"
Replied the angel. Abou spoke more low,
But cheerily still; and said: "I pray thee, then,
Write me as one that loves his fellow-men."
The angel wrote, and vanished. The next night
It came again with a great wakening light,
And shewed the names whom love of God had blessed,
And lo! Ben Adhem's name led all the rest.

THOMAS LOVE PEACOCK (1785-1866)

The War-Song of Dinas Vawr

(From "The Misfortunes of Elphin," abridged)

THE mountain sheep are sweeter,
　　But the valley sheep are fatter;
We therefore deemed it meeter

To carry off the latter.
We made an expedition;
We met an host and quelled it;
We forced a strong position,
And killed the men who held it. . . .

(From the same)

NOT drunk is he, who from the floor
Can rise alone, and still drink more:
But drunk is he who prostrate lies,
Without the power to drink or rise.

GEORGE GORDON BYRON—LORD BYRON
(1788-1824)

To the Ocean

(From "Childe Harold's Pilgrimage")

THERE is a pleasure in the pathless woods,
There is a rapture on the lonely shore,
There is society, where none intrudes
By the deep sea, and music in its roar;
I love not man the less, but nature more,
From these our interviews, in which I steal
From all I may be, or have been before,
To mingle with the universe, and feel
What I can ne'er express, yet cannot all conceal.

Roll on, thou deep and dark blue Ocean, roll!
Ten thousand fleets sweep over thee in vain;
Man marks the earth with ruin, his control
Stops with the shore; upon the watery plain
The wrecks are all thy deed, nor doth remain
A shadow of man's ravage, save his own,
When, for a moment, like a drop of rain,
He sinks into thy depths with bubbling groan,
Without a grave, unknelled, uncoffined, and unknown.

His steps are not upon thy paths, thy fields
Are not a spoil for him,—thou dost arise
And shake him from thee; the vile strength he wields
For earth's destruction thou dost all despise,
Spurning him from thy bosom to the skies,
And send'st him, shivering in thy playful spray
And howling, to his Gods, where haply lies
His petty hope in some near port or bay,
And dashest him again to earth:—there let him lay.

The armaments which thunderstrike the walls
Of rock-built cities, bidding nations quake
And monarchs tremble in their capitals,
The oak leviathans, whose huge ribs make
Their clay creator the vain title take
Of lord of thee and arbiter of war,—
These are thy toys, and, as the snowy flake,
They melt into thy yeast of waves, which mar
Alike the Armada's pride or spoils of Trafalgar.

Thy shores are empires, changed in all save thee;—
Assyria, Greece, Rome, Carthage, what are they?
Thy waters washed them power while they were free,
And many a tyrant since; their shores obey
The stranger, slave, or savage; their decay
Has dried up realms to deserts:—not so thou;
Unchangeable save to thy wild waves' play,
Times writes no wrinkle on thine azure brow;
Such as creation's dawn beheld, thou rollest now.

Thou glorious mirror, where the Almighty's form
Glasses itself in tempests; in all time,
Calm or convulsed,—in breeze, or gale, or storm,
Icing the pole, or in the torrid clime
Dark-heaving;—boundless, endless, and sublime,—
The image of Eternity,—the throne
Of the Invisible; even from out thy slime
The monsters of the deep are made; each zone
Obeys thee; thou goest forth, dread, fathomless, alone.

And I have loved thee, Ocean; and my joy
Of youthful sports was on thy breast to be
Borne, like thy bubbles, onward. From a boy
I wantoned with thy breakers,—they to me
Were a delight; and if the freshening sea
Made them a terror, 'twas a pleasing fear;
For I was as it were a child of thee,
And trusted to thy billows far and near,
And laid my hand upon thy mane,—as I do here.

The Isles of Greece

THE isles of Greece! the isles of Greece!
  Where burning Sappho loved and sung,
Where grew the arts of war and peace,
  Where Delos rose, and Phœbus sprung!
Eternal summer gilds them yet,
But all, except their sun, is set.

The Scian and the Teian muse,
  The hero's harp, the lover's lute,
Have found the fame your shores refuse:
  Their place of birth alone is mute
To sounds which echo further west
Than your sires' "Islands of the Blest."

The mountains look on Marathon—
  And Marathon looks on the sea;
And musing there an hour alone,
  I dreamed that Greece might still be free;
For standing on the Persians' grave,
I could not deem myself a slave.

A king sate on the rocky brow
  Which looks o'er sea-born Salamis;
And ships, by thousands, lay below,
  And men in nations;—all were his!
He counted them at break of day—
And when the sun set, where were they?

And where are they? and where art thou,
  My country? On thy voiceless shore
The heroic lay is tuneless now—
  The heroic bosom beats no more!
And must thy lyre, so long divine,
Degenerate into hands like mine?

'Tis something, in the dearth of fame,
  Though linked among a fettered race,
To feel at least a patriot's shame,
  Even as I sing, suffuse my face;
For what is left the poet here?
For Greeks a blush—for Greece a tear.

Must *we* but weep o'er days more blest?
  Must *we* but blush?—Our fathers bled.
Earth! render back from out thy breast
  A remnant of our Spartan dead!
Of the three hundred grant but three
To make a new Thermopylæ!

What, silent still? and silent all?
  Ah! no;—the voices of the dead
Sound like a distant torrent's fall,
  And answer, "Let one living head,
But one, arise,—we come, we come!"
'Tis but the living who are dumb.

In vain—in vain: strike other chords;
  Fill high the cup with Samian wine!
Leave battles to the Turkish hordes,
  And shed the blood of Scio's vine!
Hark! rising to the ignoble call—
How answers each bold Bacchanal!

You have the Pyrrhic dance as yet;
  Where is the Pyrrhic phalanx gone?
Of two such lessons, why forget
  The nobler and the manlier one?
You have the letters Cadmus gave—
Think ye he meant them for a slave?

Fill high the bowl with Samian wine!
  We will not think of themes like these!
It made Anacreon's song divine:
  He served—but served Polycrates—
A tyrant; but our masters then
Were still, at least, our countrymen.

The tyrant of the Chersonese
  Was freedom's best and bravest friend;
That tyrant was Miltiades!
  O that the present hour would lend
Another despot of the kind!
Such chains as his were sure to bind.

Fill high the bowl with Samian wine!
  On Suli's rock, and Parga's shore,
Exists the remnant of a line
  Such as the Doric mothers bore;
And there, perhaps, some seed is sown,
The Heracleidan blood might own.

Trust not for freedom to the Franks—
  They have a king who buys and sells;
In native swords and native ranks
  The only hope of courage dwells:
But Turkish force and Latin fraud
Would break your shield, however broad.

Fill high the bowl with Samian wine!
  Our virgins dance beneath the shade—
I see their glorious black eyes shine;
  But, gazing on each glowing maid,
My own the burning tear-drop laves,
To think such breasts must suckle slaves.

Place me on Sunium's marbled steep,
  Where nothing, save the waves and I,
May hear our mutual murmurs sweep;
  There, swan-like, let me sing and die:
A land of slaves shall ne'er be mine—
Dash down yon cup of Samian wine!

Sonnet on Chillon

ETERNAL Spirit of the chainless Mind!
  Brightest in dungeons, Liberty, thou art,
For there thy habitation is the heart—
The heart which love of thee alone can bind;
And when thy sons to fetters are consigned—
To fetters, and the damp vault's dayless gloom—
Their country conquers with their martyrdom,
And Freedom's fame finds wings on every wind.
Chillon! thy prison is a holy place,
And thy sad floor an altar; for 'twas trod,
Until his very steps have left a trace
Worn, as if thy cold pavement were a sod,
By Bonnivard!—May none those marks efface!
For they appeal from tyranny to God.

"She Walks in Beauty"

SHE walks in beauty, like the night
  Of cloudless climes and starry skies;
And all that's best of dark and bright
  Meet in her aspect and her eyes:
Thus mellowed to that tender light
  Which heaven to gaudy day denies.

One shade the more, one ray the less,
  Had half impaired the nameless grace
Which waves in every raven tress
  Or softly lightens o'er her face;
Where thoughts serenely sweet express
  How pure, how dear their dwelling-place.

And on that cheek, and o'er that brow
  So soft, so calm, yet eloquent,
The smiles that win, the tints that glow,
  But tell of days in goodness spent,
A mind at peace with all below,
  A heart whose love is innocent!

So, We'll Go No More a Roving

SO, we'll go no more a roving
    So late into the night,
Though the heart be still as loving,
    And the moon be still as bright.

For the sword outwears its sheath,
    And the soul wears out the breast,
And the heart must pause to breathe,
    And love itself have rest.

Though the night was made for loving,
    And the day returns too soon,
Yet we'll go no more a roving
    By the light of the moon.

My Boat Is on the Shore

MY boat is on the shore,
    And my bark is on the sea:
But, before I go, Tom Moore,
    Here's a double health to thee!

Here's a sigh to those that love me,
    And a smile to those who hate;
And, whatever sky's above me,
    Here's a heart for every fate.

Though the ocean roar around me,
    Yet it shall yet bear me on;
Though a desert should surround me,
    It hath springs that may be won.

Were't the last drop in the well,
    As I gasped upon the brink,
Ere my fainting spirit fell,
    'Tis to thee that I would drink.

With that water as this wine,
    The libation I would pour
Should be:—"Peace with thine and mine,
    And a health to thee, Tom Moore!"

Byron's Farewell

'TIS time this heart should be unmoved,
    Since others it hath ceased to move:
Yet, though I cannot be beloved,
    Still let me love!

My days are in the yellow leaf;
   The flowers and fruits of love are gone;
The worm, the canker, and the grief
      Are mine alone!

The fire that on my bosom preys
   Is lone as some volcanic isle;
No torch is kindled at its blaze—
      A funeral pile.

The hope, the fear, the jealous care,
   The exalted portion of the pain
And power of love, I cannot share,
      But wear the chain.

But 'tis not thus—and 'tis not here—
   Such thoughts should shake my soul, nor now,
Where glory decks the hero's bier,
      Or binds his brow.

The sword, the banner, and the field,
   Glory and Greece, around me see!
The Spartan, borne upon his shield,
      Was not more free.

Awake! (not Greece—she is awake!)
   Awake my spirit! Think through whom
Thy life-blood tracks its parent lake,
      And then strike home!

Tread those reviving passions down,
   Unworthy manhood!—Unto thee
Indifferent should the smile or frown
      Of beauty be.

If thou regret'st thy youth, why live?
   The land of honourable death
Is here:—up to the field, and give
      Away thy breath!

Seek out—less often sought than found—
   A soldier's grave, for thee the best;
Then look around and choose thy ground,
      And take thy rest.

CHARLES WOLFE (1791-1823)

The Burial of Sir John Moore After Corunna

(January 16, 1809)

NOT a drum was heard, not a funeral note,
     As his corse to the rampart we hurried;
Not a soldier discharged his farewell shot
     O'er the grave where our hero we buried.

We buried him darkly at dead of night,
     The sods with our bayonets turning,
By the struggling moonbeam's misty light
     And the lanthorn dimly burning.

No useless coffin enclosed his breast,
     Not in sheet or in shroud we wound him;
But he lay like a warrior taking his rest
     With his martial cloak around him.

Few and short were the prayers we said,
     And we spoke not a word of sorrow;
But we steadfastly gazed on the face that was dead,
     And we bitterly thought of the morrow.

We thought, as we hollowed his narrow bed
     And smoothed down his lonely pillow,
That the foe and the stranger would tread o'er his head,
     And we far away on the billow!

Lightly they'll talk of the spirit that's gone,
     And o'er his cold ashes upbraid him—
But little he'll reck, if they let him sleep on
     In the grave where a Briton has laid him.

But half of our heavy task was done
     When the clock struck the hour for retiring;
And we heard the distant and random gun
     That the foe was sullenly firing.

Slowly and sadly we laid him down,
     From the field of his fame fresh and gory;
We carved not a line, and we raised not a stone,
     But we left him alone with his glory.

PERCY BYSSHE SHELLEY (1792-1822)

To a Skylark

HAIL to thee, blithe spirit!
   Bird thou never wert,
That from heaven, or near it,
   Pourest thy full heart
In profuse strains of unpremeditated art.

Higher still and higher,
   From the earth thou springest
Like a cloud of fire;
   The blue deep thou wingest,
And singing still dost soar, and soaring ever singest.

In the golden lightning
   Of the sunken sun,
O'er which clouds are bright'ning,
   Thou dost float and run;
Like an unbodied joy whose race is just begun.

The pale purple even
   Melts around thy flight;
Like a star of heaven
   In the broad daylight
Thou art unseen, but yet I hear thy shrill delight.

Keen as are the arrows
   Of that silver sphere,
Whose intense lamp narrows
   In the white dawn clear,
Until we hardly see, we feel that it is there.

All the earth and air
   With thy voice is loud,
As, when night is bare,
   From one lonely cloud
The moon rains out her beams, and heaven is overflowed.

What thou art we know not;
   What is most like thee?
From rainbow clouds there flow not
   Drops so bright to see
As from thy presence showers a rain of melody.

Like a poet hidden
   In the light of thought,
Singing hymns unbidden
   Till the world is wrought
To sympathy with hopes and fears it heeded not:

Like a high-born maiden
  In a palace tower,
Soothing her love-laden
  Soul in secret hour
With music sweet as love, which overflows her bower:

Like a glow-worm golden
  In a dell of dew,
Scattering unbeholden
  Its aerial hue
Among the flowers and grass, which screen it from the
  view:

Like a rose embowered
  In its own green leaves,
By warm winds deflowered,
  Till the scent it gives
Makes faint with too much sweet these heavy-wingèd
  thieves:

Sound of vernal showers
  On the twinkling grass,
Rain-awakened flowers,
  All that ever was
Joyous, and clear, and fresh, thy music doth surpass.

Teach us, sprite or bird,
  What sweet thoughts are thine:
I have never heard
  Praise of love or wine
That panted forth a flood of rapture so divine.

Chorus hymeneal,
  Or triumphal chaunt,
Matched with thine would be all
  But an empty vaunt—
A thing wherein we feel there is some hidden want.

What objects are the fountains
  Of thy happy strain?
What fields, or waves, or mountains?
  What shapes of sky or plain?
What love of thine own kind? what ignorance of pain?

With thy clear keen joyance
  Languor cannot be:
Shadow of annoyance
  Never came near thee:
Thou lovest; but ne'er knew love's sad satiety.

Waking or asleep,
Thou of death must deem
Things more true and deep
Than we mortals dream,
Or how could thy notes flow in such a crystal stream?

We look before and after,
And pine for what is not:
Our sincerest laughter
With some pain is fraught;
Our sweetest songs are those that tell of saddest
thought.

Yet if we could scorn
Hate, and pride, and fear;
If we were things born
Not to shed a tear,
I know not how thy joy we ever should come near.

Better than all measures
Of delightful sound,
Better than all treasures
That in books are found,
Thy skill to poet were, thou scorner of the ground!

Teach me half the gladness
That thy brain must know,
Such harmonious madness
From my lips would flow,
The world should listen then, as I am listening now.

Ode to the West Wind

I

O wild West Wind, thou breath of Autumn's being,
Thou from whose unseen presence the leaves dead
Are driven, like ghosts from an enchanter fleeing,

Yellow, and black, and pale, and hectic red,
Pestilence-stricken multitudes! O thou
Who chariotest to their dark wintry bed

The wingèd seeds, where they lie cold and low,
Each like a corpse within its grave, until
Thine azure sister of the Spring shall blow

Her clarion o'er the dreaming earth, and fill
(Driving sweet buds like flocks to feed in air)
  With living hues and odours plain and hill;

Wild Spirit, which art moving everywhere;
Destroyer and preserver; hear, O hear!

II

Thou on whose stream, 'mid the steep sky's commotion,
  Loose clouds like earth's decaying leaves are shed,
Shook from the tangled boughs of heaven and ocean,

  Angels of rain and lightning! there are spread
On the blue surface of thine airy surge,
  Like the bright hair uplifted from the head

Of some fierce Mænad, even from the dim verge
  Of the horizon to the zenith's height,
The locks of the approaching storm. Thou dirge

  Of the dying year, to which this closing night
Will be the dome of a vast sepulchre,
  Vaulted with all thy congregated might

Of vapors, from whose solid atmosphere
Black rain, and fire, and hail will burst: O hear!

III

Thou who didst waken from his summer dreams
  The blue Mediterranean, where he lay,
Lulled by the coil of his crystàlline streams.

  Beside a pumice isle in Baiæ's bay,
And saw in sleep old palaces and towers
  Quivering within the wave's intenser day,

All overgrown with azure moss, and flowers
  So sweet, the sense faints picturing them! Thou
For whose path the Atlantic's level powers

  Cleave themselves into chasms, while far below
The sea-blooms and the oozy woods which wear
  The sapless foliage of the ocean, know

Thy voice, and suddenly grow gray with fear,
And tremble and despoil themselves: O hear!

IV

If I were a dead leaf thou mightest bear;
    If I were a swift cloud to fly with thee;
A wave to pant beneath thy power, and share

    The impulse of thy strength, only less free
Than thou, O uncontrollable! if even
    I were as in my boyhood, and could be

The comrade of thy wanderings over heaven,
    As then, when to outstrip thy skiey speed
Scarce seemed a vision—I would ne'er have striven

    As thus with thee in prayer in my sore need.
O! lift me as a wave, a leaf, a cloud!
    I fall upon the thorns of life! I bleed!

A heavy weight of hours has chained and bowed
One too like thee—tameless, and swift, and proud.

V

Make me thy lyre, even as the forest is:
    What if my leaves are falling like its own?
The tumult of thy mighty harmonies

    Will take from both a deep, autumnal tone,
Sweet though in sadness. Be thou, Spirit fierce,
    My spirit! Be thou me, impetuous one!

Drive my dead thoughts over the universe,
    Like withered leaves, to quicken a new birth;
And, by the incantation of this verse,

    Scatter, as from an unextinguished hearth
Ashes and sparks, my words among mankind!
    Be through my lips to unawakened earth

The trumpet of a prophecy! O Wind,
If Winter comes, can Spring be far behind?

From "Adonais"

PEACE, peace! he is not dead, he doth not sleep—
    He hath awakened from the dream of life—
'Tis we, who, lost in stormy visions keep,
With phantoms an unprofitable strife,
And in mad trance, strike with our spirit's knife

Invulnerable nothings. *We* decay
Like corpses in a charnel; fear and grief
Convulse us and consume us day by day,
And cold hopes swarm like worms within our living clay.

He has outsoared the shadow of our night;
Envy and calumny and hate and pain,
And that unrest which men miscall delight,
Can touch him not and torture not again;
From the contagion of the world's slow stain
He is secure, and now can never mourn
A heart grown cold, a head grown gray in vain;
Nor, when the spirit's self has ceased to burn,
With sparkless ashes load an unlamented urn. . . .

He is made one with Nature: there is heard
His voice in all her music, from the moan
Of thunder, to the song of night's sweet bird;
He is a presence to be felt and known
In darkness and in light, from herb and stone,
Spreading itself where'er that Power may move
Which has withdrawn his being to its own;
Which wields the world with never-wearied love,
Sustains it from beneath, and kindles it above.

He is a portion of the loveliness
Which once he made more lovely: he doth bear
His part, while the one Spirit's plastic stress
Sweeps through the dull dense world, compelling there,
All new successions to the forms they wear;
Torturing the unwilling dross that checks its flight
To its own likeness, as each mass may bear,
And bursting in its beauty and its might
From trees and beasts and men into the Heaven's light.

The splendors of the firmament of time
May be eclipsed, but are extinguished not;
Like stars to their appointed height they climb,
And death is a low mist which cannot blot
The brightness it may veil. When lofty thought
Lifts a young heart above its mortal lair,
And love and life contend in it, for what
Shall be its earthly doom, the dead live there
And move like winds of light on dark and stormy air.

The inheritors of unfulfilled renown
Rose from their thrones, built beyond mortal thought,
Far in the Unapparent. Chatterton

Rose pale,—his solemn agony had not
Yet faded from him; Sidney, as he fought
And as he fell and as he lived and loved,
Sublimely mild, a Spirit without spot,
Arose; and Lucan, by his death approved;
Oblivion as they rose shrank like a thing reproved. . . .

Here pause: these graves are all too young as yet
To have outgrown the sorrow which consigned
Its charge to each; and if the seal is set,
Here, on one fountain of a mourning mind,
Break it not thou! too surely shalt thou find
Thine own well full, if thou returnest home,
Of tears and gall. From the world's bitter wind
Seek shelter in the shadow of the tomb.
What Adonais is, why fear we to become?

The One remains, the many change and pass;
Heaven's light forever shines, Earth's shadows fly;
Life, like a dome of many-coloured glass,
Stains the white radiance of Eternity,
Until Death tramples it to fragments.—Die,
If thou wouldst be with that which thou dost seek!
Follow where all is fled!—Rome's azure sky,
Flowers, ruins, statues, music, words, are weak
The glory they transfuse with fitting truth to speak.

Why linger, why turn back, why shrink, my Heart?
Thy hopes are gone before; from all things here
They have departed; thou shouldst now depart!
A light is passed from the revolving year,
And man, and woman: and what still is dear
Attracts to crush, repels to make thee wither.
The soft sky smiles,—the low wind whispers near;
'Tis Adonais calls! oh, hasten thither,
No more let Life divide what Death can join together.

That Light whose smile kindles the Universe,
That Beauty in which all things work and move,
That Benediction which the eclipsing Curse
Of birth can quench not, that sustaining Love
Which through the web of being blindly wove
By man and beast and earth and air and sea,
Burns bright or dim, as each are mirrors of
The fire for which all thirst, now beams on me,
Consuming the last clouds of cold mortality.

The breath whose might I have invoked in song
Descends on me; my spirit's bark is driven

Far from the shore, far from the trembling throng
Whose sails were never to the tempest given;
The massy earth and spherèd skies are riven!
I am borne darkly, fearfully, afar;
Whilst, burning through the inmost veil of Heaven,
The soul of Adonais, like a star,
Beacons from the abode where the Eternal are.

To Night

SWIFTLY walk o'er the western wave,
        Spirit of Night!
Out of the misty eastern cave
Where, all the long and lone daylight,
Thou wovest dreams of joy and fear,
Which make thee terrible and dear,
        Swift be thy flight!

Wrap thy form in a mantle gray,
        Star-inwrought!
Blind with thine hair the eyes of Day;
Kiss her until she be wearied out,
Then wander o'er city, and sea, and land,
        Come, long-sought!

When I arose and saw the dawn,
        I sighed for thee;
When light rode high, and the dew was gone,
And noon lay heavy on flower and tree,
And the weary Day turned to his rest,
Lingering like an unloved guest,
        I sighed for thee.

Thy brother Death came, and cried,
        "Would'st thou me?"
Thy sweet child Sleep, the filmy-eyed,
Murmured like a noontide bee,
"Shall I nestle near thy side?
Would'st thou me?"—And I replied,
        "No, not thee."

Death will come when thou art dead,
        Soon, too soon—
Sleep will come when thou art fled;
Of neither would I ask the boon
I ask of thee, belovèd Night—
Swift be thine approaching flight,
        Come soon, soon!

Lines to an Indian Air

I arise from dreams of thee
  In the first sweet sleep of night,
When the winds are breathing low,
And the stars are shining bright,
I arise from dreams of thee,
And a spirit in my feet
Has led me—who knows how?
To thy chamber window, sweet!

The wandering airs they faint
On the dark, the silent stream;
The champak odours fail
Like sweet thoughts in a dream;
The nightingale's complaint,
It dies upon her heart,
As I must die on thine,
O belovèd as thou art!

O lift me from the grass!
I die, I faint, I fail!
Let thy love in kisses rain
On my lips and eyelids pale.
My cheek is cold and white, alas!
My heart beats loud and fast;
Oh! press it close to thine again,
Where it must break at last.

To ———

ONE word is too often profaned
  For me to profane it,
One feeling too falsely disdained
  For thee to disdain it.
One hope is too like despair
  For prudence to smother,
And Pity from thee more dear
  Than that from another.

I can give not what men call love;
  But wilt thou accept not
The worship the heart lifts above
  And the Heavens reject not:
The desire of the moth for the star,
  Of the night for the morrow,
The devotion to something afar
  From the sphere of our sorrow?

Music, When Soft Voices Die

MUSIC, when soft voices die,
  Vibrates in the memory;
Odours, when sweet violets sicken,
Live within the sense they quicken.

Rose leaves, when the rose is dead,
Are heaped for the belovèd's bed;
And so thy thoughts, when thou art gone,
Love itself shall slumber on.

Hellas

THE world's great age begins anew,
  The golden years return,
The earth doth like a snake renew
  Her winter weeds outworn:
Heaven smiles, and faiths and empires gleam
Like wrecks of a dissolving dream.

A brighter Hellas rears its mountains
  From waves serener far;
A new Peneus rolls his fountains
  Against the morning star;
Where fairer Tempes bloom, there sleep
Young Cyclads on a sunnier deep.

A loftier Argo cleaves the main,
  Fraught with a later prize;
Another Orpheus sings again,
  And loves, and weeps, and dies;
A new Ulysses leaves once more
Calypso for his native shore.

O write no more the tale of Troy,
  If earth Death's scroll must be—
Nor mix with Laian rage the joy
  Which dawns upon the free,
Although a subtler Sphinx renew
Riddles of death Thebes never knew.

Another Athens shall arise,
  And to remoter time
Bequeath, like sunset to the skies,
  The splendour of its prime;
And leave, if naught so bright may live,
All earth can take or Heaven can give.

Saturn and Love their long repose
  Shall burst, more bright and good
Than all who fell, than One who rose,
  Than many unsubdued:
Not gold, not blood, their altar dowers,
But votive tears and symbol flowers.

O cease! must hate and death return?
  Cease! must men kill and die?
Cease! drain not to its dregs the urn
  Of bitter prophecy!
The world is weary of the past—
O might it die or rest at last!

From "Prometheus Unbound"

TO suffer woes which Hope thinks infinite;
  To forgive wrongs darker than death or night;
To defy Power, which seems omnipotent;
To love, and bear; to hope till Hope creates
From its own wreck the thing it contemplates;
  Neither to change, nor falter, nor repent;
This, like thy glory, Titan, is to be
Good, great and joyous, beautiful and free;
This is alone Life, Joy, Empire, and Victory.

JOHN KEATS (1795-1821)

On First Looking into Chapman's Homer

MUCH have I travelled in the realms of gold,
  And many goodly states and kingdoms seen;
Round many western islands have I been
Which bards in fealty to Apollo hold.
Oft of one wide expanse had I been told
  That deep-browed Homer ruled as his demesne:
Yet did I never breathe its pure serene
Till I heard Chapman speak out loud and bold:
Then felt I like some watcher of the skies
  When a new planet swims into his ken;
Or like stout Cortez, when with eagle eyes
  He stared at the Pacific—and all his men
Looked at each other with a wild surmise—
  Silent, upon a peak in Darien.

"When I Have Fears"

WHEN I have fears that I may cease to be
　　Before my pen has gleaned my teeming brain,
Before high-piled books in charact'ry
Hold like rich garners the full-ripened grain;
When I behold, upon the night's starred face,
Huge cloudy symbols of a high romance,
And think that I may never live to trace
Their shadows, with the magic hand of chance;
And when I feel, fair creature of an hour!
That I shall never look upon thee more,
Never have relish in the fairy power
Of unreflecting love!—then on the shore
　Of the wide world I stand alone, and think
　Till Love and Fame to nothingness do sink.

Fragment of an Ode to Maia

MOTHER of Hermes! and still youthful Maia!
　　May I sing to thee
As thou wast hymnèd on the shores of Baia?
　　Or may I woo thee
In earlier Sicilian? or thy smiles
Seek as they once were sought, in Grecian isles,
By bards who died content on pleasant sward,
　Leaving great verse unto a little clan?
O give me their old vigour! and unheard
　Save of the quiet primrose, and the span
　　　Of heaven, and few ears,
Rounded by thee, my song shall die away
　　　Content as theirs,
Rich in the simple worship of a day.

From "The Eve of St. Agnes"

ST. AGNES' Eve—Ah, bitter chill it was!
　　The owl, for all his feathers, was a-cold;
The hare limped trembling through the frozen grass,
And silent was the flock in woolly fold:
Numb were the Beadsman's fingers, while he told
His rosary, and while his frosted breath,
Like pious incense from a censer old,
Seemed taking flight for heaven, without a death,
Past the sweet Virgin's picture, while his prayer he saith.

His prayer he saith, this patient, holy man;
Then takes his lamp, and riseth from his knees,
And back returneth, meager, barefoot, wan,
Along the chapel aisle by slow degrees:
The sculptured dead on each side, seem to freeze,
Emprisoned in black, purgatorial rails:
Knights, ladies, praying in dumb orat'ries,
He passeth by; and his weak spirit fails
To think how they may ache in icy hoods and mails. . . .

A casement high and triple-arched there was,
All garlanded with carven imageries
Of fruits, and flowers, and bunches of knot-grass,
And diamonded with panes of quaint device,
Innumerable of stains and splendid dyes,
As are the tiger-moth's deep-damasked wings;
And in the midst, 'mong thousand heraldries,
And twilight saints, and dim emblazonings,
A shielded scutcheon blushed with blood of queens and
        kings.

Full on this casement shone the wintry moon,
And threw warm gules on Madeline's fair breast,
As down she knelt for Heaven's grace and boon;
Rose-bloom fell on her hands, together pressed,
And on her silver cross soft amethyst,
And on her hair a glory, like a saint:
She seemed a splendid angel, newly dressed,
Save wings, for heaven:—Porphyro grew faint:
She knelt, so pure a thing, so free from mortal taint.

Anon his heart revives: her vespers done,
Of all its wreathèd pearls her hair she frees;
Unclasps her warmèd jewels one by one;
Loosens her fragrant bodice; by degrees
Her rich attire creeps rustling to her knees:
Half-hidden, like a mermaid in seaweed,
Pensive awhile she dreams awake, and sees,
In fancy, fair St. Agnes in her bed,
But dares not look behind, or all the charm is fled.

Soon, trembling in her soft and chilly nest,
In sort of wakeful swoon, perplexed she lay,
Until the poppied warmth of sleep oppressed
Her soothèd limbs, and soul fatigued away;
Flown, like a thought, until the morrow-day;
Blissfully havened both from joy and pain;
Clasped like a missal where swart Paynims pray;
Blinded alike from sunshine and from rain,
As though a rose should shut, and be a bud again.

JOHN KEATS

Stolen to this paradise, and so entranced,
Porphyro gazed upon her empty dress,
And listened to her breathing, if it chanced
To wake into a slumberous tenderness;
Which when he heard, that minute did he bless
And breathed himself: then from the closet crept
Noiseless as fear in a wide wilderness,
And over the hushed carpet, silent, stept,
And 'tween the curtains peeped, where, lo—how fast she
    slept.

Then by the bed-side, where the faded moon
Made a dim, silver twilight, soft he set
A table, and, half anguished, threw thereon
A cloth of woven crimson, gold, and jet:—
O for some drowsy Morphean amulet!
The boisterous, midnight, festive clarion,
The kettle-drum, and far-heard clarionet,
Affray his ears, though but in dying tone:—
The hall-door shuts again, and all the noise is gone.

And still she slept an azure-lidded sleep,
In blanchèd linen, smooth and lavendered,
While he forth from the closet brought a heap
Of candied apple, quince, and plum, and gourd;
With jellies soother than the creamy curd,
And lucent syrops, tinct with cinnamon;
Manna and dates, in argosy transferred
From Fez; and spicèd dainties, every one,
From silken Samarcand to cedared Lebanon.

These delicates he heaped with glowing hand
On golden dishes and in baskets bright
Of wreathèd silver: sumptuous they stand
In the retirèd quiet of the night,
Filling the chilly room with perfume light—
"And now, my love, my seraph fair, awake!
Thou art my heaven, and I thine eremite:
Open thine eyes, for meek St. Agnes' sake,
Or I shall drowse beside thee, so my soul doth ache."

Thus whispering, his warm, unnervèd arm
Sank in her pillow. Shaded was her dream
By the dusk curtains:—'twas a midnight charm
Impossible to melt as icèd stream:
The lustrous salvers in the moonlight gleam;
Broad golden fringe upon the carpet lies:
It seemed he never, never could redeem
From such a steadfast spell his lady's eyes
So mused awhile, entoiled in woofèd phantasies.

Awakening up, he took her hollow lute,—
Tumultuous,—and, in chords that tenderest be,
He played an ancient ditty, long since mute,
In Provence called, "La belle dame sans merci":
Close to her ear touching the melody;—
Wherewith disturbed, she uttered a soft moan:
He ceased—she panted quick—and suddenly
Her blue affrayèd eyes wide open shone:
Upon his knees he sank, pale as smooth-sculptured stone.

Ode on a Grecian Urn

THOU still unravished bride of quietness,
    Thou foster-child of Silence and slow Time,
Sylvan historian, who canst thus express
    A flowery tale more sweetly than our rhyme:
What leaf-fringed legend haunts about thy shape
    Of deities or mortals, or of both,
       In Tempe or the dales of Arcady?
    What men or gods are these? What maidens loth?
What mad pursuit? What struggle to escape?
    What pipes and timbrels? What wild ecstasy?

Heard melodies are sweet, but those unheard
    Are sweeter; therefore, ye soft pipes, play on;
Not to the sensual ear, but, more endured,
    Pipe to the spirit ditties of no tone:
Fair youth, beneath the trees, thou canst not leave
    Thy song, nor ever can those trees be bare;
       Bold Lover, never, never canst thou kiss,
Though winning near the goal—yet, do not grieve;
    She cannot fade, though thou hast not thy bliss,
For ever wilt thou love, and she be fair!

Ah, happy, happy boughs! that cannot shed
    Your leaves, nor ever bid the Spring adieu;
And, happy melodist, unwearièd,
    For ever piping songs for ever new;
More happy love! more happy, happy love!
    For ever warm and still to be enjoyed,
       For ever panting and for ever young;
All breathing human passion far above,
    That leaves a heart high-sorrowful and cloyed,
    A burning forehead, and a parching tongue.

Who are these coming to the sacrifice?
    To what green altar, O mysterious priest,
Lead'st thou that heifer lowing at the skies,
    And all her silken flanks with garlands dressed?
What little town by river or sea-shore,
    Or mountain-built with peaceful citadel,

Is emptied of its folk, this pious morn?
And, little town, thy streets for evermore
    Will silent be; and not a soul, to tell
        Why thou art desolate, can e'er return.

O Attic shape! fair attitude! with brede
    Of marble men and maidens overwrought,
With forest branches and the trodden weed;
    Thou, silent form! dost tease us out of thought
As doth eternity. Cold Pastoral!
    When old age shall this generation waste,
        Thou shalt remain, in midst of other woe
Than ours, a friend to man, to whom thou say'st,
    "Beauty is truth, truth beauty,"—that is all
        Ye know on earth, and all ye need to know.

On Melancholy

NO, no, go not to Lethe, neither twist
        Wolf's-bane, tight-rooted, for its poisonous wine;
Nor suffer thy pale forehead to be kiss'd
    By nightshade, ruby grape of Proserpine;
Make not your rosary of yew-berries,
    Nor let the beetle nor the death-moth be
        Your mournful Psyche, nor the downy owl
A partner in your sorrow's mysteries;
    For shade to shade will come too drowsily,
    And drown the wakeful anguish of the soul.

But when the melancholy fit shall fall
    Sudden from heaven like a weeping cloud,
That fosters the droop-headed flowers all,
    And hides the green hill in an April shroud;
Then glut thy sorrow on a morning rose,
    Or on the rainbow of the salt sand-wave,
        Or on the wealth of globed peonies;
Or if thy mistress some rich anger shows,
    Emprison her soft hand, and let her rave,
        And feed deep, deep upon her peerless eyes.

She dwells with Beauty—Beauty that must die;
    And Joy, whose hand is ever at his lips
Bidding adieu; and aching Pleasure nigh,
    Turning to poison while the bee-mouth sips:
Ay, in the very temple of Delight
    Veil'd Melancholy has her sovran shrine,
        Though seen of none save him whose strenuous tongue
            Can burst Joy's grape against his palate fine:
His soul shall taste the sadness of her might,
    And be among her cloudy trophies hung.

La Belle Dame Sans Merci

O what can ail thee, knight-at-arms,
  Alone and palely loitering?
The sedge has withered from the lake,
  And no birds sing.

O what can ail thee, knight-at-arms
  So haggard and so woe-begone?
The squirrel's granary is full,
  And the harvest's done.

I see a lily on thy brow
  With anguish moist and fever-dew,
And on thy cheeks a fading rose
  Fast withereth too.

I met a lady in the meads,
  Full beautiful—a fairy's child,
Her hair was long, her foot was light,
  And her eyes were wild.

I made a garland for her head,
  And bracelets too, and fragrant zone;
She looked at me as she did love,
  And made sweet moan.

I set her on my pacing steed
  And nothing else saw all day long,
For sidelong would she bend, and sing
  A fairy's song.

She found me roots of relish sweet,
  And honey wild and manna-dew,
And sure in language strange she said,
  "I love thee true."

She took me to her elfin grot,
  And there she wept and sighed full sore;
And there I shut her wild, wild eyes
  With kisses four.

And there she lullèd me asleep.
  And there I dreamed—Ah! woe betide!
The latest dream I ever dreamed
  On the cold hill's side.

I saw pale kings and princes too,
  Pale warriors, death-pale were they all:
They cried—"La belle dame sans merci
  Hath thee in thrall!"

I saw their starved lips in the gloam
  With horrid warning gapèd wide,
And I awoke and found me here
  On the cold hill's side.

And this is why I sojourn here
  Alone and palely loitering,
Though the sedge is withered from the lake,
  And no birds sing.

Ode to Psyche

O Goddess! hear these tuneless numbers, wrung
    By sweet enforcement and remembrance dear,
And pardon that thy secrets should be sung
  Even into thine own soft-conchèd ear:
Surely I dreamed to-day, or did I see
  The wingèd Psyche with awakened eyes?
I wandered in a forest thoughtlessly,
  And, on a sudden, fainting with surprise,
Saw two fair creatures, couchèd side by side
  In deepest grass, beneath the whispering roof
  Of leaves and trembled blossoms, where there ran
    A brooklet, scarce espied:
'Mid hushed, cool-rooted flowers fragrant-eyed,
  Blue, silver-white, and hudded Tyrian,
They lay calm-breathing on the bedded grass;
  Their arms embracèd, and their pinions too;
  Their lips touched not, but had not bade adieu,
As if disjoinèd by soft-handed slumber,
And ready still past kisses to outnumber
  At tender eye-dawn of aurorean love:
    The wingèd boy I knew;
But who wast thou, O happy, happy dove?
    His Psyche true!

O latest-born and loveliest vision far
  Of all Olympus' faded hierarchy!
Fairer than Phœbe's sapphire-regioned star,
  Or Vesper, amorous glow-worm of the sky;
Fairer than these, though temple thou hast none,
    Nor altar heaped with flowers;

Nor Virgin-choir to make delicious moan
    Upon the midnight hours;
No voice, no lute, no pipe, no incense sweet
    From chain-swung censer teeming;
No shrine, no grove, no oracle, no heat
    Of pale-mouthed prophet dreaming.

O brightest! though too late for antique vows,
    Too, too late for the fond believing lyre,
When holy were the haunted forest boughs,
    Holy the air, the water, and the fire;
Yet even in these days so far retired
    From happy pieties, thy lucent fans,
    Fluttering among the faint Olympians,
I see, and sing, by my own eyes inspired.
So let me be thy choir, and make a moan
    Upon the midnight hours!
Thy voice, thy lute, thy pipe, thy incense sweet
    From swingèd censer teeming:
Thy shrine, thy grove, thy oracle, thy heat
    Of pale-mouthed prophet dreaming.

Yes, I will be thy priest, and build a fane
    In some untrodden region of my mind,
Where branchèd thoughts, new-grown with pleasant pain,
    Instead of pines shall murmur in the wind:
Far, far around shall those dark-clustered trees
    Fledge the wild-ridgèd mountains steep by steep;
And there by zephyrs, streams, and birds, and bees,
    The moss-lain Dryads shall be lulled to sleep;
And in the midst of this wide quietness
A rosy sanctuary will I dress
With the wreathed trellis of a working brain,
    With buds, and bells, and stars without a name,
With all the gardener Fancy e'er could feign,
    Who, breeding flowers, will never breed the same;
And there shall be for thee all soft delight
    That shadowy thought can win,
A bright torch, and a casement ope at night,
    To let the warm Love in!

Ode to a Nightingale

MY heart aches, and a drowsy numbness pains
    My sense, as though of hemlock I had drunk,
Or emptied some dull opiate to the drains
    One minute past, and Lethe-wards had sunk:
'Tis not through envy of thy happy lot,
    But being too happy in thy happiness,—

That thou, light-wingèd Dryad of the trees,
  In some melodious plot
Of beechen green, and shadows numberless,
  Singest of summer in full-throated ease.

O for a draught of vintage, that hath been
  Cooled a long age in the deep-delvèd earth,
Tasting of Flora and the country green,
  Dance, and Provençal song, and sunburnt mirth!
O for a beaker full of the warm South,
  Full of the true, the blushful Hippocrene,
    With beaded bubbles winking at the brim,
      And purple-stainèd mouth;
That I might drink, and leave the world unseen,
  And with thee fade away into the forest dim:

Fade far away, dissolve, and quite forget
  What thou among the leaves hast never known,
The weariness, the fever, and the fret,
  Here, where men sit and hear each other groan;
Where palsy shakes a few, sad, last gray hairs,
  Where youth grows pale, and specter-thin, and dies;
    Where but to think is to be full of sorrow
      And leaden-eyed despairs;
Where Beauty cannot keep her lustrous eyes,
  Or new Love pine at them beyond to-morrow.

Away! away! for I will fly to thee,
  Not charioted by Bacchus and his pards,
But on the viewless wings of Poesy,
  Though the dull brain perplexes and retards:
Already with thee! tender is the night,
  And haply the Queen-Moon is on her throne,
    Clustered around by all her starry Fays;
      But here there is no light,
Save what from heaven is with the breezes blown
  Through verdurous glooms and winding mossy ways

I cannot see what flowers are at my feet,
  Nor what soft incense hangs upon the boughs,
But, in embalmèd darkness, guess each sweet
  Wherewith the seasonable month endows
The grass, the thicket, and the fruit-tree wild;
  White hawthorn, and the pastoral eglantine;
    Fast-fading violets covered up in leaves;
      And mid-May's eldest child,
The coming musk-rose, full of dewy wine,
  The murmurous haunt of flies on summer eves.

Darkling I listen; and, for many a time
I have been half in love with easeful Death,
Called him soft names in many a musèd rhyme,
To take into the air my quiet breath;
Now more than ever seems it rich to die,
To cease upon the midnight with no pain,
While thou art pouring forth thy soul abroad
In such an ecstasy!
Still wouldst thou sing, and I have ears in vain—
To thy high requiem become a sod.

Thou wast not born for death, immortal Bird!
No hungry generations tread thee down;
The voice I hear this passing night was heard
In ancient days by emperor and clown:
Perhaps the self-same song that found a path
Through the sad heart of Ruth, when, sick for home,
She stood in tears amid the alien corn;
The same that oft-times hath
Charmed magic casements, opening on the foam
Of perilous seas, in faery lands forlorn.

Forlorn! the very word is like a bell
To toll me back from thee to my sole self!
Adieu! the fancy cannot cheat so well
As she is famed to do, deceiving elf.
Adieu! adieu! thy plaintive anthem fades
Past the near meadows, over the still stream,
Up the hill-side; and now 'tis buried deep
In the next valley-glades:
Was it a vision, or a waking dream?
Fled is that music:—Do I wake or sleep?

To Autumn

SEASON of mists and mellow fruitfulness!
Close bosom-friend of the maturing sun;
Conspiring with him how to load and bless
With fruit the vines that round the thatch-eaves run;
To bend with apples the mossed cottage-trees,
And fill all fruit with ripeness to the core;
To swell the gourd, and plump the hazel-shells
With a sweet kernel; to set budding more,
And still more, later flowers for the bees,
Until they think warm days will never cease,
For Summer has o'erbrimmed their clammy cells.

Who hath not seen thee oft amid thy store?
Sometimes whoever seeks abroad may find
Thee sitting careless on a granary floor,
Thy hair soft-lifted by the winnowing wind;
Or on a half-reaped furrow sound asleep,
Drowsed with the fume of poppies, while thy hook
Spares the next swath and all its twinèd flowers;
And sometimes like a gleaner thou dost keep
Steady thy laden head across a brook;
Or by a cider-press, with patient look,
Thou watchest the last oozings, hours by hours.

Where are the songs of Spring? Ay, where are they?
Think not of them, thou hast thy music too.
While barrèd clouds bloom the soft-dying day
And touch the stubble-plains with rosy hue;
Then in a wailful choir the small gnats mourn
Among the river sallows, borne aloft
Or sinking as the light wind lives or dies;
And full-grown lambs loud bleat from hilly bourn;
Hedge-crickets sing, and now with treble soft
The redbreast whistles from a garden-croft,
And gathering swallows twitter in the skies.

Last Sonnet

BRIGHT Star! would I were steadfast as thou art—
   Not in lone splendour hung aloft the night,
And watching, with eternal lids apart,
Like Nature's patient, sleepless Eremite,
The moving waters at their priest-like task
Of pure ablution round earth's human shores,
Or gazing on the new soft-fallen mask
Of snow upon the mountains and the moors—
No—yet still steadfast, still unchangeable,
Pillowed upon my fair love's ripening breast,
To feel for ever its soft fall and swell,
Awake for ever in a sweet unrest,
   Still, still to hear her tender-taken breath,
   And so live ever—or else swoon to death.

GEORGE DARLEY (1795-1846)
From "Sylvia"

WHO wants a gown
      Of purple fold,
Embroidered down
      The seams with gold?
         See here!—a Tulip richly laced
         To please a royal fairy's taste!

Who wants a cap
    Of crimson grand?
By great good hap
    I've one on hand:
        Look, sir!—a Cock's-comb, flowering red,
        'Tis just the thing, sir, for your head!

Who wants a frock
    Of vestal hue?
Or snowy smock?—
    Fair maid, do you?
        O me!—a Ladysmock so white!
        Your bosom's self is not more bright!

Who wants to sport
    A slender limb?
I've every sort
    Of hose for him:
        Both scarlet, striped, and yellow ones:
        This Woodbine makes such pantaloons!

Who wants—(hush! hush!)
    A box of paint?
'Twill give a blush,
    Yet leave no taint:
        This Rose with natural rouge is fill'd,
        From its own dewy leaves distill'd.

HARTLEY COLERIDGE (1796-1849)

Song

SHE is not fair to outward view
    As many maidens be,
Her loveliness I never knew
    Until she smiled on me;
Oh! then I saw her eye was bright,
A well of love, a spring of light.

But now her looks are coy and cold,
    To mine they ne'er reply,
And yet I cease not to behold
    The love-light in her eye:
Her very frowns are fairer far
Than smiles of other maidens are.

THOMAS HOOD (1799-1845)
The Song of the Shirt

WITH fingers weary and worn,
　　With eyelids heavy and red,
A woman sat, in unwomanly rags,
　　Plying her needle and thread,—
　　　　Stitch—stitch—stitch!
In poverty, hunger, and dirt;
　　And still with a voice of dolorous pitch
She sang the "Song of the Shirt!"

"Work—work—work
　　While the cock is crowing aloof!
And work—work—work
　　Till the stars shine through the roof!
It's oh! to be a slave
　　Along with the barbarous Turk,
Where woman has never a soul to save,
　　If this is Christian work!

"Work—work—work
　　Till the brain begins to swim!
Work—work—work
　　Till the eyes are heavy and dim!
Seam, and gusset, and band,
　　Band, and gusset, and seam,—
Till over the buttons I fall asleep,
　　And sew them on in a dream!

"O men with sisters dear!
　　O men with mothers and wives!
It is not linen you're wearing out,
　　But human creatures' lives!
　　　　Stitch—stitch—stitch,
　　In poverty, hunger and dirt,—
Sewing at once, with a double thread,
　　A shroud as well as a shirt!

"But why do I talk of death,—
　　That phantom of grisly bone
I hardly fear his terrible shape,
　　It seems so like my own,—
It seems so like my own
　　Because of the fasts I keep;
O God! that bread should be so dear,
　　And flesh and blood so cheap!

"Work—work—work!
　　My labour never flags;

And what are its wages? A bed of straw,
  A crust of bread—and rags.
That shattered roof—and this naked floor—
  A table—a broken chair—
And a wall so blank my shadow I thank
  For sometimes falling there!

"Work—work—work
  From weary chime to chime!
Work—work—work
  As prisoners work for crime!
Band, and gusset, and seam,
  Seam, and gusset, and band,—
Till the heart is sick and the brain benumbed,
  As well as the weary hand.

"Work—work—work
  In the dull December light!
And work—work—work
  When the weather is warm and bright!
While underneath the eaves
  The brooding swallows cling,
As if to show me their sunny backs,
  And twit me with the Spring.

"Oh but to breathe the breath
  Of the cowslip and primrose sweet,—
With the sky above my head,
  And the grass beneath my feet!
For only one short hour
  To feel as I used to feel,
Before I knew the woes of want
  And the walk that costs a meal!

"Oh but for one short hour,—
  A respite, however brief!
No blessèd leisure for love or hope,
  But only time for grief!
A little weeping would ease my heart;
  But in their briny bed
My tears must stop, for every drop
  Hinders needle and thread!"

With fingers weary and worn,
  With eyelids heavy and red,
A woman sat, in unwomanly rags,
  Plying her needle and thread,—
    Stitch—stitch—stitch!
  In poverty, hunger, and dirt;
And still with a voice of dolorous pitch—
Would that its tone could reach the rich!—
  She sang this "Song of the Shirt!"

The Bridge of Sighs

ONE more Unfortunate,
    Weary of breath,
Rashly importunate,
    Gone to her death!

Take her up tenderly,
    Lift her with care;
Fashioned so slenderly,
    Young, and so fair!

Look at her garments
Clinging like cerements:
Whilst the wave constantly
    Drips from her clothing;
Take her up instantly,
    Loving, not loathing.

Touch her not scornfully;
Think of her mournfully,
    Gently and humanly;
Not of the stains of her;
All that remains of her
    Now is pure womanly.

Make no deep scrutiny
Into her mutiny
    Rash and undutiful;
Past all dishonour,
Death has left on her
    Only the beautiful.

Still, for all slips of hers,
    One of Eve's family—
Wipe those poor lips of hers
    Oozing so clammily.

Loop up her tresses
    Escaped from the comb,
Her fair auburn tresses;
Whilst wonderment guesses
    Where was her home?

Who was her father?
    Who was her mother?
Had she a sister?
    Had she a brother?

Or was there a dearer one
Still, and a nearer one
    Yet, than all other?

Alas! for the rarity
Of Christian charity
    Under the sun!
O, it was pitiful!
Near a whole city full,
    Home she had none.

Sisterly, brotherly,
Fatherly, motherly
    Feelings had changed;
    Love, by harsh evidence,
Thrown from its eminence;
Even God's providence
    Seeming estranged.

Where the lamps quiver
So far in the river,
    With many a light
From window and casement,
From garret to basement,
She stood, with amazement,
    Houseless by night.

The bleak wind of March
    Made her tremble and shiver;
But not the dark arch
Or the black flowing river:
Mad from life's history,
Glad to death's mystery,
    Swift to be hurled—
Anywhere, anywhere
    Out of the world!

In she plunged boldly—
No matter how coldly
    The rough river ran—
Over the brink of it,
Picture it,—think of it,
    Dissolute Man!
Lave in it,—drink of it,
    Then, if you can!

Take her up tenderly,
    Lift her with care;
Fashioned so slendely,
    Young, and so fair!

Ere her limbs frigidly
Stiffen too rigidly,
  Decently, kindly,
Smooth and compose them;
And her eyes, close them,
  Staring so blindly!

Dreadfully staring
  Through muddy impurity,
As when with the daring
Last look of despairing,
  Fixed on futurity.

Perishing gloomily,
Spurred by contumely,
Cold inhumanity,
Burning insanity,
  Into her rest.—
Cross her hands humbly
As if praying dumbly,
  Over her breast!

Owning her weakness,
  Her evil behaviour,
And leaving, with meekness,
  Her sins to her Saviour!

Fair Ines

O saw ye not fair Ines?
    She's gone into the West,
To dazzle when the sun is down,
  And rob the world of rest:
She took our daylight with her,
  The smiles that we love best,
With morning blushes on her cheek,
  And pearls upon her breast.

O turn again, fair Ines,
  Before the fall of night,
For fear the Moon should shine alone,
  And stars unrivaled bright;
And blessèd will the lover be
  That walks beneath their light,
And breathes the love against thy cheek
  I dare not even write!

Would I had been, fair Ines,
  That gallant cavalier,

Who rode so gaily by thy side,
　And whispered thee so near!
Were there no bonny dames at home,
　Or no true lovers here,
That he should cross the seas to win
　The dearest of the dear?

I saw thee, lovely Ines,
　Descend along the shore,
With bands of noble gentlemen,
　And banners waved before;
And gentle youth and maidens gay,
　And snowy plumes they wore:
It would have been a beauteous dream,—
　If it had been no more!

Alas, alas! fair Ines,
　She went away with song,
With Music waiting on her steps,
　And shoutings of the throng;
But some were sad, and felt no mirth,
　But only Music's wrong,
In sounds that sang Farewell, farewell,
　To her you've loved so long.

Farewell, farewell, fair Ines!
　That vessel never bore
So fair a lady on its deck,
　Nor danced so light before,—
Alas for pleasure on the sea,
　And sorrow on the shore!
The smile that blessed one lover's heart
　Has broken many more!

Silence

THERE is a silence where hath been no sound,
　There is a silence where no sound may be,
In the cold grave,—under the deep, deep sea,
Or in wide desert where no life is found,
Which hath been mute, and still must sleep profound;
No voice is hush'd—no life treads silently,
But clouds and cloudy shadows wander free,
That never spoke, over the idle ground:
But in green ruins, in the desolate walls
Of antique palaces, where Man hath been,
Though the dun fox a wild hyæna calls,
And owls that flit continually between,
Shriek to the echo, and the low winds moan—
There the true Silence is, self-conscious and alone.

THOMAS BABINGTON MACAULAY, LORD MACAULAY (1800-1859)

From "Horatius"

THEN out spake brave Horatius,
    The Captain of the Gate:
"To every man upon this earth
Death cometh soon or late.
And how can man die better
Than facing fearful odds
For the ashes of his fathers
    And the temples of his Gods,

"And for the tender mother
    Who dandled him to rest,
And for the wife who nurses
    His baby at her breast,
And for the holy maidens
    Who feed the eternal flame,—
To save them from false Sextus
    That wrought the deed of shame?

"Hew down the bridge, Sir Consul,
    With all the speed ye may;
I, with two more to help me,
    Will hold the foe in play.
In yon strait path a thousand
    May well be stopped by three:
Now who will stand on either hand,
    And keep the bridge with me?"

Then out spake Spurius Lartius,—
    A Ramnian proud was he:
"Lo, I will stand at thy right hand,
    And keep the bridge with thee."
And out spake strong Herminius,—
    Of Titan blood was he:
"I will abide on thy left side,
    And keep the bridge with thee."

"Horatius," quoth the Consul,
    "As thou sayest so let it be."
And straight against that great array
    Forth went the dauntless Three.
For Romans in Rome's quarrel
    Spared neither land nor gold,
Nor son nor wife, nor limb nor life,
    In the brave days of old.

>   Then none was for a party;
>   Then all were for the state;
>   Then the great man helped the poor,
>   And the poor man loved the great:
>   Then lands were fairly portioned;
>   Then spoils were fairly sold:
>   The Romans were like brothers
>   In the brave days of old.

SIR HENRY TAYLOR (1800-1886)

Elena's Song

> QUOTH tongue of neither maid nor wife
>   To heart of neither wife nor maid—
> Lead we not here a jolly life
>   Betwixt the shine and shade?
>
> Quoth heart of neither maid nor wife
>   To tongue of neither wife nor maid—
> Thou wagg'st, but I am worn with strife,
>   And feel like flowers that fade.

WILLIAM BARNES (1801-1886)

The Woodlands

> O spread ageän your leaves an' flow'rs
>   Lwonesome woodlands! zunny woodlands!
> Here underneath the dewy show'rs
>   O warm-air'd spring-time zunny woodlands!
> As when, in drong or open ground,
> Wi' happy bwoyish heart I vound
> The twitt'ren birds a buildèn round
> Your high-bough'd hedges, zunny woodlands!
>
> You gie'd me life, you gie'd me jäy,
>   Lwonesome woodlands! zunny woodlands!
> You gie'd me health, as in my pläy
>   I rambled through ye, zunny woodlands!
> You gie'd me freedom, vor to rove
> In airy meäd or sheädy grove
> You gie'd me smilèn Fanny's love,
>   The best ov all o't, zunny woodlands!

My vu'st shrill skylark whiver'd high,
  Lwonesome woodlands! zunny woodlands!
To zing below your deep-blue sky
  An' white spring-clouds, O zunny woodlands!
An' boughs o' trees that woonce stood here,
Wer glossy green the happy-year
That gie'd me woone I lov'd so dear,
  An' now ha lost, O zunny woodlands!

O let me rove ageän unspied,
  Lwonesome woodlands! zunny woodlands!
Along your green-bough'd hedges' zide,
  As then I rambled, zunny woodlands!
An' where the missèn trees woonce stood,
Or tongues woonce rung among the wood,
My memory shall meäke em good,
  Though you've a-lost em, zunny woodlands!

JOHN HENRY NEWMAN (1801-1890)
The Pillar of the Cloud

LEAD, kindly Light, amid the encircling gloom,
      Lead Thou me on!
The night is dark, and I am far from home—
      Lead Thou me on!
Keep Thou my feet; I do not ask to see
The distant scene,—one step enough for me.

I was not ever thus, nor prayed that Thou
      Shouldst lead me on.
I loved to choose and see my path; but now
      Lead Thou me on!
I loved the garish day, and, spite of fears,
Pride ruled my will: remember not past years.

So long Thy power hath blessed me, sure it still
      Will lead me on,
O'er moor and fen, o'er crag and torrent, till
      The night is gone;
And with the morn those angel faces smile
Which I have loved long since, and lost awhile.

WINTHROP MACKWORTH PRAED (1802-1839)
Fairy Song

HE has conn'd the lesson now;
      He has read the book of pain:
There are furrows on his brow;
      I must make it smooth again.

Lo! I knock the spurs away;
  Lo! I loosen belt and brand;
Hark! I hear the courser neigh
  For his stall in Fairy-Land.

Bring the cap, and bring the vest;
  Buckle on his sandal shoon;
Fetch his memory from the chest
  In the treasury of the moon.

I have taught him to be wise
  For a little maiden's sake;—
Lo! he opens his glad eyes,
  Softly, slowly: Minstrel, wake!

JAMES CLARENCE MANGAN (1803-1849)

Dark Rosaleen

O my dark Rosaleen,
    Do not sigh, do not weep!
The priests are on the ocean green,
  They march along the deep.
There's wine from the royal Pope
  Upon the ocean green,
And Spanish ale shall give you hope,
  My dark Rosaleen!
  My own Rosaleen!
Shall glad your heart, shall give you hope,
Shall give you health, and help, and hope,
  My dark Rosaleen!

Over hills and through dales
  Have I roamed for your sake;
All yesterday I sailed the sails
  On river and on lake.
The Erne, at its highest flood,
  I dashed across unseen,
For there was lightning in my blood,
  My dark Rosaleen!
  My own Rosaleen!
Oh! there was lightning in my blood,
Red lightning lightened through my blood,
  My dark Rosaleen!

All day long, in unrest,
  To and fro do I move.
The very soul within my breast
  Is wasted for you, love!

The heart in my bosom faints
  To think of you, my Queen,
My life of life, my saint of saints,
  My dark Rosaleen!
  My own Rosaleen!
To hear your sweet and sad complaints,
My life, my love, my saint of saints,
  My dark Rosaleen!

Woe and pain, pain and woe,
  Are my lot, night and noon,
To see your bright face clouded so,
  Like to the mournful moon.
But yet will I rear your throne
  Again in golden sheen;
'Tis you shall reign, shall reign alone
  My dark Rosaleen!
  My own Rosaleen!
'Tis you shall have the golden throne,
'Tis you shall reign, and reign alone,
  My dark Rosaleen!

Over dews, over sands,
  Will I fly for your weal:
Your holy, delicate white hands
  Shall girdle me with steel.
At home in your emerald bowers,
  From morning's dawn till e'en,
You'll pray for me, my flower of flowers,
  My dark Rosaleen!
  My own Rosaleen!
You'll think of me through daylight's hours,
My virgin flower, my flower of flowers,
  My dark Rosaleen!

I could scale the blue air,
  I could plough the high hills,
Oh, I could kneel all night in prayer,
  To heal your many ills!
And one beamy smile from you
  Would float like light between
My toils and me, my own, my true,
  My dark Rosaleen!
  My own Rosaleen!
Would give me life and soul anew,
A second life, a soul anew,
  My dark Rosaleen!

Oh! the Erne shall run red
　With redundance of blood,
The earth shall rock beneath our tread,
　And flames wrap hill and wood,
And gun-peal and slogan-cry
　Wake many a glen serene,
Ere you shall fade, ere you shall die,
　My dark Rosaleen!
　My own Rosaleen!
The Judgment Hour must first be nigh,
Ere you shall fade, ere you can die,
　My dark Rosaleen!

THOMAS LOVELL BEDDOES (1803-1849)
Dream-Pedlary

IF there were dreams to sell,
　　What would you buy?
Some cost a passing bell;
　Some a light sigh,
That shakes from Life's fresh crown
Only a rose-leaf down.

If there were dreams to sell,
Merry and sad to tell,
And the crier rang the bell,
　What would you buy?

ELIZABETH BARRETT BROWNING (1806-1861)
From "Sonnets from the Portuguese"

I

I thought once how Theocritus had sung
　Of the sweet years, the dear and wished-for years,
Who each one in a gracious hand appears
To bear a gift for mortals, old or young:
And, as I mused it in his antique tongue,
I saw, in gradual vision through my tears,
The sweet, sad years, the melancholy years,
Those of my own life, who by turns had flung
A shadow across me.　Straightway I was 'ware,
So weeping, how a mystic Shape did move
Behind me, and drew me backward by the hair;
And a voice said in mastery, while I strove,—
"Guess now who holds thee?"—"Death," I said.　But, there,
The silver answer rang,—"Not Death, but Love."

III

Unlike are we, unlike, O princely Heart!
Unlike our uses and our destinies.
Our ministering two angels look surprise
On one another, as they strike athwart
Their wings in passing. Thou, bethink thee, art
A guest for queens to social pageantries,
With gages from a hundred brighter eyes
Than tears even can make mine, to play thy part
Of chief musician. What hast *thou* to do
With looking from the lattice-lights at me,
A poor, tired, wandering singer, singing through
The dark, and leaning up a cypress tree?
The chrism is on thine head,—on mine, the dew,—
And Death must dig the level where these agree.

VI

Go from me. Yet I feel that I shall stand
Henceforward in thy shadow. Nevermore
Alone upon the threshold of my door
Of individual life, I shall command
The uses of my soul, nor lift my hand
Serenely in the sunshine as before,
Without the sense of that which I forbore,—
Thy touch upon the palm. The widest land
Doom takes to part us, leaves thy heart in mine
With pulses that beat double. What I do
And what I dream include thee, as the wine
Must taste of its own grapes. And when I sue
God for myself, He hears that name of thine,
And sees within my eyes the tears of two.

XIV

If thou must love me, let it be for naught
Except for love's sake only. Do not say
"I love her for her smile—her look—her way
Of speaking gently,—for a trick of thought
That falls in well with mine, and certes brought
A sense of pleasant ease on such a day"—
For these things in themselves, Belovèd, may
Be changed, or change for thee,—and love, so wrought,
May be unwrought so. Neither love me for
Thine own dear pity's wiping my cheeks dry,—
A creature might forget to weep, who bore
Thy comfort long, and lose thy love thereby!
But love me for love's sake, that evermore
Thou may'st love on, through love's eternity.

XVIII

I never gave a lock of hair away
To a man, Dearest, except this to thee,
Which now upon my fingers thoughtfully
I ring out to the full brown length and say
"Take it." My day of youth went yesterday;
My hair no longer bounds to my foot's glee,
Nor plant I it from rose or myrtle-tree,
As girls do, any more: it only may
Now shade on two pale cheeks the mark of tears,
Taught drooping from the head that hangs aside
Through sorrow's trick. I thought the funeral-shears
Would take this first, but Love is justified,—
Take it thou,—finding pure, from all those years,
The kiss my mother left here when she died.

XLIII

How do I love thee? Let me count the ways.
I love thee to the depth and breadth and height
My soul can reach, when feeling out of sight
For the ends of Being and ideal Grace.
I love thee to the level of everyday's
Most quiet need, by sun and candle-light.
I love thee freely, as men strive for Right;
I love thee purely, as they turn from Praise.
I love thee with the passion put to use
In my old griefs, and with my childhood's faith.
I love thee with a love I seemed to lose
With my lost saints,—I love thee with the breath,
Smiles, tears, of all my life!—and, if God choose,
I shall but love thee better after death.

A Denial

WE have met late—it is too late to meet,
    O friend, not more than friend!
Death's forecome shroud is tangled round my feet,
And if I step or stir, I touch the end.
    In this last jeopardy
Can I approach thee,—I, who cannot move?
How shall I answer thy request for love?
    Look in my face and see.

"I might have loved thee in some former days.
    Oh, then, my spirits had leapt
As now they sink, at hearing thy love-praise!

Before these faded cheeks were overwept,
   Had this been asked of me,
To love thee with my whole strong heart and head,—
I should have said still . . . Yes, but *smiled* and said,
   'Look in my face and see!'

"But now . . . God sees me, God, who took my heart
   And drowned it in life's surge.
In all your wide warm earth I have no part—
A light song overcomes me like a dirge.
   Could love's great harmony
The saints keep step to when their bonds are loose,
Not weigh me down? am *I* a wife to choose?
   Look in my face and see—

"While I behold, as plain as one who dreams,
   Some woman of full worth,
Whose voice, as cadenced as a silver stream's,
Shall prove the fountain-soul which sends it forth,
   One younger, more thought-free
And fair and gay, than I, thou must forget,
With brighter eyes than these . . . which are not wet—
   Look in my face and see!

"So farewell thou, whom I have known too late
   To let thee come so near.
Be counted happy while men call thee great,
And one beloved woman feels thee dear!—
   Not I!—that cannot be,
I am lost, I am changed,—I must go farther where
The change shall take me worse, and no one dare
   Look in my face and see."

A Musical Instrument

WHAT was he doing, the great god Pan,
      Down in the reeds by the river?
Spreading ruin and scattering ban,
Splashing and paddling with hoofs of a goat,
And breaking the golden lilies afloat
      With the dragon-fly on the river.

He tore out a reed, the great god Pan,
   From the deep cool bed of the river:
The limpid water turbidly ran,
And the broken lilies a-dying lay,
And the dragon-fly had fled away,
      Ere he brought it out of the river.

High on the shore sat the great god Pan,
　While turbidly flowed the river;
And hacked and hewed as a great god can,
With his hard bleak steel at the patient reed,
Till there was not a sign of a leaf indeed
　　To prove it fresh from the river.

He cut it short, did the great god Pan,
　(How tall it stood in the river!)
Then drew the pith, like the heart of a man,
Steadily from the outside ring,
And notched the poor dry empty thing
　　In holes, as he sat by the river.

"This is the way," laughed the great god Pan,
　(Laughed while he sat by the river,)
"The only way, since gods began
To make sweet music, they could succeed."
Then, dropping his mouth to a hole in the reed,
　　He blew in power by the river.

Sweet, sweet, sweet, O Pan!
　Piercing sweet by the river!
Blinding sweet, O great god Pan!
The sun on the hill forgot to die,
And the lilies revived, and the dragon-fly
　　Came back to dream on the river.

Yet half a beast is the great god Pan,
　To laugh as he sits by the river,
Making a poet out of a man:
The true gods sigh for the cost and pain,—
For the reed which grows nevermore again
　　As a reed with the reeds in the river.

EDWARD FITZGERALD (1809-1883)

From "The Rubáiyát of Omar Kháyyám"

COME, fill the Cup, and in the fire of Spring
　Your Winter-garment of Repentance fling:
　　The Bird of Time has but a little way
To flutter—and the Bird is on the Wing.

Whether at Naishápúr or Babylon,
Whether the Cup with sweet or bitter run,
　The Wine of Life keeps oozing drop by drop,
The Leaves of Life keep falling one by one.

A Book of Verses underneath the Bough,
A Jug of Wine, a Loaf of Bread—and Thou
  Beside me singing in the Wilderness—
Oh, Wilderness were Paradise enow!

Some for the Glories of this World; and some
Sigh for the Prophet's Paradise to come;
  Ah, take the Cash, and let the Credit go,
Nor heed the rumble of a distant Drum!

The Worldly Hope men set their Hearts upon
Turns Ashes—or it prospers; and anon,
  Like Snow upon the Desert's dusty Face,
Lighting a little hour or two—was gone.

Think, in this battered caravanserai
Whose portals are alternate Night and Day,
  How Sultán after Sultán with his Pomp
Abode his destined Hour, and went his way.

They say the Lion and the Lizard keep
The Courts where Jamshyd gloried and drank deep:
  And Bahrám, that great Hunter—the Wild Ass
Stamps o'er his Head, but cannot break his Sleep.

I sometimes think that never blows so red
The Rose as where some buried Cæsar bled;
  That every Hyacinth the Garden wears
Dropped in her Lap from some once lovely Head.

And this reviving Herb whose tender Green
Fledges the River-Lip on which we lean—
  Ah, lean upon it lightly! for who knows
From what once lovely Lip it springs unseen!

Ah, my Beloved, fill the Cup that clears
To-DAY of past Regret and future Fears:
  To-MORROW!—Why, To-morrow I may be
Myself with Yesterday's Seven thousand Years.

For some we loved, the loveliest and the best
That from his Vintage rolling Time hath pressed,
  Have drunk their Cup a Round or two before,
And one by one crept silently to rest.

And we that now make merry in the Room
They left, and Summer dresses in new bloom,
  Ourselves must we beneath the Couch of Earth
Descend—ourselves to make a Couch—for whom?

Ah, make the most of what we yet may spend,
Before we too into the Dust descend;
   Dust into Dust, and under Dust, to lie,
Sans Wine, sans Song, sans Singer, and—sans End!

I sent my Soul through the Invisible
Some letter of that After-life to spell:
   And by and by my Soul returned to me,
And answered, "I Myself am Heaven and Hell."

Heaven but the Vision of fulfilled Desire,
And Hell the Shadow from a Soul on fire
   Cast on the Darkness into which Ourselves
So late emerged from, shall so soon expire.

We are no other than a moving row
Of magic Shadow-shapes that come and go
   Round with the Sun-illumined Lantern held
In Midnight by the Master of the Show;

But helpless Pieces of the Game He plays
Upon this Checker-board of Nights and Days;
   Hither and thither moves, and checks, and slays,
And one by one back in the Closet lays.

The Ball no question makes of Ayes and Noes,
But Here or There, as strikes the Player, goes;
   And He that tossed you down into the Field,
He knows about it all—HE knows—HE knows!

The Moving Finger writes; and, having writ,
Moves on: nor all your Piety nor Wit
   Shall lure it back to cancel half a Line
Nor all your Tears wash out a Word of it

And that inverted Bowl they call the Sky,
Whereunder crawling cooped we live and die,
   Lift not your hands to *It* for help—for It
As impotently moves as you or I. . . .

What! out of senseless Nothing to provoke
A conscious Something to resent the yoke
   Of unpermitted Pleasure, under pain
Of Everlasting Penalties, if broke!

What! from his helpless Creature be repaid
Pure Gold for what he lent him dross-allayed—
   Sue for a Debt we never did contract,
And cannot answer—Oh the sorry trade!

Oh Thou, who didst with pitfall and with gin
Beset the Road I was to wander in,
　Thou wilt not with Predestined Evil round
Enmesh, and then impute my Fall to Sin!

Oh Thou, who Man of Baser Earth didst make,
And even with Paradise devise the Snake:
　For all the Sin wherewith the Face of Man
Is blackened—Man's forgiveness give—and take!

Ah, with the Grape my fading Life provide,
And wash the Body whence the Life has died,
　And lay me, shrouded in the living Leaf,
By some not unfrequented Garden-side.

That even my buried Ashes such a snare
Of Vintage shall fling up into the Air
　As not a True-believer passing by
But shall be overtaken unaware.

Indeed the Idols I have loved so long
Have done my credit in the World much wrong:
　Have drowned my Glory in a shallow Cup,
And sold my reputation for a Song.

Indeed, indeed, Repentance oft before
I swore—but was I sober when I swore?
　And then, and then came Spring, and Rose-in-hand
My thread-bare Penitence apieces tore.

And much as Wine has played the Infidel,
And robbed me of my Robe of Honour—Well,
　I often wonder what the Vintners buy
One half so precious as the stuff they sell.

Yet Ah, that Spring should vanish with the Rose!
That Youth's sweet-scented manuscript should close!
　The Nightingale that in the branches sang,
Ah whence, and whither flown again, who knows!

Would but the Desert of the Fountain yield
One glimpse—if dimly, yet indeed, revealed,
　To which the fainting Traveler might spring,
As springs the trampled herbage of the field!

Would but some wingèd Angel ere too late
Arrest the yet unfolded Roll of Fate,
　And make the stern Recorder otherwise
Enregister, or quite obliterate!

Ah Love! could you and I with Him conspire
To grasp this sorry Scheme of Things entire,
  Would not we shatter it to bits—and then
Remold it nearer to the Heart's desire!

*   *   *   *   *

Yon rising Moon that looks for us again—
How oft hereafter will she wax and wane;
  How oft hereafter rising look for us
Through this same Garden—and for *one* in vain!

And when like her, oh Sákí, you shall pass
Among the Guests Star-scattered on the Grass,
  And in your joyous errand reach the spot
Where I made One—turn down an empty Glass!

ALFRED, LORD TENNYSON (1809-1892)

The Lady of Shalott

PART I

ON either side the river lie
  Long fields of barley and of rye,
That clothe the wold and meet the sky;
And through the field the road runs by
    To many-towered Camelot;
And up and down the people go,
Gazing where the lilies blow
Round an island there below,
    The island of Shalott.

Willows whiten, aspens quiver,
Little breezes dusk and shiver
Through the wave that runs for ever
By the island in the river
    Flowing down to Camelot.
Four gray walls, and four gray towers,
Overlook a space of flowers,
And the silent isle embowers
    The Lady of Shalott.

By the margin, willow-veiled,
Slide the heavy barges trailed
By slow horses; and unhailed
The shallop flitteth silken-sailed
    Skimming down to Camelot:

But who hath seen her wave her hand?
Or at the casement seen her stand?
Or is she known in all the land,
    The Lady of Shalott?

Only reapers, reaping early
In among the bearded barley,
Hear a song that echoes cheerly
From the river winding clearly,
    Down to towered Camelot:
And by the moon the reaper weary,
Piling sheaves in uplands airy,
Listening, whispers " 'Tis the fairy
    Lady of Shalott."

PART II

There she weaves by night and day
A magic web with colours gay.
She has heard a whisper say,
A curse is on her if she stay
    To look down to Camelot.
She knows not what the curse may be,
And so she weaveth steadily,
And little other care hath she,
    The Lady of Shalott.

And moving through a mirror clear
That hangs before her all the year,
Shadows of the world appear.
There she sees the highway near
    Winding down to Camelot:
There the river eddy whirls,
And there the surly village-churls,
And the red cloaks of market girls,
    Pass onward from Shalott.

Sometimes a troop of damsels glad,
An abbot on an ambling pad,
Sometimes a curly shepherd-lad
Or long-haired page in crimson clad,
    Goes by to towered Camelot;
And sometimes through the mirror blue
The knights come riding two and two:
She hath no loyal knight and true,
    The Lady of Shalott.

But in her web she still delights
To weave the mirror's magic sights,

For often through the silent nights
A funeral, with plumes and lights
    And music, went to Camelot:
Or when the moon was overhead,
Came two young lovers lately wed;
"I am half sick of shadows," said
    The Lady of Shalott.

PART III

A bow-shot from her bower-eaves,
He rode between the barley-sheaves,
The sun came dazzling through the leaves,
And flamed upon the brazen greaves
    Of bold Sir Lancelot.
A red-cross knight for ever kneeled
To a lady in his shield,
That sparkled on the yellow field,
    Beside remote Shalott.

The gemmy bridle glittered free,
Like to some branch of stars we see
Hung in the golden Galaxy.
The bridle bells rang merrily
    As he rode down to Camelot:
And from his blazoned baldric slung
A mighty silver bugle hung,
And as he rode his armour rung,
    Beside remote Shalott.

All in the blue unclouded weather
Thick-jeweled shone the saddle-leather,
The helmet and the helmet-feather
Burned like one burning flame together,
    As he rode down to Camelot;
As often through the purple night,
Below the starry clusters bright,
Some bearded meteor, trailing light,
    Moves over still Shalott.

His broad clear brow in sunlight glowed;
On burnished hooves his war-horse trode;
From underneath his helmet flowed
His coal-black curls as on he rode,
    As he rode down to Camelot.
From the bank and from the river
He flashed into the crystal mirror,
"Tirra lirra," by the river
    Sang Sir Lancelot.

She left the web, she left the loom,
She made three paces through the room,
She saw the water-lily bloom,
She saw the helmet and the plume,
    She looked down to Camelot.
Out flew the web and floated wide;
The mirror cracked from side to side;
"The curse is come upon me!" cried
    The Lady of Shalott.

PART IV

In the stormy east-wind straining,
The pale yellow woods were waning,
The broad stream in his banks complaining,
Heavily the low sky raining
    Over towered Camelot;
Down she came and found a boat
Beneath a willow left afloat,
And round about the prow she wrote
    The Lady of Shalott.

And down the river's dim expanse—
Like some bold seër in a trance,
Seeing all his own mischance—
With a glassy countenance
    Did she look to Camelot.
And at the closing of the day
She loosed the chain, and down she lay;
The broad stream bore her far away,
    The Lady of Shalott.

Lying, robed in snowy white
That loosely flew to left and right—
The leaves upon her falling light—
Through the noises of the night
    She floated down to Camelot:
And as the boat-head wound along
The willowy hills and fields among,
They heard her singing her last song,
    The Lady of Shalott.

Heard a carol, mournful, holy,
Chanted loudly, chanted lowly,
Till her blood was frozen slowly,
And her eyes were darkened wholly,
    Turned to towered Camelot;
For ere she reached upon the tide
The first house by the water-side,
Singing in her song she died,
    The Lady of Shalott.

Under tower and balcony,
By garden-wall and gallery,
A gleaming shape she floated by,
Dead-pale between the houses high,
    Silent into Camelot.
Out upon the wharfs they came,
Knight and burgher, lord and dame,
And round the prow they read her name,
    The Lady of Shalott.

Who is this? and what is here?
And in the lighted palace near
Died the sound of royal cheer;
And they crossed themselves for fear,
    All the knights at Camelot:
But Lancelot mused a little space;
He said, "She has a lovely face;
God in His mercy lend her grace,
    The Lady of Shalott."

The Lotos-Eaters

"COURAGE!" he said, and pointed toward the land,
    This mounting wave will roll us shoreward soon."
In the afternoon they came unto a land
In which it seemèd always afternoon.
All round the coast the languid air did swoon,
Breathing like one that hath a weary dream.
Full-faced above the valley stood the moon;
And, like a downward smoke, the slender stream
Along the cliff to fall and pause and fall did seem.

A land of streams! some, like a downward smoke,
Slow-dropping veils of thinnest lawn, did go;
And some through wavering lights and shadows broke,
Rolling a slumberous sheet of foam below.
They saw the gleaming river seaward flow
From the inner land: far off, three mountain-tops,
Three silent pinnacles of agèd snow,
Stood sunset-flushed; and, dewed with showery drops,
Up-clomb the shadowy pine above the woven copse.

The charmèd sunset lingered low adown
In the red West: through mountain clefts the dale
Was seen far inland, and the yellow down
Bordered with palm, and many a winding vale
And meadow, set with slender galingale;
A land where all things always seemed the same!
And round about the keel with faces pale,

Dark faces pale against that rosy flame,
The mild-eyed melancholy Lotos-eaters came.

Branches they bore of that enchanted stem,
Laden with flower and fruit, whereof they gave
To each, but whoso did receive of them
And taste, to him the gushing of the wave
Far, far away did seem to mourn and rave
On alien shores; and if his fellow spake,
His voice was thin, as voices from the grave;
And deep-asleep he seemed, yet all awake,
And music in his ears his beating heart did make.

They sat them down upon the yellow sand,
Between the sun and moon upon the shore;
And sweet it was to dream of Father-land,
Of child, and wife, and slave; but evermore
Most weary seemed the sea, weary the oar,
Weary the wandering fields of barren foam.
Then some one said, "We will return no more;"
And all at once they sang, "Our island home
Is far beyond the wave; we will no longer roam."

Song of the Lotos-Eaters

THERE is sweet music here that softer falls
      Than petals from blown roses on the grass,
Or night-dews on still waters between walls
Of shadowy granite, in a gleaming pass;
Music that gentlier on the spirit lies,
Than tired eyelids upon tired eyes;
Music that brings sweet sleep down from the blissful skies.
Here are cool mosses deep,
And thro' the moss the ivies creep,
And in the stream the long-leaved flowers weep,
And from the craggy ledge the poppy hangs in sleep.

Why are we weigh'd upon with heaviness,
And utterly consumed with sharp distress,
While all things else have rest from weariness?
All things have rest: why should we toil alone,
We only toil, who are the first of things,
And make perpetual moan,
Still from one sorrow to another thrown:
Nor ever fold our wings,
And cease from wanderings,
Nor steep our brows in slumber's holy balm;
Nor harken what the inner spirit sings,
"There is no joy but calm!"—
Why should we only toil, the roof and crown of things?

Lo! in the middle of the wood,
The folded leaf is woo'd from out the bud
With winds upon the branch, and there
Grows green and broad, and takes no care,
Sun-steep'd at noon, and in the moon
Nightly dew-fed; and turning yellow
Falls, and floats adown the air.
Lo! sweeten'd with the summer light,
The full-juiced apple, waxing over-mellow,
Drops in a silent autumn night.
All its allotted length of days,
The flower ripens in its place,
Ripens and fades, and falls, and hath no toil,
Fast-rooted in the fruitful soil.

Hateful is the dark-blue sky,
Vaulted o'er the dark-blue sea.
Death is the end of life; ah, why
Should life all labour be?
Let us alone. Time driveth onward fast,
And in a little while our lips are dumb.
Let us alone. What is it that will last?
All things are taken from us, and become
Portions and parcels of the dreadful Past.
Let us alone. What pleasure can we have
To war with evil? Is there any peace
In ever climbing up the climbing wave?
All things have rest, and ripen toward the grave
In silence; ripen, fall and cease:
Give us long rest or death, dark death, or dreamful ease.

How sweet it wert, hearing the downward stream,
With half-shut eyes ever to seem
Falling asleep in a half-dream!
To dream and dream, like yonder amber light,
Which will not leave the myrrh-bush on the height;
To hear each other's whisper'd speech;
Eating the Lotos day by day,
To watch the crisping ripples on the beach,
And tender curving lines of creamy spray;
To lend our hearts and spirits wholly
To the influence of mild-minded melancholy;
To muse and brood and live again in memory,
With those old faces of our infancy
Heap'd over with a mound of grass,
Two handfuls of white dust, shut in an urn of brass!

Dear is the memory of our wedded lives,
And dear the last embraces of our wives
And their warm tears: but all hath suffer'd change;

For surely now our household hearths are cold:
Our sons inherit us: our looks are strange:
And we should come like ghosts to trouble joy.
Or else the island princes over-bold
Have eat our substance, and the minstrel sings
Before them of the ten years' war in Troy,
And our great deeds, as half-forgotten things.
Is there confusion in the little isle?
Let what is broken so remain.
The Gods are hard to reconcile:
'Tis hard to settle order once again.
There is confusion worse than death,
Trouble on trouble, pain on pain,
Long labour unto agèd breath,
Sore task to hearts worn out with many wars
And eyes grow dim with gazing on the pilot-stars.
But, propt on beds of amaranth and moly,
How sweet (while warm airs lull us, blowing lowly)
With half-dropt eyelids still,
Beneath a heaven dark and holy,
To watch the long bright river drawing slowly
His waters from the purple hill—
To hear the dewy echoes calling
From cave to cave thro' the thick-twinèd vine—
To watch the emerald-colour'd water falling
Thro' many a wov'n acanthus-wreath divine!
Only to hear and see the far-off sparkling brine,
Only to hear were sweet, stretch'd out beneath the pine.

The Lotos blooms below the barren peak:
The Lotos blows by every winding creek:
All day the wind breathes low with mellower tone:
Thro' every hollow cave and alley lone
Round and round the spicy downs the yellow Lotos-dust is
    blown.
We have had enough of action, and of motion we,
Roll'd to starboard, roll'd to larboard, when the surge was
    seething free,
Where the wallowing monster spouted his foam-fountains in
    the sea.
Let us swear an oath, and keep it with an equal mind,
In the hollow Lotos-land to live and lie reclined
On the hills like Gods together, careless of mankind.
For they lie beside their nectar, and the bolts are hurl'd
Far below them in the valleys, and the clouds are lightly
    curl'd
Round their golden houses, girdled with the gleaming world:
Where they smile in secret, looking over wasted lands,
Blight and famine, plague and earthquake, roaring deeps and
    fiery sands,

Clanging fights, and flaming towns, and sinking ships, and
    praying hands.
But they smile, they find a music centred in a doleful song
Steaming up, a lamentation and an ancient tale of wrong,
Like a tale of little meaning tho' the words are strong;
Chanted from an ill-used race of men that cleave the soil,
Sow the seed, and reap the harvest with enduring toil,
Storing yearly little dues of wheat, and wine and oil;
Till they perish and they suffer—some, 'tis whisper'd—down
    in hell
Suffer endless anguish, others in Elysian valleys dwell,
Resting weary limbs at last on beds of asphodel.
Surely, surely, slumber is more sweet than toil, the shore
Than labour in the deep mid-ocean, wind and wave and oar;
O rest ye, brother mariners, we will not wander more.

Song

I

A spirit haunts the year's last hours
    Dwelling amid these yellowing bowers:
        To himself he talks;
For at eventide, listening earnestly,
At his work you may hear him sob and sigh
        In the walks;
    Earthward he boweth the heavy stalks
Of the mouldering flowers:
    Heavily hangs the broad sunflower
        Over its grave i' the earth so chilly;
    Heavily hangs the hollyhock,
        Heavily hangs the tigerlily.

II

The air is damp, and hushed, and close,
As a sick man's room when he taketh repose
        An hour before death;
My very heart faints and my whole soul grieves
At the moist rich smell of the rotting leaves,
        And the breath
        Of the fading edges of box beneath,
And the year's last rose.
    Heavily hangs the broad sunflower
        Over its grave i' the earth so chilly;
    Heavily hangs the hollyhock,
        Heavily hangs the tigerlily.

From "In Memoriam"

STRONG Son of God, immortal Love,
  Whom we, that have not seen thy face,
 By faith, and faith alone, embrace,
Believing where we cannot prove;

Thine are these orbs of light and shade;
  Thou madest Life in man and brute;
  Thou madest Death, and lo, thy foot
Is on the skull which thou hast made.

Thou wilt not leave us in the dust:
  Thou madest man, he knows not why,
  He thinks he was not made to die;
And thou hast made him: thou art just.

Thou seemest human and divine,
  The highest, holiest manhood, thou.
  Our wills are ours, we know not how;
Our wills are ours, to make them thine.

Our little systems have their day;
  They have their day and cease to be;
  They are but broken lights of thee,
And thou, O Lord, art more than they.

We have but faith: we cannot know,
  For knowledge is of things we see;
  And yet we trust it comes of thee,
A beam in darkness: let it grow.

Let knowledge grow from more to more,
  But more of reverence in us dwell;
  That mind and soul, according well,
May make one music as before,

But vaster. We are fools and slight;
  We mock thee when we do not fear:
  But help thy foolish ones to bear;
Help thy vain worlds to bear thy light.

Forgive what seem'd my sin in me,
  What seem'd my worth since I began;
  For merit lives from man to man,
And not from man, O Lord, to thee.

Forgive my grief for one removed,
  Thy creature, whom I found so fair.

I trust he lives in thee, and there
I find him worthier to be loved.

Forgive these wild and wandering cries,
  Confusions of a wasted youth;
  Forgive them where they fail in truth,
And in thy wisdom make me wise.

I

I held it truth, with him who sings
  To one clear harp in divers tones,
  That men may rise on stepping stones
Of their dead selves to higher things.

But who shall so forecast the years,
  And find in loss a gain to match?
  Or reach a hand thro' time to catch
The far-off interest of tears?

Let Love clasp Grief lest both be drown'd,
  Let darkness keep her raven gloss.
  Ah, sweeter to be drunk with loss,
To dance with Death, to beat the ground,

Than that the victor Hours should scorn
  The long result of love, and boast,
  "Behold the man that loved and lost,
But all he was is overworn."

IX

Fair ship, that from the Italian shore
  Sailest the placid ocean-plains
  With my lost Arthur's loved remains,
Spread thy full wings, and waft him o'er.

So draw him home to those that mourn
  In vain; a favorable speed
  Ruffle thy mirror'd mast, and lead
Thro' prosperous floods his holy urn.

All night no ruder air perplex
  Thy sliding keel, till Phospor, bright
  As our pure love, thro' early light
Shall glimmer on the dewy decks.

Sphere all your lights around, above;
  Sleep, gentle heavens, before the prow;
  Sleep, gentle winds, as he sleeps now,
My friend, the brother of my love;

My Arthur, whom I shall not see
  Till all my widow'd race be run;
  Dear as the mother to the son,
More than my brothers are to me.

XXVII

I envy not in any moods
  The captive void of noble rage,
  The linnet born within the cage,
That never knew the summer woods;

I envy not the beast that takes
  His license in the field of time,
  Unfetter'd by the sense of crime,
To whom a conscience never wakes;

Nor, what may count itself as blest,
  The heart that never plighted troth
  But stagnates in the weeds of sloth;
Nor any want-begotten rest.

I hold it true, whate'er befall;
  I feel it, when I sorrow most;
  'Tis better to have loved and lost
Than never to have loved at all.

LIV

O, yet we trust that somehow good
  Will be the final goal of ill,
  To pangs of nature, sins of will,
Defects of doubt, and taints of blood;

That nothing walks with aimless feet;
  That not one life shall be destroyed,
  Or cast as rubbish to the void,
When God hath made the pile complete;

That not a worm is cloven in vain;
  That not a moth with vain desire
  Is shrivell'd in a fruitless fire,
Or but subserves another's gain.

Behold, we know not anything;
  I can but trust that good shall fall
  At last—far off—at last, to all,
And every winter change to spring.

So runs my dream; but what am I?
  An infant crying in the night;
  An infant crying for the light,
And with no language but a cry.

XCVI

You say, but with no touch of scorn,
  Sweet-hearted, you, whose light-blue eyes
  Are tender over drowning flies,
You tell me, doubt is Devil-born.

I know not: one indeed I knew
  In many a subtle question versed,
  Who touch'd a jarring lyre at first,
But ever strove to make it true;

Perplext in faith, but pure in deeds,
  At last he beat his music out.
  There lives more faith in honest doubt,
Believe me, than in half the creeds.

He fought his doubts and gathered strength,
  He would not make his judgment blind,
  He faced the spectres of the mind
And laid them; thus he came at length

To find a stronger faith his own,
  And Power was with him in the night,
  Which makes the darkness and the light,
And dwells not in the light alone,

But in the darkness and the cloud,
  As over Sinai's peaks of old,
  While Israel made their gods of gold,
Altho' the trumpet blew so loud.

CVI

Ring out, wild bells, to the wild sky,
  The flying cloud, the frosty light:
  The year is dying in the night;
Ring out, wild bells, and let him die.

Ring out the old, ring in the new,
  Ring, happy bells, across the snow:
  The year is going, let him go;
Ring out the false, ring in the true.

Ring out the grief that saps the mind,
  For those that here we see no more;
  Ring out the feud of rich and poor,
Ring in redress to all mankind.

Ring out a slowly dying cause,
  And ancient forms of party strife;
  Ring in the nobler modes of life,
With sweeter manners, purer laws.

Ring out the want, the care, the sin,
  The faithless coldness of the times;
  Ring out, ring out, my mournful rhymes,
But ring the fuller minstrel in.

Ring out false pride in place and blood,
  The civic slander and the spite;
  Ring in the love of truth and right;
Ring in the common love of good.

Ring out old shapes of foul disease;
  Ring out the narrowing lust of gold;
  Ring out the thousand wars of old,
Ring in the thousand years of peace.

Ring in the valiant man and free,
  The larger heart, the kindlier hand;
  Ring out the darkness of the land,
Ring in the Christ that is to be.

    .   .   .

Again the feast, the speech, the glee,
  The shade of passing thought, the wealth
  Of words and wit, the double health,
The crowning cup, the three-times-three,

And last the dance;—till I retire.
  Dumb is that tower which spake so loud,
  And high in heaven the streaming cloud,
And on the downs a rising fire:

And rise, O moon, from yonder down,
  Till over down and over dale
  All night the shining vapor sail
And pass the silent-lighted town,

The white-faced walls, the glancing rills,
  And catch at every mountain head,
  And o'er the friths that branch and spread
Their sleeping silver thro' the hills;

And touch with shade the bridal doors,
  With tender gloom the roof, the wall,
  And breaking let the splendor fall
To spangle all the happy shores

By which they rest, and ocean sounds,
  And, star and system rolling past,
  A soul shall draw from out the vast
And strike his being into bounds,

And movèd thro' life of lower phase,
  Result in man, be born and think,
  And act and love, a closer link
Betwixt us and the crowing race

Of those that, eye to eye, shall look
  On knowledge; under whose command
  Is Earth and Earth's, and in their hand
Is Nature like an open book;

No longer half-akin to brute,
  For all we thought and loved and did,
  And hoped and suffer'd, is but seed
Of what in them is flower and fruit;

Whereof the man that with me trod
  This planet was a nobler type
  Appearing ere the times were ripe,
That friend of mind who lives in God,

That God, which ever lives and loves,
  One God, one law, one element,
  And one far-off divine event,
To which the whole creation moves.

"Come into the Garden, Maud"

COME into the garden, Maud,
  For the black bat, night, has flown,
Come into the garden, Maud,
  I am here at the gate alone;
And the woodbine spices are wafted abroad,
  And the musk of the rose is blown.

For a breeze of morning moves,
  And the planet of Love is on high,
Beginning to faint in the light that she loves
  On a bed of daffodil sky,
To faint in the light of the sun she loves,
  To faint in his light, and to die.

All night have the roses heard
   The flute, violin, bassoon;
All night has the casement jessamine stirred
   To the dancers dancing in tune;
Till a silence fell with the waking bird,
   And a hush with the setting moon.

I said to the lily, "There is but one
   With whom she has heart to be gay.
When will the dancers leave her alone?
   She is weary of dance and play."
Now half to the setting moon are gone,
   And half to the rising day;
Low on the sand and loud on the stone
   The last wheel echoes away.

I said to the rose, "The brief night goes
   In babble and revel and wine.
O young lord-lover, what sighs are those,
   For one that will never be thine?
But mine, but mine," so I sware to the rose,
   "For ever and ever, mine."

And the soul of the rose went into my blood,
   As the music clashed in the hall:
And long by the garden lake I stood,
   For I heard your rivulet fall
From the lake to the meadow and on to the wood,
   Our wood, that is dearer than all;

From the meadow your walks have left so sweet
   That whenever a March-wind sighs
He sets the jewel-print of your feet
   In violets blue as your eyes,
To the woody hollows in which we meet
   And the valleys of Paradise.

The slender acacia would not shake
   One long milk-bloom on the tree;
The white lake-blossom fell into the lake
   As the pimpernel dozed on the lea;
But the rose was awake all night for your sake,
   Knowing your promise to me;
The lilies and roses were all awake,
   They sighed for the dawn and thee.

Queen rose of the rosebud garden of girls,
   Come hither the dances are done,
In gloss of satin and glimmer of pearls,
   Queen lily and rose in one;
Shine out, little head, sunning over with curls,
   To the flowers, and be their sun.

There has fallen a splendid tear
   From the passion-flower at the gate.
She is coming, my dove, my dear;
   She is coming, my life, my fate;
The red rose cries, "She is near, she is near";
   And the white rose weeps, "She is late";
The larkspur listens, "I hear, I hear";
   And the lily whispers, "I wait."

She is coming, my own, my sweet;
   Were it ever so airy a tread,
My heart would hear her and beat,
   Were it earth in an earthy bed;
My dust would hear her and beat,
   Had I lain for a century dead;
Would start and tremble under her feet,
   And blossom in purple and red.

"O That 'Twere Possible"

O THAT 'twere possible
   After long grief and pain
To find the arms of my true love
   Round me once again!

When I was wont to meet her
   In the silent woody places
Of the land that gave me birth,
   We stood tranced in long embraces
Mixed with kisses sweeter, sweeter
   Than anything on earth.

A shadow flits before me,
   Not thou, but like to thee.
Ah, Christ, that it were possible
   For one short hour to see
The souls we loved, that they might tell us
   What and where they be!

From "The Princess"

I

NOW sleeps the crimson petal, now the white;
   Nor waves the cypress in the palace walk;
Nor winks the gold fin in the porphyry font:
The firefly wakens: waken thou with me.

Now droops the milkwhite peacock like a ghost,
And like a ghost she glimmers on to me.

Now lies the Earth all Danaë to the stars,
And all thy heart lies open unto me.

Now slides the silent meteor on, and leaves
A shining furrow, as thy thoughts in me.

Now folds the lily all her sweetness up,
And slips into the bosom of the lake:
So fold thyself, my dearest, thou, and slip
Into my bosom and be lost in me.

II

Come down, O maid, from yonder mountain height:
What pleasure lives in height (the shepherd sang),
In height and cold, the splendour of the hills?
But cease to move so near the Heavens, and cease
To glide a sunbeam by the blasted Pine,
To sit a star upon the sparkling spire;
And come, for Love is of the valley, come,
For Love is of the valley, come thou down
And find him: by the happy threshold, he,
Or hand in hand with Plenty in the maize,
Or red with spirted purple of the vats,
Or foxlike in the vine; nor cares to walk
With Death and Morning on the silver horns,
Nor wilt thou snare him in the white ravine,
Nor find him dropt upon the firths of ice,
That huddling slant in furrow-cloven falls
To roll the torrent out of dusky doors:
But follow; let the torrent dance thee down
To find him in the valley; let the wild
Lean-headed Eagles yelp alone, and leave
The monstrous ledges there to slope, and spill
Their thousand wreaths of dangling water-smoke,
That like a broken purpose waste in air:
So waste not thou; but come; for all the vales
Await thee; azure pillars of the hearth
Arise to thee; the children call, and I
Thy shepherd pipe, and sweet is every sound,
Sweeter thy voice, but every sound is sweet;
Myriads of rivulets hurrying thro' the lawn,
The moan of doves in immemorial elms,
And murmuring of innumerable bees.

SALEM COLLEGE
LIBRARY
Winston-Salem, N. C.

The Splendour Falls on Castle Walls

THE splendour falls on castle walls
        And snowy summits old in story:
The long light shakes across the lakes,
        And the wild cataract leaps in glory.
Blow, bugle, blow, set the wild echoes flying,
Blow, bugle; answer, echoes, dying, dying, dying.

O hark, O hear! how thin and clear,
        And thinner, clearer, farther going!
O sweet and far from cliff and scar
        The horns of Elfland faintly blowing!
Blow, let us hear the purple glens replying:
Blow, bugle; answer, echoes, dying, dying, dying.

O love, they die in yon rich sky,
        They faint on hill or field or river:
Our echoes roll from soul to soul,
        And grow for ever and for ever.
Blow, bugle, blow, set the wild echoes flying,
And answer, echoes, answer, dying, dying, dying.

Tears, Idle Tears

TEARS, idle tears, I know not what they mean,
        Tears from the depth of some divine despair
Rise in the heart, and gather to the eyes,
In looking on the happy Autumn-fields,
And thinking of the days that are no more.

Fresh as the first beam glittering on a sail,
That brings our friends up from the underworld,
Sad as the last which reddens over one
That sinks with all we love below the verge;
So sad, so fresh, the days that are no more.

Ah, sad and strange as in dark summer dawns
The earliest pipe of half-awaken'd birds
To dying ears, when unto dying eyes
The casement slowly grows a glimmering square;
So sad, so strange, the days that are no more.

Dear as remember'd kisses after death,
And sweet as those by hopeless fancy feign'd
On lips that are for others; deep as love,
Deep as first love, and wild with all regret;
O Death in Life, the days that are no more.

O Swallow, Swallow

O Swallow, Swallow, flying, flying South,
      Fly to her and fall upon her gilded eaves,
And tell her, tell her what I tell to thee.

O tell her, Swallow, that thou knowest each,
That bright and fierce and fickle is the South,
And dark and true and tender is the North.

O Swallow, Swallow, if I could follow, and light
Upon her lattice, I would pipe and trill,
And cheep and twitter twenty million loves.

O were I thou that she might take me in,
And lay me on her bosom, and her heart
Would rock the snowy cradle till I died.

Why lingereth she to clothe her heart with love,
Delaying as the tender ash delays
To clothe herself when all the woods are green?

O tell her, Swallow, that thy brood is flown:
Say to her, I do but wanton in the South,
But in the North long since my nest is made.

O tell her, brief is life but love is long,
And brief the sun of summer in the North,
And brief the moon of beauty in the South.

O Swallow, flying from the golden woods,
Fly to her, and pipe and woo her, and make her mine,
And tell her, tell her, that I follow thee.

Home They Brought Her Warrior Dead

HOME they brought her warrior dead:
      She nor swoon'd, nor utter'd cry:
All her maidens, watching, said,
      "She must weep or she will die."

Then they praised him, soft and low,
      Call'd him worthy to be loved,
Truest friend and noblest foe;
      Yet she neither spoke nor moved.

Stole a maiden from her place,
      Lightly to the warrior stept,
Took the face-cloth from the face;
      Yet she neither moved nor wept.

Rose a nurse of ninety years,
Set his child upon her knee—
Like summer tempest came her tears—
"Sweet my child, I live for thee."

"Break, Break, Break"

BREAK, break, break,
  On thy cold gray stones, O Sea!
And I would that my tongue could utter
  The thoughts that arise in me.

O, well for the fisherman's boy,
  That he shouts with his sister at play!
O, well for the sailor lad,
  That he sings in his boat on the bay!

And the stately ships go on,
  To their haven under the hill;
But O for the touch of a vanished hand,
  And the sound of a voice that is still!

Break, break, break,
  At the foot of thy crags, O Sea!
But the tender grace of a day that is dead
  Will never come back to me.

The Charge of the Light Brigade

[Balaclava, October 25, 1852]

HALF a league, half a league,
  Half a league onward,
All in the valley of Death
  Rode the six hundred.
"Forward, the Light Brigade!
Charge for the guns!" he said:
Into the valley of Death
  Rode the six hundred.

"Forward, the Light Brigade!"
Was there a man dismayed?
Not though the soldier knew
  Some one had blundered:
Theirs not to make reply,
Theirs not to reason why,
Theirs but to do and die:
Into the valley of Death
  Rode the six hundred.

Cannon to right of them,
Cannon to left of them,
Cannon in front of them
    Volleyed and thundered;
Stormed at with shot and shell,
Boldly they rode and well,
Into the jaws of Death,
Into the mouth of Hell
    Rode the six hundred.

Flashed all their sabres bare,
Flashed as they turned in air
Sabring the gunners there,
Charging an army, while
    All the world wondered:
Plunged in the battery-smoke
Right through the line they broke;
Cossack and Russian
Reeled from the sabre-stroke,
    Shattered and sundered.
Then they rode back, but not,
    Not the six hundred.

Cannon to right of them,
Cannon to left of them,
Cannon behind them
    Volleyed and thundered;
Stormed at with shot and shell,
While horse and hero fell,
They that had fought so well
Came through the jaws of Death,
Back from the mouth of Hell,
All that was left of them,
    Left of six hundred.

When can their glory fade?
O the wild charge they made!
    All the world wondered.
Honor the charge they made!
Honor the Light Brigade,
    Noble six hundred!

Ulysses

IT little profits that an idle king,
    By this still hearth, among these barren crags,
Matched with an agèd wife, I mete and dole
Unequal laws unto a savage race,
That hoard, and sleep, and feed, and know not me.
I cannot rest from travel: I will drink
Life to the lees. All times I have enjoyed

Greatly, have suffered greatly, both with those
That loved me, and alone; on shore, and when
Through scudding drifts the rainy Hyades
Vexed the dim sea. I am become a name;
For always roaming with a hungry heart
Much have I seen and known,—cities of men
And manners, climates, councils, governments,
Myself not least, but honored of them all;
And drunk delight of battle with my peers,
Far on the ringing plains of windy Troy.
I am part of all that I have met;
Yet all experience is an arch wherethrough
Gleams that untravelled world, whose margin fades
For ever and for ever when I move.
How dull it is to pause, to make an end,
To rust unburnished, not to shine in use!
As though to breathe were life. Life piled on life
Were all too little, and of one to me
Little remains: but every hour is saved
From that eternal silence, something more,
A bringer of new things; and vile it were
For some three suns to store and hoard myself,
And this gray spirit yearning in desire
To follow knowledge like a sinking star,
Beyond the utmost bound of human thought.
   This is my son, mine own Telemachus,
To whom I leave the sceptre and the isle—
Well-loved of me, discerning to fulfil
This labor, by slow prudence to make mild
A rugged people, and through soft degrees
Subdue them to the useful and the good.
Most blameless is he, centred in the sphere
Of common duties, decent not to fail
In offices of tenderness, and pay
Meet adoration to my household gods,
When I am gone. He works his work, I mine.
   There lies the port; the vessel puffs her sail:
There gloom the dark, broad seas. My mariners,
Souls that have toiled, and wrought, and thought with me—
That ever with a frolic welcome took
The thunder and the sunshine, and opposed
Free hearts, free foreheads—you and I are old;
Old age hath yet his honour and his toil;
Death closes all: but something ere the end,
Some work of noble note, may yet be done,
Not unbecoming men that strove with gods.
The lights begin to twinkle from the rocks:
The long day wanes: the slow moon climbs: the deep
Moans round with many voices. Come, my friends,

'Tis not too late to seek a newer world.
Push off, and sitting well in order smite
The sounding furrows; for my purpose holds
To sail beyond the sunset, and the baths
Of all the western stars, until I die.
It may be that the gulfs will wash us down:
It may be we shall touch the Happy Isles,
And see the great Achilles, whom we knew.
Though much is taken, much abides; and though
We are not now that strength which in old days
Moved earth and heaven; that which we are, we are;—
One equal temper of heroic hearts,
Made weak by time and fate, but strong in will
To strive, to seek, to find, and not to yield.

Crossing the Bar

SUNSET and evening star,
    And one clear call for me!
And may there be no moaning of the bar
    When I put out to sea,

But such a tide as moving seems asleep,
    Too full for sound and foam,
When that which drew from out the boundless
        deep
    Turns again home.

Twilight and evening bell,
    And after that the dark!
And may there be no sadness of farewell,
    When I embark;

For tho' from out our bourne of Time and place
    The flood may bear me far,
I hope to see my Pilot face to face
    When I have crost the bar.

The Silent Voices

WHEN the dumb Hour, clothed in black,
    Brings the Dreams about my bed,
Call me not so often back,
Silent Voices of the dead,
Toward the lowland ways behind me,
And the sunlight that is gone!
Call me rather, silent voices,
Forward to the starry track
Glimmering up the heights beyond me
On, and always on!

WILLIAM   MAKEPEACE   THACKERAY
(1811-1863)

The Age of Wisdom

GO, pretty page, with the dimpled chin,
   That never has known the barber's shear,
All your wish is woman to win,
This is the way that boys begin,—
   Wait till you come to Forty Year.

Curly gold locks cover foolish brains,
   Billing and cooing is all your cheer;
Sighing, and singing of midnight strains,
Under Bonnybell's window-panes,—
   Wait till you come to Forty Year.

Forty times over let Michaelmas pass,
   Grizzling hair the brain does clear—
Then you know a boy is an ass,
Then you know the worth of a lass,
   Once you have come to Forty Year.

Pledge me round; I bid ye declare,
   All good fellows whose beards are gray,
Did not the fairest of the fair
Common grow and wearisome ere
   Ever a month was passed away?

The reddest lips that ever have kissed,
   The brightest eyes that ever have shone,
May pray and whisper, and we not list,
Or look away and never be missed,
   Ere yet ever a month is gone.

Gillian's dead, God rest her bier,
   How I loved her twenty years syne!
Marian's married, but I sit here,
Alone and merry at Forty Year,
   Dipping my nose in the Gascon wine.

The Sorrows of Werther

WERTHER had a love for Charlotte
      Such as words could never utter;
Would you know how first he met her?
She was cutting bread-and-butter.

Charlotte was a married lady,
    And a moral man was Werther,
And, for all the wealth of Indies,
    Would do nothing for to hurt her.

So he sighed and pined and ogled,
    And his passion boiled and bubbled,
Till he blew his silly brains out,
    And no more was by it troubled.

Charlotte, having seen his body
    Borne before her on a shutter,
Like a well-conducted person,
    Went on cutting Bread-and-Butter.

The End of the Play

THE play is done; the curtain drops,
    Slow falling, to the prompter's bell:
A moment yet the actor stops
And looks around to say farewell.
It is an irksome word and task,
And when he's laughed and said his say,
He shows as he removes the mask,
A face that's anything but gay.

One word, ere yet the evening ends,
Let's close it with a parting rhyme,
And pledge a hand to all young friends,
As fits the merry Christmas-time.
On Life's wide scene you, too, have parts,
That Fate ere long shall bid you play;
Good-night! with honest, gentle hearts
A kindly greeting go alway.
        *   *   *   *   *

Come wealth or want, come good or ill,
Let young and old accept their part,
And bow before the Awful Will,
And bear it with an honest heart,
Who misses, or who wins the prize.
Go, lose or conquer if you can;
But if you fail or if you rise,
Be each, pray God, a gentleman.

A gentleman or old or young!
(Bear kindly with my humble lays)
The sacred chorus first was sung
Upon the first of Christmas days.
The shepherds heard it overhead—
The joyful angels raised it then:
Glory to Heaven on high, it said,
And peace on earth to gentle men.

My song, save this, is little worth;
I lay the weary pen aside,
And wish you health and love and mirth,
As fits the solemn Christmas-tide.
As fits the holy Christmas birth,
Be this, good friends, our carol still—
Be peace on earth, be peace on earth,
To men of gentle will.

EDWARD LEAR (1812-1888)

The Owl and the Pussy-Cat

THE Owl and the Pussy-cat went to sea
    In a beautiful pea-green boat:
They took some honey, and plenty of money
    Wrapped up in a five-pound note.
The Owl looked up to the stars above,
    And sang to a small guitar,
"O lovely Pussy, O Pussy, my love,
    What a beautiful Pussy you are,
            You are,
            You are!
    What a beautiful Pussy you are!"

Pussy said to the Owl, "You elegant fowl,
    How charmingly sweet you sing!
Oh! let us be married; too long we have tarried:
    But what shall we do for a ring?"
They sailed away, for a year and a day,
    To the land where the bong-tree grows;
And there in a wood a Piggy-wig stood,
    With a ring at the end of his nose,
            His nose,
            His nose,
    With a ring at the end of his nose.

"Dear Pig, are you willing to sell for one shilling
    Your ring?"   Said the Piggy, "I will."
So they took it away, and were married next day
    By the Turkey who lives on the hill.
They dined on mince and slices of quince,
    Which they ate with a runcible spoon;
And hand in hand, on the edge of the sand,
    They danced by the light of the moon,
            The moon,
            The moon,
    They danced by the light of the moon.

ROBERT BROWNING (1812-1889)

From "Cavalier Tunes"

KENTISH Sir Byng stood for his King,
   Bidding the crop-headed Parliament swing:
And, pressing a troop unable to stoop,
And see the rogues flourish and honest folk droop,
Marched them along, fifty-score strong,
Great-hearted gentlemen, singing this song.

God for King Charles! Pym and such carles
To the Devil that prompts 'em their treasonous parles!
Cavaliers, up! Lips from the cup,
Hands from the pasty, nor bite take nor sup
Till you're—

   Chorus.—Marching along, fifty-score strong,
      Great-hearted gentlemen, singing this song.

Hampton to hell, and his obsequies' knell.
Serve Hazelrig, Fiennes, and young Harry as well!
England, good cheer! Rupert is near!
Kentish and loyalists, keep we not here.

   Chorus.—Marching along, fifty-score strong,
      Great-hearted gentlemen, singing this song?

Then, God for King Charles! Pym and his snarls
To the Devil that pricks on such pestilent carles!
Hold by the right, you double your might;
So, onward to Nottingham, fresh from the fight.

   Chorus.—Marching along, fifty-score strong,
      Great-hearted gentlemen, singing this song!

Home Thoughts, from Abroad

I

OH, to be in England
   Now that April's there,
And whoever wakes in England
Sees, some morning, unaware,
That the lowest boughs and the brushwood sheaf
Round the elm-tree bole are in tiny leaf,
While the chaffinch sings on the orchard bough
In England—now!

II

And after April, when May follows,
And the whitethroat builds, and all the swallows!
Hark, where my blossomed pear-tree in the hedge
Leans to the field and scatters on the clover
   Blossoms and dewdrops—at the bent spray's edge—
That's the wise thrush; he sings each song twice over,
Lest you should think he never could recapture
The first fine careless rapture!

Song from "Pippa Passes"

THE year's at the spring,
   And day's at the morn;
Morning's at seven;
The hill-side's dew-pearled;
The lark's on the wing;
The snail's on the thorn;
God's in His Heaven—
All's right with the world!

Evelyn Hope

I

BEAUTIFUL Evelyn Hope is dead!
   Sit and watch by her side an hour.
That is her book-shelf, this her bed;
   She plucked that piece of geranium-flower,
Beginning to die too, in the glass;
   Little has yet been changed, I think:
The shutters are shut, no light may pass
   Save two long rays through the hinge's chink.

II

Sixteen years old when she died!
   Perhaps she had scarcely heard my name;
It was not her time to love; beside,
   Her life had many a hope and aim,
Duties enough and little cares,
   And now was quiet, now astir,
Till God's hand beckoned unawares,—
   And the sweet white brow is all of her.

III

Is it too late then, Evelyn Hope?
  What, your soul was pure and true,
The good stars met in your horoscope,
  Made you of spirit, fire and dew—
And, just because I was thrice as old
  And our paths in the world diverged so wide,
Each was nought to each, must I be told?
  We were fellow mortals, nought beside?

IV

No, indeed! for God above
  Is great to grant, as mighty to make,
And creates the love to reward the love:
  I claim you still, for my own love's sake!
Delayed it may be for more lives yet,
  Through worlds I shall traverse, not a few:
Much is to learn, much to forget
  Ere the time be come for taking you.

V

But the time will come,—at last it will,
  When, Evelyn Hope, what meant, I shall say,
In the lower earth, in the years long still,
  That body and soul so pure and gay?
Why your hair was amber, I shall divine,
  And your mouth of your own geranium's red—
And what you would do with me, in fine,
  In the new life come in the old one's stead.

VI

I have lived, I shall say, so much since then,
  Given up myself so many times,
Gained me the gains of various men,
  Ransacked the ages, spoiled the climes;
Yet one thing, one, in my soul's full scope,
  Either I missed or itself missed me:
And I want and find you, Evelyn Hope!
  What is the issue? let us see!

VII

I loved you, Evelyn, all the while.
  My heart seemed full as it could hold?
There was place and to spare for the frank young smile,
  And the red young mouth, and the hair's young gold.
So hush,—I will give you this leaf to keep:
  See, I shut it inside the sweet cold hand!
There, that is our secret: go to sleep!
  You will wake, and remember, and understand.

Porphyria's Lover

THE rain set early in to-night,
  The sullen wind was soon awake,
It tore the elm-tops down for spite,
  And did its worst to vex the lake:
  I listened with heart fit to break,
When glided in Porphyria; straight
  She shut the cold out and the storm,
And kneeled and made the cheerless grate
  Blaze up, and all the cottage warm;
  Which done, she rose, and from her form
Withdrew the dripping cloak and shawl,
  And laid her soiled gloves by, untied
Her hat and let the damp hair fall,
  And, last, she sat down by my side
  And called me. When no voice replied,
She put my arm about her waist,
  And made her smooth white shoulder bare,
And all her yellow hair displaced,
  And, stooping, made my cheek lie there,
  And spread, o'er all, her yellow hair,
Murmuring how she loved me—she
  Too weak, for all her heart's endeavour,
To set its struggling passion free
  From pride, and vainer ties dissever,
  And give herself to me for ever.
But passion sometimes would prevail,
  Nor could to-night's gay feast restrain
A sudden thought of one so pale
  For love of her, and all in vain:
  So, she was come through wind and rain.
Be sure I looked up at her eyes
  Happy and proud; at last I knew
Porphyria worshipped me; surprise
  Made my heart swell, and still it grew
  While I debated what to do.
That moment she was mine, mine, fair,
  Perfectly pure and good: I found
A thing to do, and all her hair
  In one long yellow string I wound
  Three times her little throat around,
And strangled her. No pain felt she;
  I am quite sure she felt no pain.
As a shut bud that holds a bee,
  I warily oped her lids: again
  Laughed the blue eyes without a stain.
And I untightened next the tress
  About her neck; her cheek once more

Blushed bright beneath my burning kiss:
   I propped her head up as before,
   Only, this time my shoulder bore
Her head, which droops upon it still:
   The smiling rosy little head,
So glad it has its utmost will,
   That all it scorned at once is fled,
   And I, its love, am gained instead!
Porphyria's love: she guessed not how
   Her darling one wish would be heard.
And thus we sit together now,
   And all night long we have not stirred,
   And yet God has not said a word!

A Toccata of Galuppi's

OH Galuppi, Baldassaro, this is very sad to find!
   I can hardly misconceive you; it would prove me deaf
      and blind;
But although I take your meaning, 'tis with such a heavy
   mind!

Here you come with your old music, and here's all the good
   it brings.
What, they lived once thus at Venice where the merchants
   were the kings,
Where St. Mark's is, where the Doges used to wed the sea
   with rings?

Ay, because the sea's the street there; and 'tis arched by
   . . . . what you call
. . . Shylock's bridge with houses on it, where they kept the
   carnival:
I was never out of England—it's as if I saw it all.

Did young people take their pleasure when the sea was warm
   in May?
Balls and masks begun at midnight, burning ever to midday,
When they made up fresh adventures for the morrow, do
   you say?

Was a lady such a lady, cheeks so round and lips so red,—
On her neck the small face buoyant, like a bell-flower on its
   bed,
O'er the breast's superb abundance where a man might base
   his head?

Well, and it was graceful of them—they'd break talk off
    and afford
—She, to bite her mask's black velvet—he, to finger on his
    sword,
While you sat and played Toccatas, stately at the clavichord?

What? Those lesser thirds so plaintive, sixths diminished,
    sigh on sigh,
Told them something? Those suspensions, those solutions
    —"Must we die?"
Those commiserating sevenths—"Life might last! we can but
    try!"

"Were you happy?"—"Yes"—"And are you still as happy?"
    "Yes. And you?"
—"Then, more kisses!"—"Did *I* stop them, when a million
    seemed so few?"
Hark! the dominant's persistence, till it must be answered to!

So, an octave struck the answer. Oh, they praised you, I
    dare say!
"Brave Galuppi! that was music! good alike at grave and
    gay!
I can always leave off talking, when I hear a master play."

Then they left you for their pleasure: till in due time, one by
    one,
Some with lives that came to nothing, some with deeds as
    well undone,
Death came tacitly and took them where they never see
    the sun.

But when I sit down to reason, think to take my stand nor
    swerve,
While I triumph o'er a secret wrung from nature's close
    reserve,
In you come with your cold music, till I creep through every
    nerve.

Yes, you, like a ghostly cricket, creaking where a house was
    burned:
"Dust and ashes, dead and done with, Venice spent what
    Venice earned!
The soul, doubtless, is immortal—where a soul can be dis-
    cerned.

"Yours for instance: you know physics, something of ge-
    ology,

Mathematics are your pastime; souls shall rise in their de-
    gree;
Butterflies may dread extinction,—you'll not die, it cannot be!

"As for Venice and her people, merely born to bloom and
    drop,
Here on earth they bore their fruitage, mirth and folly were
    the crop;
What of soul was left, I wonder, when the kissing had to
    stop?

"Dust and ashes!" So you creak it, and I want the heart
    to scold.
Dear dead women, with such hair, too—what's become of
    all the gold
Used to hang and brush their bosoms? I feel chilly and
    grown old.

A Grammarian's Funeral

Shortly After the Revival of Learning in Europe

LET us begin and carry up this corpse,
        Singing together.
Leave we the common crofts, the vulgar thorpes
        Each in its tether
Sleeping safe on the bosom of the plain,
        Cared-for till cock-crow:
Look out if yonder be not day again
        Rimming the rock-row!
That's the appropriate country; there, man's thought,
        Rarer, intenser,
Self-gathered for an outbreak, as it ought,
        Chafes in the censer.
Leave we the unlettered plain its herd and crop;
        Seek we sepulture
On a tall mountain, citied to the top,
        Crowded with culture!
All the peaks soar, but one the rest excels;
        Clouds overcome it:
No! yonder sparkle is the citadel's
        Circling its summit.
Thither our path lies: wind we up the heights;
        Wait ye the warning?
Our low life was the level's and the night's;
        He's for the morning.
Step to a tune, square chests, erect each head,
        'Ware the beholders!
This is our master, famous, calm and dead,
        Borne on our shoulders.

Sleep, crop and herd! sleep, darkling thorpe and croft,
    Safe from the weather!
He, whom we convoy to his grave aloft,
    Singing together,
He was a man born with thy face and throat,
    Lyric Apollo!
Long he lived nameless: how should Spring take note
    Winter would follow?
Till lo, the little touch, and youth was gone!
    Cramped and diminished,
Moaned he, "New measures, other feet anon!
    My dance is finished?"
No, that's the world's way: (keep the mountain-side,
    Make for the city!)
He knew the signal, and stepped on with pride
    Over men's pity;
Left play for work, and grappled with the world
    Bent on escaping:
"What's in the scroll," quoth he, "thou keepest furled?
    Show me their shaping,
Theirs who most studied man, the bard and sage,—
    Give!"—So, he gowned him,
Straight got by heart that book to its last page:
    Learnèd, we found him.
Yea, but we found him bald too, eyes like lead,
    Accents uncertain:
"Time to taste life," another would have said,
    "Up with the curtain!"
This man said rather, "Actual life comes next?
    Patience a moment!
Grant I have mastered learning's crabbed text,
    Still there's the comment.
Let me know all! Prate not of most or least,
    Painful or easy!
Even to the crumbs I'd fain eat up the feast,
    Ay, nor feel queasy."
Oh, such a life as he resolved to live,
    When he had learned it,
When he had gathered all books had to give!
    Sooner, he spurned it.
Imagine the whole, then execute the parts—
    Fancy the fabric
Quite, ere you build, ere steel strike fire from quartz,
    Ere mortar dab brick!
(Here's the town-gate reached: there's the market-place
    Gaping before us.)
Yea, this in him was the peculiar grace
    (Hearten our chorus!)

That before living he'd learn how to live—
    No end to learning:
Earn the means first—God surely will contrive
    Use for our earning.
Others mistrust and say, "But time escapes:
    Live now or never!"
He said, "What's time? Leave Now for dogs and apes!
    Man has Forever."
Back to his book then: deeper drooped his head:
    Calculus racked him:
Leaden before, his eyes grew dross of lead:
    Tussis attacked him.
"Now, master, take a little rest!"—not he!
    (Caution redoubled,
Step two abreast, the way winds narrowly!)
    Not a whit troubled,
Back to his studies, fresher than at first,
    Fierce as a dragon
He (soul-hydroptic with a sacred thirst)
    Sucked at the flagon.
Oh, if we draw a circle premature,
    Heedless of far gain,
Greedy for quick returns of profit, sure
    Bad is our bargain!
Was it not great? did not he throw on God,
    (He loves the burthen)—
God's task to make the heavenly period
    Perfect the earthen?
Did not he magnify the mind, show clear
    Just what it all meant?
He would not discount life, as fools do here,
    Paid by instalment.
He ventured neck or nothing—heaven's success
    Found, or earth's failure:
"Wilt thou trust death or not?" He answered "Yes!
    Hence with life's pale lure!"
That low man seeks a little thing to do,
    Sees it and does it:
This high man, with a great thing to pursue,
    Dies ere he knows it.
This low man goes on adding one to one,
    His hundred's soon hit:
This high man, aiming at a million,
    Misses an unit.
That, has the world here—should he need the next,
    Let the world mind him!
This, throws himself on God, and unperplexed
    Seeking shall find him.
So, with the throttling hands of death at strife,
    Ground he at grammar;

Still, through the rattle, parts of speech were rife:
    While he could stammer
He settled *Hoti's* business—let it be!—
    Properly based *Oun*—
Gave us the doctrine of the enclitic *De*,
    Dead from the waist down.
Well, here's the platform, here's the proper place:
    Hail to your purlieus,
All ye highfliers of the feathered race,
    Swallows and curlews!
Here's the top-peak; the multitude below
    Live, for they can, there:
This man decided not to Live but Know—
    Bury this man there?
Here—here's his place, where meteors shoot, clouds form,
    Lightnings are loosened,
Stars come and go! Let joy break with the storm,
    Peace let the dew send!
Lofty designs must close in like effects:
    Loftily lying,
Leave him—still loftier than the world suspects,
    Living and dying.

The Last Ride Together

I said—Then, dearest, since 'tis so,
  Since now at length my fate I know,
Since nothing all my love avails,
Since all, my life seem'd meant for, fails,
  Since this was written and needs must be—
My whole heart rises up to bless
Your name in pride and thankfulness!
Take back the hope you gave,—I claim
Only a memory of the same,
—And this beside, if you will not blame;
  Your leave for one more last ride with me.

My mistress bent that brow of hers,
Those deep dark eyes where pride demurs
When pity would be softening through,
Fix'd me a breathing-while or two
  With life or death in the balance: right!
The blood replenish'd me again;
My last thought was at least not vain:
I and my mistress, side by side
Shall be together, breathe and ride,
So, one day more am I deified.
  Who knows but the world may end to-night?

Hush! if you saw some western cloud
All billowy-bosom'd, over-bow'd
By many benedictions—sun's
And moon's and evening-star's at once—
   And so, you, looking and loving best,
Conscious grew, your passion drew
Cloud, sunset, moonrise, star-shine too,
Down on you, near and yet more near,
Till flesh must fade for heaven was here!—
Thus leant she and linger'd—joy and fear!
   Thus lay she a moment on my breast.

Then we began to ride. My soul
Smooth'd itself out, a long-cramp'd scroll
Freshening and fluttering in the wind.
Past hopes already lay behind.
   What need to strive with a life awry?
Had I said that, had I done this,
So might I gain, so might I miss.
Might she have loved me? just as well
She might have hated, who can tell!
Where had I been now if the worst befell?
   And here we are riding, she and I.

Fail I alone, in words and deeds?
Why, all men strive and who succeeds?
We rode; it seem'd my spirit flew,
Saw other regions, cities new,
   As the world rush'd by on either side.
I thought,—All labour, yet no less
Bear up beneath their unsuccess.
Look at the end of work, contrast
The petty done, the undone vast,
This present of theirs with the hopeful past!
   I hoped she would love me; here we ride.

What hand and brain went ever pair'd?
What heart alike conceived and dared?
What act proved all its thought had been?
What will but felt the fleshly screen?
   We ride and I see her bosom heave.
There's many a crown for who can **reach.**
Ten lines, a statesman's life in each!
The flag stuck on a heap of bones,
A soldier's doing! what atones?
They scratch his name on the Abbey-stones.
   My riding is better, by their leave.

What does it all mean, poet? Well,
Your brains beat into rhythm, you tell
What we felt only; you express'd
You hold things beautiful the best,
    And pace them in rhyme so, side by side.
'Tis something, nay 'tis much: but then,
Have you yourself what's best for men?
Are you—poor, sick, old ere your time—
Nearer one whit your own sublime
Than we who never have turn'd a rhyme?
    Sing, riding's a joy! For me, I ride.

And you, great sculptor—so, you gave
A score of years to Art her slave,
And that's your Venus, whence we turn
To yonder girl that fords the burn!
    You acquiesce, and shall I repine?
What, man of music, you grown gray
With notes and nothing else to say,
Is this your sole praise from a friend,
"Greatly his opera's strains intend,
But in music we know how fashions end!"
    I gave my youth: but we ride, in fine.

Who knows what's fit for us? Had fate
Proposed bliss here should sublimate
My being—had I sign'd the bond—
Still one must lead some life beyond,
    Have a bliss to die with, dim-descried.
This foot once planted on the goal,
This glory-garland round my soul,
Could I descry such? Try and test!
I sink back shuddering from the quest.
Earth being so good, would heaven seem best?
    Now, heaven and she are beyond this ride.

And yet—she has not spoke so long!
What if heaven be that, fair and strong
At life's best, with our eyes upturn'd
Whither life's flower is first discern'd,
    We, fix'd so, ever should so abide?
What if we still ride on, we two
With life for ever old yet new,
Changed not in kind but in degree,
The instant made eternity,—
And heaven just prove that I and she
    Ride, ride together, for ever ride?

Memorabilia

(1792-1822)

AH, did you once see Shelley plain,
    And did he stop and speak to you,
And did you speak to him again?
    How strange it seems and new!

But you were living before that,
    And also you were living after;
And the memory I started at—
    My starting moves your laughter!

I crossed a moor, with a name of its own
    And a certain use in the world no doubt,
Yet a hand's-breadth of it shines alone
    'Mid the blank miles round about:

For there I picked up on the heather
    And there I put inside my breast
A molted feather, an eagle-feather!
    Well, I forget the rest.

Parting at Morning

ROUND the cape of a sudden came the sea,
    And the sun looked over the mountain's rim:
And straight was a path of gold for him,
And the need of a world of men for me.

Song

From "In a Gondola"

THE moth's kiss, first!
    Kiss me as if you made believe
You were not sure, this eve,
How my face, your flower, had pursed
Its petals up; so, here and there
You brush it, till I grow aware
Who wants me, and wide ope I burst.

The bee's kiss, now!
Kiss me as if you entered gay
My heart at some noonday,
A bud that dares not disallow
The claim, so all is rendered up,
And passively its shattered cup
Over your head to sleep I bow.

Summum Bonum

ALL the breath and the bloom of the year in the bag of one
    bee:
  All the wonder and wealth of the mine in the heart of one
    gem:
In the core of one pearl all the shade and the shine of the sea:
  Breath and bloom, shade and shine,—wonder, wealth, and
    —how far above them—
       Truth, that's brighter than gem,
       Trust, that's purer than pearl,—
Brightest truth, purest trust in the universe—all were for me
    In the kiss of one girl.

Prospice

DEAR death?—to feel the fog in my throat,
    The mist in my face,
When the snows begin, and the blasts denote
    I am nearing the place,
The power of the night, the press of the storm,
    The post of the foe;
Where he stands, the Arch Fear in a visible form,
    Yet the strong man must go:
For the journey is done and the summit attained,
    And the barriers fall,
Though a battle's to fight ere the guerdon be gained,
    The reward of it all.
I was ever a fighter, so—one fight more,
    The best and the last!
I would hate that death bandaged my eyes, and forbore,
    And bade me creep past.
No! let me taste the whole of it, fare like my peers
    The heroes of old,
Bear the brunt, in a minute pay glad life's arrears
    Of pain, darkness and cold.
For sudden the worst turns the best to the brave,
    The black minute's at end,
And the elements' rage, the fiend-voices that rave,
    Shall dwindle, shall blend,
Shall change, shall become first a peace out of pain,
    Then a light, then thy breast.
O thou soul of my soul! I shall clasp thee again,
    And with God be the rest!

Epilogue

From "Asolando"

AT the midnight in the silence of the sleep-time,
  When you set your fancies free,
Will they pass to where—by death, fools think, imprisoned—
Low he lies who once so loved you, whom you loved so,
    —Pity me?

Oh to love so, be so loved, yet so mistaken!
  What had I on earth to do
With the slothful, with the mawkish, the unmanly?
Like the aimless, helpless, hopeless, did I drivel
    —Being—who?

One who never turned his back but marched breast forward,
  Never doubted clouds would break,
Never dreamed, though right were worsted, wrong would
    triumph,
Held we fall to rise, are baffled to fight better,
    Sleep to wake.

No, at noonday in the bustle of man's work-time
  Greet the unseen with a cheer!
Bid him forward, breast and back as either should be,
"Strive and thrive!" cry "Speed,—fight on, fare ever
    There as here!"

EMILY BRONTË (1818-1848)

The Prisoner

STILL let my tyrants know, I am not doom'd to wear
  Year after year in gloom and desolate despair;
A messenger of Hope comes every night to me,
And offers for short life, eternal liberty.

He comes with Western winds, with evening's wandering airs,
With that clear dusk of heaven that brings the thickest stars:
Winds take a pensive tone, and stars a tender fire,
And visions rise, and change, that kill me with desire.

Desire for nothing known in my maturer years,
When Joy grew mad with awe, at counting future tears:
When, if my spirit's sky was full of flashes warm,
I knew not whence they came, from sun or thunder-storm.

But first, a hush of peace—a soundless calm descends;
The struggle of distress and fierce impatience ends.
Mute music soothes my breast—unutter'd harmony
That I could never dream, till Earth was lost to me.

Then dawns the Invisible; the Unseen its truth reveals;
My outward sense is gone, my inward essence feels;
Its wings are almost free—its home, its harbour found;
Measuring the gulf, it stoops, and dares the final bound.

O dreadful is the check—intense the agony—
When the ear begins to hear, and the eye begins to see;
When the pulse begins to throb—the brain to think again—
The soul to feel the flesh, and the flesh to feel the chain.

Yet I would lose no sting, would wish no torture less;
The more that anguish racks, the earlier it will bless;
And robed in fires of hell, or bright with heavenly shine,
If it but herald Death, the vision is divine.

Last Lines

NO coward soul is mine,
　　No trembler in the world's storm-troubled
　　　　sphere:
　I see Heaven's glories shine,
And faith shines equal, arming me from fear.

　O God within my breast,
Almighty, ever-present Deity!
　Life—that in me has rest,
As I—undying Life—have power in Thee!

　Vain are the thousand creeds
That move men's hearts: unutterably vain;
　Worthless as wither'd weeds,
Or idlest froth amid the boundless main,

　To waken doubt in one
Holding so fast by thine infinity;
　So surely anchor'd on
The steadfast rock of immortality.

　With wide-embracing love
Thy Spirit animates eternal years,
　Pervades and broods above,
Changes, sustains, dissolves, creates, and rears.

Though earth and man were gone,
And suns and universes ceased to be,
   And Thou were left alone,
Every existence would exist in Thee.

   There is not room for Death,
Nor atom that his might could render void:
   Thou—Thou art Being and Breath,
And what Thou art may never be destroy'd.

GEORGE ELIOT (1819-1880)

"Oh, May I Join the Choir Invisible"

OH, may I join the choir invisible
   Of those immortal dead who live again
In minds made better by their presence; live
In pulses stirred to generosity,
In deeds of daring rectitude, in scorn
For miserable aims that end with self,
In thoughts sublime that pierce the night like stars,
And with their mild persistence urge man's search
To vaster issues. . . .

. . . This is life to come,
Which martyred men have made more glorious
For us who strive to follow. May I reach
That purest heaven, be to other souls
The cup of strength in some great agony,
Enkindle generous ardour, feed pure love,
Beget the smiles that have no cruelty,
Be the sweet presence of a good diffused,
And in diffusion ever more intense.
So shall I join the choir invisible
Whose music is the gladness of the world.
                                                Abridged.

CHARLES KINGSLEY (1819-1875)

The Sands of Dee

"O Mary, go and call the cattle home,
      And call the cattle home,
   And call the cattle home
   Across the sands of Dee!"
The western wind was wild and dank with foam,
   And all alone went she.

The western tide crept up along the sand,
 And o'er and o'er the sand,
 And round and round the sand,
As far as eye could see.
The rolling mist came down and hid the land:
And never home came she.

"Oh! is it weed, or fish, or floating hair—
 A tress of golden hair,
 A drownèd maiden's hair
Above the nets at sea?
Was never salmon yet that shone so fair
 Among the stakes on Dee."

They rowed her in across the rolling foam,
 The cruel crawling foam,
 The cruel hungry foam,
To her grave beside the sea:
But still the boatmen hear her call the cattle home
 Across the sands of Dee!

The Three Fishers

THREE fishers went sailing away to the West,
 Away to the West as the sun went down;
Each thought on the woman who loved him the best,
 And the children stood watching them out of the town;
For men must work, and women must weep,
And there's little to earn, and many to keep,
 Though the harbor bar be moaning.

Three wives sat up in the lighthouse tower
 And they trimmed the lamps as the sun went down;
They looked at the squall, and they looked at the shower,
 And the night-rack came rolling up ragged and brown.
But men must work, and women must weep,
Though storms be sudden, and waters deep,
 And the harbor bar be moaning.

Three corpses lay out on the shining sands
 In the morning gleam as the tide went down,
And the women are weeping and wringing their hands
 For those who will never come home to the town;
For men must work, and women must weep,
And the sooner it's over, the sooner to sleep;
 And good-by to the bar and its moaning.

ARTHUR HUGH CLOUGH (1819-1861)

"Say Not, the Struggle Naught Availeth"

SAY not, the struggle naught availeth,
  The labour and the wounds are vain,
The enemy faints not, nor faileth,
  And as things have been they remain.

If hopes were dupes, fears may be liars;
  It may be, in yon smoke concealed,
Your comrades chase e'en now the fliers,
  And, but for you, possess the field.

For while the tired waves, vainly breaking,
  Seem here no painful inch to gain,
Far back, through creeks and inlets making,
  Comes silent, flooding in, the main.

And not by eastern windows only,
  When daylight comes, comes in the light;
In front, the sun climbs slow, how slowly,
  But westward, look, the land is bright.

FREDERICK LOCKER-LAMPSON (1821-1895)

The Unrealised Ideal

MY only Love is always near,—
  In country or in town
I see her twinkling feet, I hear
  The whisper of her gown.

She foots it ever fair and young,
  Her locks are tied in haste,
And one is o'er her shoulder flung,
  And hangs below her waist.

She ran before me in the meads;
  And down this world-worn track
She leads me on; but while she leads
  She never gazes back.

And yet her voice is in my dreams,
  To witch me more and more;
That wooing voice! Ah me, it seems
  Less near me than of yore.

Lightly I sped when hope was high,
    And youth beguiled the chase;
I follow—follow still; but I
    Shall never see her Face.

At Her Window

BEATING Heart! we come again
        Where my Love reposes:
This is Mabel's window-pane;
    These are Mabel's roses.

Is she nested? Does she kneel
    In the twilight stilly,
Lily clad from throat to heel,
    She, my virgin Lily?

Soon the wan, the wistful stars,
    Fading, will forsake her;
Elves of light, on beamy bars,
    Whisper then, and wake her.

Let this friendly pebble plead
    At her flowery grating;
If she hear me will she heed?
    Mabel, I am waiting.

Mabel will be deck'd anon,
    Zoned in bride's apparel;
Happy zone! O hark to yon
    Passion-shaken carol!

Sing thy song, thou trancèd thrush,
    Pipe thy best, thy clearest;—
Hush, her lattice moves, O hush—
    Dearest Mabel!—dearest . . .

MATTHEW ARNOLD (1822-1888)
Quiet Work

ONE lesson, Nature, let me learn of thee,
    One lesson which in every wind is blown,
One lesson of two duties kept at one,
Though the loud world proclaim their enmity—

Of toil unsevered from tranquillity!
Of labour, that in lasting fruit outgrows
Far noisier schemes, accomplished in repose,
Too great for haste, too high for rivalry!

Yes! while on earth a thousand discords ring,
Man's fitful uproar mingling with his toil,
Still do thy sleepless ministers move on,
Their glorious tasks in silence perfecting;
Still working, blaming still our vain turmoil,
Labourers that shall not fail, when man is gone.

Requiescat

STREW on her roses, roses,
    And never a spray of yew.
In quiet she reposes:
    Ah! would that I did too.

Her mirth the world required:
    She bathed it in smiles of glee.
But her heart was tired, tired,
    And now they let her be.

Her life was turning, turning,
    In mazes of heat and sound.
But for peace her soul was yearning,
    And now peace laps her round.

Her cabin'd, ample Spirit,
    It flutter'd and fail'd for breath.
To-night it doth inherit
    The vasty Hall of Death.

Dover Beach

THE sea is calm to-night.
    The tide is full, the moon lies fair
Upon the straits;—on the French coast the light
Gleams and is gone; the cliffs of England stand,
Glimmering and vast, out in the tranquil bay.
Come to the window, sweet is the night-air!
Only, from the long line of spray
Where the sea meets the moon-blanched land,
Listen! you hear the grating roar
Of pebbles which the waves draw back, and fling,
At their return, up the high strand,
Begin, and cease, and then again begin,
With tremulous cadence slow, and bring
The eternal note of sadness in.

Sophocles long ago
Heard it on the Ægean, and it brought
Into his mind the turbid ebb and flow
Of human misery; we
Find also in the sound a thought,
Hearing it by this distant northern sea.

The sea of faith
Was once, too, at the full, and round earth's shore
Lay like the folds of a bright girdle furled.
But now I only hear
Its melancholy, long, withdrawing roar,
Retreating, to the breath
Of the night-wind, down the vast edges drear
And naked shingles of the world.

Ah, love, let us be true
To one another! for the world, which seems
To lie before us like a land of dreams,
So various, so beautiful, so new,
Hath really neither joy, nor love, nor light,
Nor certitude, nor peace nor help for pain;
And we are here as on a darkling plain
Swept with confused alarms of struggle and flight,
Where ignorant armies clash by night.

Morality

WE cannot kindle when we will
    The fire which in the heart resides;
The spirit bloweth and is still,
In mystery our soul abides.
    But tasks in hours of insight willed
    Can be through hours of gloom fulfilled.

With aching hands and bleeding feet
We dig and heap, lay stone on stone;
We bear the burden and the heat
Of the long day, and wish 'twere done.
    Not till the hours of light return
    All we have built do we discern.

Then, when the clouds are off the soul,
When thou dost bask in Nature's eye,
Ask, how *she* viewed thy self-control,
Thy struggling, tasked morality—
    Nature, whose free, light, cheerful air,
    Oft made thee, in thy gloom, despair.

And she, whose answer thou dost dread.
Whose eye thou wast afraid to seek,
See, on her face a glow is spread,
A strong emotion on her cheek!
  "Ah, child," she cries, "that strife divine,
  Whence was it, for it is not mine?

"There is no effort on *my* brow—
I do not strive, I do not weep;
I rush with the swift spheres and glow
In joy, and when I will, I sleep.
  Yet that severe, that earnest air,
  I saw, I felt it once—but where?

"I knew not yet the gauge of time,
Nor wore the manacles of space;
I felt it in some other clime,
I saw it in some other place.
  'Twas when the heavenly house I trod,
  And lay upon the breast of God."

The Scholar-Gipsy

G O, for they call you, Shepherd, from the hill;
   Go, Shepherd, and untie the wattled cotes:
No longer leave thy wistful flock unfed,
Nor let thy bawling fellows rack their throats,
  Nor the cropped grasses shoot another head.
    But when the fields are still,
And the tired men and dogs all gone to rest,
  And only the white sheep are sometimes seen
  Cross and recross the strips of moon-blanched green;
Come, Shepherd, and again begin the quest.

Here, where the reaper was at work of late,
  In this high field's dark corner, where he leaves
His coat, his basket, and his earthen cruise,
And in the sun all morning binds the sheaves,
  Then here, at noon, comes back his stores to use;
    Here will I sit and wait,
While to my ear from uplands far away
  The bleating of the folded flocks is borne,
  With distant cries of reapers in the corn—
All the live murmur of a summer's day.

Screened is this nook o'er the high, half-reaped field,
  And here till sundown, Shepherd, will I be.
    Through the thick corn the scarlet poppies peep,

And round green roots and yellowing stalks I see
　Pale blue convolvulus in tendrils creep:
　　And air-swept lindens yield
Their scent, and rustle down their perfumed showers
　Of bloom on the bent grass where I am laid,
　And bower me from the August sun with shade;
And the eye travels down to Oxford's towers:

And near me on the grass lies Glanvil's book—
　Come, let me read the oft-read tale again:
　　The story of that Oxford scholar poor,
Of pregnant parts and quick inventive brain,
　Who, tired of knocking at Preferment's door,
　　One summer morn forsook
His friends, and went to learn the Gipsy lore,
　And roamed the world with that wild brotherhood,
　And came, as most men deemed, to little good,
But came to Oxford and his friends no more.

But once, years after, in the country lanes,
　Two scholars, whom at college erst he knew,
　　Met him, and of his way of life inquired.
Whereat he answered that the Gipsy crew,
　His mates, had arts to rule as they desired
　　The workings of men's brains;
And they can bind them to what thoughts they will:
　"And I," he said, "the secret of their art,
　When fully learned, will to the world impart:
But it needs Heaven-sent moments for this skill!"

This said, he left them, and returned no more,
　But rumors hung about the country-side,
　　That the lost Scholar long was seen to stray,
Seen by rare glimpses, pensive and tongue-tied,
　In hat of antique shape, and cloak of gray,
　　The same the Gipsies wore.
Shepherds had met him on the Hurst in spring;
　At some lone alehouse in the Berkshire moors,
　On the warm ingle-bench, the smock-frocked boors
Had found him seated at their entering.

But, 'mid their drink and clatter, he would fly:
　And I myself seem half to know thy looks,
　　And put the shepherds, Wanderer, on thy trace;
And boys who in lone wheatfields scare the rooks
　I ask if thou hast passed their quiet place;
　　Or in my boat I lie
Moored to the cool bank in the summer heats,
　'Mid wide grass meadows which the sunshine fills,
　And watch the warm green-muffled Cumner hills,
And wonder if thou haunt'st their shy retreats.

For most, I know, thou lov'st retirèd ground.
  Thee, at the ferry, Oxford riders blithe,
    Returning home on summer nights, have met
  Crossing the stripling Thames at Bablock-hithe,
    Trailing in the cool stream thy fingers wet,
      As the slow punt swings round:
  And leaning backwards in a pensive dream,
    And fostering in thy lap a heap of flowers
    Plucked in shy fields and distant Wychwood bowers,
  And thine eyes resting on the moonlit stream:

And then they land, and thou art seen no more.
  Maidens who from the distant hamlets come
    To dance around the Fyfield elm in May,
  Oft through the darkening fields have seen thee roam,
    Or cross a stile into the public way.
      Oft thou hast given them store
  Of flowers—the frail-leafed, white anemone—
    Dark bluebells drenched with dews of summer eves,
    And purple orchises with spotted leaves—
  But none has words she can report of thee.

And, above Godstow Bridge, when hay-time's here
  In June, and many a scythe in sunshine flames,
    Men who through those wide fields of breezy grass
  Where black-winged swallows haunt the glittering Thames,
    To bathe in the abandoned lasher pass,
      Have often passed thee near
  Sitting upon the river bank o'ergrown:
    Marked thine outlandish garb, thy figure spare,
    Thy dark vague eyes, and soft abstracted air;
  But, when they came from bathing, thou wert gone.

At some lone homestead in the Cumner hills,
  Where at her open door the housewife darns,
    Thou hast been seen, or hanging on a gate
  To watch the threshers in the mossy barns.
    Children, who early range these slopes and late
      For cresses from the rills,
  Have known thee watching, all an April day,
    The springing pastures and the feeding kine;
    And marked thee, when the stars come out and shine,
  Through the long dewy grass move slow away.

In autumn, on the skirts of Bagley Wood,
  Where most the Gipsies by the turf-edged way
    Pitch their smoked tents, and every bush you see
  With scarlet patches tagged and shreds of gray,
    Above the forest-ground called Thessaly—
      The blackbird picking food

Sees thee, nor stops his meal, nor fears at all;
So often has he known thee past him stray
Rapt, twirling in thy hand a withered spray,
And waiting for the spark from Heaven to fall.

And once, in winter, on the causeway chill
Where home through flooded fields foot-travelers go,
Have I not passed thee on the wooden bridge
Wrapped in thy cloak and battling with the snow,
Thy face towards Hinksey and its wintry ridge?
And thou hast climbed the hill
And gained the white brow of the Cumner range;
Turned once to watch, while thick the snowflakes fall,
The line of festal light in Christ Church hall—
Then sought thy straw in some sequestered grange.

But what—I dream! Two hundred years are flown
Since first thy story ran through Oxford halls,
And the grave Glanvil did the tale inscribe
That thou wert wandered from the studious walls
To learn strange arts, and join a Gipsy tribe:
And thou from earth art gone
Long since, and in some quiet churchyard laid;
Some country nook, where o'er thy unknown grave
Tall grasses and white flowering nettles wave—
Under a dark red-fruited yew-tree's shade.

—No, no, thou hast not felt the lapse of hours.
For what wears out the life of mortal men?
'Tis that from change to change their being rolls
'Tis that repeated shocks, again, again,
Exhaust the energy of strongest souls,
And numb the elastic powers.
Till having used our nerves with bliss and teen,
And tired upon a thousand schemes our wit,
To the just-pausing Genius we remit
Our worn-out life, and are—what we have been.

Thou hast not lived, why shouldst thou perish, so?
Thou hadst *one* aim, *one* business, *one* desire;
Else wert thou long since numbered with the dead—
Else hadst thou spent, like other men, thy fire.
The generations of thy peers are fled,
And we ourselves shall go;
But thou possessest an immortal lot,
And we imagine thee exempt from age
And living as thou liv'st on Glanvil's page,
Because thou hadst—what we, alas, have not!

For early didst thou leave the world, with powers
  Fresh, undiverted to the world without,
    Firm to their mark, not spent on other things;
  Free from the sick fatigue, the languid doubt,
    Which much to have tried, in much been baffled, brings.
      O Life unlike to ours!
Who fluctuate idly without term or scope,
  Of whom each strives, nor knows for what he strives,
  And each half lives a hundred different lives;
Who wait like thee, but not, like thee, in hope.

Thou waitest for the spark from Heaven: and we,
  Vague half-believers of our casual creeds,
    Who never deeply felt, nor clearly willed,
  Whose insight never has borne fruit in deeds,
    Whose weak resolves never have been fulfilled;
      For whom each year we see
Breeds new beginnings, disappointments new;
  Who hesitate and falter life away,
  And lose to-morrow the ground won to-day—
Ah, do not we, Wanderer, await it too?

Yes, we await it, but it still delays,
  And then we suffer; and amongst us One,
    Who most has suffered, takes dejectedly
His seat upon the intellectual throne;
    And all his store of sad experience he
      Lays bare of wretched days;
Tells us his misery's birth and growth and signs,
  And how the dying spark of hope was fed,
  And how the breast was soothed, and how the head,
And all his hourly varied anodynes.

This for our wisest: and we others pine,
  And wish the long unhappy dream would end,
    And waive all claim to bliss, and try to bear,
With close-lipped Patience for our only friend,
    Sad Patience, too near neighbour to Despair:
      But none has hope like thine.
Thou through the fields and through the woods dost stray,
  Roaming the country-side, a truant boy,
  Nursing thy project in unclouded joy,
And every doubt long blown by time away.

O born in days when wits were fresh and clear,
  And life ran gaily as the sparkling Thames;
    Before this strange disease of modern life,
  With its sick hurry, its divided aims,
    Its heads o'ertaxed, its palsied hearts, was rife—
      Fly hence, our contact fear!

Still fly, plunge deeper in the bowering wood!
  Averse, as Dido did with gesture stern
    From her false friend's approach in Hades turn,
Wave us away, and keep thy solitude.

Still nursing the unconquerable hope,
  Still clutching the inviolable shade,
    With a free onward impulse brushing through,
By night, the silvered branches of the glade—
    Far on the forest-skirts, where none pursue,
      On some mild pastoral slope
Emerge, and resting on the moonlit pales,
  Freshen thy flowers, as in former years,
  With dew, or listen with enchanted ears,
From the dark dingles, to the nightingales.

But fly our paths, our feverish contact fly!
  For strong the infection of our mental strife,
    Which, though it gives no bliss, yet spoils for rest;
And we should win thee from thy own fair life,
    Like us distracted, and like us unblest.
      Soon, soon thy cheer would die,
Thy hopes grow timorous, and unfixed thy powers,
  And thy clear aims be cross and shifting made:
  And then thy glad perennial youth would fade,
Fade, and grow old at last, and die like ours.

Then fly our greetings, fly our speech and smiles!
  —As some grave Tyrian trader, from the sea,
    Descried at sunrise an emerging prow
Lifting the cool-haired creepers stealthily,
    The fringes of a southward-facing brow
      Among the Ægean isles;
And saw the merry Grecian coaster come,
  Freighted with amber grapes, and Chian wine,
  Green bursting figs, and tunnies steeped in brine;
And knew the intruders on his ancient home,

The young light-hearted Masters of the waves;
  And snatched his rudder, and shook out more sail,
    And day and night held on indignantly
O'er the blue Midland waters with the gale,
  Betwixt the Syrtes and soft Sicily,
    To where the Atlantic raves
Outside the Western Straits, and unbent sails
  There, where down cloudy cliffs, through sheets of foam,
  Shy traffickers, the dark Iberians come;
And on the beach undid his corded bales.

Thyrsis

A Monody, to commemorate the author's friend,
ARTHUR HUGH CLOUGH, *who died at Florence,* 1861.

HOW changed is here each spot man makes or fills!
 In the two Hinkseys nothing keeps the same;
The village-street its haunted mansion lacks,
And from the sign is gone Sibylla's name,
 And from the roofs the twisted chimney-stacks—
 Are ye too changed, ye hills!
See, 'tis no foot of unfamiliar men
 To-night from Oxford up your pathway strays!
Here came I often, often, in old days—
Thyrsis and I; we still had Thyrsis then.

Runs it not here, the track by Childsworth Farm,
 Past the high wood, to where the elm-tree crowns
 The hill behind whose ridge the sunset flames?
The signal-elm, that looks on Ilsley Downs,
 The Vale, the three lone weirs, the youthful Thames?—
 This winter-eve is warm,
Humid the air! leafless, yet soft as spring,
 The tender purple spray on copse and briers!
 And that sweet city with her dreaming spires
She needs not June for beauty's heightening,

Lovely, all times she lies, lovely to-night!—
 Only, methinks, some loss of habit's power
 Befalls me wandering through this upland dim.
Once pass'd I blindfolded here, at any hour;
 Now seldom come I, since I came with him.
 That single elm-tree bright
Against the west—I miss it! is it gone?
 We prized it dearly; while it stood, we said,
 Our friend, the Gipsy-Scholar, was not dead;
While the tree lived, he in these fields lived on.

Too rare, too rare, grow now my visits here,
 But once I knew each field, each flower, each stick;
 And with the country-folk acquaintance made
By barn in threshing-time, by new-built rick.
 Here, too, our shepherd-pipes we first assay'd.
 Ah me! this many a year
My pipe is lost, my shepherd's-holiday!
 Needs must I lose them, needs with heavy heart
 Into the world and wave of men depart;
But Thyrsis of his own will went away.

It irk'd him to be here, he could not rest.
  He loved each simple joy the country yields,
    He loved his mates; but yet he could not keep,
For that a shadow lower'd on the fields,
    Here with the shepherds and the silly sheep.
      Some life of men unblest
He knew, which made him droop, and fill'd his head.
  He went; his piping took a troubled sound
    Of storms that rage outside our happy ground;
He could not wait their passing, he is dead.

So, some tempestuous morn in early June,
  When the year's primal burst of bloom is o'er,
    Before the roses and the longest day—
When garden-walks and all the grassy floor
    With blossoms red and white of fallen May
      And chestnut flowers are strewn—
So have I heard the cuckoo's parting cry,
  From the wet field, through the vext garden-trees,
  Come with the volleying rain and tossing breeze:
  The bloom is gone, and with the bloom go I!

Too quick despairer, wherefore wilt thou go?
  Soon will the high Midsummer pomps come on,
    Soon will the musk carnations break and swell,
Soon shall we have gold-dusted snapdragon,
    Sweet-William with his homely cottage-smell,
      And stocks in fragrant blow;
Roses that down the alleys shine afar,
  And open, jasmine-muffled lattices,
  And groups under the dreaming garden-trees,
And the full moon, and the white evening-star.

He hearkens not! light comer, he is flown!
  What matters it? next year he will return,
    And we shall have him in the sweet spring-days,
With whitening hedges, and uncrumpling fern,
    And blue-bells trembling by the forest-ways,
      And scent of hay new-mown.
But Thyrsis never more we swains shall see;
  See him come back, and cut a smoother reed,
  And blow a strain the world at last shall heed—
For Time, not Corydon, hath conquer'd thee!

Alack, for Corydon no rival now!—
  But when Sicilian shepherds lost a mate,
    Some good survivor with his flute would go,
Piping a ditty sad for Bion's fate;

And cross the unpermitted ferry's flow,
   And relax Pluto's brow,
And make leap up with joy the beauteous head
Of Proserpine, among whose crowned hair
Are flowers first open'd on Sicilian air,
And flute his friend, like Orpheus, from the dead.

O easy access to the hearer's grace
   When Dorian shepherds sang to Proserpine!
   For she herself had trod Sicilian fields,
She knew the Dorian water's gush divine,
   She knew each lily white which Enna yields,
      Each rose with blushing face;
She loved the Dorian pipe, the Dorian strain.
   But ah, of our poor Thames she never heard!
   Her foot the Cumner cowslips never stirr'd;
And we should tease her with our plaint in vain!

Well! wind-dispersed and vain the word will be,
   Yet, Thyrsis, let me give my grief its hour
      In the old haunt, and find our tree-topp'd hill!
Who, if not I, for questing here hath power?
   I know the wood which hides the daffodil,
      I know the Fyfield tree,
I know what white, what purple fritillaries
   The grassy harvest of the river-fields
   Above by Ensham, down by Sandford, yields,
And what sedged brooks are Thames's tributaries;

I know these slopes; who knows them if not I?—
   But many a dingle on the loved hill-side,
      With thorns once studded, old, white-blossom'd trees,
Where thick the cowslips grew, and far descried
   High tower'd the spikes of purple orchises,
      Hath since our day put by
The coronals of that forgotten time;
   Down each green bank hath gone the plough-boy's team,
   And only in the hidden brookside gleam
Primroses, orphans of the flowery prime.

Where is the girl, who by the boatman's door,
   Above the locks, above the boating throng,
      Unmoor'd our skiff when through the Wytham flats,
Red loosestrife and blond meadow-sweet among,
   And darting swallows and light water-gnats,
      We track'd the shy Thames shore?
Where are the mowers, who, as the tiny swell
   Of our boat passing heaved the river-grass,
   Stood with suspended scythe to see us pass?—
They all are gone, and thou art gone as well!

Yes, thou art gone! and round me too the night
  In ever-nearing circle weaves her shade.
    I see her veil draw soft across the day,
  I feel her slowly chilling breath invade
    The cheek grown thin, the brown hair sprent with grey;
      I feel her finger light
  Laid pausefully upon life's headlong train;—
    The foot less prompt to meet the morning dew,
    The heart less bounding at emotion new,
  And hope, once crush'd, less quick to spring again.

And long the way appears, which seem'd so short
  To the less practised eye of sanguine youth;
    And high the mountain-tops, in cloudy air,
  The mountain-tops where is the throne of Truth,
    Tops in life's morning-sun so bright and bare!
      Unbreachable the fort
  Of the long-batter'd world uplifts its wall;
    And strange and vain the earthly turmoil grows,
    And near and real the charm of thy repose,
  And night as welcome as a friend would fall.

But hush! the upland hath a sudden loss
  Of quiet!—Look, adown the dusk hillside,
    A troop of Oxford hunters going home,
  As in old days, jovial and talking, ride!
    From hunting with the Berkshire hounds they come.
      Quick! let me fly, and cross
  Into yon farther field—'Tis done; and see,
    Back'd by the sunset, which doth glorify
    The orange and pale violet evening-sky,
  Bare on its lonely ridge, the Tree! the Tree!

I take the omen! Eve lets down her veil,
  The white fog creeps from bush to bush about,
    The west unflushes, the high stars grow bright,
  And in the scatter'd farms the lights come out;
    I cannot reach the signal-tree to-night,
      Yet, happy omen, hail!
  Hear it from thy broad lucent Arno-vale
    (For there thine earth-forgetting eyelids keep
    The morningless and unawakening sleep
  Under the flowery oleanders pale),

Hear it, O Thyrsis, still our tree is there!—
  Ah, vain! These English fields, this upland dim,
    These brambles pale with mist engarlanded,
  That lone, sky-pointing tree, are not for him;
    To a boon southern country he is fled,
      And now in happier air,

Wandering with the great Mother's train divine
  (And purer or more subtle soul than thee,
  I trow, the mighty Mother doth not see)
Within a folding of the Apennine,

Thou hearest the immortal chants of old!—
  Putting his sickle to the perilous grain
  In the hot cornfield of the Phrygian king,
For thee the Lityerses-song again
  Young Daphnis with his silver voice doth sing;
    Sings his Sicilian fold,
His sheep, his hapless love, his blinded eyes—
  And how a call celestial round him rang,
  And heavenward from the fountain-brink he sprang,
And all the marvel of the golden skies.

There thou art gone, and me thou leavest here
  Sole in these fields! yet will I not despair.
  Despair I will not, while I yet descry
Under mild canopy of English air
  That lonely tree against the western sky.
    Still, still these slopes, 'tis clear,
Our Gipsy-Scholar haunts, outliving thee!
  Fields where soft sheep from cages pull the hay,
  Woods with anemonies in flower till May,
Know him a wanderer still; then why not me?

A fugitive and gracious light he seeks,
  Shy to illumine; and I seek it too.
  This does not come with houses or with gold,
With place, with honour, and a flattering crew;
  'Tis not in the world's market bought and sold—
    But the smooth-slipping weeks
Drop by, and leave its seeker still untired;
  Out of the heed of mortals he is gone,
  He wends unfollow'd, he must house alone;
Yet on he fares, by his own heart inspired.

Thou too, O Thyrsis, on like quest wast bound!
  Thou wanderedst with me for a little hour!
    Men gave thee nothing; but this happy quest,
If men esteem'd thee feeble, gave thee power,
  If men procured thee trouble, gave thee rest.
    And this rude Cumner ground
Its fir-topped Hurst, its farms, its quiet fields,
  Here cam'st thou in thy jocund youthful time,
  Here was thine height of strength, thy golden prime!
And still the haunt beloved a virtue yields.

What though the music of thy rustic flute
  Kept not for long its happy, country tone;
    Lost it too soon, and learnt a stormy note
Of men contention-tost, of men who groan,
    Which task'd thy pipe too sore, and tired thy throat—
    It fail'd, and thou wast mute!
Yet hadst thou alway visions of our light,
  And long with men of care thou couldst not stay,
  And soon thy foot resumed its wandering way,
Left human haunt, and on alone till night.

Too rare, too rare, grow now my visits here!
  'Mid city-noise, not, as with thee of yore,
    Thyrsis! in reach of sheep-bells is my home.
  —Then through the great town's harsh, heart-wearying roar
    Let in thy voice a whisper often come
      To chase fatigue and fear:
    Why faintest thou? I wander'd till I died.
    Roam on! The light we sought is shining still.
    Dost thou ask proof? Our tree yet crowns the hill,
Our Scholar travels yet the loved hillside.

From "Empedocles on Etna"

WE would have inward peace,
    Yet will not look within;
We would have misery cease,
Yet will not cease from sin;
We want all pleasant ends, but will use no harsh means;

    We do not what we ought,
    What we ought not, we do,
    And lean upon the thought
    That chance will bring us through;
But our own acts for good or ill are mightier powers.

    Yet, even when man forsakes
    All sin,—is just, is pure,
    Abandons all which makes
    His welfare insecure,—
Other existences there are, that clash with ours.

    Like us, the lightning-fires
    Love to have scope and play;
    The stream, like us, desires
    An unimpeded way;
Like us, the Libyan wind delights to roam at large.

Streams will not curb their pride
The just man not to entomb,
Nor lightnings go aside
To give his virtues room;
Nor is that wind less rough which blows a good.

Nature, with equal mind,
Sees all her sons at play;
Sees man control the wind,
The wind sweep man away;
Allows the proudly-riding and the foundering bark.
    *   *   *   *   *   *   *

Is it so small a thing
To have enjoy'd the sun,
To have lived light in the spring,
To have loved, to have thought, to have done;
To have advanced true friends, and beat down baffling foes;

That we must feign a bliss
Of doubtful future date,
And while we dream on this
Lose all our present state,
And relegate to worlds yet distant our repose?

Not much, I know, you prize
What pleasures may be had,
Who look on life with eyes
Estranged, like mine, and sad:
And yet the village churl feels the truth more than you;

Who's loth to leave this life
Which to him little yields:
His hard-task'd sunburnt wife,
His often-labour'd fields;
The boors with whom he talk'd, the country spots he knew.

I say, Fear not! life still
Leaves human effort scope.
But since life teems with ill,
Nurse no extravagant hope.
Because thou must not dream, thou need'st not then despair.

Shakespeare

OTHERS abide our question. Thou art free.
   We ask and ask—Thou smilest and art still,
Out-topping knowledge. For the loftiest hill,
Who to the stars uncrowns his majesty,
Planting his steadfast footsteps in the sea,

Making the heaven of heavens his dwelling-place,
Spares but the cloudy border of his base
To the foiled searching of mortality;
And thou, who didst the stars and sunbeams know,
Self-schooled, self-scanned, self-honoured, self-secure,
Didst tread on earth unguessed at.—Better so!
All pains the immortal spirit must endure,
All weakness which impairs, all griefs which bow,
Find their sole speech in that victorious brow.

From "Lines Written in Kensington Gardens"

CALM Soul of all things! make it mine
  To feel, amid the city's jar,
That there abides a peace of thine,
Man did not make, and cannot mar.

The will to neither strive nor cry,
The power to feel with others give.
Calm, calm me more; nor let me die
Before I have begun to live.

The Buried Life

LIGHT flows our war of mocking words; and yet
  Behold, with tears mine eyes are wet!
I feel a nameless sadness o'er me roll.
Yes, yes, we know that we can jest,
We know, we know, that we can smile!
But there's a something in this breast,
To which thy light words bring no rest,
And thy gay smiles no anodyne;
Give me thy hand, and hush awhile,
And turn those limpid eyes on mine,
And let me read there, love! thy inmost soul.

Alas! is even love too weak
To unlock the heart and let it speak?
Are even lovers powerless to reveal
To one another what indeed they feel?
I knew the mass of common men concealed
Their thoughts, for fear that if revealed
They would by other men be met
With blank indifference, or with blame reproved;
I knew they lived and moved
Tricked in disguises, alien to the rest
Of men, and alien to themselves—and yet
The same heart beats in every human breast!

But we, my love! doth a like spell benumb
Our hearts, our voices? Must we, too, be dumb?
Ah, well for us, if even we,
Even for a moment, can get free
Our heart, and have our lips unchained;
For that which seals them hath been deep ordained!
Fate, which foresaw
How frivolous a baby man would be,—
By what distractions he would be possessed,
How he would pour himself in every strife,
And well-nigh change his own identity,—
That it might keep from his capricious play
His genuine self, and force him to obey
Even in his own despite his being's law,
Bade through the deep recesses of our breast
The unregarded river of our life
Pursue with indiscernible flow its way;
And that we should not see
The buried stream, and seem to be
Eddying at large in blind uncertainty,
Though driving on with it eternally.

But often, in the world's most crowded streets,
But often, in the din of strife,
There rises an unspeakable desire
After the knowledge of our buried life,
A thirst to spend our fire and restless force
In tracking out our true, original course;
A longing to inquire
Into the mystery of this heart which beats
So wild, so deep in us,—to know
Whence our lives come, and where they go.
And many a man in his own breast then delves,
But deep enough, alas! none ever mines.
And we have been on many thousand lines,
And we have shown, on each, spirit and power;
But hardly have we, for one little hour,
Been on our own line, have we been ourselves,—
Hardly had skill to utter one of all
The nameless feelings that course throughout
                    our breast,
But they course on forever unexpressed.
And long we try in vain to speak and act
Our hidden self, and what we say and do
Is eloquent, is well—but 'tis not true!
And then we will no more be racked
With inward striving, and demand
Of all the thousand nothings of the hour
Their stupefying power,
Ah, yes, and they benumb us at our call!

Yet still, from time to time, vague and forlorn,
From the soul's subterranean depth upborne
As from an infinitely distant land,
Come airs, and floating echoes and convey
A melancholy into all our day.

Only—but this is rare—
When a beloved hand is laid in ours,
When, jaded with the rush and glare
Of the interminable hours,
Our eyes can in another's eyes read clear,
When our world-deafened ear
Is by the tones of a loved voice caressed,—
A bolt is shot back somewhere in our breast,
And a lost pulse of feeling stirs again.
The eye sinks inward, and the heart lies plain,
And what we mean, we say, and what we would,
      we know.

A man becomes aware of his life's flow,
And hears its winding murmur, and he sees
The meadows where it glides, the sun, the breeze.

And there arrives a lull in the hot race
Wherein he doth forever chase
The flying and elusive phantom, rest.
An air of coolness plays upon his face,
And an unwonted calm pervades his breast;
And then he thinks he knows
The hills where his life rose,
And the sea where it goes.

WILLIAM (JOHNSON) CORY (1823-1892)

Heraclitus

THEY told me, Heraclitus, they told me you were dead,
    They brought me bitter news to hear and bitter tears to
      shed.
I wept as I remember'd how often you and I
Had tired the sun with talking and sent him down the sky.

And now that thou art lying, my dear old Carian guest,
A handful of grey ashes, long, long ago at rest,
Still are thy pleasant voices, thy nightingales, awake;
For Death, he taketh all away, but them he cannot take.

Remember

YOU come not, as aforetime, to the headstone every day,
And I, who died, I do not chide because, my friend, you
play;
Only, in playing, think of him who once was kind and dear,
And if you see a beauteous thing, just say, he is not here.

COVENTRY PATMORE (1823-1896)

Winter

I, singularly moved
To love the lovely that are not beloved,
Of all the Seasons, most
Love Winter, and to trace
The sense of the Trophonian pallor on her face.
It is not death, but plenitude of peace;
And the dim cloud that does the world enfold
Hath less the characters of dark and cold
Than warmth and light asleep,
And correspondent breathing seems to keep
With the infant harvest, breathing soft below
Its eider coverlet of snow.
Nor is in field or garden anything
But, duly look'd into, contains serene
The substance of things hoped for, in the Spring,
And evidence of Summer not yet seen.
On every chance-mild day
That visits the moist shaw,
The honeysuckle, 'sdaining to be crost
In urgence of sweet life by sleet or frost,
'Voids the time's law
With still increase
Of leaflet new, and little, wandering spray;
Often, in sheltering brakes,
As one from rest disturb'd in the first hour,
Primrose or violet bewilder'd wakes,
And deems 'tis time to flower;
Though not a whisper of her voice he hear,
The buried bulb does know
The signals of the year,
And hails far Summer with his lifted spear.
The gorse-field dark, by sudden, gold caprice,
Turns, here and there, into a Jason's fleece;
Lilies, that soon in Autumn slipp'd their gowns of green,
And vanish'd into earth,
And came again, ere Autumn died, to birth,
Stand full-array'd, amidst the wavering shower,
And perfect for the Summer, less the flower;

In nook of pale or crevice of crude bark,
Thou canst not miss,
If close thou spy, to mark
The ghostly chrysalis,
That, if thou touch it, stirs in its dream dark;
And the flush'd Robin, in the evenings hoar,
Does of Love's Day, as if he saw it, sing;
But sweeter yet than dream or song of Summer or Spring
Are Winter's sometimes smiles, that seem to well
From infancy ineffable;
Her wandering, languorous gaze,
So unfamiliar, so without amaze,
On the elemental, chill adversity,
The uncomprehended rudeness; and her sigh
And solemn, gathering tear,
And look of exile from some great repose, the sphere
Of ether, moved by ether only, or
By something still more tranquil.

The Toys

MY little Son, who looked from thoughtful eyes
And moved and spoke in quiet grown-up wise,
Having my law the seventh time disobeyed,
I struck him and dismissed
With hard words and unkissed,
—His Mother, who was patient, being dead.
Then, fearing lest his grief should hinder sleep,
I visited his bed,
But found him slumbering deep,
With darkened eyelids, and their lashes yet
From his late sobbing wet.
And I, with moan,
Kissing away his tears, left others of my own;
For, on a table drawn beside his head,
He had put, within his reach,
A box of counters and a red-veined stone,
A piece of glass abraded by the beach,
And six or seven shells,
A bottle with bluebells,
And two French copper coins, ranged there with careful art,
To comfort his sad heart.
So when that night I prayed
To God, I wept, and said:
Ah, when at last we lie with trancèd breath,
Not vexing Thee in death,
And Thou rememberest of what toys
We made our joys,
How weakly understood

Thy great commanded good,
Then, fatherly not less
Than I whom Thou hast moulded from the clay,
Thou'lt leave Thy wrath, and say,
"I will be sorry for their childishness."

Departure

IT was not like your great and gracious ways!
   Do you, that have naught other to lament,
Never, my Love, repent
Of how, that July afternoon,
You went,
With sudden, unintelligible phrase,
And frightened eye,
Upon your journey of so many days
Without a single kiss, or a good-bye?
I knew, indeed, that you were parting soon;
And so we sate, within the low sun's rays,
You whispering to me, for your voice was weak,
Your harrowing praise.
Well, it was well
To hear you such things speak,
And I could tell
What made your eyes a glowing gloom of love,
As a warm South-wind sombers a March grove.

And it was like your great and gracious ways
To turn your talk on daily things, my Dear,
Lifting the luminous, pathetic lash
To let the laughter flash,
Whilst I drew near,
Because you spoke so low that I could scarcely hear.
But all at once to leave me at the last,
More at the wonder than the loss aghast,
With huddled, unintelligible phrase,
And frightened eye,
And go your journey of all days
With not one kiss, or a good-bye,
And the only loveless look the look with which you passed:
'Twas all unlike your great and gracious ways.

WILLIAM ALLINGHAM (1824-1889)

THESE little songs
   Found here and there,
Floating in air
By forest and lea,

Or hill-side heather,
In houses and throngs,
Or down by the sea—
Have come together,
How I can't tell: . . .
But the best in the songs,
Whatever it be,
To you, and to me,
And to no one belongs.

The Fairies

UP the airy mountain,
   Down the rushy glen,
We daren't go a-hunting
  For fear of little men;
Wee folk, good folk,
  Trooping all together;
Green jacket, red cap,
  And white owl's feather!

Down along the rocky shore
  Some make their home,
They live on crispy pancakes
  Of yellow tide foam;
Some in the reeds
  Of the black mountain lake,
With frogs for their watch-dogs,
  All night awake.

High on the hill-top
  The old king sits;
He is now so old and gray
  He's nigh lost his wits.
With a bridge of white mist
  Columbkill he crosses,
On his stately journeys
  From Slieveleague to Rosses:

Or going up with music
  On cold starry nights,
To sup with the Queen
  Of the gay Northern lights.
They stole little Bridget
  For seven years long;
When she came down again
  Her friends were all gone.

They took her lightly back,
  Between the night and morrow,
They thought that she was fast asleep,
  But she was dead with sorrow.
They have kept her ever since
  Deep within the lake,
On a bed of flag-leaves,
  Watching till she wake.

By the craggy hill-side,
  Through the mosses bare,
They have planted thorn-trees
  For pleasure here and there.
Is any man so daring
  As dig them up in spite,
He shall find their sharpest thorns
  In his bed at night.

Up the airy mountain,
  Down the rushy glen,
We daren't go a-hunting
  For fear of little men;
Wee folk, good folk,
  Trooping all together;
Green jacket, red cap,
  And white owl's feather!

SYDNEY DOBELL (1824-1874)

The Orphan's Song

I had a little bird,
  I took it from the nest;
I prest it, and blest it,
And nurst it in my breast.

I set it on the ground,
I danced round and round,
And sang about it so cheerly,
With "Hey my little bird, and ho my little bird,
And oh but I love thee dearly!"

I make a little feast
Of food soft and sweet,
I hold it in my breast,
And coax it to eat;

I pit, and I pat,
I call it this and that,
And sing about it so cheerly,
With "Hey my little bird, and ho my little bird,
And oh but I love thee dearly!"

I may kiss, I may sing,
But I can't make it feed,
It taketh no heed
Of any pleasant thing.

I scolded, and I socked,
But it minded not a whit,
Its little mouth was locked,
And I could not open it.

Tho' with pit, and with pat,
And with this, and with that,
I sang about it so cheerly,
With "Hey my little bird, and ho my little bird,
And oh but I love thee dearly!"

But when the day was done,
And the room was at rest,
And I sat all alone
With my birdie in my breast,

And the light had fled,
And not a sound was heard,
Then my little bird
Lifted up its head,

And the little mouth
Loosed its sullen pride,
And it opened, it opened,
With a yearning strong and wide.

Swifter than I speak
I brought it food once more,
But the poor little beak
Was locked as before.

I sat down again,
And not a creature stirred,
I laid the little bird
Again where it had lain;

And again when nothing stirred,
And not a word I said,
Then my little bird
Lifted up its head,
And the little beak
Loosed its stubborn pride,
And it opened, it opened,
With a yearning strong and wide.

It lay in my breast,
It uttered no cry,
'Twas famished, 'twas famished,
And I couldn't tell why.

I couldn't tell why,
But I saw that it would die,
For all that I kept dancing round and round,
And sing above it so cheerly,
With "Hey my little bird, and ho my little bird,
And oh but I love thee dearly!"

I never look sad,
I hear what people say,
I laugh when they are gay
And they think I am glad.

My tears never start,
I never say a word,
But I think that my heart
Is like that little bird.

Every day I read,
And I sing, and I play,
But thro' the long day
It taketh no heed.

It taketh no heed
Of any pleasant thing,
I know it doth not read,
I know it doth not sing.

With my mouth I read,
With my hands I play,
My shut heart is shut,
Coax it how you may.

You may coax it how you may
While the day is broad and bright,
But in the dead night
When the guests are gone away,

And no more the music sweet
Up the house doth pass,
Nor the dancing feet
Shake the nursery glass;

And I've heard my aunt
Along the corridor,
And my uncle gaunt
Lock his chamber door;

And upon the stair
All is hushed and still,
And the last wheel
Is silent in the square;

And the nurses snore,
And the dim sheets rise and fall,
And the lamplight's on the wall,
And the mouse is on the floor;

And the curtains of my bed
Are like a heavy cloud,
And the clock ticks loud,
And sounds are in my head;

And little Lizzie sleeps
Softly at my side,
It opens, it opens,
With a yearning strong and wide!

It yearns in my breast,
It utters no cry,
'Tis famished, 'tis famished,
And I feel that I shall die,
I feel that I shall die,
And none will know why.
Tho' the pleasant life is dancing round and round
And singing about me so cheerly,
With "Hey my little bird, and ho my little bird,
And oh but I love thee dearly!"

The Ballad of Keith of Ravelston

THE murmur of the mourning ghost
      That keeps the shadowy kine,
"O Keith of Ravelston,
   The sorrows of thy line!"

Ravelston, Ravelston,
  The merry path that leads
Down the golden morning hill,
  And through the silver meads;

Ravelston, Ravelston,
  The stile beneath the tree,
The maid that kept her mother's kine,
  The song that sang she!

She sang her song, she kept her kine,
  She sat beneath the thorn,
When Andrew Keith of Ravelston
  Rode through the Monday morn.

His henchmen sing, his hawk-bells ring,
  His belted jewels shine;
O Keith of Ravelston,
  The sorrows of thy line!

Year after year, where Andrew came,
  Comes evening down the glade,
And still there sits a moonshine ghost
  Where sat the sunshine maid.

Her misty hair is faint and fair,
  She keeps the shadowy kine;
O Keith of Ravelston,
  The sorrows of thy line!

I lay my hand upon the stile,
  The stile is lone and cold,
The burnie that goes babbling by
  Says naught that can be told.

Yet, stranger! here, from year to year,
  She keeps her shadowy kine;
O Keith of Ravelston,
  The sorrows of thy line!

Step out three steps, where Andrew stood—
  Why blanch thy cheeks for fear?
The ancient stile is not alone,
  'Tis not the burn I hear!

She makes her immemorial moan,
  She keeps her shadowy kine;
O Keith of Ravelston,
  The sorrows of thy line!

DANTE GABRIEL ROSSETTI (1828-1882)

The Blessed Damozel

THE blessed damozel leaned out
    From the gold bar of Heaven;
Her eyes were deeper than the depth
    Of waters stilled at even;
She had three lilies in her hand,
    And the stars in her hair were seven.

Her robe, ungirt from clasp to hem,
    No wrought flowers did adorn,
But a white rose of Mary's gift,
    For service sweetly worn;
Her hair that lay along her back
    Was yellow like ripe corn.

Herseemed she scarce had been a day
    One of God's choristers;
The wonder was not yet quite gone
    From that still look of hers;
Albeit, to them she left, her day
    Had counted as ten years.

(To one, it is ten years of years.
    . . . Yet now, and in this place,
Surely she leaned o'er me—her hair
    Fell all about my face. . . .
Nothing: the autumn fall of leaves.
    The whole year sets apace.)

It was the rampart of God's house
    That she was standing on;
By God built over the sheer depth
    The which is Space begun;
So high, that looking downward thence
    She scarce could see the sun.

It lies in Heaven, across the flood
    Of ether, as a bridge.
Beneath, the tides of day and night
    With flame and darkness ridge
The void, as low as where this earth
    Spins like a fretful midge.

Around her, lovers, newly met
    'Mid deathless love's acclaims,
Spoke evermore among themselves
    Their heart-remembered names;

And the souls mounting up to God
   Went by her like thin flames.

And still she bowed herself and stooped
   Out of the circling charm;
Until her bosom must have made
   The bar she leaned on warm,
And the lilies lay as if asleep
   Along her bended arm.

From the fixed place of Heaven she saw
   Time like a pulse shake fierce
Through all the worlds. Her gaze still strove
   Within the gulf to pierce
Its path; and now she spoke as when
   The stars sang in their spheres.

The sun was gone now; the curled moon
   Was like a little feather
Fluttering far down the gulf; and now
   She spoke through the still weather.
Her voice was like the voice the stars
   Had when they sang together.

(Ah sweet! Even now, in that bird's song,
   Strove not her accents there,
Fain to be hearkened? When those bells
   Possessed the mid-day air,
Strove not her steps to reach my side
   Down all the echoing stair?)

"I wish that he were come to me,
   For he will come," she said.
"Have not I prayed in Heaven?—on earth,
   Lord, Lord, has he not prayed?
Are not two prayers a perfect strength?
   And shall I feel afraid?

"When round his head the aureole clings,
   And he is clothed in white,
I'll take his hand and go with him
   To the deep wells of light;
As unto a stream we will step down,
   And bathe there in God's sight.

"We two will stand beside that shrine,
   Occult, withheld, untrod,
Whose lamps are stirred continually
   With prayer sent up to God;

And see our old prayers, granted, melt
  Each like a little cloud.

"We two will lie i' the shadow of
  That living mystic tree
Within whose secret growth the Dove
  Is sometimes felt to be,
While every leaf that His plumes touch
  Saith His Name audibly.

"And I myself will teach to him,
  I myself, lying so,
The songs I sing here; which his voice
  Shall pause in, hushed and slow,
And find some knowledge at each pause,
  Or some new thing to know."

(Alas! we two, we two, thou say'st!
  Yea, one wast thou with me
That once of old. But shall God lift
  To endless unity
The soul whose likeness with thy soul
  Was but its love for thee?)

"We two," she said, "will seek the groves
  Where the lady Mary is,
With her five handmaidens, whose names
  Are five sweet symphonies,
Cecily, Gertrude, Magdalen,
  Margaret and Rosalys.

"Circlewise sit they, with bound locks
  And foreheads garlanded;
Into the fine cloth white like flame
  Weaving the golden thread,
To fashion the birth-robes for them
  Who are just born, being dead.

"He shall fear, haply, and be dumb:
  Then will I lay my cheek
To his, and tell about our love,
  Not once abashed or weak:
And the dear Mother will approve
  My pride, and let me speak.

"Herself shall bring us, hand in hand,
  To Him round whom all souls
Kneel, the clear-ranged unnumbered heads
  Bowed with their aureoles:

And angels meeting us shall sing
　　To their cithern and citoles.

"There will I ask of Christ the Lord
　　Thus much for him and me:—
Only to live as once on earth
　　With Love, only to be,
As then awhile, for ever now
　　Together, I and he."

She gazed and listened and then said,
　　Less sad of speech than mild,—
"All this is when he comes." She ceased.
　　The light thrilled towards her, filled
With angels in strong level flight.
　　Her eyes prayed, and she smiled.

(I saw her smile.) But soon their path
　　Was vague in distant spheres:
And then she cast her arms along
　　The golden barriers,
And laid her face between her hands,
　　And wept. (I heard her tears.)

The Sonnet

A sonnet is a moment's monument,—
　　Memorial from the Soul's eternity
To one dead deathless hour. Look that it be,
Whether for lustral rite or dire portent,
Of its own arduous fulness reverent:
Carve it in ivory or in ebony,
As Day or Night may rule; and let Time see
Its flowering crest impearled and orient.
A Sonnet is a coin: its face reveals
The soul,—its converse, to what Power 'tis due:—
Whether for tribute to the august appeals
Of Life, or dower in Love's high retinue,
It serve; or, 'mid the dark wharf's cavernous breath,
In Charon's palm it pay the toll to Death.

Sonnets from "The House of Life"

IV

LOVESIGHT

WHEN do I see thee most, belovèd one?
　　When in the light the spirits of mine eyes
Before thy face their altar, solemnize
The worship of that Love through thee made known?

Or when in the dusk hours, (we two alone,)
Close-kissed and eloquent of still replies
Thy twilight-hidden glimmering visage lies,
And my soul only sees thy soul its own?
O love, my love! if I no more should see
Thyself, nor on the earth the shadow of thee,
Nor images of thine eyes in any spring,—
How then should sound upon Life's darkening slope
The ground-whirl of the perished leaves of Hope,
The wind of Death's imperishable wing?

V

HEART'S HOPE

By what word's power, the key of paths untrod,
Shall I the difficult deeps of Love explore,
Till parted waves of Song yield up the shore
Even as that sea which Israel crossed dryshod?
For lo! in some poor rhythmic period,
Lady, I fain would tell how evermore
Thy soul I know not from thy body, nor
Thee from myself, neither our love from God.
Yea, in God's name, and Love's, and thine, would I
Draw from one loving heart such evidence
As to all hearts all things shall signify;
Tender as dawn's first lull-fire, and intense
As instantaneous penetrating sense,
In Spring's birth-hour, of other Springs gone by.

XXVI

MID-RAPTURE

Thou lovely and belovèd, thou my love;
Whose kiss seems still the first; whose summoning eyes,
Even now, as for our love-world's new sunrise,
Shed very dawn; whose voice, attuned above
All modulation of the deep-bowered dove,
Is like a hand laid softly on the soul;
Whose hand is like a sweet voice to control
Those worn tired brows it hath the keeping of:—
What word can answer to thy word,—what gaze
To thine, which now absorbs within its sphere
My worshipping face, till I am mirrored there
Light-circled in a heaven of deep-drawn rays?
What clasp, what kiss mine inmost heart can prove,
O lovely and belovèd, O my love?

XXXIV

THE DARK GLASS

Not I myself know all my love for thee:
How should I reach so far, who cannot weigh
To-morrow's dower by gage of yesterday?
Shall birth and death, and all dark names that be
As doors and windows bared to some loud sea,
Lash deaf mine ears and blind my face with spray;
And shall my sense pierce love,—the last relay
And ultimate outpost of eternity?
Lo! what am I to Love, the lord of all?
One murmuring shell he gathers from the sand,—
One little heart-flame sheltered in his hand.
Yet through thine eyes he grants me clearest call
And veriest touch of powers primordial
That any hour-girt life may understand.

LXXVIII

BODY'S BEAUTY

Of Adam's first wife, Lilith, it is told
(The witch he loved before the gift of Eve,)
That, ere the snake's, her sweet tongue could deceive,
And her enchanted hair was the first gold.
And still she sits, young while the earth is old,
And, subtly of herself contemplative,
Draws men to watch the bright web she can weave,
Till heart and body and life are in its hold.
The rose and poppy are her flowers: for where
Is he not found, O Lilith! whom shed scent
And soft-shed kisses and soft sleep shall snare?
Lo! as that youth's eyes burned at thine, so went
Thy spell through him, and left his straight neck bent,
And round his heart one strangling golden hair.

A Superscription

LOOK in my face; my name is Might-have-been;
    I am also called No-more, Too-late, Farewell;
Unto thine ear I hold the dead-sea shell
Cast up thy Life's foam-fretted feet between;
Unto thine eyes the glass where that is seen
Which had Life's form and Love's, but by my spell
Is now a shaken shadow intolerable,
Of ultimate things unuttered the frail screen.
Mark me, how still I am! But should there dart

One moment through thy soul the soft surprise
Of that winged Peace which lulls the breath of sighs,—
Then shalt thou see me smile, and turn apart
Thy visage to mine ambush at thy heart
Sleepless with cold commemorative eyes.

The Ballade of Dead Ladies, from the French of François Villon, 1450

TELL me now in what hidden way is
  Lady Flora the lovely Roman?
Where's Hipparchia, and where is Thais,
  Neither of them the fairer woman?
  Where is Echo, beheld of no man,
Only heard on river and mere,—
  She whose beauty was more than human? . . .
But where are the snows of yester-year?

Where's Héloise, the learnèd nun,
  For whose sake Abeilard, I ween,
Lost manhood and put priesthood on?
  (From Love he won such dule and teen!)
  And where, I pray you, is the Queen
Who willed that Buridan should steer
  Sewed in a sack's mouth down the Seine? . . .
But where are the snows of yester-year?

White Queen Blanche, like a queen of lilies,
  With a voice like any mermaiden,—
Bertha Broadfoot, Beatrice, Alice,
  And Ermengarde the lady of Maine,—
  And that good Joan whom Englishmen
At Rouen doomed and burned her there,—
  Mother of God, where are they then? . . .
But where are the snows of yester-year?

Nay, never ask this week, fair lord,
  Where they are gone, nor yet this year,
Except with this for an overword,—
  But where are the snows of yester-year?

One Girl (A Combination from "Sappho")

I

LIKE the sweet apple which reddens upon the topmost
    bough,
  A-top on the topmost twig,—which the pluckers forgot,
    somehow,—

Forgot it not, nay, but got it not, for none could get it till
   now.

II

Like the wild hyacinth flower which on the hills is found,
Which the passing feet of the shepherds for ever tear and
   wound,
Until the purple blossom is trodden into the ground.

GEORGE MEREDITH (1828-1909)
Love in the Valley

UNDER yonder beech-tree single on the green-sward,
   Couched with her arms behind her golden head,
Knees and tresses folded to slip and ripple idly,
   Lies my young love sleeping in the shade.
Had I the heart to slide an arm beneath her,
   Press her parting lips as her waist I gather slow,
Waking in amazement she could not but embrace me:
   Then would she hold me and never let me go?

Shy as the squirrel and wayward as the swallow,
   Swift as the swallow along the river's light
Circleting the surface to meet his mirrored winglets,
   Fleeter she seems in her stay than in her flight,
Shy as the squirrel that leaps among the pine-tops,
   Wayward as the swallow overhead at set of sun,
She whom I love is hard to catch and conquer,
   Hard, but O the glory of the winning were she won!

When her mother tends her before the laughing mirror,
   Tying up her laces, looping up her hair,
Often she thinks, were this wild thing wedded,
   More love should I have, and much less care.
When her mother tends her before the lighted mirror,
   Loosening her laces, combing down her curls,
Often she thinks, were this wild thing wedded,
   I should miss but one for many boys and girls.

Heartless she is as the shadow in the meadows,
   Flying to the hills on a blue and breezy noon.
No, she is athirst and drinking up her wonder:
   Earth to her is young as the slip of the new moon.
Deals she an unkindness, 'tis but her rapid measure,
   Even as in a dance; and her smile can heal no less:
Like the swinging May-cloud that pelts the flowers with hail-
   stones
   Off a sunny border, she was made to bruise and bless.

Lovely are the curves of the white owl sweeping
  Wavy in the dusk lit by one large star.
Lone on the fir-branch, his rattle-note unvaried,
  Brooding o'er the gloom, spins the brown eve-jar.
Darker grows the valley, more and more forgetting:
  So were it with me if forgetting could be willed.
Tell the grassy hollow that holds the bubbling well-spring,
  Tell it to forget the source that keeps it filled.

Stepping down the hill with her fair companions,
  Arm in arm, all against the raying West,
Boldly she sings, to the merry tune she marches;
  Brave in her shape, and sweeter unpossessed.
Sweeter, for she is what my heart first awaking
  Whispered the world was; morning light is she.
Love that so desires would fain keep her changeless;
  Fain would fling the net, and fain have her free.

Happy, happy time, when the white star hovers
  Low over dim fields fresh with bloomy dew,
Near the face of dawn, that draws athwart the darkness,
  Threading it with color, like yewberries the yew.
Thicker crowd the shades as the grave East deepens
  Glowing, and with crimson a long cloud swells.
Maiden still the morn is; and strange she is, and secret;
  Strange her eyes; her cheeks are cold as cold sea-shells.

Sunrays, leaning on our southern hills and lighting
  Wild cloud-mountains that drag the hills along,
Oft ends the day of your shifting brilliant laughter
  Chill as a dull face frowning on a song.
Ay, but shows the South-west a ripple-feathered bosom
  Blown to silver while the clouds are shaken and ascend
Scaling the mid-heavens as they stream, there comes a sunset
  Rich, deep like love in beauty without end.

When at dawn she sighs, and like an infant to the window
  Turns grave eyes craving light, released from dreams,
Beautiful she looks, like a white water-lily
  Bursting out of bud in havens of the streams.
When from bed she rises clothed from neck to ankle
  In her long nightgown sweet as boughs of May,
Beautiful she looks, like a tall garden-lily
  Pure from the night, and splendid for the day.

Mother of the dews, dark eye-lashed twilight,
  Low-lidded twilight, o'er the valley's brim,
Rounding on thy breast sings the dew-delighted skylark,
  Clear as though the dewdrops had their voice in him.

Hidden where the rose-flush drinks the rayless planet,
  Fountain-full he pours the spraying fountain-showers.
Let me hear her laughter, I would have her ever
  Cool as dew in twilight, the lark above the flowers.

All the girls are out with their baskets for the primrose;
  Up lanes, woods through, they troop in joyful bands.
My sweet leads: she knows not why, but now she loiters,
  Eyes the bent anemones, and hangs her hands.
Such a look will tell that the violets are peeping,
  Coming the rose: and unaware a cry
Springs in her bosom for odours and for colour,
  Covert and the nightingale; she knows not why.

Kerchiefed head and chin she darts between her tulips,
  Streaming like a willow gray in arrowy rain:
Some bend beaten cheek to gravel, and their angel
  She will be; she lifts them, and on she speeds again.
Black the driving rain cloud breasts the iron gateway:
  She is forth to cheer a neighbour lacking mirth.
So when sky and grass met rolling dumb for thunder
  Saw I once a white dove, sole light of earth.

Prim little scholars are the flowers of her garden,
  Trained to stand in rows, and asking if they please.
I might love them well but for loving more the wild ones:
  O my wild ones! they tell me more than these.
You, my wild one, you tell of honied field-rose,
  Violet, blushing eglantine in life; and even as they,
They by the wayside are earnest of your goodness,
  You are of life's, on the banks that line the way.

Peering at her chamber the white crowns the red rose,
  Jasmine winds the porch with stars two and three.
Parted is the window; she sleeps; the starry jasmine
  Breathes a falling breath that carries thoughts of me.
Sweeter unpossessed, have I said of her my sweetest?
  Not while she sleeps: while she sleeps the jasmine breathes,
Luring her to love: she sleeps; the starry jasmine
  Bears me to her pillow under white rose-wreaths.

Yellow with birdfoot-trefoil are the grass-glades;
  Yellow with cinquefoil of the dew-gray leaf;
Yellow with stonecrop; the moss-mounds are yellow;
  Blue-necked the wheat sways, yellowing to the sheaf.
Green-yellow bursts from the copse the laughing yaffle;
  Sharp as a sickle is the edge of shade and shine:
Earth in her heart laughs looking at the heavens,
  Thinking of the harvest: I look and think of mine.

This I may know: her dressing and undressing
  Such a change of light shows as when the skies in sport
Shift from cloud to moonlight; or edging over thunder
  Slips a ray of sun; or sweeping into port
White sails furl; or on the ocean borders
  White sails lean along the waves leaping green.
Visions of her shower before me, but from eyesight
  Guarded she would be like the sun were she seen.

Front door and back of the mossed old farmhouse
  Open with the morn, and in a breezy link
Freshly sparkles garden to stripe-shadowed orchard,
  Green across a rill where on sand the minnows wink.
Busy in the grass the early sun of summer
  Swarms, and the blackbird's mellow fluting notes
Call my darling up with round and roguish challenge:
  Quaintest, richest carol of all the singing throats!

Cool was the woodside; cool as her white dairy
  Keeping sweet the cream-pan; and there the boys from
    school,
Cricketing below, rushed brown and red with sunshine;
  O the dark translucence of the deep-eyed cool!
Spying from the farm, herself she fetched a pitcher
  Full of milk, and tilted for each in turn the beak.
Then a little fellow, mouth up and on tiptoe,
  Said, "I will kiss you": she laughed and leaned her cheek.

Doves of the fir-wood walling high our red roof
  Through the long noon coo, crooning through the coo.
Loose droop the leaves, and down the sleepy roadway
  Sometimes pipes a chaffinch; loose droops the blue.
Cows flap a slow tail knee-deep in the river,
  Breathless, given up to sun and gnat and fly.
Nowhere is she seen; and if I see her nowhere,
  Lightning may come, straight rains and tiger sky.

O the golden sheaf, the rustling treasure-armful!
  O the nutbrown tresses nodding interlaced!
O the treasure-tresses one another over
  Nodding! O the girdle slack about the waist!
Slain are the poppies that shot their random scarlet
  Quick amid the wheat-ears: wound about the waist,
Gathered, see these brides of Earth one blush of ripeness!
  O the nutbrown tresses nodding interlaced.

Large and smoky red the sun's cold disk drops,
  Clipped by naked hills, on violet shaded snow:
Eastward large and still lights up a bower of moonrise,
  Whence at her leisure steps the moon aglow.

Nightlong on black print-branches our beech-tree
Gazes in this whiteness: nightlong could I.
Here may life on death or death on life be painted.
Let me clasp her soul to know she cannot die!

Gossips count her faults; they scour a narrow chamber
Where there is no window, read not heaven or her.
"When she was a tiny," one agèd woman quavers,
Plucks at my heart and leads me by the ear.
Faults she had once as she learned to run and tumbled:
Faults of feature some see, beauty not complete.
Yet, good gossips, beauty that makes holy
Earth and air, may have faults from head to feet.

Hither she comes; she comes to me; she lingers,
Deepens her brown eyebrows, while in new surprise
High rise the lashes in wonder of a stranger;
Yet am I the light and living of her eyes.
Something friends have told her fills her heart to brimming,
Nets her in her blushes, and wounds her, and tames.—
Sure of her haven, O like a dove alighting,
Arms up, she dropped: our souls were in our names.

Soon will she lie like a white frost sunrise.
Yellow oats and brown wheat, barley pale as rye,
Long since your sheaves have yielded to the thresher,
Felt the girdle loosened, seen the tresses fly.
Soon will she lie like a blood-red sunset.
Swift with the to-morrow, green-winged Spring!
Sing from the South-west, bring her back the truants,
Nightingale and swallow, song and dipping wing.

Soft new beech-leaves, up to beamy April
Spreading bough on bough a primrose mountain, you,
Lucid in the moon, raise lilies to the skyfields,
Youngest green transfused in silver shining through:
Fairer than the lily, than the wild white cherry:
Fair as in image my seraph love appears
Borne to me by dreams when dawn is at my eyelids:
Fair as in the flesh she swims to me on tears.

Could I find a place to be alone with heaven,
I would speak my heart out: heaven is my need.
Every woodland tree is flushing like the dogwood,
Flashing like the whitebeam, swaying like the reed.
Flushing like the dogwood crimson in October;
Streaming like the flag-reed South-west blown;
Flashing as in gusts the sudden-lighted whitebeam:
All seem to know what is for heaven alone.

Lucifer in Starlight

O N a starr'd night Prince Lucifer uprose.
⠀⠀⠀Tired of his dark dominion swung the fiend
⠀⠀Above the rolling ball in cloud part screen'd,
Where sinners hugg'd their sceptre of repose.
Poor prey to his hot fit of pride were those.
⠀⠀⠀And now upon his western wing he lean'd,
⠀⠀Now his huge bulk o'er Afric's sands careen'd,
Now the black planet shadow'd Arctic snows.
Soaring thru wider zones that prick'd his scars
⠀⠀With memory of the old revolt from Awe,
He reach'd the middle height, and at the stars,
Which are the brain of heaven, he look'd, and sank.
Around the ancient track march'd, rank on rank,
⠀⠀The army of unalterable law.

From "Modern Love"

I

B Y this he knew she wept with waking eyes:
⠀⠀That, at his hand's light quiver by her head,
The strange low sobs that shook their common bed
Were called into her with a sharp surprise,
And strangled mute, like little gaping snakes,
Dreadfully venomous to him. She lay
Stone-still, and the long darkness flowed away
With muffled pulses. Then as midnight makes
Her giant heart of Memory and Tears
Drink the pale drug of silence, and so beat
Sleep's heavy measure, they from head to feet
Were moveless, looking through their dead black years,
By vain regret scrawled over the blank wall.
Like sculptured effigies they might be seen
Upon their marriage-tomb, the sword between;
Each wishing for the sword that severs all.

XLI

How many a thing which we cast to the ground,
When others pick it up becomes a gem!
We grasp at all the wealth it is to them;
And by reflected light its worth is found.
Yet for us still 'tis nothing! and that zeal
Of false appreciation quickly fades.
This truth is little known to human shades,
How rare from their own instinct 'tis to feel!
They waste the soul with spurious desire,

That is not the ripe flame upon the bough.
We two have taken up a lifeless vow
To rob a living passion: dust for fire!
Madam is grave, and eyes the clock that tells
Approaching midnight. We have struck despair
Into two hearts. O, look we like a pair
Who for fresh nuptials joyfully yield all else?

XLVII

We saw the swallows gathering in the sky,
And in the osier-isle we heard their noise.
We had not to look back on summer joys,
Or forward to a summer of bright dye:
But in the largeness of the evening earth
Our spirits grew as we went side by side.
The hour became her husband and my bride.
Love that had robbed us so, thus blessed our dearth!
The pilgrims of the year waxed very loud
In multitudinous chatterings, as the flood
Full brown came from the West, and like pale blood
Expanded to the upper crimson cloud.
Love that had robbed us of immortal things,
This little moment mercifully gave,
Where I had seen across the twilight wave
The swan sail with her young beneath her wings.

XLIX

He found her by the ocean's moaning verge,
Nor any wicked change in her discerned;
And she believed his old love had returned,
Which was her exultation, and her scourge.
She took his hand, and walked with him, and seemed
The wife he sought, though shadow-like and dry.
She had one terror, lest her heart should sigh,
And tell her loudly she no longer dreamed.
She dared not say, "This is my breast: look in."
But there's a strength to help the desperate weak.
That night he learned how silence best can speak
The awful things when Pity pleads for Sin.
About the middle of the night her call
Was heard, and he came wondering to the bed.
"Now kiss me, dear! it may be, now!" she said.
Lethe had passed those lips, and he knew all.

L

Thus piteously Love closed what he begat:
The union of this ever-diverse pair!
These two were rapid falcons in a snare,
Condemned to do the flitting of the bat.
Lovers beneath the singing sky of May,
They wandered once; clear as the dew on flowers:

But they fed not on the advancing hours:
Their hearts held cravings for the buried day.
Then each applied to each that fatal knife,
Deep questioning, which probes to endless dole.
Ah, what a dusty answer gets the soul
When hot for certainties in this our life!—
In tragic hints here see what evermore
Moves dark as yonder midnight ocean's force,
Thumping like ramping hosts of warrior horse,
To throw that faint thin line upon the shore!

CHRISTINA G. ROSSETTI (1830-1894)

A Birthday

MY heart is like a singing bird
    Whose nest is in a watered shoot;
My heart is like an apple-tree
    Whose boughs are bent with thickest fruit;
My heart is like a rainbow shell
    That paddles in a halcyon sea;
My heart is gladder than all these
    Because my love is come to me.

Raise me a dais of silk and down,
    Hang it with vair and purple dyes;
Carve it in doves, and pomegranates,
    And peacocks with a hundred eyes;
Work it in gold and silver grapes,
    In leaves and silver fleurs-de-lys;
Because the birthday of my life
    Is come, my love is come to me.

Up-Hill

DOES the road wind up-hill all the way?
    Yes, to the very end.
Will the day's journey take the whole long day?
    From morn till night, my friend.

But is there for the night a resting-place?
    A roof for when the slow dark hours begin.
May not the darkness hide it from my face?
    You cannot miss that inn.

Shall I meet other wayfarers at night?
    Those who have gone before.
Then must I knock, or call when just in sight?
    They will not keep you standing at that door.

Shall I find comfort, travel-sore and weak?
  Of labour you shall find the sum.
Will there be beds for me and all who seek?
  Yea, beds for all who come.

Song

WHEN I am dead, my dearest,
    Sing no sad songs for me;
Plant thou no roses at my head,
    Nor shady cypress-tree:
Be the green grass above me
    With showers and dewdrops wet;
And if thou wilt, remember,
    And if thou wilt, forget.

I shall not see the shadows,
    I shall not feel the rain;
I shall not hear the nightingale
    Sing on, as if in pain:
And dreaming through the twilight
    That doth not rise nor set,
Haply I may remember
    And haply may forget.

Rest

O earth, lie heavily upon her eyes:
    Seal her sweet eyes weary of watching, Earth;
  Lie close around her; leave no room for mirth
With its harsh laughter, nor for sound of sighs.
She hath no questions, she hath no replies.
    Hush'd in and curtain'd with a blessèd dearth
    Of all that irk'd her from the hour of birth;
With stillness that is almost Paradise.
Darkness more clear than noonday holdeth her,
    Silence more musical than any song;
Even her very heart has ceased to stir:
Until the morning of Eternity
Her rest shall not begin nor end, but be;
    And when she wakes she will not think it long.

Remember

REMEMBER me when I am gone away,
    Gone far away into the silent land,
  When you can no more hold me by the hand.
Nor I half turn to go, yet turning stay.

Remember me when no more day by day
  You tell me of our future that you plann'd:
Only remember me; you understand
It will be late to counsel then or pray.
Yet if you should forget me for a while
  And afterwards remember, do not grieve:
For if the darkness and corruption leave
  A vestige of the thoughts that once I had,
Better by far you should forget and smile
  Than that you should remember and be sad.

THOMAS EDWARD BROWN (1830-1897)

My Garden

A garden is a lovesome thing, God wot!
  Rose plot,
    Fringed pool,
  Ferned grot—
    The veriest school
    Of peace; and yet the fool
Contends that God is not—
Not God! in gardens! when the eve is cool?
  Nay, but I have a sign:
  'Tis very sure God walks in mine.

LEWIS CARROLL (Pseud. of C. L. Dodgson) (1832-1898)

Jabberwocky

'TWAS brillig, and the slithy toves
  Did gyre and gimble in the wabe;
All mimsy were the borogoves,
  And the mome raths outgrabe.

"Beware the Jabberwock, my son!
  The jaws that bite, the claws that catch!
Beware the Jubjub bird, and shun
  The frumious Bandersnatch!"

He took his vorpal sword in hand:
  Long time the manxome foe he sought—
So rested he by the tum-tum tree,
  And stood awhile in thought.

And as in uffish thought he stood,
  The Jabberwock, with eyes of flame,
Came whiffling through the tulgey wood,
  And burbled as it came!

One, two! One, two! And through and through
  The vorpal blade went snicker-snack!

He left it dead, and with its head
   He went galumphing back.

"And hast thou slain the Jabberwock?
   Come to my arms, my beamish boy!
O frabjous day! Callooh! Callay!"
   He chortled in his joy.

'Twas brillig, and the slithy toves
   Did gyre and gimble in the wabe;
All mimsy were the borogroves,
   And the mome raths outgrabe.

SIR EDWIN ARNOLD (1832-1904)

We Are the Voices of the Whispering Wind

WE are the voices of the wandering wind,
   Which moan for rest and rest can never find;
Lo! as the wind is, so is mortal life,
A moan, a sigh, a sob, a storm, a strife.

Wherefore and whence we are ye cannot know,
Nor where life springs nor whither life doth go;
We are as ye are, ghosts from the inane,
What pleasure have we of our changeful pain?

What pleasure hast thou of thy changeful bliss?
Nay, if love lasted, there were joy in this;
But life's way is the wind's way, all these things,
Are but brief voices breathed on shifting strings.

JAMES THOMSON (1834-1882)

From "The City of Dreadful Night"

THE chambers of the mansions of my heart,
   In every one whereof thine image dwells,
Are black with grief eternal for thy sake.

The inmost oratory of my soul,
Wherein thou ever dwellest quick or dead,
Is black with grief eternal for thy sake.

I kneel beside thee and I clasp the cross,
With eyes forever fixed upon that face,
So beautiful and dreadful in its calm.

I kneel here patient as thou liest there;
As patient as a statue carved in stone,
Of adoration and eternal grief.

While thou dost not awake I cannot move;
And something tells me thou wilt never wake,
And I alive feel turning into stone.

The Vine

THE wine of Love is music,
    And the feast of Love is song:
And when Love sits down to the banquet,
    Love sits long:

Sits long and arises drunken,
    But not with the feast and the wine;
He reeleth with his own heart,
    That great, rich Vine.

Give a Man a Horse He Can Ride

GIVE a man a horse he can ride,
    Give a man a boat he can sail;
And his rank and wealth, his strength and health
    Nor sea nor shore shall fail.

Give a man a pipe he can smoke,
    Give a man a book he can read;
And his home is bright with a calm delight,
    Though the rooms be poor indeed.

Give a man a girl he can love,
    As I, O my Love, love thee;
And his hand is great with the pulse of Fate,
    At home, on land, on sea.

WILLIAM MORRIS (1834-1896)

Prelude to "The Earthly Paradise"

OF Heaven or Hell I have no power to sing,
    I cannot ease the burden of your fears,
Or make quick-coming death a little thing,
Or bring again the pleasure of past years,
Nor for my words shall ye forget your tears,
Or hope again for aught that I can say,
The idle singer of an empty day.

But rather, when aweary of your mirth,
From full hearts still unsatisfied ye sigh,
And, feeling kindly unto all the earth,
Grudge every minute as it passes by,
Made the more mindful that the sweet days die,—
Remember me a little then, I pray,
The idle singer of an empty day.

The heavy trouble, the bewildering care
That weighs us down who live and earn our bread,
These idle verses have no power to bear;
So let me sing of names rememberèd,
Because they, living not, can ne'er be dead,
Or long time take their memory quite away
From us poor singers of an empty day.

Dreamer of dreams, born out of my due time,
Why should I strive to set the crooked straight?
Let it suffice me that my murmuring rhyme
Beats with light wing against the ivory gate,
Telling a tale not too importunate
To those who in the sleepy region stay,
Lulled by the singer of an empty day.

Folk say, a wizard to a northern king
At Christmas-tide such wondrous things did show,
That through one window men beheld the spring,
And through another saw the summer glow,
And through a third the fruited vines a-row,
While still, unheard, but in its wonted way,
Piped the drear wind of that December day.

So with this Earthly Paradise it is,
If ye will read aright, and pardon me,
Who strive to build a shadowy isle of bliss
Midmost the beating of the steely sea,
Where tossed about all hearts of men must be;
Whose ravening monsters mighty men shall slay,
Not the poor singer of an empty day.

Love is Enough

LOVE is enough: though the world be a-waning,
    And the woods have no voice but the voice of complaining,
Though the sky be too dark for dim eyes to discover
The gold-cups and daisies fair blooming thereunder,
Though the hills be held shadows, and the sea a dark wonder,
    And this day draw a veil over all deeds pass'd over,
Yet their hands shall not tremble, their feet shall not falter;
The wind shall not weary, the fear shall not alter
    These lips and these eyes of the loved and the lover.

The Nymph's Song to Hylas, from "The Life and Death of Jason"

I know a little garden-close
  Set thick with lily and red rose,
Where I would wander if I might
From dewy dawn to dewy night,
And have one with me wandering.

And though within it no birds sing,
And though no pillared house is there,
And though the apple boughs are bare
Of fruit and blossom, would to God,
Her feet upon the green grass trod,
And I beheld them as before!

There comes a murmur from the shore,
And in the place two fair streams are,
Drawn from the purple hills afar,
Drawn down unto the restless sea;
The hills whose flowers ne'er fed the bee,
The shore no ship has ever seen,
Still beaten by the billows green,
Whose murmur comes unceasingly
Unto the place for which I cry.

For which I cry both day and night,
For which I let slip all delight,
That maketh me both deaf and blind,
Careless to win, unskilled to find,
And quick to lose what all men seek.

Yet tottering as I am, and weak,
Still have I left a little breath
To seek within the jaws of death
An entrance to that happy place;
To seek the unforgotten face
Once seen, once kissed, once reft from me
Anigh the murmuring of the sea.

Song of Orpheus, from "The Life and Death of Jason"

O surely now the fisherman
  Draws homeward through the water wan
Across the bay we know so well,
And in the sheltered chalky dell
The shepherd stirs: and now afield

They drive the team, with white wand peeled,
Muttering across the barley-head
At daily toil and dreary-head.

And midst them all, perchance, my love
Is waking, and doth gently move
And stretch her soft arms out to me,
Forgetting thousand leagues of sea;
And now her body I behold,
Unhidden but by hair of gold,
And now the silver waters kiss,
The crown of all delight and bliss.
And now I see her bind her hair
And don upon her raiment fair,
And now before the altar stand,
With incense in her outstretched hand,
   To supplicate the Gods for me;
   Ah! one day landing from the sea,
   Amid the maidens shall I hear
   Her voice in praise, and see her near,
   Holding the gold-wrapt laurel crown,
   'Midst of the shouting, wondering town!

JOHN LEICESTER WARREN, LORD DE TABLEY
(1835-1895)

From "Orestes"

L ET us go up and look him in the face—
   We are but as he made us: the disgrace
Of this, our imperfection, is his own—
And unabashed in that fierce stare and blaze
Front him and say,
"We come not to atone,
To cringe and moan:
God, vindicate thy way.
Erase the staining sorrow we have known,
Thou, whom ill things obey;
And give our clay
Some master bliss imperial as thine own:
Or wipe us quite away,
Far from the ray of thine eternal throne.
Dream not we love this sorrow of our breath,
Hope not we wince or palpitate at death;
Slay us, for thine is nature and thy slave:
Draw down her clouds to be our sacrifice,
And heap unmeasured mountain for our grave,
With peaks of fire and ice.

Flicker one cord of lightning, north to south,
And mix in awful glories wood and cloud;
We shall have rest, and find
Illimitable darkness for our shroud;
We shall have peace, then, surely, when thy mouth
Breathes us away into the darkness blind,
Then only kind.

From "Hymn to Astarte"

WHAT foreland fledged with myrrh,
    Vocal with myriad bees,
What pine-sequestered spur,
  What lone declivities,
    Will draw thee to descend,
    Creation's cradle-friend?

The sun feeds at thy smiles,
  The wan moon glows thereby.
The dædal ocean isles
  Terraced in rosemary,
    The brushwood in the bed
    Of the dry torrent head.

The rolling river brink
  With plumy sedges grey,
The ford where foxes drink,
  The creek where others play—
    Year upwards—all of them—
    To grasp thy raiment's hem.

SIR WILLIAM SCHWENCK GILBERT (1836-1911)

The Yarn of the "Nancy Bell"

'TWAS on the shores that round our coast
  From Deal to Ramsgate span,
That I found alone, on a piece of stone,
  An elderly naval man.

His hair was weedy, his beard was long,
  And weedy and long was he,
And I heard this wight on the shore recite,
  In a singular minor key:

"Oh, I am a cook and a captain bold,
  And the mate of the *Nancy* brig,
And a bo'sun tight, and a midshipmite
  And the crew of the captain's gig."

And he shook his fists and he tore his hair
  Till I really felt afraid,
For I couldn't help thinking the man had been drinking
  And so I simply said:

"Oh, elderly man, it's little I know,
  Of the duties of men of the sea,
And I'll eat my hand if I understand
  How you can possibly be

"At once a cook and a captain bold
  And the mate of the *Nancy* brig,
And a bo'sun tight and a midshipmite,
  And a crew of the captain's gig."

Then he gave a hitch to his trousers, which
  Is a trick all seamen larn,
And having got rid of a thumping quid,
  He spun this painful yarn:

" 'Twas in the good ship *Nancy Bell*
  That we sailed to the Indian sea,
And there on a reef we came to grief,
  Which has often occurred to me.

"And pretty nigh all o' the crew was drowned
  (There was seventy-seven o' soul),
And only ten of the *Nancy's* men
  Said 'Here!' to the muster roll.

"There was me and the cook and the captain bold,
  And the mate of the *Nancy* brig,
And the bo'sun tight an' a midshipmite,
  And the crew of the captain's gig.

"For a month we'd neither wittles nor drink,
  Till a-hungry we did feel,
So, we drawed a lot, and, accordin', shot
  The captain for our meal.

"The next lot fell to the *Nancy's* mate,
  And a delicate dish he made:
Then our appetite with the midshipmite
  We seven survivors stayed.

"And then we murdered the bo'sun tight,
  And he much resembled pig;
Then we wittled free, did the cook and me,
  On the crew of the captain's gig.

"Then only the cook and me was left,
  And the delicate question, 'which
Of us goes to the kettle?' arose,
  And we argued it out as sich.

"For I loved that cook as a brother, I did,
  And the cook he worshipped me;
But we'd both be blowed if we'd either be stowed
  In the other chap's hold, you see.

" 'I'll be eat if you dines off me,' says Tom.
  'Yes, that,' says I, " 'you'll be,'—
" 'I'm boiled if I die, my friend,' quoth I,
  And 'exactly so,' says he.

"Says he, 'Dear James, to murder me
  Were a foolish thing to do,
For don't you see that you can't cook *me*,
  While I can—and will—cook *you!*'

"So, he boils the water, and takes the salt
  And the pepper in portions true
(Which he never forgot), and some chopped shalot,
  And some sage and parsley, too.

" 'Come here,' says he, with a proper pride,
  Which his smiling features tell,
' 'Twill soothing be if I let you see
  How extremely nice you'll smell.'

"And he stirred it round and round and round,
  And he sniffed at the foaming froth;
When I ups with his heels, and smothers his squeals
  In the scum of the boiling broth.

"And I eat that cook in a week or less,
  And—as I eating be
The last of his chops, why I almost drops,
  For a wessel in sight I see.
   *   *   *   *   *   *   *
"And I never larf, and I never smile,
  And I never lark nor play,
But I set and croak, and a single joke
  I have—which is to say:

"Oh, I am a cook and a captain bold,
  And the mate of the *Nancy* brig,
And a bo'sun tight, and a midshipmite,
  And the crew of the captain's gig!"

To the Terrestrial Globe

By a Miserable Wretch

R OLL on, thou ball, roll on!
      Through pathless realms of Space
            Roll on!
What though I'm in a sorry case?
What though I cannot meet my bills?
What though I suffer toothache's ills?
What though I swallow countless pills?
      Never *you* mind!
            Roll on!

Roll on, thou ball, roll on!
Through seas of inky air
            Roll on!
It's true I've got no shirts to wear;
It's true my butcher's bill is due;
It's true my prospects all look blue—
But don't let that unsettle you!
      Never *you* mind!
            Roll on!   (*It rolls on*)

THEODORE WATTS-DUNTON (1836-1914)

From "The Coming of Love"

B ENEATH the loveliest dream there coils a fear:
      Last night came she whose eyes are memories now;
Her far-off gaze seemed all forgetful how
Love dimmed them once, so calm they shone and clear.
"Sorrow," I said, "has made me old, my dear;
'Tis I, indeed, but grief can change the brow:
Beneath my load a seraph's neck might bow,
Vigils like mine would blanch an angel's hair."
Oh, then I saw, I saw the sweet lips move!
I saw the love-mists thickening in her eyes—
I heard a sound as if a murmuring dove
Felt lonely in the dells of Paradise;
But when upon my neck she fell, my love,
Her hair smelt sweet of whin and woodland spice.

ALGERNON CHARLES SWINBURNE (1837-1909)

From "The Triumph of Time"

I will go back to the great sweet mother,—
      Mother and lover of men, the Sea.
I will go down to her, I and none other,
      Close with her, kiss her, and mix her with me;

Cling to her, strive with her, hold her fast;
O fair white mother, in days long past
Born without sister, born without brother,
    Set free my soul as thy soul is free.

O fair green-girdled mother of mine,
    Sea, that art clothed with the sun and the rain,
Thy sweet hard kisses are strong like wine,
    Thy large embraces are keen like pain.
Save me and hide me with all thy waves,
Find me one grave of thy thousand graves,
Those pure cold populous graves of thine,
    Wrought without hand in a world without stain.

I shall sleep, and move with the moving ships,
    Change as the winds change, veer in the tide;
My lips will feast on the foam of thy lips,
    I shall rise with thy rising, with thee subside;
Sleep, and not know if she be, if she were,
Filled full with life to the eyes and hair,
As a rose is fulfilled to the rose-leaf tips
    With splendid summer and perfume and pride.

This woven raiment of nights and days,
    Were it once cast off and unwound from me,
Naked and glad would I walk in thy ways,
    Alive and aware of thy waves and thee;
Clear of the whole world, hidden at home,
Clothed with the green, and crowned with the foam,
A pulse of the life of thy straits and bays,
    A vein in the heart of the streams of the Sea.

Fair mother, fed with the lives of men,
    Thou art subtle and cruel of heart, men say;
Thou hast taken, and shalt not render again;
    Thou art full of thy dead, and cold as they.
But death is the worst that comes of thee;
Thou art fed with our dead, O Mother, O Sea,
But when hast thou fed on our hearts? or when
    Having given us love, hast thou taken away?

O tender-hearted, O perfect lover,
    Thy lips are bitter, and sweet thine heart.
The hopes that hurt and the dreams that hover,
    Shall they not vanish away and apart?
But thou, thou art sure, thou art older than earth;
Thou art strong for death and fruitful of birth;
Thy depths conceal and thy gulfs discover;
    From the first thou wert; in the end thou art.

Chorus from "Atalanta in Calydon"

WHEN the hounds of spring are on winter's traces,
    The mother of months in meadow or plain
Fills the shadows and windy places
    With lisp of leaves and ripple of rain;
And the brown bright nightingale amorous
Is half assuaged for Itylus,
For the Thracian ships and the foreign faces,
    The tongueless vigil, and all the pain.

Come with bows bent and with emptying of quivers,
    Maiden most perfect, lady of light,
With a noise of winds and many rivers,
    With a clamor of waters, and with might;
Bind on thy sandals, O thou most fleet,
Over the splendour and speed of thy feet;
For the faint east quickens, the wan west shivers,
    Round the feet of the day and the feet of the night.

Where shall we find her, how shall we sing to her,
    Fold our hands round her knees, and cling?
O that man's heart were as fire and could spring to her,
    Fire, or the strength of the streams that spring!
For the stars and the winds are unto her
As raiment, as songs of the harp-player;
For the risen stars and the fallen cling to her,
    And the southwest-wind and the west-wind sing.

For winter's rains and ruins are over,
    And all the season of snows and sins;
The days dividing lover and lover,
    The light that loses, the night that wins;
And time remembered is grief forgotten,
And frosts are slain and flowers begotten,
And in green underwood and cover
    Blossom by blossom the spring begins.

The full streams feed on flower of rushes,
    Ripe grasses trammel a travelling foot,
The faint fresh flame of the young year flushes
    From leaf to flower and flower to fruit;
And fruit and leaf are as gold and fire,
And the oat is heard above the lyre,
And the hoofèd heel of a satyr crushes
    The chestnut-husk at the chestnut-root.

And Pan by noon and Bacchus by night,
    Fleeter of foot than the fleet-foot kid,

Follows with dancing and fills with delight
　　The Mænad and the Bassarid;
And soft as lips that laugh and hide
The laughing leaves of the trees divide,
And screen from seeing and leave in sight
　　The god pursuing, the maiden hid.

The ivy falls with the Bacchanal's hair
　　Over her eyebrows hiding her eyes;
　　The wild vine slipping down leaves bare
　　Her bright breast shortening into sighs;
The wild vine slips with the weight of its leaves,
But the berried ivy catches and cleaves
To the limbs that glitter, the feet that scare
　　The wolf that follows, the fawn that flies.

The Garden of Prosperine

HERE, where the world is quiet,
　　　　Here, where all trouble seems
Dead winds' and spent waves' riot
　　In doubtful dreams of dreams,
I watch the green field growing
For reaping folk and sowing,
For harvest-time and mowing,
　　A sleepy world of streams.

I am tired of tears and laughter,
　　And men that laugh and weep;
Of what may come hereafter
　　For men that sow to reap:
I am weary of days and hours,
Blown buds of barren flowers,
Desires and dreams and powers,
　　And everything but sleep.

Here life has death for neighbour,
　　And far from eye or ear
Wan waves and wet winds labour,
　　Weak ships and spirits steer;
They drive adrift, and whither
They wot not who make thither;
But no such winds blow hither,
　　And no such things grow here.

No growth of moor or coppice,
　　No heather-flower or vine,

But bloomless buds of poppies,
  Green grapes of Proserpine,
Pale beds of blowing rushes,
Where no leaf blooms or blushes
Save this whereout she crushes
  For dead men deadly wine.

Pale, without name or number,
  In fruitless fields of corn,
They bow themselves and slumber
  All night till light is born;
And like a soul belated,
In hell and heaven unmated,
By cloud and mist abated
  Comes out of darkness morn.

Though one were strong as seven,
  He too with death shall dwell,
Nor wake with wings in heaven,
  Nor weep for pains in hell;
Though one were fair as roses,
His beauty clouds and closes;
And well though love reposes,
  In the end it is not well.

Pale, beyond porch and portal,
  Crowned with calm leaves, she stands
Who gathers all things mortal
  With cold immortal hands;
Her languid lips are sweeter
Than Love's, who fears to greet her,
To men that mix and meet her
  From many times and lands.

She waits for each and other,
  She waits for all men born;
Forgets the earth her mother,
  The life of fruits and corn;
And spring and seed and swallow
Take wing for her and follow
Where summer song rings hollow
  And flowers are put to scorn.

There go the loves that wither,
  The old loves with wearier wings;
And all dead years draw thither,
  And all disastrous things;
Dead dreams of days forsaken,
Blind buds that snows have shaken,

Wild leaves that winds have taken,
  Red strays of ruined springs.

We are not sure of sorrow,
  And joy was never sure;
To-day will die to-morrow;
  Time stoops to no man's lure;
And Love, grown faint and fretful.
With lips but half regretful
Sighs, and with eyes forgetful
  Weeps that no loves endure.

From too much love of living,
  From hope and fear set free,
We thank with brief thanksgiving
  Whatever gods may be,
That no life lives forever;
That dead men rise up never;
That even the weariest river
  Winds somewhere safe to sea.

Then star nor sun shall waken,
  Nor any change of light:
Nor sound of waters shaken,
  Nor any sound or sight:
Nor wintry leaves nor vernal,
Nor days nor things diurnal;
Only the sleep eternal
  In an eternal night.

Ave Atque Vale

IN MEMORY OF CHARLES BAUDELAIRE

Nous devrions pourtant lui porter quelques fleurs;
Les morts, les pauvres morts, ont de grandes douleurs,
Et quand Octobre souffle, émondeur des vieux arbres,
Son vent mélancolique a l'entour de leurs marbres,
Certe, ils doivent trouver les vivants bien ingrats.
            Les Fleurs du Mal.

I

SHALL I strew on thee rose or rue or laurel,
  Brother, on this that was the veil of thee?
Or quiet sea-flower moulded by the sea,
Or simplest growth of meadow-sweet or sorrel,
  Such as the summer-sleepy Dryads weave,
  Waked up by snow-soft sudden rains at eve?

Or wilt thou rather, as on earth before,
  Half-faded fiery blossoms, pale with heat
  And full of bitter summer, but more sweet
To thee than gleanings of a northern shore
  Trod by no tropic feet?

II

For always thee the fervid languid glories
  Allured of heavier suns in mightier skies;
  Thine ears knew all the wandering watery sighs
Where the sea sobs round Lesbian promontories,
  The barren kiss of piteous wave to wave
  That knows not where is that Leucadian grave
Which hides too deep the supreme head of song.
  Ah, salt and sterile as her kisses were,
  The wild sea winds her and the green gulfs bear
Hither and thither, and vex and work her wrong,
  Blind gods that cannot spare.

III

Thou sawest, in thine old singing season, brother,
  Secrets and sorrows unbeheld of us:
  Fierce loves, and lovely leaf-buds poisonous,
Bare to thy subtler eye, but for none other
  Blowing by night in some unbreathed-in clime;
  The hidden harvest of luxurious time,
Sin without shape, and pleasure without speech;
  And where strange dreams in a tumultuous sleep
  Make the shut eyes of stricken spirits weep;
And with each face thou sawest the shadow on each,
  Seeing as men sow men reap.

IV

O sleepless heart and sombre soul unsleeping,
  That were athirst for sleep and no more life
  And no more love, for peace and no more strife!
Now the dim gods of death have in their keeping
  Spirit and body and all the springs of song,
  Is it well now where love can do no wrong,
Where stingless pleasure has no foam or fang
  Behind the unopening closure of her lips?
  Is it not well where soul from body slips
And flesh from bone divides without a pang
  As dew from flower-bell drips?

V

It is enough: the end and the beginning
  Are one thing to thee, who art past the end.
  O hand unclasped of unbeholden friend,
For thee no fruits to pluck, no palms for winning,

No triumph and no labour and no lust,
Only dead yew-leaves and a little dust.
O quiet eyes wherein the light saith nought,
Whereto the day is dumb, nor any night
With obscure finger silences your sight,
Nor in your speech the sudden soul speaks thought,
Sleep, and have sleep for light.

VI

Now all strange hours and all strange loves are over,
Dreams and desires and sombre songs and sweet,
Hast thou found place at the great knees and feet
Of some pale Titan-woman like a lover,
Such as thy vision here solicited,
Under the shadow of her fair vast head,
The deep division of prodigious breasts,
The solemn slope of mighty limbs asleep,
The weight of awful tresses that still keep
The savor and shade of old-world pine-forests
Where the wet hill-winds weep?

VII

Hast thou found any likeness for thy vision?
O gardener of strange flowers, what bud, what bloom,
Hast thou found sown, what gathered in the gloom?
What of despair, of rapture, of derision,
What of life is there, what of ill or good?
Are the fruits gray like dust or bright like blood?
Does the dim ground grow any seed of ours,
The faint fields quicken and terrene root,
In low lands where the sun and moon are mute
And all the stars keep silence? Are there flowers
At all, or any fruit?

VIII

Alas, but though my flying song flies after,
O sweet strange elder singer, thy more fleet
Singing, and footprints of thy fleeter feet,
Some dim derision of mysterious laughter
From the blind tongueless warders of the dead,
Some gainless glimpse of Proserpine's veiled head,
Some little sound of unregarded tears
Wept by effaced unprofitable eyes,
And from pale mouths some cadence of dead sighs—
These only, these the hearkening spirit hears,
Sees only such things rise.

IX

Thou art far too far for wings of words to follow,
  Far too far off for thought or any prayer.
  What ails us with thee, who art wind and air?
What ails us gazing where all seen is hollow?
  Yet with some fancy, yet with some desire,
  Dreams pursue death as winds a flying fire,
Our dreams pursue our dead and do not find.
  Still, and more swift than they, the thin flame flies,
  The low light fails us in elusive skies,
Still the foiled earnest ear is deaf, and blind
  Are still the eluded eyes.

X

Not thee, O never thee, in all time's changes,
  Not thee, but this the sound of thy sad soul,
  The shadow of thy swift spirit, this shut scroll
I lay my hand on, and not death estranges
  My spirit from communion of thy song—
  These memories and these melodies that throng
Veiled porches of a Muse funereal—
  These I salute, these touch, these clasp and fold
  As though a hand were in my hand to hold,
Or through mine ears a mourning musical
  Of many mourners rolled.

XI

I among these, I also, in such station
  As when the pyre was charred, and piled the sods,
  And offering to the dead made, and their gods,
The old mourners had, standing to make libation,
  I stand, and to the gods and to the dead
  Do reverence without prayer or praise, and shed
Offering to these unknown, the gods of gloom,
  And what of honey and spice my seed-lands bear,
  And what I may of fruits in this chilled air,
And lay, Orestes-like, across the tomb
  A curl of severed hair.

XII

But by no hand nor any treason stricken,
  Not like the low-lying head of Him, the King,
  The flame that made of Troy a ruinous thing,
Thou liest and on this dust no tears could quicken.
  There fall no tears like theirs that all men hear
  Fall tear by sweet imperishable tear
Down the opening leaves of holy poet's pages.
  Thee not Orestes, not Electra mourns;
  But bending us-ward with memorial urns
The most high Muses that fulfil all ages
  Weep, and our God's heart yearns.

XIII

For, sparing of his sacred strength, not often
   Among us darkling here the lord of light
   Makes manifest his music and his might
In hearts that open and in lips that soften
   With the soft flame and heat of songs that shine.
   Thy lips indeed he touched with bitter wine,
And nourished them indeed with bitter bread;
   Yet surely from his hand thy soul's food came,
   The fire that scarred thy spirit at his flame
Was lighted, and thine hungering heart he fed
   Who feeds our hearts with fame.

XIV

Therefore he too now at thy soul's sunsetting,
   God of all suns and songs, he too bends down
   To mix his laurel with thy cypress crown
And save thy dust from blame and from forgetting.
   Therefore he too, seeing all thou wert and art,
   Compassionate, with sad and sacred heart,
Mourns thee of many his children the last dead,
   And hallows with strange tears and alien sighs
   Thine unmelodious mouth and sunless eyes
And over thine irrevocable head
   Sheds light from the under skies.

XV

And one weeps with him in the ways Lethean,
   And stains with tears her changing bosom chill;
   That obscure Venus of the hollow hill,
That thing transformed which was the Cytherean,
   With lips that lost their Grecian laugh divine
   Long since, and face no more called Erycine
A ghost, a bitter and luxurious god,
   Thee also with fair flesh and singing spell
   Did she, a sad and second prey, compel
Into the footless places once more trod,
   And shadows hot from hell.

XVI

And now no sacred staff shall break in blossom,
   No choral salutation lure to light
   A spirit sick with perfume and sweet night
And love's tired eyes and hands and barren bosom.
   There is no help for these things; none to mend,
   And none to mar; not all our songs, O friend,

Will make death clear or make life durable.
　Howbeit with rose and ivy and wild vine
　And with wild notes about this dust of thine
At least I fill the place where white dreams dwell
　And wreathe an unseen shrine.

XVII

Sleep; and if life was bitter to thee, pardon,
　If sweet, give thanks; thou hast no more to live
　And to give thanks is good, and to forgive.
Out of the mystic and the mournful garden
　Where all day through thine hands in barren braid
　Wove the sick flowers of secrecy and shade,
Green buds of sorrow and sin, and remnants gray,
　Sweet-smelling, pale with poison, sanguine-hearted,
　Passions that sprang from sleep and thoughts that
　　started,
Shall death not bring us all as thee one day
　Among the days departed?

XVIII

For thee, O now a silent soul, my brother,
　Take at my hands this garland, and farewell.
　Thin is the leaf, and chill the wintry smell,
And chill the solemn earth, a fatal mother,
　With sadder than the Niobean womb,
　And in the hollow of her breasts a tomb.
Content thee, howsoe'er, whose days are done:
　There lies not any troublous thing before,
　Nor sight nor sound to war against thee more,
For whom all winds are quiet as the sun,
　All waters as the shore.

From Prologue to "Tristram of Lyonesse"

LOVE, that is first and last of all things made,
　The light that has the living world for shade,
The spirit that for temporal veil has on
The souls of all men woven in unison,
One fiery raiment with all lives inwrought
And lights of sunny and starry deed and thought,
And always through new act and passion new
Shines the divine same body and beauty through,
The body spiritual of fire and light
That is to worldly noon as noon to night;
Love, that is flesh upon the spirit of man

And spirit within the flesh whence breath began;
Love, that keeps all the choir of lives in chime;
Love, that is blood within the veins of time;
That wrought the whole world without stroke of hand,
Shaping the breadth of sea, the length of land,
And with the pulse and motion of his breath
Through the great heart of the earth strikes life and death
The sweet twain chords that made the sweet tune live
Through day and night of things alternative,
Through silence and through sound of stress and strife,
And ebb and flow of dying death and life;
Love, that sounds loud or light in all men's ears,
Whence all men's eyes take fire from sparks of tears,
That binds on all men's feet or chains or wings;
Love, that is root and fruit of terrene things;
Love, that the whole world's waters shall not drown,
The whole world's fiery forces not burn down;
Love, that what time his own hands guard his head
The whole world's wrath and strength shall not strike dead;
Love, that if once his own hands make his grave
The whole world's pity and sorrow shall not save;
Love that for very life shall not be sold,
Nor bought nor bound with iron nor with gold;
So strong that heaven, could love bid heaven farewell,
Would turn to fruitless and unflowering hell;
So sweet that hell, to hell could love be given,
Would turn to splendid and sonorous heaven;
Love that is fire within thee and light above,
And lives by grace of nothing but of love;
Through many and lovely thoughts and much desire
Led these twain to the life of tears and fire;
Through many and lovely days and much delight
Led these twain to the lifeless life of night.
   Yea, but what then? albeit all this were thus,
And soul smote soul and left it ruinous,
And love led love as eyeless men lead men,
Through chance by chance to deathward—
   Ah, what then?
Hath love not likewise led them further yet,
Out through the years where memories rise and set,
Some large as suns, some moon-like warm and pale,
Some starry-sighted, some through clouds that sail
Seen as red flame through special float of fume,
Each with the blush of its own spectral bloom
On the fair face of its own coloured light,
Distinguishable in all the host of night,
Divisible from all the radiant rest
And separable in splendour? Hath the best
Light of love's all, of all that burn and move,

A better heaven than heaven is? Hath not love
Made for all these their sweet particular air
To shine in, their own beams and names to bear,
Their ways to wander and their wards to keep,
Till story and song and glory and all things sleep?
Hath he not plucked from death of lovers dead
Their musical soft memories, and kept red
The rose of their remembrance in men's eyes,
The sunsets of their stories in his skies,
The blush of their dead blood in lips that speak
Of their dead lives, and in the listener's cheek
That trembles with the kindling pity lit
In gracious hearts for some sweet fever-fit,
A fiery pity enkindled of pure thought
By tales that make their honey out of nought,
The faithless faith that lives without belief
Its light life through, the griefless ghost of grief?
Yea, as warm night refashions the sere blood
In storm-struck petal or in sun-struck bud,
With tender hours and tempering dew to cure
The hunger and thirst of day's distemperature
And ravin of the dry discolouring hours,
Hath he not bid relume their flameless flowers
With summer fire and heat of lamping song,
And bid the short-lived things, long dead, live long,
And thought remake their wan funereal fames,
And the sweet shining signs of women's names
That mark the months out and the weeks anew
He moves in changeless change of seasons through
To fill the days up of his dateless year
Flame from Queen Helen to Queen Guenevere?
For first of all the sphery signs whereby
Love severs light from darkness, and most high,
In the white front of January there glows
The rose-red sign of Helen like a rose:
And gold-eyed as the shore flower shelterless
Whereon the sharp-breathed sea blows bitterness,
A storm-star that the seafarers of love
Strain their wind-wearied eyes for glimpses of,
Shoots keen through February's grey frost and damp
The lamplike star of Hero for a lamp;
The star that Marlowe sang into our skies
With mouth of gold, and morning in his eyes;
And in clear March across the rough blue sea
The signal sapphire of Alcyone
Makes bright the blown brows of the windfoot year;
And shining like a sunbeam-smitten tear
Full ere it fall, the fair next sign in sight
Burns opal-wise with April-coloured light

When air is quick with song and rain and flame,
My birth-month star that in love's heaven hath name
Iseult, a light of blossom and beam and shower,
My singing sign that makes the song-tree flower;
Next like a pale and burning pearl beyond
The rose-white sphere of flower-named Rosamond
Signs the sweet head of Maytime; and for June
Flares like an angered and storm-reddening moon
Her signal sphere, whose Carthaginian pyre
Shadowed her traitor's flying sail with fire;
Next, glittering as the wine-bright jacinth-stone,
A star south-risen that first to music shone,
The keen girl-star of golden Juliet bears
Light northward to the month whose forehead wears
Her name for flower upon it, and his trees
Mix their deep English song with Veronese;
And like an awful sovereign chrysolite
Burning, the supreme fire that blinds the night,
The hot gold head of Venus kissed by Mars,
A sun-flower among small sphered flowers of stars,
The light of Cleopatra fills and burns
The hollow of heaven whence ardent August yearns;
And fixed and shining as the sister-shed
Sweet tears for Phaethon disorbed and dead,
The pale bright autumn's amber-coloured sphere,
That through September sees the saddening year
As love sees change through sorrow, hath to name
Francesca's; and the star that watches flame
The embers of the harvest overgone
Is Thisbe's, slain of love in Babylon,
Set in the golden girdle of sweet signs
A blood-bright ruby; last save one light shines
An Eastern wonder of sphery chrysopras,
The star that made men mad, Angelica's;
And latest named and lordliest, with a sound
Of swords and harps in heaven that ring it round,
Last love-light and last love-song of the year's,
Gleams like a glorious emerald Guenevere's.

A Match

IF love were what the rose is,
    And I were like the leaf,
Our lives would grow together
In sad or singing weather,
Blown fields or flowerful closes,
    Green pleasure or gray grief;
If love were what the rose is,
    And I were like the leaf.

If I were what the words are,
  And love were like the tune,
With double sound and single
Delight our lips would mingle,
With kisses glad as birds are
  That get sweet rain at noon;
If I were what the words are,
  And love were like the tune.

If you were life, my darling,
  And I your love were death,
We'd shine and snow together
Ere March made sweet the weather
With daffodil and starling
  And hours of fruitful breath;
If you were life, my darling,
  And I your love were death.

If you were thrall to sorrow,
  And I were page to joy,
We'd play for lives and seasons
With loving looks and treasons
And tears of night and morrow
  And laughs of maid and boy;
If you were thrall to sorrow,
  And I were page to joy.

If you were April's lady
  And I were lord in May,
We'd throw with leaves for hours
And draw for day with flowers,
Till day like night were shady
  And night were bright like day;
If you were April's lady,
  And I were lord in May.

If you were queen of pleasure,
  And I were king of pain,
We'd hunt down love together,
Pluck out his flying-feather,
And teach his feet a measure,
  And find his mouth a rein;
If you were queen of pleasure,
  And I were king of pain.

The Oblation

ASK nothing more of me, sweet;
  All I can give you, I give.
Heart of my heart, were it more,
More would be laid at your feet:
  Love that should help you to live,
    Song that should spur you to soar.

All things were nothing to give
  Once to have sense of you more,
    Touch you and taste of you, sweet,
Think you and breathe you and live,
  Swept of your wings as they soar
    Trodden by chance of your feet.

I that have love and no more
  Give you but love of you, sweet:
    He that hath more, let him give;
He that hath wings let him soar;
  Mine is the heart at your feet
    Here, that must love you to live.

THOMAS HARDY (1840-   )

In the Moonlight

A lonely workman, standing there
  In a dream, why do you stare and stare
At her grave, as no other grave there were?

"If your great gaunt eyes so importune
Her soul by the shine of this corpse-cold moon,
Maybe you'll raise her phantom soon!"

"Why, fool, it is what I would rather see
Than all the living folk there be;
But alas, there is no such joy for me!"

"Ah—she was one you loved, no doubt,
Through good and evil, through rain and drought,
And when she passed, all your sun went out?"

"Nay: she was the woman I did not love,
Whom all the others were ranked above,
Whom during her life I thought nothing of."

The Man He Killed

"HAD he and I but met
       By some old ancient inn,
We should have sat us down to wet
    Right many a nipperkin!

"But ranged as infantry,
    And staring face to face,
I shot at him as he at me,
    And killed him in his place.

"I shot him dead because—
    Because he was my foe,
Just so: my foe of course he was;
    That's clear enough; although

"He thought he'd 'list, perhaps,
    Off-hand like—just as I—
Was out of work—had sold his traps—
    No other reason why.

"Yes; quaint and curious war is!
    You shoot a fellow down
You'd treat if met where any bar is,
    Or help to half-a-crown."

WILFRID SCAWEN BLUNT (1840-1922)

To One Who Would Make a Confession

OH! leave the past to bury its own dead.
    The past is naught to us, the present all.
What need of last year's leaves to strew Love's bed?
What need of ghost to grace a festival?
I would not, if I could, those days recall,
Those days not ours. For us the feast is spread,
The lamps are lit, and music plays withal.
Then let us love and leave the rest unsaid.
This island is our home. Around it roar
Great gulfs and oceans, channels, straits and seas.
What matter in what wreck we reached the shore,
So we both reached it? We can mock at these.
    Oh! leave the past, if past indeed there be;
    I would not know it; I would know but thee.

To Manon, on His Fortune in Loving Her

I did not choose thee, dearest. It was Love
 That made the choice, not I. Mine eyes were blind
As a rude shepherd's who to some lone grove
His offering brings and cares not at whose shrine
He bends his knee. The gifts alone were mine;
The rest was Love's. He took me by the hand,
And fired the sacrifice, and poured the wine,
And spoke the words I might not understand.
 I was unwise in all but the dear chance
Which was my fortune, and the blind desire
Which led my foolish steps to Love's abode,
And youth's sublime unreason'd prescience
Which raised an altar and inscribed in fire
Its dedication: *To the Unknown God.*

From "Esther"

A little honey! Ay, a little sweet,
 A little pleasure when the years were young,
A joyous measure trod by dancing feet,
A tale of folly told by a loved tongue,—
These are the things by which our hearts are wrung
More than by tears. Oh, I would rather laugh,
So I had not to choose those tales among
Which was most laughable. Man's nobler self
Resents mere sorrow. I would rather sit
With just the common crowd that watch the play
And mock at harlequin and the clown's wit,
And call it tragedy and go my way.
I should not err, because the tragic part
Lay not in these, but sealed in my own heart.

AUSTIN DOBSON (1840-   )

A Garden Song

HERE, in this sequestered close
 Bloom the hyacinth and rose;
Here beside the modest stock
Flaunts the flaring hollyhock;
Here, without a pang, one sees
Ranks, conditions, and degrees.

All the seasons run their race
In this quiet resting-place;
Peach, and apricot, and fig
Here will ripen, and grow big;
Here is store and overplus,—
More had not Alcinoüs!

Here, in alleys cool and green,
Far ahead the thrush is seen;
Here along the southern wall
Keeps the bee his festival;
All is quiet else—afar
Sounds of toil and turmoil are.

Here be shadows large and long;
Here be spaces meet for song;
Grant, O garden-god, that I,
Now that none profane is nigh,—
Now that mood and moment please,
Find the fair Pierides!

The Ladies of St. James's

A PROPER NEW BALLAD OF THE COUNTRY AND THE TOWN

Phyllida amo ante alias.—VIRGIL

THE ladies of St. James's
    Go swinging to the play;
Their footmen run before them,
    With a "Stand by! Clear the way!"
But Phyllida, my Phyllida!
    She takes her buckled shoon,
When we go out a-courting
    Beneath the harvest moon.

The ladies of St. James's
    Wear satin on their backs;
They sit all night at *Ombre,*
    With candles all of wax:
But Phyllida, my Phyllida!
    She dons her russet gown,
And runs to gather May dew
    Before the world is down.

The ladies of St. James's!
    They are so fine and fair,
You'd think a box of essences
    Was broken in the air:

SALEM COLLEGE LIBRARY
Winston-Salem, N. C.

But Phyllida, my Phyllida!
　The breath of heath and furze
When breezes blow at morning,
　Is not so fresh as hers.

The ladies of St. James's!
　They're painted to the eyes;
Their white it stays for ever
　Their red it never dies:
But Phyllida, my Phyllida!
　Her color comes and goes;
It trembles to a lily,—
　It wavers to a rose.

The ladies of St. James's!
　You scarce can understand
The half of all their speeches,
　Their phrases are so grand:
But Phyllida, my Phyllida!
　Her shy and simple words
Are clear as after rain-drops
　The music of the birds.

The ladies of St. James's!
　They have their fits and freaks;
They smile on you—for seconds,
　They frown on you—for weeks:
But Phyllida, my Phyllida!
　Come either storm or shine,
From Shrove-tide unto Shrove-tide,
　Is always true—and mine.

My Phyllida! my Phyllida!
　I care not though they heap
The hearts of all St. James's,
　And give me all to keep;
I care not whose the beauties
　Of all the world may be,
For Phyllida—for Phyllida
　Is all the world to me!

The Ballade of Prose and Rhyme

WHEN the ways are heavy with mire and rut,
　In November fogs, in December snows,
When the North Wind howls, and the doors are shut,—
　There is place and enough for the pains of prose;
　But whenever a scent from the whitethorn blows,

And the jasmine-stars at the casement climb,
    And a Rosalind-face at the lattice shows,
Then hey!—for the ripple of laughing rhyme!

When the brain gets dry as an empty nut,
    When the reason stands on its squarest toes,
When the mind (like a beard) has a "formal cut,"—
    There is place and enough for the pains of prose;
    But whenever the May-blood stirs and glows,
And the young year draws to the "golden prime,"
    And Sir Romeo sticks in his ear a rose,—
Then hey—for the ripple of laughing rhyme!

In a theme where the thoughts have a pedant-strut,
    In a changing quarrel of "Ayes" and "Noes,"
In a starched procession of "If" and "But,"—
    There is place and enough for the pains of prose;
    But whenever a soft glance softer grows,
And the light hours dance to the trysting-time,
    And the secret is told "that no one knows,"—
Then hey!—for the ripple of laughing rhyme!

ENVOY

In the work-a-day world,—for its needs and woes,
There is place and enough for the pains of prose;
But whenever the May-bells clash and chime,
Then hey!—for the ripple of laughing rhyme!

In After Days

(Rondeau)

IN after days when grasses high
    O'er top the stone where I shall lie,
    Though ill or well the world adjust
    My slender claim to honoured dust,
I shall not question nor reply.

I shall not see the morning sky;
I shall not hear the night-wind sigh;
    I shall be mute, as all men must
        In after days!

But yet, now living, fain were I
That some one then should testify,
    Saying—"He held his pen in trust
    To Art, not serving shame or lust."
Will none?—Then let my memory die
        In after days!

Triolet

I intended an Ode,
    And it turned to a Sonnet.
It began *à la mode,*
I intended an Ode;
But Rose crossed the road
    In her latest new bonnet;
I intended an Ode;
    And it turned to a Sonnet.

ROBERT BUCHANAN (1841-1901)

Judas Iscariot

'TWAS the soul of Judas Iscariot,
    Strange, and sad, and tall,
Stood all alone at dead of night
    Before a lighted hall.

And the world was white with snow,
    And his foot-marks black and damp,
And the ghost of the silver moon arose,
    Holding her yellow lamp.

And the icicles were on the eaves,
    And the walls were deep with white,
And the shadows of the guests within
    Pass'd on the window light.

The shadows of the wedding-guests
    Did strongly come and go,
And the body of Judas Iscariot
    Lay stretch'd along the snow.

The body of Judas Iscariot
    Lay stretched along the snow;
'Twas the soul of Judas Iscariot
    Ran swiftly to and fro.

To and fro, and up and down,
    He ran so swiftly there,
As round and round the frozen Pole
    Glideth the lean white bear.

. . . 'Twas the Bridegroom sat at the table-head,
    And the lights burnt bright and clear—
"Oh, who is that," the Bridegroom said,
    "Whose weary feet I hear?"

'Twas one looked from the lighted hall,
    And answer'd soft and slow,
"It is a wolf runs up and down
    With a black track in the snow."

The Bridegroom in his robe of white
    Sat at the table-head—
"Oh, who is that who moans without?"
    The blessed Bridegroom said.

'Twas one look'd from the lighted hall,
    And answer'd fierce and low,
" 'Tis the soul of Judas Iscariot
    Gliding to and fro."

'Twas the soul of Judas Iscariot
    Did hush itself and stand,
And saw the Bridegroom at the door
    With a light in his hand.

The Bridegroom stood in the open door,
    And he was clad in white,
And far within the Lord's Supper
    Was spread so broad and bright.

The Bridegroom shaded his eyes and look'd,
    And his face was bright to see—
"What dost thou here at the Lord's Supper
    With thy body's sins?" said he.

'Twas the soul of Judas Iscariot
    Stood black, and sad, and bare—
"I have wander'd many nights and days;
    There is no light elsewhere."

'Twas the wedding guests cried out within,
    And their eyes were fierce and bright—
"Scourge the soul of Judas Iscariot
    Away into the night!"

The Bridegroom stood in the open door,
    And he waved his hands and slow,
And the third time that he waved his hands
    The air was thick with snow.

And of every flake of falling snow,
    Before it touch'd the ground,
There came a dove, and a thousand doves
    Made sweet sound.

'Twas the soul of Judas Iscariot
  Floated away full fleet,
And the wings of the doves that bare it off
  Were like its winding-sheet.

'Twas the bridegroom stood at the open door,
  And beckon'd, smiling sweet;
'Twas the soul of Judas Iscariot
  Stole in, and fell at his feet.

"The Holy Supper is spread within,
  And the many candles shine,
And I have waited long for thee
  Before I pour'd the wine."

The supper wine is pour'd at last,
  The lights burn bright and fair,
Iscariot washes the Bridegroom's feet,
  And dries them with his hair.

F. W. H. MYERS (1843-1901)

The Inner Light

LO, if some pen should write upon your rafter
  MENE and MENE in the folds of flame,
Think you could any memories thereafter
  Wholly retrace the couplet as it came?

Lo, if some strange, intelligible thunder
  Sang to the earth the secret of a star,
Scarce could ye catch, for terror and for wonder,
  Shreds of the story that was pealed so far.

Scarcely I catch the words of His revealing,
  Hardly I hear Him, dimly understand,
Only the Power that is within me pealing
  Lives on my lips and beckons to my hand.

Whoso has felt the Spirit of the Highest
  Cannot confound nor doubt Him nor deny:
Yea, with one voice, O world, though thou deniest,
  Stand thou on that side, for on this am I.

Rather the earth shall doubt when her retrieving
  Pours in the rain and rushes from the sod,
Rather than he for whom the great conceiving
  Stirs in his soul to quicken into God.

Ay, though thou then shouldst strike from him his glory,
   Blind and tormented, maddened and alone,
Even on the cross would he maintain his story,
   Yes, and in hell would whisper, I have known.

ARTHUR O'SHAUGHNESSY (1844-1881)

Ode

WE are the music makers,
      And we are the dreamers of dreams,
Wandering by lone sea-breakers,
   And sitting by desolate streams;—
World-losers and world-forsakers,
   On whom the pale moon gleams:
Yet we are the movers and shakers
   Of the world for ever, it seems.

With wonderful deathless ditties
We build up the world's great cities,
   And out of a fabulous story
   We fashion an empire's glory:
One man with a dream, at pleasure,
   Shall go forth and conquer a crown;
And three with a new song's measure
   Can trample a kingdom down.

We, in the ages lying
   In the buried past of the earth,
Built Nineveh with our sighing,
   And Babel itself in our mirth;
And o'erthrew them with prophesying
   To the old of the new world's worth;
For each age is a dream that is dying,
   Or one that is coming to birth. . . .
                                   Abridged.

Song

HAS summer come without the rose,
      Or left the bird behind?
Is the blue changed above thee,
   O world! or am I blind?
Will you change every flower that grows,
   Or only change this spot,
Where she who said, I love thee,
   Now says, I love thee not?

The skies seemed true above thee,
　The rose true on the tree;
The bird seemed true the summer through,
　But all proved false to me.
World! is there one good thing in you,
　Life, love, or death—or what?
Since lips that sang, I love thee,
　Have said, I love thee not?

I think the sun's kiss will scarce fall
　Into one flower's gold cup;
I think the bird will miss me,
　And give the summer up.
O sweet place! desolate in tall
　Wild grass, have you forgot
How her lips loved to kiss me,
　Now that they kiss me not?

Be false or fair above me,
　Come back with any face,
Summer!—do I care what you do?
　You cannot change one place—
The grass, the leaves, the earth, the dew,
　The grave I make the spot—
Here, where she used to love me,
　Here, where she loves me not.

Song

I made another garden, yea,
　For my new love:
I left the dead rose where it lay,
　And set the new above.
Why did the summer not begin?
　Why did my heart not haste?
My old love came and walked therein,
　And laid the garden waste.

She entered with her weary smile,
　Just as of old;
She looked around a little while,
　And shivered at the cold.
Her passing touch was death to all,
　Her passing look a blight:
She made the white rose-petals fall,
　And turned the red rose white.

Her pale robe, clinging to the grass,
  Seemed like a snake
That bit the grass and ground, alas!
  And a sad trail did make.
She went up slowly to the gate;
  And there, just as of yore,
She turned back at the last to wait,
  And say farewell once more.

Song from "Chartivel"

HATH any loved you well, down there,
  Summer or winter through?
Down there, have you found any fair
  Laid in the grave with you?
Is death's long kiss a richer kiss
  Than mine was wont to be—
Or have you gone to some far bliss
  And quite forgotten me?

What soft enamouring of sleep
  Hath you in some soft way?
What charmed death holdeth you with deep
  Strange lure by night and day?
A little space below the grass,
  Out of the sun and shade;
But worlds away from me, alas,
  Down there where you are laid?

My bright hair's waved and wasted gold,
  What is it now to thee—
Whether the rose-red life I hold
  Or white death holdeth me?
Down there you love the grave's own green,
  And evermore you rave
Of some sweet seraph you have seen
  Or dreamt of in the grave. . . .

                              Abridged.

ROBERT BRIDGES (1844-   )

I love all beauteous things,
    i seek and adore them;
God hath no better praise,
And man in his hasty days
  Is honoured for them.

I, too, will something make
And joy in the making;
Altho' to-morrow it seem
Like the empty words of a dream
Remembered on waking.

I have loved flowers that fade;
Within whose magic tents
Rich hues have marriage made
With sweet unmemoried scents:
A honeymoon delight,—
A joy of love at sight,
That ages in an hour:—
My song be like a flower!

I have loved airs that die
Before their charm is writ
Along a liquid sky
Trembling to welcome it.
Notes, that with pulse of fire
Proclaim the spirit's desire,
Then die, and are nowhere:—
My song be like an air!

Die, song, die like a breath,
And wither as a bloom:
Fear not a flowery death,
Dread not an airy tomb!
Fly with delight, fly hence!
'Twas thine love's tender sense
To feast, now on thy bier
Beauty shall shed a tear.

Elegy on a Lady Whom Grief for the Death of Her Betrothed Killed

ASSEMBLE, all ye maidens, at the door,
And all ye loves, assemble, far and wide
Proclaim the bridal, that proclaimed before
Hath been deferred to this late eventide:
For on this night the bride,
The days of her betrothal over,
Leaves the parental hearth for evermore:
To-night the bride goes forth to meet her lover.

Reach down the wedding vesture, that has lain
Yet all unvisited, the silken gown:
Bring out the bracelets, and the golden chain

Her dearer friends provided: sere and brown
  Bring out the festal crown,
 And set it on her forehead lightly:
  Though it be withered, twine no wreath again;
This only is the crown she can wear rightly.

Cloak her in ermine, for the night is cold,
And wrap her warmly, for the night is long,
In pious hands the flaming torches hold,
While her attendants, chosen from among
  Her faithful virgin throng,
  May lay her in her cedar litter,
 Decking her coverlet with sprigs of gold,
Roses, and lilies white that best befit her.

Sound flute and tabor, that the bridal be
Not without music, nor with these alone;
But let the viol lead the melody,
With lesser intervals, and plaintive moan
  Of sinking semitone;
  And, all in choir, the virgin voices
 Rest not from singing in skilled harmony
The song that aye the bridegroom's ear rejoices.

Let the priests go before, arrayed in white,
And let the dark-stoled minstrels follow slow,
Next they that bear her, homeward on this night,
And then the maidens, in a double row,
  Each singing soft and low,
  And each on high a torch upstaying:
 Unto her lover lead her forth with light,
With music, and with singing, and with praying.

'Twas at this sheltering hour he nightly came,
And found her trusty window open wide,
And knew the signal of the timorous flame,
That long the restless curtain would not hide
  Her form that stood beside;
  As scarce she dare to be delighted,
 Listening to that sweet tale, that is no shame
To faithful lovers, that their hearts have plighted.

But now for many days the dewy grass
Has shown no markings of his feet at morn:
And watching she has seen no shadow pass
The moonlit walk, and heard no music borne
  Upon her ear forlorn.
  In vain has she looked out to greet him;
 He has not come, he will not come, alas!
So let us bear her out where she must meet him.

Now to the river bank the priests are come:
The bark is ready to receive its freight:
Let some prepare her place therein, and some
Embark the litter with its slender weight:
    The rest stand by in state,
      And sing her a safe passage over;
    While she is oared across to her new home
Into the arms of her expectant lover.

And thou, O lover, that art on the watch,
Where, on the banks of the forgetful streams,
The pale indifferent ghosts wander, and snatch
The sweeter moments of their broken dreams,—
    Thou, when the torchlight gleams,
      When thou shall see the slow procession,
    And when thine ears the fitful music catch,
Rejoice, for thou art near to thy possession.

Nightingales

B EAUTIFUL must be the mountains whence ye come,
  And bright in the fruitful valleys the streams, wherefrom
    Ye learn your song:
Where are those starry woods? O might I wander there,
  Among the flowers, which in that heavenly air
    Bloom the year long!

Nay, barren are those mountains and spent the streams:
Our song is the voice of desire, that haunts our dreams,
    A throe of the heart,
Whose pining visions dim, forbidden hopes profound,
  No dying cadence nor long sigh can sound,
    For all our art.

Alone, aloud in the raptured ear of men
We pour our dark nocturnal secret; and then,
    As night is withdrawn
From these sweet-springing meads and bursting boughs of
  May,
  Dream, while the innumerable choir of day
    Welcome the dawn.

A Passer-By

W HITHER, O splendid ship, thy white sails crowding,
    Leaning across the bosom of the urgent West,
That fearest nor sea rising, nor sky clouding,
  Whither away, fair rover, and what thy quest?
  Ah, soon, when Winter has all our vales opprest,

When skies are cold and misty, and hail is hurling,
  Wilt thou glide on the blue Pacific, or rest
In a summer haven asleep, thy white sails furling.

I there before thee, in the country that well thou knowest,
  Already arrived am inhaling the odorous air:
I watch thee enter unerringly where thou goest,
  And anchor queen of the strange shipping there,
  Thy sails for awnings spread, thy masts bare;
Nor is aught from the foaming reef to the snow-capped,
    grandest
  Peak, that is over the feathery palms more fair
Than thou, so upright, so stately, and still thou standest.

And yet, O splendid ship, unhail'd and nameless,
  I know not if, aiming a fancy, I rightly divine
That thou hast a purpose joyful, a courage blameless,
  Thy port assured in a happier land than mine.
  But for all I have given thee, beauty enough is thine,
As thou, aslant with trim tackle and shrouding,
  From the proud nostril curve of a prow's line
In the offing scatterest foam, thy white sails crowding.

ANDREW LANG (1844-1891)
The Odyssey

A S one that for a weary space has lain
      Lulled by the song of Circe and her wine
  In gardens near the pale of Proserpine,
Where that Ææan isle forgets the main,
And only the low lutes of love complain,
  And only shadows of wan lovers pine,
  As such an one were glad to know the brine
Salt on his lips, and the large air again—
So gladly, from the songs of modern speech
  Men turn, and see the stars, and feel the free
    Shrill wind beyond the close of heavy flowers,
    And through the music of the languid hours
They hear like Ocean on a western beach
  The surge and thunder of the Odyssey.

Lost Love

W HO wins his Love shall lose her,
      Who loses her shall gain,
  For still the spirit wooes her,
    A soul without a stain;
  And Memory still pursues her
    With longings not in vain!

He loses her who gains her,
  Who watches day by day
The dust of time that stains her,
  The griefs that leave her gray,
The flesh that yet enchains her
  Whose grace hath passed away!

Oh, happier he who gains not
  The Love some seem to gain:
The joy that custom stains not
  Shall still with him remain,
The loveliness that wanes not,
  The Love that ne'er can wane.

In dreams she grows not older
  The lands of Dream among,
Though all the world wax colder,
  Though all the songs be sung,
In dreams doth he behold her
  Still fair and kind and young.

Ballade of Middle Age

OUR youth began with tears and sighs,
    With seeking what we could not find;
Our verses all were threnodies,
    In elegiacs still we whined;
    Our ears were deaf, our eyes were blind,
We sought and knew not what we sought.
    We marvel, now we look behind:
Life's more amusing than we thought!

Oh, foolish youth, untimely wise!
    Oh, phantoms of the sickly mind!
  What? not content with seas and skies,
    With rainy clouds and southern wind,
    With common cares and faces kind,
With pains and joys each morning brought?
    Ah, old, and worn, and tired we find
Life's more amusing than we thought!

Though youth "turns spectre-thin and dies,"
    To mourn for youth we're not inclined;
We set our souls on salmon flies,
    We whistle where we once repined.
    Confound the woes of human-kind!
By Heaven we're "well deceived," I wot;
    Who hum, contented or resigned,
"Life's more amusing than we thought"!

ENVOY
O nate mecum, worn and lined
Our faces show, but *that* is naught:
   Our hearts are young 'neath wrinkled rind:
Life's more amusing than we thought!

EUGENE LEE-HAMILTON (1845-1907)
Idle Charon

THE shores of Styx are lone forevermore,
   And not one shadowy form upon the steep
Looms through the dusk, as far as eyes can sweep,
To call the ferry over as of yore;
But tintless rushes, all about the shore,
   Have hemm'd the old boat in, where, lock'd in sleep,
   Hoar-bearded Charon lies; while pale weeds creep
With tightening grasp all round the unused oar.

For now in the world of Life strange rumors run
   That now the Soul departs not with the breath,
But that the Body and the Soul are one;
   And in the loved one's mouth, now, after death,
The widow puts no obol, nor the son,
   To pay the ferry in the world beneath.

Baudelaire

A Paris gutter of the good old times,
   Black and putrescent in its stagnant bed,
Save where the shamble oozings fringe it red,
Or scaffold trickles, or nocturnal crimes.
It holds dropped gold; dead flowers from tropic climes;
Gems true and false, by midnight maskers shed;
Old pots of rouge; old broken phials that spread
Vague fumes of musk, with fumes from slums and slimes.
And everywhere, as glows the set of day,
There floats upon the winding fetid mire
The gorgeous iridescence of decay:
A wavy film of colour, gold and fire,
Trembles all through it as you pick your way,
And streaks of purple that are straight from Tyre.

GRANT ALLEN (1848-1901)
A Prayer

A crowned Caprice is god of this world:
   On his stony breast are his white wings **furled.**
No ear to listen, no eye to see,
No heart to feel for a man hath he.

But his pitiless arm is swift to smite;
And his mute lips utter one word of might,
Mid the clash of gentler souls and rougher,
"Wrong must thou do, or wrong must suffer."
Then grant, oh! dumb blind god, at least that we
Rather the sufferers than the doers be.

EDMUND GOSSE (1849-   )

To Austin Dobson

NEIGHBOUR of the near domain,
    Stay awhile your passing wain!
Though to give is more your way,
Take a gift from me to-day!
From my homely store I bring
Signs of my poor husbanding;—
Here a spike of purple phlox,
Here a spicy bunch of stocks,
Mushrooms from my moister fields,
Apples that my orchard yields,—
Nothing,—for the show they make,
Something,—for the donor's sake;
Since for ten years we have been
Best of neighbours ever seen;
We have fronted evil weather,
Nip of critic's frost, together;
We have shared laborious days,
Shared the pleasantness of praise;
Brother not more close to brother,
We have cheered and helped each other:
Till so far the fields of each
Into the other's stretch and reach,
That perchance when both are gone
Neither may be named alone.

Impression

IN these restrained and careful times
    Our knowledge petrifies our rhymes;
Ah! for that reckless fire men had
When it was witty to be mad;

When wild conceits were piled in scores,
And lit by flaming metaphors,
When all was crazed and out of tune,—
Yet throbbed with music of the moon.

If we could dare to write as ill
As some whose voices haunt us still,
Even we, perchance, might call our own
Their deep enchanting undertone.

We are too diffident and nice,
Too learnèd and too over-wise,
Too much afraid of faults to be
The flutes of bold sincerity.

For, as this sweet life passes by,
We blink and nod with critic eye;
We've no words rude enough to give
Its charm so frank and fugitive.

The green and scarlet of the Park,
The undulating streets at dark,
The brown smoke blown across the blue,
This colored city we walk through;—

The pallid faces full of pain,
The field-smell of the passing wain,
The laughter, longing, perfume, strife,
The daily spectacle of life;—

Ah! how shall this be given to rhyme,
By rhymesters of a knowing time?
Ah! for the age when verse was clad,
Being godlike, to be bad and mad.

WILLIAM ERNEST HENLEY (1849-1903)

Invictus

OUT of the night that covers me,
    Black as the pit from pole to pole,
I thank whatever gods may be
    For my unconquerable soul.

In the fell clutch of circumstance
    I have not winced nor cried aloud.
Under the bludgeonings of chance
    My head is bloody, but unbowed.

Beyond this place of wrath and tears
    Looms but the Horror of the shade,
And yet the menace of the years
    Finds and shall find me unafraid.

It matters not how strait the gate,
  How charged with punishments the scroll,
I am the master of my fate:
  I am the captain of my soul.

From "In Hospital"

Operation

YOU are carried in a basket,
    Like a carcass from the shambles,
  To the theatre, a cockpit
  Where they stretch you on a table.

Then they bid you close your eyelids,
  And they mask you with a napkin,
  And the anaesthetic reaches
  Hot and subtle through your being.

And you gasp and reel and shudder
  In a rushing, swaying rapture,
  While the voices at your elbow
  Fade—receding—fainter—farther.

Lights about you shower and tumble,
  And your blood seems crystallizing—
  Edged and vibrant, yet within you
  Racked and hurried back and forward.

Then the lights grow fast and furious,
  And you hear a noise of waters,
  And you wrestle, blind and dizzy,
  In an agony of effort.

Till a sudden lull accepts you,
  And you sound an utter darkness . . .
  And awaken . . . with a struggle . . .
  On a hushed, attentive audience.

"A Late Lark Twitters from the Quiet Skies"

A late lark twitters from the quiet skies;
    And from the west,
  Where the sun, his day's work ended,
  Lingers as in content,
  There falls on the old, gray city
  An influence luminous and serene,
  A shining peace.

The smoke ascends
In a rosy-and-golden haze. The spires
Shine, and are changed. In the valley
Shadows rise. The lark sings on. The sun,
Closing his benediction,
Sinks, and the darkening air
Thrills with a sense of the triumphing night—
Night with her train of stars
And her great gift of sleep.

So be my passing!
My task accomplished and the long day done,
My wages taken, and in my heart
Some late lark singing,
Let me be gathered to the quiet west,
The sundown splendid and serene,
Death.

From "London Voluntaries"

DOWN through the ancient Strand
    The Spirit of October, mild and boon
And sauntering, takes his way
This golden end of afternoon,
As though the corn stood yellow in all the land
And the ripe apples dropped to the harvest moon.

Lo! the round sun, half down the western slope—
Seen as along an enlarged telescope—
Lingers and lolls, loath to be done with day:
Gifting the long, lean, lanky street
And its abounding confluences of being
With aspects generous and bland:
Making a thousand harnesses to shine
As with new ore from some enchanted mine,
And every horse's coat so full of sheen
He looks new-tailored, and every 'bus feels clean,
And never a hansom but is worth the feeing;
And every jeweller within the pale
Offers a real Arabian Night for sale;
And even the roar
Of the strong streams of toil that pause and pour
Eastward and westward sounds suffused—
Seems as it were bemused
And blurred, and like the speech
Of lazy seas upon a lotus-eating beach—
With this enchanted lustrousness,
This mellow magic that (as a man's caress
Brings back to some faded face beloved before

A heavenly shadow of the grace it wore
Ere the poor eyes were minded to beseech)
Old things transfigures, and you hail and bless
Their looks of long-lapsed loveliness once more;
Till the sedate and mannered elegance
Of Clement's is all tinctured with romance;
The while the fanciful, formal, finicking charm
Of Bride's, that madrigal in stone,
Glows flushed and warm
And beauteous with a beauty not its own;
And the high majesty of Paul's
Uplifts a voice of living light, and calls—
Calls to his millions to behold and see
How goodly this his London Town can be!
For earth and sky and air
Are golden everywhere,
And golden with a gold so suave and fine
The looking on it lifts the heart like wine.
Trafalgar Square
(The fountains volleying golden glaze)
Gleams like an angel market. . . .

Out of the poisonous East,
Over a continent of blight,
Like a maleficent Influence released
From the most squalid cellarage of hell,
The Wind-Fiend, the abominable—
The hangman wind that tortures temper and light—
Comes slouching, sullen and obscene,
Hard on the skirts of the embittered night:
And in a cloud unclean
Of excremental humours, roused to strife
By the operation of some ruinous change
Wherever his evil mandate run and range
Into a dire intensity of life,
A craftsman at his bench, he settles down
To the grim job of throttling London Town. . . .
And Death the while—
Death, with his well-worn, lean, professional smile,
Death in his threadbare working trim—
Comes to your bedside, unannounced and bland,
And with expert, inevitable hand
Feels at your windpipe, fingers you in the lung,
Or flicks the clot well into the labouring heart:
Thus signifying unto old and young,
However hard of mouth or wild of whim,
'Tis time—'tis time by his ancient watch—to part
With books and women and talk and drink and art:
And you go humbly after him

To a mean suburban lodging: on the way
To what or where
Not Death, who is old and very wise, can say:
And you—how should you care
So long as, unreclaimed of hell,
The Wind-Fiend, the insufferable,
Thus vicious and thus patient sits him down
To the black job of lurking London Town?

Abridged.

THEOPHILE MARZIALS (1850-   )

A Tragedy

SHE was only a woman, famished for loving,
    Mad with devotion, and such slight things;
And he was a very great musician,
    And used to finger his fiddle-strings.

Her heart's sweet gamut is cracking and breaking
    For a look, for a touch,—for such slight things;
But he's such a very great musician
    Grimacing and fingering his fiddle-strings.

ROBERT LOUIS STEVENSON (1850-1894)

Romance

I will make you brooches and toys for your delight
    Of bird-song at morning and star-shine at night.
I will make a palace fit for you and me,
Of green days in forests and blue days at sea.

I will make my kitchen, and you shall keep your room,
Where white flows the river and bright blows the broom,
And you shall wash your linen and keep your body white
In rainfall at morning and dewfall at night.

And this shall be for music when no one else is near,
The fine song for singing, the rare song to hear!
That only I remember, that only you admire,
Of the broad road that stretches and the roadside fire.

Happy Thought

THE world is so full of a number of things,
    I'm sure we should all be as happy as kings.

In the Highlands

IN the highlands, in the country places,
  Where the old plain men have rosy faces,
And the young fair maidens
  Quiet eyes;
Where essential silence cheers and blesses,
And for ever in the hill-recesses
Her more lovely music
  Broods and dies.—

O to mount again where erst I haunted;
Where the old red hills are bird-enchanted,
And the low green meadows
  Bright with sward;
And when even dies, the million-tinted,
And the night has come, and planets glinted,
Lo, the valley hollow
  Lamp-bestarred!

O to dream, O to awake and wander
There, and with delight to take and render,
Through the trance of silence,
  Quiet breath!
Lo! for there, among the flowers and grasses,
Only the mightier movement sounds and passes;
Only winds and rivers,
  Life and Death.

Requiem

UNDER the wide and starry sky
  Dig the grave and let me lie.
Glad did I live and gladly die,
  And I laid me down with a will.

This be the verse you grave for me:
Here he lies where he longed to be;
Home is the sailor, home from sea,
  And the hunter home from the hill.

PHILIP BOURKE MARSTON (1850-1887)

IT must have been for one of us, my own,
  To drink this cup and eat this bitter bread.
Had not my tears upon thy face been shed,
Thy tears had dropped on mine; if I alone
Did not walk now, thy spirit would have known

My loneliness; and did my feet not tread
This weary path and steep, thy feet had bled
For mine, and thy mouth had for mine made moan:

And so it comforts me, yea, not in vain,
   To think of thine eternity of sleep;
   To know thine eyes are tearless though mine weep:
And when this cup's last bitterness I drain,
   One thought shall still its primal sweetness keep,—
Thou hadst the peace and I the undying pain.

ALICE MEYNELL (1853-1922)

Renouncement

I must not think of thee; and, tired yet strong,
   I shun the love that lurks in all delight—
The love of thee—and in the blue heaven's height,
And in the dearest passage of a song.
Oh, just beyond the fairest thoughts that throng
This breast, the thought of thee waits hidden yet bright;
But it must never, never come in sight;
I must stop short of thee the whole day long.
But when sleep comes to close each difficult day,
When night gives pause to the long watch I keep,
And all my bonds I needs must loose apart,
Must doff my will as raiment laid away,—
With the first dream that comes with the first sleep
I run, I run, I am gathered to thy heart.

The Lady of the Lambs

SHE walks—the lady of my delight—
   A shepherdess of sheep.
Her flocks are thoughts. She keeps them white;
   She guards them from the steep.
She feeds them on the fragrant height,
   And folds them in for sleep.

She roams maternal hills and bright,
   Dark valleys safe and deep.
Her dreams are innocent at night;
   The chastest stars may peep.
She walks—the lady of my delight—
   A shepherdess of sheep.

She holds her little thoughts in sight,
　　Though gay they run and leap.
She is so circumspect and right;
　　She has her soul to keep.
She walks—the lady of my delight—
　　A shepherdess of sheep.

"FIONA MACLEOD" (1856-1905)

(Pseud. of William Sharp)

Mo-lennav-a-chree

EILIDH, Eilidh, Eilidh, dear to me, dear and sweet,
　　In dreams I am hearing the sound of your little running
　　　　feet—
The sound of your running feet that like the sea-hoofs beat
A music by day an' night, Eilidh, on the sands of my heart,
　　my Sweet!

Eilidh, blue i' the eyes, flower-sweet as children are,
And white as the canna that blows with the hill-breast wind
　　afar,
Whose is the light in thine eyes—the light of a star?—a star
That sitteth supreme where the starry lights of heaven a glory
　　are.

Eilidh, Eilidh, Eilidh, put off your wee hands from the heart
　　o' me,
It is pain they are making there, where no more pain should
　　be:
For little running feet, an' wee white hands, an' croodlin' as
　　of the sea,
Bring tears to my eyes, Eilidh, tears, tears, out of the heart
　　o' me—
　　　　　Mo-lennav-a-chree,
　　　　　Mo-lennav-a-chree!

OSCAR WILDE (1856-1900)

Hélas

TO drift with every passion, till my soul
　　Is a stringed lute on which all winds can play,
Is it for this that I have given away
Mine ancient wisdom and austere control?
Methinks my life is a twice-written scroll,
Scrawled over on some boyish holiday
With idle songs for pipe or virelay,
Which do but mar the secret of the whole.

Surely there was a time I might have trod
The sunlight heights, and from life's dissonance
Struck one clear chord to reach the ears of God!
Is that time dead? Lo! with a little rod
I did but touch the honey of romance,
And must I lose a soul's inheritance?

The Ballad of Reading Gaol

I

HE did not wear his scarlet coat,
  For blood and wine are red,
And blood and wine were on his hands
  When they found him with the dead,
The poor dead woman whom he loved,
  And murdered in her bed.

He walked amongst the Trial Men
  In a suit of shabby gray;
A cricket cap was on his head,
  And his step seemed light and gay;
But I never saw a man who looked
  So wistfully at the day.

I never saw a man who looked
  With such a wistful eye
Upon that little tent of blue
  Which prisoners call the sky,
And at every drifting cloud that went
  With sails of silver by.

I walked, with other souls in pain,
  Within another ring,
And was wondering if the man had done
  A great or little thing,
When a voice behind me whispered low,
  "That fellow's got to swing."

Dear Christ! the very prison walls
  Suddenly seemed to reel,
And the sky above my head became
  Like a casque of scorching steel;
And, though I was a soul in pain,
  My pain I could not feel.

I only knew what hunted thought
  Quickened his step, and why
He looked upon the garish day
  With such a wistful eye:
The man had killed the thing he loved,
  And so he had to die

Yet each man kills the thing he loves,
  By each let this be heard,
Some do it with a bitter look,
  Some with a flattering word,
The coward does it with a kiss,
  The brave man with a sword!

Some kill their love when they are young,
  And some when they are old;
Some strangle with the hands of Lust,
  Some with the hands of Gold:
The kindest use a knife, because
  The dead so soon grow cold.

Some love too little, some too long,
  Some sell, and others buy;
Some do the deed with many tears,
  And some without a sigh:
For each man kills the thing he loves,
  Yet each man does not die.

He does not die a death of shame
  On a day of dark disgrace,
Nor have a noose about his neck,
  Nor a cloth upon his face,
Nor drop feet foremost through the floor
  Into an empty space.

He does not sit with silent men
  Who watch him night and day;
Who watch him when he tries to weep,
  And when he tries to pray;
Who watch him lest himself should rob
  The prison of its prey.

He does not wake at dawn to see
  Dread figures throng his room,
The shivering Chaplain robed in white,
  The Sheriff stern with gloom,
And the Governor all in shiny black,
  With the yellow face of Doom.

He does not rise in piteous haste
  To put on convict-clothes,
While some coarse-mouthed Doctor gloats, and
    notes
  Each new and nerve-twitched pose,
Fingering a watch whose little ticks
  Are like horrible hammer-blows.

He does not know that sickening thirst
   That sands one's throat, before
The hangman with his gardener's gloves
   Slips through the padded door,
And binds one with three leathern thongs,
   That the throat may thirst no more.

He does not bend his head to hear
   The Burial Office read,
Nor, while the terror of his soul
   Tells him he is not dead,
Cross his own coffin, as he moves
   Into the hideous shed.

He does not stare upon the air
   Through a little roof of glass:
He does not pray with lips of clay
   For his agony to pass;
Nor feel upon his shuddering cheek
   That kiss of Caiaphas.

II

Six weeks our guardsman walked the yard,
   In the suit of shabby gray:
His cricket cap was on his head,
   And his step seemed light and gay,
But I never saw a man who looked
   So wistfully at the day.

I never saw a man who looked
   With such a wistful eye
Upon that little tent of blue
   Which prisoners call the sky,
And at every wandering cloud that trailed
   Its raveled fleeces by.

He did not wring his hands, as do
   Those witless men who dare
To try to rear the changeling Hope
   In the cave of black Despair:
He only looked upon the sun,
   And drank the morning air.

He did not wring his hands nor weep,
   Nor did he peek or pine,
But he drank the air as though it held
   Some healthful anodyne;
With open mouth he drank the sun
   As though it had been wine!

And I and all the souls in pain,
　Who tramped the other ring,
Forgot if we ourselves had done
　A great or little thing,
And watched with gaze of dull amaze
　The man who had to swing.

And strange it was to see him pass
　With a step so light and gay,
And strange it was to see him look
　So wistfully at the day,
And strange it was to think that he
　Had such a debt to pay.

For oak and elm have pleasant leaves
　That in the spring-time shoot:
But grim to see is the gallows-tree,
　With its adder-bitten root,
And, green or dry, a man must die
　Before it bears its fruit!

The loftiest place is that seat of grace
　For which all wordlings try:
But who would stand in hempen band
　Upon a scaffold high,
And through a murderer's collar take
　His last look at the sky?

It is sweet to dance to violins
　When Love and Life are fair:
To dance to flutes, to dance to lutes
　Is delicate and rare:
But it is not sweet with nimble feet
　To dance upon the air!

So with curious eyes and sick surmise
　We watched him day by day,
And wondered if each one of us
　Would end the self-same way,
For none can tell to what red Hell
　His sightless soul may stray.

At last the dead man walked no more
　Amongst the Trial Men,
And I knew that he was standing up
　In the black dock's dreadful pen,
And that never would I see his face
　In God's sweet world again.

Like two doomed ships that pass in storm,
    We had crossed each other's way:
But we made no sign, we said no word,
    We had no word to say;
For we did not meet in the holy night,
    But in the shameful day.

A prison wall was round us both,
    Two outcast men we were:
The world had thrust us from its heart,
    And God from out his care:
And the iron gin that waits for Sin
    Had caught us in its snare.

III

In Debtor's Yard the stones are hard,
    And the dripping wall is high,
So it was there he took the air
    Beneath the leaden sky,
And by each side a Warder walked,
    For fear the man might die.

Or else he sat with those who watched
    His anguish night and day;
Who watched him when he rose to weep,
    And when he crouched to pray;
Who watched him lest himself should rob
    Their scaffold of its prey.

The Governor was strong upon
    The Regulations Act:
The Doctor said that Death was but
    A scientific fact:
And twice a day the Chaplain called,
    And left a little tract.

And twice a day he smoked his pipe,
    And drank his quart of beer:
His soul was resolute, and held
    No hiding-place for fear;
He often said that he was glad
    The hangman's hands were near.

But why he said so strange a thing
    No Warder dared to ask:
For he to whom a watcher's doom
    Is given as his task,
Must set a lock upon his lips,
    And make his face a mask.

Or else he might be moved, and try
   To comfort or console:
And what should Human Pity do
   Pent up in Murderers' Hole?
What word of grace in such a place
   Could help a brother's soul?

With slouch and swing around the ring
   We trod the Fools' Parade!
We did not care: we knew we were
   The Devil's Own Brigade:
And shaven head and feet of lead
   Make a merry masquerade.

We tore the tarry rope to shreds
   With blunt and bleeding nails;
We rubbed the doors, and scrubbed the floors,
   And cleaned the shining rails:
And, rank by rank, we soaped the plank,
   And clattered with the pails.

We sewed the sacks, we broke the stones,
   We turned the dusty drill:
We banged the tins, and bawled the hymns,
   And sweated on the mill:
But in the heart of every man
   Terror was lying still.

So still it lay that every day
   Crawled like a weed-clogged wave:
And we forgot the bitter lot
   That waits for fool and knave,
Till once, as we tramped in from work,
   We passed an open grave.

With yawning mouth the yellow hole
   Gaped for a living thing;
The very mud cried out for blood
   To the thirsty asphalt ring:
And we knew that ere one dawn grew fair,
   Some prisoner had to swing.

Right in we went, with soul intent
   On Death and Dread and Doom:
The hangman, with his little bag,
   Went shuffling through the gloom:
And each man trembled as he crept
   Into his numbered tomb.

That night the empty corridors
  Were full of forms of Fear,
And up and down the iron town
  Stole feet we could not hear,
And through the bars that hide the stars
  White faces seemed to peer.

He lay as one who lies and dreams
  In a pleasant meadow-land,
The watchers watched him as he slept,
  And could not understand
How one could sleep so sweet a sleep
  With a hangman close at hand.

But there is no sleep when men must weep
  Who never yet have wept:
So we—the fool, the fraud, the knave—
  That endless vigil kept,
And through each brain on hands of pain
  Another's terror crept.

Alas! it is a fearful thing
  To feel another's guilt!
For, right within, the sword of Sin
  Pierced to its poisoned hilt,
And as molten lead were the tears we shed
  For the blood we had not spilt.

The Warders with their shoes of felt
  Crept by each padlocked door,
And peeped and saw, with eyes of awe,
  Gray figures on the floor,
And wondered why men knelt to pray
  Who never prayed before.

All through the night we knelt and prayed,
  Mad mourners of a corse!
The troubled plumes of midnight were
  The plumes upon a hearse:
And bitter wine upon a sponge
  Was the savor of Remorse.

The gray cock crew, the red cock crew,
  But never came the day;
And crooked shapes of terror crouched
  In the corners where we lay:
And each evil sprite that walks by night
  Before us seemed to play.

They glided past, they glided fast,
  Like travelers through a mist:
They mocked the moon in a rigadoon
  Of delicate turn and twist,
And with formal pace and loathsome grace
  The phantoms kept their tryst.

With mop and mow, we saw them go,
  Slim shadows hand and hand:
About, about, in ghostly rout
  They trod a saraband:
And the damned grotesques made arabesques,
  Like the wind upon the sand!

With pirouettes of marionettes
  They tripped on pointed tread:
But with flutes of Fear they filled the ear,
  As their grisly masque they led,
And loud they sang, and long they sang,
  For they sang to wake the dead.

"Oho!" they cried, "The world is wide,
  But fettered limbs go lame!
And once, or twice, to throw the dice
  Is a gentlemanly game,
But he does not win who plays with Sin
  In the Secret House of Shame."

No things of air these antics were,
  That frolicked with such glee:
To men whose lives were held in gyves,
  And whose feet might not go free,
Ah! wounds of Christ! they were living things,
  Most terrible to see.

Around, around, they waltzed and wound;
  Some wheeled in smirking pairs;
With the mincing step of a demirep
  Some sidled up the stairs:
And with subtle sneer, and fawning leer,
  Each helped us at our prayers.

The morning wind began to moan,
  But still the night went on;
Through its giant loom the web of gloom
  Crept till each thread was spun:
And, as we prayed, we grew afraid
  Of the Justice of the Sun.

The moaning wind went wandering round
  The weeping prison-wall:
Till like a wheel of turning steel
  We felt the minutes crawl:
O moaning wind! what had we done
  To have such a seneschal?

At last I saw the shadowed bars,
  Like a lattice wrought in lead,
Move right across the whitewashed wall
  That faced my three-planked bed,
And I knew that somewhere in the world
  God's dreadful dawn was red.

At six o'clock we cleaned our cells,
  At seven all was still,
But the sough and swing of a mighty wing
  The prison seemed to fill,
For the Lord of Death with icy breath,
  Had entered in to kill.

He did not pass in purple pomp,
  Nor ride a moon-white steed.
Three yards of cord and a sliding board
  Are all the gallows' need:
So with rope of shame the Herald came
  To do the secret deed.

We were as men who through a fen
  Of filthy darkness grope:
We did not dare to breathe a prayer,
  Or to give our anguish scope:
Something was dead in each of us,
  And what was dead was Hope.

For Man's grim Justice goes its way,
  And will not swerve aside:
It slays the weak, it slays the strong,
  It has a deadly stride:
With iron heel it slays the strong,
  The monstrous parricide!

We waited for the stroke of eight:
  Each tongue was thick with thirst:
For the stroke of eight is the stroke of **Fate**
  That makes a man accursed,
And Fate will use a running noose
  For the best man and the worst.

We had no other thing to do,
   Save to wait for the sign to come:
So, like things of stone in a valley lone,
   Quiet we sat and dumb:
But each man's heart beat thick and quick,
   Like a madman on a drum!

With sudden shock, the prison-clock
   Smote on the shivering air,
And from all the jail rose up a wail
   Of impotent despair,
Like the sound that frightened marshes hear
   From some leper in his lair.

And as one sees most dreadful things
   In the crystal of a dream,
We saw the greasy hempen rope
   Hooked to the blackened beam,
And heard the prayer the hangman's snare
   Strangled into a scream.

And all the woe that moved him so
   That he gave that bitter cry,
And the wild regrets, and the bloody sweats,
   None knew so well as I:
For he who lives more lives than one
   More deaths than one must die.

IV

There is no chapel on the day
   On which they hang a man:
The Chaplain's heart is far too sick,
   Or his face is far too wan,
Or there is that written in his eyes
   Which none should look upon.

So they kept us close till nigh on noon,
   And then they rang the bell,
And the Warders with their jingling keys
   Opened each listening cell,
And down the iron stair we tramped,
   Each from his separate Hell.

Out into God's sweet air we went,
   But not in wonted way,
For this man's face was white with fear,
   And that man's face was gray,
And I never saw sad men who looked
   So wistfully at the day.

I never saw sad men who looked
    With such a wistful eye
Upon that little tent of blue
    We prisoners call the sky,
And at every careless cloud that passed
    In happy freedom by.

But there were those amongst us all
    Who walked with downcast head,
And knew that, had each got his due,
    They should have died instead:
He had but killed a thing that lived,
    Whilst they had killed the dead.

For he who sins a second time
    Wakes a dead soul to pain,
And draws it from its spotted shroud,
    And makes it bleed again,
And makes it bleed great gouts of blood,
    And makes it bleed in vain!

Like ape or clown, in monstrous garb
    With crooked arrows starred,
Silently we went round and round
    The slippery asphalt yard;
Silently we went round and round
    And no man spoke a word.

Silently we went round and round,
    And through each hollow mind
The Memory of dreadful things
    Rushed like a dreadful wind,
And Honor stalked before each man,
    And Terror crept behind.

The Warders strutted up and down,
    And kept their herd of brutes,
Their uniforms were spick and span,
    They wore their Sunday suits,
But we knew the work they had been at,
    By the quicklime on their bocts.

For where a grave had opened wide,
    There was no grave at all:
Only a stretch of mud and sand
    By the hideous prison-wall,
And all the while the burning lime
    That the man should have his pall.

For he has a pall, this wretched man,
    Such as few men can claim:
Deep down below a prison-yard,
    Naked for greater shame,
He lies, with fetters on each foot,
    Wrapped in a sheet of flame!

And all the while the burning lime
    Eats flesh and bone away,
It eats the brittle bone by night,
    And the soft flesh by day,
It eats the flesh and bone by turns,
    But it eats the heart alway.

For three long years they will not sow
    Or root or seedling there:
For three long years the unblessed spot
    Will sterile be and bare,
And look upon the wondering sky
    With unreproachful stare.

They think a murderer's heart would taint
    Each simple seed they sow.
It is not true! God's kindly earth
    Is kindlier than men know,
And the red rose would but blow more red,
    The white rose whiter blow.

Out of his mouth a red, red rose!
    Out of his heart a white!
For who can say by what strange way
    Christ brings his will to light,
Since the barren staff the pilgrim bore
    Bloomed in the great Pope's sight?

But neither milk-white rose nor red
    May bloom in prison air;
The shard, the pebble, and the flint,
    Are what they give us there:
For flowers have been known to heal
    A common man's despair.

So never will wine-red rose or white
    Petal by petal, fall
On that stretch of mud and sand that lies
    By that hideous prison-wall,
To tell the men who tramp the yard
    That God's Son died for all.

Yet though the hideous prison-wall
  Still hems him round and round,
And a spirit may not walk by night
  That is with fetters bound,
And a spirit may but weep that lies
  In such unholy ground,

He is at peace—this wretched man—
  At peace, or will be soon:
There is no thing to make him mad,
  Nor does Terror walk at noon,
For the lampless Earth in which he lies
  Has neither Sun nor Moon.

They hanged him as a beast is hanged:
  They did not even toll
A requiem that might have brought
  Rest to his startled soul,
But hurriedly they took him out,
  And hid him in a hole.

They stripped him of his canvas clothes,
  And gave him to the flies:
They mocked the swollen purple throat,
  And the stark and staring eyes:
And with laughter loud they heaped the shroud
  In which their convict lies.

The Chaplain would not kneel to pray
  By his dishonoured grave:
Nor mark it with that blessed Cross
  That Christ for sinners gave,
Because the man was one of those
  Whom Christ came down to save.

Yet all is well; he has but passed
  To Life's appointed bourne:
And alien tears will fill for him
  Pity's long-broken urn,
For his mourners will be outcast men,
  And outcasts always mourn.

v

I know not whether Laws be right,
  Or whether Laws be wrong;
All that we know who lie in jail
  Is that the wall is strong;
And that each day is like a year,
  A year whose days are long.

But this I know, that every Law
  That men have made for Man,
Since first Man took his brother's life,
  And this sad world began,
But straws the wheat and saves the chaff
  With a most evil fan.

This too I know—and wise it were
  If each could know the same—
That every prison that men build
  Is built with bricks of shame,
And bound with bars lest Christ should see
  How men their brothers maim.

With bars they blur the gracious moon,
  And blind the goodly sun:
And they do well to hide their Hell,
  For in it things are done
That Son of God nor son of Man
  Ever should look upon!

The vilest deeds like poison weeds
  Bloom well in prison-air:
It is only what is good in Man
  That wastes and withers there:
Pale Anguish keeps the heavy gate,
  And the Warder is Despair.

For they starve the little frightened child,
  Till it weeps both night and day:
And they scourge the weak, and flog the fool,
  And gibe the old and gray,
And some grow mad, and all grow bad,
  And none a word may say.

Each narrow cell in which we dwell
  Is a foul and dark latrine,
And the fetid breath of living Death
  Chokes up each grated screen,
And all, but Lust, is turned to dust
  In Humanity's machine.

The brackish water that we drink
  Creeps with a loathsome slime,
And the bitter bread they weigh in scales
  Is full of chalk and lime,
And Sleep will not lie down, but walks
  Wild-eyed, and cries to Time.

But though lean Hunger and green Thirst
  Like asp with adder fight,
We have little care of prison fare,
  For what chills and kills outright
Is that every stone one lifts by day
  Becomes one's heart by night.

With midnight always in one's heart,
  And twilight in one's cell,
We turn the crank, or tear the rope,
  Each in his separate Hell,
And the silence is more awful far
  Than the sound of a brazen bell.

And never a human voice comes near
  To speak a gentle word:
And the eye that watches through the door
  Is pitiless and hard:
And by all forgot, we rot and rot,
  With soul and body marred.

And thus we rust Life's iron chain,
  Degraded and alone:
And some men curse, and some men weep,
  And some men make no moan:
But God's eternal Laws are kind
  And break the heart of stone.

And every human heart that breaks,
  In prison-cell or yard,
Is as that broken box that gave
  Its treasure to the Lord,
And filled the unclean leper's house
  With the scent of costliest nard.

Ah! happy they whose hearts can break
  And peace of pardon win!
How else may man make straight his plan
  And cleanse his soul from Sin?
How else but through a broken heart
  May Lord Christ enter in?

And he of the swollen purple throat,
  And the stark and staring eyes,
Waits for the holy hands that took
  The Thief to Paradise:
And a broken and a contrite heart
  The Lord will not despise.

The man in red who reads the Law
  Gave him three weeks of life,
Three little weeks in which to heal
  His soul of his soul's strife,
And cleanse from every blot of blood
  The hand that held the knife.

And with tears of blood he cleansed the hand,
  The hand that held the steel:
For only blood can wipe out blood,
  And only tears can heal:
And the crimson stain that was of Cain
  Became Christ's snow-white seal.

VI

In Reading gaol by Reading town
  There is a pit of shame,
And in it lies a wretched man
  Eaten by teeth of flame,
In a burning winding-sheet he lies
  And his grave has got no name.

And there, till Christ call forth the dead,
  In silence let him lie:
No need to waste the foolish tear,
  Or heave the windy sigh:
The man had killed the thing he loved,
  And so he had to die.

And all men kill the thing they love,
  By all let this be heard,
Some do it with a bitter look,
  Some with a flattering word,
The coward does it with a kiss,
  The brave man with a sword!

Requiescat

TREAD lightly, she is near,
    Under the snow;
Speak gently, she can hear
    The daisies grow.

All her bright golden hair
    Tarnished with rust,
She that was young and fair
    Fallen to dust.

Lily-like, white as snow,
  She hardly knew
She was a woman, so
  Sweetly she grew.

Coffin-board, heavy stone,
  Lie on her breast;
I vex my heart alone,
  She is at rest.

Peace, peace; she cannot hear
  Lyre or sonnet;
All my life's buried here—
  Heap earth upon it.

Sonnet to Liberty

NOT that I love thy children, whose dull eyes
    See nothing but their own unlovely woe,
Whose minds know nothing, nothing care to know,—
But that the roar of thy Democracies,
Thy reigns of Terror, thy great Anarchies,
Mirror my wildest passions like the sea
And give my rage a brother——! Liberty!
For this sake only do thy dissonant cries
Delight my discreet soul, else might all kings
By bloody knout or treacherous cannonades
Rob nations of their rights inviolate
And I remain unmoved—and yet, and yet,
These Christs that die upon the barricades,
God knows it I am with them, in some things.

On the Recent Sale by Auction of Keats' Love Letters

THESE are the letters which Endymion wrote
    To one he loved in secret and apart,
And now the brawlers of the auction mart
Bargain and bid for each poor blotted note,
Aye! for each separate pulse of passion quote
    The merchant's price. I think they love not art
    Who break the crystal of a poet's heart
That small and sickly eyes may glare and gloat.

Is it not said that many years ago,
    In a far Eastern town, some soldiers ran
    With torches through the midnight, and began
To wrangle for mean raiment, and to throw
    Dice for the garments of a wretched man.
Not knowing the God's wonder, or His woe.

The Harlot's House

WE caught the tread of dancing feet,
  We loitered down the moonlit street,
And stopped beneath the Harlot's house.

Inside, above the din and fray,
We heard the loud musicians play
The "Treues Liebes Herz," of Strauss.

Like strange mechanical grotesques,
Making fantastic arabesques,
The shadows raced across the blind.

We watched the ghostly dances spin
To sound of horn and violin,
Like black leaves wheeling in the wind.

Like wire-pulled automatons,
Slim silhouetted skeletons
Went sidling through the slow quadrille,

Then took each other by the hand,
And danced a stately saraband;
Their laughter echoed thin and shrill.

Sometimes a clock-work puppet pressed
A phantom lover to her breast,
Sometimes they seemed to try to sing.

Sometimes a horrible marionette
Came out, and smoked its cigarette
Upon the steps, like a live thing.

Then turning to my love I said,
"The dead are dancing with the dead,
The dust is whirling with the dust."

But she, she heard the violin,
And left my side and entered in:
Love passed into the house of lust.

Then suddenly the tune went false,
The dancers wearied of the waltz,
The shadows ceased to wheel and whirl,

And down the long and silent street,
The dawn with silver-sandalled feet,
Crept like a frightened girl.

JOHN DAVIDSON (1857-1909)

A Ballad of a Nun

FROM Eastertide to Eastertide
   For ten long years her patient knees
Engraved the stones—the fittest bride
   Of Christ in all the diocese.

She conquered every earthly lust:
   The abbess loved her more and more;
And, as mark of perfect trust,
   Made her the keeper of the door.

High on a hill the convent hung,
   Across a duchy looking down;
Where everlasting mountains flung
   Their shadows over tower and town.

The jewels of their lofty snows
   In constellations flashed at night;
Above their crests the moon arose;
   The deep earth shuddered with delight.

Long ere she left her cloudy bed,
   Still dreaming in the orient land.
On many a mountain's happy head
   Dawn lightly laid her rosy hand.

The adventurous sun took Heaven by storm;
   Clouds scattered largesses of rain;
The sounding cities, rich and warm,
   Smouldered and glittered in the plain.

Sometimes it was a wandering wind.
   Sometimes the fragrance of the pine,
Sometimes the thought how others sinned,
   That turned her sweet blood into wine.

Sometimes she heard a serenade
   Complaining sweetly far away:
She said, "A young man woos a maid";
   And dreamt of love till break of day.

Then would she ply her knotted scourge
   Until she swooned: but evermore
She had the same red sin to purge,
   Poor, passionate keeper of the door!

For still night's starry scroll unfurled,
　And still the day came like a flood:
It was the greatness of the world
　That made her long to use her blood.

In winter-time when Lent drew nigh,
　And hill and plain were wrapped in snow,
She watched beneath the frosty sky
　The nearest city nightly glow.

Like peals of airy bells outworn
　Faint laughter died above her head
In gusts of broken music borne:
　"They keep the Carnival," she said.

Her hungry heart devoured the town:
　"Heaven save me by a miracle!
Unless God sends an angel down,
　Thither I go though it were Hell."

She dug her nails deep in her breast,
　Sobbed, shrieked, and straight withdrew the bar:
A fledgling flying from the nest,
　A pale moth rushing to a star.

Fillet and veil in strips she tore;
　Her golden tresses floated wide;
The ring and bracelet that she wore
　As Christ's betrothed, she cast aside.

"Life's dearest meaning I shall probe;
　Lo! I shall taste of love at last!
Away!" She doffed her outer robe,
　And sent it sailing down the blast.

Her body seemed to warm the wind;
　With bleeding feet o'er ice she ran;
"I leave the righteous God behind;
　I go to worship sinful man."

She reached the sounding city's gate;
　No question did the warder ask:
He passed her in: "Welcome, wild mate!"
　He thought her some fantastic mask.

Half-naked through the town she went;
　Each footstep left a bloody mark;
Crowds followed her with looks intent;
　Her bright eyes made the torches dark.

Alone and watching in the street
  There stood a grave youth nobly dressed;
To him she knelt and kissed his feet;
  Her face her great desire confessed.

Straight to his house the nun he led:
  "Strange lady, what would you with me?"
"Your love, your love, sweet lord," she said;
  "I bring you my virginity."

He healed her bosom with a kiss;
  She gave him all her passion's hoard;
And sobbed and murmured ever, "This
  Is life's great meaning, dear, my lord.

"I care not for my broken vow;
  Though God should come in thunder soon,
I am sister to the mountains now,
  And sister to the sun and moon."

Through all the towns of Belmarie
  She made a progress like a queen.
"She is," they said, "whate'er she be,
  The strangest woman ever seen.

"From fairyland she must have come,
  Or else she is a mermaiden."
Some said she was a ghoul, and some
  A heathen goddess born again.

But soon her fire to ashes burned;
  Her beauty changed to haggardness;
Her golden hair to silver turned;
  The hour came of her last caress.

At midnight from her lonely bed
  She rose, and said, "I have had my will."
The old ragged robe she donned, and fled
  Back to the convent on the hill.

Half-naked as she went before,
  She hurried to the city wall,
Unnoticed in the rush and roar
  And splendour of the carnival.

No question did the warder ask:
  Her ragged robe, her shrunken limb,
Her dreadful eyes! "It is no mask;
  It is a she-wolf, gaunt and grim!"

She ran across the icy plain;
  Her worn blood curdled in the blast;
Each footstep left a crimson stain;
  The white-faced moon looked on aghast.

She said between her chattering jaws,
  "Deep peace is mine, I cease to strive;
Oh, comfortable convent laws,
  That bury foolish nuns alive!

"A trowel for my passing-bell,
  A little bed within the wall,
A coverlet of stones; how well
  I there shall keep the Carnival!"

Like tired bells chiming in their sleep,
  The wind faint peals of laughter bore;
She stopped her ears and climbed the steep,
  And thundered at the convent door.

It opened straight; she entered in,
  And at the wardress' feet fell prone:
"I come to purge away my sin;
  Bury me, close me up in stone."

The wardress raised her tenderly;
  She touched her wet and fast-shut eyes:
"Look, sister; sister, look at me;
  Look, can you see through my disguise?"

She looked and saw her own sad face,
  And trembled, wondering, "Who art thou?"
"God sent me down to fill your place:
  I am the Virgin Mary now."

And with the word, God's mother shone:
  The wanderer whispered, "Mary, hail!"
The vision helped her to put on
  Bracelet and fillet, ring and veil.

"You are sister to the mountains now,
  And sister to the day and night;
Sister to God." And on the brow
  She kissed her thrice, and left her sight.

While dreaming in her cloudy bed,
  Far in the crimson orient land,
On many a mountain's happy head
  Dawn lightly laid her rosy hand.

Butterflies

AT sixteen years she knew no care;
   How could she, sweet and pure as light?
And there pursued her everywhere
   Butterflies all white.

A lover looked. She dropped her eyes
   That glowed like pansies wet with dew;
And lo, there came from out the skies
   Butterflies all blue.

Before she guessed her heart was gone;
   The tale of love was swiftly told;
And all about her wheeled and shone
   Butterflies all gold.

Then he forsook her one sad morn;
   She wept and sobbed, "Oh, love, come back!"
There only came to her forlorn
   Butterflies all black.

From "The Testament of John Davidson"

NONE should outlive his power. . . . Who kills
   Himself subdues the conqueror of kings:
Exempt from death is he who takes his life:
My time has come. . . .
            By my own will alone
The ethereal substance, which I am. attained,
And now by my own sovereign will, forgoes,
Self-consciousness: and thus are men supreme.
No other living thing can choose to die.
This franchise and this high prerogative
I show the world:—Men are the Universe
Aware at last, and must not live in fear,
Slaves of the seasons, padded, bolstered up,
Clystered and drenched and dieted and drugged;
Or hateful victims of senility,
Toothless and like an infant checked and schooled;
Or in the dungeon of a sick room drained
By some tabescent horror in their prime;
But when the tide of life begins to turn,
Before the treason of the ebbing wave
Divulges refuse and the barren shore,
Upon the very period of the flood,
Stand out to sea and bend our weathered sail,
Against the sunset, valiantly resolved
To win the heaven of eternal night.

From "Fleet Street Eclogues"

AT early dawn through London you must go
   Until you come where long black hedgerows grow,
With pink buds pearled, with here and there a tree,
   And gates and stiles; and watch good country folk;
   And scent the spicy smoke
Of withered weeds that burn where gardens be;
And in a ditch perhaps a primrose see.
The rocks shall stalk the plough, larks mount the skies,
   Blackbirds and speckled thrushes sing aloud,
   Hid in the warm white cloud
Mantling the thorn, and far away shall rise
The milky low of cows and farmyard cries.
From windy heavens the climbing sun shall shine,
   And February greet you like a maid
   In russet-cloak arrayed;
And you shall take her for your mistress fine,
And pluck a crocus for her valentine.

E. NESBIT (MRS. HUBERT BLAND) (1858-   )

IF on some balmy summer night
   You rowed across the moon-path white,
And saw the shining sea grow fair
With silver scales and golden hair—
What would you do?
                  I would be wise
And shut my ears and shut my eyes,
Lest I should leap into the tide
And clasp the sea-maid as I died.
But, if you thus were strong to flee
From sweet spells woven of moon and sea,
Are you quite sure that you would reach,
Without one backward look the beach?
   I might look back, my dear, and then
Row straight into the snare again;
Or, if I safely got away—
Regret it to my dying day.

WILLIAM WATSON (1858-   )

Song

APRIL, April,
   Laugh thy girlish laughter;
Then, the moment after,
Weep thy girlish tears!

April, that mine ears
Like a lover greetest,
If I tell thee, sweetest,
All my hopes and fears,
April, April,
Laugh thy golden laughter,
But, the moment after,
Weep thy golden tears!

From "Wordsworth's Grave"

I

THE old rude church, with bare, bald tower, is here;
  Beneath its shadow high-born Rotha flows;
Rotha, remembering well who slumbers near,
  And with cool murmur lulling his repose.

Rotha, remembering well who slumbers near.
  His hills, his lakes, his streams are with him yet.
Surely the heart that reads her own heart clear
  Nature forgets not soon: 'tis we forget.

We that with vagrant soul his fixity
  Have slighted; faithless, done his deep faith wrong;
Left him for poorer loves, and bowed the knee
  To misbegotten strange new gods of song.

Yet, led by hollow ghost or beckoning elf
  Far from her homestead to the desert bourn,
The vagrant soul returning to herself
  Wearily wise, must needs to him return.

To him and to the powers that with him dwell:—
  Inflowings that divulged not whence they came;
And that secluded Spirit unknowable,
  The mystery we make darker with a name:

The Somewhat which we name but cannot know,
  Even as we name a star and only see
His quenchless flashings forth, which ever show
  And ever hide him, and which are not he.

II

Poet who sleepest by this wandering wave!
  When thou wast born, what birth-gift hadst thou then?
To thee what wealth was that the Immortals gave,
  The wealth thou gavest in thy turn to men?

Not Milton's keen, translunar music thine;
  Not Shakespeare's cloudless, boundless human view;
Not Shelley's flush of rose on peaks divine;
  Nor yet the wizard twilight Coleridge knew.

What hadst thou that could make so large amends
  For all thou hadst not and thy peers possessed,
Motion and fire, swift means to radiant ends?—
  Thou hadst, for weary feet, the gift of rest.

From Shelley's dazzling glow or thunderous haze,
  From Byron's tempest-anger, tempest-mirth,
Men turned to thee and found—not blast and blaze,
  Tumult of tottering heavens, but peace on earth.

Nor peace that grows by Lethe, scentless flower,
  There in white languors to decline and cease;
But peace whose names are also rapture, power,
  Clear sight, and love: for these are parts of peace.
                                        Abridged.

From "Epigrams"

THE beasts in field are glad, and have not wit
  To know why leap'd their hearts when spring-time
    shone.
Man looks at his own bliss, considers it,
Weighs it with curious fingers; and 'tis gone.

THINK not thy wisdom can illume away
  The ancient tanglement of night and day.
Enough, to acknowledge both, and both revere:
They see not clearliest who see all things clear.

MOMENTOUS to himself as I to me
  Hath each man been that ever woman bore;
Once, in a lightning-flash of sympathy,
  I *felt* this truth, an instant, and no more.

(*After Reading "Tamberlaine the Great"*)

I close your Marlowe's page, my Shakespeare's ope.
  How welcome—after gong and cymbal's din—
The continuity, the long slow slope
  And vast curves of the gradual violin!

(*Shelley and Harriet Westbrook*)

A great star stoop'd from heaven and loved a flower
   Grown in earth's garden—loved it for an hour:
Let eyes which trace his orbit in the spheres
Refuse not, to a ruin'd rosebud, tears.

(*To a Foolish Wise Man*)

THE world's an orange—thou hast suck'd its juice;
   But wherefore all this pomp and pride and puffing?
Somehow a goose is none the less a goose
   Though moon and stars be minc'd to yield it stuffing.

Autumn

THOU burden of all songs the earth hath sung,
   Thou retrospect in Time's reverted eyes,
   Thou metaphor of everything that dies,
That dies ill-starred, or dies beloved and young
   And therefore blest and wise,—
O be less beautiful, or be less brief,
   Thou magic splendour, strange, and full of fear!
   In vain her pageant shall the Summer rear?
At thy mute signal, leaf by golden leaf,
   Crumbles the gorgeous year.

Ah, ghostly as remembered mirth, the tale
   Of Summer's bloom, the legend of the Spring!
   And thou, too, flutterest an impatient wing,
Thou presence yet more fugitive and frail,
   Thou most unbodied thing,
Whose very being is thy going hence,
   And passage and departure all thy theme;
   Whose life doth still a splendid dying seem,
And thou at height of thy magnificence
   A figment and a dream.

Stilled is the virgin rapture that was June,
   And cold is August's panting heart of fire;
   And in the storm-dismantled forest-choir
For thine own elegy thy winds attune
   Their wild and wizard lyre:
And poignant grows the charm of thy decay,
   The pathos of thy beauty, and the sting,
   Thou parable of greatness vanishing!
For me, thy woods of gold and skies of grey
   With speech fantastic ring.

For me, to dreams resigned, there come and go,
  'Twixt mountains draped and hooded night and morn,
Elusive notes in wandering wafture borne,
From undiscoverable lips that blow
    An immaterial horn;
And spectral seem thy winter-boding trees,
  Thy ruinous bowers and drifted foliage wet—
O Past and Future in sad bridal met,
O voice of everything that perishes,
    And soul of all regret!

Nightmare (*Written During Apparent Imminence of War*)

IN a false dream I saw the Foe prevail.
  The war was ended: the last smoke had rolled
Away: and we, erewhile the strong and bold,
Stood broken, humbled, withered, weak and pale,
And moaned, "Our greatness is become a tale
To tell our children's babes when we are old.
They shall put by their playthings to be told
How England once, before the years of bale,
Throned above trembling, puissant, grandiose, calm,
Held Asia's richest jewel in her palm;
And with unnumbered isles barbaric she
The broad hem of her glistening robe impearled;
Then, when she wound her arms about the world,
And had for vassal the obsequious sea."

To the Sultan

CALIPH, I did thee wrong. I hailed thee late
  "Abdul the Damned", and would recall my word.
It merged thee with the unillustrious herd
Who crowd the approaches to the infernal gate—
Spirits gregarious, equal in their state
As is the innumerable ocean bird,
Gannet or gull, whose wandering plaint is heard
On Ailsa or Iona desolate.
For, in a world where cruel deeds abound,
The merely damned are legion: with such souls
Is not each hollow and cranny of Tophet crammed?
Thou, with the brightest of Hell's aureoles
Dost shine supreme, incomparably crowned,
Immortally, beyond all mortals, damned.

ALFRED EDWARD HOUSMAN (1859-   )

From "A Shropshire Lad"

"IS my team ploughing,
    That I was used to drive
And hear the harness jingle
    When I was man alive?"

Ay, the horses trample,
    The harness jingles now;
No change though you lie under
    The land you used to plough.

"Is football playing
    Along the river shore,
With lads to chase the leather,
    Now I stand up no more?"

Ay, the ball is flying,
    The lads play heart and soul;
The goal stands up, the keeper
    Stands up to keep the goal.

"Is my girl happy,
    That I thought hard to leave,
And has she tired of weeping
    As she lies down at eve?"

Ay, she lies down lightly,
    She lies not down to weep:
Your girl is well contented.
    Be still, my lad, and sleep.

"Is my friend hearty,
    Now I am thin and pine,
And has he found to sleep in
    A better bed than mine?"

Yes, lad, I lie easy,
    I lie as lads would choose;
I cheer a dead man's sweetheart,
    Never ask me whose.

The Power of Malt

WHY, if 'tis dancing you would be,
    There's brisker pipes than poetry.
Say, for what were hop-yards meant,

Or why was Burton built on Trent?
Oh, many a peer of England brews
Livelier liquor than the Muse,
And malt does more than Milton can
To justify God's ways to man.
Ale, man, ale's the stuff to drink
For fellows whom it hurts to think:
Look into the pewter pot
To see the world as the world's not.

With Rue My Heart Is Laden

WITH rue my heart is laden
    For golden friends I had,
For many a rose-lipt maiden
    And many a lightfoot lad.

By brooks too broad for leaping
    The lightfoot boys are laid;
The rose-lipt girls are sleeping
    In fields where roses fade.

FRANCIS THOMPSON (1860-1907)

The Hound of Heaven

I fled Him, down the nights and down the days;
    I fled Him, down the arches of the years;
I fled Him, down the labyrinthine ways
    Of my own mind; and in the midst of tears
I hid from Him, and under running laughter.
        Up vistaed hopes I sped;
        And shot, precipitated
Adown Titanic glooms of chasmed fears,
From those strong Feet that followed, followed after.
        But with unhurrying chase,
        And unperturbèd pace,
    Deliberate speed, majestic instancy,
        They beat—and a Voice beat
        More instant than the Feet—
    "All things betray thee, who betrayest Me."

        I pleaded, outlaw-wise,
By many a hearted casement, curtained red,
    Trellised with intertwining charities;
(For, though I knew His love Who followèd,
        Yet was I sore adread
Lest, having Him, I must have naught beside);

But, if one little casement parted wide,
    The gust of His approach would clash it to.
Fear wist not to evade, as Love wist to pursue.
Across the margent of the world I fled,
    And troubled the gold gateways of the stars,
    Smiting for shelter on their clangèd bars;
        Fretted to dulcet jars
And silvern chatter the pale ports o' the moon.
I said to dawn, Be sudden; to eve, Be soon;
    With thy young skiey blossoms heap me over
        From this tremendous Lover!
Float thy vague veil about me, lest He see!
    I tempted all His servitors, but to find
My own betrayal in their constancy,
In faith to Him their fickleness to me,
    Their traitorous trueness, and their loyal deceit.
To all swift things for swiftness did I sue;
    Clung to the whistling mane of every wind.
    But whether they swept, smoothly fleet,
    The long savannahs of the blue;
        Or whether, Thunder-driven,
    They clanged his chariot 'thwart a heaven
Plashy with flying lightnings round the spurn o' their feet:—
    Fear wist not to evade, as Love wist to pursue.
        Still with unhurrying chase,
        And unperturbèd pace,
    Deliberate speed, majestic instancy,
        Came on the following Feet,
        And a Voice above their beat—
    "Naught shelters thee, who wilt not shelter Me."

I sought no more that after which I strayed
    In face of man or maid;
But still within the little children's eyes
    Seems something, something that replies;
They at least are for me, surely for me!
I turned me to them very wistfully;
But, just as their young eyes grew sudden fair
    With dawning answers there,
Their angel plucked them from me by the hair.
"Come then, ye other children, Nature's—share
With me" (said I) "your delicate fellowship;
        Let me greet you lip to lip,
        Let me twine you with caresses,
            Wantoning
        With our Lady Mother's vagrant tresses,
            Banqueting
        With her in her wind-walled palace,
        Underneath her azure daïs,
        Quaffing, as your taintless way is,

From a chalice
Lucent-weeping out of the dayspring."
            So it was done:
I in their delicate fellowship was one—
Drew the bolt of Nature's secrecies.
I knew all the swift importings
        On the wilful face of skies,
        I knew how the clouds arise
        Spumèd of the wild sea-snortings;
            All that's born or dies
        Rose and drooped with—made them shapers
Of mine own moods, or wailful or divine—
        With them joyed and was bereaven.
        I was heavy with the even,
        When she lit her glimmering tapers
        Round the day's dead sanctities.
        I laughed in the morning's eyes.
I triumphed and I saddened with all weather,
        Heaven and I wept together,
        And its sweet tears were salt with mortal mine;
        Against the red throb of its sunset-heart
            I laid my own to beat,
            And share commingling heat;
But not by that, by that, was eased my human smart.
In vain my tears were wet on Heaven's gray cheek.
For ah! we know not what each other says,
        These things and I; in sound I speak—
Their sound is but their stir, they speak by silences.
Nature, poor stepdame, cannot slake my drouth;
        Let her, if she would owe me,
Drop yon blue bosom-veil of sky, and show me
        The breasts o' her tenderness:
Never did any milk of hers once bless
        My thirsting mouth.
        Nigh and dry draws the chase,
        With unperturbèd pace,
        Deliberate speed, majestic instancy;
            And past those noisèd Feet
            A voice comes yet more fleet—
        "Lo! naught contents thee, who content'st not Me."

Naked I wait Thy love's uplifted stroke!
My harness piece by piece Thou hast hewn from me,
        And smitten me to my knee;
        I am defenseless utterly.
        I slept, methinks, and woke,
And, slowly gazing, find me stripped in sleep.
In the rash lustihood of my young powers,
        I shook the pillaring hours

And pulled my life upon me; grimed with smears
I stand amid the dust o' the mounded years—
My mangled youth lies dead beneath the heap.
My days have crackled and gone up in smoke,
Have puffed and burst as sun-starts on a stream.
    Yea, faileth now each dream
The dreamer, and the lute the lutanist;
Even the linked fantasies, in whose blossomy twist
I swung the earth a trinket at my wrist,
Are yielding; cords of all too weak account
For earth with heavy griefs so overplussed.
    Ah! is Thy love indeed
A weed, albeit an amaranthine weed,
Suffering no flowers except its own to mount?
    Ah! must—
    Designer infinite!—
Ah! must Thou char the wood ere Thou canst limn with it?
My freshness spent its wavering shower i' the dust:
And now my heart is as a broken fount,
Wherein tear-drippings stagnate, spilt down ever
    From the dank thoughts that shiver
Upon the sighful branches of my mind.
    Such is; what is to be?
The pulp so bitter, how shall taste the rind?
I dimly guess what Time in mists confounds;
Yet ever and anon a trumpet sounds
From the hid battlements of Eternity;
Those shaken mists a space unsettle, then
Round the half-glimpsèd turrets slowly wash again.
    But not ere him who summoneth
    I first have seen, enwound
With glooming robes purpureal, cypress-crowned;
His name I know, and what his trumpet saith.
Whether man's heart or life it be that yields
    Thee harvest, must Thy harvest fields
    Be dunged with rotten death?

    Now of that long pursuit
    Comes on at hand the bruit;
That Voice is round me like a bursting sea.
    "And is thy earth so marred,
    Shattered in shard on shard?
Lo, all things fly thee, for thou flyest Me!
    Strange, piteous, futile thing,
Wherefore should any set thee love apart?
Seeing none but I makes much of naught" (He said),
"And human love needs human meriting:
    How hast thou merited—
Of all man's clotted clay the dingiest clot?
    Alack, thou knowest not

How little worthy of any love thou art!
Whom wilt thou find to love ignoble thee
    Save Me, save only Me?
All which I took from thee, I did but take,
    Not for thy harms,
But just that thou might'st seek it in My arms.
    All which thy child's mistake
Fancies as lost, I have stored for thee at home;
    Rise, clasp My hand, and come!"
        Halts by me that footfall:
        Is my gloom, after all,
    Shade of His hand, outstretched caressingly?
        "Ah, fondest, blindest, weakest,
        I am He Whom thou seekest!
Thou dravest love from thee, who dravest Me."

To a Snowflake

WHAT heart could have thought you?—
    Past our devisal
(O filigree petal!)
Fashioned so purely
Fragilely, surely,
From what Paradisal
Imagineless metal,
Too costly for cost?
Who hammered you, wrought you,
From argentine vapour?—
"God was my shaper,
Passing surmisal,
He hammered, He wrought me,
From curled silver vapour,
To lust of His Mind:—
Thou could'st not have thought me!
So purely, so palely,
Tinily, surely,
Mightily, frailly
Insculped and embossed,
With His hammer of wind
And His graver of frost."

Arab Love-Song

THE hunchèd camels of the night
    Trouble the bright
And silver waters of the moon.
The maiden of the moon will soon
Through Heaven stray and sing,
Star gathering.

Now while the dark about our love is strewn,
Light of my dark, blood of my heart, O come!
And night will catch her breath up, and be dumb.

Leave thy father, leave thy mother
And thy brother;
Leave the black tents of thy tribe apart!
Am I not thy father and thy brother,
And thy mother?
And thou—what needest with thy tribe's black tents
Who hast the red pavilion of my heart?

Daisy

WHERE the thistle lifts a purple crown
Six foot out of the turf,
And the harebell shakes on the windy hill—
O the breath of the distant surf!—

The hills look over on the South,
And southward dreams the sea,
And with the sea-breeze hand in hand
Came innocence and she.

Where 'mid the gorse the raspberry
Red for the gatherer springs,
Two children did we stray and talk
Wise, idle, childish things.

She listened with big-lipped surprise,
Breast-deep 'mid flower and spine:
Her skin was like a grape, whose veins
Run snow instead of wine.

She knew not those sweet words she spake,
Nor knew her own sweet way;
But there's never a bird, so sweet a song
Thronged in whose throat that day.

Oh, there were flowers in Storrington
On the turf and on the spray;
But the sweetest flower on Sussex hills
Was the daisy-flower that day!

Her beauty smoothed earth's furrowed face
She gave me tokens three:—
A look, a word of her winsome mouth,
And a wild raspberry.

A berry red, a guileless look,
   A still word,—strings of sand!
And yet they made my wild, wild heart
   Fly down to her little hand.

For standing artless as the air,
   And candid as the skies,
She took the berries with her hand,
   And the love with her sweet eyes.

The fairest things have fleetest end,
   Their scent survives their close:
But the rose's scent is bitterness
   To him that loved the rose.

She looked a little wistfully,
   Then went her sunshine way:—
The sea's eye had a mist on it,
   And the leaves fell from the day.

She went her unremembering way,
   She went and left in me
The pang of all the partings gone
   And partings yet to be.

She left me marvelling why my soul
   Was sad that she was glad;
At all the sadness in the sweet,
   The sweetness in the sad.

Still, still I seemed to see her, still
   Look up with soft replies,
And take the berries with her hand,
   And the love with her lovely eyes.

Nothing begins, and nothing ends,
   That is not paid with moan;
For we are born in others' pain,
   And perish in our own.

ROBINSON KAY LEATHER

Advice to a Boy

BOY, should you meet a pretty wench
   unseen, alone, at twilight hour,
      ask not her name;
for on the crowded street at noon
she ill could brook the glare and gaze,

and Jack and Bill would call her plain,
and it were nothing but a dream,
    and you would wake.

Ask no forget-me-not, nor name
a trysting-place, for she will change,
    and you will change:
but if upon your memory
no single detail you imprint,
perchance will come into your mind
her witchery all unawares,
    at twilight hour.

CHARLES G. D. ROBERTS (1860-   )
Recessional

NOW along the solemn heights
  Fade the Autumn's altar-lights;
Down the great earth's glimmering chancel
Glide the days and nights.

Little kindred of the grass,
Like a shadow in a glass
  Falls the dark and falls the stillness;
We must rise and pass.

We must rise and follow, wending
Where the nights and days have ending,—
  Pass in order pale and slow
Unto sleep extending.

Little brothers of the clod,
Soul of fire and seed of sod,
  We must fare into the silence
At the knees of God.

Little comrades of the sky
Wing to wing we wander by
  Going, going, going, going,
Softly as a sigh.

Hark, the moving shapes confer,
Globe of dew and gossamer,
  Fading and ephemeral spirits
In the dusk astir.

Moth and blossom, blade and bee,
Worlds must go as well as we,
  In the long procession joining
Mount, and star, and sea.

Toward the shadowy brink we climb
Where the round year rolls sublime,
    Rolls, and drops, and falls forever
In the vast of time;

Like a plummet plunging deep
Past the utmost reach of sleep,
    Till remembrance has no longer
Care to laugh or weep.

An Epitaph on a Husbandman

HE who would start and rise
        Before the crowing cocks—
No more he lifts his eyes,
    Whoever knocks.

He who before the stars
    Would call the cattle home,—
They wait about the bars
    For him to come.

Him at whose hearty calls
    The farmstead woke again
The horses in their stalls
    Expect in vain.

Busy, and blithe, and bold,
    He laboured for the morrow,—
The plough his hands would hold
    Rusts in the furrow.

His fields he had to leave,
    His orchards cool and dim;
The clods he used to cleave
    Now cover him.

But the green, growing things
    Lean kindly to his sleep,—
White roots and wandering strings,
    Closer they creep.

Because he loved them long
    And with them bore his part,
Tenderly now they throng
    About his heart.

The Cricket

OH, to be a cricket,
    That's the thing!
To scurry in the grass
    And to have one's fling!
And it's oh, to be a cricket
In the warm thistle-thicket,
    Where the sun-winds pass,
    Winds a-wing,
And the bumble-bees hang humming
    Hum and swing,
And the honey-drops are coming!

Abridged.

The Frosted Pane

ONE night came Winter noiselessly and leaned
    Against my window-pane.
In the deep stillness of his heart convened
    The ghosts of all his slain.

Leaves and ephemera, and stars of earth,
    And fugitives of grass,—
White spirits loosed from bonds of mortal birth,
    He drew them on the glass.

JUSTIN HUNTLY McCARTHY (1860-   )

To Omar Kháyyám

OMAR, dear Sultan of the Persian Song,
    Familiar Friend whom I have loved so long,
    Whose Volume made my pleasant Hiding-place
From this fantastic World of Right and Wrong.

My Youth lies buried in thy Verses: lo,
I read, and as the haunted Numbers flow,
    My Memory turns in anguish to the Face
That leaned o'er Omar's pages long ago.

Alas for Me, alas for all who weep
And wonder at the Silence dark and deep
    That girdles round this little Lamp in space
No wiser than when Omar fell asleep.

Rest in thy Grave beneath the crimson rain
Of heart-desired Roses. Life is vain,
    And vain the trembling Legends we may trace
Upon the open Book that shuts again.

If I Were King (After Villon)

IF I were king—ah, love, if I were king!
  What tributary nations would I bring
    To stoop before your sceptre and to swear
    Allegiance to your lips and eyes and hair.
Beneath your feet what treasures I would fling:—

The stars should be your pearls upon a string,
The world a ruby for your finger ring,
    And you should have the sun and moon to wear
            If I were king.

Let these wild dreams and wilder words take wing,
Deep in the woods I hear a shepherd sing
    A simple ballad to a sylvan air,
    Of love that ever finds your face more fair.
I could not give you any godlier thing
            If I were king.

BLISS CARMAN (1861-   )

Spring Song

MAKE me over, Mother April,
  When the sap begins to stir! . . .
When thy flowery hand delivers
All the mountain-prisoned rivers,
And thy great heart beats and quivers
To revive the days that were,
Make me over, Mother April,
When the sap begins to stir! . . .

Set me in the urge and tide-drift
Of the streaming hosts a-wing!
Breast of scarlet, throat of yellow,
Raucous challenge, wooings mellow—
Every migrant is my fellow,
Making northward with the spring.
Set me in the urge and tide-drift
Of the streaming hosts a-wing! . . .

Make me over, Mother April,
When the sap begins to stir!
Fashion me from swamp or meadow,
Garden plot or ferny shadow,
Hyacirth or humble burr!
Make me over, Mother April,
When the sap begins to stir!

Let me hear the far, low summons,
When the silver winds return;
Rills that run and streams that stammer,
Goldenwing with his loud hammer,
Icy brooks that brawl and clamor,
Where the Indian willows burn;
Let me hearken to the calling,
When the silver winds return. . . .

For I have no choice of being,
When the sap begins to climb,—
Strong insistence, sweet intrusion,
Vasts and verges of illusion,—
So I win, to time's confusion,
The one perfect pearl of time,
Joy and joy and joy forever,
Till the sap forgets to climb! . . .

Let me taste the old immortal
Indolence of life once more;
Not recalling nor foreseeing,
Let the great slow joys of being
Well my heart through as of yore!
Let me taste the old immortal
Indolence of life once more!

Give me the old drink for rapture,
The delirium to drain,
All my fellows drank in plenty
At the Three Score Inns and Twenty
From the mountains to the main!
Give me the old drink for rapture,
The delirium to drain!

Only make me over, April,
When the sap begins to stir!
Make me man or make me woman,
Make me oaf or ape or human,
Cup of flower or cone of fir;
Make me anything but neuter
When the sap begins to stir!

Abridged.

Ballad of John Camplejohn

"WHAT do you sell, John Camplejohn,
    In Bay-Street by the sea?"
"Oh, turtle-shell is what I sell
    In great variety.

"Trinkets and combs and rosaries,
  All keepsakes of the sea;
'Tis choose and buy what takes the eye
  In such a treasury."

" 'Tis none of these, John Camplejohn,
  Tho' curious they be:
But something more I'm looking for,
  In Bay-Street by the sea,

"Where can I buy the magic charm
  Of the Bahamian Sea,
That fills mankind with peace of mind
  And soul's felicity?

"Now what do you sell, John Camplejohn,
  In Bay-Street by the sea,
Tinged with that true and native blue,
  Of lapis lazuli?

"Look from your door and tell me now
  The colour of the sea—
Where can I buy the wondrous dye
  And take it home with me?

"And where can I buy that rustling sound
  In this city by the sea,
Of the plumy palms in their high blue calms;
  Or the stately poise and free?

"Of the bearers who go up and down
  Silent as mystery,
Burden on head, with naked tread
  In the white streets by the sea?

"And where can I buy, John Camplejohn,
  In Bay-Street by the sea?
The sunlight's fall on the old pink wall
  Or the gold of the orange tree?"

"Ah, that is more than I've heard tell
  In Bay-Street by the sea,
Since I began, my roving man,
  A trafficker to be.

"As sure as I'm John Camplejohn,
  And Bay-Street's by the sea,
Those things for gold have not been sold
  Within my memory.

"But what would you give, my roving man,
    From countries over the sea,
For the things you name the life of the same,
    And the power to bid them be?"

"I'd give my hand, John Camplejohn,
    In Bay-Street by the sea,
For the smallest dower of that dear power,
    To paint the things I see."

"My roving man, I never heard,
    On any land or sea,
Under the sun, of any one
    Could sell that power to thee."

"'Tis sorry news, John Camplejohn,
    If this be destiny,
That every mart should know that art,
    Yet none can sell it me.

"But look you here's the Grace of God;
    There's neither price nor fee,
Duty nor toil, that can control
    The power to love and see.

"To each his luck, John Camplejohn,
    No less, and as for me,
Give me the pay of an idle day
    In Bay-Street by the sea."

Envoy

Have little care that Life is brief,
And less that Art is long.
Success is in the silences
Though fame is in the song. . . .

                                        Abridged.

KATHARINE TYNAN HINKSON (1861-   )

The Desire

GIVE me no mansions ivory white
    Nor palaces of pearl and gold;
Give me a child for all delight,
    Just four years old.

Give me no wings of rosy shine
Nor snowy raiment, fold on fold,
Give me a little boy all mine,
    Just four years old.

Give me no gold and starry crown
Nor harps, nor palm branches unrolled;
Give me a nestling head of brown,
    Just four years old.

Give me a cheek that's like the peach,
Two arms to clasp me from the cold;
And all my heaven's within my reach,
    Just four years old.

Dear God, You give me from Your skies
A little paradise to hold,
As Mary once her Paradise,
    Just four years old.

SIR OWEN SEAMAN (1861-   )
To a Boy-Poet of the Decadence

(Showing curious reversal of epigram—*"La nature l'a fait sanglier; la civilisation l'a réduit
à l'état de cochon."*)

BUT, my good little man, you have made a mistake
    If you really are pleased to suppose
That the Thames is alight with the lyrics you make;
    We could all do the same if we chose.

From Solomon down, we may read, as we run,
    On the ways of a man and a maid;
There is nothing that's new to us under the sun,
    And certainly not in the shade.

The erotic affairs that you fiddle aloud
    Are as vulgar as coin of the mint;
And you merely distinguish yourself from the crowd
    By the fact that you put 'em in print.

You're a 'prentice, my boy, in the primitive stage,
    And you itch, like a boy, to confess:
When you know a bit more of the arts of the age
    You will probably talk a bit less.

For your dull little vices we don't care a fig,
  It is *this* that we deeply deplore:
You were cast for a common or usual pig,
  But you play the invincible bore.

MAURICE HEWLETT (1861-   )

Flos Virginum

W HERE is a holier thing
        In a fair world apparell'd for our bliss
Than the pure influence
That dwells in a girl's heart
And beams from her quiet eyes?
Earth has no ministering
So lovely, so acceptable or wise,
Withal so frail as this;
Which, if man win, it needeth all his art,
Lest uncouth violence,
Rough mastery, or the tyrannies of earth,
Should maim or shatter out
With ill-timed speech or flout
Her wistful-tender'd balm at very birth.

Her Motherhood to be
She hides in her child-bosom, as a seed
That creepeth to be flower
Long ere it feeleth light:
She nurtureth her lover.
Within her arms made free,
Upon her heart made restful, given over
To her most gentle deed,
He lieth watcht upon by her grave sight;
And she liveth her hour,
Contented to be Mother to this child,
Given before her time
Assurance whence to climb
Up to her real throne of Godhead mild. . . .

.   .   .   .

Ah, frailer than a breath,
Sullied sooner, more fatally than glass!
If such most desolate
Pitiful lot be hers,
That a brute-soul possess
And goad her to her death;
Death were more welcome than the piteousness

Of life, for she would pass
Up to the stars, the silent messengers
Of God who from his seat
Weepeth for beauty driven down by dearth
Of love to peak and fail,
To wring hands and turn pale,
Eyeing dismay'd the shock of her soul's worth.

SIR HENRY NEWBOLT (1862-   )

Drake's Drum

(Sir Francis Drake, 1540?-1596)

DRAKE, he's in his hammock an' a thousand mile away,
    (Capten, art tha sleepin' there below?),
Slung atween the round shot in Nombre Dios Bay,
    An' dreamin' arl the time o' Plymouth Hoe.
Yarnder lumes the Island, yarnder lie the ships,
    Wi' sailor lads a-dancin' heel-an'-toe,
An' the shore-lights flashin', an' the night-tide dashin',
    He sees et arl so plainly as he saw et long ago.

Drake he was a Devon man, an' ruled the Devon seas,
    (Capten, art tha sleepin' there below?),
Rovin' though his death fell, he went wi' heart at ease,
    An' dreamin' arl the time o' Plymouth Hoe.
"Take my drum to England, hang et by the shore,
    Strike et when your powder's runnin' low;
If the Dons sight Devon, I'll quit the port o' Heaven,
    An' drum them up the Channel as we drummed them long
      ago."

Drake he's in his hammock till the great Armadas come,
    (Capten, art tha sleepin' there below?),
Slung atween the round shot, listenin' for the drum,
    An' dreamin' arl the time o' Plymouth Hoe.
Call him on the deep sea, call him up the Sound,
    Call him when ye sail to meet the foe;
Where the old trade's plyin' an' the old flag flyin',
    They shall find him ware an' wakin', as they found him
      long ago!

Messmates

HE gave us all a good-by cheerily
    At the first dawn of day;
We dropped him down the side full drearily
    When the light died away.

It's a dead dark watch that he's a-keeping there,
And a long, long night that lags a-creeping there,
Where the Trades and the tides roll over him
    And the great ships go by.

He's there alone with green seas rocking him,
    For a thousand miles around;
He's there alone with dumb things mocking him,
    And we're homeward bound.
It's a long, lone watch that he's a-keeping there,
And a dead cold night that lags a-creeping there,
While the months and the years roll over him
    And the great ships go by.

I wonder if the tramps come near enough,
    As they thrash to and fro,
And the battleships' bells ring clear enough
    To be heard down below;
If through all the lone watch that he's a-keeping there,
And the long, cold night that lags a-creeping there,
The voices of the sailor-men shall comfort him
    When the great ships go by.

ARTHUR CHRISTOPHER BENSON (1862-   )
Prelude

HUSHED is each shout:
    The reverent people wait,
To see the sacred pomp stream out
    Beside the temple gate.

The bull with garlands hung,
    Stern priests in vesture grim:
With rolling voices swiftly sung—
    Peals out the jocund hymn.

In front, behind, beside,
    Beneath the chimney towers,
Pass boys that fling the censer wide,
    And striplings scattering flowers.

Victim or minister
    I dare not claim to be,
But in the concourse and the stir,
    There shall be room for me.

The victim feels the stroke:
    The priests are bowed in prayer:—
I feed the porch with fragrant smoke,
    Strew roses on the stair.

NORMAN GALE (1862-   )

A Love-Song

O to think, O to think as I see her stand there
   With the rose that I plucked, in her glorious hair,
   In the robe that I love,
   So demure and so neat,
I am lord of her lips and her eyes and her feet.

O to think, O to think when the last hedge is leapt,
When the blood is awakened that dreamingly slept,
   I shall make her heart throb
   In its cradle of lace,
As the lord of her hair and her breast and her face.

O to think, O to think when our wedding-bells ring,
When our love's at the summer but life's at the spring,
   I shall guard her asleep
   As my hound guards her glove,
Being lord of her life and her heart and her love!

A Creed

GOD sends no message by me. I am mute
      When Wisdom crouches in her farthest cave;
I love the organ, but must touch the lute. . . .

No controversies thrust me to the ledge
   Of dangerous schools and doctrines hard to learn;
Give me the whitethroat whistling in the hedge.

Why should I fret myself to find out nought?
   Dispute can blight the soul's eternal corn
And choke its richness with the tares of thought.

I am content to know that God is great,
   And Lord of fish and fowl, of air and sea,—
Some little points are misty. Let them wait. . . .

Abridged.

VICTOR PLARR (1863-   )

Epitaphium Citharistriæ

STAND not uttering sedately
      Trite oblivious praise above her!
Rather say you saw her lately
   Lightly kissing her last lover.

Whisper not "There is a reason
  Why we bring her no white blossom:"
Since the snowy bloom's in season,
  Strow it on her sleeping bosom:

Oh, for it would be a pity
  To o'erpraise her or to flout her:
She was wild, and sweet, and witty—
  Let's not say dull things about her.

ROSAMUND MARRIOTT WATSON (1863-   )

Requiescat

BURY me deep when I am dead,
  Far from the woods where sweet birds sing;
Lap me in sullen stone and lead,
Lest my poor dust should feel the Spring.

Never a flower be near me set,
Nor starry cup nor slender stem,
Anemone nor violet,
Lest my poor dust remember them.

And you—wherever you may fare—
Dearer than birds, or flowers, or dew—
Never, ah me, pass never there,
Lest my poor dust should dream of you.

SIR ARTHUR T. QUILLER-COUCH (1863-   )

The Splendid Spur

NOT on the neck of prince or hound,
  Nor on a woman's finger twined,
May gold from the deriding ground
  Keep sacred that we sacred bind:
        Only the heel
        Of splendid steel
Shall stand secure on sliding fate,
When golden navies weep their freight.

The scarlet hat, the laureled stave
  Are measures, not the springs, of worth;
In a wife's lap, as in a grave,
  Man's airy notions mix with earth.
        Seek other spur
        Bravely to stir
The dust in this loud world, and tread
Alp-high among the whispering dead.

Trust in thyself,—then spur amain:
So shall Charybdis wear a grace,
Grim Ætna laugh, the Libyan plain
Take roses to her shriveled face.
This orb—this round
Of sight and sound—
Count it the lists that God hath built
For haughty hearts to ride a-tilt.

HERBERT P. HORNE (1864-   )

A Song

BE not too quick to carve our rhyme
And hearts, upon the tree of Time;
Lest one swift year prove, in its run,
They were but lines, and poorly done.
That longest lived, which longest grows
In stillness, and by sure degrees:
So rest you, Sweet;
That, going hence with calmer feet,
We may be friends, when friends are foes,
And old days merely histories.

Upon Returning a Silk Handkerchief

TINGED with my kisses go, go thou to her,
And bid her bind thee round her faultless throat;
Till thou, close-lying o'er the charmed stir
Of her white breast, grow warm and seem to float
Away into the golden noon, the still,
Deep sunlight of her. Oh, sleep on! 'Tis thine,
Love's summer day. No, not June's thronged hours
So glad are, when the songs of birds fulfil
Earth, and the breezes in the grass decline,
Held by the scent of many thousand flowers.

Yet loose that flood of kisses, which thou hast,
Into her bosom, and through all her hair;
Whispering, it is my utmost wealth amassed
For her, being fairest: nor do thou forbear,
Until she feel my spirit, like a blush,
Steal by her shoulder and frail neck; for when
The gorgeous scarlet, burning, shall have moved
Over her cheek, the little after-hush
Will tell to her, that I am happy then,
God! for how short a time, and she is loved.

Loved? Wherefore loved that never, but in thought,
  May be possessed? Is it, that thus might grow
From out a look, a touch, long past to naught,
  My Beatrice, and my perfect love; and so
Dwell with me here, although the while I guess,
  'Tis but a dream, which only does me wrong?
    O wretched truth! and yet the hour, that girds
My pensive nature with her loveliness,
  Would bitter be, as 'tis unto this Song
    To wed these thoughts too stern for dainty words.

Would 'twere no dream, this dream; this long, devout,
  Untiring worship, vainly yet essayed;
This absolute love; then were the torturing doubt,
  The troubled ocean of the soul allayed:
Desire would have her lust, and we have ease.
  Here, from her everlasting thirst; nor pine
    Vainly; but feel the fret, the harrowed breath,
The throbbing heart, that will not, will not cease,
  Stilled into marble, Greek-like, calm, divine,
    Remembering not the past. Stay! This is Death.

Sonnet

If I could come again to that dear place
Where once I came, where Beauty lived and moved,
Where, by the sea, I saw her face to face,
That soul alive by which the world has loved;
If, as I stood at gaze among the leaves,
She would appear again, as once before,
While the red herdsman gathered up his sheaves
And brimming waters trembled up the shore;
If, as I gazed, her Beauty that was dumb,
In that old time, before I learned to speak,
Would lean to me and revelation come,
Words to the lips and colour to the cheek,
Joy with its searing-iron would burn me wise.
I should know all; all powers, all mysteries.

WILLIAM BUTLER YEATS (1865-   )

The Lake Isle of Innisfree

I will arise and go now, and go to Innisfree,
    And a small cabin build there, of clay and wattles made:
Nine bean rows will I have there, a hive for the honey bee,
    And live alone in the bee-loud glade.

And I shall have some peace there, for peace comes dropping
    slow,
  Dropping from the veils of the morning to where the cricket
    sings;
There midnight's all a glimmer, and noon a purple glow,
  And evening full of the linnet's wings.

I will arise and go now, for always, night and day,
  I hear lake-water lapping with low sounds by the shore;
While I stand on the roadway, or on the pavements gray,
  I hear it in the deep heart's core.

"When You Are Old"

WHEN you are old and gray and full of sleep,
    And nodding by the fire, take down this book,
And slowly read and dream of the soft look
Your eyes had once, and of their shadows deep;

How many loved your moments of glad grace,
And loved your beauty with love false or true;
But one man loved the pilgrim soul in you,
And loved the sorrows of your changing face.

And bending down beside the glowing bars
Murmur, a little sadly, how love fled
And paced upon the mountains overhead
And hid his face amid a crowd of stars.

The Cap and Bells

A jester walked in the garden;
    The garden had fallen still;
He bade his soul rise upward
And stand at her window-sill.

It rose in a straight blue garment,
When owls began to call:
It had grown wise-tongued by thinking
Of a quiet and light foot-fall;

But the young queen would not listen;
She rose in her pale night gown;
She drew in the heavy casement
And push'd the latches down.

He bade his heart go to her, .
When the owls call'd out no more:
In a red and quivering garment
It sang to her through the door.

It had grown sweet-tongued by dreaming
Of a flutter of flower-like hair;
But she took up her fan from the table
And waved it off on the air.

"I have cap and bells," he pondered,
"I will send them to her and die";
And when the morning whiten'd
He left them where she went by.

She laid them upon her bosom,
Under a cloud of her hair,
And her red lips sang them a love-song,
Till stars grew out of the air.

She open'd her door and her window,
And the heart and the soul came through,
To her right hand came the red one,
To her left hand came the blue.

They set up a noise like crickets,
A chattering wise and sweet,
And her hair was a folded flower,
And the quiet of love in her feet.

ARTHUR SYMONS (1865-   )

At the Stage-Door

K ICKING my heels in the street,
    Here at the edge of the pavement I wait, and my feet
Paw at the ground like the horses' hoofs in the street.

Under the archway sheer,
Sudden and black as a hole in the placarded wall,
Faces flicker and veer,
Wavering out of the darkness into the light,
Wavering back into night;
Under the archway, suddenly seen, the curls
And thin, bright faces of girls,
Roving eyes, and smiling lips, and the glance
Seeking, finding perchance,
Here at the edge of the pavement, there by the wall,
One face, out of them all.

Steadily, face after face,
Cheeks with the blush of the paint yet lingering, eyes
Still with their circle of black . . .
But hers, but hers?

Rose-leaf cheeks, and flower-soft lips, and the grace
Of the vanishing Spring come back,
And a child's heart blithe in the sudden and sweet surprise,
Subtly expectant, that stirs
In the smile of her heart to my heart, of her eyes to my eyes.

Asking Forgiveness

I did not know; child, child, I did not know,
   Who now in lonely wayfare go,
Who wander lonely of you, O my child,
And by myself exiled.
I did not know, but, O white soul of youth,
So passionate of truth,
So amorous of duty, and so strong
To suffer, all but wrong,
Is there for me no pity, who am weak?
Spare me this silence, speak!
I did not know: I wronged you; I repent:
But will you not relent?
Must I still wander, outlawed, and go on
The old weary ways alone,
As in the old, intolerable days
Before I saw your face,
The doubly darkened ways since you withdraw
Your light, that was my law?
I charge you by your soul, pause, ere you hurl
Sheer to destruction, girl,
A poor soul that had midway struggled out,
Still midway clogged about,
And for the love of you had turned his back
Upon the miry track,
That had been as a grassy wood-way, dim
With violet-beds, to him.
I wronged you, but I loved you; and to me
Your love was purity;
I rose, because you called me, and I drew
Nearer to God, in you.
I fall, and if you leave me, I must fall
To that last depth of all,
Where not the miracle of even your eyes
Can bid the dead arise.
I charge you that you save not your own sense
Of lilied innocence,
By setting, at the roots of that fair stem,
A murdered thing, to nourish them.

After Love

TO part now, and, parting now,
  Never to meet again;
To have done for ever, I and thou,
With joy, and so with pain.

It is too hard, too hard to meet
If we must love no more;
Those other meetings were too sweet
That went before.

And I would have, now love is over,
An end to all, an end:
I cannot, having been your lover,
Stoop to become your friend!

RUDYARD KIPLING (1865-   )

Mandalay

BY the old Moulmein Pagoda, lookin' eastward to the sea,
  There's a Burma girl a-settin', an' I know she thinks
    o' me;
For the wind is in the palm trees, an' the temple bells they say:
"Come you back, you British soldier; come you back to Man-
    dalay!"

Come you back to Mandalay,
Where the old Flotilla lay:
Can't you 'ear their paddles chunkin' from Rangoon to Man-
    dalay?
Oh, the road to Mandalay,
Where the flyin'-fishes play,
An' the dawn comes up like thunder outer China 'crost the
    Bay!

'Er petticut was yaller an' 'er little cap was green,
An' 'er name was Supi-yaw-lat—jes' the same as Theebaw's
    Queen,
An' I seed her fust a-smokin' of a whackin' white cheroot,
An' a-wastin' Christian kisses on an 'eathen idol's foot:
  Bloomin' idol made o' mud—
  Wot they called the Great Gawd Budd—
  Plucky lot she cared for idols when I kissed 'er where she
    stud!
On the road to Mandalay—

When the mist was on the rice-fields an' the sun was droppin'
      slow,
She'd git 'er little banjo an' she'd sing *"Kulla-lo-lo!"*
With 'er arm upon my shoulder, an' 'er cheek agin my cheek,
We useter watch the steamers an' the *hathis* pilin' teak.
    Elephints a-pilin' teak.
    In the sludgy, squdgy creek,
      Where the silence 'ung that 'eavy you was 'arf afraid to
          speak!
On the road to Mandalay—

But that's all shove be'ind me—long ago an' fur away,
An' there ain't no 'buses runnin' from the Benk to Mandalay;
An' I'm learnin' 'ere in London what the ten-year sodger tells:
"If you've 'eard the East a-callin', why, you won't 'eed nothin'
      else."
    No! you won't 'eed nothin' else
    But them spicy garlic smells
An' the sunshine an' the palm trees an' the tinkly temple
      bells!
On the road to Mandalay—

I am sick o' wastin' leather on these gutty pavin'-stones,
An' the blasted Henglish drizzle wakes the fever in my bones;
Though I walks with fifty 'ousemaids outer Chelsea to the
      Strand,
An' they talks a lot o' lovin', but wot do they understand?
    Beefy face an' grubby 'and—
    Law! wot *do* they understand?
I've a neater, sweeter maiden in a cleaner, greener land!
On the road to Mandalay—

Ship me somewheres east of Suez where the best is like the
      worst,
Where there aren't no Ten Commandments, an' a man can
      raise a thirst;
For the temple bells are callin', an' it's there that I would
      be—
By the old Moulmein Pagoda, lookin' lazy at the sea—
    On the road to Mandalay,
    Where the old Flotilla lay,
      With our sick beneath the awnings when we went to Man-
          dalay!
    Oh, the road to Mandalay,
    Where the flyin'-fishes play,
An' the dawn comes up like thunder outer China 'crost the
      Bay!

Danny Deever

WHAT are the bugles blowin' for?" said Files-on-Parade.
  To turn you out, to turn you out," the Color-Sergeant
    said.
"What makes you look so white, so white?" said Files-on-
    Parade.
"I'm dreadin' what I've got to watch," the Color-Sergeant
    said.
  For they're hangin' Danny Deever, you can 'ear the Dead
    March play,
  The regiment's in 'ollow square—they're hangin' him to-day;
  They've taken of his buttons off an' cut his stripes away,
  An' they're hangin' Danny Deever in the mornin'.

"What makes the rear-rank breathe so 'ard?" said Files-on-
    Parade.
"It's bitter cold, it's bitter cold," the Color-Sergeant said.
  "What makes that front-rank man fall down?" says Files-
    on-Parade.
"A touch o' sun, a touch o' sun," the Color-Sergeant said.
  They're hangin' Danny Deever, they are marchin' of 'im
    round,
  They 'ave 'alted Danny Deever by 'is coffin on the ground;
  An' 'e'll swing in 'arf a minute for a sneakin' shootin'
    hound—
  O they're hangin' Danny Deever in the mornin'!

"'Is cot was right-'and cot to mine," said Files-on-Parade.
"'E's sleepin' out an' far to-night," the Color-Sergeant said.
  "I've drunk 'is beer a score o' times," said Files-on-Parade.
"'E's drinkin' bitter beer alone," the Color-Sergeant said.
  They are hangin' Danny Deever, you must mark 'im to 'is
    place,
  For 'e shot a comrade sleepin'—you must look 'im in the
    face;
  Nine 'undred of 'is county an' the regiment's disgrace,
  While they're hangin' Danny Deever in the mornin'.

"What's that so black agin the sun?" said Files-on-Parade.
"It's Danny fightin' 'ard fur life," the Color-Sergeant said.
"What's that that whimpers over'ead?" said Files-on-Parade.
"It's Danny's soul that's passin' now," the Color-Sergeant said.
  For they're done with Danny Deever, you can 'ear the quick-
    step play,
  The regiment's in column, an' they're marchin' us away;
  Ho! the young recruits are shakin', an' they'll want their
    beer to-day,
  After hangin' Danny Deever in the mornin'.

Recessional

GOD of our fathers, known of old—
    Lord of our far-flung battle line—
Beneath whose awful hand we hold
    Dominion over palm and pine—
Lord God of Hosts, be with us yet,
Lest we forget—lest we forget!

The tumult and the shouting dies—
    The Captains and the Kings depart—
Still stands Thine ancient sacrifice,
    An humble and a contrite heart.
Lord God of Hosts, be with us yet,
Lest we forget—lest we forget!

Far-called, our navies melt away—
    On dune and headland sinks the fire—
Lo, all our pomp of yesterday
    Is one with Nineveh and Tyre!
Judge of the Nations, spare us yet,
Lest we forget—lest we forget!

If, drunk with sight of power, we loose
    Wild tongues that have not Thee in awe—
Such boasting as the Gentiles use,
    Or lesser breeds without the Law—
Lord God of Hosts, be with us yet,
Lest we forget—lest we forget!

For heathen heart that puts her trust
    In reeking tube and iron shard—
All valiant dust that builds on dust,
    And guarding calls not Thee to guard,—
For frantic boast and foolish word,
Thy Mercy on Thy People, Lord! AMEN.

The Vampire, as Suggested by the Painting by Philip Burne-Jones

A fool there was and he made his prayer
            (Even as you and I!)
To a rag and a bone and a hank of hair
(We called her the woman who did not care),
But the fool he called her his lady fair
            (Even as you and I!)

Oh the years we waste and the tears we waste,
  And the work of our head and hand,
Belong to the woman who did not know
(And now we know that she never could know)
  And did not understand.

A fool there was and his goods he spent
          (Even as you and I!)
Honor and faith and a sure intent
(And it wasn't the least what the lady meant),
But a fool must follow his natural bent
          (Even as you and I!)
Oh the toil we lost and the spoil we lost,
  And the excellent things we planned,
Belong to the woman who didn't know why
(And now we know she never knew why)
  And did not understand.

The fool was stripped to his foolish hide
          (Even as you and I!)
Which she might have seen when she threw him aside,—
(But it isn't on record the lady tried)
So some of him lived but the most of him died—
          (Even as you and I!)

And it isn't the shame and it isn't the blame
  That stings like a white-hot brand.
It's coming to know that she never knew why
(Seeing at last she could never know why)
  And never could understand.

The Story of Uriah

"Now there were two men in one city; the one rich and the
            other poor."

JACK BARRETT went to Quetta,
      Because they told him to.
He left his wife at Simla
      On three-fourths his monthly screw:
Jack Barrett died at Quetta
      Ere the next month's pay he drew.

Jack Barrett went to Quetta,
      He didn't understand
The reason of his transfer
      From the pleasant mountain-land:
The season was September,
      And it killed him out of hand.

Jack Barrett went to Quetta
  And there gave up the ghost,
Attempting two men's duty
  In that very healthy post;
And Mrs. Barrett mourned for him
  Five lively months at most.

Jack Barrett's bones at Quetta
  Enjoy profound repose;
But I shouldn't be astonished
  If *now* his spirit knows
The reason of his transfer
  From the Himalayan snows.

And, when the Last Great Bugle Call
  Adown the Hurnai throbs,
When the last grim joke is entered
  In the big black Books of Jobs,
And Quetta's graveyards give again
  Their victims to the air,
I shouldn't like to be the man
  Who sent Jack Barrett there.

L'Envoi

THERE'S a whisper down the field where the year has
    shot her yield,
  And the ricks stand grey to the sun,
Singing:—'Over then, come over, for the bee has quit the
    clover
  And your English summer's done.'
      You have heard the beat of the off-shore wind,
      And the thresh of the deep-sea rain;
      You have heard the song—how long! how long?
      Pull out on the trail again!

    Ha' done with the Tents of Shem, dear lass,
    We've seen the seasons through,
    And it's time to turn on the old trail, our own trail,
      the out trail,
    Pull out, pull out, on the Long Trail—the trail that is
      always new.

It's North you may run to the rime-ringed sun
  Or South to the blind Horn's hate;
Or East all the way into Mississippi Bay,
  Or West to the Golden Gate;

Where the blindest bluffs hold good, dear lass,
  And the wildest tales are true,
And the men bulk big on the old trail, our own trail, the out
    trail,
And life runs large on the Long Trail—the trail that is always

The days are sick and cold, and the skies are grey and old,
   And the twice-breathed airs blow damp;
And I'd sell my tired soul for the bucking beam-sea roll
   Of a black Bilbao tramp;

   With her load-line over her hatch, dear lass,
   And a drunken Dago crew,
   And her nose held down on the old trail, our own trail,
      the out trail
   From Cadiz Bar on the Long Trail—the trail that is al-
      ways new.

There be triple ways to take, of the eagle or the snake,
   Or the way of a man with a maid;
But the sweetest way to me is a ship's upon the sea
   In the heel of the North-East Trade.

   Can you hear the crash on her bows, dear lass,
   And the drum of the racing screw,
   As she ships it green on the old trail, our own trail, the
      out trail,
   As she lifts and 'scends on the Long Trail—the trail that
      is always new?

See the shaking funnels roar, with the Peter at the fore,
   And the fenders grind and heave,
And the derricks clack and grate as the tackle hooks the crate,
   And the fall-rope whines through the sheave;

   It's 'Gang-plank up and in,' dear lass,
   It's 'Hawsers warp her through!'
   And it's 'All clear aft' on the old trail, our own trail, the
      out trail,
   We're backing down on the Long Trail—the trail that is
      always new.

Oh, the mutter overside, when the port-fog holds us tied,
   And the syrens hoot their dread!
When foot by foot we creep o'er the hueless, viewless deep
   To the sob of the questing lead!

   It's down by the Lower Hope, dear lass,
   With the Gunfleet Sands in view,
   Till the Mouse swings green on the old trail, our own
      trail, the out trail,
   And the Gull Light lifts on the Long Trail—the trail that
      is always new.

Oh, the blazing tropic night, when the wake's a welt of light
   That holds the hot sky tame,
And the steady fore-foot snores through the planet-powdered
      floors
   Where the scared whale flukes in flame!

Her plates are scarred by the sun, dear lass,
Her ropes are taut with the dew,
For we're booming down on the old trail, our own trail,
  the out trail,
We're sagging south on the Long Trail—the trail that is
  always new.

Then home, get her home where the drunken rollers comb,
  And the shouting seas drive by,
And the engines stamp and ring and the wet bows reel and
    swing,
  And the Southern Cross rides high!

Yes, the old lost stars wheel back, dear lass,
That blaze in the velvet blue.
They're all old friends on the old trail, our own trail, the
  out trail,
They're God's own guides on the Long Trail—the trail
  that is always new.

Fly forward, O my heart, from the Foreland to the Start—
  We're steaming all too slow,
And it's twenty thousand mile to our little lazy isle
  Where the trumpet-orchids blow!

You have heard the call of the off-shore wind
And the voice of the deep-sea rain—
You have heard the song—how long! how long?
Pull out on the trail again!

The Lord knows what we may find, dear lass,
And the Deuce knows what we may do—
But we're back once more on the old trail, our own trail, the
  out trail,
We're down, hull-down on the Long Trail—the trail that is
  always new.

HERBERT TRENCH (1865-   )

A Charge

IF thou hast squandered years to grave a gem
    Commissioned by thy absent Lord, and while
  'Tis incomplete,
Others would bribe thy needy skill to them—
    Dismiss them to the street!

Shouldst thou at last discover Beauty's grove,
  At last be panting on the fragrant verge,
    But in the track,
Drunk with divine possession, thou meet Love—
    Turn, at her bidding, back.

When round thy ship in tempest Hell appears,
  And every specter mutters up more dire
    To snatch control
And loose to madness thy deep-kenneled Fears—
    Then to the helm, O Soul!

Last, if upon the cold, green-mantling sea,
  Thou cling, alone with Truth, to the last spar,
    Both castaway,
And one must perish—let it not be he
    Whom thou art sworn to obey.

"I Heard a Soldier"

I HEARD a soldier sing some trifle
  Out in the sun-dried veldt alone:
He lay and cleaned his grimy rifle
  Idly, behind a stone.

"If after death, love, comes a waking,
And in their camp so dark and still
The men of dust hear bugles, breaking
  Their halt upon the hill,

"To me the slow and silver pealing
  That then the last high trumpet pours
Shall softer than the dawn come stealing,
  For, with its call, comes yours!"

What grief of love had he to stifle,
  Basking so idly by his stone,
That grimy soldier with his rifle
  Out in the veldt, alone?

LAURENCE HOPE (ADELA NICOLSON) (1865-1904)

Ashore

BUT I came from the dancing place,
  The night-wind met me face to face—

A wind off the harbor, cold and keen,
"I know," it whistled, "where thou hast been."

A faint voice fell from the stars above—
"Thou? whom we lighted to shrines of Love!"

I found when I reached my lonely room
A faint sweet scent in the unlit gloom.

And this was the worst of all to bear,
For some one had left white lilac there.

The flower you loved, in times that were.

LIONEL JOHNSON (1867-1902)

Cadwith

MY windows open to the autumn night,
   In vain I watched for sleep to visit me;
How should sleep dull mine ears, and dim my sight,
Who saw the stars and listened to the sea?

Ah, how the city of our God is fair!
If, without sea, and starless though it be,
For joy of the majestic beauty there
Men shall not miss the stars, nor mourn the sea.

By the Statue of King Charles at Charing Cross

SOMBRE and rich, the skies,
   Great glooms and starry plains;
Gently the night wind sighs;
Else a vast silence reigns.

The splendid silence clings
Around me: and around
The saddest of all Kings,
Crown'd, and again discrown'd.

Comely and calm, he rides
Hard by his own Whitehall.
Only the night wind glides:
No crowds, nor rebels, brawl.

Gone, too, his Court: and yet,
The stars his courtiers are:
Stars in their stations set;
And every wandering star.

Alone he rides, alone,
The fair and fatal King:
Dark night is all his own,
That strange and solemn thing.

Which are more full of fate:
The stars; or those sad eyes?
Which are more still and great:
Those brows, or the dark skies?

Although his whole heart yearn
In passionate tragedy,
Never was face so stern
With sweet austerity.

Vanquish'd in life, his death
By beauty made amends:
The passing of his breath
Won his defeated ends.

Brief life, and hapless? Nay:
Through death, life grew sublime.
Speak after sentence? Yea:
And to the end of time.

Armour'd he rides, his head
Bare to the stars of doom;
He triumphs now, the dead,
Beholding London's gloom.

Our wearier spirit faints,
Vex'd in the world's employ:
His soul was of the saints;
And art to him was joy.

King, tried in fires of woe!
Men hunger for thy grace:
And through the night I go,
Loving thy mournful face.

Yet, when the city sleeps,
When all the cries are still,
The stars and heavenly deep
Work out a perfect will.

The Precept of Silence

I know you: solitary griefs,
  Desolate passions, aching hours!
I know you: tremulous beliefs,
  Agonized hopes, and ashen flowers!

The winds are sometimes sad to me;
  The starry spaces full of fear:
Mine is the sorrow on the sea,
  And mine the sigh of places drear.

Some players upon plaintive strings
  Publish their wistfulness abroad:
I have not spoken of these things,
  Save to one man, and unto God.

ERNEST DOWSON (1867-1900)

Non Sum Qualis Eram Bonae Sub Regno Cynaræ

LAST night, ah, yesternight, betwixt her lips and mine
  There fell thy shadow, Cynara! thy breath was shed
Upon my soul between the kisses and the wine;
And I was desolate and sick of an old passion,
    Yea, I was desolate and bowed my head.
I have been faithful to thee, Cynara! in my fashion.

All night upon mine heart I felt her warm heart beat,
Night-long within mine arms in love and sleep she lay;
Surely the kisses of her bought red mouth were sweet;
But I was desolate and sick of an old passion,
    When I awoke and found the dawn was gray:
I have been faithful to thee, Cynara! in my fashion.

I have forgot much, Cynara! gone with the wind,
Flung roses, roses riotously with the throng,
Dancing, to put thy pale, lost lilies out of mind;
But I was desolate and sick of an old passion,
    Yea, all the time, because the dance was long:
I have been faithful to thee, Cynara! in my fashion.

I cried for madder music and for stronger wine,
But when the feast is finished and the lamps expire,
Then falls thy shadow, Cynara! the night is thine;
And I am desolate and sick of an old passion,
    Yea, hungry for the lips of my desire:
I have been faithful to thee, Cynara! in my fashion.

Dregs

THE fire is out, and spent the warmth thereof,
(This is the end of every song man sings!)
The golden wine is drunk, the dregs remain,
Bitter as wormwood and as salt as pain;
And health and hope have gone the way of love
Into that drear oblivion of lost things.
Ghosts go along with us until the end;
This was a mistress, this, perhaps, a friend.
With pale, indifferent eyes, we sit and wait
For the dropped curtain and the closing gate:
This is the end of all the songs man sings.

Extreme Unction

UPON the eyes, the lips, the feet,
On all the passages of sense,
The atoning oil is spread with sweet
Renewal of lost innocence.

The feet that lately ran so fast
To meet desire, are soothly sealed;
The eyes, that were so often cast
On vanity, are touched and healed.

From troubles, sights and sounds set free,
In such a twilight hour of breath,
Shall one retrace his life, or see,
Through shadows, the true face of death?

Vials of mercy! Sacring oils!
I know not where nor when they come,
Nor through what wanderings and toils
To crave of you Viaticum.

Yet, when the walls of flesh grow weak,
In such an hour, it well may be,
Through mist and darkness, light will break,
And each anointed sense will see.

"A. E." (GEORGE WILLIAM RUSSELL) (1867-   )

A Memory of Earth

IN the west dusk silver sweet,
Down the violet-scented ways,
As I moved with quiet feet
I was met by mighty days.

On the hedge the hanging dew
  Glass'd the eve and stars and skies;
While I gazed a madness grew
  Into thunder'd battle-cries.

Where the hawthorn glimmered white
  Flashed the spear and fell the stroke,
Ah, what faces pale and bright
  Where the dazzling battle broke!

There a hero-hearted queen
  With young beauty lit the van.
Gone! the darkness flowed between
  All the ancient wars of man.

While I paced the valley's gloom,
  Where the rabbits patter'd near,
Shone a temple and a tomb
  With a legend carven clear:

Time put by a myriad fates
That her day might dawn in glory:
Death made wide a million gates
So to close her tragic story.

The Gift

I thought, beloved, to have brought to you,
  A gift of quietness and ease and peace,
Cooling your brow as with the mystic dew
  Dropping from twilight trees.

Homeward I go not yet; the darkness grows;
Not mine the voice to still with peace divine:
From the first fount the stream of quiet flows
  Thru other hearts than mine.

Yet of my night I give to you my stars,
And of my sorrow here the sweetest gains,
And out of hell, beyond its iron bars,
  My scorn of all its pains.

The Burning-Glass

A shaft of fire that falls like dew,
  And melts and maddens all my blood,
From out thy spirit flashes through
  The burning glass of womanhood.

Only so far; here must I stay:
  Nearer I miss the light, the fire;
I must endure the torturing ray,
  And with all beauty, all desire.

Ah, time long must the effort be,
  And far the way that I must go
To bring my spirit unto thee,
  Behind the glass, within the glow.

STEPHEN PHILLIPS (1868-1915)

I in the greyness rose;
    I could not sleep for thinking of one dead.
Then to the chest I went,
    Where lie the things of my beloved spread.

Quickly these I took;
    A little glove, a sheet of music torn,
Paintings, ill-done, perhaps;
    Then lifted up a dress that she had worn.

And now I came to where
    Her letters are; they lie beneath the rest;
And read them in the haze;
    She spoke of many things, was sore opprest.

But these things moved me not;
    Not when she spoke of being parted quite,
Or being misunderstood,
    Or growing weary of the world's great fight.

Not even when she wrote
    Of our dear child, and the handwriting swerved;
Not even then I shook:
    Not even by such words was I unnerved.

I thought, she is at peace;
    Whither the child is gone, she, too, has passed.
And a much-needed rest
    Is fallen upon her, she is still at last.

But when at length I took
    From under all those letters one small sheet,
Folded and writ in haste;
    Why did my heart with sudden sharpness beat?

Alas! it was not sad!
　Her saddest words I had read calmly o'er.
Alas! it had no pain!
　Her painful words, all these I knew before.

A hurried, happy line!
　A little jest, too slight for one so dead:
This did I not endure:
　Then with a shuddering heart no more I read.

From "Marpessa"

O brief and breathing creature, wilt thou cease
　Once having been? Thy doom doth make thee rich,
And the low grave doth make thee exquisite.
But if thou'lt live with me, then will I kiss
Warm immortality into thy lips;
And I will carry thee above the world,
To share my ecstasy of flinging beams,
And scattering without intermission joy.
And thou shalt know that first leap of the sea
Toward me; the grateful upward look of earth,
Emerging roseate from her bath of dew,—
We two in heaven dancing,—Babylon
Shall flash and murmur, and cry from under us,
And Nineveh catch fire, and at our feet
Be hurled with her inhabitants, and all
Adoring Asia kindle and hugely bloom;—
We two in heaven running,—continents
Shall lighten, ocean unto ocean flash,
And rapidly laugh till all this world is warm.
Or since thou art a woman, thou shalt have
More tender tasks; to steal upon the sea,
A long expected bliss to tossing men.
Or build upon the evening sky some wished
And glorious metropolis of cloud.
Thou shalt persuade the harvest and bring on
The deeper green; or silently attend
The fiery funeral of foliage old,
Connive with Time serene and the good hours.
Or,—for I know thy heart,—a dearer toil,—
To lure into the air a face long sick,
To gild the brow that from its dead looks up,
To shine on the unforgiven of this world;
With slow sweet surgery restore the brain,
And to dispel shadows and shadowy fear.
When he had spoken, humbly Idas said:
"After such argument what can I plead?
Or what pale promise make? Yet since it is

In women to pity rather than to aspire,
A little I will speak. I love thee then
Not only for thy body packed with sweet
Of all this world, that cup of brimming June,
That jar of violet wine set in the air,
That palest rose sweet in the night of life;
Nor for that stirring bosom all besieged
By drowsing lovers, or thy perilous hair;
Nor for that face that might indeed provoke
Invasion of old cities; no, nor all
Thy freshness stealing on me like strange sleep.
Not for this only do I love thee, but
Because Infinity upon thee broods;
And thou art full of whispers and of shadows.
Thou meanest what the sea had striven to say
So long, and yearned up the cliffs to tell;
Thou art what all the winds have uttered not,
What the still night suggesteth to the heart.
Thy voice is like to music heard ere birth,
Some spirit lute touched on a spirit sea;
Thy face remembered is from other worlds,
It has been died for, though I know not when,
It has been sung of, though I know not where.
It has the strangeness of the luring West,
And of sad sea-horizons; beside thee
I am aware of other times and lands,
Of birth far-back, of lives in many stars.
O beauty lone and like a candle clear
In this dark country of the world! Thou art
My woe, my early light, my music dying."

From "Herod"

*H*EROD.   Pour out those pearls,
     And give me in my hand that bar of gold.
I heard an angel crying from the Sun,
For glory, for more glory on the earth;
And here I'll build the wonder of the world.
I have conceived a Temple that shall stand
Up in such splendour that men bright from it
Shall pass with a light glance the pyramids. . . .
I dreamed last night of a dome of beaten gold
To be a counter-glory to the Sun.
There shall the eagle blindly dash himself,
There the first beam shall stifle, and there the moon
Shall aim all night her argent archery;
And it shall be the tryst of sundered stars,
The haunt of dead and dreaming Solomon;
Shall send a light upon the lost in Hell,

And flashings upon faces without hope—
And I will think in gold and dream in silver,
Imagine in marble and in bronze conceive,
Till it shall dazzle pilgrim nations.
And stammering tribes from undiscovered lands,
Allure the living God out of the bliss,
And all the streaming seraphim from heaven.

LAURENCE BINYON (1869-   )

"O World, Be Nobler"

O World, be nobler, for her sake!
        If she but knew thee what thou art,
What wrongs are borne, what deeds are done
In thee, beneath thy daily sun,
    Know'st thou not that her tender heart
For pain and very shame would break?
O World, be nobler, for her sake!

LORD ALFRED DOUGLAS (1870-   )

The Dead Poet

I dreamed of him last night, I saw his face
    All radiant and unshadowed of distress,
And as of old, in music measureless,
I heard his golden voice and marked him trace
Under the common thing the hidden grace,
And conjure wonder out of emptiness,
Till mean things put on beauty like a dress
And all the world was an enchanted place.
And then methought outisde a fast-locked gate
I mourned the loss of unrecorded words,
Forgotten tales and mysteries half said.
Wonders that might have been articulate,
And voiceless thoughts like murdered singing birds.
And so I woke and knew that he was dead.

OLIVE CUSTANCE (LADY ALFRED DOUGLAS)

O! do you hear the rain
        Beat on the glass in vain?
So my tears beat against fate's feet
In vain . . . in vain . . . in vain.

O! do you see the skies
As gray as your grave eyes?
O! do you hear the wind, my dear,
That sighs and sighs and sighs? . . .

. . . Tired as this twilight seems
My soul droops sad with dreams . . .
You cannot know where we two go
In dreams . . . in dreams . . . in dreams.

You only watch the light,
Sinking away from night . . .
In silver mail all shadowy pale,
The moon shines white, *so* white. . . .

. . . O! if we two were wise
Your eyes would leave the skies
And look into my eyes!
And I who wistful stand, . . .
One foot in fairy land,
Would catch Love by the hand.

DOLLIE RADFORD

I could not through the burning day
    In hope prevail,
Beside my task I could not stay
    If love should fail.

Nor underneath the evening sky,
    When labours cease,
Fold both my tired hands and lie
    At last in peace.

Ah! what to me in death or life
    Could then avail!
I dare not ask for rest or strife
    If love should fail.

THOMAS STURGE MOORE (1870-   )
A Duet

"FLOWERS nodding gaily, scent in air,
    Flowers posied, flowers for the hair,
Sleepy flowers, flowers bold to stare——"
        "O pick me some!"
"Shells with lip, or tooth, or bleeding gum,
Tell-tale shells, and shells that whisper *Come,*
Shells that stammer, blush, and yet are dumb——"
        "O let me hear."
Eyes so black they draw one trembling near,
Brown eyes, caverns flooded with a tear,
Cloudless eyes, blue eyes so windy clear——"
        "O look at me."

"Kisses sadly blown across the sea,
Darkling kisses, kisses fair and free,
Bob-a-cherry kisses 'neath a tree——"
      "O give me one!"
Thus sang a king and queen in Babylon.

HILAIRE BELLOC (1870-   )

The Early Morning

THE moon on the one hand, the dawn on the other:
      The moon is my sister, the dawn is my brother.
The moon on my left hand, the dawn on my right.
My brother, good morning: my sister, good-night.

COL. JOHN McCRAE (1872-1918)

In Flanders' Fields

IN Flanders' fields the poppies blow
      Between the crosses, row on row,
That mark our place, and in the sky
The larks still singing bravely fly,
Scarce heard amid the guns below.

We are the dead. Short days ago
We lived, felt dawn, saw sun-set glow,
Loved and were loved, and now we lie
            In Flanders' fields.

Take up our quarrel with the foe!
To you, from failing hands we throw
The torch—be yours to hold it high!
If ye break faith with us who die,
We shall not sleep, tho poppies grow
            In Flanders' fields.

DORA SIGERSON SHORTER (1873-   )

Ireland

'TWAS the dream of a God,
      And the mould of His hand,
That you shook 'neath this stroke,
That you trembled and broke
      To this beautiful land.

Here He loosed from His hold
   A brown tumult of wings,
Till the wind on the sea
Bore the strange melody
   Of an island that sings.

He made you all fair,
   You in purple and gold,
You in silver and green,
Till no eye that has seen
   Without love can behold.

I have left you behind
   In the path of the past,
With the white breath of flowers,
With the best of God's hours,
   I have left you at last.

WALTER DE LA MARE (1873-   )

The Listeners

"**I**S there anybody there?" said the Traveller,
   Knocking on the moonlit door;
And his horse in the silence champed the grasses
   Of the forest's ferny floor:
And a bird flew up out of the turret,
   Above the Traveller's head:
And he smote upon the door again a second time;
   "Is there anybody there?" he said.
But no one descended to the Traveller;
   No head from the leaf-fringed sill
Leaned over and looked into his grey eyes,
   Where he stood perplexed and still.
But only a host of phantom listeners
   That dwelt in the lone house then
Stood listening in the quiet of the moonlight
   To that voice from the world of men:
Stood thronging the faint moonbeams on the dark stair,
   That goes down to the empty hall,
Hearkening in an air stirred and shaken
   By the lonely Traveller's call.
And he felt in his heart their strangeness,
   Their stillness answering his cry,
While his horse moved, cropping the dark turf,
   'Neath the starred and leafy sky;
For he suddenly smote on the door, even
   Louder, and lifted his head:—

"Tell them I came, and no one answered,
    That I kept my word," he said.
Never the least stir made the listeners,
    Though every word he spake
Fell echoing through the shadowiness of the still house
    From the one man left awake:
Ay, they heard his foot upon the stirrup,
    And the sound of iron on stone,
And how the silence surged softly backward,
    When the plunging hoofs were gone.

Queen Djenira

WHEN Queen Djenira slumbers through
        The sultry noon's repose,
From out her dreams, as soft she lies,
    A faint thin music flows.

Her lovely hands lie narrow and pale
    With gilded nails, her head
Couched in its banded nets of gold
    Lies pillowed on her bed.

The little Nubian boys who fan
    Her cheeks and tresses clear,
Wonderful, wonderful, wonderful voices
    Seem afar to hear.

They slide their eyes, and nodding, say,
    "Queen Djenira walks to-day
The courts of the lord Pthamasar
    Where the sweet birds of Psuthys are."

And those of earth about her porch
    Of shadow cool and grey
Their sidelong beaks in silence lean,
    And silent flit away.

An Epitaph

HERE lies a most beautiful lady,
    Light of step and heart was she;
I think she was the most beautiful lady
That ever was in the West Country.
But beauty vanishes; beauty passes;
However rare—rare it be;
And when I crumble, who will remember
This lady of the West Country?

JOHN MASEFIELD (1874-   )

Flesh, I Have Knocked at Many a Dusty Door

FLESH, I have knocked at many a dusty door,
  Gone down full many a windy midnight lane,
Probed in old walls and felt along the floor,
Pressed in blind hope the lighted window-pane.
But useless all, though sometimes, when the moon
Was full in heaven and the sea was full,
Along my body's alleys came a tune
Played in the tavern by the Beautiful.
Then for an instant I have felt at point
To find and seize her, whosoe'er she be,
Whether some saint whose glory does anoint
Those whom she loves, or but a part of me,
Or something that the things not understood
Make for their uses out of flesh and blood.

There, on the darkened deathbed, dies the brain
That flared three several times in seventy years;
It cannot lift the silly hand again,
Nor speak, nor sing, it neither sees nor hears.
And muffled mourners put it in the ground
And then go home, and in the earth it lies,
Too dark for vision and too deep for sound,
The million cells that made a good man wise.
Yet for a few short years an influence stirs
A sense or wraith or essence of him dead,
Which makes insensate things its ministers
To those beloved, his spirit's daily bread;
Then that, too, fades; in book or deed a spark
Lingers, then that, too, fades; then all is dark.

Roses are beauty, but I never see
Those blood drops from the burning heart of June
Glowing like thought upon the living tree,
Without a pity that they die so soon,
Die into petals, like those roses old,
Those women, who were summer in men's hearts
Before the smile upon the Sphinx was cold,
Or sand had hid the Syrian and his arts.
O myriad dust of beauty that lies thick
Under our feet that not a single grain
But stirred and moved in beauty and was quick
For one brief moon and died nor lived again;
But when the moon rose lay upon the grass
Pasture to living beauty, life that was.

SALEM COLLEGE
LIBRARY
Winston-Salem, N. C.

The other form of Living does not stir;
Where the seed chances there it roots and grows,
To suck what makes the lily or the fir
Out of the earth and from the air that blows.
Great power of Will that little thing the seed
Has, all alone in earth, to plan the tree,
And, though the mud oppresses, to succeed,
And put out branches where the birds may be.
Then the wind blows it, but the bending boughs
Exult like billows, and their million green
Drink the all-living sunlight in carouse,
Like dainty harts where forest wells are clean.
While it, the central plant, which looks o'er miles,
Draws milk from the earth's breast, and sways, and smiles.

I saw her like a shadow on the sky
In the last light, a blur upon the sea,
Then the gale's darkness put the shadow by,
But from one grave that island talked to me;
And, in the midnight, in the breaking storm,
I saw its blackness and a blinking light,
And thought, "So death obscures your gentle form,
So memory strives to make the darkness bright;
And, in that heap of rocks, your body lies,
Part of the island till the planet ends,
My gentle comrade, beautiful and wise,
Part of this crag this bitter surge offends,
While I, who pass, a little obscure thing,

War with this force, and breathe, and am its king."
You will remember me in days to come
With love, or pride, or pity, or contempt;
So will my friends (not many friends, yet some)
When this my life will be a dream out-dreamt;
And one, remembering friendship by the fire,
And one, remembering love time in the dark,
And one, remembering unfulfilled desire,
Will sigh, perhaps, yet be beside the mark;
For this my body with its wandering ghost
Is nothing solely but an empty grange,
Dark in a night that owls inhabit most,
Yet when the king rides by there comes a change;
The windows gleam, the cresset's fiery hair
Blasts the blown branch and beauty lodges there.

Ships

I CANNOT tell their wonder nor make known
  Magic that once thrilled through me to the bone;
But all men praise some beauty, tell some tale,

Vent a high mood which makes the rest seem pale,
Pour their heart's blood to flourish one green leaf,
Follow some Helen for her gift of grief,
And fail in what they mean, whate'er they do:
You should have seen, man cannot tell to you
The beauty of the ships of that my city.

That beauty now is spoiled by the sea's pity;
For one may haunt the pier a score of times,
Hearing St. Nicholas bells ring out the chimes,
Yet never see the proud ones swaying home
With mainyards backed and bows a cream of foam,
Those bows so lovely curving, cut so fine,
Those coulters of the many-bubbled brine,
As once, long since, when all the docks were filled
With that sea-beauty man has ceased to build.

Yet, though their splendor may have ceased to be
Each played her sovereign part in making me;
Now I return my thanks with heart and lips
For the great queenliness of all those ships.

And first the first bright memory, still so clear,
An autumn evening in a golden year,
When in the last lit moments before dark
The *Chepica,* a steel-gray lovely barque,
Came to anchor near us on the flood,
Her trucks aloft in sun-glow red as blood.

Then come so many ships that I could fill
Three docks with their fair hulls remembered still,
Each with her special memory's special grace,
Riding the sea, making the waves give place
To delicate high beauty; man's best strength,
Noble in every line in all their length.
Ailsa, Genista, ships with long jibbooms,
The *Wanderer* with great beauty and strange dooms,
Liverpool (mightiest then) superb, sublime,
The *California* huge, as slow as time.
The *Copley* swift, the perfect *J. T. North,*
The loveliest barque my city has sent forth,
Dainty *John Lockett* well remembered yet,
The splendid *Argus* with her sky-sail set,
Stalwart *Drumcliff,* white-blocked, majestic *Sierras,*
Divine bright ships, the water's standard-bearers;
Melpomene, Euphrosyne, and their sweet
Sea-troubling sisters of the Fernie fleet;
Corunna (in whom my friend died) and the old
Long since loved *Esmeralda,* long since sold.

Centurion passed in Rio, *Glaucus* spoken,
Aladdin burnt, the *Bidston* water-broken,
Yola, in whom my friend sailed, *Dawpool* trim,
Fierce-bowed *Egeria* plunging to the swim,
Stanmore wide-sterned, sweet *Cupica,* tall *Bard,*
Queen in all harbors with her moon-sail yard.

Though I tell many, there must still be others,
McVickar Marshall's ships and Fernie Brothers',
Lochs, Counties, Shires, Drums, the countless lines
Whose house-flags once were all familiar signs
At high main-trucks on Mersey's windy ways
When sunlight made the wind-white water blaze.
Their names bring back old mornings, when the docks
Shone with their house-flags and their painted blocks,
Their raking masts below the Custom House
And all the marvellous beauty of their bows.

Familiar steamers, too, familiar steamers,
Shearing Atlantic roller-tops to streamers,
Umbria, Etruria, noble, still at sea,
The grandest, then, that man had brought to be.
Majestic, City of Paris, City of Rome,
Forever jealous racers, out and home.

The *Alfred Holt's* blue smoke-stacks down the stream,
The fair *Loanda* with her bows a-cream.
Booth liners, Anchor liners, Red Star liners,
The marks and styles of countless ship-designers,
The *Magdalena, Puno, Potosi,*
Lost *Cotopaxi,* all well-known to me.

These splendid ships, each with her grace, her glory,
Her memory of old song or comrade's story,
Still in my mind the image of life's need,
Beauty in hardest action, beauty indeed.
"They built great ships and sailed them" sounds most
     brave,
Whatever arts we have or fail to have.
I touch my country's mind, I come to grips
With half her purpose, thinking of these ships:
That art untouched by softness, all that line
Drawn ringing hard to stand the test of brine;
That nobleness and grandeur, all that beauty
Born of a many life and bitter duty;
That splendor of fine bows which yet could stand
The shock of rollers never checked by land;
That art of masts, sail-crowded, fit to break,
Yet stayed to strength and backstayed into rake;

The life demanded by that art, the keen
Eye-puckered, hard-cased seamen, silent, lean.
They are grander than all the art of towns;
Their tests are tempests and the sea that drowns.
They are my country's line, her great art done
By strong brains laboring on the thought unwon.
They mark our passage as a race of men—
Earth will not see such ships as those again.

Cargoes

QUINQUIREME of Nineveh from distant Ophir,
 Rowing home to haven in sunny Palestine,
With a cargo of ivory,
And apes and peacocks,
Sandalwood, cedarwood, and sweet white wine.

Stately Spanish galleon coming from the Isthmus
Dipping through the Tropics by the palm-green shores,
With a cargo of diamonds,
Emeralds, amethysts,
Topazes, and cinnamon, and gold moidores.

Dirty British coaster with a salt-caked smoke stack,
Butting through the Channel in the mad March days,
With a cargo of Tyne coal,
Road-rails, pig-lead,
Firewood, iron-ware, and cheap tin trays.

Sea-Fever

I must go down to the seas again, to the lonely sea and
 the sky,
And all I ask is a tall ship and a star to steer her by;
And the wheel's kick and the wind's song and the white sail's
 shaking,
And a grey mist on the sea's face and a grey dawn breaking.

I must go down to the seas again, for the call of the running
 tide
Is a wild call and a clear call that may not be denied;
And all I ask is a windy day with the white clouds flying,
And the flung spray and the blown spume, and the sea-gulls
 crying.

I must go down to the seas again, to the vagrant gypsy life,
To the gull's way and the whale's way where the wind's like
 a whetted knife;
And all I ask is a merry yarn from a laughing fellow-rover,
And quiet sleep and a sweet dream when the long trick's
 over.

Prayer

WHEN the last sea is sailed, when the last shallow's
    charted,
When the last field is reaped, and the last harvest stored,
When the last fire is out and the last guest departed,
Grant the last prayer that I shall pray, be good to me, O Lord.

And let me pass in a night at sea, a night of storm and
    thunder,
In the loud crying of the wind through sail and rope and spar,
Send me a ninth great peaceful wave to drown and roll me
    under
To the cold tunny-fish's home where the drowned galleons are.

And in the dim green quiet place far out of sight and hearing,
Grant I may hear at whiles the wash and thresh of the sea-
    foam
About the fine keen bows of the stately clippers steering
Towards the lone northern star and the fair ports of home.

GORDON BOTTOMLEY (1874-   )

In Memoriam

A. M. W.

September, 1910

(For a Solemn Music)

Out of a silence
The voice of music speaks.

When words have no more power,
When tears can tell no more,
The heart of all regret
Is uttered by a falling wave
Of melody.

No more, no more
The voice that gathered us
Shall hush us with deep joy;
But in this hush,
Out of its silence,
In the awaking of music,
It shall return.
For music can renew
Its gladness and communion,
Until we also sink,
Where sinks the voice of music,
Into a silence.

GILBERT KEITH CHESTERTON (1874-   )
From "The Ballad of the White Horse"

U P over windy wastes and up
     Went Alfred over the shaws,
Shaken of the joy of giants,
     The joy without a cause.

In the slopes away to the western bays,
     Where blows not ever a tree,
He washed his soul in the west wind
     And his body in the sea.

And he set to rhyme his ale-measures
     And he sang aloud his laws;
Because of the joy of the giants,
     The joy without a cause.

For the King went gathering Wessex men
     As grain out of the chaff;
The few that were alive to die,
Laughing, as littered skulls that lie
After lost battles turn to the sky
     An everlasting laugh.

The King went gathering Christian men
     As wheat out of the husk;
Eldred the Franklin by the sea,
And Mark, the man from Italy,
And Golan of the Sacred Tree,
     From the old tribe on Usk.

The rook croaked homeward heavily,
     The west was clear and warm,
The smoke of evening food and ease
Rose like a blue tree in the trees
     When he came to Eldred's farm.

But Eldred's farm was fallen awry,
     Like an old cripple's bones,
And Eldred's tools were red with rust;
And on his well was a green crust,
And purple thistles upward thrust
     Between the kitchen stones.

But smoke of some good feasting
     Went upwards evermore,
And Eldred's doors stood wide apart
For loitering foot or labouring cart;
And Eldred's great and foolish heart
     Stood open, like his door.

A mighty man was Eldred;
  A bulk for casks to fill;
His face a dreaming furnace,
  His body a walking hill.

In the old wars of Wessex
  His sword had sunken deep,
But all his friends, he sighed and said,
Were broken about Ethelred;
And between the deep drink and the dead
  He had fallen upon sleep.

"Come not to me, King Alfred,
  Save always for the ale;
Why should my harmless hinds be slain
Because the chiefs cry once again,
As in all fights, that we shall gain,
  And in all fights we fail.

"Your scalds still thunder and prophesy
  That crown that never comes;
Friend, I will watch the certain things,
Swine, and slow moons like silver rings,
  And the ripening of the plums."

Glencoe

THE star-crowned cliffs seem hinged upon the sky,
  The clouds are floating rags across them curled,
They open to us like the gates of God
Cloven in the last great wall of all the world.

I looked, and saw the valley of my soul
Where naked crests fight to achieve the skies,
Where no grain grows nor wine, no fruitful thing,
Only big words and stony blasphemies.

But you have clothed with mercy like a moss
The barren violence of its primal wars,
Sterile although they be and void of rule,
You know my shapeless crags have loved the stars.

How shall I thank you, O courageous heart,
That of this wasteful world you had no fear;
But bade it blossom in clear faith and sent
Your fair flower-feeding rivers: even as here

The peat burns brimming from their cups of stone
Glow brown and blood-red down the vast decline
As if Christ stood on yonder clouded peak
And turned its thousand waters into wine.

EDWARD THOMAS (1878-1917)

The Unknown

SHE is most fair,
    And when they see her pass
The poets' ladies
Look no more in the glass
But after her.

On a bleak moor
Running under the moon
She lures a poet,
Once proud or happy, soon
Far from his door.

Beside a train,
Because they saw her go,
Or failed to see her,
Travellers and watchers know
Another pain.

The simple lack
Of her is more to me
Than others' presence,
Whether life splendid be
Or utter black.

I have not seen,
I have no news of her;
I can tell only
She is not here, but there
She might have been.

She is to be kissed
Only perhaps by me;
She may be seeking
Me and no other: she
May not exist.

THOMAS MACDONAGH (1878-1916)

To His Ideal

Translated from the Irish of Padraic Pearse

NAKED I saw thee,
    O beauty of beauty!
And I blinded my eyes
For fear I should flinch.

I heard thy music,
O sweetness of sweetness!
And I shut my ears
For fear I should fail.

I kissed thy lips,
O sweetness of sweetness!
And I hardened my heart
For fear of my ruin.

I blinded my eyes,
And my ears I shut;
I hardened my heart,
And my love I quenched.

I turned my back
On the dream I had shaped,
And to this road before me
My face I turned.

I set my face
To the road here before me;
To the work that I see,
To the death that I shall meet.

WILFRID WILSON GIBSON (1878-   )
Daily Bread

ALL life moving to one measure—
    Daily bread, daily bread—
Bread of life, and bread of labour,
Bread of bitterness and sorrow,
Hand-to-mouth, and no to-morrow,
Death for housemate, death for neighbor . . .
"Yet when all the babes are fed,
Love, are there no crumbs to treasure?"

RALPH HODGSON (1878?-)
The Mystery

HE came and took me by the hand
    Up to a red rose tree,
He kept His meaning to Himself
    But gave a rose to me.

I did not pray Him to lay bare
    The mystery to me:
Enough the rose was Heaven to smell,
    And His own face to see.

HAROLD MONRO (1879-   )

Youth in Arms

HAPPY boy, happy boy,
    David the immortal-willed,
Youth a thousand times
Slain, but not once killed,
Swaggering again to-day
In the old contemptuous way;

Leaning backward from your thigh
Up against the tinselled bar—
Lust and ashes! is it you?
Laughing, boasting, there you are!
First we hardly rerognized you
In your modern avatar.

Soldier, rifle, brown khaki—
Is your blood as happy so?
Where's your sling or painted shield,
Helmet, you're going to the wars—
Well, you're going to the wars—
That is all you need to know.

Graybeards plotted. They were sad.
Death was in their wrinkled eyes.
At their tables—with their maps,
Plans and calculations—wise
They all seemed; for well they knew
How ungrudgingly Youth dies.

At their green official baize
They debated all the night
Plans for your adventurous days
Which you followed with delight,
Youth in all your wanderings,
David of a thousand slings.

ALFRED NOYES (1880-   )

Haunted in Old Japan

MUSIC of the star-shine shimmering o'er the sea
    Mirror me no longer in the dusk of memory:
Dim and white the rose-leaves drift along the shore.
Wind among the roses, blow no more!

All along the purple creek, lit with silver foam,
Silent, silent voices, cry no more of home!
Soft beyond the cherry-trees, o'er the dim lagoon,
Dawns the crimson lantern of the large low moon.

We that loved in April, we that turned away
Laughing ere the wood-dove crooned across the May,
Watch the withered rose-leaves drift along the shore.
Wind among the roses, blow no more!

We the Sons of Reason, we that chose to bride
Knowledge, and rejected the Dream that we denied,
We that chose the Wisdom that triumphs for an hour,
We that let the young love perish like a flower. . . .

We that hurt the kind heart, we that went astray,
We that in the darkness idly dreamed of day. . . .
. . . Ah! The dreary rose-leaves drift along the shore.
Wind among the roses, blow no more!

Lonely starry faces, wonderful and white,
Yearning with a cry across the dim sweet night,
All our dreams are blown a-drift as flowers before a fan,
All our hearts are haunted in the heart of old Japan.

Haunted, haunted, haunted—we that mocked and sinned
Hear the vanished voices wailing down the wind,
Watch the ruined rose-leaves drift along the shore.
Wind among the roses, blow no more!

All along the purple creek, lit with silver foam,
Sobbing, sobbing voices, cry no more of home!
Soft beyond the cherry-trees, o'er the dim lagoon,
Dawns the crimson lantern of the large low moon.

A Japanese Love-Song

THE young moon is white,
    But the willows are blue:
Your small lips are red,
    But the great clouds are gray:
The waves are so many
    That whisper to you;
But my love is only
    One flight of spray.

The bright drops are many,
  The dark wave is one:
The dark wave subsides,
  And the bright sea remains!
And wherever, O singing
  Maid, you run,
You are one with the world
  For all your pains.

Tho' the great skies are dark,
  And your small feet are white,
Tho' your wide eyes are blue
  And the closed poppies red,
Tho, the kisses are many
  That colour the night,
They are linkèd like pearls
  On one golden thread.

Were the gray clouds not made
  For the red of your mouth;
The ages for flight
  Of the butterfly years;
The sweet of the peach
  For the pale lips of drouth,
The sunlight of smiles
  For the shadow of tears?

Love, Love is the thread
  That has pierced them with bliss!
All their hues are but notes
  In one world-wide tune:
Lips, willows and waves,
  We are one as we kiss,
And your face and the flowers
  Faint away in the moon.

FRANCIS LEDWIDGE (1881-1917)

The Wife of Llew

A ND Gwydion said to Math, when it was Spring:
  "Come now and let us make a wife for Llew."
And so they broke broad boughs yet moist with dew,
And in a shadow made a magic ring:
They took the violet and the meadow-sweet
To form her pretty face, and for her feet

They built a mound of daisies on a wing,
And for her voice they made a linnet sing
In the wide poppy blowing for her mouth.
And over all they chanted twenty hours.
And Llew came singing from the azure south
And bore away his wife of birds and flowers.

Growing Old

WE'LL fill a Provence bowl and pledge us deep
    The memory of the far ones and between
The soothing pipes, in heavy-lidded sleep,
Perhaps we'll dream the things that once have been.
'Tis only noon and still too soon to die,
Yet we are growing old, my heart and I.

A hundred books are ready in my head
To open out where Beauty bent a leaf.
What do we want with Beauty? We are wed
Like ancient Proserpine to dismal grief.
And we are changing with the hours that fly,
And growing odd and old, my heart and I.

Across a bed of bells the river flows,
And roses dawn, but not for us; we want
The new thing ever as the old thing grows
Spectral and weary on the hills we haunt.
And that is why we feast, and that is why
We're growing odd and old, my heart and I.

JOHN DRINKWATER (1882-   )
A Man's Daughter

THERE is an old woman who looks each night
    Out of the wood.
She has one tooth, that isn't too white.
    She isn't too good.

She came from the north looking for me,
    About my jewel.
Her son, she says, is tall as can be;
    But, men say, cruel.

My girl went northward, holiday making,
    And a queer man spoke
At the woodside once when night was breaking,
    And her heart broke.

For ever since she has pined and pined,
    A sorry maid;
Her fingers are slack as the wool they wind,
    Or her girdle-braid.

So now shall I send her north to wed,
  Who here may know
Only the little house of the dead
  To ease her woe?

Or keep her for fear of that old woman,
  As a bird quick-eyèd,
And her tall son who is hardly human,
  At the woodside?

She is my babe and my daughter dear,
  How well, how well.
Her grief to me is a fourfold fear,
  Tongue cannot tell.

And yet I know that far in that wood
  Are crumbling bones,
And a mumble mumble of nothing that's good,
  In heathen tones.

And I know that frail ghosts flutter and sigh
  In brambles there,
And never a bird or beast to cry—
  Beware, beware.

While threading the silent thickets go
  Mother and son,
Where scrupulous berries never grow,
  And airs are none.

And her deep eyes peer at eventide
  Out of the wood,
And her tall son waits by the dark woodside,
  For maidenhood.

And the little eyes peer, and peer, and peer;
  And a word is said,
And some house knows, for many a year,
  But years of dread.

RICHARD MIDDLETON (1882-1911)
To A. C. M.

THOU art my dream, but for my last delight
    Thou art transformed to sweetest shape by day,
  And o'er the rosy hills and far away,
There pass the sombre fancies of my night,
  With their sad lips and eyelids red with tears,
  And their dominion of my barren years.

I am as one who goes to meet the dawn
  After a night of sorrow, where she takes
  The meadows with her silver feet, and wakes
The drowsy daisies on the dewy lawn;
  Upon my forehead falls her healing kiss,
  Night has her balm, but none so sweet as this.

Yet that dim spirit of imagined things
  And love desired that filled the shadowy way
  With wistful laughter of young fauns at play,
Gleam of quick feet and tumult of faint wings—
  Has touched thy lips with sleep-wrought memories,
  And set a star-lit wonder in thine eyes.

So while I marvel still how fair thou art
  With thy day-roses, there remains with me
  The glory of the night's tranquillity,
Dream within dream, heart upon sleeping heart,
  As though we wandered where the moon doth keep
  Upon the frosty hills her silent sleep.

Thou hast been given the magic of all hours,
  Day's joys, night's wonder, in thy little hands
  Thou hast the gifts of all desirous lands;
What may I give thee then? these sunlit flowers,
  These blossoms of the night to thee belong,
  And thine is all the merit of my song.

Heyst-sur-Mer

UNDER the arch of summer
    The great black ships go by,
The sun is like a bead of blood
Upon the wounded sky,
The girls are dancing, dancing,
And night falls tenderly.

Would I were on a great ship
With the wind upon my face,
And the water's music in my ears,
And the rigging's song of grace,
Would I were on a great ship
Bound to a new place.

Where trees are and flowers are
And breakers on the shore,
Where a child might find all the dreams

That he had known before,
Where I should be at peace at last
And the girls would dance no more.

Under the arch of summer
The great black ships go by,
There is a madness in the wind,
A wonder in the sky,
And the girls are dancing, dancing . . .
No peace, no peace have I.

JAMES JOYCE (1882-   )

Golden Hair

L EAN out of the window
     Goldenhair,
I heard you singing
    A merry air.

My book was closed,
    I read no more,
Watching the fire dance
    On the floor.

I have left my book,
    I have left my room,
For I heard you singing
    Through the gloom.

Singing and singing
    A merry air,
Lean out of the window,
    Goldenhair.

W. M. LETTS (1882-   )

F OR England's sake men give their lives
    And we cry "Brave."
But braver yet
The hearts that break and live
Having no more to give,
Mothers, sweethearts and wives.
Let none forget
Or with averted head
Pass this great sorrow by—
These would how thankfully be dead
Yet may not die.

The Spires of Oxford

I saw the spires of Oxford
  As I was passing by,
The grey spires of Oxford
  Against a pearl-grey sky;
My heart was with the Oxford men
  Who went abroad to die.

The years go fast in Oxford,
  The golden years and gay;
The hoary colleges look down
  On careless boys at play,
But when the bugles sounded—War!
  They put their games away.

They left the peaceful river,
  The cricket field, the quad,
The shaven lawns of Oxford
  To seek a bloody sod.
They gave their merry youth away
  For country and for God.

God rest you, happy gentlemen,
  Who laid your good lives down,
Who took the khaki and the gun
  Instead of cap and gown.
God bring you to a fairer place
  Than even Oxford town.

LASCELLES ABERCROMBIE (1884-

From "Marriage Song"

I

COME up, dear chosen morning, come,
  Blessing the air with light,
And bid the sky repent of being dark:
Let all the spaces round the world be white,
And give the earth her green again.
Into new hours of beautiful delight,
Out of the shadow where she has lain,
Bring the earth awake for glee,
Shining with dews as fresh and clear
As my beloved's voice upon the air.
For now, O morning chosen of all days, on thee
A wondrous duty lies:
There was an evening that did loveliness foretell;
Thence upon thee, O chosen morn, it fell

To fashion into perfect destiny
The radiant prophecy.
For in an evening of young moon, that went
Filling the moist air with a rosy fire,
I and my beloved knew our love;
And knew that thou, O morning, wouldst arise
To give us knowledge of achieved desire.
For, standing stricken with astonishment,
Half terrified in the delight,
Even as the moon did into clear air move
And made a golden light,
Lo there, croucht up against it, a dark hill,
A monstrous back of earth, a spine
Of hunchèd rock, furred with great growth of pine,
Lay like a beast, snout in its paws, asleep;
Yet in its sleeping seemed it miserable,
As though strong fear must always keep
Hold of its heart, and drive its blood in dream.
Yea, for to our new love, did it not seem,
That dark and quiet length of hill,
The sleeping grief of the world?—Out of it we
Had like imaginations stept to be
Beauty and golden wonder; and for the lovely fear
Of coming perfect joy, had changed
The terror that dreamt there!
And now the golden moon had turned
To shining white, white as our souls that burned
With vision of our prophecy assured:
Suddenly white was the moon; but she
At once did on a woven modesty
Of cloud, and soon went in obscured:
And we were dark, and vanisht that strange hill.
But yet it was not long before
There opened in the sky a narrow door,
Made with pearl lintel and pearl sill;
And the earth's night seem'd pressing there,—
All as a beggar on some festival would peer,—
To gaze into a room of light beyond,
The hidden silver splendour of the moon.
Yea, and we also, we
Long gazed wistfully
Towards thee, O morning, come at last,
And towards the light that thou wilt pour upon us soon!

.   .   .   .

IV

For wonderfully to live I now begin:
So that the darkness which accompanies
Our being here, is fasten'd up within

The power of light that holdeth me;
And from these shining chains, to see
My joy with bold misliking eyes,
The shrouded figure will not dare arise.
For henceforth, from to-night,
I am wholly gone into the bright
Safety of the beauty of love:
Not only all my waking vigours plied
Under the searching glory of love,
But knowing myself with love all satisfied
Even when my life is hidden in sleep;
As high clouds, to themselves that keep
The moon's white company, are all possest
Silverly with the presence of their guest;
Or as a darken'd room
That hath within it roses, whence the air
And quietness are taken everywhere
Deliciously by sweet perfume.

Balkis

From "Emblems of Love"

BALKIS was in her marble town,
    And shadow over the world came down.
Whiteness of walls, towers and piers,
That all day dazzled eyes to tears,
Turned from being white-golden flame,
And like the deep-sea blue became.
Balkis into her garden went;
Her spirit was in discontent
Like a torch in restless air.
Joylessly she wandered where,
And saw her city's azure white
Lying under the great night,
Beautiful as the memory
Of a worshipping world would be
In the mind of a god, in the hour
When he must kill his outward power;
And, coming to a pool where trees
Grew in double greeneries
Saw herself, as she went by
The water, walking beautifully,
And saw the stars shine in the glance
Of her eyes, and her own fair countenance
Passing, pale and wonderful,
Across the night that filled the pool.
And cruel was the grief that played
With the queen's spirit; and she said:

"What do I hear, reigning alone?
For to be unloved is to be alone.
There is no man in all my land
Dare my longing understand;
The whole folk like a peasant bows
Lest its look should meet my brows
And be harmed by this beauty of mine.
I burn their brains as I were sign
Of God's beautiful anger sent
To master them with punishment
Of beauty that must pour distress
On hearts grown dark with ugliness.
But it is I am the punished one.
Is there no man, is there none,
In whom my beauty will but move
The lust of a delighted love;
In whom some spirit of God so thrives
That we may wed our lonely lives?
Is there no man, is there none?"
She said, "I will go to Solomon."

JAMES ELROY FLECKER (1884-1915)

To a Poet a Thousand Years Hence

I who am dead a thousand years,
    And wrote this sweet archaic song,
Send you my words for messengers
    The way I shall not pass along.
I care not if you bridge the seas,
    Or ride secure the cruel sky,
Or build consummate palaces
    Of metal or of masonry.

But have you wine and music still,
    And statues and a bright-eyed love,
And foolish thoughts of good and ill,
    And prayers to them that sit above?

How shall we conquer? Like a wind
    That falls at eve our fancies blow,
And old Mœonides the blind
    Said it three thousand years ago.

O friend, unseen, unborn, unknown,
    Student of our sweet English tongue,
Read out my words at night, alone:
    I was a poet, I was young.

Since I can never see your face,
And never shake you by the hand,
I send my soul through time and space
To greet you. You will understand.

RUPERT BROOKE (1887-1915)

The Hill

BREATHLESS, we flung us on the windy hill,
    Laughed in the sun, and kissed the lovely grass.
You said, "Through glory and ecstasy we pass;
Wind, sun, and earth remain, the birds sing still,
When we are old, are old. . . ." "And when we die
    All's over that is ours; and life burns on
Through other lovers, other lips," said I,
—"Heart of my heart, our heaven is now, is won!"
"We are Earth's best, that learnt her lesson here.
    Life is our cry. We have kept the faith!" we said;
"We shall go down with unreluctant tread
Rose-crowned into the darkness!" . . . Proud we were,
And laughed, that had such brave true things to say.
—And then you suddenly cried, and turned away.

Peace

NOW, God be thanked Who has matched us with His hour,
    And caught our youth, and wakened us from sleeping,
With hand made sure, clear eye, and sharpened power,
To turn, as swimmers into cleanness leaping,
Glad from a world grown old and cold and weary,
    Leave the sick hearts that honour could not move,
And half-men, and their dirty songs and dreary,
    And all the little emptiness of love!

Oh! we, who have known shame, we have found release
    there,
Where there's no ill, no grief, but sleep has mending,
    Naught broken save this body, lost but breath;
Nothing to shake the laughing heart's long peace there
    But only agony, and that has ending;
And the worst friend and enemy is but Death.

The Dead

BLOW out, you bugles, over the rich Dead!
    There's none of these so lonely and poor of old,
    But dying, has made us rarer gifts than gold.
These laid the world away; poured out the red

Sweet wine of youth; gave up the years to be
  Of work and joy, and that unhoped serene,
That men call age; and those who would have been,
Their sons, they gave, their immortality.

Blow, bugles, blow! They brought us, for our dearth,
  Holiness, lacked so long, and Love, and Pain.
Honour has come back, as a king, to earth,
  And paid his subjects with a royal wage;
And Nobleness walks in our ways again;
  And we have come into our heritage.

The Soldier

IF I should die, think only this of me:
    That there's some corner of a foreign field
That is for ever England. There shall be
  In that rich earth a richer dust concealed;
A dust whom England bore, shaped, made aware,
  Gave, once, her flowers to love, her ways to roam,
A body of England's, breathing English air,
  Washed by the rivers, blest by suns of home.

And think, this heart, all evil shed away,
  A pulse in the eternal mind, no less
    Gives somewhere back the thoughts by England given;
Her sights and sounds; dreams happy as her day;
  And laughter, learnt of friends; and gentleness,
    In hearts at peace, under an English heaven.

JAMES STEPHENS

Deirdre

DO not let any woman read this verse;
    It is for men, and after them their sons
And their sons' sons.

The time comes when our hearts sink utterly;
When we remember Deirdre and her tale,
And that her lips are dust.

Once she did tread the earth: men took her hand;
They looked into her eyes and said their say,
And she replied to them.

More than a thousand years it is since she
Was beautiful: she trod the waving grass;
She saw the clouds.

A thousand years! The grass is still the same,
The clouds as lovely as they were that time
When Deirdre was alive.

But there has never been a woman born
Who was so beautiful, not one so beautiful
Of all the women born.

Let all men go apart and mourn together;
No man can ever love her; not a man
Can ever be her lover.

No man can bend before her: no man say—
What could one say to her? There are no words
That one could say to her!

Now she is but a story that is told
Beside the fire! No man can ever be
The friend of that poor queen.

The Snare, to A. E.

I hear a sudden cry of pain!
    There is a rabbit in a snare:
Now I hear the cry again,
    But I cannot tell from where.

But I cannot tell from where
    He is calling out for aid;
Crying on the frightened air,
    Making everything afraid.

Making everything afraid,
    Wrinkling up his little face,
As he cries again for aid:
    And I cannot find the place!

And I cannot find the place
    Where his paw is in the snare:
Little one! Oh, little one!
    I am searching everywhere.

D. H. LAWRENCE (1885-   )

All of Roses

I

BY the Isar, in the twilight
    We were wandering and singing;
By the Isar, in the evening
We climbed the huntsman's ladder and sat swinging

In the fir-tree overlooking the marshes;
While river met with river, and the ringing
Of their pale-green glacier-water filled the evening.

By the Isar, in the twilight
We found our warm wild roses
Hanging red at the river; and simmering
Frogs were singing, and over the river closes
Was scent of roses, and glimmering
In the twilight, our kisses across the roses
Met, and her face, and my face, were roses.

II

When she rises in the morning
I linger to watch her.
She stands in silhouette against the window,
And the sunbeams catch her
Glistening white on the shoulders;
While down her sides, the mellow
Golden shadow glows, and her breasts
Swing like full-blown yellow
Gloire de Dijon roses.

She drips herself with water,
And her shoulders
Glisten as silver, they crumple up
Like wet and shaken roses, and I listen
For the rustling of their white, unfolding petals.
In the window full of sunlight
She stirs her golden shadow,
And flashes all herself as sun-bright
As if roses fought with roses.

III

Just a few of the roses we gathered from the Isar
Are fallen, and their mauve-red petals on the cloth
Float like boats on a river, waiting
For a fairy-wind to wake them from their sloth.
She laughs at me across the table, saying
She loves me; and I blow a little boat
Rocking down the shoals between the tea-cups
And so kiss-beladen that it scarce can float.

IV

Now like a rose come tip-toe out of bud
I see the woman's soul steal in her eyes,
And wide in ecstasy I sit and watch
The unknown flower issued magic-wise.

And day by day out of the envious bud
My treasure softly slips uncurled,
And day by day my happiness vibrates
In wide and wider circles round the world.

SIEGFRIED SASSOON (1886-   )

To These I Turn, in These I Trust

TO these I turn, in these I trust;
    Brother Lead and sister Steel.
To his blind power I make appeal;
I guard her beauty clean from rust.
He skins and burns and loves the air,
And splits a skull to win my praise;
But up the nobly marching days
She glitters naked, cold and fair.

Sweet Sister, grant your soldier this;
That in good fury he may feel
The body where he sets his heel
Quail from your downward darting kiss.

RICHARD ALDINGTON (1892-   )

After Two Years

SHE is all so slight
    And tender and white
    As a May morning.
She walks without hood
At dusk. It is good
    To hear her sing.
It is God's will
That I shall love her still
    As He loves Mary.
And night and day
I will go forth to pray
    That she love me.

She is as gold
Lovely, and far more cold.
    Do thou pray with me,
For if I win grace
To kiss twice her face
    God has done well to me.

ROBERT NICHOLS (1893-   )

The Full Heart

ALONE on the shore in the pause of the night-time
   I stand and I hear the long wind blow light;
I view the constellations, quietly, quietly burning;
I hear the wave fall in the hush of the night.

Long after I am dead, ended this bitter journey,
Many another whose heart holds no light
Shall your solemn sweetness, hush, awe and comfort,
O my companions, Wind, Waters, Stars, and Night.

ROBERT GRAVES

Not Dead

WALKING through trees to cool my heat and pain,
   I know that David's with me here again.
All that is simple, happy, strong, he is.
Caressingly I stroke
Rough bark of the friendly oak.
A brook goes babbling by: the voice is his,
Turf burns with pleasant smoke;
I laugh at chaffinch and at primroses.
All that is simple, happy, strong, he is.
Over the whole wood in a little while
Breaks his slow smile.

INDEX OF FIRST LINES

A

539

J

K

L

O

Y

INDEX OF TITLES

553

INDEX OF AUTHORS

INDEX OF AUTHORS

INDEX OF AUTHORS

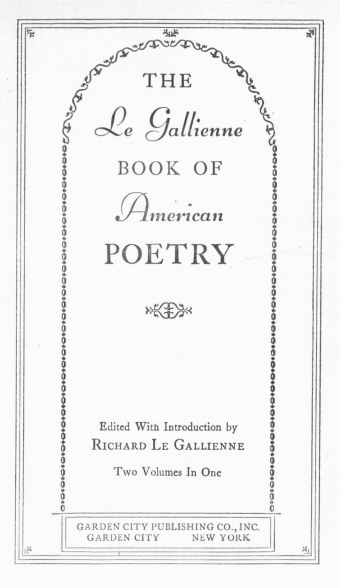

THE
Le Gallienne
BOOK OF
American
POETRY

Edited With Introduction by
RICHARD LE GALLIENNE

Two Volumes In One

GARDEN CITY PUBLISHING CO., INC.
GARDEN CITY   NEW YORK

THE LE GALLIENNE BOOK OF AMERICAN VERSE

Copyright, 1925, by
BONI & LIVERIGHT, INC.

Printed in the United States of America

THE MODERN BOOK OF AMERICAN VERSE

CONTENTS

CONTENTS

CONTENTS

CONTENTS

CONTENTS

CONTENTS

CONTENTS

CONTENTS

CONTENTS

CONTENTS

CONTENTS

CONTENTS

CONTENTS

CONTENTS

CONTENTS

THE MODERN BOOK OF AMERICAN VERSE

INTRODUCTION

In the making of a collection of this kind poetic excellence cannot be the only consideration. Along with the best must be included no little of the worst— from the artistic standpoint. The representative poetry of all nations includes both. Some verse, however bad, by its chronological position, its historical associations, its mere popularity, has its place in all such national anthologies. Such books are not for the supercilious, but no good critic is ever supercilious. Whatever his personal predilections, the true critic finds nothing that is human foreign to him, realising that in literature too it takes all kinds to make a world. Any poetry, however "homely," sentimental, or provincial, that has won the ear of a people, or touched its heart, has its place i' the story, in the case of such a popular collection as this aims to be. Therefore, no popular "favourite," however chap-fallen, or outmoded, has been consciously omitted from this "Book of American Verse," which attempts to illustrate the whole course of American poetry in dull periods as well as in bright, and as represented by real poets as well as by men and women who were often but commonplace versifiers, accidentally and temporarily "famous." On the whole, however, I believe that little will be found included here which will not have some quality of poetical entertainment for the humane, sympathetic reader—associative value at least.

INTRODUCTION

There are four American poets that are also world-poets: Emerson, Longfellow, Poe, Walt Whitman, and to these should, I think, be added Bret Harte. These, with the exception of Poe, are also the most distinctively American. Poe belongs to the Palace of Art. He might have been born anywhere; but the others could hardly have come out of any other country but America. The originality of Emerson is not perhaps sufficiently appreciated. The spiritual element in Whitman's broader, grosser, more specifically national genius, comes largely from Emerson, as from Whitman has come the new energy, the revolutionary freedom, which vitalizes all modern poetry written in the English language. Though our recent renaissance of poetry has produced no great poet, there is in it a breath of new life, felt as an animating quality in the work of the smallest modern poet that is a poet at all—and that breath comes from Walt Whitman. He is pre-eminently the poet of the modern world.

With many, to appreciate Whitman and Poe is to belittle Longfellow. But this, of course, is merely stupid. Contemporary taste runs so narrowly towards the intellectual, the bizarre, and the perverse, that it is bored with anything wholesome and homely. The modern reader of poetry is too much of an absinthe-drinker, turning up his nose at honest beer. But, indeed, Longfellow's verse has not infrequently the quality of a delicate light wine. It is far from being without charm, and occasionally, indeed, achieves magic. It is also pervaded with unobtrusive culture and a fine humanism. As a balladist, idyllist and lyrist, Longfellow had considerable gifts, and Amer-

ica is in his debt for two great services. In *Hiawatha,*
Evangeline, and *The Courtship of Miles Standish,* he
has written the legend of American history with something of epic breadth, and his poetry generally is filled
with gentle entertainment of great variety, which has
still its attractiveness for those who do not conceive
of poetry as inspired only by erotomania and delirium
tremens. Longfellow's other service to his countrymen was in his being a bridge between them and European literature, particularly Spanish and Italian, and
in the satisfaction he brought them for that general
homesickness for European life and culture, which is
still an American characteristic. To Bret Harte we
owe not merely his own, which still remains the best,
but all succeeding poetry written in American dialect
and story, and embodying that humour which all the
world regards as peculiarly American. Of other distinctively American poets that are not world-poets
too, I am sorry for the man who cannot appreciate
the cosmic nature-love of Bryant, or the homely,
rugged piety of Whittier, or the learned, philosophic
muses of such scholarly poets as T. W. Parsons and
Richard Henry Stoddard, as well as the sweeping harmonies of Lanier, and the fantasy and delicate art of
Aldrich. For the rest of the vast multitude of vari-
ously gifted singers gathered here, one has but to
glance down the "Contents" pages to be struck by the
immense number of clever, and even brilliant and
beautiful things that even the "minor poets" of
"these States" have produced. The humorous poets
are particularly good and numerous, but there is many
a lovely lyric too, many striking expressions of the

joy and sorrow and beauty of life, deep-rooted in humanity, and done with a fine artistry. In love-poetry and nature-poetry alike this volume is rich. But to discriminate amongst its contents would pass the bounds of this brief preface. Much will be already known to many readers, and those to whom the extent and variety of American poetry is yet to be discovered will, I think, be surprised at the gamut of themes spanned in this volume, and the many modes of skilful execution. As for the more recent poets, I am in the hopes that my selections from them will be sufficiently comprehensive to demonstrate, what is well-known to their unprejudiced readers, that contemporary American poetry is at present the most vital and original being written in the English tongue. For the moment, at all events, it looks as though the future of English poetry is to be in America. The tremendous, eager, wide-spread interest in poetry which has spread like wild-fire over the country during the last ten years, seems in itself to be something of a portent. However we may laugh at the veritable jungle-growth of Poetry Societies, they are an encouraging sign. And I couldn't help smiling just now, as I glanced at Professor Woodberry's article on "American Literature" in the eleventh edition of "The Encyclopedia Britannica" (published 1910-11) and read his conclusion. "The imaginative life is feeble," he says, "and when felt is crude"; and then he adds, "The poet's pulse is imperceptible." That, you see, was fifteen years ago. Professor Woodberry could hardly find "the poetic pulse" imperceptible now.

INTRODUCTION

In making this collection I have gratefully to acknowledge my great indebtedness to Stedman's well-known anthology, as well as to Mr. Burton Stevenson's vast thesaurus, "The Home-Book of Verse."

RICHARD LE GALLIENNE.

THE MODERN BOOK OF AMERICAN VERSE

PHILIP FRENEAU (1752-1832)

From "Female Frailty"

SONG OF THYRSIS

The turtle on yon withered bough,
That lately mourned her murdered mate,
Has found another comrade now—
Such changes all await!
Again her drooping plume is drest,
Again she's willing to be blest
And takes her lover to her nest.
If nature has decreed it so
With all above, and all below,
  Let us like them forget our woe,
   And not be killed with sorrow.
If I should quit your arms to-night
And chance to die before 'twas light—
I would advise you—and you might—
   Love again to-morrow.

The Wild Honeysuckle

Fair flower, that dost so comely grow,
 Hid in this silent, dull retreat,
Untouched thy honied blossoms blow,
 Unseen thy little branches greet:
  No roving foot shall crush thee here,
  No busy hand provoke a tear.

By Nature's self in white arrayed,
 She bade thee shun the vulgar eye,
And planted here the guardian shade,
 And sent soft waters murmuring by;
  Thus quietly thy summer goes,
  Thy days declining to repose.

Smit with those charms, that must decay,
 I grieve to see your future doom;
They died—nor were those flowers more gay,

1

The flowers that did in Eden bloom;
  Unpitying frosts and Autumn's power
  Shall leave no vestige of this flower.

From morning suns and evening dews
  At first thy little being came;
If nothing once, you nothing lose,
  For when you die you are the same;
    The space between is but an hour,
    The frail duration of a flower.

The Parting Glass

The man that joins in life's career
And hopes to find some comfort here,
To rise above this earthly mass,—
The only way's to drink his glass.

But still, on this uncertain stage
Where hopes and fears the soul engage,
And while, amid the joyous band,
Unheeded flows the measured sand,
Forget not as the moments pass
That time shall bring the parting glass!

In spite of all the mirth I've heard,
This is the glass I always feared,
The glass that would the rest destroy,
The farewell cup, the close of joy.

With you, whom reason taught to think,
I could for ages sit and drink;
But with the fool, the sot, the ass,
I haste to take the parting glass.

The luckless wight, that still delays
His draught of joys to future days,
Delays too long—for then, alas!
Old age steps up, and—breaks the glass!

The nymph who boasts no borrowed charms,
Whose sprightly wit my fancy warms,—
What though she tends this country inn,
And mixes wine, and deals out gin?
With such a kind, obliging lass,
I sigh to take the parting glass.

With him who always talks of gain
(Dull Momus, of the plodding train),
The wretch who thrives by others' woes,
And carries grief where'er he goes,—
With people of this knavish class
The first is still my parting glass.

With those that drink before they dine,
With him that apes the grunting swine,
Who fills his page with low abuse,
And strives to act the gabbling goose
Turned out by fate to feed on grass—
Boy, give me quick the parting glass.

The man whose friendship is sincere,
Who knows no guilt, and feels no fear,—
It would require a heart of brass
With him to take the parting glass.

With him who quaffs his pot of ale,
Who holds to all an even scale,
Who hates a knave in each disguise,
And fears him not—whate'er his size—
With him, well pleased my days to pass,
May heaven forbid the Parting Glass!

To a Honey Bee

Thou, born to sip the lake or spring,
  Or quaff the waters of the stream,
Why hither come, on vagrant wing?
  Does Bacchus tempting seem,—
    Did he for you this glass prepare?
    Will I admit you to a share?

Did storms harass or foes perplex,
  Did wasps or king-birds bring dismay,—
Did wars distress, or labors vex,
  Or did you miss your way?
    A better seat you could not take
    Than on the margin of this lake.

Welcome!—I hail you to my glass:
  All welcome here you find;
Here let the cloud of trouble pass,
  Here be all care resigned.
    This fluid never fails to please,
    And drown the griefs of men or bees.

What forced you here we cannot know,
  And you will scarcely tell,
But cheery we would have you go
  And bid a glad farewell:
    On lighter wings we bid you fly,—
    Your dart will now all foes defy.

Yet take not, oh! too deep a drink,
  And in this ocean die;
Here bigger bees than you might sink,
  Even bees full six feet high.
    Like Pharaoh, then, you would be said
    To perish in a sea of red.

Do as you please, your will is mine;
  Enjoy it without fear,
And your grave will be this glass of wine,
  Your epitaph—a tear;
    Go, take your seat in Charon's boat;
    We'll tell the hive, you died afloat.

AUTHOR UNKNOWN

The Yankee Man-of-War

'Tis of a gallant Yankee ship that flew the Stripes and Stars,
And the whistling wind from the west-nor'-west blew through
    the pitch-pine spars;
With her starboard tacks aboard, my boys, she hung upon the
    gale;
Of an autumn night we raised the light on the old Head of
    Kinsale.

It was a clear and cloudless night, and the wind blew steady
    and strong,
As gayly over the sparkling deep our good ship bowled along;
With the foaming seas beneath her bow the fiery waves she
    spread,
And bending low her bosom of snow, she buried her lee cat-
    head.

There was no talk of short'ning sail by him who walked the
    poop,
And under the press of her pond'ring jib, the boom bent like
    a hoop!
And the groaning water-ways told the strain that held her
    stout main-tack,
But he only laughed as he glanced aloft at a white and silvery
    track.

The mid-tide meets in the Channel waves that flow from shore
    to shore.
And the mist hung heavy upon the land from Featherstone to
    Dunmore.
And that sterling light in Tusker Rock where the old bell
    tolls each hour,
And the beacon light that shone so bright was quench'd on
    Waterford Tower.

The mighty ropes our good ship wore were her whole top-
    sails three,
Her spanker and her standing jib—the courses being free,
"Now, lay aloft! my heroes bold, not a moment must be
    passed!"
And royals and top-gallant sails were quickly on each mast.

What looms upon our starboard bow? What hangs upon the
    breeze?
'Tis time our good ship hauled her wind abreast the old
    Saltees,
For by her ponderous press of sail and by her consorts four
We saw our morning visitor was a British man-of-war.

Up spake our noble Captain then, as a shot ahead of us
    past—
"Haul snug your flowing courses! lay your topsail to the
    mast!"
Those Englishmen gave three loud hurrahs from the deck of
    their covered ark,
And we answered back by a solid broadside from the decks
    of our patriot bark.

"Out booms! out booms!" our skipper cried, "out booms and
    give her sheet,"
And the swiftest keel that was ever launched shot ahead of
    the British fleet,
And amidst a thundering shower of shot, with stun'-sails
    hoisting away,
Down the North Channel Paul Jones did steer just at the
    break of day.

TIMOTHY DWIGHT (1752-1817)

The Smooth Divine

There smiled the smooth Divine, unused to wound
The sinner's heart with hell's alarming sound.
No terrors on his gentle tongue attend;
No grating truths the nicest ear offend.

That strange new-birth, that methodistic grace,
Nor in his heart nor sermons found a place.
Plato's fine tales he clumsily retold,
Trite, fireside, moral seesaws, dull as old,—
His Christ and Bible placed at good remove,
Guilt hell-deserving, and forgiving love.
'Twas best, he said, mankind should cease to sin:
Good fame required it; so did peace within.
Their honors, well he knew, would ne'er be driven;
But hoped they still would please to go to heaven.
Each week he paid his visitation dues;
Coaxed, jested, laughed; rehearsed the private news;
Smoked with each goody, thought her cheese excelled;
Her pipe he lighted, and her baby held.
Or placed in some great town, with lacquered shoes,
Trim wig, and trimmer gown, and glistening hose,
He bowed, talked politics, learned manners mild,
Most meekly questioned, and most smoothly smiled;
At rich men's jests laughed loud, their stories praised,
Their wives' new patterns gazed, and gazed, and gazed;
Most daintily on pampered turkeys dined,
Nor shrunk with fasting, nor with study pined:
Yet from their churches saw his brethren driven,
Who thundered truth, and spoke the voice of heaven,
Chilled trembling guilt in Satan's headlong path,
Charmed the feet back, and roused the ear of death.
"Let fools," he cried, "starve on, while prudent I
Snug in my nest shall live, and snug shall die."

ST. GEORGE TUCKER (1752-1828)

Days of My Youth

Days of my youth,
    Ye have glided away;
Hairs of my youth,
    Ye are frosted and gray;
Eyes of my youth,
    Your keen sight is no more;
Cheeks of my youth,
    Ye are furrowed all o'er;
Strength of my youth,
    All your vigor is gone;
Thoughts of my youth,
    Your gay visions are flown.
Days of my youth,
    I wish not your recall;

Hairs of my youth,
    I'm content ye should fall;
Eyes of my youth,
    You much evil have seen;
Cheeks of my youth,
    Bathed in tears have you been;
Thoughts of my youth,
    You have led me astray;
Strength of my youth,
    Why lament your decay?

Days of my age,
    Ye will shortly be past;
Pains of my age,
    Yet awhile ye can last;
Joys of my age,
    In true wisdom delight;
Eyes of my age,
    Be religion your light;
Thoughts of my age,
    Dread ye not the cold sod;
Hopes of my age,
    Be ye fixed on your God.

ALEXANDER WILSON (1766-1813)

The Fisherman's Hymn

The osprey sails above the sound,
  The geese are gone, the gulls are flying;
The herring shoals swarm thick around,
  The nets are launched, the boats are plying;
    Yo ho, my hearts! let's seek the deep,
      Raise high the song, and cheerily wish her,
    Still as the bending net we sweep,
      "God bless the fish-hawk and the fisher!"

She brings us fish—she brings us spring,
  Good times, fair weather, warmth, and plenty,
Fine stores of shad, trout, herring, ling,
  Sheepshead and drum, and old-wives dainty.
    Yo ho, my hearts! let's seek the deep,
      Ply every oar, and cheerily wish her,
    Still as the bending net we sweep,
      "God bless the fish-hawk and the fisher!"

She rears her young on yonder tree,
  She leaves her faithful mate to mind 'em;

Like us, for fish, she sails to sea,
  And, plunging, shows us where to find 'em.
  Yo ho, my hearts! let's seek the deep,
    Ply every oar, and cheerily wish her,
    While the slow bending net we sweep,
    "God bless the fish-hawk and the fisher!"

JOSEPH HOPKINSON (1770-1842)

Hail, Columbia!

Hail, Columbia! happy land!
Hail, ye heroes! heaven-born band!
  Who fought and bled in Freedom's cause,
  Who fought and bled in Freedom's cause,
And when the storm of war was gone,
Enjoyed the peace your valor won.
  Let independence be our boast,
  Ever mindful what it cost;
  Ever grateful for the prize,
  Let its altar reach the skies.

        Firm, united, let us be,
        Rallying round our Liberty;
        As a band of brothers joined,
        Peace and safety we shall find.

Immortal patriots! rise once more:
Defend your rights, defend your shore:
  Let no rude foe, with impious hand,
  Let no rude foe, with impious hand,
Invade the shrine where sacred lies
Of toil and blood the well-earned prize.
  While offering peace sincere and just,
  In Heaven we place a manly trust,
  That truth and justice will prevail,
  And every scheme of bondage fail.

        Firm, united, etc.

Sound, sound, the trump of Fame!
Let WASHINGTON's great name
  Ring through the world with loud applause,
  Ring through the world with loud applause;
Let every clime to Freedom dear,
Listen with a joyful ear.
  With equal skill, and godlike power,
  He governed in the fearful hour

Of horrid war; or guides, with ease,
The happier times of honest peace.

Firm, united, etc.

Behold the chief who now commands,
Once more to serve his country, stands—
    The rock on which the storm will beat,
    The rock on which the storm will beat;
But, armed in virtue firm and true,
His hopes are fixed on Heaven and you.
    When hope was sinking in dismay,
    And glooms obscured Columbia's day,
    His steady mind, from changes free,
    Resolved on death or liberty.

        Firm, united, let us be,
        Rallying round our Liberty;
        As a band of brothers joined,
        Peace and safety we shall find.

JAMES KIRKE PAULDING (1779-1860)

The Old Man's Carousal

Drink! drink! to whom shall we drink?
To a friend or a mistress? Come, let me think!
To those who are absent, or those who are here?
To the dead that we loved, or the living still dear?
Alas! when I look, I find none of the last!
The present is barren,—let's drink to the past!

Come! here's to the girl with a voice sweet and low,
The eye all of fire and the bosom of snow,
Who erewhile, in the days of my youth that are fled,
Once slept on my bosom, and pillowed my head!
Would you know where to find such a delicate prize?
Go seek in yon church-yard, for there she lies.

And here's to the friend, the one friend of my youth,
With a head full of genius, a heart full of truth,
Who traveled with me in the sunshine of life,
And stood by my side in its peace and its strife!
Would you know where to seek for a blessing so rare?
Go drag the lone sea, you may find him there.

And here's to a brace of twin cherubs of mine,
With hearts like their mother's, as pure as this wine,

Who came but to see the first act of the play,
Grew tired of the scene, and then both went away.
Would you know where this brace of bright cherubs have
    hied?
Go seek them in heaven, for there they abide.

A bumper, my boys! to a gray-headed pair,
Who watched o'er my childhood with tenderest care.
God bless them, and keep them, and may they look down
On the head of their son, without tear, sigh, or frown!
Would you know whom I drink to? go seek 'mid the dead,
You will find both their names on the stone at their head.

And here's—but alas! the good wine is no more,
The bottle is emptied of all its bright store;
Like those we have toasted, its spirit is fled,
And nothing is left of the light that it shed.
Then, a bumper of tears, boys! the banquet here ends.
With a health to our dead, since we've no living friends.

WASHINGTON ALLSTON (1779-1843)

America to Great Britain

All hail! thou noble land,
    Our Father's native soil!
Oh, stretch thy mighty hand,
    Gigantic grown by toil,
O'er the vast Atlantic wave to our shore!
    For thou with magic might
    Canst reach to where the light
    Of Phœbus travels bright
        The world o'er!

The Genius of our clime,
    From his pine-embattled steep,
Shall hail the guest sublime;
    While the Tritons of the deep
With their conchs the kindred league shall proclaim.
    Then let the world combine,—
    O'er the main our naval line
    Like the milky-way shall shine
        Bright in fame!

Though ages long have past
    Since our Fathers left their home,
Their pilot in the blast,
    O'er untravelled seas to roam,
Yet lives the blood of England in our veins!

And shall we not proclaim
That blood of honest fame
Which no tyranny can tame
   By its chains?

While the language free and bold
   Which the bard of Avon sung,
In which our Milton told
   How the vault of heaven rung
When Satan, blasted, fell with his host;—
   While this, with reverence meet,
   Ten thousand echoes greet,
   From rock to rock repeat
      Round our coast;—

While the manners, while the arts,
   That mould a nation's soul,
Still cling around our hearts,—
   Between let Ocean roll,
Our joint communion breaking with the Sun:
   Yet still from either beach
   The voice of blood shall reach,
   More audible than speech,
      "We are One."

FRANCIS SCOTT KEY (1780-1843)

The Star-Spangled Banner

O say, can you see, by the dawn's early light,
   What so proudly we hailed at the twilight's last gleaming—
Whose broad stripes and bright stars, through the perilous
   fight,
   O'er the ramparts we watched were so gallantly streaming?
And the rocket's red glare, the bombs bursting in air,
Gave proof through the night that our flag was still there;
O! say, does that star-spangled banner yet wave
O'er the land of the free, and the home of the brave?

On that shore dimly seen through the mists of the deep,
   Where the foe's haughty host in dread silence reposes,
What is that which the breeze, o'er the towering steep,
   As it fitfully blows, now conceals, now discloses?
Now it catches the gleam of the morning's first beam,
In full glory reflected now shines on the stream;
'Tis the star-spangled banner; O long may it wave
O'er the land of the free, and the home of the brave!

And where is that band who so vauntingly swore
   That the havoc of war and the battle's confusion

SALEM COLLEGE
LIBRARY
Winston-Salem, N. C.

A home and a country should leave us no more?
   Their blood has washed out their foul footsteps' pollution.
No refuge could save the hireling and slave
From the terror of flight, or the gloom of the grave;
And the star-spangled banner in triumph doth wave
O'er the land of the free, and the home of the brave.

O! thus be it ever, when freemen shall stand
   Between their loved homes and the war's desolation!
Blest with victory and peace, may the heav'n-rescued land
   Praise the power that hath made and preserved us a nation.
Then conquer we must, when our cause it is just,
And this be our motto—"In God is our trust":
And the star-spangled banner in triumph shall wave
O'er the land of the free, and the home of the brave.

DANIEL WEBSTER (1782-1852)

On the Death of My Son Charles

My son, thou wast my heart's delight,
   Thy morn of life was gay and cheery;
That morn has rushed to sudden night,
   Thy father's house is sad and dreary.

I held thee on my knee, my son!
   And kissed thee laughing, kissed thee weeping;
But ah! thy little day is done,
   Thou'rt with thy angel sister sleeping.

The staff, on which my years should lean,
   Is broken, ere those years come o'er me;
My funeral rites thou shouldst have seen,
   But thou art in the tomb before me.

Thou rear'st to me no filial stone,
   No parent's grave with tears beholdest;
Thou art my ancestor, my son!
   And stand'st in Heaven's account the oldest.

On earth my lot was soonest cast,
   Thy generation after mine,
Thou hast thy predecessor past;
   Earlier eternity is thine.

I should have set before thine eyes
   The road to Heaven, and showed it clear;
But thou untaught spring'st to the skies,
   And leav'st thy teacher lingering here.

Sweet Seraph, I would learn of thee,
  And hasten to partake thy bliss!
And oh! to thy world welcome me,
  As first I welcomed thee to this.

Dear Angel, thou art safe in heaven;
  No prayers for thee need more be made;
Oh! let thy prayers for those be given
  Who oft have blessed thy infant head.

My father! I beheld thee born,
  And led thy tottering steps with care;
Before me risen to Heaven's bright morn,
  My son! my father! guide me there.

JOHN PIERPONT (1785-1866)

Warren's Address to the American Soldiers

Stand! the ground's your own, my braves!
Will ye give it up to slaves?
Will ye look for greener graves?
  Hope ye mercy still?
What's the mercy despots feel?
Hear it in that battle-peal!
Read it on yon bristling steel!
  Ask it,—ye who will.

Fear ye foes who kill for hire?
Will ye to your homes retire?
Look behind you! they're a-fire!
  And, before you, see
Who have done it!—From the vale
On they come!—And will ye quail?—
Leaden rain and iron hail
  Let their welcome be!

In the God of battles trust!
Die we may,—and die we must;
But, O, where can dust to dust
  Be consigned so well,
As where Heaven its dews shall shed
On the martyred patriot's bed,
And the rocks shall raise their head,
  Of his deeds to tell!

The Ballot

A weapon that comes down as still
  As snowflakes fall upon the sod;
But executes a freeman's will,
  As lightning does the will of God.

SAMUEL WOODWORTH (1785-1842)

The Old Oaken Bucket

How dear to this heart are the scenes of my childhood,
  When fond recollection presents them to view!
The orchard, the meadow, the deep-tangled wild-wood,
  And every loved spot which my infancy knew!
The wide-spreading pond, and the mill that stood by it,
  The bridge and the rock where the cataract fell,
The cot of my father, the dairy-house nigh it,
  And e'en the rude bucket that hung in the well—
The old oaken bucket, the iron-bound bucket,
The moss-covered bucket which hung in the well.

That moss-covered vessel I hailed as a treasure,
  For often at noon, when returned from the field,
I found it the source of an exquisite pleasure,
  The purest and sweetest that nature can yield.
How ardent I seized it, with hands that were glowing,
  And quick to the white-pebbled bottom it fell;
Then soon, with the emblem of truth overflowing,
  And dripping with coolness, it rose from the well—
The old oaken bucket, the iron-bound bucket,
The moss-covered bucket arose from the well.

How sweet from the green mossy brim to receive it,
  As poised on the curb it inclined to my lips!
Not a full blushing goblet could tempt me to leave it,
  The brightest that beauty or revelry sips.
And now, far removed from the loved habitation,
  The tear of regret will intrusively swell,
As fancy reverts to my father's plantation,
  And sighs for the bucket that hangs in the well—
The old oaken bucket, the iron-bound bucket,
The moss-covered bucket that hangs in the well!

RICHARD HENRY DANA (1787-1879)

The Little Beach-Bird

Thou little bird, thou dweller by the sea,
  Why takest thou its melancholy voice,
    And with that boding cry
    Why o'er the waves dost fly?
O, rather, bird, with me
  Through the fair land rejoice!

Thy flitting form comes ghostly dim and pale,
  As driven by a beating storm at sea;
    Thy cry is weak and scared,
    As if thy mates had shared
The doom of us: Thy wail,—
  What doth it bring to me?

Thou call'st along the sand, and haunt'st the surge,
  Restless and sad; as if, in strange accord
    With the motion and the roar
    Of waves that drive to shore,
One spirit did ye urge—
  The Mystery—the Word.

Of thousands, thou, both sepulchre and pall,
  Old Ocean! A requiem o'er the dead
    From out thy gloomy cells
    A tale of mourning tells,—
Tells of man's woe and fall,
  His sinless glory fled.

Then turn thee, little bird, and take thy flight
  Where the complaining sea shall sadness bring
    Thy spirit never more;
    Come, quit with me the shore,
And on the meadows light
  Where birds for gladness sing!

EMMA HART WILLARD (1787-1870)

Rocked in the Cradle of the Deep

Rocked in the cradle of the deep
I lay me down in peace to sleep;
Secure I rest upon the wave,
For thou, O Lord! hast power to save.
I know thou wilt not slight my call,
For Thou dost mark the sparrow's fall;

And calm and peaceful shall I sleep,
Rocked in the cradle of the deep.

When in the dead of night I lie
And gaze upon the trackless sky,
The star-bespangled heavenly scroll,
The boundless waters as they roll,—
I feel thy wondrous power to save
From perils of the stormy wave:
Rocked in the cradle of the deep,
I calmly rest and soundly sleep.

And such the trust that still were mine,
Though stormy winds swept o'er the brine,
Or though the tempest's fiery breath
Roused me from sleep to wreck and death.
In ocean cave, still safe with Thee
The germ of immortality!
And calm and peaceful shall I sleep,
Rocked in the cradle of the deep.

RICHARD HENRY WILDE (1789-1847)

To the Mocking-bird

Who shall thy gay buffoonery describe?
Winged mimic of the woods! thou motley fool!
Thine ever ready notes of ridicule
Pursue thy fellows still with jest and gibe.
Wit, sophist, songster, Yorick of thy tribe,
Thou sportive satirist of Nature's school,
To thee the palm of scoffing we ascribe,
Arch-mocker and mad Abbot of Misrule!
For such thou art by day—but all night long
Thou pourest a soft, sweet, pensive, solemn strain,
As if thou didst in this thy moonlight song
Like to the melancholy Jacques complain,
Musing on falsehood, folly, vice, and wrong,
And sighing for thy motley coat again.

JAMES FENIMORE COOPER (1789-1851)

My Brigantine

My brigantine!
Just in thy mould and beauteous in thy form,
Gentle in roll and buoyant on the surge,
Light as the sea-fowl rocking in the storm,
In breeze and gale thy onward course we urge,
My water-queen!

Lady of mine!
More light and swift than thou none thread the sea,
With surer keel or steadier on its path;
We brave each waste of ocean-mystery
And laugh to hear the howling tempest's wrath,
  For we are thine!

My brigantine!
Trust to the mystic power that points thy way,
Trust to the eye that pierces from afar,
Trust to the red meteors that around thee play,
And, fearless, trust the Sea-Green Lady's Star,
  Thou bark divine!

FITZ-GREENE HALLECK (1790-1867)

Marco Bozzaris

At midnight, in his guarded tent,
  The Turk was dreaming of the hour
When Greece, her knee in suppliance bent,
  Should tremble at his power:
In dreams, through camp and court, he bore
The trophies of a conqueror;
  In dreams his song of triumph heard;
Then wore his monarch's signet ring:
Then pressed that monarch's throne—a king;
As wild his thoughts, and gay of wing,
  As Eden's garden bird.

At midnight, in the forest shades,
  Bozzaris ranged his Suliote band,
True as the steel of their tried blades,
  Heroes in heart and hand.
There had the Persian's thousands stood,
There had the glad earth drunk their blood
  On old Plataea's day;
And now there breathed that haunted air
The sons of sires who conquered there,
With arm to strike and soul to dare,
  As quick, as far as they.

An hour passed on—the Turk awoke;
  That bright dream was his last;
He woke—to hear his sentries shriek,
"To arms! they come! the Greek! the Greek!"

He woke—to die midst flame, and smoke,
And shout, and groan, and sabre-stroke,
  And death-shots falling thick and fast
As lightnings from the mountain-cloud;
And heard, with voice as trumpet loud,
  Bozzaris cheer his band:
"Strike—till the last armed foe expires;
Strike—for your altars and your fires;
Strike—for the green graves of your sires;
  God—and your native land!"

They fought—like brave men, long and well;
  They piled that ground with Moslem slain,
They conquered—but Bozzaris fell,
  Bleeding at every vein.
His few surviving comrades saw
His smile when rang their proud hurrah,
  And the red field was won;
Then saw in death his eyelids close
Calmly, as to a night's repose,
  Like flowers at set of sun.

Come to the bridal-chamber, Death!
  Come to the mother's, when she feels,
For the first time, her first-born's breath;
  Come when the blessed seals
That close the pestilence are broke,
And crowded cities wail its stroke;
Come in consumption's ghastly form,
The earthquake shock, the ocean storm;
Come when the heart beats high and warm
  With banquet-song, and dance, and wine;
And thou art terrible—the tear,
The groan, the knell, the pall, the bier,
And all we know, or dream, or fear
  Of agony, are thine.

But to the hero, when his sword
  Has won the battle for the free,
Thy voice sounds like a prophet's word;
And in its hollow tones are heard
  The thanks of millions yet to be.
Come, when his task of fame is wrought—
Come, with her laurel-leaf, blood-bought—
  Come in her crowning hour—and then
Thy sunken eye's unearthly light
To him is welcome as the sight
  Of sky and stars to prisoned men;

Thy grasp is welcome as the hand
Of brother in a foreign land;
Thy summons welcome as the cry
That told the Indian isles were nigh
　　To the world-seeking Genoese,
When the land wind, from woods of palm,
And orange-groves, and fields of balm,
　　Blew o'er the Haytian seas.

Bozzaris! with the storied brave
　　Greece nurtured in her glory's time,
Rest thee—there is no prouder grave,
　　Even in her own proud clime.
She wore no funeral-weeds for thee,
　　Nor bade the dark hearse wave its plume
Like torn branch from death's leafless tree
In sorrow's pomp and pageantry,
　　The heartless luxury of the tomb;
But she remembers thee as one
Long loved and for a season gone;
For thee her poet's lyre is wreathed,
Her marble wrought, her music breathed;
For thee she rings the birthday bells;
Of thee her babe's first lisping tells;
For thine her evening prayer is said
At palace-couch and cottage-bed;
Her soldier, closing with the foe,
Gives for thy sake a deadlier blow;
His plighted maiden, when she fears
For him the joy of her young years,
Thinks of thy fate, and checks her tears;
　　And she, the mother of thy boys,
Though in her eye and faded cheek
Is read the grief she will not speak,
　　The memory of her buried joys,
And even she who gave thee birth,
Will, by their pilgrim-circled hearth,
　　Talk of thy doom without a sigh;
For thou art Freedom's now, and Fame's:
One of the few, the immortal names,
　　That were not born to die.

JOHN HOWARD PAYNE (1791-1852)

Home, Sweet Home

'Mid pleasures and palaces though we may roam,
Be it ever so humble, there's no place like home;

A charm from the sky seems to hallow us there,
Which, seek through the world, is ne'er met with elsewhere.
    Home! Home! sweet, sweet Home!
There's no place like Home! there's no place like Home!

An exile from home, splendor dazzles in vain;
O, give me my lowly thatched cottage again!
The birds singing gayly, that came at my call,—
Give me them,—and the peace of mind, dearer than all!
    Home! Home! sweet, sweet Home!
There's no place like Home! there's no place like Home!

How sweet 'tis to sit 'neath a fond father's smile,
And the cares of a mother to soothe and beguile!
Let others delight 'mid new pleasures to roam,
But give me, oh, give me, the pleasures of home!
    Home! Home! sweet, sweet Home!
There's no place like Home! there's no place like Home!

To thee I'll return, overburdened with care;
The heart's dearest solace will smile on me there;
No more from that cottage again will I roam;
Be it ever so humble, there's no place like home.
    Home! Home! sweet, sweet Home!
There's no place like Home! there's no place like Home!

LYDIA HUNTLEY SIGOURNEY (1791-1865)

Indian Names

Ye say, they all have pass'd away,
  That noble race and brave;
That their light canoes have vanish'd
  From off the crested wave;
That, 'mid the forests where they roam'd,
  There rings no hunter's shout;
But their name is on your waters,—
  Ye may not wash it out.

'Tis where Ontario's billow
  Like Ocean's surge is curl'd;
Where strong Niagara's thunders wake
  The echo of the world;
Where red Missouri bringeth
  Rich tributes from the West,
And Rappahannock sweetly sleeps
  On green Virginia's breast.

Ye say, their cone-like cabins,
    That cluster'd o'er the vale,
Have fled away, like wither'd leaves
    Before the Autumn gale:
But their memory liveth on your hills,
    Their baptism on your shore;
Your everlasting rivers speak
    Their dialect of yore.

Old Massachusetts wears it
    Within her lordly crown,
And broad Ohio bears it
    'Mid all her young renown;
Connecticut hath wreathed it
    Where her quiet foliage waves,
And bold Kentucky breathed it hoarse
    Through all her ancient caves.

Wachuset hides its lingering voice
    Within his rocky heart,
And Alleghany graves its tone
    Throughout his lofty chart;
Monadnock, on his forehead hoar,
    Doth seal the sacred trust;
Your mountains build their monument,
    Though ye destroy their dust.

WILLIAM CULLEN BRYANT (1794-1878)

Thanatopsis

To him who in the love of Nature holds
Communion with her visible forms, she speaks
A various language; for his gayer hours
She has a voice of gladness, and a smile
And eloquence of beauty, and she glides
Into his darker musings, with a mild
And healing sympathy, that steals away
Their sharpness, ere he is aware. When thoughts
Of the last bitter hour come like a blight
Over thy spirit, and sad images
Of the stern agony, and shroud, and pall,
And breathless darkness, and the narrow house,
Make thee to shudder and grow sick at heart;—
Go forth, under the open sky, and list
To Nature's teachings, while from all around—
Earth and her waters, and the depths of air—
Comes a still voice:—

Yet a few days, and thee
The all-beholding sun shall see no more
In all his course; nor yet in the cold ground,
Where thy pale form was laid with many tears,
Nor in the embrace of ocean, shall exist
Thy image. Earth, that nourished thee, shall claim
Thy growth, to be resolved to earth again,
And, lost each human trace, surrendering up
Thine individual being, shalt thou go
To mix forever with the elements,
To be a brother to the insensible rock
And to the sluggish clod, which the rude swain
Turns with his share, and treads upon. The oak
Shall send his roots abroad, and pierce thy mould.

Yet not to thine eternal resting-place
Shalt thou retire alone, nor couldst thou wish
Couch more magnificent. Thou shalt lie down
With patriarchs of the infant world—with kings,
The powerful of the earth—the wise, the good,
Fair forms, and hoary seers of ages past,
All in one mighty sepulchre. The hills
Rock-ribbed and ancient as the sun,—the vales
Stretching in pensive quietness between;
The venerable woods—rivers that move
In majesty, and the complaining brooks
That make the meadows green; and, poured round all,
Old Ocean's gray and melancholy waste,—
Are but the solemn decorations all
Of the great tomb of man. The golden sun,
The planets, all the infinite host of heaven,
Are shining on the sad abodes of death
Through the still lapse of ages. All that tread
The globe are but a handful to the tribes
That slumber in its bosom.—Take the wings
Of morning, pierce the Barcan wilderness,
Or lose thyself in the continuous woods
Where rolls the Oregon, and hears no sound,
Save his own dashings—yet the dead are there;
And millions in those solitudes, since first
The flight of years began, have laid them down
In their last sleep—the dead reign there alone.
So shalt thou rest, and what if thou withdraw
In silence from the living, and no friend
Take note of thy departure? All that breathe
Will share thy destiny. The gay will laugh
When thou art gone, the solemn brood of care
Plod on, and each one as before will chase

His favorite phantom; yet all these shall leave
Their mirth and their employments, and shall come
And make their bed with thee. As the long train
Of ages glides away, the sons of men—
The youth in life's fresh spring, and he who goes
In the full strength of years, matron and maid,
The speechless babe, and the gray-headed man—
Shall one by one be gathered to thy side,
By those, who in their turn shall follow them.

So live, that when thy summons comes to join
The innumerable caravan which moves
To that mysterious realm, where each shall take
His chamber in the silent halls of death,
Thou go not, like the quarry-slave at night,
Scourged to his dungeon, but, sustained and soothed
By an unfaltering trust, approach thy grave
Like one who wraps the drapery of his couch
About him, and lies down to pleasant dreams.

To a Waterfowl

Whither, midst falling dew,
While glow the heavens with the last steps of day,
Far, through their rosy depths, dost thou pursue
Thy solitary way?

Vainly the fowler's eye
Might mark thy distant flight to do thee wrong,
As, darkly painted on the crimson sky,
Thy figure floats along.

Seek'st thou the plashy brink
Of weedy lake, or marge of river wide,
Or where the rocking billows rise and sink
On the chafed ocean side?

There is a Power whose care
Teaches thy way along that pathless coast—
The desert and illimitable air—
Lone wandering, but not lost.

All day thy wings have fanned,
At that far height, the cold, thin atmosphere,
Yet stoop not, weary, to the welcome land,
Though the dark night is near.

And soon that toil shall end;
Soon shalt thou find a summer home, and rest,

And scream among thy fellows; reeds shall bend,
    Soon, o'er thy sheltered nest.

Thou'rt gone! the abyss of heaven
Hath swallowed up thy form; yet on my heart
Deeply hath sunk the lesson thou hast given,
    And shall not soon depart.

He, who, from zone to zone,
Guides through the boundless sky thy certain flight,
In the long way that I must tread alone
    Will lead my steps aright.

The Snow-Shower

Stand here by my side and turn, I pray,
  On the lake below thy gentle eyes;
The clouds hang over it, heavy and gray,
  And dark and silent the water lies;
And out of that frozen mist the snow
In wavering flakes begins to flow;
    Flake after flake
They sink in the dark and silent lake.

See how in a living swarm they come
  From the chambers beyond that misty veil;
Some hover awhile in air, and some
  Rush prone from the sky like summer hail.
All, dropping swiftly or settling slow,
Meet, and are still in the depths below;
    Flake after flake
Dissolved in the dark and silent lake.

Here delicate snow-stars, out of the cloud,
  Come floating downward in airy play,
Like spangles dropped from the glistening crowd
  That whiten by night the Milky Way;
There broader and burlier masses fall;
The sullen water buries them all—
    Flake after flake—
All drowned in the dark and silent lake.

And some, as on tender wings they glide
  From their chilly birth-cloud, dim and gray,
Are joined in their fall, and, side by side,
  Come clinging along their unsteady way;
As friend with friend, or husband with wife,
Makes hand in hand the passage of life;
    Each mated flake
Soon sinks in the dark and silent lake.

Lo! while we are gazing, in swifter haste
  Stream down the snows, till the air is white,
As, myriads by myriads madly chased,
  They fling themselves from their shadowy height.
The fair, frail creatures of middle sky,
What speed they make, with their grave so nigh;
        Flake after flake
To lie in the dark and silent lake!

I see in thy gentle eyes a tear;
  They turn to me in sorrowful thought;
Thou thinkest of friends, the good and dear,
  Who were for a time and now are not;
Like these fair children of cloud and frost,
That glisten a moment and then are lost—
        Flake after flake,—
All lost in the dark and silent lake.

Yet look again, for the clouds divide;
  A gleam of blue on the water lies;
And far away, on the mountain-side,
  A sunbeam falls from the opening skies.
But the hurrying host that flew between
The cloud and the water, no more is seen;
        Flake after flake,
At rest in the dark and silent lake.

The Planting of the Apple-Tree

  Come, let us plant the apple-tree.
Cleave the tough greensward with the spade;
Wide let its hollow bed be made;
There gently lay the roots, and there
Sift the dark mould with kindly care,
  And press it o'er them tenderly,
As, round the sleeping infant's feet,
We softly fold the cradle-sheet;
  So plant we the apple-tree.

  What plant we in this apple-tree?
Buds, which the breath of summer days
Shall lengthen into leafy sprays;
Boughs where the thrush, with crimson breast,
Shall haunt and sing and hide her nest;
  We plant, upon the sunny lea,
A shadow for the noontide hour,
A shelter from the summer shower,
  When we plant the apple-tree.

What plant we in this apple-tree?
Sweets for a hundred flowery springs
To load the May-wind's restless wings,
When, from the orchard row, he pours
Its fragrance through our open doors;
    A world of blossoms for the bee,
Flowers for the sick girl's silent room,
For the glad infant sprigs of bloom,
    We plant with the apple-tree.

What plant we in this apple-tree?
Fruits that shall swell in sunny June,
And redden in the August noon,
And drop, when gentle airs come by,
That fan the blue September sky,
    While children come, with cries of glee,
And seek them where the fragrant grass
Betrays their bed to those who pass,
    At the foot of the apple-tree.

And when, above this apple-tree,
The winter stars are quivering bright,
And winds go howling through the night,
Girls, whose young eyes o'erflow with mirth,
Shall peel its fruit by cottage-hearth,
    And guests in prouder homes shall see,
Heaped with the grape of Cintra's vine
And golden orange of the line,
    The fruit of the apple-tree.

The fruitage of this apple-tree
Winds and our flag of stripe and star
Shall bear to coasts that lie afar,
Where men shall wonder at the view,
And ask in what fair groves they grew;
    And sojourners beyond the sea
Shall think of childhood's careless day,
And long, long hours of summer play,
    In the shade of the apple-tree.

Each year shall give this apple-tree
A broader flush of roseate bloom,
A deeper maze of verdurous gloom,
And loosen, when the frost-clouds lower,
The crisp brown leaves in thicker shower.
    The years shall come and pass, but we
Shall hear no longer, where we lie,
The summer's songs, the autumn's sigh,
    In the boughs of the apple-tree.

And time shall waste this apple-tree.
Oh, when its aged branches throw
Thin shadows on the ground below,
Shall fraud and force and iron will
Oppress the weak and helpless still?
What shall the tasks of mercy be,
Amid the toils, the strifes, the tears
Of those who live when length of years
    Is wasting this little apple-tree?

"Who planted this old apple-tree?"
The children of that distant day
Thus to some aged man shall say;
And, gazing on its mossy stem,
The gray-haired man shall answer them:
"A poet of the land was he,
Born in the rude but good old times;
'Tis said he made some quaint old rhymes,
    On planting the apple-tree."

JOSEPH RODMAN DRAKE (1795-1820)

From "The Culprit Fay"

THE FAY'S SENTENCE

The monarch sat on his judgment-seat,
    On his brow the crown imperial shone,
The prisoner Fay was at his feet,
    And his peers were ranged around the throne.
He waved his sceptre in the air;
    He looked around and calmly spoke;
His brow was grave and his eye severe,
    But his voice in a softened accent broke:

"Fairy! Fairy! list and mark,
    Thou hast broke thine elfin chain,
Thy flame-wood lamp is quenched and dark,
    And thy wings are dyed with a deadly stain—
Thou hast sullied thine elfin purity
In the glance of a mortal maiden's eye,
Thou hast scorned our dread decree,
And thou shouldst pay the forfeit high,
But well I know her sinless mind
Is pure as the angel forms above,
Gentle and meek, and chaste and kind,
Such as a spirit well might love;
Fairy! had she spot or taint,

Bitter had been thy punishment.
Tied to the hornet's shardy wings;
Tossed on the pricks of nettle's stings;
Or seven long ages doomed to dwell
With the lazy worm in the walnut-shell;
Or every night to writhe and bleed
Beneath the tread of the centipede;
Or bound in a cobweb dungeon dim,
Your jailer a spider huge and grim,
Amid the carrion bodies to lie,
Of the worm, and the bug, and the murdered fly;
These it had been your lot to bear,
Had a stain been found on the earthly fair.
Now list, and mark our mild decree—
Fairy, this your doom must be:

"Thou shalt seek the beach of sand
Where the water bounds the elfin land,
Thou shalt watch the oozy brine
Till the sturgeon leaps in the bright moonshine,
Then dart the glistening arch below,
And catch a drop from his silver bow.
The water-sprites will wield their arms
    And dash around, with roar and rave,
And vain are the woodland spirits' charms,
    They are the imps that rule the wave.
Yet trust thee in thy single might,—
If thy heart be pure and thy spirit right,
Thou shalt win the warlock fight.

"If the spray-bead gem be won,
    The stain of thy wing is washed away,
But another errand must be done
    Ere thy crime be lost for aye;
Thy flame-wood lamp is quenched and dark,
Thou must re-illumine its spark.
Mount thy steed and spur him high
To the heaven's blue canopy;
And when thou seest a shooting star,
Follow it fast, and follow it far—
The last faint spark of its burning train
Shall light the elfin lamp again.
Thou hast heard our sentence, Fay;
Hence! to the water-side, away!"

The American Flag

When Freedom from her mountain height
    Unfurled her standard to the air,

She tore the azure robe of night,
  And set the stars of glory there.
She mingled with its gorgeous dyes
The milky baldric of the skies,
And striped its pure celestial white
With streakings of the morning light;
Then from his mansion in the sun
She called her eagle bearer down,
And gave into his mighty hand
The symbol of her chosen land.

Majestic monarch of the cloud,
  Who rear'st aloft thy regal form,
To hear the tempest trumpings loud
And see the lightning lances driven,
  When strive the warriors of the storm,
And rolls the thunder-drum of heaven,
Child of the sun! to thee 'tis given
  To guard the banner of the free,
To hover in the sulphur smoke,
To ward away the battle stroke,
And bid its blendings shine afar,
Like rainbows on the cloud of war,
  The harbingers of victory!

Flag of the brave! thy folds shall fly,
The sign of hope and triumph high,
When speaks the signal trumpet tone,
And the long line comes gleaming on.
Ere yet the life-blood, warm and wet,
Has dimmed the glistening bayonet,
Each soldier eye shall brightly turn
To where thy sky-born glories burn,
And, as his springing steps advance,
Catch war and vengeance from the glance.
And when the cannon-mouthings loud,
Heave in wild wreaths the battle shroud,
  And gory sabres rise and fall
Like shoots of flame on midnight's pall,
  Then shall thy meteor glances glow,
And cowering foes shall shrink beneath
  Each gallant arm that strikes below
That lovely messenger of death.

Flag of the seas! on ocean wave
Thy stars shall glitter o'er the brave;
When death, careering on the gale,
Sweeps darkly round the bellied sail,

And frighted waves rush wildly back
Before the broadside's reeling rack,
Each dying wanderer of the sea
Shall look at once to heaven and thee,
And smile to see thy splendors fly
In triumph o'er his closing eye.

Flag of the free heart's hope and home!
 By angel hands to valor given;
Thy stars have lit the welkin dome,
 And all thy hues were born in heaven.
Forever float that standard sheet!
 Where breathes the foe but falls before us,
With Freedom's soil beneath our feet,
 And Freedom's banner streaming o'er us?

JAMES GATES PERCIVAL (1795-1856)

Elegiac

O, it is great for our country to die, where ranks are contending!
 Bright is the wreath of our fame; glory awaits us for
  aye,—
Glory, that never is dim, shining on with light never ending,—
 Glory that never shall fade, never, O never, away!
O, it is sweet for our country to die! How softly reposes
 Warrior youth on his bier, wet by the tears of his love,
Wet by a mother's warm tears. They crown him with garlands of roses,
 Weep, and then joyously turn, bright where he triumphs
  above.

Not to the shades shall the youth descend, who for country
  hath perished;
 Hebe awaits him in heaven, welcomes him there with her
  smile;
There, at the banquet divine, the patriot spirit is cherished;
 Gods love the young who ascend pure from the funeral pile.

Not to Elysian fields, by the still, oblivious river;
 Not to the isles of the blest, over the blue, rolling sea;
But on Olympian heights shall dwell the devoted forever;
 There shall assemble the good, there the wise, valiant, and
  free.

O, then, how great for our country to die, in the front rank
  to perish,
 Firm with our breast to the foe, victory's shout in our ear!

Long they our statues shall crown, in songs our memory
    cherish;
We shall look forth from our heaven, pleased the sweet
    music to hear.

MARIA GOWEN BROOKS (1795-1845)
Song of Egla

Day in melting purple dying,
Blossoms all around me sighing,
Fragrance from the lilies straying,
Zephyr with my ringlets playing,
        Ye but waken my distress:
        I am sick of loneliness.

Thou to whom I love to hearken,
Come ere night around me darken:
Though thy softness but deceive me,
Say thou'rt true, and I'll believe thee.
        Veil, if ill, thy soul's intent:
        Let me think it innocent!

Save thy toiling, spare thy treasure:
All I ask is friendship's pleasure:
Let the shining ore lie darkling;
Bring no gem in lustre sparkling;
        Gifts and gold are nought to me:
        I would only look on thee;

Tell to thee the high-wrought feeling,
Ecstasy but in revealing;
Paint to thee the deep sensation,
Rapture in participation,
        Yet but torture, if comprest
        In a lone unfriended breast.

Absent still? Ah, come and bless me!
Let these eyes again caress thee.
Once, in caution, I could fly thee.
Now I nothing could deny thee.
        In a look if death there be,
        Come, and I will gaze on thee!

AMOS BRONSIN ALCOTT (1799-1888)
Wendell Phillips

People's Attorney, servant of the Right!
Pleader for all shades of the solar ray,

Complexions dusky, yellow, red, or white;
Who, in thy country's and thy time's despite,
Hast only questioned, What will Duty say?
And followed swiftly in her narrow way:
Tipped is thy tongue with golden eloquence,
All honeyed accents fall from off thy lips,—
Each eager listener his full measure sips,
Yet runs to waste the sparkling opulence,—
The scorn of bigots, and the worldling's flout.
If Time long held thy merit in suspense,
Hastening repentant now, with pen devout,
Impartial History dare not leave thee out.

GRENVILLE MELLEN (1799-1841)

From an "Ode on the Celebration of the Battle of Bunker Hill, June 17, 1825"

THE LONELY BUGLE GRIEVES

The trump hath blown,
  And now upon that reeking hill
Slaughter rides screaming on the vengeful ball;
  While with terrific signal shrill,
The vultures, from their bloody eyries flown,
    Hang o'er them like a pall.
  Now deeper roll the maddening drums,
    And the mingling host like ocean heaves:
    While from the midst a horrid wailing comes,
And high above the fight the lonely bugle grieves!

ALBERT GORTON GREENE (1802-1868)

Old Grimes

Old Grimes is dead; that good old man
  We never shall see more:
He used to wear a long black coat,
  All buttoned down before.

His heart was open as the day,
  His feelings all were true;
His hair was some inclined to gray—
  He wore it in a queue.

Whene'er he heard the voice of pain,
  His breast with pity burned;

The large, round head upon his cane
   From ivory was turned.

Kind words he ever had for all;
   He knew no base design:
His eyes were dark and rather small,
   His nose was aquiline.

He lived at peace with all mankind,
   In friendship he was true;
His coat had pocket-holes behind,
   His pantaloons were blue.

Unharmed, the sin which earth pollutes
   He passed securely o'er,
And never wore a pair of boots
   For thirty years or more.

But good old Grimes is now at rest,
   Nor fears misfortune's frown:
He wore a double-breasted vest—
   The stripes ran up and down.

He modest merit sought to find,
   And pay it its desert:
He had no malice in his mind,
   No ruffles on his shirt.

His neighbors he did not abuse—
   Was sociable and gay:
He wore large buckles on his shoes,
   And changed them every day.

His knowledge, hid from public gaze,
   He did not bring to view,
Nor make a noise, town-meeting days,
   As many people do.

His worldly goods he never threw
   In trust to fortune's chances,
But lived (as all his brothers do)
   In easy circumstances.

Thus undisturbed by anxious cares,
   His peaceful moments ran;
And everybody said he was
   A fine old gentleman.

EDWARD COATE PINKNEY (1802-1828)

Votive Song

I burn no incense, hang no wreath,
  On this thine early tomb:
Such cannot cheer the place of death,
  But only mock its gloom.
Here odorous smoke and breathing flower
  No grateful influence shed;
They lose their perfume and their power,
  When offered to the dead.

And if, as is the Afghan's creed,
  The spirit may return,
A disembodied sense to feed,
  On fragrance, near its urn,—
It is enough that she, whom thou
  Didst love in living years,
Sits desolate beside it now,
  And fall these heavy tears.

GEORGE POPE MORRIS (1802-1864)

Woodman, Spare That Tree

Woodman, spare that tree!
  Touch not a single bough!
In youth it sheltered me,
  And I'll protect it now.
'Twas my forefather's hand
  That placed it near his cot;
There, woodman, let it stand,
  Thy axe shall harm it not.

That old familiar tree,
  Whose glory and renown
Are spread o'er land and sea—
  And wouldst thou hew it down?
Woodman, forbear thy stroke!
  Cut not its earth-bound ties;
Oh, spare that aged oak
  Now towering to the skies!

When but an idle boy,
  I sought its grateful shade;

In all their gushing joy
 Here, too, my sisters played.
My mother kissed me here;
 My father pressed my hand—
Forgive this foolish tear,
 But let that old oak stand.

My heart-strings round thee cling,
 Close as thy bark, old friend!
Here shall the wild-bird sing,
 And still thy branches bend.
Old tree! the storm still brave!
 And, woodman, leave the spot;
While I've a hand to save,
 Thy axe shall harm it not.

RALPH WALDO EMERSON (1803-1882)

The Problem

I like a church; I like a cowl;
I love a prophet of the soul;
And on my heart monastic aisles
Fall like sweet strains, or pensive smiles:
Yet not for all his faith can see
Would I that cowled churchman be.
Why should the vest on him allure,
Which I could not on me endure?

Not from a vain or shallow thought
His awful Jove young Phidias brought;
Never from lips of cunning fell
The thrilling Delphic oracle;
Out from the heart of nature rolled
The burdens of the Bible old;
The litanies of nations came,
Like the volcano's tongue of flame,
Up from the burning core below,—
The canticles of love and woe:
The hand that rounded Peter's dome
And groined the aisles of Christian Rome
Wrought in a sad sincerity;
Himself from God he could not free;
He builded better than he knew;
The conscious stone to beauty grew.

Knowest thou what wove yon woodbird's nest
Of leaves and feathers from her breast?
Or how the fish outbuilt her shell,
Painting with morn each annual cell?
Or how the sacred pine-tree adds
To her old leaves new myriads?
Such and so grew these holy piles,
Whilst love and terror laid the tiles.
Earth proudly wears the Parthenon,
As the best gem upon her zone
And Morning opes with haste her lids
To gaze upon the Pyramids;
O'er England's abbeys bends the sky,
As on its friends, with kindred eye;
For out of Thought's interior sphere
These wonders rose to upper air;
And Nature gladly gave them place,
Adopted them into her race,
And granted them an equal date
With Andes and with Ararat.

These temples grew as grows the grass;
Art might obey, but not surpass.
The passive Master lent his hand
To the vast soul that o'er him planned;
And the same power that reared the shrine
Bestrode the tribes that knelt within.
Ever the fiery Pentecost
Girds with one flame the countless host,
Trances the heart through chanting choirs,
And through the priest the mind inspires.
The word unto the prophet spoken
Was writ on tables yet unbroken;
The word by seers or sibyls told,
In groves of oak, or fanes of gold,
Still floats upon the morning wind,
Still whispers to the willing mind.
One accent of the Holy Ghost
The heedless world hath never lost.
I know what say the fathers wise,—
The Book itself before me lies,
Old Chrysostom, best Augustine,
And he who blent both in his line,
The younger Golden Lips or mines,
Taylor, the Shakespeare of divines.
His words are music in my ear,
I see his cowlëd portrait dear;
And yet, for all his faith could see,
I would not the good bishop be.

Bacchus

Bring me wine, but wine which never grew
In the belly of the grape,
Or grew on vine whose tap-roots, reaching through
Under the Andes to the Cape,
Suffered no savor of the earth to 'scape.

Let its grapes the morn salute
From a nocturnal root,
Which feels the acrid juice
Of Styx and Erebus;
And turns the woe of Night,
By its own craft, to a more rich delight.

We buy ashes for bread;
We buy diluted wine;
Give me of the true,—
Whose ample leaves and tendrils curled
Among the silver hills of heaven
Draw everlasting dew;
Wine of wine,
Blood of the world,
Form of forms, and mold of statures,
That I intoxicated,
And by the draught assimilated,
May float at pleasure through all natures;
The bird-language rightly spell,
And that which roses say so well.

Wine that is shed
Like the torrents of the sun
Up the horizon walls,
Or like the Atlantic streams, which run
When the South Sea calls.

Water and bread,
Food which needs no transmuting,
Rainbow-flowering, wisdom-fruiting,
Wine which is already man,
Food which teach and reason can.

Wine which Music is,—
Music and wine are one,—
That I, drinking this,
Shall hear far Chaos talk with me;
Kings unborn shall walk with me;
And the poor grass shall plot and plan
What it will do when it is man.

Quickened so, will I unlock
Every crypt of every rock.

I thank the joyful juice
For all I know;—
Winds of remembering
Of the ancient being blow,
And seeming-solid walls of use
Open and flow.

Pour, Bacchus! the remembering wine;
Retrieve the loss of me and mine!
Vine for vine be antidote,
And the grape requite the lote!
Haste to cure the old despair,—
Reason in Nature's lotus drenched,
The memory of ages quenched;
Give them again to shine;
Let wine repair what this undid;
And where the infection slid,
A dazzling memory revive;
Refresh the faded tints,
Recut the agèd prints,
And write my old adventures with the pen
Which on the first day drew,
Upon the tablets blue,
The dancing Pleiads and eternal men.

The Snow-Storm

Announced by all the trumpets of the sky,
Arrives the snow, and, driving o'er the fields,
Seems nowhere to alight: the whited air
Hides hills and woods, the river, and the heaven,
And veils the farm-house at the garden's end.
The sled and traveller stopped, the courier's feet
Delayed, all friends shut out, the house-mates sit
Around the radiant fireplace, enclosed
In a tumultuous privacy of storm.

Come see the north wind's masonry.
Out of an unseen quarry evermore
Furnished with tile, the fierce artificer
Curves his white bastions with projected roof
Round every windward stake, or tree, or door.
Speeding, the myriad-handed, his wild work
So fanciful, so savage, naught cares he
For number or proportion. Mockingly,

On coop or kennel he hangs Parian wreaths;
A swan-like form invests the hidden thorn;
Fills up the farmer's lane from wall to wall,
Maugre the farmer's sighs; and at the gate
A tapering turret overtops the work.
And when his hours are numbered, and the world
Is all his own, retiring, as he were not,
Leaves, when the sun appears, astonished Art
To mimic in slow structures, stone by stone,
Built in an age, the mad wind's night-work,
The frolic architecture of the snow.

From "Saadi"

Trees in groves,
Kine in droves,
In ocean sport the scaly herds,
Wedge-like cleave the air the birds,
To northern lakes fly wind-borne ducks,
Browse the mountain sheep in flocks,
Men consort in camp and town,
But the poet dwells alone.

Brahma

If the red slayer think he slays,
    Or if the slain think he is slain,
They know not well the subtle ways
    I keep, and pass, and turn again.

Far or forgot to me is near;
    Shadow and sunlight are the same;
The vanished gods to me appear;
    And one to me are shame and fame.

They reckon ill who leave me out;
    When me they fly, I am the wings;
I am the doubter and the doubt,
    And I the hymn the Brahmin sings.

The strong gods pine for my abode,
    And pine in vain the sacred Seven;
But thou, meek lover of the good!
    Find me, and turn thy back on heaven.

The Rhodora

ON BEING ASKED, WHENCE IS THE FLOWER

In May, when sea-winds pierced our solitudes,
I found the fresh Rhodora in the woods,

Spreading its leafless blooms in a damp nook,
To please the desert and the sluggish brook.
The purple petals, fallen in the pool,
Made the black water with their beauty gay;
Here might the red-bird come, his plumes to cool,
And court the flower that cheapens his array.
Rhodora! if the sages ask thee why
This charm is wasted on the earth and sky,
Tell them, dear, that if eyes were made for seeing,
Then Beauty is its own excuse for being:
Why thou wert there, O rival of the Rose!
I never thought to ask, I never knew:
But in my simple ignorance suppose
The self-same Power that brought me there brought you.

Forbearance

Hast thou named all the birds without a gun?
Loved the wood-rose, and left it on its stalk?
At rich men's tables eaten bread and pulse?
Unarmed, faced danger with a heart of trust?
And loved so well a high behavior,
In man or maid, that thou from speech refrained,
Nobility more nobly to repay?
O, be my friend, and teach me to be thine!

Merlin

Thy trivial harp will never please
Or fill my craving ear;
Its chords should ring as blows the breeze,
Free, peremptory, clear.
No jingling serenader's art,
Nor tinkle of piano strings,
Can make the wild blood start
In its mystic springs.
The kingly bard
Must smite the chords rudely and hard,
As with hammer or with mace;
That they may render back
Artful thunder, which conveys
Secrets of the solar track,
Sparks of the supersolar blaze.
Merlin's blows are strokes of fate,
Chiming with the forest tone,
When boughs buffet boughs in the wood;
Chiming with the gasp and moan
Of the ice-imprisoned flood;
With the pulse of manly hearts;

With the voice of orators;
With the din of city arts;
With the cannonade of wars;
With the marches of the brave;
And prayers of might from martyr's cave.

Great is the art,
Great be the manners, of the bard.
He shall not his brain encumber
With the coil of rhythm and number;
But, leaving rule and pale forethought,
He shall aye climb
For his rhyme.
"Pass in, pass in," the angels say,
"Into the upper doors,
Nor count compartments of the floors,
But mount to paradise
By the stairway of surprise."

Blameless master of the games,
King of sport that never shames,
He shall daily joy dispense
Hid in song's sweet influence.
Forms more cheerly live and go,
What time the subtle mind
Sings aloud the tune whereto
Their pulses beat,
And march their feet,
And their members are combined.

By Sybarites beguiled,
He shall no task decline;
Merlin's mighty line
Extremes of nature reconciled,
Bereaved a tyrant of his will,
And made the lion mild.
Songs can the tempest still,
Scattered on the stormy air,
Mould the year to fair increase,
And bring in poetic peace.

He shall not seek to weave,
In weak, unhappy times,
Efficacious rhymes;
Wait his returning strength.
Bird that from the nadir's floor
To the zenith's top can soar.—
The soaring orbit of the muse exceeds that
    journey's length.

Nor profane affect to hit
Or compass that, by meddling wit,
Which only the propitious mind
Publishes when 'tis inclined.

There are open hours
When the God's will sallies free,
And the dull idiot might see
The flowing fortunes of a thousand years;
Sudden, at unawares,
Self-moved, fly-to the doors,
Nor sword of angels could reveal
What they conceal.

Days

Daughters of Time, the hypocritic Days,
Muffled and dumb like barefoot dervishes,
And marching single in an endless file,
Bring diadems and fagots in their hands.
To each they offer gifts after his will,
Bread, kingdoms. stars, and sky that holds them all.
I, in my pleachëd garden, watched the pomp,
Forgot my morning wishes, hastily
Took a few herbs and apples, and the Day
Turned and departed silent. I, too late,
Under her solemn fillet saw the scorn.

"Give All to Love"

Give all to love;
Obey thy heart;
Friends, kindred, days,
Estate, good-fame,
Plans, credit, and the Muse,—
Nothing refuse.

'Tis a brave master;
Let it have scope:
Follow it utterly,
Hope beyond hope:
High and more high
It dives into noon,
With wing unspent,
Untold intent;
But it is a god,
Knows its own path
And the outlets of the sky.

It was never for the mean;
It requireth courage stout.
Souls above doubt,
Valor unbending,
It will reward,—
They shall return
More than they were,
And ever ascending.

Leave all for love;
Yet, hear me, yet,
One word more thy heart behoved,
One pulse more of firm endeavor,—
Keep thee to-day,
To-morrow, forever,
Free as an Arab
Of thy beloved.

Cling with life to the maid;
But when the surprise,
First vague shadow of surmise,
Flits across her bosom young,
Of a joy apart from thee,
Free be she, fancy-free;
Nor thou detain her vesture's hem,
Nor the palest rose she flung
From her summer diadem.

Though thou loved her as thyself,
As a self of purer clay,
Though her parting dims the day,
Stealing grace from all alive;
Heartily know,
When half-gods go,
The gods arrive.

Concord Hymn

SUNG AT THE COMPLETION OF THE BATTLE MONUMENT,
APRIL 19, 1836

By the rude bridge that arched the flood,
  Their flag to April's breeze unfurled,
Here once the embattled farmers stood,
  And fired the shot heard round the world.

The foe long since in silence slept;
  Alike the conqueror silent sleeps;

And Time the ruined bridge has swept
   Down the dark stream which seaward creeps.

On this green bank, by this soft stream,
   We set to-day a votive stone;
That memory may their deed redeem,
   When, like our sires, our sons are gone.

Spirit, that made those heroes dare
   To die, and leave their children free,
Bid Time and Nature gently spare
   The shaft we raise to them and thee.

Ode

SUNG IN THE TOWN HALL, CONCORD, JULY 4, 1857

O tenderly the haughty day
   Fills his blue urn with fire;
One morn is in the mighty heaven,
   And one in our desire.

The cannon booms from town to town,
   Our pulses beat not less,
The joy-bells chime their tidings down,
   Which children's voices bless.

For He that flung the broad blue fold
   O'er-mantling land and sea,
One third part of the sky unrolled
   For the banner of the free.

The men are ripe of Saxon kind
   To build an equal state,—
To take the statute from the mind
   And make of duty fate.

United States! the ages plead,—
   Present and Past in under-song,—
Go put your creed into your deed,
   Nor speak with double tongue.

For sea and land don't understand
   Nor skies without a frown
See rights for which the one hand fights
   By the other cloven down.

Be just at home; then write your scroll
   Of honor o'er the sea,

And bid the broad Atlantic roll
  A ferry of the free.

And henceforth there shall be no chain,
  Save underneath the sea
The wires shall murmur through the main
  Sweet songs of liberty.

The conscious stars accord above,
  The waters wild below,
And under, through the cable wove,
  Her fiery errands go.

For He that worketh high and wise,
  Nor pauses in His plan,
Will take the sun out of the skies
  Ere freedom out of man.

Good-Bye

Good-bye, proud world! I'm going home:
Thou art not my friend, and I'm not thine.
Long through thy weary crowds I roam;
A river-ark on the ocean brine,
Long I've been tossed like the driven foam;
But now, proud world! I'm going home.

Good-bye to Flattery's fawning face;
To Grandeur with his wise grimace;
To upstart Wealth's averted eye;
To supple Office, low and high;
To crowded halls, to court and street;
To frozen hearts and hasting feet;
To those who go, and those who come;
Good-bye, proud world! I'm going home.

I am going to my own hearth-stone,
Bosomed in yon green hills alone,—
A secret nook in a pleasant land,
Whose groves the frolic fairies planned;
Where arches green, the livelong day,
Echo the blackbird's roundelay,
And vulgar feet have never trod—
A spot that is sacred to thought and God.

O, when I am safe in my sylvan home,
I tread on the pride of Greece and Rome;
And when I am stretched beneath the pines,

Where the evening star so holy shines,
I laugh at the lore and the pride of man,
At the sophist schools, and the learned clan;
For what are they all, in their high conceit,
When man in the bush with God may meet?

SARAH HELEN WHITMAN (1803-1878)

Sonnets

FROM THE SERIES RELATING TO EDGAR ALLAN POE

3

On our lone pathway bloomed no earthly hopes:
Sorrow and death were near us, as we stood
Where the dim forest, from the upland slopes,
Swept darkly to the sea. The enchanted wood
Thrilled, as by some foreboding terror stirred;
And as the waves broke on the lonely shore,
In their low monotone, methought I heard
A solemn voice that sighed, "Ye meet no more."
There, while the level sunbeams seemed to burn
Through the long aisles of red, autumnal gloom,—
Where stately, storied cenotaphs inurn
Sweet human hopes, too fair on Earth to bloom,—
Was the bud reaped, whose petals pure and cold
Sleep on my heart till Heaven the flower unfold.

4

If thy sad heart, pining for human love,
In its earth solitude grew dark with fear,
Lest the high Sun of Heaven itself should prove
Powerless to save from that phantasmal sphere
Wherein thy spirit wandered,—if the flowers
That pressed around thy feet, seemed but to bloom
In lone Gethsemanes, through starless hours,
When all who loved had left thee to thy doom,—
Oh, yet believe that, in that hollow vale
Where thy soul lingers, waiting to attain
So much of Heaven's sweet grace as shall avail
To lift its burden of remorseful pain,
My soul shall meet thee, and its Heaven forego
Till God's great love, on both, one hope, one
    Heaven bestow.

NATHANIEL PARKER WILLIS (1806-1867)

Unseen Spirits

The shadows lay along Broadway,
  'Twas near the twilight-tide,
And slowly there a lady fair
  Was walking in her pride.
Alone walked she; but, viewlessly,
  Walked spirits at her side.

Peace charmed the street beneath her feet,
  And Honor charmed the air;
And all astir looked kind on her,
  And called her good as fair,
For all God ever gave to her
  She kept with chary care.

She kept with care her beauties rare
  From lovers warm and true,
For her heart was cold to all but gold,
  And the rich came not to woo—
But honored well are charms to sell
  If priests the selling do.

Now walking there was one more fair—
  A slight girl, lily-pale;
And she had unseen company
  To make the spirit quail:
'Twixt Want and Scorn she walked forlorn,
  And nothing could avail.

No mercy now can clear her brow
  For this world's peace to pray;
For, as love's wild prayer dissolved in air,
  Her woman's heart gave way!—
But the sin forgiven by Christ in heaven
  By man is cursed alway!

CHARLES FENNO HOFFMAN (1806-1884)

Monterey

We were not many—we who stood
  Before the iron sleet that day—

Yet many a gallant spirit would
Give half his years if he then could
    Have been with us at Monterey.

Now here, now there, the shot, it hailed
    In deadly drifts of fiery spray,
Yet not a single soldier quailed
When wounded comrades round them wailed
    Their dying shout at Monterey.

And on—still on our column kept
    Through walls of flame its withering way;
Where fell the dead, the living stept,
Still charging on the guns which swept
    The slippery streets of Monterey.

The foe himself recoiled aghast,
    When, striking where he strongest lay,
We swooped his flanking batteries past,
And braving full their murderous blast,
    Stormed home the towers of Monterey.

Our banners on those turrets wave;
    And there our evening bugles play;
Where orange boughs above their grave
Keep green the memory of the brave
    Who fought and fell at Monterey.

We are not many,—we who pressed
    Beside the brave who fell that day;
But who of us has not confessed
He'd rather share their warrior rest
    Than not have been at Monterey?

HENRY WADSWORTH LONGFELLOW (1807-1882)

Hymn to the Night

I heard the trailing garments of the Night
    Sweep through her marble halls!
I saw her sable skirts all fringed with light
    From the celestial walls!

I felt her presence, by its spell of might,
    Stoop o'er me from above;
The calm, majestic presence of the Night,
    As of the one I love.

I heard the sounds of sorrow and delight,
  The manifold, soft chimes,
That fill the haunted chambers of the Night,
  Like some old poet's rhymes.

From the cool cisterns of the midnight air
  My spirit drank repose;
The fountain of perpetual peace flows there,—
  From those deep cisterns flows.

O holy Night! from thee I learn to bear
  What man has borne before!
Thou layest thy finger on the lips of Care,
  And they complain no more.

Peace! Peace! Orestes-like I breathe this prayer!
  Descend with broad-winged flight,
The welcome, the thrice-prayed for, the most fair,
  The best-belovèd Night!

A Psalm of Life

WHAT THE HEART OF THE YOUNG MAN SAID TO THE
PSALMIST

Tell me not, in mournful numbers,
  Life is but an empty dream!—
For the soul is dead that slumbers,
  And things are not what they seem.

Life is real! Life is earnest!
  And the grave is not its goal;
Dust thou art, to dust returnest,
  Was not spoken of the soul.

Not enjoyment, and not sorrow,
  Is our destined end or way;
But to act, that each to-morrow
  Find us farther than to-day.

Art is long, and Time is fleeting,
  And our hearts, though stout and brave,
Still, like muffled drums, are beating
  Funeral marches to the grave.

In the world's broad field of battle,
  In the bivouac of Life,
Be not like dumb, driven cattle!
  Be a hero in the strife!

Trust no Future, howe'er pleasant!
Let the dead Past bury its dead!
Act,—act in the living Present!
Heart within, and God o'erhead!

Lives of great men all remind us
We can make our lives sublime,
And, departing, leave behind us
Footprints on the sands of time;

Footprints, that perhaps another,
Sailing o'er life's solemn main,
A forlorn and shipwrecked brother,
Seeing, shall take heart again.

Let us, then, be up and doing,
With a heart for any fate;
Still achieving, still pursuing,
Learn to labor and to wait.

The Skeleton in Armor

"Speak! speak! thou fearful guest!
Who, with thy hollow breast
Still in rude armor drest,
Comest to daunt me!
Wrapt not in Eastern balms,
But with thy fleshless palms
Stretched, as if asking alms,
Why dost thou haunt me?"

Then from those cavernous eyes
Pale flashes seemed to rise,
As when the Northern skies
Gleam in December;
And, like the water's flow
Under December's snow,
Came a dull voice of woe
From the heart's chamber.

"I was a Viking old!
My deeds, though manifold,
No Skald in song has told,
 No Saga taught thee!
Take heed that in thy verse
Thou dost the tale rehearse,
Else dread a dead man's curse;
For this I sought thee.

"Far in the Northern Land,
By the wild Baltic's strand,
I, with my childish hand,
    Tamed the gerfalcon;
And, with my skates fast-bound,
Skimmed the half-frozen Sound,
That the poor whimpering hound
    Trembled to walk on.

"Oft to his frozen lair
Tracked I the grisly bear,
While from my path the hare
    Fled like a shadow;
Oft through the forest dark
Followed the were-wolf's bark,
Until the soaring lark
    Sang from the meadow.

"But when I older grew,
Joining a corsair's crew,
O'er the dark sea I flew
    With the marauders.
Wild was the life we led;
Many the souls that sped,
Many the hearts that bled,
    By our stern orders.

"Many a wassail-bout
Wore the long Winter out;
Often our midnight shout
    Set the cocks crowing,
As we the Berserk's tale
Measured in cups of ale,
Draining the oaken pail
    Filled to o'erflowing.

"Once as I told in glee
Tales of the stormy sea,
Soft eyes did gaze on me,
    Burning yet tender;
And as the white stars shine
On the dark Norway pine,
On that dark heart of mine
    Fell their soft splendor.

"I wooed the blue-eyed maid,
Yielding, yet half afraid,
And in the forest's shade
    Our vows were plighted.

Under its loosened vest
Fluttered her little breast,
Like birds within their nest
    By the hawk frighted.

"Bright in her father's hall
Shields gleamed upon the wall,
Loud sang the minstrels all,
    Chanting his glory;
When of old Hildebrand
I asked his daughter's hand,
Mute did the minstrels stand
    To hear my story.

"While the brown ale he quaffed,
Loud then the champion laughed,
And as the wind-gusts waft
    The sea-foam brightly,
So the loud laugh of scorn,
Out of those lips unshorn,
From the deep drinking-horn
    Blew the foam lightly.

"She was a Prince's child,
I but a Viking wild,
And though she blushed and smiled,
    I was discarded!
Should not the dove so white
Follow the sea-mew's flight?
Why did they leave that night
    Her nest unguarded?

"Scarce had I put to sea,
Bearing the maid with me,—
Fairest of all was she
    Among the Norsemen!—
When on the white sea-strand,
Waving his armëd hand,
Saw we old Hildebrand,
    With twenty horsemen.

"Then launched they to the blast,
Bent like a reed each mast,
Yet we were gaining fast,
    When the wind failed us;
And with a sudden flaw
Came round the gusty Skaw,
So that our foe we saw
    Laugh as he hailed us.

"And as to catch the gale
Round veered the flapping sail,
'Death!' was the helmsman's hail,
   'Death without quarter!'
Midships with iron keel
Struck we her ribs of steel;
Down her black hulk did reel
   Through the black water!

"As with his wings aslant,
Sails the fierce cormorant,
Seeking some rocky haunt,
   With his prey laden,
So toward the open main,
Beating to sea again,
Through the wild hurricane,
   Bore I the maiden.

"Three weeks we westward bore,
And when the storm was o'er,
Cloud-like we saw the shore
   Stretching to leeward;
There for my lady's bower
Built I the lofty tower,
Which, to this very hour,
   Stands looking seaward.

"There lived we many years;
Time dried the maiden's tears;
She had forgot her fears,
   She was a mother;
Death closed her mild blue eyes;
Under that tower she lies;
Ne'er shall the sun arise
   On such another.

"Still grew my bosom then,
Still as a stagnant fen!
Hateful to me were men,
   The sunlight hateful!
In the vast forest here,
Clad in my warlike gear,
Fell I upon my spear,
   Oh, death was grateful!

"Thus, seamed with many scars,
Bursting these prison bars,
Up to its native stars
   My soul ascended!

There from the flowing bowl
Deep drinks the warrior's soul,
Skoal! to the Northland! *skoal!"*
Thus the tale ended.

The Village Blacksmith

Under a spreading chestnut-tree
  The village smithy stands;
The smith, a mighty man is he,
  With large and sinewy hands;
And the muscles of his brawny arms
  Are strong as iron bands.

His hair is crisp, and black, and long,
  His face is like the tan;
His brow is wet with honest sweat,
  He earns whate'er he can,
And looks the whole world in the face,
  For he owes not any man.

Week in, week out, from morn till night,
  You can hear his bellows blow;
You can hear him swing his heavy sledge
  With measured beat and slow,
Like a sexton ringing the village bell,
  When the evening sun is low.

And children coming home from school
  Look in at the open door;
They love to see the flaming forge,
  And hear the bellows roar,
And catch the burning sparks that fly
  Like chaff from a threshing-floor.

He goes on Sunday to the church,
  And sits among his boys;
He hears the parson pray and preach,
  He hears his daughter's voice,
Singing in the village choir,
  And it makes his heart rejoice.

It sounds to him like her mother's voice,
  Singing in Paradise!
He needs must think of her once more,
  How in the grave she lies;
And with his hard, rough hand he wipes
  A tear out of his eyes.

Toiling,—rejoicing,—sorrowing,
    Onward through life he goes;
Each morning sees some task begun,
    Each evening sees its close;
Something attempted, something done,
    Has earned a night's repose.

Thanks, thanks to thee, my worthy friend,
    For the lesson thou hast taught!
Thus at the flaming forge of life
    Our fortunes must be wrought;
Thus on its sounding anvil shaped
    Each burning deed and thought!

From "Tales of a Wayside Inn"

PRELUDE

A youth was there, of quiet ways,
A student of old books and days,
To whom all tongues and lands were known,
And yet a lover of his own;
With many a social virtue graced,
And yet a friend of solitude;
A man of such a genial mood
The heart of all things he embraced,
And yet of such fastidious taste,
He never found the best too good.
Books were his passion and delight,
And in his upper room at home
Stood many a rare and sumptuous tome,
In vellum bound, with gold bedight,
Great volumes garmented in white,
Recalling Florence, Pisa, Rome.
He loved the twilight that surrounds
The border-land of old romance;
Where glitter hauberk, helm, and lance,
And banner waves, and trumpet sounds,
And ladies ride with hawk on wrist,
And mighty warriors sweep along,
Magnified by the purple mist,
The dusk of centuries and of song.
The chronicles of Charlemagne,
Of Merlin and the Mort d'Arthure,
Mingled together in his brain
With tales of Flores and Blanchefleur,
Sir Ferumbras, Sir Eglamour,
Sir Launcelot, Sir Morgadour,
Sir Guy, Sir Bevis, Sir Gawain.

From "The Spanish Student"

SERENADE

Stars of the summer night!
    Far in yon azure deeps,
Hide, hide your golden light!
    She sleeps!
My lady sleeps!
    Sleeps!

Moon of the summer night!
    Far down yon western steeps,
Sink, sink in silver light!
    She sleeps!
My lady sleeps!
    Sleeps!

Wind of the summer night!
    Where yonder woodbine creeps,
Fold, fold thy pinions light!
    She sleeps!
My lady sleeps!
    Sleeps!

Dreams of the summer night!
    Tell her, her lover keeps
Watch! while in slumbers light
    She sleeps!
My lady sleeps!
    Sleeps!

The Arrow and the Song

I shot an arrow into the air,
It fell to earth, I knew not where;
For, so swiftly it flew, the sight
Could not follow it in its flight.

I breathed a song into the air,
It fell to earth, I knew not where;
For who has sight so keen and strong
That it can follow the flight of song?

Long, long afterward, in an oak
I found the arrow, still unbroke;
And the song, from beginning to end,
I found again in the heart of a friend.

Song of the Silent Land

FROM THE GERMAN OF SALIS

Into the Silent Land!
Ah! who shall lead us thither?
Clouds in the evening sky more darkly gather,
And shattered wrecks lie thicker on the strand.
Who leads us with a gentle hand
Thither, oh, thither,
Into the Silent Land?

Into the Silent Land!
To you, ye boundless regions
Of all perfection! Tender morning-visions
Of beauteous souls! The Future's pledge and band!
Who in Life's battle firm doth stand,
Shall bear Hope's tender blossoms
Into the Silent Land!

O Land! O Land!
For all the broken-hearted
The mildest herald by our fate allotted,
Beckons, and with inverted torch doth stand
To lead us with a gentle hand
To the land of the great Departed,
Into the Silent Land!

(After von Salis-Seewis.)

From "Evangeline"

A TALE OF ACADIE

This is the forest primeval. The murmuring pines and the
    hemlocks,
Bearded with moss, and in garments green, indistinct in the
    twilight,
Stand like Druids of old, with voices sad and prophetic,
Stand like harpers hoar, with beards that rest on their bosoms.
Loud from its rocky caverns, the deep-voiced neighboring
    ocean
Speaks, and in accents disconsolate answers the wail of the
    forest.

  This is the forest primeval; but where are the hearts that
    beneath it

Leaped like the roe, when he hears in the woodland the voice
   of the huntsman?
Where is the thatch-roofed village, the home of Acadian
   farmers,—
Men whose lives glided on like rivers that water the wood-
   lands,
Darkened by shadows of earth, but reflecting an image of
   heaven?
Waste are those pleasant farms, and the farmers forever de-
   parted!
Scattered like dust and leaves, when the mighty blasts of
   October
Seize them, and whirl them aloft, and sprinkle them far o'er
   the ocean.
Naught but tradition remains of the beautiful village of
   Grand-Pré.

   Ye who believe in affection that hopes, and endures, and
      is patient,
Ye who believe in the beauty and strength of woman's de-
   votion,
List to the mournful tradition still sung by the pines of the
   forest;
List to a Tale of Love in Acadie, home of the happy.

From "The Building of the Ship"

THE REPUBLIC

Thou, too, sail on, O Ship of State!
Sail on, O UNION, strong and great!
Humanity with all its fears,
With all the hopes of future years,
Is hanging breathless on thy fate!
We know what Master laid thy keel,
What Workmen wrought thy ribs of steel,
Who made each mast, and sail, and rope,
What anvils rang, what hammers beat,
In what a forge and what a heat
Were shaped the anchors of thy hope!
Fear not each sudden sound and shock,
'Tis of the wave and not the rock;
'Tis but the flapping of the sail,
And not a rent made by the gale!
In spite of rock and tempest's roar,
In spite of false lights on the shore,
Sail on, nor fear to breast the sea!

Our hearts, our hopes, are all with thee,
Our hearts, our hopes, our prayers, our tears,
Our faith triumphant o'er our fears,
Are all with thee,—are all with thee!

"The Song of Hiawatha"

INTRODUCTION

Should you ask me, whence these stories?
Whence these legends and traditions,
With the odors of the forest,
With the dew and damp of meadows,
With the curling smoke of wigwams,
With the rushing of great rivers,
With their frequent repetitions,
And their wild reverberations,
As of thunder in the mountains?
   I should answer, I should tell you,
"From the forests and the prairies,
From the great lakes of the Northland,
From the land of the Ojibways,
From the land of the Dacotahs,
From the mountains, moors, and fen-lands,
Where the heron, the Shuh-shuh-gah,
Feeds among the reeds and rushes.
I repeat them as I heard them
From the lips of Nawadaha,
The musician, the sweet singer."
   Should you ask where Nawadaha
Found these songs, so wild and wayward,
Found these legends and traditions,
I should answer, I should tell you,
   "In the bird's-nests of the forest,
In the lodges of the beaver,
In the hoof-prints of the bison,
In the eyrie of the eagle!
   "All the wild-fowl sang them to him,
In the moorlands and the fen-lands,
In the melancholy marshes;
Chetowaik, the plover, sang them,
Mahng, the loon, the wild-goose, Wawa,
The blue heron, the Shuh-shuh-gah,
And the grouse, the Mushkodasa!"
   If still further you should ask me,
Saying, "Who was Nawadaha?
Tell us of this Nawadaha,"

I should answer your inquiries
Straightway in such words as follow:
"In the Vale of Tawasentha,
In the green and silent valley,
By the pleasant watercourses,
Dwelt the singer Nawadaha.
Round about the Indian village
Spread the meadows and the cornfields,
And beyond them stood the forest,
Stood the groves of singing pine-trees,
Green in Summer, white in Winter,
Ever sighing, ever singing.

"And the pleasant watercourses,
You could trace them through the valley,
By the rushing in the Spring-time,
By the alders in the Summer,
By the white fog in the Autumn,
By the black line in the Winter;
And beside them dwelt the singer,
In the vale of Tawasentha,
In the green and silent valley.

"There he sang of Hiawatha,
Sang the Song of Hiawatha,
Sang his wondrous birth and being,
How he prayed and how he fasted,
How he lived, and toiled, and suffered,
That the tribes of men might prosper,
That he might advance his people!"

Ye who love the haunts of Nature,
Love the sunshine of the meadow,
Love the shadow of the forest,
Love the wind among the branches,
And the rain-shower and the snow-storm,
And the rushing of great rivers
Through their palisades of pine-trees,
And the thunder in the mountains,
Whose innumerable echoes
Flap like eagles in their eyries;—
Listen to these wild traditions,
To this Song of Hiawatha!

Ye who love a nation's legends,
Love the ballads of a people,
That like voices from afar off
Waving like a hand that beckons,
Call to us to pause and listen,
Speak in tones so plain and childlike,
Scarcely can the ear distinguish
Whether they are sung or spoken;—

Listen to this Indian Legend,
To this Song of Hiawatha!
    Ye whose hearts are fresh and simple,
Who have faith in God and Nature,
Who believe, that in all ages
Every human heart is human,
That in even savage bosoms
There are longings, yearnings, strivings
For the good they comprehend not,
That the feeble hands and helpless,
Groping blindly in the darkness,
Touch God's right hand in that darkness
And are lifted up and strengthened;—
Listen to this simple story,
To this Song of Hiawatha!
    Ye who, sometimes, in your rambles
Through the green lanes of the country,
Where the tangled barberry-bushes
Hang their tufts of crimson berries
Over stone walls gray with mosses,
Pause by some neglected graveyard,
For a while to muse, and ponder
On a half-effaced inscription,
Written with little skill of song-craft,
Homely phrases, but each letter
Full of hope, and yet of heart-break,
Full of all the tender pathos
Of the Here and the Hereafter;—
Stay and read this rude inscription,
Read this Song of Hiawatha!

My Lost Youth

Often I think of the beautiful town
    That is seated by the sea;
Often in thought go up and down
The pleasant streets of that dear old town,
    And my youth comes back to me.
        And a verse of a Lapland song
        Is haunting my memory still:
    "A boy's will is the wind's will,
And the thoughts of youth are long, long thoughts."

I can see the shadowy lines of its trees,
    And catch, in sudden gleams,
The sheen of the far-surrounding seas,
And islands that were the Hesperides

Of all my boyish dreams.
  And the burden of that old song,
  It murmurs and whispers still:
  "A boy's will is the wind's will,
And the thoughts of youth are long, long thoughts."

I remember the black wharves and the slips,
  And the sea-tides tossing free;
And Spanish sailors with bearded lips,
And the beauty and mystery of the ships,
  And the magic of the sea.
    And the voice of that wayward song
    Is singing and saying still:
    "A boy's will is the wind's will,
And the thoughts of youth are long, long thoughts."

I remember the bulwarks by the shore,
  And the fort upon the hill;
The sunrise gun, with its hollow roar,
The drum-beat repeated o'er and o'er,
  And the bugle wild and shrill.
    And the music of that old song
    Throbs in my memory still:
    "A boy's will is the wind's will,
And the thoughts of youth are long, long thoughts."

I remember the sea-fight far away,
  How it thundered o'er the tide!
And the dead captains, as they lay
In their graves, o'erlooking the tranquil bay
  Where they in battle died.
    And the sound of that mournful song
    Goes through me with a thrill:
    "A boy's will is the wind's will,
And the thoughts of youth are long, long thoughts."

I can see the breezy dome of groves,
  The shadows of Deering's Woods;
And the friendships old and the early loves
Come back with a Sabbath sound, as of doves
  In quiet neighborhoods.
    And the verse of that sweet old song,
    It flutters and murmurs still:
    "A boy's will is the wind's will,
And the thoughts of youth are long, long thoughts."

I remember the gleams and glooms that dart
  Across the school-boy's brain;
The song and the silence in the heart,

That in part are prophecies, and in part
  Are longings wild and vain.
    And the voice of that fitful song
    Sings on, and is never still:
    "A boy's will is the wind's will,
And the thoughts of youth are long, long thoughts."

There are things of which I may not speak;
  There are dreams that cannot die;
There are thoughts that make the strong heart weak,
And bring a pallor into the cheek,
  And a mist before the eye.
    And the words of that fatal song
    Come over me like a chill:
    "A boy's will is the wind's will,
And the thoughts of youth are long, long thoughts."

Strange to me now are the forms I meet
  When I visit the dear old town;
But the native air is pure and sweet,
And the trees that o'ershadow each well-known street,
  As they balance up and down,
    Are singing the beautiful song,
    Are sighing and whispering still:
    "A boy's will is the wind's will,
And the thoughts of youth are long, long thoughts."

And Deering's Woods are fresh and fair,
  And with joy that is almost pain
My heart goes back to wander there,
And among the dreams of the days that were,
  I find my lost youth again.
    And the strange and beautiful song,
    The groves are repeating it still:
    "A boy's will is the wind's will,
And the thoughts of youth are long, long thoughts."

The Reaper and the Flowers

There is a Reaper, whose name is Death,
  And, with his sickle keen,
He reaps the bearded grain at a breath,
  And the flowers that grow between.

"Shall I have naught that is fair?" saith he;
  "Have naught but the bearded grain?
Though the breath of these flowers is sweet to me,
  I will give them all back again."

He gazed at the flowers with tearful eyes,
  He kissed their drooping leaves;
It was for the Lord of Paradise
  He bound them in his sheaves.

"My Lord has need of these flowerets gay,"
  The Reaper said, and smiled;
"Dear tokens of the earth are they,
  Where He was once a child.

"They shall all bloom in fields of light,
  Transplanted by my care,
And saints, upon their garments white,
  These sacred blossoms wear."

And the mother gave, in tears and pain,
  The flowers she most did love;
She knew she should find them all again
  In the fields of light above.

Oh, not in cruelty, not in wrath,
  The Reaper came that day;
'Twas an angel visited the green earth,
  And took the flowers away.

"The Day Is Done"

The day is done, and the darkness
  Falls from the wings of Night,
As a feather is wafted downward
  From an eagle in his flight.

I see the lights of the village
  Gleam through the rain and the mist,
And a feeling of sadness comes o'er me
  That my soul cannot resist:

A feeling of sadness and longing,
  That is not akin to pain,
And resembles sorrow only
  As the mist resembles rain.

Come, read to me some poem,
  Some simple and heartfelt lay,
That shall soothe this restless feeling,
  And banish the thoughts of day.

Not from the grand old masters,
  Not from the bards sublime,

Whose distant footsteps echo
  Through the corridors of Time.

For, like strains of martial music,
  Their mighty thoughts suggest
Life's endless toil and endeavor;
  And to-night I long for rest.

Read from some humbler poet,
  Whose songs gushed from his heart,
As showers from the clouds of summer,
  Or tears from the eyelids start;

Who, through long days of labor,
  And nights devoid of ease,
Still heard in his soul the music
  Of wonderful melodies.

Such songs have power to quiet
  The restless pulse of care,
And come like the benediction
  That follows after prayer.

Then read from the treasured volume
  The poem of thy choice,
And lend to the rhyme of the poet
  The beauty of thy voice;

And the night shall be filled with music,
  And the cares, that infest the day,
Shall fold their tents, like the Arabs,
  And as silently steal away.

Chaucer

An old man in a lodge within a park;
The chamber walls depicted all around
With portraitures of huntsman, hawk, and hound,
And the hurt deer. He listeneth to the lark,
Whose song comes with the sunshine through the **dark**
Of painted glass in leaden lattice bound;
He listeneth and he laugheth at the sound,
Then writeth in a book like any clerk.
He is the poet of the dawn, who wrote
The Canterbury Tales, and his old age
Made beautiful with song; and as I read
I hear the crowing cock, I hear the note
Of lark and linnet, and from every page
Rise odors of ploughed field or flowery mead.

The Cross of Snow

In the long, sleepless watches of the night,
  A gentle face—the face of one long dead—
  Looks at me from the wall, where round its head
The night-lamp casts a halo of pale light.
Here in this room she died; and soul more white
  Never through martyrdom of fire was led
  To its repose; nor can in books be read
The legend of a life more benedight.
There is a mountain in the distant West
  That, sun-defying, in its deep ravines,
  Displays a cross of snow upon its side.
Such is the cross I wear upon my breast
  These eighteen years, through all the changing scenes
  And seasons, changeless since the day she died.

Nature

As a fond mother, when the day is o'er,
  Leads by the hand her little child to bed,
  Half willing, half reluctant to be led,
  And leave his broken playthings on the floor,
Still gazing at them through the open door,
  Nor wholly reassured and comforted
  By promises of others in their stead,
  Which, though more splendid, may not please him more;
So Nature deals with us, and takes away
  Our playthings one by one, and by the hand
  Leads us to rest so gently that we go
Scarce knowing if we wish to go or stay,
  Being too full of sleep to understand
  How far the unknown transcends the what we know.

JOHN GREENLEAF WHITTIER (1807-1892)

Proem

(WRITTEN TO INTRODUCE THE FIRST GENERAL
COLLECTION OF HIS POEMS)

    I love the old melodious lays
Which softly melt the ages through,
    The songs of Spenser's golden days,
    Arcadian Sidney's silvery phrase,
Sprinkling our noon of time with freshest morning dew.

    Yet, vainly in my quiet hours
To breathe their marvellous notes I try;

I feel them, as the leaves and flowers
In silence feel the dewy showers,
And drink with glad, still lips the blessing of the sky.

The rigor of a frozen clime,
The harshness of an untaught ear,
The jarring words of one whose rhyme
Beat often Labor's hurried time,
Or Duty's rugged march through storm and strife, are here.

Of mystic beauty, dreamy grace,
No rounded art the lack supplies;
Unskilled the subtle lines to trace,
Or softer shades of Nature's face,
I view her common forms with unanointed eyes.

Nor mine the seer-like power to show
The secrets of the heart and mind;
To drop the plummet-line below
Our common world of joy and woe,
A more intense despair or brighter hope to find.

Yet here at least an earnest sense
Of human right and weal is shown;
A hate of tyranny intense,
And hearty in its vehemence,
As if my brother's pain and sorrow were my own.

O Freedom! if to me belong
Nor mighty Milton's gift divine,
Nor Marvell's wit and graceful song,
Still with a love as deep and strong
As theirs, I lay, like them, my best gifts on thy shrine!

The Farewell

OF A VIRGINIA SLAVE MOTHER TO HER DAUGHTERS SOLD INTO SOUTHERN BONDAGE

Gone, gone,—sold and gone,
To the rice-swamp dank and lone.
Where the slave-whip ceaseless swings,
Where the noisome insect stings,
Where the fever demon strews
Poison with the falling dews,
Where the sickly sunbeams glare
Through the hot and misty air;
Gone, gone,—sold and gone,
To the rice-swamp dank and lone,
From Virginia's hills and waters;
Woe is me, my stolen daughters!

Gone, gone,—sold and gone,
  To the rice-swamp dank and lone.
There no mother's eye is near them,
There no mother's ear can hear them;
Never, when the torturing lash
Seams their back with many a gash,
Shall a mother's kindness bless them,
Or a mother's arms caress them.
  Gone, gone,—sold and gone,
  To the rice-swamp dank and lone,
  From Virginia's hills and waters;
  Woe is me, my stolen daughters!

Gone, gone,—sold and gone,
  To the rice-swamp dank and lone.
O, when weary, sad, and slow,
From the fields at night they go,
Faint with toil, and racked with pain,
To their cheerless homes again,
There no brother's voice shall greet them;
There no father's welcome meet them.
  Gone, gone,—sold and gone,
  To the rice-swamp dank and lone,
  From Virginia's hills and waters;
  Woe is me, my stolen daughters!

Gone, gone,—sold and gone,
  To the rice-swamp dank and lone.
From the tree whose shadow lay
On their childhood's place of play;
From the cool spring where they drank;
Rock, and hill, and rivulet bank;
From the solemn house of prayer,
And the holy counsels there;
  Gone, gone,—sold and gone,
  To the rice-swamp dank and lone,
  From Virginia's hills and waters;
  Woe is me, my stolen daughters!

Gone, gone,—sold and gone,
  To the rice-swamp dank and lone.
Toiling through the weary day,
And at night the spoiler's prey.
Oh, that they had earlier died,
Sleeping calmly, side by side,
Where the tyrant's power is o'er,
And the fetter galls no more!
  Gone, gone,—sold and gone,

To the rice-swamp dank and lone,
From Virginia's hills and waters;
Woe is me, my stolen daughters!

Gone, gone,—sold and gone,
  To the rice-swamp dank and lone.
By the holy love He beareth;
By the bruisèd reed He spareth;
Oh, may He, to whom alone
All their cruel wrongs are known,
Still their hope and refuge prove,
With a more than mother's love.
  Gone, gone,—sold and gone,
  To the rice-swamp dank and lone,
  From Virginia's hills and waters;
  Woe is me, my stolen daughters!

The Barefoot Boy

Blessings on thee, little man,
Barefoot boy, with cheek of tan!
With thy turned-up pantaloons,
And thy merry whistled tunes;
With thy red lip, redder still
Kissed by strawberries on the hill;
With the sunshine on thy face,
Through thy torn brim's jaunty grace;
From my heart I give thee joy,—
I was once a barefoot boy!
Prince thou art,—the grown-up man
Only is republican.
Let the million-dollared ride!
Barefoot, trudging at his side,
Thou hast more than he can buy
In the reach of ear and eye,—
Outward sunshine, inward joy:
Blessings on thee, barefoot boy!

Oh for boyhood's painless play,
Sleep that wakes in laughing day,
Health that mocks the doctor's rules,
Knowledge never learned of schools,
Of the wild bee's morning chase,
Of the wild flower's time and place,
Flight of fowl and habitude
Of the tenants of the wood;
How the tortoise bears his shell,
How the woodchuck digs his cell,
And the ground-mole sinks his well;

How the robin feeds her young,
How the oriole's nest is hung;
Where the whitest lilies blow,
Where the freshest berries grow,
Where the ground-nut trails its vine,
Where the wood-grape's clusters shine;
Of the black wasp's cunning way,
Mason of his walls of clay,
And the architectural plans
Of gray hornet artisans!
For, eschewing books and tasks,
Nature answers all he asks;
Hand in hand with her he walks,
Face to face with her he talks,
Part and parcel of her joy,—
Blessings on the barefoot boy!

Oh for boyhood's time of June,
Crowding years in one brief moon,
When all things I heard or saw,
Me, their master, waited for.
I was rich in flowers and trees,
Humming-birds and honey-bees;
For my sport the squirrel played,
Plied the snouted mole his spade;
For my taste the blackberry cone
Purpled over hedge and stone;
Laughed the brook for my delight
Through the day and through the night,—
Whispering at the garden wall,
Talked with me from fall to fall;
Mine the sand-rimmed pickerel pond,
Mine the walnut slopes beyond,
Mine, on bending orchard trees,
Apples of Hesperides!
Still as my horizon grew,
Larger grew my riches too;
All the world I saw or knew
Seemed a complex Chinese toy,
Fashioned for a barefoot boy!

Oh for festal dainties spread,
Like my bowl of milk and bread;
Pewter spoon and bowl of wood,
On the door-stone, gray and rude!
O'er me, like a regal tent,
Cloudy-ribbed, the sunset bent,
Purple-curtained, fringed with gold,
Looped in many a wind-swung fold;

While for music came the play
Of the pied frogs' orchestra;
And, to light the noisy choir,
Lit the fly his lamp of fire.
I was monarch: pomp and joy
Waited on the barefoot boy!

Cheerily, then, my little man,
Live and laugh, as boyhood can!
Though the flinty slopes be hard,
Stubble-speared the new-mown sward,
Every morn shall lead thee through
Fresh baptisms of the dew;
Every evening from thy feet
Shall the cool wind kiss the heat:
All too soon these feet must hide
In the prison cells of pride,
Lose the freedom of the sod,
Like a colt's for work be shod,
Made to tread the mills of toil,
Up and down in ceaseless moil:
Happy if their track be found
Never on forbidden ground;
Happy if they sink not in
Quick and treacherous sands of sin.
Ah! that thou couldst know thy joy,
Ere it passes, barefoot boy!

Maud Muller

Maud Muller on a summer's day
Raked the meadow sweet with hay.

Beneath her torn hat glowed the wealth
Of simple beauty and rustic health.

Singing, she wrought, and her merry glee
The mock-bird echoed from his tree.

But when she glanced to the far-off town,
White from its hill-slope looking down,

The sweet song died, and a vague unrest
And a nameless longing filled her breast,—

A wish that she hardly dared to own,
For something better than she had known.

The Judge rode slowly down the lane,
Smoothing his horse's chestnut mane.

He drew his bridle in the shade
Of the apple-trees, to greet the maid,

And asked a draught from the spring that flowed
Through the meadow across the road.

She stooped where the cool spring bubbled up,
And filled for him her small tin cup,

And blushed as she gave it, looking down
On her feet so bare, and her tattered gown.

"Thanks!" said the Judge; "a sweeter draught
From a fairer hand was never quaffed."

He spoke of the grass and flowers and trees,
Of the singing birds and the humming bees;

Then talked of the haying, and wondered whether
The cloud in the west would bring foul weather.

And Maud forgot her brier-torn gown
And her graceful ankles bare and brown;

And listened, while a pleased surprise
Looked from her long-lashed hazel eyes.

At last, like one who for delay
Seeks a vain excuse, he rode away.

Maud Muller looked and sighed: "Ah me!
That I the Judge's bride might be!

"He would dress me up in silks so fine,
And praise and toast me at his wine.

"My father should wear a broadcloth coat;
My brother should sail a painted boat.

"I'd dress my mother so grand and gay,
And the baby should have a new toy each day.

"And I'd feed the hungry and clothe the poor,
And all should bless me who left our door."

The Judge looked back as he climbed the hill,
And saw Maud Muller standing still.

"A form more fair, a face more sweet,
Ne'er hath it been my lot to meet.

"And her modest answer and graceful air
Show her wise and good as she is fair.

"Would she were mine, and I to-day,
Like her, a harvester of hay;

"No doubtful balance of rights and wrongs,
Nor weary lawyers with endless tongues,

"But low of cattle and song of birds,
And health and quiet and loving words."

But he thought of his sisters, proud and cold,
And his mother, vain of her rank and gold.

So, closing his heart, the Judge rode on,
And Maud was left in the field alone.

But the lawyers smiled that afternoon,
When he hummed in court an old love-tune;

And the young girl mused beside the well
Till the rain on the unraked clover fell.

He wedded a wife of richest dower,
Who lived for fashion, as he for power.

Yet oft, in his marble hearth's bright glow,
He watched a picture come and go;

And sweet Maud Muller's hazel eyes
Looked out in their innocent surprise.

Oft, when the wine in his glass was red,
He longed for the wayside well instead;

And closed his eyes on his garnished rooms
To dream of meadows and clover-blooms.

And the proud man sighed, with a secret pain,
"Ah, that I were free again!

"Free as when I rode that day,
Where the barefoot maiden raked her hay."

She wedded a man unlearned and poor,
And many children played round her door.

But care and sorrow, and childbirth pain,
Left their traces on heart and brain.

And oft, when the summer sun shone hot
On the new-mown hay in the meadow lot,

And she heard the little spring brook fall
Over the roadside, through the wall,

In the shade of the apple-tree again
She saw a rider draw his rein;

And, gazing down with timid grace,
She felt his pleased eyes read her face.

Sometimes her narrow kitchen walls
Stretched away into stately halls;

The weary wheel to a spinet turned,
The tallow candle an astral burned,

And for him who sat by the chimney lug,
Dozing and grumbling o'er pipe and mug,

A manly form at her side she saw,
And joy was duty and love was law.

Then she took up her burden of life again,
Saying only, "It might have been."

Alas for maiden, alas for Judge,
For rich repiner and household drudge!

God pity them both! and pity us all,
Who vainly the dreams of youth recall.

For of all sad words of tongue or pen,
The saddest are these: "It might have been!"

Ah, well! for us all some sweet hope lies
Deeply buried from human eyes;

And, in the hereafter, angels may
Roll the stone from its grave away!

Barbara Frietchie

(SEPTEMBER 13, 1862)

Up from the meadows rich with corn,
Clear in the cool September morn,

The clustered spires of Frederick stand
Green-walled by the hills of Maryland.

Round about them orchards sweep,
Apple and peach tree fruited deep,

Fair as the garden of the Lord
To the eyes of the famished rebel horde,

On that pleasant morn of the early fall
When Lee marched over the mountain-wall;

Over the mountains winding down,
Horse and foot, into Frederick town.

Forty flags with their silver stars,
Forty flags with their crimson bars,

Flapped in the morning wind: the sun
Of noon looked down, and saw not one.

Up rose old Barbara Frietchie then,
Bowed with her fourscore years and ten;

Bravest of all in Frederick town,
She took up the flag the men hauled down;

In her attic window the staff she set,
To show that one heart was loyal yet.

Up the street came the rebel tread.
Stonewall Jackson riding ahead.

Under his slouched hat left and right
He glanced; the old flag met his sight.

"Halt!"—the dust-brown ranks stood fast,
"Fire!"—out blazed the rifle-blast.

It shivered the window, pane and sash;
It rent the banner with seam and gash.

Quick as it fell, from the broken staff
Dame Barbara snatched the silken scarf.

She leaned far out on the window-sill,
And shook it forth with a royal will.

"Shoot, if you must, this old gray head,
But spare your country's flag," she said.

A shade of sadness, a blush of shame,
Over the face of the leader came;

The nobler nature within him stirred
To life at that woman's deed and word;

"Who touches a hair of yon gray head
Dies like a dog! March on!" he said.

All day long through Frederick street
Sounded the tread of marching feet:

All day long that free flag tossed
Over the heads of the rebel host.

Ever its torn folds rose and fell
On the loyal winds that loved it well;

And through the hill-gaps sunset light
Shone over it with a warm good-night.

Barbara Frietchie's work is o'er,
And the Rebel rides on his raids no more.

Honor to her! and let a tear
Fall, for her sake, on Stonewall's bier.

Over Barbara Frietchie's grave,
Flag of Freedom and Union, wave!

Peace and order and beauty draw
Round thy symbol of light and law;

And ever the stars above look down
On thy stars below in Frederick town!

Brown of Ossawatomie

(DECEMBER 2, 1859)

John Brown of Ossawatomie spake on his dying day:
"I will not have to shrive my soul a priest in Slavery's pay.
But let some poor slave-mother whom I have striven to free,
With her children, from the gallows-stair put up a prayer
for me!"

John Brown of Ossawatomie, they led him out to die;
And lo! a poor slave-mother with her little child pressed
nigh.

Then the bold, blue eye grew tender, and the old harsh face
    grew mild,
As he stooped between the jeering ranks and kissed the
    negro's child!

The shadows of his stormy life that moment fell apart;
And they who blamed the bloody hand forgave the loving
    heart.
That kiss from all its guilty means redeemed the good intent,
And round the grisly fighter's hair the martyr's aureole bent!

Perish with him the folly that seeks through evil good!
Long live the generous purpose unstained with human blood!
Not the raid of midnight terror, but the thought which un-
    derlies;
Not the borderer's pride of daring, but the Christian sacri-
    fice.

Nevermore may yon Blue Ridges the Northern rifle hear,
Nor see the light of blazing homes flash on the negro's spear;
But let the free-winged angel Truth their guarded passes
    scale,
To teach that right is more than might, and justice more
    than mail!

So vainly shall Virginia set her battle in array;
In vain her trampling squadrons knead the winter snow with
    clay.
She may strike the pouncing eagle, but she dares not harm
    the dove;
And every gate she bars to Hate, shall open wide to Love!

The Eternal Goodness

O friends! with whom my feet have trod
    The quiet aisles of prayer,
Glad witness to your zeal for God
    And love of man I bear.

I trace your lines of argument;
    Your logic linked and strong
I weigh as one who dreads dissent,
    And fears a doubt as wrong.

But still my human hands are weak
    To hold your iron creeds:
Against the words ye bid me speak
    My heart within me pleads.

Who fathoms the Eternal Thought?
　Who talks of scheme and plan?
The Lord is God! He needeth not
　The poor device of man.

I walk with bare, hushed feet the ground
　Ye tread with boldness shod;
I dare not fix with mete and bound
　The love and power of God.

Ye praise His justice; even such
　His pitying love I deem:
Ye seek a king; I fain would touch
　The robe that hath no seam.

Ye see the curse which overbroods
　A world of pain and loss;
I hear our Lord's beatitudes
　And prayer upon the cross.

More than your schoolmen teach, within
　Myself, alas! I know:
Too dark ye cannot paint the sin,
　Too small the merit show.

I bow my forehead to the dust,
　I veil mine eyes for shame,
And urge, in trembling self-distrust,
　A prayer without a claim.

I see the wrong that round me lies,
　I feel the guilt within;
I hear, with groan and travail-cries,
　The world confess its sin.

Yet, in the maddening maze of things,
　And tossed by storm and flood,
To one fixed trust my spirit clings;
　I know that God is good!

Not mine to look where cherubim
　And seraphs may not see,
But nothing can be good in Him
　Which evil is in me.

The wrong that pains my soul below
　I dare not throne above,
I know not of His hate,—I know
　His goodness and His love.

I dimly guess from blessings known
　　Of greater out of sight,
And, with the chastened Psalmist, own
　　His judgments too are right.

I long for household voices gone,
　　For vanished smiles I long,
But God hath led my dear ones on,
　　And He can do no wrong.

I know not what the future hath
　　Of marvel or surprise,
Assured alone that life and death
　　His mercy underlies.

And if my heart and flesh are weak
　　To bear an untried pain,
The bruisëd reed He will not break,
　　But strengthen and sustain.

No offering of my own I have,
　　Nor works my faith to prove;
I can but give the gifts He gave,
　　And plead His love for love.

And so beside the Silent Sea
　　I wait the muffled oar;
No harm from Him can come to me
　　On ocean or on shore.

I know not where His islands lift
　　Their fronded palms in air;
I only know I cannot drift
　　Beyond His love and care.

O brothers! if my faith is vain,
　　If hopes like these betray,
Pray for me that my feet may gain
　　The sure and safer way.

And Thou, O Lord! by whom are seen
　　Thy creatures as they be,
Forgive me if too close I lean
　　My human heart on Thee!

SAMUEL FRANCIS SMITH (1808-1895)

America

My country, 'tis of thee,
Sweet land of liberty,
　　Of thee I sing;

Land where my fathers died,
Land of the pilgrims' pride,
From every mountain-side
    Let freedom ring.

My native country, thee,
Land of the noble free,—
    Thy name I love;
I love thy rocks and rills,
Thy woods and templed hills;
My heart with rapture thrills
    Like that above.

Let music swell the breeze,
And ring from all the trees,
    Sweet freedom's song;
Let mortal tongues awake,
Let all that breathe partake,
Let rocks their silence break,—
    The sound prolong.

Our fathers' God, to Thee,
Author of liberty,
    To Thee I sing;
Long may our land be bright
With freedom's holy light;
Protect us by thy might,
    Great God our King.

EDGAR ALLAN POE (1809-1849)

To Helen

Helen, thy beauty is to me
    Like those Nicæan barks of yore,
That gently, o'er a perfumed sea,
    The weary, wayworn wanderer bore
    To his own native shore.

On desperate seas long wont to roam,
    Thy hyacinth hair, thy classic face,
Thy Naiad airs, have brought me home
    To the glory that was Greece
    And the grandeur that was Rome.

Lo! in yon brilliant window-niche
    How statue-like I see thee stand,
The agate lamp within thy hand!
    Ah, Psyche, from the regions which
    Are Holy Land!

The Raven

Once upon a midnight dreary, while I pondered, weak and
    weary,
Over many a quaint and curious volume of forgotten lore,—
While I nodded, nearly napping, suddenly there came a tap-
    ping,
As of some one gently rapping, rapping at my chamber door.
" 'Tis some visitor," I muttered, "tapping at my chamber door:
    Only this and nothing more."

Ah, distinctly I remember it was in the bleak December,
And each separate dying ember wrought its ghost upon the
    floor.
Eagerly I wished the morrow;—vainly I had sought to borrow
From my books surcease of sorrow—sorrow for the lost
    Lenore,
For the rare and radiant maiden whom the angels name
    Lenore:
    Nameless here for evermore.

And the silken sad uncertain rustling of each purple curtain
Thrilled me—filled me with fantastic terrors never felt be-
    fore;
So that now, to still the beating of my heart, I stood repeating
" 'Tis some visitor entreating entrance at my chamber door,
Some late visitor entreating entrance at my chamber door:
    This it is and nothing more."

Presently my soul grew stronger; hesitating then no longer,
"Sir," said I, "or Madam, truly your forgiveness I implore;
But the fact is I was napping, and so gently you came rapping,
And so faintly you came tapping, tapping at my chamber door,
That I scarce was sure I heard you"—here I opened wide the
    door:—
    Darkness there and nothing more.

Deep into that darkness peering, long I stood there wonder-
    ing, fearing,
Doubting, dreaming dreams no mortals ever dared to dream
    before;
But the silence was unbroken, and the stillness gave no token,
And the only word there spoken was the whispered word,
    "Lenore?"
This I whispered, and an echo murmured back the word,
    "Lenore":
    Merely this and nothing more.

Back into the chamber turning, all my soul within me burning,
Soon again I heard a tapping somewhat louder than before.
"Surely," said I, "surely that is something at my window
  lattice;
Let me see, then, what thereat is, and this mystery explore;
Let my heart be still a moment and this mystery explore:
  'Tis the wind and nothing more."

Open here I flung the shutter, when, with many a flirt and
  flutter,
In there stepped a stately Raven of the saintly days of yore.
Not the least obeisance made he; not a minute stopped or
  stayed he;
But, with mien of lord or lady, perched above my chamber
  door,
Perched upon a bust of Pallas just above my chamber door:
  Perched, and sat, and nothing more.

Then this ebony bird beguiling my sad fancy into smiling
By the grave and stern decorum of the countenance it wore,—
"Though thy crest be shorn and shaven, thou," I said, "art
  sure no craven,
Ghastly grim and ancient Raven wandering from the Nightly
  shore:
Tell me what thy lordly name is on the Night's Plutonian
  shore!"
  Quoth the Raven, "Nevermore."

Much I marvelled this ungainly fowl to hear discourse so
  plainly,
Though its answer little meaning—little relevancy bore;
For we cannot help agreeing that no living human being
Ever yet was blessed with seeing bird above his chamber
  door,
Bird or beast upon the sculptured bust above his chamber
  door,
  With such name as "Nevermore."

But the Raven, sitting lonely on the placid bust, spoke only
That one word, as if his soul in that one word he did outpour.
Nothing further then he uttered, not a feather then he flut-
  tered,
Till I scarcely more than muttered,—"Other friends have
  flown before;
On the morrow *he* will leave me, as my Hopes have flown
  before."
  Then the bird said, "Nevermore."

Startled at the stillness broken by reply so aptly spoken,
"Doubtless," said I, "what it utters is its only stock and
  store,
Caught from some unhappy master whom unmerciful Disaster
Followed fast and followed faster till his songs one burden
  bore:
Till the dirges of his Hope that melancholy burden bore
  Of 'Never—nevermore.' "

But the Raven still beguiling all my fancy into smiling,
Straight I wheeled a cushioned seat in front of bird and bust
  and door;
Then, upon the velvet sinking, I betook myself to linking
Fancy unto fancy, thinking what this ominous bird of yore,
What this grim, ungainly, ghastly, gaunt, and ominous bird
  of yore
  Meant in croaking "Nevermore."

This I sat engaged in guessing, but no syllable expressing
To the fowl whose fiery eyes now burned into my bosom's
  core;
This and more I sat divining, with my head at ease reclining
On the cushion's velvet lining that the lamp-light gloated o'er
But whose velvet violet lining with the lamp-light gloating o'er
  She shall press, ah, nevermore!

Then, methought, the air grew denser, perfumed from an
  unseen censer
Swung by seraphim whose foot-falls tinkled on the tufted
  floor.
"Wretch," I cried, "thy God hath lent thee—by these angels
  he hath sent thee
Respite—respite and nepenthe from thy memories of Lenore!
Quaff, oh quaff this kind nepenthe, and forget this lost
  Lenore!"
  Quoth the Raven, "Nevermore."

"Prophet!" said I, "thing of evil! prophet still, if bird or
  devil!
Whether Tempter sent, or whether tempest tossed thee here
  ashore,
Desolate yet all undaunted, on this desert land enchanted—
On this home by Horror haunted—tell me truly, I implore:
Is there—is there balm in Gilead?—tell me—tell me, I
  implore!"
  Quoth the Raven, "Nevermore."

"Prophet!" said I, "thing of evil—prophet still, if bird or
  devil!

By that Heaven that bends above us, by that God we both
    adore,
Tell this soul with sorrow laden if, within the distant Aidenn,
It shall clasp a sainted maiden whom the angels name Lenore:
Clasp a rare and radiant maiden whom the angels name
    Lenore!"
Quoth the Raven, "Nevermore."

"Be that word our sign of parting, bird or fiend!" I shrieked,
    upstarting:
"Get thee back into the tempest and the Night's Plutonian
    shore!
Leave no black plume as a token of that lie thy soul hath
    spoken!
Leave my loneliness unbroken! quit the bust above my door!
Take thy beak from out my heart, and take thy form from
    off my door!"
Quoth the Raven, "Nevermore."

And the Raven, never flitting, still is sitting, still is sitting,
On the pallid bust of Pallas just above my chamber door;
And his eyes have all the seeming of a demon's that is
    dreaming,
And the lamp-light o'er him streaming throws his shadow on
    the floor:
And my soul from out that shadow that lies floating on the
    floor
    Shall be lifted—nevermore!

To One in Paradise

Thou wast all that to me, love,
    For which my soul did pine:
A green isle in the sea, love,
    A fountain and a shrine
All wreathed with fairy fruits and flowers,
    And all the flowers were mine.

Ah, dream too bright to last!
    Ah, starry Hope, that didst arise
But to be overcast!
    A voice from out the Future cries,
"On! on!"—but o'er the Past
    (Dim gulf!) my spirit hovering lies
Mute, motionless, aghast.

For, alas! alas! with me
    The light of Life is o'er!
No more—no more—no more—

(Such language holds the solemn sea
  To the sands upon the shore)
Shall bloom the thunder-blasted tree,
  Or the stricken eagle soar.

And all my days are trances,
  And all my nightly dreams
Are where thy gray eye glances,
  And where thy footstep gleams—
In what ethereal dances,
  By what eternal streams.

The City in the Sea

Lo! Death has reared himself a throne
In a strange city lying alone
Far down within the dim West,
Where the good and the bad and the worst and
    the best
Have gone to their eternal rest.
There shrines and palaces and towers
(Time-eaten towers that tremble not)
Resemble nothing that is ours.
Around, by lifting winds forgot,
Resignedly beneath the sky
The melancholy waters lie.
No rays from the holy heaven come down
On the long night-time of that town;
But light from out the lurid sea
Streams up the turrets silently,
Gleams up the pinnacles far and free:
Up domes, up spires, up kingly halls,
Up fanes, up Babylon-like walls,
Up shadowy long-forgotten bowers
Of sculptured ivy and stone flowers,
Up many and many a marvellous shrine
Whose wreathèd friezes intertwine
The viol, the violet, and the vine.

Resignedly, beneath the sky
The melancholy waters lie.
So blend the turrets and shadows there
That all seem pendulous in air,
While from a proud tower in the town
Death looks gigantically down.

There open fanes and gaping graves
Yawn level with the luminous waves;
But not the riches there that lie

In each idol's diamond eye,—
Not the gaily-jewelled dead,
Tempt the waters from their bed;
For no ripples curl, alas,
Along that wilderness of glass;
No swellings tell that winds may be
Upon some far-off happier sea;
No heavings hint that winds have been
On seas less hideously serene!

But lo, a stir is in the air!
The wave—there is a movement there!
As if the towers had thrust aside,
In slightly sinking, the dull tide;
As if their tops had feebly given
A void within the filmy Heaven!
The waves have now a redder glow,
The hours are breathing faint and low;
And when, amid no earthly moans,
Down, down, that town shall settle hence,
Hell, rising from a thousand thrones,
Shall do it reverence.

Israfel

And the angel Israfel, whose heart-strings are a lute, and who has the sweetest voice of all God's creatures.—
KORAN.

In Heaven a spirit doth dwell
    Whose heart-strings are a lute;
None sing so wildly well
As the angel Israfel,
And the giddy stars (so legends tell),
Ceasing their hymns, attend the spell
    Of his voice, all mute.

Tottering above
    In her highest noon,
    The enamoured moon
Blushes with love,
    While, to listen, the red levin
    (With the rapid Pleiads, even,
    Which were seven)
    Pauses in Heaven.

And they say (the starry cnoir
    And the other listening things)
That Israfel's fire

Is owing to that lyre
  By which he sits and sings,
The trembling living wire
  Of those unusual strings.

But the skies that angel trod,
  Where deep thoughts are a duty,
Where Love's a grown-up God,
Where the Houri glances are
  Imbued with all the beauty
Which we worship in a star.

Therefore thou art not wrong,
  Israfel, who despisest
An unimpassioned song;
To thee the laurels belong,
  Best bard, because the wisest:
Merrily live, and long!

The ecstasies above
  With thy burning measures suit:
Thy grief, thy joy, thy hate, thy love,
  With the fervor of thy lute:
  Well may the stars be mute!

Yes, Heaven is thine; but this
  Is a world of sweets and sours;
  Our flowers are merely—flowers,
And the shadow of thy perfect bliss
  Is the sunshine of ours.

If I could dwell
Where Israfel
  Hath dwelt,.and he where I,
He might not sing so wildly well
  A mortal melody,
While a bolder note than this might swell
  From my lyre within the sky.

Annabel Lee

It was many and many a year ago,
  In a kingdom by the sea,
That a maiden there lived whom you may know
  By the name of Annabel Lee;
And this maiden she lived with no other thought
  Than to love and be loved by me.

I was a child and she was a child,
  In this kingdom by the sea,
But we loved with a love that was more than love,
  I and my Annabel Lee;
With a love that the wingéd seraphs of heaven
  Coveted her and me.

And this was the reason that, long ago,
  In this kingdom by the sea,
A wind blew out of a cloud, chilling
  My beautiful Annabel Lee;
So that her highborn kinsmen came
  And bore her away from me,
To shut her up in a sepulchre
  In this kingdom by the sea.

The angels, not half so happy in heaven,
  Went envying her and me;
Yes! that was the reason (as all men know,
  In this kingdom by the sea)
That the wind came out of the cloud by night,
  Chilling and killing my Annabel Lee.

But our love it was stronger by far than the love
  Of those who were older than we,
  Of many far wiser than we;
And neither the angels in heaven above,
  Nor the demons down under the sea,
Can ever dissever my soul from the soul
  Of the beautiful Annabel Lee:
For the moon never beams, without bringing me dreams
  Of the beautiful Annabel Lee;

And the stars never rise, but I feel the bright eyes
  Of the beautiful Annabel Lee;
And so, all the night-tide, I lie down by the side
Of my darling—my darling—my life and my bride,
  In her sepulchre there by the sea,
  In her tomb by the sounding sea.

Ulalume

The skies they were ashen and sober;
  The leaves they were crispéd and sere,
  The leaves they were withering and sere;
It was night in the lonesome October
  Of my most immemorial year;
It was night by the dim lake of Auber,
  In the misty mid region of Weir:
It was down by the dank tarn of Auber,
  In the ghoul-haunted woodland of Weir.

Here once, through an alley Titanic
    Of cypress, I roamed with my Soul—
    Of cypress, with Psyche, my Soul.
These were days when my heart was volcanic
    As the scoriac rivers that roll,
    As the lavas that restlessly roll
Their sulphurous currents down Yaanek
    In the ultimate climes of the pole,
That groan as they roll down Mount Yaanek
    In the realms of the boreal pole.

Our talk had been serious and sober,
    But our thoughts they were palsied and sere,
    Our memories were treacherous and sere,
For we knew not the month was October,
    And we marked not the night of the year,
    (Ah, night of all nights in the year!)
We noted not the dim lake of Auber
    (Though once we had journeyed down here),
Remembered not the dank tarn of Auber
    Nor the ghoul-haunted woodland of Weir.

And now, as the night was senescent
    And star-dials pointed to morn,
    As the star-dials hinted of morn,
At the end of our path a liquescent
    And nebulous lustre was born,
Out of which a miraculous crescent
    Arose with a duplicate horn,
Astarte's bediamonded crescent
    Distinct with its duplicate horn.

And I said—"She is warmer than Dian:
    She rolls through an ether of sighs,
    She revels in a region of sighs:
She has seen that the tears are not dry on
    These cheeks, where the worm never dies,
And has come past the stars of the Lion
    To point us the path to the skies,
    To the Lethean peace of the skies:
Come up, in despite of the Lion,
    To shine on us with her bright eyes:
Come up through the lair of the Lion,
    With love in her luminous eyes."

But Psyche, uplifting her finger,
    Said—"Sadly this star I mistrust,
    Her pallor I strangely mistrust:
Oh, hasten!—oh, let us not linger!
    Oh, fly!—let us fly!—for we must."

In terror she spoke, letting sink her
    Wings until they trailed in the dust;
In agony sobbed, letting sink her
    Plumes till they trailed in the dust,
    Till they sorrowfully trailed in the dust.

I replied—"This is nothing but dreaming:
    Let us on by this tremulous light!
    Let us bathe in this crystalline light!
Its sibyllic splendor is beaming
    With hope and in beauty to-night:
    See, it flickers up the sky through the night!
Ah, we safely may trust to its gleaming,
    And be sure it will lead us aright:
We safely may trust to a gleaming
    That cannot but guide us aright,
    Since it flickers up to Heaven through the night."

Thus I pacified Psyche and kissed her,
    And tempted her out of her gloom,
    And conquered her scruples and gloom;
And we passed to the end of the vista,
    But were stopped by the door of a tomb,
    By the door of a legended tomb;
And I said—"What is written, sweet sister,
    On the door of this legended tomb?"
    She replied—"Ulalume—Ulalume—
    'Tis the vault of thy lost Ulalume!"

Then my heart it grew ashen and sober
    As the leaves that were crispèd and sere,
    As the leaves that were withering and sere,
And I cried—"It was surely October
    On this very night of last year
    That I journeyed—I journeyed down here,
    That I brought a dread burden down here:
    On this night of all nights in the year,
    Ah, what demon has tempted me here?
Well I know, now, this dim lake of Auber,
    This misty mid region of Weir:
Well I know, now, this dank tarn of Auber,
    This ghoul-haunted woodland of Weir."

OLIVER WENDELL HOLMES (1809-1894)

The Last Leaf

I saw him once before,
As he passed by the door,

And again
The pavement stones resound,
As he totters o'er the ground
    With his cane.

They say that in his prime,
Ere the pruning-knife of Time
    Cut him down,
Not a better man was found
By the Crier on his round
    Through the town.

But now he walks the streets,
And he looks at all he meets
    Sad and wan,
And he shakes his feeble head,
That it seems as if he said,
    "They are gone."

The mossy marbles rest
On the lips that he has prest
    In their bloom,
And the names he loved to hear
Have been carved for many a year
    On the tomb.

My grandmamma has said—
Poor old lady, she is dead
    Long ago—
That he had a Roman nose,
And his cheek was like a rose
    In the snow;

But now his nose is thin,
And it rests upon his chin
    Like a staff,
And a crook is in his back,
And a melancholy crack
    In his laugh.

I know it is a sin
For me to sit and grin
    At him here;
But the old three-cornered hat,
And the breeches, and all that,
    Are so queer!

And if I should live to be
The last leaf upon the tree
    In the spring,

Let them smile, as I do now,
At the old forsaken bough
Where I cling.

The Height of the Ridiculous

I wrote some lines once on a time
In wondrous merry mood,
And thought, as usual, men would say
They were exceeding good.

They were so queer, so very queer,
I laughed as I would die;
Albeit, in the general way,
A sober man am I.

I called my servant, and he came;
How kind it was of him
To mind a slender man like me,
He of the mighty limb.

"These to the printer," I exclaimed,
And, in my humorous way,
I added (as a trifling jest,)
"There'll be the devil to pay."

He took the paper, and I watched,
And saw him peep within;
At the first line he read, his face
Was all upon the grin.

He read the next; the grin grew broad,
And shot from ear to ear;
He read the third; a chuckling noise
I now began to hear.

The fourth; he broke into a roar;
The fifth; his waistband split;
The sixth; he burst five buttons off,
And tumbled in a fit.

Ten days and nights, with sleepless eye,
I watched that wretched man,
And since, I never dare to write
As funny as I can.

A Logical Story—The Deacon's Masterpiece, or the Won-
derful "One-Hoss Shay"

Have you heard of the wonderful one-hoss shay,
That was built in such logical way
It ran a hundred years to a day,
And then, of a sudden, it—ah, but stay,
I'll tell you what happened without delay,
Scaring the parson into fits,
Frightening people out of their wits,—
Have you ever heard of that, I say?

Seventeen hundred and fifty-five.
Georgius Secundus was then alive,—
Snuffy old drone from the German hive.
That was the year when Lisbon-town
Saw the earth open and gulp her down,
And Braddock's army was done so brown,
Left without a scalp to its crown.
It was on the terrible Earthquake-day
That the Deacon finished the one-hoss shay.

Now in building of chaises, I tell you what,
There is always *somewhere* a weakest spot,—
In hub, tire, felloe, in spring or thill,
In panel, or crossbar, or floor, or sill,
In screw, bolt, thoroughbrace,—lurking still,
Find it somewhere you must and will,—
Above or below, or within or without,—
And that's the reason, beyond a doubt,
That a chaise *breaks down,* but doesn't *wear out.*

But the Deacon swore (as Deacons do,
With an "I dew vum," or an "I tell *yeou,*")
He would build one shay to beat the taown
'N' the keounty 'n' all the kentry raoun';
It should be so built that it *couldn'* break daown:
"Fur," said the Deacon, "'t's mighty plain
Thut the weakes' place mus' stan' the strain;
'N' the way t' fix it, uz I maintain,
          Is only jest
T' make that place uz strong uz the rest."

So the Deacon inquired of the village folk
Where he could find the strongest oak,
That couldn't be split nor bent nor broke,—
That was for spokes and floor and sills;
He sent for lancewood to make the thills;
The crossbars were ash, from the straightest trees,
The panels of white-wood, that cuts like cheese,
But lasts like iron for things like these;
The hubs of logs from the "Settler's ellum,"—

Last of its timber,—they couldn't sell 'em,
Never an axe had seen their chips,
And the wedges flew from between their lips,
Their blunt ends frizzled like celery-tips;
Step and prop-iron, bolt and screw,
Spring, tire, axle, and linchpin too,
Steel of the finest, bright and blue;
Thoroughbrace bison-skin, thick and wide;
Boot, top, dasher, from tough old hide
Found in the pit when the tanner died.
That was the way he "put her through."
"There!" said the Deacon, "naow she'll dew!"

Do! I tell you, I rather guess
She was a wonder, and nothing less!
Colts grew horses, beards turned gray,
Deacon and deaconess dropped away,
Children and grandchildren—where were they?
But there stood the stout old one-hoss shay
As fresh as on Lisbon-earthquake-day!

EIGHTEEN HUNDRED;—it came and found
The Deacon's masterpiece strong and sound.
Eighteen hundred increased by ten;
"Hahnsum kerridge," they called it then.
Eighteen hundred and twenty came;—
Running as usual; much the same.
Thirty and Forty at last arrive,
And then come Fifty, and FIFTY-FIVE.

Little of all we value here
Wakes on the morn of its hundredth year
Without both feeling and looking queer.
In fact, there's nothing that keeps its youth,
So far as I know, but a tree and truth.
(This is a moral that runs at large;
Take it.—You're welcome.—No extra charge.)

FIRST OF NOVEMBER,—the Earthquake-day,—
There are traces of age in the one-hoss shay.
A general flavor of mild decay,
But nothing local, as one may say.
There couldn't be,—for the Deacon's art
Had made it so like in every part
That there wasn't a chance for one to start.
For the wheels were just as strong as the thills,
And the floor was just as strong as the sills,
And the panels just as strong as the floor,
And the whipple-tree neither less nor more,

And the back-crossbar as strong as the fore,
And spring and axle and hub *encore*.
And yet, *as a whole*, it is past a doubt
In another hour it will be *worn out!*

First of November, Fifty-five!
This morning the parson takes a drive.
Now, small boys, get out of the way!
Here comes the wonderful one-hoss shay,
Drawn by a rat-tailed, ewe-necked bay.
"Huddup!" said the parson.—Off went they.

The parson was working his Sunday's text,—
Had got to *fifthly,* and stopped perplexed
At what the—Moses—was coming next.
All at once the horse stood still,
Close by the meet'n'-house on the hill.
First a shiver, and then a thrill,
Then something decidedly like a spill,—
And the parson was sitting upon a rock,
At half past nine by the meet'n'-house clock,—
Just the hour of the Earthquake shock!
What do you think the parson found,
When he got up and stared around?
The poor old chaise in a heap or mound,
As if it had been to the mill and ground!
You see, of course, if you're not a dunce,
How it went to pieces all at once,—
All at once, and nothing first,—
Just as bubbles do when they burst.

End of the wonderful one-hoss shay.
Logic is logic. That's all I say.

The Living Temple

Not in the world of light alone,
Where God has built his blazing throne,
Nor yet alone in earth below,
With belted seas that come and go,
And endless isles of sunlit green,
Is all thy Maker's glory seen:
Look in upon thy wondrous frame,—
Eternal wisdom still the same!
The smooth, soft air with pulse-like waves
Flows murmuring through its hidden caves,
Whose streams of brightening purple rush,
Fired with a new and livelier blush,

While all their burden of decay
The ebbing current steals away,
And red with Nature's flame they start
From the warm fountains of the heart.

No rest that throbbing slave may ask,
Forever quivering o'er his task,
While far and wide a crimson jet
Leaps forth to fill the woven net
Which in unnumbered crossing tides
The flood of burning life divides,
Then, kindling each decaying part,
Creeps back to find the throbbing heart.

But warmed with that unchanging flame
Behold the outward moving frame,
Its living marbles jointed strong
With glistening band and silvery thong,
And linked to reason's guiding reins
By myriad rings in trembling chains,
Each graven with the threaded zone
Which claims it as the master's own.

See how yon beam of seeming white
Is braided out of seven-hued light,
Yet in those lucid globes no ray
By any chance shall break astray.
Hark how the rolling surge of sound,
Arches and spirals circling round,
Wakes the hushed spirit through thine ear
With music it is heaven to hear.

Then mark the cloven sphere that holds
All thought in its mysterious folds;
That feels sensation's faintest thrill,
And flashes forth the sovereign will;
Think on the stormy world that dwells
Locked in its dim and clustering cells!
The lightning gleams of power it sheds
Along its hollow glassy threads!

O Father! grant thy love divine
To make these mystic temples thine!
When wasting age and wearying strife
Have sapped the leaning walls of life,
When darkness gathers over all,
And the last tottering pillars fall,
Take the poor dust thy mercy warms,
And mould it into heavenly forms!

The Chambered Nautilus

This is the ship of pearl, which, poets feign,
    Sails the unshadowed main,—
    The venturous bark that flings
On the sweet summer wind its purpled wings
In gulfs enchanted, where the Siren sings,
    And coral reefs lie bare,
Where the cold sea-maids rise to sun their streaming hair.

Its webs of living gauze no more unfurl;
    Wrecked is the ship of pearl!
    And every chambered cell,
Where its dim dreaming life was wont to dwell,
As the frail tenant shaped his growing shell,
    Before thee lies revealed,—
Its irised ceiling rent, its sunless crypt unsealed!

Year after year beheld the silent toil
    That spread his lustrous coil;
    Still, as the spiral grew.
He left the past year's dwelling for the new,
Stole with soft step its shining archway through,
    Built up its idle door,
Stretched in his last-found home, and knew the old no
        more.

Thanks for the heavenly message brought by thee,
    Child of the wandering sea,
    Cast from her lap, forlorn!
From thy dead lips a clearer note is born
Than ever Triton blew from wreathëd horn!
    While on mine ear it rings,
Through the deep caves of thought I hear a voice that
        sings :—

Build thee more stately mansions, O my soul,
    As the swift seasons roll!
    Leave thy low-vaulted past!
Let each new temple, nobler than the last,
Shut thee from heaven with a dome more vast,
    Till thou at length art free,
Leaving thine outgrown shell by life's unresting sea!

ALBERT PIKE (1809-1891)

Dixie

I wish I was in de land ob cotton,
Old times dar am not forgotten;

Look away, look away, look away, Dixie land!
In Dixie land whar I was born in,
Early on one frosty mornin',
　　Look away, look away, look away, Dixie land!

Chorus—Den I wish I was in Dixie! Hooray! Hooray!
　　　　In Dixie's land we'll took our stand, to lib
　　　　　　an' die in Dixie,
　　　　　　Away, away, away down south in Dixie!
　　　　　　Away, away, away down south in Dixie!

Old missus marry Will de weaber,
William was a gay deceaber,
When he put his arm around 'er,
He looked as fierce as a forty-pounder.

His face was sharp as a butcher cleaber,
But dat did not seem to greab 'er;
Will run away, missus took a decline, O
Her face was the color of bacon rhine, O.

While missus libbed, she libbed in clover,
When she died, she died all over;
How could she act de foolish part,
An' marry a man to break her heart?

FRANCES SARGENT OSGOOD (1811-1850)

To Sleep

Come to me, angel of the weary hearted!
　　Since they my loved ones, breathed upon by thee,
Unto thy realms unreal have departed,
　　I too may rest—even I: ah! haste to me.

I dare not bid thy darker, colder brother
　　With his more welcome offering appear,
For those sweet lips at morn will murmur, "Mother,"
　　And who shall soothe them if I be not near?

Bring me no dream, dear Sleep, though visions glowing
　　With hues of heaven thy wand enchanted shows;
I ask no glorious boon of thy bestowing,
　　Save that most true, most beautiful,—repose.

I have no heart to roam in realms of Faëry,
　　To follow Fancy at her elfin call:

I am too wretched—too soul-worn and weary;
  Give me but rest, for rest to me is all.

Paint not the Future to my fainting spirit,
  Though it were starred with glory like the skies;
There is no gift immortals may inherit,
  That could rekindle hope in these cold eyes.

And for the Past—the fearful Past—ah! never
  Be Memory's downcast gaze unveiled by thee:
Would thou couldst bring oblivion forever
  Of all that is, that has been, and will be!

ROBERT HINCKLEY MESSINGER (1811-1874)

A Winter Wish

  Old wine to drink!
    Ay, give the slippery juice
That drippeth from the grape thrown loose
    Within the tun;
Plucked from beneath the cliff
Of sunny-sided Teneriffe,
    And ripened 'neath the blink
    Of India's sun!
Tempered with well-boiled water!
    Peat whiskey hot,
These make the long night shorter,—
    Forgetting not
Good stout old English porter.

  Old wood to burn!
Ay, bring the hill-side beech
From where the owlets meet and screech,
    And ravens croak;
The crackling pine, and cedar sweet;
Bring too a clump of fragrant peat,
    Dug 'neath the fern;
    The knotted oak,
    A fagot, too, perhaps,
Whose bright flame, dancing, winking,
Shall light us at our drinking;
    While the oozing sap
Shall make sweet music to our thinking.

  Old books to read!
Ay, bring those nodes of wit,

The brazen-clasped, the vellum writ,
    Time-honored tomes!
The same my sire scanned before,
The same my grandsire thumbëd o'er,
The same his sire from college bore,
    The well-earned meed
        Of Oxford's domes:
        Old Homer blind,
Old Horace, rake Anacreon, by
Old Tully, Plautus, Terence lie;
Mort Arthur's olden minstrelsie,
Quaint Burton, quainter Spenser, ay!
And Gervase Markham's venerie—
    Nor leave behind
The holye Book by which we live and die.

    Old friends to talk!
Ay, bring those chosen few,
The wise, the courtly, and the true,
    So rarely found;
Him for my wine, him for my stud,
Him for my easel, distich, bud
    In mountain walk!
    Bring Walter good,
With soulful Fred, and learned Will,
And thee, my alter ego (dearer still
    For every mood).

These add a bouquet to my wine!
These add a sparkle to my pine!
    If these I tine,
Can books, or fire, or wine be good?

CHRISTOPHER PEARSE CRANCH (1813-1892)

The Pines and the Sea

Beyond the low marsh-meadows and the beach,
Seen through the hoary trunks of windy pines,
The long blue level of the ocean shines.
The distant surf, with hoarse, complaining speech,
Out from its sandy barrier seems to reach;
And while the sun behind the woods declines,
The moaning sea with sighing boughs combines,
And waves and pines make answer, each to each.
O melancholy soul, whom far and near,

In life, faith, hope, the same sad undertone
Pursues from thought to thought! thou needs must hear
An old refrain, too much, too long thine own:
'Tis thy mortality infects thine ear;
The mournful strain was in thyself alone.

JONES VERY (1813-1880)

The Dead

I see them,—crowd on crowd they walk the earth,
Dry leafless trees no autumn wind laid bare;
And in their nakedness find cause for mirth,
And all unclad would winter's rudeness dare;
No sap doth through their clattering branches flow,
Whence springing leaves and blossoms bright appear;
Their hearts the living God have ceased to know
Who gives the springtime to the expectant year.
They mimic life, as if from Him to steal
His glow of health to paint the livid cheek;
They borrow words for thoughts they cannot feel,
That with a seeming heart their tongue may speak;
And in their show of life more dead they live
Than those that to the earth with many tears they give.

EPES SARGENT (1813-1880)

A Life on the Ocean Wave

A life on the ocean wave,
    A home on the rolling deep,
Where the scattered waters rave,
    And the winds their revels keep!
Like an eagle caged, I pine
    On this dull, unchanging shore:
Oh! give me the flashing brine,
    The spray and the tempest's roar!

Once more on the deck I stand
    Of my own swift-gliding craft:
Set sail! farewell to the land!
    The gale follows fair abaft.
We shoot through the sparkling foam
    Like an ocean-bird set free;—
Like the ocean-bird, our home
    We'll find far out on the sea.

The land is no longer in view,
　The clouds have begun to frown;
But with a stout vessel and crew,
　We'll say, Let the storm come down!
And the song of our hearts shall be,
　While the winds and the waters rave,
A home on the rolling sea!
　A life on the ocean wave!

JOHN GODFREY SAXE (1816-1887)

Early Rising

"God bless the man who first invented sleep!"
　So Sancho Pansa said, and so say I:
And bless him, also, that he didn't keep
　His great discovery to himself; nor try
To make it—as the lucky fellow might—
A close monopoly by patent-right.

Yes—bless the man who first invented sleep
　(I really can't avoid the iteration),
But blast the man, with curses loud and deep,
　Whate'er the rascal's name, or age, or station,
Who first invented, and went round advising,
That artificial cut-off, early rising.

"Rise with the lark, and with the lark to bed,"
　Observes some solemn, sentimental owl;
Maxims like these are very cheaply said;
　But, ere you make yourself a fool or fowl,
Pray just inquire about his rise and fall,
And whether larks have any beds at all!

The time for honest folks to be a-bed
　Is in the morning, if I reason right;
And he who cannot keep his precious head
　Upon his pillow till it's fairly light,
And so enjoy his forty morning winks,
Is up to knavery—or else he drinks!

Thompson, who sung about the "Seasons," said
　It was a glorious thing to *rise* in season;
But then he said it lying—in his bed,
　At ten o'clock A.M.,—the very reason
He wrote so charmingly. The simple fact is,
His preaching wasn't sanctioned by his practice.

'Tis, doubtless, well to be sometimes awake,—
  Awake to duty, and awake to truth,—
But when, alas! a nice review we take
  Of our best deeds and days, we find, in sooth,
The hours that leave the slightest cause to weep
Are those we passed in childhood or asleep!

'Tis beautiful to leave the world awhile
  For the soft visions of the gentle night;
And free, at last, from mortal care or guile,
  To live as only in the angels' sight,
In sleep's sweet realm so cosily shut in,
Where, at the worst, we only *dream* of sin!

So let us sleep, and give the Maker praise.
  I like the lad who, when his father thought
To clip his morning nap by hackneyed phrase
  Of vagrant worm by early songster caught,
Cried, "Served him right!—it's not at all surprising;
The worm was punished, sir, for early rising!"

HENRY DAVID THOREAU (1817-1862)

Inspiration

If with light head erect I sing,
Though all the Muses lend their force,
From my poor love of anything,
The verse is weak and shallow as its source.

But if with bended neck I grope
Listening behind me for my wit,
With faith superior to hope,
More anxious to keep back than forward it,—

Making my soul accomplice there
Unto the flame my heart hath lit,
Then will the verse forever wear,—
Time cannot bend the line which God has writ.

I hearing get, who had but ears,
And sight, who had but eyes before;
I moments live, who lived but years,
And truth discern, who knew but learning's lore.

Now chiefly is my natal hour,
And only now my prime of life;

Of manhood's strength it is the flower,
'Tis peace's end, and war's beginning strife.

It comes in summer's broadest noon,
By a gray wall, or some chance place,
Unseasoning time, insulting June,
And vexing day with its presuming face.

I will not doubt the love untold
Which not my worth nor want hath bought,
Which wooed me young, and wooes me old,
And to this evening hath me brought.

Mist

Low-anchored cloud,
Newfoundland air,
Fountain-head and source of rivers,
Dew-cloth, dream-drapery,
And napkin spread by fays;
Drifting meadow of the air,
Where bloom the daisied banks and violets,
And in whose fenny labyrinth
The bittern booms and heron wades;
Spirit of lakes and seas and rivers,—
Bear only perfumes and the scent
Of healing herbs to just men's fields.

WILLIAM ELLERY CHANNING (1818-1901)

From "A Poet's Hope"

Lady, there is a hope that all men have,—
Some mercy for their faults, a grassy place
To rest in, and a flower-strown, gentle grave;
Another hope which purifies our race,
That, when that fearful bourne forever past,
They may find rest,—and rest so long to last.

I seek it not, I ask no rest for ever,
My path is onward to the farthest shores,—
Upbear me in your arms, unceasing river,
That from the soul's clear fountain swiftly pours,
Motionless not, until the end is won,
Which now I feel hath scarcely felt the sun.

To feel, to know, to soar unlimited
Mid throngs of light-winged angels sweeping far,
And pore upon the realms unvisited

That tessellate the unseen, unthought star,—
To be the thing that now I feebly dream,
Flashing within my faintest, deepest gleam.

Ah! caverns of my soul! how thick your shade,
Where flows that life by which I faintly see:—
Wave your bright torches, for I need your aid,
Golden-eyed demons of my ancestry!
Your son though blinded hath a light within,
A heavenly fire which ye from suns did win.

And, lady, in thy hope my life will rise
Like the air-voyager, till I upbear
These heavy curtains of my filmy eyes
Into a lighter, more celestial air:
A mortal's hope shall bear me safely on,
Till I the higher region shall have won.

O Time! O Death! I clasp you in my arms,
For I can soothe an infinite cold sorrow,
And gaze contented on your icy charms
And that wild snow-pile which we call to-morrow;
Sweep on, O soft and azure-lidded sky,
Earth's waters to your gentle gaze reply.

I am not earth-born, though I here delay;
Hope's child, I summon infiniter powers,
And laugh to see the mild and sunny day
Smile on the shrunk and thin autumnal hours;
I laugh, for hope hath happy place with me,—
If my bark sinks, 'tis to another sea.

JAMES RUSSELL LOWELL (1819-1891)

She Came and Went

As a twig trembles, which a bird
  Lights on to sing, then leaves unbent,
So is my memory thrilled and stirred;—
  I only know she came and went.

As clasps some lake, by gusts unriven,
  The blue dome's measureless content,
So my soul held that moment's heaven;—
  I only know she came and went.

As, at one bound, our swift spring heaps
  The orchards full of bloom and scent,

So clove her May my wintry sleeps;—
I only know she came and went.

An angel stood and met my gaze,
    Through the low doorway of my tent;
The tent is struck, the vision stays;—
    I only know she came and went.

Oh, when the room grows slowly dim,
    And life's last oil is nearly spent,
One gush of light these eyes will brim,
    Only to think she came and went.

From "The Vision of Sir Launfal"

For a cap and bells our lives we pay,
Bubbles we buy with a whole soul's tasking;
'Tis heaven alone that is given away,
'Tis only God may be had for the asking;
No price is set on the lavish summer;
June may be had by the poorest comer.

And what is so rare as a day in June?
    Then, if ever, come perfect days;
Then Heaven tries earth if it be in tune,
    And over it softly her warm ear lays;
Whether we look or whether we listen,
We hear life murmur or see it glisten;
Every clod feels a stir of might,
    An instinct within it that reaches and towers,
And, groping blindly above it for light,
    Climbs to a soul in grass and flowers;
The flush of life may well be seen
    Thrilling back over hills and valleys;
The cowslip startles in meadows green,
    The buttercup catches the sun in its chalice,
And there's never a leaf nor a blade too mean
    To be some happy creature's palace;
The little bird sits at his door in the sun,
    Atilt like a blossom among the leaves,
And lets his illumined being o'errun
    With the deluge of summer it receives;
His mate feels the eggs beneath her wings,
And the heart in her dumb breast flutters and sings;
He sings to the wide world and she to her nest,—
In the nice ear of Nature which song is the best?

Now is the high-tide of the year,
    And whatever of life hath ebbed away
Comes flooding back with a ripply cheer,

Into every bare inlet and creek and bay;
Now the heart is so full that a drop overfills it,
We are happy now because God wills it;
No matter how barren the past may have been,
'Tis enough for us now that the leaves are green;
We sit in the warm shade and feel right well
How the sap creeps up and the blossoms swell;
We may shut our eyes, but we cannot help knowing
That skies are clear and grass is growing;
The breeze comes whispering in our ear,
That dandelions are blossoming near,
    That maize has sprouted, that streams are flowing,
That the river is bluer than the sky,
That the robin is plastering his house hard by;
And if the breeze kept the good news back,
For other couriers we should not lack;
    We could guess it all by yon heifer's lowing,—
And hark! how clear bold chanticleer,
Warmed with the new wine of the year,
    Tells all in his lusty crowing!

From "The Biglow Papers"

What Mr. Robinson Thinks

Guvener B. is a sensible man;
  He stays to his home an' looks arter his folks;
He draws his furrer ez straight ez he can,
  An' into nobody's tater-patch pokes;
      But John P.
      Robinson he
    Sez he wunt vote fer Guvener B.

My! aint it terrible? Wut shall we du?
  We can't never choose him o' course,—thet's flat;
Guess we shall hev to come round, (don't you?)
  An' go in fer thunder an' guns, an' all that;
      Fer John P.
      Robinson he
    Sez he wunt vote fer Guvener B.

Gineral C. is a dreffle smart man:
  He's ben on all sides thet give places or pelf;
But consistency still wuz a part of his plan,—
  He's ben true to *one* party,—an' thet is himself;—
      So John P.
      Robinson he
    Sez he shall vote fer Gineral C.

Gineral C. he goes in fer the war;
  He don't vally princerple morn'n an old cud;
Wut did God make us raytional creeturs fer.
  But glory an' gunpowder, plunder an' blood?
        So John P.
        Robinson he
    Sez he shall vote fer Gineral C.

We were gittin' on nicely up here to our village,
  With good old idees o' wut's right an' wut aint,
We kind o' thought Christ went agin war an' pillage,
  An' thet eppyletts worn't the best mark of a saint;
        But John P.
        Robinson he
    Sez this kind o' thing's an exploded idee.

The side of our country must ollers be took,
  An' Presidunt Polk, you know, *he* is our country.
An' the angel thet writes all our sins in a book
  Puts the *debit* to him, an' to us the *per contry;*
        An' John P.
        Robinson he
    Sez this is his view o' the thing to a T.

Parson Wilbur he calls all these argimunts lies;
  Sez they're nothin' on airth but jest *fee, faw, fum;*
An thet all this big talk of our destinies
  Is half on it ign'ance, an' t'other half rum;
        But John P.
        Robinson he
    Sez it aint no sech thing; an', of course, so must we.

Parson Wilbur sez *he* never heerd in his life
  Thet th' Apostles rigged out in their swaller-tail coats,
An' marched round in front of a drum an' a fife,
  To git some on 'em office, an' some on 'em votes;
        But John P.
        Robinson he
    Sez they didn't know everythin' down in Judee.

Wal, it's a marcy we've gut folks to tell us
  The rights an' the wrongs o' these matters, I vow,—
God sends country lawyers, an' other wise fellers,
  To start the world's team wen it gits in a slough;
        Fer John P.
        Robinson he
    Sez the world'll go right, ef he hollers out Gee!

From "Ode Recited at the Harvard Commemoration"
JULY 21, 1865

I

Weak-winged is song,
Nor aims at that clear-ethered height
Whither the brave deed climbs for light:
    We seem to do them wrong,
Bringing our robin's-leaf to deck their hearse
Who in warm life-blood wrote their nobler verse,
Our trivial song to honor those who come
With ears attuned to strenuous trump and drum,
And shaped in squadron-strophes their desire,
Live-battle-odes whose lines were steel and fire:
    Yet sometimes feathered words are strong,
A gracious memory to buoy up and save
From Lethe's dreamless ooze, the common grave
    Of the unventurous throng.

II

To-day our Reverend Mother welcomes back
Her wisest Scholars, those who understood
The deeper teaching of her mystic tome,
And offered their fresh lives to make it good:
    No lore of Greece or Rome,
No science peddling with the names of things,
Or reading stars to find inglorious fates,
    Can lift our life with wings
Far from Death's idle gulf that for the many waits
    And lengthen out our dates
With that clear fame whose memory sings
In manly hearts to come, and nerves them and dilates:
Nor such thy teaching, Mother of us all!
    Not such the trumpet-call
    Of thy diviner mood,
    That could thy sons entice
From happy homes and toils, the fruitful nest
Of those half-virtues which the world calls best,
    Into War's tumult rude;
    But rather far that stern device
The sponsors chose that round thy cradle stood
    In the dim, unventured wood,
    The VERITAS that lurks beneath
    The letter's unprolific sheath,
Life of whate'er makes life worth living,
Seed-grain of high emprise, immortal food,
One heavenly thing whereof earth hath the giving.

III

Many loved Truth, and lavished life's best oil
  Amid the dust of books to find her,
Content at last, for guerdon of their toil,
    With the cast mantle she hath left behind her.
  Many in sad faith sought for her,
  Many with crossed hands sighed for her;
    But these, our brothers, fought for her,
    At life's dear peril wrought for her,
    So loved her that they died for her,
    Tasting the raptured fleetness
    Of her divine completeness:
      Their higher instinct knew
Those love her best who to themselves are true,
And what they dare to dream of, dare to do;
    They followed her and found her
    Where all may hope to find,
Not in the ashes of the burnt-out mind,
But beautiful, with danger's sweetness round her.
    Where faith made whole with deed
    Breathes its awakening breath
    Into the lifeless creed,
    They saw her plumed and mailed,
    With sweet, stern face unveiled,
And all-repaying eyes, look proud on them in death.

IV

Our slender life runs rippling by, and glides
  Into the silent hollow of the past;
    What is there that abides
To make the next age better for the last?
    Is earth too poor to give us
Something to live for here that shall outlive us?
    Some more substantial boon
Than such as flows and ebbs with Fortune's fickle moon?
    The little that we see
    From doubt is never free;
    The little that we do
    Is but half-nobly true;
    With our laborious hiving
What men call treasure, and the gods call dross,
  Life seems a jest of Fate's contriving,
  Only secure in every one's conniving,
A long account of nothings paid with loss,
Where we poor puppets, jerked by unseen wires,
After our little hour of strut and rave,

With all our pasteboard passions and desires,
Loves, hates, ambitions, and immortal fires,
Are tossed pell-mell together in the grave.
But stay! no age was e'er degenerate,
Unless men held it at too cheap a rate,
For in our likeness still we shape our fate.
   Ah, there is something here
  Unfathomed by the cynic's sneer,
  Something that gives our feeble light
   A high immunity from Night,
  Something that leaps life's narrow bars
To claim its birthright with the hosts of heaven;
  A seed of sunshine that can leaven
Our earthly dullness with the beams of stars,
    And glorify our clay
With light from fountains elder than the Day;
  A conscience more divine than we,
  A gladness fed with secret tears,
  A vexing, forward-reaching sense
Of some more noble permanence;
   A light across the sea,
Which haunts the soul and will not let it be,
Still beaconing from the heights of undegenerate years.

VI

   Such was he, our Martyr-Chief,
   Whom late the Nation he had led,
   With ashes on her head,
Wept with the passion of an angry grief:
Forgive me, if from present things I turn
To speak what in my heart will beat and burn,
And hang my wreath on his world-honored urn.

   Nature, they say, doth dote,
   And cannot make a man
   Save on some worn-out plan,
   Repeating us by rote:
For him her Old-World moulds aside she threw,
And, choosing sweet clay from the breast
   Of the unexhausted West,
With stuff untainted shaped a hero new,
Wise, steadfast in the strength of God, and true.
   How beautiful to see
Once more a shepherd of mankind indeed,
Who loved his charge, but never loved to lead;
One whose meek flock the people joyed to be,
   Not lured by any cheat of birth,
   But by his clear-grained human worth,

SALEM COLLEGE
LIBRARY
Winston-Salem, N. C.

And brave old wisdom of sincerity!
    They knew that outward grace is dust;
    They could not choose but trust
In that sure-footed mind's unfaltering skill,
    And supple-tempered will
That bent like perfect steel to spring again and thrust.
His was no lonely mountain-peak of mind,
Thrusting to thin air o'er our cloudy bars,
A sea-mark now, now lost in vapors blind;
Broad prairie rather, genial, level-lined,
Fruitful and friendly for all human kind,
Yet also nigh to heaven and loved of loftiest stars.
    Nothing of Europe here,
Or, then, of Europe fronting mornward still,
    Ere any names of Serf and Peer
    Could Nature's equal scheme deface
    And thwart her genial will;
Here was a type of the true elder race,
And one of Plutarch's men talked with us face to face.
    I praise him not; it were too late;
And some innative weakness there must be
In him who condescends to victory
Such as the Present gives, and cannot wait,
    Safe in himself as in a fate.
    So always firmly he:
    He knew to bide his time,
    And can his fame abide.
Still patient in his simple faith sublime,
    Till the wise years decide.
  Great captains, with their guns and drums,
    Disturb our judgment for the hour,
    But at last silence comes;
These all are gone, and, standing like a tower,
  Our children shall behold his fame,
The kindly-earnest, brave, foreseeing man,
Sagacious, patient, dreading praise, not blame,
New birth of our new soil, the first American.

IX

    But is there hope to save
Even this ethereal essence from the grave?
What ever 'scaped Oblivion's subtle wrong
Save a few clarion names, or golden threads of song?
    Before my musing eye
The mighty ones of old sweep by,
Disvoicèd now and insubstantial things,
As noisy once as we; poor ghosts of kings,
Shadows of empire wholly gone to dust,
And many races, nameless long ago.

To darkness driven by that imperious gust
Of ever-rushing Time that here doth blow:
O visionary world, condition strange,
Where naught abiding is but only Change,
Where the deep-bolted stars themselves still shift and
          range!
Shall we to more continuance make pretence?
Renown builds tombs; a life-estate is Wit;
          And, bit by bit,
The cunning years steal all from us but woe;
Leaves are we, whose decays no harvest sow.
          But, when we vanish hence,
Shall they lie forceless in the dark below,
Save to make green their little length of sods,
Or deepen pansies for a year or two,
Who now to us are shining-sweet as gods?
Was dying all they had the skill to do?
That were not fruitless: but the Soul resents
Such short-lived service, as if blind events
Ruled without her, or earth could so endure;
She claims a more divine investiture
Of longer tenure than Fame's airy rents;
Whate'er she touches doth her nature share;
Her inspiration haunts the ennobled air,
          Gives eyes to mountains blind,
Ears to the deaf earth, voices to the wind,
And her clear trump sings succor everywhere
By lonely bivouacs to the wakeful mind;
For soul inherits all that soul could dare:
          Yea, Manhood hath a wider span
And larger privilege of life than man.
The single deed, the private sacrifice,
So radiant now through proudly-hidden tears,
Is covered up erelong from mortal eyes
With thoughtless drift of the deciduous years;
But that high privilege that makes all men peers,
That leap of heart whereby a people rise
          Up to a noble anger's height,
And, flamed on by the Fates, not shrink, but grow more
          bright,
That swift validity in noble veins,
Of choosing danger and disdaining shame,
          Of being set on flame
By the pure fire that flies all contact base
But wraps its chosen with angelic might,
          These are imperishable gains,
Sure as the sun, medicinal as light,
These hold great futures in their lusty reins
And certify to earth a new imperial race.

JULIA WARD HOWE (1819-1910)

Battle-Hymn of the Republic

Mine eyes have seen the glory of the coming of the Lord:
He is trampling out the vintage where the grapes of wrath
     are stored;
He hath loosed the fateful lightning of His terrible swift
     sword:
     His truth is marching on.

I have seen Him in the watch-fires of a hundred circling
     camps;
They have builded Him an altar in the evening dews and
     damps;
I can read His righteous sentence by the dim and flaring
     lamps.
     His day is marching on.

I have read a fiery gospel, writ in burnished rows of steel:
"As ye deal with my contemners, so with you my grace shall
     deal;
Let the Hero, born of woman, crush the serpent with his heel,
     Since God is marching on."

He has sounded forth the trumpet that shall never call retreat;
He is sifting out the hearts of men before His judgment-seat:
Oh! be swift, my soul, to answer Him! be jubilant, my feet!
     Our God is marching on.

In the beauty of the lilies Christ was born across the sea,
With a glory in His bosom that transfigures you and me:
As He died to make men holy, let us die to make men free,
     While God is marching on.

WALT WHITMAN (1819-1892)

One's-self I Sing

One's-self I sing, a simple separate person,
Yet utter the word Democratic, the word En-Masse.

Of physiology from top to toe I sing,
Not physiognomy alone nor brain alone is worthy for the
     Muse,
     I say the Form complete is worthier far,
The Female equally with the Male I sing.

Of Life immense in passion, pulse, and power,
Cheerful, for freest action form'd under the laws divine,
The Modern Man I sing.

As I Ponder'd in Silence

As I ponder'd in silence,
Returning upon my poems, considering, lingering long,
A Phantom arose before me with distrustful aspect,
Terrible in beauty, age, and power,
The genius of poets of old lands,
As to me directing like flame its eyes,
With finger pointing to many immortal songs,
And menacing voice, *What singest thou?* it said,
*Know'st thou not there is but one theme for ever-enduring
    bards?*
And that is the theme of War, the fortune of battles,
The making of perfect soldiers.
Be it so, then I answer'd,
*I too haughty Shade also sing war, and a longer and greater
    one than any,*
*Waged in my book with varying fortune, with flight, advance
    and retreat, victory deferr'd and wavering,*
*(Yet methinks certain, or as good as certain, at the last), the
    field the world,*
For life and death, for the Body and for the eternal Soul,
Lo, I too am come, chanting the chant of battles,
I above all promote brave soldiers.

To You

Stranger, if you passing meet me and desire to speak to me,
    why should you not speak to me?
And why should I not speak to you?

From "The Song of Myself"

I celebrate myself, and sing myself,
And what I assume you shall assume,
For every atom belonging to me as good belongs to you.

I loaf and invite my soul,
I lean and loaf at my ease observing a spear of summer
    grass.

My tongue, every atom of my blood, formed from this soil,
    this air,

Born here of parents born here from parents the same, and
    their parents the same,
I, now thirty-seven years old in perfect health begin,
Hoping to cease not till death.

Creeds and schools in abeyance,
Retiring back awhile sufficed at what they are, but never for-
    gotten,
I harbor for good or bad, I permit to speak at every hazard,
Nature without check with original energy.

   .   .   .   .   .

A child said *What is the grass?* fetching it to me with full
    hands;
How could I answer the child? I do not know what it is any
    more than he.

I guess it must be the flag of my disposition, out of hopeful
    green stuff woven.

Or I guess it is the handkerchief of the Lord,
A scented gift and remembrancer designedly dropped,
Bearing the owner's name someway in the corners, that we
    may see and remark, and say *Whose?*

Or I guess the grass is itself a child, the produced babe of
    the vegetation.

Or I guess it is a uniform hieroglyphic,
And it means, Sprouting alike in broad zones and narrow
    zones,
Growing among black folks as among white,
Kanuck, Tuckahoe, Congressman, Cuff, I give them the same,
    I receive them the same.

And now it seems to me the beautiful uncut hair of graves.

Tenderly will I use you curling grass,
It may be you transpire from the breasts of young men,
It may be if I had known them I would have loved them,
It may be you are from old people, or from offspring taken
    soon out of their mothers' laps,
And here you are the mothers' laps.

This grass is very dark to be from the white heads of old
    mothers,
Darker than the colorless beards of old men,
Dark to come from under the faint red roofs of mouths.

O I perceive after all so many uttering tongues,
And I perceive they do not come from the roofs of mouths
    for nothing.

I wish I could translate the hints about the dead young men
    and women,
And the hints about old men and mothers, and the offspring
    taken soon out of their laps.

What do you think has become of the young and old men?
And what do you think has become of the women and
    children?

They are alive and well somewhere,
The smallest sprout shows there is really no death,
And if ever there was it led forward life, and does not wait
    at the end to arrest it,
And ceased the moment life appeared.

All goes onward and outward, nothing collapses,
And to die is different from what any one supposed, and
    luckier.

.   .   .   .   .   .

Who goes there? hankering, gross, mystical, nude;
How is it that I extract strength from the beef I eat?

What is a man anyhow? what am I? what are you?
All I mark as my own you shall offset it with your own,
Else it were time lost listening to me.

I do not snivel that snivel the world over,
That months are vacuums and the ground but wallow and
    filth.

Whimpering and truckling, fold with powders for invalids,
    conformity goes to the fourth-remov'd,
I wear my hat as I please indoors or out.

Why should I pray? why should I venerate and be cere-
    monious?

Having pried through the strata, analysed to a hair, counsell'd
    with doctors and calculated close,
I find no sweeter fat than sticks to my own bones.

In all people I see myself, none more and not one a barley-
   corn less,
And the good or bad I say of myself I say of them.

I know I am solid and sound,
To me the converging objects of the universe perpetually
   flow,
All are written to me, and I must get what the writing means.

. . . . . .

I know I am deathless,
I know this orbit of mine cannot be swept by a carpenter's
   compass,
I know I shall not pass like a child's carlacue cut with a
   burnt stick at night.

. . . . . .

One world is away and by far the largest to me, and that is
   myself,
And whether I come to my own to-day or in ten thousand
   or ten million years,
I can cheerfully take it now, or with equal cheerfulness I
   can wait.
My foothold is tenoned and mortised in granite,
I laugh at what you call dissolution,
And I know the amplitude of time.

. . . . . .

I am the poet of the Body and I am the poet of the Soul,
The pleasures of heaven are with me and the pains of hell
   are with me,
The first I graft and increase upon myself, the latter I
   translate into a new tongue.

I am the poet of the woman the same as the man,
And I say it is as great to be a woman as to be a man,
And I say there is nothing greater than the mother of men.

. . . . . .

I understand the large hearts of heroes,
The courage of present times and all times,
How the skipper saw the crowded and rudderless wreck of
   the steamship, and Death chasing it up and down the
   storm,

How he knuckled tight and gave not back an inch, and was
  faithful of days and faithful of nights,
And chalked in large letters on a board, *Be of good cheer,
  we will not desert you;*
How he followed with them and tacked with them three days
  and would not give it up,
How he saved the drifting company at last,
How the lank loose-gowned women looked when boated from
  the side of their prepared graves,
How the silent old-faced infants, and the lifted sick, and the
  sharp-lipped unshaved men;
All this I swallow, it tastes good, I like it well, it becomes
  mine,
I am the man, I suffered, I was there.

      .   .   .   .   .   .

Agonies are one of my changes of garments,
I do not ask the wounded person how he feels, I myself
  become the wounded person,
My hurts turn livid upon me as I lean on a cane and observe.

      .   .   .   .   .   .

Walt Whitman, a kosmos, of Manhattan the son,
Turbulent, fleshy, sensual, eating, drinking, and breeding,
No sentimentalist, no stander above men and women or apart
  from them,
No more modest than immodest.

Unscrew the locks from the doors!
Unscrew the doors themselves from their jambs!
Whoever degrades another degrades me,
And whatever is done or said returns at last to me.

Through me the afflatus surging and surging, through me
  the current and index.

I speak the pass-word primeval, I give the sign of democracy,
By God! I will accept nothing which all cannot have their
  counterpart of on the same terms.

      .   .   .   .   .   .

I believe in the flesh and the appetites,
Seeing, hearing, feeling, are miracles, and each part and tag
  of me is a miracle.

Divine am I inside and out, and I make holy whatever I
   touch or am touch'd from,
The scent of these arm-pits aroma finer than prayer,
This head more than churches, bibles, and all the creeds.

.　　　.　　　.　　　.　　　.　　　.

I think I could turn and live with animals, they are so placid
   and self-contain'd,
I stand and look at them long and long.

They do not sweat and whine about their condition,
They do not lie awake in the dark and weep for their sins,
They do not make me sick discussing their duty to God,
Not one is dissatisfied, not one is demented with the mania
   of owning things,
Not one kneels to another, nor to his kind that lived thousands
   of years ago.
Not one is respectable or unhappy over the whole earth.

So they show their relations to me and I accept them,
They bring me tokens of myself, they evince them plainly in
   their possession.

.　　　.　　　.　　　.　　　.　　　.

It is time to explain myself—let us stand up.

What is known I strip away,
I launch all men and women forward with me into the
   Unknown.

The clock indicates the moment—but what does eternity
   indicate?
We have thus far exhausted trillions of winters and summers,
There are trillions ahead, and trillions ahead of them.

Births have brought us richness and variety,
And other births will bring us richness and variety.

I do not call one greater and one smaller,
That which fills its period and place is equal to any.

.　　　.　　　.　　　.　　　.

My feet strike an apex of the apices of the stars,
On every step bunches of ages, and larger bunches between
   the steps,
All below duly travelled, and still I mount and mount.

Rise after rise bow the phantoms behind me,
Afar down I see the huge first Nothing, I know I was even
    there,
I waited unseen and always, and slept through the lethargic
    mist,
And took my time, and took no hurt from the fetid carbon.

Long I was hugged close—long and long.

Immense have been the preparations for me,
Faithful and friendly the arms that have helped me.
Cycles ferried my cradle, rowing and rowing like cheerful
    boatmen,
For room to me stars kept aside in their own rings,
They sent influences to look after what was to hold me.

Before I was born out of my mother generations guided me,
My embryo has never been torpid, nothing could overlay it.

For it the nebula cohered to an orb,
The long slow strata piled to rest it on,
Vast vegetables gave it sustenance,
Monstrous sauroids transported it in their mouths and de-
    posited it with care.

All forces have been steadily employed to complete and
    delight me,
Now on this spot I stand with my robust soul.

        .   .   .   .   .   .

This day before dawn I ascended a hill and look'd at the
    crowded heaven,
And I said to my spirit, *When we become the enfolders of
    those orbs, and the pleasure and knowledge of everything
    in them, shall we be fill'd and satisfied then?*
And my spirit said, *No, we but level that lift to pass and
    continue beyond.*

        .   .   .   .   .   .

And as to you, Death, and you, bitter hug of mortality, it is
    idle to try to alarm me.

To his work without flinching the accoucheur comes,
I see the elder-hand pressing, receiving, supporting,
I recline by the sills of the exquisite flexible doors,
And mark the outlet, and mark the relief and escape.

And as to you, Corpse, I think you are good manure, but that
    does not offend me,
I smell the white roses sweet-scented and growing,
I reach to the leafy lips, I reach to the polish'd breasts of
    melons.

And as to you, Life, I reckon you are the leavings of many
    deaths,
(No doubt I have died myself ten thousand times before).

I hear you whispering there, O stars of heaven,
O suns—O grass of graves—O perpetual transfers and pro-
    motions,
If you do not say anything how can I say anything?

.   .   .   .   .   .

The spotted hawk swoops by and accuses me, he complains
    of my gab and my loitering.

I too am not a bit tamed, I too am untranslatable,
I sound my barbaric yawp over the roofs of the world.

The last scud of day holds back for me,
It flings my likeness after the rest and true as any on the
    shadow'd wilds,
It coaxes me to the vapour and the dusk.

I depart as air, I shake my white locks at the runaway sun,
I effuse my flesh in eddies, and drift it in lacy jags.
I bequeath myself to the dirt to grow from the grass I love,
If you want me again look for me under your boot-soles.

You will hardly know who I am or what I mean,
But I shall be good health to you nevertheless,
And filter and fibre your blood.

Failing to fetch me at first keep encouraged,
Missing me one place search another,
I stop somewhere waiting for you.

When I Heard at the Close of the Day

When I heard at the close of the day how my name had been
    receiv'd with plaudits in the capitol, still it was not a
    happy night for me that follow'd,
And else when I carous'd, or when my plans were accom-
    plish'd, still I was not happy,

But the day when I rose at dawn from the bed of perfect
    health, refresh'd, singing, inhaling the ripe breath of
    autumn,
When I saw the full moon in the west grow pale and dis-
    appear in the morning light,
When I wander'd alone over the beach, and undressing bathed,
    laughing with the cool waters, and saw the sun rise,
And when I thought how my dear friend, my lover, was on
    his way coming, O then I was happy,
O then each breath tasted sweeter, and all that day my food
    nourish'd me more, and the beautiful day pass'd well,
And the next came with equal joy, and with the next at
    evening came my friend,
And that night while all was still I heard the waters roll
    slowly continually up the shores,
I heard the hissing rustle of the liquid and sands as directed
    to me whispering to congratulate me,
For the one I love most lay sleeping by me under the same
    cover in the cool night,
In the stillness in the autumn moonbeams his face was inclined
    toward me,
And his arm lay lightly around my breast—and that night I
    was happy.

Song of the Open Road

Afoot and light-hearted, I take to the open road,
Healthy, free, the world before me,
The long brown path before me, leading wherever I choose.

Henceforth I ask not good-fortune, I myself am good-
    fortune,
Henceforth I whimper no more, postpone no more, need
    nothing,
Done with indoor complaints, libraries, querulous criticisms,
Strong and content I travel the open road.

The earth, that is sufficient;
I do not want the constellations any nearer;
I know they are very well where they are;
I know they suffice for those who belong to them.

    •   •   •   •   •   •

You road I enter upon and look around, I believe you are not
    all that is here,
I believe that much unseen is also here.

    •   •   •   •   •   •

From this hour, freedom!
From this hour I ordain myself loos'd of limits and imag-
  inary lines,
Going where I list, my own master, total and absolute,
Listening to others, and considering well what they say,
Pausing, searching, receiving, contemplating,
Gently, but with undeniable will, divesting myself of the
  holds that would hold me.

I inhale great draughts of space;
The east and the west are mine, and the north and the south
  are mine.

I am larger, better than I thought;
I did not know I held so much goodness.

All seems beautiful to me;
I can repeat over to men and women, You have done such
  good to me I would do the same to you.
I will recruit for myself and you as I go;
I will scatter myself among men and women as I go;
I will toss the new gladness and roughness among them;
Whoever denies me, it shall not trouble me;
Whoever accepts me, he or she shall be blessed, and shall bless
  me.

     .   .   .   .

Now if a thousand perfect men were to appear, it would not
  amaze me;

Now if a thousand beautiful forms of women appear'd, it
  would not astonish me.

Now I see the secret of the making of the best persons,
It is to grow in the open air, and to eat and sleep with the
  earth.

     .   .   .   .

Allons! whoever you are, come travel with me!
Travelling with me, you find what never tires.

The earth never tires,
The earth is rude, silent, incomprehensible at first, Nature is
  rude and incomprehensible at first,
Be not discouraged, keep on, there are divine things well
  envelop'd,

I swear to you there are divine things more beautiful than
    words can tell.

Allons! we must not stop here,
However sweet these laid-up stores, however convenient this
    dwelling, we cannot remain here,
However shelter'd this port and however calm these waters,
    we must not anchor here,
However welcome the hospitality that surrounds us, we are
    permitted to receive it but a little while.

. . . . . .

Allons! the inducements shall be greater,
We will sail pathless and wild seas,
We will go where winds blow, waves dash, and the Yankee
    clipper speeds by under full sail.

Allons! with power, liberty, the earth, the elements,
Health, defiance, gaiety, self-esteem, curiosity;
Allons! from all formules!
From your formules, O bat-eyed and materialistic priests.

The stale cadaver blocks up the passage—the burial waits
    no longer.

. . . . . .

Listen! I will be honest with you;
I do not offer the old smooth prizes, but offer rough new
    prizes,
These are the days that must happen to you:
You shall not heap up what is call'd riches,
You shall scatter with lavish hand all that you earn or achieve,
You but arrive at the city to which you were destin'd, you
    hardly settle yourself to satisfaction before you are
    call'd by an irresistible call to depart,
You shall be treated to the ironical smiles and mockings of
    those who remain behind you;
What beckonings of love you receive, you shall only answer
    with passionate kisses of parting,
You shall not allow the hold of those who spread their
    reach'd hands toward you.

. . . . . .

Allons! after the GREAT COMPANIONS, and to belong to them!
They too are on the road—they are the swift and majestic
    men—they are the greatest women,

Enjoyers of calms of seas and storms of seas,
Sailors of many a ship, walkers of many a mile of land.

. . . . . .

Allons! through struggles and wars!
The goal that was named cannot be countermanded.

Have the past struggles succeeded?
What has succeeded? yourself? your nation? Nature?
Now understand me well—it is provided in the essence of
    things that from any fruition of success, no matter what,
    shall come forth something to make a greater struggle
    necessary.

My call is the call of battle, I nourish active rebellion,
He going with me must go well arm'd,
He going with me goes often with spare diet, poverty, angrv
    enemies, desertions.

. . . . . .

Allons! the road is before us!
It is safe—I have tried it—my own feet have tried it well—
Allons! be not detain'd!

Let the paper remain on the desk unwritten, and the book on
    the shelf unopen'd!
Let the tools remain in the workshop! let the money remain
    unearn'd!
Let the school stand! mind not the cry of the teacher!
Let the preacher preach in his pulpit! let the lawyer plead
    in the court, and the judge expound the law.

Mon enfant! I give you my hand!
I give you my love more precious than money,
I give you myself before preaching or law;
Will you give me yourself? will you come travel with me?
Shall we stick by each other as long as we live?

From "A Song of Joys"

O to make the most jubilant song!
Full of music—full of manhood, womanhood, infancy!
Full of common employments—full of grain and trees.

O for the voices of animals—O for the swiftness and balance
    of fishes!
O for the dropping of raindrops in a song!
O for the sunshine and motion of waves in a song!

O the joy of my spirit—it is uncaged—it darts like lightning!
It is not enough to have this globe or a certain time,
I will have thousands of globes and all time.

Beautiful Women

Women sit or move to and fro, some old, some young,
The young are beautiful—but the old are more beautiful
    than the young.

The Dresser

1

An old man bending, I come, among new faces,
Years looking backward, resuming, in answer to children,
Come tell us, old man, as from young men and maidens that
    love me,
(Arous'd and angry, I'd thought to beat the alarum, and
    urge relentless war,
But soon my fingers fail'd me, my face droop'd and I resign'd
    myself,
To sit by the wounded and soothe them, or silently watch the
    dead;)
Years hence of these scenes, of these furious passions, these
    chances,
Of unsurpass'd heroes (was one side so brave? the other was
    equally brave;)
Now be witness again—paint the mightiest armies of earth;
Of those armies, so rapid, so wondrous, what saw you to
    tell us?
What stays with you latest and deepest? of curious panics,
Of hard-fought engagements, or sieges tremendous, what
    deepest remains?

2

O maidens and young men I love, and that love me,
What you ask of my days, those the strangest and sudden
    your talking recalls;
Soldier alert I arrive, after a long march, cover'd with sweat
    and dust;

In the nick of time I come, plunge in the fight, loudly shout
in the rush of successful charge;
Enter the captur'd works—yet lo, like a swift-running river
they fade,
Pass and are gone, they fade—I dwell not on soldiers' perils
or soldiers' joys,
(Both I remember well—many the hardships, few the joys, yet
I was content).

But in silence, in dreams' projections,
While the world of gain and appearance and mirth goes on,
So soon what is over forgotten, and waves wash the imprints
off the sand,
In nature's reverie sad, with hinged knees returning, I enter
the doors—(while for you up there,
Whoever you are, follow me without noise, and be of strong
heart).

3

Bearing the bandages, water and sponge,
Straight and swift to my wounded I go,
Where they lie on the ground, after the battle brought in;
Where their priceless blood reddens the grass, the ground;
Or to the rows of the hospital tent, or under the roof'd hos-
pital;
To the long rows of cots, up and down, each side, I return;
To each and all, one after another, I draw near—not one do
I miss;
An attendant follows, holding a tray—he carries a refuse pail,
Soon to be fill'd with clotted rags and blood, emptied, and
fill'd again.

I onward go, I stop,
With hinged knees and steady hand, to dress wounds;
I am firm with each—the pangs are sharp, yet unavoidable;
One turns to me his appealing eyes—(poor boy! I never knew
you,
Yet I think I could not refuse this moment to die for you,
if that would save you).

4

On, on I go!—(open doors of time! open hospital doors!)
The crush'd head I dress, (poor crazed hand, tear not the
bandage away),
The neck of the cavalry-man, with the bullet through and
through, I examine;

Hard the breathing rattles, quite glazed already the eye, yet
    life struggles hard;
(Come sweet death! be persuaded O beautiful death!
In mercy come quickly).

From the stump of the arm, the amputated hand,
I undo the clotted lint, remove the slough, wash off the mat-
    ter and blood;
Back on his pillow the soldier bends, with curv'd neck, and
    side-falling head,
His eyes are closed, his face is pale, he dares not look on the
    bloody stump,
And has not yet look'd on it.

I dress a wound in the side, deep, deep,
But a day or two more, for see the frame all wasted and sink-
    ing,
And the yellow-blue countenance see.

I dress the perforated shoulder, the foot with the bullet-
    wound,
Cleanse the one with a gnawing and putrid gangrene, so sick-
    ening, so offensive,
While the attendant stands behind aside me holding the tray
    and pail.

I am faithful, I do not give out,
The fractur'd thigh, the knee, the wound in the abdomen,
These and more I dress with impassive hand (yet deep in my
    breast a fire, a burning flame).

5

Thus in silence in dreams' projections,
Returning, resuming, I thread my way through the hospitals,
The hurt and wounded I pacify with soothing hand,
I sit by the restless all the dark night, some are so young,
Some suffer so much, I recall the experience sweet and sad,
(Many a soldier's loving arms about this neck have cross'd
    and rested,
Many a soldier's kiss dwells on these bearded lips).

From "By Blue Ontario's Shore"

Give me the pay I have served for,
Give me to sing the songs of the great Idea, take all the rest,
I have loved the earth, sun, animals, I have despised riches,
I have given alms to every one that ask'd, stood up for the
    stupid and crazy, devoted my income and labor to others,

Hated tyrants, argued not concerning God, had patience and
  indulgence toward the people, taken off my hat to nothing
  known or unknown,
Gone freely with powerful uneducated persons and with the
  young, and with the mothers of families,
Read these leaves to myself in the open air, tried them by trees,
  stars, rivers,
Dismiss'd whatever insulted my own soul or defiled my body,
Claim'd nothing to myself which I have not carefully claim'd
  for others on the same terms,
Sped to the camps, and comrades found and accepted from
  every State,
(Upon this breast has many a dying soldier lean'd to breathe
  his last,
This arm, this hand, this voice, have nourish'd, rais'd, restored,
To life recalling many a prostrate form) ;
I am willing to wait to be understood by the growth of the
  taste of myself,
Rejecting none, permitting all.

"O Captain! My Captain!"

(ABRAHAM LINCOLN, 1809-1865)

O Captain! my Captain! our fearful trip is done,
The ship has weathered every rack, the prize we sought is
  won,
The port is near, the bells I hear, the people all exulting,
While follow eyes the steady keel, the vessel grim and daring;
    But O heart! heart! heart!
      O the bleeding drops of red,
    Where on the deck my Captain lies,
      Fallen cold and dead.

O Captain! my Captain! rise up and hear the bells;
Rise up—for you the flag is flung—for you the bugle trills,
For you bouquets and ribboned wreaths—for you the shores
  a-crowding,
For you they call, the swaying mass, their eager faces turning;
    Here Captain! dear father!
      This arm beneath your head!
    It is some dream that on the deck
      You've fallen cold and dead.

My Captain does not answer, his lips are pale and still,
My father does not feel my arm, he has no pulse nor will,
The ship is anchored safe and sound, its voyage closed and
  done,

From fearful trip the victor ship comes in with object won;
   Exult O shores, and ring O bells!
   But I, with mournful tread,
   Walk the deck my Captain lies,
   Fallen cold and dead.

"When Lilacs Last in the Dooryard Bloomed"

PRESIDENT LINCOLN'S BURIAL HYMN

I

When lilacs last in the dooryard bloomed,
And the great star early drooped in the western sky in the
   night,
I mourned, and yet shall mourn with ever-returning spring.

O ever-returning spring, trinity sure to me you bring,
Lilac blooming perennial and drooping star in the west,
And thought of him I love.

II

O powerful, western, fallen star!
O shades of night—O moody, tearful night!
O great star disappeared—O the black murk that hides the
   star!
O cruel hands that hold me powerless—O helpless soul of me!
O harsh surrounding cloud that will not free my soul!

III

In the dooryard fronting an old farmhouse, near the whitewashed palings,
Stands the lilac-bush, tall-growing, with heart-shaped leaves
   of rich green,
With many a pointed blossom, rising, delicate, with the perfume strong I love,
With every leaf a miracle—and from this bush in the dooryard,
With delicate-colored blossoms, and heart-shaped leaves of
   rich green,
A sprig with its flower I break.

IV

In the swamp in secluded recesses,
A shy and hidden bird is warbling a song.

Solitary the thrush,
The hermit withdrawn to himself, avoiding the settlements,
Sings by himself a song.

Song of the bleeding throat,
Death's outlet song of life—(for well, dear brother, I know
If thou wast not gifted to sing, thou wouldst surely die).

V

Over the breast of the spring, the land, amid cities,
Amid lanes and through old woods, where lately the violets
    peeped from the ground, spotting the gray debris,
Amid the grass in the fields each side of the lanes, passing the
    endless grass,
Passing the yellow-speared wheat, every grain from its shroud
    in the dark-brown fields uprisen,
Passing the apple-tree blows of white and pink in the or-
    chards,
Carrying a corpse to where it shall rest in the grave,
Night and day journeys a coffin.

VI

Coffin that passes through lanes and streets,
Through day and night, with the great cloud darkening the
    land,
With the pomp of the inlooped flags, with the cities draped
    in black,
With the show of the States themselves, as of crape-veiled
    women standing,
With processions long and winding, and the flambeaus of the
    night,
With the countless torches lit—with the silent sea of faces and
    the unbared heads,
With the waiting depot, the arriving coffin, and the somber
    faces,
With dirges through the night, with the thousand voices
    rising strong and solemn;
With all the mournful voices of the dirges poured around
    the coffin,
The dim-lit churches and the shuddering organs—Where amid
    these you journey,
With the tolling, tolling bells' perpetual clang;
Here, coffin that slowly passes,
I give you my sprig of lilac.

VII

(Nor for you, for one, alone;
Blossoms and branches green to coffins all I bring:

For fresh as the morning—thus would I carol a song for you,
  O sane and sacred death.

All over bouquets of roses,
O death, I cover you over with roses and early lilies;
But mostly and now the lilac that blooms the first,
Copious I break, I break the sprigs from the bushes;
With loaded arms I come, pouring for you,
For you, and the coffins all of you, O death.)

VIII

O western orb, sailing the heaven!
Now I know what you must have meant, as a month since we
  walked,
As we walked up and down in the dark blue so mystic,
As we walked in silence the transparent shadowy night,
As I saw you had something to tell as you bent to me night
  after night,
As you drooped from the sky low down, as if to my side,
  (while the other stars all looked on,)
As we wandered together the solemn night, (for something,
  I know not what, kept me from sleep,)
As the night advanced, and I saw on the rim of the west ere
  you went, how full you were of woe;
As I stood on the rising ground in the breeze in the cool
  transparent night,
As I watched where you passed, and was lost in the nether-
  ward black of the night,
As my soul, in its trouble, dissatisfied, sank, as where you, sad
  orb,
Concluded, dropped in the night, and was gone.

IX

Sing on, there in the swamp!
O singer bashful and tender! I hear your notes—I hear your
  call,
I hear—I come presently—I understand you;
But a moment I linger, for the lustrous star has detained me,
The star, my departing comrade, holds and detains me.

X

O how shall I warble myself for the dead one there I loved?
And how shall I deck my song for the large sweet soul that
  has gone?
And what shall my perfume be, for the grave of him I love?

Sea-winds blown from east and west,
Blown from the Eastern sea and blown from the Western
    sea, till there on the prairies meeting,
These and with these and the breath of my chant,
I'll perfume the grave of him I love.

XI

O what shall I hang on the chamber walls?
And what shall the pictures be that I hang on the walls,
To adorn the burial-house of him I love?

Pictures of growing spring and farms and homes,
With the Fourth-month eve at sundown, and the gray smoke
    lucid and bright,
With floods of the yellow gold of the gorgeous, indolent,
    sinking sun, burning, expanding the air,
With the fresh sweet herbage under foot, and the pale green
    leaves of the trees prolific,
In the distance the flowing glaze, the breast of the river,
    with a wind-dapple here and there,
With ranging hills on the banks, with many a line against the
    sky, and shadows,
And the city at hand, with dwellings so dense, and stacks of
    chimneys,
And all the scenes of life, and the workshops, and the work-
    men homeward returning.

XII

Lo, body and soul—this land,
Mighty Manhattan, with spires, and the sparkling and hurry-
    ing tides and the ships,
The varied and ample land, the South and the North in the
    light, Ohio's shores and flashing Missouri,
And ever the far-spreading prairies covered with grass and
    corn.

Lo, the most excellent sun so calm and haughty,
The violet and purple morn with just-felt breezes,
The gentle, soft-born, measureless light,
The miracle, spreading, bathing all, the fulfilled noon,
The coming eve delicious, the welcome night and the stars,
Over my cities shining all, enveloping man and land.

XIII

Sing on, sing on, you gray-brown bird,
Sing from the swamps, the recesses, pour your chant from
    the bushes,

Limitless out of the dusk, out of the cedars and pines.
Sing on, dearest brother—warble your reedy song;
Loud human song, with voice of uttermost woe.

O liquid and free and tender!
O wild and loose to my soul—O wondrous singer!
You only I hear—yet the star holds me, (but will soon de-
    part,)
Yet the lilac with mastering odor holds me.

XIV

Now while I sat in the day and looked forth,
In the close of the day with its light and the fields of spring,
    and the farmer preparing his crops,
In the large unconscious scenery of my land with its lakes
    and forests,
In the heavenly aerial beauty, (after the perturbed winds
    and the storms,)
Under the arching heavens of the afternoon swift passing,
    and the voices of children and women,
The many-moving sea-tides, and I saw the ships how they
    sailed,
And the summer approaching with richness, and the fields
    all busy with labor,
And the infinite separate houses, how they all went on, each
    with its meals and minutia of daily usages,
And the streets, how their throbbings throbbed, and the cities
    pent—lo, then and there,
Falling upon them all and among them all, enveloping me
    with the rest,
Appeared the cloud, appeared the long black trail,
And I knew death, its thought, and the sacred knowledge of
    death.

Then with the knowledge of death as walking one side of me,
And the thought of death close-walking the other side of me,
And I in the middle as with companions, and as holding the
    hands of companions,
I fled forth to the hiding receiving night that talks not,
Down to the shores of the water, the path by the swamp in
    the dimness,
To the solemn shadowy cedars and ghostly pines so still.

And the singer so shy to the rest received me,
The gray-brown bird I know received us comrades three,
And he sang what seemed the carol of death, and a verse for
    him I love.

From deep secluded recesses,
From the fragrant cedars and the ghostly pines so still,
Came the carol of the bird.

And the charm of the carol rapt me,
As I held as if by their hands my comrades in the night,
And the voice of my spirit tallied the song of the bird.

DEATH CAROL

Come, lovely and soothing Death,
Undulate round the world, serenely arriving, arriving,
In the day, in the night, to all, to each,
Sooner or later delicate death.

Praised be the fathomless universe,
For life and joy, and for objects and knowledge curious,
And for love, sweet love—but praise! praise! praise!
For the sure-enwinding arms of cool-enfolding death.

Dark Mother, always gliding near, with soft feet,
Have none chanted for thee a chant of fullest welcome?
Then I chant it for thee, I glorify thee above all,
I bring thee a song that when thou must indeed come, come
*   unfalteringly.*

Approach, strong Deliveress!
When it is so, when thou hast taken them, I joyously sing the
*   dead,*
Lost in the loving floating ocean of thee,
Laved in the flood of thy bliss, O Death.

From me to thee glad serenades,
Dances for thee I propose, saluting thee—adornments and
*   feastings for thee,*
And the sights of the open landscape and the high-spread sky
*   are fitting,*
And life and the fields, and the huge and thoughtful night.

The night in silence under many a star,
The ocean shore and the husky whispering wave whose voice I
*   know,*
And the soul turning to thee, O vast and well-veiled Death,
And the body gratefully nestling close to thee.

Over the tree-tops I float thee a song!

Over the rising and sinking waves—over the myriad fields and
*   the prairies wide,*
Over the dense-packed cities all, and the teeming wharves and
*   ways,*
I float this carol with joy, with joy to thee, O Death.

XV

To the tally of my soul,
Loud and strong kept up the gray-brown bird,
With pure deliberate notes, spreading, filling the night.

Loud in the pines and cedars dim,
Clear in the freshness moist, and the swamp-perfume;
And I with my comrades there in the night.

While my sight that was bound in my eyes unclosed,
As to long panoramas of visions.

I saw askant the armies,
And I saw, as in noiseless dreams, hundreds of battle-flags,
Borne through the smoke of the battles and pierced with mis-
    siles I saw them,
And carried hither and yon through the smoke, and torn
    and bloody,
And at last but a few shreds left on the staffs, (and all in
    silence,)
And the staffs all splintered and broken.

I saw battle corpses, myriads of them,
And the white skeletons of young men—I saw them;
I saw the debris and debris of all the dead soldiers of the war;
But I saw they were not as was thought,
They themselves were fully at rest, they suffered not,
The living remained and suffered, the mother suffered,
And the wife and the child and the musing comrade suffered,
And the armies that remained suffered.

XVI

Passing the visions, passing the night,
Passing, unloosing the hold of my comrades' hands,
Passing the song of the hermit bird, and the tallying song of
    my soul,
Victorious song, death's outlet song, yet varying, ever-altering
    song,

As low and wailing, yet clear the notes, rising and falling,
 flooding the night,
Sadly sinking and fainting, as warning and warning, and yet
 again bursting with joy,
Covering the earth and filling the spread of the heaven,
As that powerful psalm in the night I heard from recesses,
Passing, I leave thee, lilac with heart-shaped leaves,
I leave thee there in the dooryard, blooming, returning with
 spring.

I cease from my song for thee,
From my gaze on thee in the west, fronting the west, com-
 muning with thee,
O comrade lustrous, with silver face in the night.

Yet each I keep, and all, retrievements out of the night,
The song, the wondrous chant of the gray-brown bird,
And the tallying chant, the echo aroused in my soul,
With the lustrous and drooping star with the countenance
 full of woe,
With the lilac tall, and its blossoms of mastering odor;
With the holders holding my hand hearing the call of the
 bird,
Comrades mine and I in the midst, and their memory ever
 to keep, for the dead I loved so well,
For the sweetest, wisest soul of all my days and lands—and
 this for his dear sake,
Lilac and star and bird, twined with the chant of my soul,
There in the fragrant pines and the cedars dusk and dim.

To a Common Prostitute

Be composed—be at ease with me—I am Walt Whitman,
 liberal and lusty as Nature,
Not till the sun excludes you do I exclude you,
Not till the waters refuse to glisten for you and the leaves
 to rustle for you, do my words refuse to glisten and
 rustle for you.

My girl, I appoint with you an appointment, and I charge
 you that you make preparation to be worthy to meet me,
And I charge you that you be patient and perfect till I come.

Till then I salute you with a significant look that you do not
 forget me.

From "So Long"

Camerado, this is no book,
Who touches this touches a man,
(Is it night? are we here together alone?)
It is I you hold and who holds you,
I spring from the pages into your arms—decease calls me
    forth.

O how your fingers drowse me,
Your breath falls around me like dew, your pulse lulls the
    tympans of my ears,
I feel immerged from head to foot,
Delicious, enough.

Enough O deed impromptu and secret,
Enough O gliding present—enough O summ'd-up past.

Dear friend whoever you are take this kiss,
I give it especially to you, do not forget me,
I feel like one who has done work for the day to retire awhile,
I receive now again of my many translations, from my ava-
    taras ascending, while others doubtless await me,
An unknown sphere more real than I dream'd, more direct,
    darts awakening rays about me, *So long!*
Remember my words, I may again return,
I love you, I depart from materials,
I am as one disembodied, triumphant, dead.

Good-bye My Fancy!

Good-bye my Fancy!
Farewell dear mate, dear love!
I'm going away, I know not where,
Or to what fortune, or whether I may ever see you again,
So Good-bye my Fancy.

Now for my last—let me look back a moment;
The slower fainter ticking of the clock is in me,
Exit, nightfall, and soon the heart-thud stopping.

Long have we lived, joy'd, caress'd together;
Delightful!—now separation—Good-bye my Fancy.

Yet let me not be too hasty,
Long indeed have we lived, slept, filter'd, become really
    blended into one;
Then if we die we die together, (yes, we'll remain one,)

If we go anywhere we'll go together to meet what happens,
May-be we'll be better off and blither, and learn something,
May-be it is yourself now really ushering me to the true
songs, (who knows?)
May-be it is you the mortal knob really undoing, turning—so
now finally,
Good-bye—and hail! my Fancy.

Darest Thou Now, O Soul

Darest thou now, O soul,
Walk out with me toward the unknown region,
Where neither ground is for the feet nor any path to follow?

No map there, nor guide,
Nor voice sounding, nor touch of human hand,
Nor face with blooming flesh, nor lips, nor eyes, are in that
land.

I know it not, O soul!
Nor dost thou, all is a blank before us,—
All waits undreamed of in that region, that inaccessible land.

Till when the tie is loosened,
All but the ties eternal, Time and Space,
Nor darkness, gravitation, sense, nor any bounds bounding us.

Then we burst forth, we float,
In Time and Space, O soul! prepared for them,
Equal, equipped at last, (O joy! O fruit of all!) them to fulfil,
O soul!

THOMAS DUNN ENGLISH (1819-1902)

Ben Bolt

Don't you remember sweet Alice, Ben Bolt,—
Sweet Alice whose hair was so brown,
Who wept with delight when you gave her a smile,
And trembled with fear at your frown?
In the old church-yard in the valley, Ben Bolt,
In a corner obscure and alone,
They have fitted a slab of the granite so gray,
And Alice lies under the stone.

Under the hickory tree, Ben Bolt,
Which stood at the foot of the hill,
Together we've lain in the noonday shade,
And listened to Appleton's mill.

The mill-wheel has fallen to pieces, Ben Bolt,
 The rafters have tumbled in,
And a quiet which crawls round the walls as you gaze
 Has followed the olden din.

Do you mind of the cabin of logs, Ben Bolt,
 At the edge of the pathless wood,
And the button-ball tree with its motley limbs,
 Which nigh by the doorstep stood?
The cabin to ruin has gone, Ben Bolt,
 The tree you would seek for in vain;
And where once the lords of the forest waved
 Are grass and the golden grain.

And don't you remember the school, Ben Bolt,
 With the master so cruel and grim,
And the shaded nook in the running brook
 Where the children went to swim?
Grass grows on the master's grave, Ben Bolt,
 The spring of the brook is dry,
And of all the boys who were schoolmates then
 There are only you and I.

There is change in the things I loved, Ben Bolt,
 They have changed from the old to the new;
But I feel in the deeps of my spirit the truth,
 There never was change in you.
Twelvemonths twenty have past, Ben Bolt,
 Since first we were friends—yet I hail
Your presence a blessing, your friendship a truth,
 Ben Bolt of the salt-sea gale.

JOSIAH GILBERT HOLLAND (1819-1881)

Daniel Gray

If I shall ever win the home in heaven
For whose sweet rest I humbly hope and pray,
In the great company of the forgiven
I shall be sure to find old Daniel Gray.

I knew him well; in truth, few knew him better;
For my young eyes oft read for him the Word,
And saw how meekly from the crystal letter
He drank the life of his beloved Lord.

Old Daniel Gray was not a man who lifted
On ready words his freight of gratitude,
Nor was he called as one among the gifted,
In the prayer-meetings of his neighborhood.

He had a few old-fashioned words and phrases,
Linked in with sacred texts and Sunday rhymes;
And I suppose that in his prayers and graces
I've heard them all at least a thousand times.

I see him now—his form, his face, his motions,
His homespun habit, and his silver hair,—
And hear the language of his trite devotions,
Rising behind the straight-backed kitchen chair.

I can remember how the sentence sounded—
"Help us, O Lord, to pray and not to faint!"
And how the "conquering and to conquer," rounded
The loftier aspirations of the saint.

He had some notions that did not improve him:
He never kissed his children—so they say;
And finest scenes and fairest flowers would move him
Less than a horse-shoe picked up in the way.

He had a hearty hatred of oppression,
And righteous words for sin of every kind;
Alas, that the transgressor and transgression
Were linked so closely in his honest mind!

He could see naught but vanity in beauty,
And naught but weakness in a fond caress,
And pitied men whose views of Christian duty
Allowed indulgence in such foolishness.

Yet there were love and tenderness within him;
And I am told that when his Charley died,
Nor nature's need nor gentle words could win him
From his fond vigils at the sleeper's side.

And when they came to bury little Charley
They found fresh dew-drops sprinkled in his hair,
And on his breast a rose-bud gathered early,
And guessed, but did not know, who placed it there.

Honest and faithful, constant in his calling,
Strictly attendant on the means of grace,
Instant in prayer, and fearful most of falling,
Old Daniel Gray was always in his place.

A practical old man, and yet a dreamer,
He thought that in some strange, unlooked-for way,
His mighty Friend in Heaven, the great Redeemer,
Would honor him with wealth some golden day.

This dream he carried in a hopeful spirit
Until in death his patient eye grew dim,
And his Redeemer called him to inherit
The heaven of wealth long garnered up for him.

So, if I ever win the home in heaven
For whose sweet rest I humbly hope and pray,
In the great company of the forgiven
I shall be sure to find old Daniel Gray.

HERMAN MELVILLE (1819-1891)

The Enviable Isles

Through storms you reach them and from storms are free
  Afar descried, the foremost drear in hue,
But, nearer, green; and, on the marge, the sea
  Makes thunder low and mist of rainbowed dew.

But, inland,—where the sleep that folds the hills
A dreamier sleep, the trance of God, instils,—
  On uplands hazed, in wandering airs aswoon,
Slow-swaying palms salute love's cypress tree
  Adown in vale where pebbly runlets croon
A song to lull all sorrow and all glee.

Sweet-fern and moss in many a glade are here,
  Where, strown in flocks, what cheek-flushed myriads lie
Dimpling in dream, unconscious slumberers mere,
  While billows endless round the beaches die.

THOMAS WILLIAM PARSONS (1819-1892)

On a Bust of Dante

See, from this counterfeit of him
Whom Arno shall remember long,
  How stern of lineament, how grim,
The father was of Tuscan's song:
There but the burning sense of wrong,

Perpetual care and scorn, abide;
Small friendship for the lordly throng;
Distrust of all the world beside.

Faithful if this wan image be,
No dream his life was,—but a fight!
Could any Beatrice see
A lover in that anchorite?
To that cold Ghibelline's gloomy sight
Who could have guessed the visions came
Of Beauty, veiled with heavenly light,
In circles of eternal flame?

The lips as Cumæ's cavern close,
The cheeks with fast and sorrow thin,
The rigid front, almost morose,
But for the patient hope within,
Declare a life whose course hath been
Unsullied still, though still severe,
Which, through the wavering days of sin,
Kept itself icy-chaste and clear.

Not wholly such his haggard look
When wandering once, forlorn, he strayed,
With no companion save his book,
To Corvo's hushed monastic shade;
Where, as the Benedictine laid
His palm upon the convent's guest,
The single boon for which he prayed
Was peace, that pilgrim's one request.

Peace dwells not here,—this rugged face
Betrays no spirit of repose;
The sullen warrior sole we trace,
The marble man of many woes.
Such was his mien when first arose
The thought of that strange tale divine,
When hell he peopled with his foes,
Dread scourge of many a guilty line.

War to the last he waged with all
The tyrant canker-worms of earth;
Baron and duke, in hold and hall,
Cursed the dark hour that gave him birth;
He used Rome's harlot for his mirth;
Plucked bare hypocrisy and crime;
But valiant souls of knightly worth
Transmitted to the rolls of Time.

O Time! whose verdicts mock our own,
The only righteous judge art thou;
    That poor old exile, sad and lone,
Is Latium's other Virgil now:
Before his name the nations bow;
    His words are parcel of mankind,
Deep in whose hearts, as on his brow,
    The marks have sunk of Dante's mind.

Into the Noiseless Country

Into the noiseless country Annie went,
    Among the silent people where no sound
Of wheel or voice or implement—no roar
    Of wind or billow moves the tranquil air:

And oft at midnight when my strength is spent
    And day's delirium in the lull is drowned
Of deepening darkness, as I kneel before
    Her palm and cross, comes to my soul this prayer,
That partly brings me back to my content,
    "Oh, that hushed forest!—soon may I be there!"

HENRY HOWARD BROWNELL (1820-1872)

The Burial of the Dane

Blue gulf all around us,
    Blue sky overhead—
Muster all on the quarter,
    We must bury the dead!

It is but a Danish sailor,
    Rugged of front and form;
A common son of the forecastle,
    Grizzled with sun and storm.

His name, and the strand he hailed from
    We know, and there's nothing more!
But perhaps his mother is waiting
    In the lonely Island of Fohr.

Still, as he lay there dying,
    Reason drifting awreck,
" 'Tis my watch," he would mutter,
    "I must go upon deck!"

Aye, on deck, by the foremast!
  But watch and lookout are done;
The Union Jack laid o'er him,
  How quiet he lies in the sun!

Slow the ponderous engine,
  Stay the hurrying shaft;
Let the roll of the ocean
  Cradle our giant craft;
Gather around the grating,
  Carry your messmate aft!

Stand in order, and listen
  To the holiest page of prayer!
Let every foot be quiet,
  Every head be bare—
The soft trade-wind is lifting
  A hundred locks of hair.

Our captain reads the service,
  (A little spray on his cheeks)
The grand old words of burial,
  And the trust a true heart seeks:—
"We therefore commit his body
  To the deep"—and, as he speaks,

Launched from the weather railing,
  Swift as the eye can mark,
The ghastly, shotted hammock
  Plunges, away from the shark,
Down, a thousand fathoms,
  Down into the dark!

A thousand summers and winters
  The stormy Gulf shall roll
High o'er his canvas coffin;
  But, silence to doubt and dole:—
There's a quiet harbor somewhere
  For the poor aweary soul.

Free the fettered engine,
  Speed the tireless shaft,
Loose to'gallant and topsail.
  The breeze is fair abaft!

Blue sea all around us,
  Blue sky bright o'erhead—
Every man to his duty,
  We have buried our dead!

THOMAS BUCHANAN READ (1822-1872)

Drifting

My soul to-day
Is far away,
Sailing the Vesuvian Bay;
My wingëd boat,
A bird afloat,
Swings round the purple peaks remote:---

Round purple peaks
It sails, and seeks
Blue inlets and their crystal creeks,
Where high rocks throw,
Through deeps below,
A duplicated golden glow.

Far, vague, and dim,
The mountains swim;
While on Vesuvius' misty brim,
With outstretched hands,
The gray smoke stands
O'erlooking the volcanic lands.

Here Ischia smiles
O'er liquid miles;
And yonder, bluest of the isles,
Calm Capri waits,
Her sapphire gates
Beguiling to her bright estates.

I heed not, if
My rippling skiff
Float swift or slow from cliff to cliff;
With dreamful eyes
My spirit lies
Under the walls of Paradise.

Under the walls
Where swells and falls
The Bay's deep breast at intervals
At peace I lie,
Blown softly by,
A cloud upon this liquid sky.

The day, so mild,
Is Heaven's own child,

With Earth and Ocean reconciled;
The airs I feel
Around me steal
Are murmuring to the murmuring keel.

Over the rail
My hand I trail
Within the shadow of the sail,
A joy intense,
The cooling sense
Glides down my drowsy indolence.

With dreamful eyes
My spirit lies
Where Summer sings and never dies,—
O'erveiled with vines
She glows and shines
Among her future oil and wines.

Her children, hid
The cliffs amid,
Are gambolling with the gambolling kid;
Or down the walls,
With tipsy calls,
Laugh on the rocks like waterfalls.

The fisher's child,
With tresses wild,
Unto the smooth, bright sand beguiled,
With glowing lips
Sings as she skips,
Or gazes at the far-off ships.

Yon deep bark goes
Where traffic blows,
From lands of sun to lands of snows;
This happier one,—
Its course is run
From lands of snow to lands of sun.

O happy ship,
To rise and dip,
With the blue crystal at your lip!
O happy crew,
My heart with you
Sails, and sails, and sings anew!

No more, no more
The worldly shore
Upbraids me with its loud uproar:
With dreamful eyes
My spirit lies
Under the walls of Paradise!

GEORGE HENRY BOKER (1823-1890)

Dirge for a Soldier

Close his eyes; his work is done!
  What to him is friend or foeman,
Rise of moon, or set of sun,
  Hand of man, or kiss of woman?
    Lay him low, lay him low,
    In the clover or the snow!
    What cares he? he cannot know:
      Lay him low!

As man may, he fought his fight,
  Proved his truth by his endeavor;
Let him sleep in solemn night,
  Sleep forever and forever.
    Lay him low, lay him low,
    In the clover or the snow!
    What cares he? he cannot know:
      Lay him low!

Fold him in his country's stars,
  Roll the drum and fire the volley!
What to him are all our wars,
  What but death bemocking folly?
    Lay him low, lay him low,
    In the clover or the snow!
    What cares he? he cannot know:
      Lay him low!

Leave him to God's watching eye,
  Trust him to the hand that made him.
Mortal love weeps idly by:
  God alone has power to aid him.
    Lay him low, lay him low,
    In the clover or the snow!
    What cares he? he cannot know:
      Lay him low!

THOMAS WENTWORTH HIGGINSON (1823-1911)

To Duty

Light of dim mornings; shield from heat and cold;
Balm for all ailments; substitute for praise;
Comrade of those who plod in lonely ways
(Ways that grow lonelier as the years wax old);
Tonic for fears; check to the over-bold;
Nurse, whose calm hand its strong restriction lays,
Kind but resistless, on our wayward days;
Mart, where high wisdom at vast price is sold;
Gardener, whose touch bids the rose-petals fall,
The thorns endure; surgeon, who human hearts
Searchest with probes, though the death-touch be given;
Spell that knits friends, but yearning lovers parts;
Tyrant relentless o'er our blisses all;—
Oh, can it be, thine other name is Heaven?

GEORGE WILLIAM CURTIS (1824-1892)

Ebb and Flow

I walked beside the evening sea,
And dreamed a dream that could not be;
The waves that plunged along the shore
Said only—"Dreamer, dream no more!"

But still the legions charged the beach;
Loud rang their battle-cry, like speech;
But changed was the imperial strain:
It murmured—"Dreamer, dream again!"

I homeward turned from out the gloom,—
That sound I heard not in my room;
But suddenly a sound, that stirred
Within my very breast, I heard.

It was my heart, that like a sea
Within my breast beat ceaselessly:
But like the waves along the shore,
It said—"Dream on!" and "Dream no more!"

CHARLES GODFREY LELAND (1824-1903)

Hans Breitmann's Party

Hans Breitmann gife a barty,
Dey had biano-blayin;

I felled in lofe mit a Merican frau,
  Her name was Madilda Yane.
She hat haar as prown ash a pretzel,
  Her eyes vas himmel-plue,
Und ven dey looket indo mine,
  Dey shplit mine heart in two.

Hans Breitmann gife a barty.
  I vent dere you'll be pound.
I valset mit Madilda Yane
  Und vent shpinnen round und round.
De pootiest Frauelein in de House,
  She vayed 'pout dwo hoondred pound,
Und efery dime she give a shoomp
  She make de vindows sound.

Hans Breitmann gife a barty,
  I dells you it cost him dear.
Dey rolled in more ash sefen kecks
  Of foost-rate Lager Beer.
Und venefer dey knocks de shpicket in,
  De Deutschers gifes a cheer.
I dinks dat so vine a barty
  Nefer coom to a het dis year.

Hans Breitmann gife a barty;
  Dere all vas Souse und Brouse,
Ven de sooper coomed in, de gompany
  Did make demselfs to house;
Dey ate das Brot und Gensy broost,
  De Bratwurst und Braten fine,
Und vash der Abendessen down
  Mit four parrels of Neckarwein.

Hans Breitmann gife a barty;
  We all cot troonk ash bigs.
I poot mine mout to a parrel of bier,
  Und emptied it oop mit a schwigs.
Und denn I gissed Madilda Yane
  Und she shlog me on de kop,
Und de gompany fited mit daple-lecks
  Dill de coonshtable made oos shtop.

Hans Breitmann gife a barty—
  Where ish dat barty now?
Where ish de lofely golden cloud
  Dat float on de moundain's prow?

Where ish de himmelstrahlende Stern—
De shtar, of de shpirit's light?
All goned afay mit de Lager Beer—
Afay in de Ewigkeit!

The Two Friends

I have two friends—two glorious friends—two better could
    not be,
And every night when midnight tolls they meet to laugh
    with me.

The first was shot by Carlist thieves—ten years ago in Spain.
The second drowned near Alicante—while I alive remain.

I love to see their dim white forms come floating through
    the night,
And grieve to see them fade away in early morning light.

The first with gnomes in the Under Land is leading a lordly
    life,
The second has married a mermaiden, a beautiful water-wife.

And since I have friends in the Earth and Sea—with a few,
    I trust, on high,
'Tis a matter of small account to me—the way that I may die.

For whether I sink in the foaming flood, or swing on the
    triple tree,
Or die in my bed, as a Christian should, is all the same to me.

BAYARD TAYLOR (1825-1878)

Song

Daughter of Egypt, veil thine eyes!
    I cannot bear their fire;
Nor will I touch with sacrifice
    Those altars of desire.
For they are flames that shun the day,
    And their unholy light
Is fed from natures gone astray
    In passion and in night.

The stars of Beauty and of Sin,
    They burn amid the dark,
Like beacons that to ruin win
    The fascinated bark.

Then veil their glow, lest I forswear
The hopes thou canst not crown,
And in the black waves of thy hair
My struggling manhood drown!

Bedouin Song

From the Desert I come to thee
On a stallion shod with fire;
And the winds are left behind
In the speed of my desire.
Under thy window I stand,
And the midnight hears my cry:
I love thee, I love but thee,
With a love that shall not die
Till the sun grows cold,
And the stars are old,
And the leaves of the Judgment
Book unfold!

Look from thy window and see
My passion and my pain;
I lie on the sands below,
And I faint in thy disdain.
Let the night-winds touch thy brow
With the heat of my burning sigh,
And melt thee to hear the vow
Of a love that shall not die
Till the sun grows cold,
And the stars are old,
And the leaves of the Judgment
Book unfold!

My steps are nightly driven,
By the fever in my breast,
To hear from thy lattice breathed
The word that shall give me rest.
Open the door of thy heart,
And open thy chamber door,
And my kisses shall teach thy lips
The love that shall fade no more
Till the sun grows cold,
And the stars are old,
And the leaves of the Judgment
Book unfold!

JULIA CAROLINE RIPLEY DORR (1825-1913)

Two Paths

A path across a meadow fair and sweet,
Where clover-blooms the lithesome grasses greet,

A path worn smooth by his impetuous feet.
A straight, swift path—and at its end, a star
Gleaming behind the lilac's fragrant bar,
And her soft eyes, more luminous by far!

A path across the meadow fair and sweet,
Still sweet and fair where blooms and grasses meet—
A path worn smooth by his reluctant feet.

A long, straight path—and, at its end, a gate
Behind whose bars she doth in silence wait
To keep the tryst, if he come soon or late!

JOHN WILLIAMSON PALMER (1825-1906)

The Fight at the San Jacinto

"Now for a brisk and cheerful fight!"
    Said Harman, big and droll,
As he coaxed his flint and steel for a light,
    And puffed at his cold clay bowl;
"For we are a skulking lot," says he,
    "Of land-thieves hereabout,
And these bold señores, two to one,
    Have come to smoke us out."

Santa Anna and Castillon,
    Almonte brave and gay,
Portilla red from Goliad,
    And Cos with his smart array.
Dulces and cigaritos,
    And the light guitar, ting-tum!
Sant' Anna courts siesta,
    And Sam Houston taps his drum.

The buck stands still in the timber—
    "Is it patter of nuts that fall?"
The foal of the wild mare whinnies—
    Did he hear the Comanche call?
In the brake by the crawling bayou
    The slinking she-wolves howl;
And the mustang's snort in the river sedge
    Has startled the paddling fowl.

A soft, low tap, and a muffled tap,
  And a roll not loud nor long—
We would not break Sant' Anna's nap,
  Nor spoil Almonte's song.
Saddles and knives and rifles!
  Lord! but the men were glad
When Deaf Smith muttered "Alamo!"
  And Karnes hissed "Goliad!"

The drummer tucked his sticks in his belt,
  And the fifer gripped his gun.
Oh, for one free, wild, Texan yell,
  As we took the slope in a run!
But never a shout nor a shot we spent,
  Nor an oath nor a prayer, that day,
Till we faced the bravos, eye to eye,
  And then we blazed away.

Then we knew the rapture of Ben Milam,
  And the glory that Travis made,
With Bowie's lunge, and Crockett's shot,
  And Fannin's dancing blade;
And the heart of the fighter, bounding free
  In his joy so hot and mad—
When Millard charged for Alamo,
  Lamar for Goliad.

Deaf Smith rode straight, with reeking spur,
  Into the shock and rout:
"I've hacked and burned the bayou bridge;
  There's no sneak's back-way out!"
Muzzle or butt for Goliad,
  Pistol and blade and fist!
Oh, for the knife that never glanced,
  And the gun that never missed!

Dulces and cigaritos,
  Song and the mandolin!
That gory swamp is a gruesome grove
  To dance fandangoes in.
We bridged the bog with the sprawling herd
  That fell in that frantic rout;
We slew and slew till the sun set red,
  And the Texan star flashed out.

RICHARD HENRY STODDARD (1825-1903)

The Witch's Whelp

Along the shore the slimy brine-pits yawn,
Covered with thick green scum; the billows rise,

And fill them to the brim with clouded foam,
And then subside, and leave the scum again.
The ribbëd sand is full of hollow gulfs,
Where monsters from the waters come and lie.
Great serpents bask at noon along the rocks,
To me no terror; coil on coil they roll
Back to their holes before my flying feet.
The Dragon of the Sea, my mother's god,
Enormous Setebos, comes here to sleep;
Him I molest not; when he flaps his wing
A whirlwind rises, when he swims the deep
It threatens to engulf the trembling isle.
　　Sometimes when winds do blow, and clouds are dark,
I seek the blasted wood whose barkless trunks
Are bleached with summer suns; the creaking trees
Stoop down to me, and swing me right and left
Through crashing limbs, but not a jot care I.
The thunder breaks above, and in their lairs
The panthers roar; from out the stormy clouds
Whose hearts are fire, sharp lightnings rain around
And split the oaks; not faster lizards run
Before the snake up the slant trunks than I,
Not faster down, sliding with hands and feet.
I stamp upon the ground, and adders rouse,
Sharp-eyed, with poisonous fangs; beneath the leaves
They couch, or under rocks, and roots of trees
Felled by the winds; through briery undergrowth
They slide with hissing tongues, beneath my feet
To writhe, or in my fingers squeezed to death.
　　There is a wild and solitary pine,
Deep in the meadows; all the island birds
From far and near fly there, and learn new songs.
Something imprisoned in its wrinkled bark
Wails for its freedom; when the bigger light
Burns in mid-heaven, and dew elsewhere is dried,
There it still falls; the quivering leaves are tongues,
And load the air with syllables of woe.
One day I thrust my spear within a cleft
No wider than its point, and something shrieked,
And falling cones did pelt me sharp as hail:
I picked the seeds that grew between their plates,
And strung them round my neck with sea-mew eggs.
　　Hard by are swamps and marshes, reedy fens
Knee-deep in water; monsters wade therein
Thick-set with plated scales; sometimes in troops
They crawl on slippery banks; sometimes they lash
The sluggish waves among themselves at war.
Often I heave great rocks from off the crags,
And crush their bones; often I push my spear

Deep in their drowsy eyes, at which they howl
And chase me inland; then I mount their humps
And prick them back again, unwieldy, slow.
At night the wolves are howling round the place,
And bats sail there athwart the silver light,
Flapping their wings; by day in hollow trees
They hide, and slink into the gloom of dens.
  We live, my mother Sycorax and I,
In caves with bloated toads and crested snakes.
She can make charms, and philters, and brew storms
And call the great Sea Dragon from his deeps.
Nothing of this know I, nor care to know.
Give me the milk of goats in gourds or shells,
The flesh of birds and fish, berries and fruit,
Nor want I more, save all day long to lie,
And hear, as now, the voices of the sea.

A Catch

Once the head is gray,
  And the heart is dead,
There's no more to do:
  Make the man a bed
Six foot under ground,
There he'll slumber sound.

Golden was my hair,
  And my heart did beat
To the viol's voice
  Like the dancers' feet.
Not colder now his blood
Who died before the flood.

Fair, and fond, and false,
  Mother, wife, and maid,
Never lived a man
  They have not betrayed.
None shall 'scape my mirth
But old Mother Earth.

Safely housed with her,
  With no company
But my brother Worm,
  Who will feed on me,
I shall slumber sound,
Deep down under ground.

The Flight of Youth

There are gains for all our losses
　　There are balms for all our pain:
But when youth, the dream, departs,
It takes something from our hearts,
　　And it never comes again.

We are stronger, and are better,
　　Under manhood's sterner reign:
Still we feel that something sweet
Followed youth, with flying feet,
　　And will never come again.

Something beautiful is vanished,
　　And we sigh for it in vain:
We behold it everywhere,
On the earth, and in the air,
　　But it never comes again.

The Jar

Day and night my thoughts incline
To the blandishments of wine:
Jars were made to drain, I think,
Wine, I know, was made to drink.

When I die, (the day be far!)
Should the potters make a jar
Out of this poor clay of mine,
Let the jar be filled with wine!

From "Threescore and Ten"

Who reach their threescore years and ten,
　　As I have mine, without a sigh,
Are either more or less than men—
　　Not such am I.

I am not of them; life to me
　　Has been a strange, bewildering dream,
Wherein I knew not things that be
　　From things that seem.

I thought, I hoped, I knew one thing,
　　And had one gift, when I was young—

The impulse and the power to sing,
    And so I sung.

    .   .   .   .   .

They left me here, they left me there,
    Went down dark pathways, one by one—
The wise, the great, the young, the fair;
    But I went on.

And I go on! And bad or good,
    The old allotted years of men
I have endured as best I could,
    Threescore and ten!

An Old Song Reversed

"There are gains for all our losses."
    So I said when I was young.
If I sang that song again,
'Twould not be with that refrain,
    Which but suits an idle tongue.

Youth has gone, and hope gone with it,
    Gone the strong desire for fame.
Laurels are not for the old.
Take them, lads. Give Senex gold.
    What's an everlasting name?

When my life was in its summer
    One fair woman liked my looks:
Now that Time has driven his plough
In deep furrows on my brow,
    I'm no more in her good books.

"There are gains for all our losses?"
    Grave beside the wintry sea,
Where my child is, and my heart,
For they would not live apart,
    What has been your gain to me?

No, the words I sang were idle,
    And will ever so remain:
Death, and Age, and vanished Youth
All declare this bitter truth,
    There's a loss for every gain!

STEPHEN COLLINS FOSTER (1826-1864)

My Old Kentucky Home, Good-Night

The sun shines bright in the old Kentucky home;
    'Tis summer, the darkeys are gay;

The corn top's ripe, and the meadow's in the bloom,
  While the birds make music all the day.
The young folks roll on the little cabin floor,
  All merry, all happy and bright;
By-'n'-by hard times comes a-knocking at the door:—
  Then my old Kentucky home, good-night!

    Weep no more, my lady,
      O, weep no more to-day!
  We will sing one song for the old Kentucky home,
    For the old Kentucky home, far away.

They hunt no more for the possum and the coon,
  On the meadow, the hill, and the shore;
They sing no more by the glimmer of the moon,
  On the bench by the old cabin door.
The day goes by like a shadow o'er the heart,
  With sorrow, where all was delight;
The time has come when the darkeys have to part:—
  Then my old Kentucky home, good-night!

The head must bow, and the back will have to bend,
  Wherever the darkey may go;
A few more days, and the trouble all will end,
  In the field where the sugar-canes grow.
A few more days for to tote the weary load,—
  No matter, 'twill never be light;
A few more days till we totter on the road:—
  Then my old Kentucky home, good-night!

    Weep no more, my lady,
      O, weep no more to-day!
  We will sing one song for the old Kentucky home,
    For the old Kentucky home, far away.

Old Folks at Home

  Way down upon de Swanee Ribber,
    Far, far away,
  Dere's wha my heart is turning ebber,
    Dere's wha de old folks stay.
  All up and down de whole creation
    Sadly I roam,
  Still longing for de old plantation,
    And for de old folks at home.

    All de world am sad and dreary,
      Eberywhere I roam;
  Oh, darkeys, how my heart grows weary,
    Far from de old folks at home!

All round de little farm I wandered
    When I was young,
Den many happy days I squandered,
    Many de songs I sung.
When I was playing wid my brudder,
    Happy was I;
Oh, take me to my kind old mudder!
    Dere let me live and die.

One little hut among de bushes,
    One dat I love,
Still sadly to my memory rushes,
    No matter where I rove.
When will I see de bees a-humming
    All round de comb?
When will I hear de banjo tumming,
    Down in my good old home?

    All de world am sad and dreary,
        Eberywhere I roam,
    Oh, darkeys, how my heart grows weary,
        Far from de old folks at home!

Massa's in de Cold Ground

Round de meadows am a-ringing
    De darkeys' mournful song,
While de mocking-bird am singing,
    Happy as de day am long.
Where de ivy am a-creeping,
    O'er de grassy mound,
Dere old massa am a-sleeping,
    Sleeping in de cold, cold ground.

    Down in de corn-field
        Hear dat mournful sound:
    All de darkeys am a-weeping,—
        Massa's in de cold, cold ground.

When de autumn leaves were falling,
    When de days were cold,
'Twas hard to hear old massa calling,
    Cayse he was so weak and old.
Now de orange tree am blooming
    On de sandy shore,
Now de summer days am coming,—
    Massa nebber calls no more.

Massa make de darkeys love him,
  Cayse he was so kind;
Now dey sadly weep above him,
  Mourning cayse he leave dem behind.
I cannot work before to-morrow,
  Cayse de tear-drop flow;
I try to drive away my sorrow,
  Pickin' on de old banjo.

Down in de corn-field
  Hear dat mournful sound:
All de darkeys am a-weeping,—
  Massa's in de cold, cold ground.

ROSE TERRY COOKE (1827-1892)

In Vain

Put every tiny robe away!
The stitches all were set with tears,
Slow, tender drops of joys; to-day
Their rain would wither hopes or fears:
Bitter enough to daunt the moth
That longs to fret this dainty cloth.

The filmy lace, the ribbons blue,
The tracery deft of flower and leaf,
The fairy shapes that bloomed and grew
Through happy moments all too brief.
The warm, soft wraps. O God! how cold
It must be in that wintry mould!

Fold carefully the broidered wool:
Its silken wreaths will ne'er grow old,
And lay the linen soft and cool
Above it gently, fold on fold.
So lie the snows on that soft breast,
Where mortal garb will never rest.

How many days in dreamed delight,
With listless fingers, working slow,
I fashioned them from morn till night
And smiled to see them slowly grow.
I thought the task too late begun;
Alas! how soon it all was done!

Go lock them in a cedar chest,
And never bring me back the key!
Will hiding lay this ghost to rest,
Or the turned lock give peace to me?
No matter!—only that I dread
Lest other eyes behold my dead.

I would have laid them in that grave
To perish too, like any weed;
But legends tell that they who save
Such garments, ne'er the like will need:
But give or burn them,—need will be;
I want but one such memory!

ETHEL LYNN BEERS (1827-1879)

All Quiet along the Potomac

"All quiet along the Potomac," they say,
  "Except now and then a stray picket
Is shot, as he walks on his beat to and fro,
  By a rifleman hid in the thicket.
'Tis nothing—a private or two now and then
  Will not count in the news of the battle;
Not an officer lost—only one of the men,
  Moaning out, all alone, the death-rattle."

All quiet along the Potomac to-night,
  Where the soldiers lie peacefully dreaming;
Their tents in the rays of the clear autumn moon,
  Or the light of the watch-fire, are gleaming.
A tremulous sigh of the gentle night-wind
  Through the forest leaves softly is creeping;
While stars up above, with their glittering eyes,
  Keep guard, for the army is sleeping.

There's only the sound of the lone sentry's tread,
  As he tramps from the rock to the fountain,
And thinks of the two in the low trundle-bed
  Far away in the cot on the mountain.
His musket falls slack; his face, dark and grim,
  Grows gentle with memories tender,
As he mutters a prayer for the children asleep,
  For their mother; may Heaven defend her!

The moon seems to shine just as brightly as then,
  That night, when the love yet unspoken
Leaped up to his lips—when low-murmured vows
  Were pledged to be ever unbroken.

Then drawing his sleeve roughly over his eyes,
  He dashes off tears that are welling,
And gathers his gun closer up to its place,
  As if to keep down the heart-swelling.

He passes the fountain, the blasted pine-tree,
  The footstep is lagging and weary;
Yet onward he goes, through the broad belt of light,
  Toward the shade of the forest so dreary.
Hark! was it the night-wind that rustled the leaves?
  Was it moonlight so wondrously flashing?
It looked like a rifle . . . "Ha! Mary, good-bye!"
  The red life-blood is ebbing and plashing.

All quiet along the Potomac to-night;
  No sound save the rush of the river;
While soft falls the dew on the face of the dead—
  The picket's off duty forever!

FRANCIS MILES FINCH (1827-1907)

The Blue and the Gray

By the flow of the inland river,
  Whence the fleets of iron have fled,
Where the blades of the grave-grass quiver,
  Asleep are the ranks of the dead:
    Under the sod and the dew,
      Waiting the judgment-day;
    Under the one, the Blue,
      Under the other, the Gray.

These in the robings of glory,
  Those in the gloom of defeat,
All with the battle-blood gory,
  In the dusk of eternity meet:
    Under the sod and the dew,
      Waiting the judgment-day;
    Under the laurel, the Blue,
      Under the willow, the Gray.

From the silence of sorrowful hours
  The desolate mourners go,
Lovingly laden with flowers
  Alike for the friend and the foe:
    Under the sod and the dew,
      Waiting the judgment-day;
    Under the roses, the Blue,
      Under the lilies, the Gray.

So with an equal splendor,
  The morning sun-rays fall,
With a touch impartially tender,
  On the blossoms blooming for all:
    Under the sod and the dew,
      Waiting the judgment-day;
    Broidered with gold, the Blue,
      Mellowed with gold, the Gray.

So, when the summer calleth,
  On forest and field of grain,
With an equal murmur falleth
  The cooling drip of the rain:
    Under the sod and the dew,
      Waiting the judgment-day;
    Wet with the rain, the Blue,
      Wet with the rain, the Gray.

Sadly, but not with upbraiding,
  The generous deed was done,
In the storm of the years that are fading
  No braver battle was won:
    Under the sod and the dew,
      Waiting the judgment-day;
    Under the blossoms, the Blue,
      Under the garlands, the Gray.

No more shall the war cry sever,
  Or the winding rivers be red;
They banish our anger forever
  When they laurel the graves of our dead!
    Under the sod and the dew,
      Waiting the judgment-day;
    Love and tears for the Blue,
      Tears and love for the Gray.

JOHN TOWNSEND TROWBRIDGE (1827-1916)

The Vagabonds

We are two travellers, Roger and I.
  Roger's my dog.—Come here, you scamp!
Jump for the gentleman,—mind your eye!

Over the table,—look out for the lamp!
  The rogue is growing a little old;

Five years we've tramped through wind and weather,
And slept out-doors when nights were cold,
    And ate and drank—and starved—together.

We've learned what comfort is, I tell you!
    A bed on the floor, a bit of rosin,
A fire to thaw our thumbs (poor fellow!
    The paw he holds up there's been frozen),
Plenty of catgut for my fiddle
    (This out-door business is bad for strings),
Then a few nice buckwheats hot from the griddle,
    And Roger and I set up for kings!

No, thank ye, Sir,—I never drink;
    Roger and I are exceedingly moral,—
Aren't we, Roger?—See him wink!—
    Well, something hot, then,—we won't quarrel.
He's thirsty, too,—see him nod his head?
    What a pity, Sir, that dogs can't talk!
He understands every word that's said,—
    And he knows good milk from water-and-chalk.

The truth is, Sir, now I reflect,
    I've been so sadly given to grog,
I wonder I've not lost the respect
    (Here's to you, Sir!) even of my dog.
But he sticks by, through thick and thin;
    And this old coat, with its empty pockets,
And rags that smell of tobacco and gin,
    He'll follow while he has eyes in his sockets.

There isn't another creature living
    Would do it, and prove, through every disaster,
So fond, so faithful, and so forgiving,
    To such a miserable, thankless master!
No, Sir!—see him wag his tail and grin!
    By George! it makes my old eyes water!
That is, there's something in this gin
    That chokes a fellow. But no matter!

We'll have some music, if you're willing,
    And Roger (hem! what a plague a cough is, Sir!)
Shall march a little— Start, you villain!
    Paws up! Eyes front! Salute your officer!
'Bout face! Attention! Take your rifle!
    (Some dogs have arms, you see!) Now hold your
Cap while the gentlemen give a trifle,
    To aid a poor old patriot soldier!

March! Halt! Now show how the rebel shakes
  When he stands up to hear his sentence.
Now tell us how many drams it takes
  To honor a jolly new acquaintance.
Five yelps,—that's five; he's mighty knowing!
  The night's before us, fill the glasses!—
Quick, Sir! I'm ill,—my brain is going!—
  Some brandy,—thank you,—there!—it passes!

Why not reform? That's easily said;
  But I've gone through such wretched treatment,
Sometimes forgetting the taste of bread,
  And scarce remembering what meat meant,
That my poor stomach's past reform;
  And there are times when, mad with thinking,
I'd sell out heaven for something warm
  To prop a horrible inward sinking.

Is there a way to forget to think?
  At your age, Sir, home, fortune, friends,
A dear girl's love,—but I took to drink,—
  The same old story; you know how it ends.
If you could have seen these classic features,—
  You needn't laugh, Sir; they were not then
Such a burning libel on God's creatures:
  I was one of your handsome men!

If you had seen *her,* so fair and young,
  Whose head was happy on this breast!
If you could have heard the songs I sung
  When the wine went round, you wouldn't have guessed
That ever I, Sir, should be straying
  From door to door, with fiddle and dog,
Ragged and penniless, and playing
  To you to-night for a glass of grog!

She's married since,—a parson's wife:
  'Twas better for her that we should part,—
Better the soberest, prosiest life
  Than a blasted home and a broken heart.
I have seen her? Once: I was weak and spent
  On the dusty road: a carriage stopped:
But little she dreamed, as on she went,
  Who kissed the coin that her fingers dropped!

You've set me talking, Sir; I'm sorry;
  It makes me wild to think of the change!
What do you care for a beggar's story?
  Is it amusing? you find it strange?

I had a mother so proud of me!
   'Twas well she died before.—Do you know
If the happy spirits in heaven can see
   The ruin and wretchedness here below?

Another glass, and strong, to deaden
   This pain; then Roger and I will start.
I wonder, has he such a lumpish, leaden,
   Aching thing in place of a heart?
He is sad sometimes, and would weep, if he could,
   No doubt remembering things that were,—
A virtuous kennel, with plenty of food.
   And himself a sober, respectable cur.

I'm better now; that glass was warming.—
   You rascal! limber your lazy feet!
We must be fiddling and performing
   For supper and bed, or starve in the street.—
Not a very gay life to lead, you think?
   But soon we shall go where lodgings are free,
And the sleepers need neither victuals nor drink:—
   The sooner, the better for Roger and me!

Midwinter

The speckled sky is dim with snow,
The light flakes falter and fall slow;
Athwart the hill-top, rapt and pale,
Silently drops a silvery veil;
And all the valley is shut in
By flickering curtains gray and thin.

But cheerily the chickadee
Singeth to me on fence and tree;
The snow sails round him as he sings,
White as the down of angels' wings.

I watch the snowflakes as they fall
On bank and brier and broken wall;
Over the orchard, waste and brown,
All noiselessly they settle down,
Tipping the apple-boughs, and each
Light quivering twig of plum and peach.
On turf and curb and bower-roof
The snow-storm spreads its ivory woof;
It paves with pearl the garden-walk;
And lovingly round tattered stalk
And shivering stem its magic weaves
A mantle fair as lily-leaves.

The hooded beehive, small and low,
Stands like a maiden in the snow;
And the old door-slab is half hid
Under an alabaster lid.

All day it snows: the sheeted post
Gleams in the dimness like a ghost;
All day the blasted oak has stood
A muffled wizard of the wood;
Garland and airy cap adorn
The sumach and the wayside thorn,
And clustering spangles lodge and shine
In the dark tresses of the pine.

The ragged bramble, dwarfed and old,
Shrinks like a beggar in the cold;
In surplice white the cedar stands,
And blesses him with priestly hands.

Still cheerily the chickadee
Singeth to me on fence and tree:
But in my inmost ear is heard
The music of a holier bird;
And heavenly thoughts as soft and white
As snow-flakes, on my soul alight,
Clothing with love my lonely heart,
Healing with peace each bruisëd part,
Till all my being seems to be
Transfigured by their purity.

CLARENCE CHATHAM COOK (1828-1900)

On One Who Died in May

Why, Death, what dost thou here,
      This time o' year?
Peach-blow and apple-blossom;
Clouds, white as my love's bosom;
   Warm wind o' the west
   Cradling the robin's nest;
Young meadows hasting their green laps to fill
With golden dandelion and daffodil:
   These are fit sights for spring;
   But, oh, thou hateful thing,
      What dost thou here?

Why, Death, what dost thou here,
    This time o' year?
Fair, at the old oak's knee,
The young anemone;
Fair, the plash places set
With dog-tooth violet;
    The first sloop-sail,
    The shad-flower pale;
Sweet are all sights,
Sweet are all sounds of spring;
But thou, thou ugly thing,
    What dost thou here?

Dark Death let fall a tear.
    Why am I here?
Oh, heart ungrateful! Will man never know
I am his friend, nor ever was his foe?
Whose the sweet season, if it be not mine?
Mine, not the bobolink's, that song divine,
Chasing the shadows o'er the flying wheat!
'Tis a dead voice, not his, that sounds so sweet.
Whose passionate heart burns in this flaming rose
But his whose passionate heart long since lay still?
Whose wan hope pales this snowlike lily tall,
    Beside the garden wall,
But his whose radiant eyes and lily grace
Sleep in the grave that crowns yon tufted hill?

    All hope, all memory,
Have their deep springs in me:
  And love, that else might fade,
  By me immortal made,
Spurns at the grave, leaps to the welcoming skies,
And burns a steadfast star to steadfast eyes.

HENRY TIMROD (1829-1867)

Quatorzain

Most men know love but as a part of life;
They hide it in some corner of the breast,
Even from themselves; and only when they rest
In the brief pauses of that daily strife,
Wherewith the world might else be not so rife,
They draw it forth (as one draws forth a toy
To soothe some ardent, kiss-exacting boy)
And hold it up to sister, child, or wife.

Ah me! why may not love and life be one?
Why walk we thus alone, when by our side,
Love, like a visible god, might be our guide?
How would the marts grow noble! and the street,
Worn like a dungeon-floor by weary feet,
Seem then a golden court-way of the Sun!

SILAS WEIR MITCHELL (1829-1914)

On a Boy's First Reading of "King Henry V"

When youth was lord of my unchallenged fate,
And time seemed but the vassal of my will,
I entertained certain guests of state—
The great of older days, who, faithful still,
Have kept with me the pact my youth had made.

And I remember how one galleon rare
From the far distance of a time long dead
Came on the wings of a fair-fortuned air,
With sound of martial music heralded,
In blazonry of storied shields arrayed.

So the *Great Harry* with high trumpetings,
The wind of victory in her burly sails!
And all her deck with clang of armor rings:
And under-flown the Lily standard trails,
And over-flown the royal Lions ramp.

The waves she rode are strewn with silent wrecks,
Her proud sea-comrades once; but ever yet
Comes time-defying laughter from her decks,
Where stands the lion-lord Plantagenet,
Large-hearted, merry, king of court and camp.

Sail on! sail on! The fatal blasts of time
That spared so few, shall thee with joy escort;
And with the stormy thunder of thy rhyme
Shalt thou salute full many a centuried port
With "Ho! for Harry and red Agincourt!"

A Decanter of Madeira, Aged 86, to George Bancroft, Aged 86, Greeting

Good Master, you and I were born
In "Teacup days" of hoop and hood,
And when the silver cue hung down,
And toasts were drunk, and wine was good;

When kin of mine (a jolly brood)
From sideboards looked, and knew full well
What courage they had given the beau,
How generous made the blushing belle.

Ah me! what gossip could I prate
Of days when doors were locked at dinners!
Believe me, I have kissed the lips
Of many pretty saints—or sinners.

Lip service have I done, alack!
I don't repent, but come what may,
What ready lips, sir, I have kissed,
Be sure at least I shall not say.

Two honest gentlemen are we,—
I Demi John, whole George are you;
When Nature grew us one in years
She meant to make a generous brew.

She bade me store for festal hours
The sun our south-side vineyard knew;
To sterner tasks she set your life,
As statesman, writer, scholar, grew.

Years eighty-six have come and gone;
At last we meet. Your health to-night.
Take from this board of friendly hearts
The memory of a proud delight.

The days that went have made you wise,
There's wisdom in my rare bouquet.
I'm rather paler than I was;
And, on my soul, you're growing gray.

I like to think, when Toper Time
Has drained the last of me and you,
Some here shall say, They both were good,—
The wine we drank, the man we knew.

EMILY DICKINSON (1830-1886)

Life

Our share of night to bear,
Our share of morning,
Our blank in bliss to fill,
Our blank in scorning.

Here a star, and there a star,
Some lose their way.
Here a mist, and there a mist,
Afterwards—day!

Parting

My life closed twice before its close;
  It yet remains to see
If Immortality unveil
  A third event to me,

So huge, so hopeless to conceive,
  As these that twice befell:
Parting is all we know of heaven,
  And all we need of hell.

Called Back

Just lost when I was saved!
Just felt the world go by!
Just girt me for the onset with eternity,
When breath blew back
And on the other side
I heard recede the disappointed tide!

Therefore, as one returned, I feel,
Odd secrets of the line to tell!
Some sailor, skirting foreign shores,
Some pale reporter from the awful doors
Before the seal!

Next time, to stay!
Next time, the things to see
By ear unheard,
Unscrutinized by eye.

Next time, to tarry,
While the ages steal,—
Slow tramp the centuries,
And the cycles wheel.

Constant

Alter? When the hills do.
Falter? When the sun
Question if his glory
Be the perfect one.

Surfeit? When the daffodil
Doth of the dew:
Even as herself, O friend!
I will of you!

Heart, We Will Forget Him

Heart, we will forget him!
  You and I, to-night!
You may forget the warmth he gave,
  I will forget the light.

When you have done, pray tell me,
  That I my thoughts may dim;
Haste! lest while you're lagging,
  I may remember him!

Chartless

I never saw a moor,
I never saw the sea;
Yet know I how the heather looks,
And what a wave must be.

I never spoke with God,
Nor visited in heaven;
Yet certain am I of the spot
As if the chart were given.

Beauty Crowds Me

Beauty crowds me till I die,
Beauty, mercy have on me!
Yet if I expire to-day
Let it be in sight of thee!

Eternity

On this wondrous sea,
Sailing silently,
  Ho! pilot, ho!
Knowest thou the shore
Where no breakers roar,
  Where the storm is o'er?

In the silent west
Many sails at rest,
    Their anchors fast;
Thither I pilot thee,—
Land, ho! Eternity!
    Ashore at last!

HELEN HUNT JACKSON (1831-1885)

Poppies in the Wheat

Along Ancona's hills the shimmering heat,
A tropic tide of air, with ebb and flow
Bathes all the fields of wheat until they glow
Like flashing seas of green, which toss and beat
Around the vines. The poppies lithe and fleet
Seem running, fiery torchmen, to and fro
To mark the shore. The farmer does not know
That they are there. He walks with heavy feet,
Counting the bread and wine by autumn's gain,
But I,—I smile to think that days remain
Perhaps to me in which, though bread be sweet
No more, and red wine warm my blood in vain,
I shall be glad remembering how the fleet,
Lithe poppies ran like torchmen with the wheat.

Habeas Corpus

My body, eh? Friend Death, how now?
    Why all this tedious pomp of writ?
Thou hast reclaimed it sure and slow
    For half a century, bit by bit.

In faith thou knowest more to-day
    Than I do, where it can be found!
This shriveled lump of suffering clay,
    To which I now am chained and bound,

Has not of kith or kin a trace
    To the good body once I bore;
Look at this shrunken, ghastly face:
    Didst ever see that face before?

Ah, well, friend Death, good friend thou art;
    Thy only fault thy lagging gait,
Mistaken pity in thy heart
    For timorous ones that bid thee wait.

Do quickly all thou hast to do,
  Nor I nor mine will hindrance make;
I shall be free when thou art through;
  I grudge thee naught that thou must take!

Stay! I have lied: I grudge thee one,
  Yes, two I grudge thee at this last,—
Two members which have faithful done
  My will and bidding in the past.

I grudge thee this right hand of mine;
  I grudge thee this quick-beating heart;
They never gave me coward sign,
  Nor played me once a traitor's part.

I see now why in olden days
  Men in barbaric love or hate
Nailed enemies' hands at wild crossways,
  Shrined leaders' hearts in costly state:

The symbol, sign, and instrument
  Of each soul's purpose, passion, strife,
Of fires in which are poured and spent
  Their all of love, their all of life.

O feeble, mighty human hand!
  O fragile, dauntless human heart!
The universe holds nothing planned
  With such sublime, transcendent art!

Yes, Death, I own I grudge thee mine
  Poor little hand, so feeble now;
Its wrinkled palm, its altered line,
  Its veins so pallid and so slow—

[Unfinished here.]

Ah, well, friend Death, good friend thou art:
  I shall be free when thou art through.
Take all there is—take hand and heart:
  There must be somewhere work to do.
    [Her last poem: 7 August, 1885.]

PAUL HAMILTON HAYNE (1831-1886)

Between the Sunken Sun and the New Moon

Between the sunken sun and the new moon,
I stood in fields through which a rivulet ran

With scarce perceptible motion, not a span
Of its smooth surface trembling to the tune
Of sunset breezes: "O delicious boon,"
I cried, "of quiet! wise is Nature's plan,
Who, in her realm, as in the soul of man,
Alternates storm with calm, and the loud noon
With dewy evening's soft and sacred lull:
Happy the heart that keeps *its* twilight hour,
And, in the depths of heavenly peace reclined,
Loves to commune with thoughts of tender power;
Thoughts that ascend, like angels beautiful,
A shining Jacob's ladder of the mind."

A Little While I Fain Would Linger Yet

A little while (my life is almost set!)
  I fain would pause along the downward way,
  Musing an hour in this sad sunset-ray,
While, Sweet! our eyes with tender tears are wet:
A little hour I fain would linger yet.

A little while I fain would linger yet,
  All for love's sake, for love that cannot tire;
  Though fervid youth be dead, with youth's desire,
And hope has faded to a vague regret,
A little while I fain would linger yet.

A little while I fain would linger here:
  Behold! who knows what strange, mysterious bars
  'Twixt souls that love may rise in other stars?
Nor can love deem the face of death is fair:
A little while I still would linger here.

A little while I yearn to hold thee fast,
  Hand locked in hand, and loyal heart to heart;
  (O pitying Christ! those woeful words, "We part!")
So ere the darkness fall, the light be past,
A little while I fain would hold thee fast.

A little while, when light and twilight meet,—
  Behind, our broken years; before, the deep
  Weird wonder of the last unfathomed sleep,—
A little while I still would clasp thee, Sweet,
A little while, when night and twilight meet.

A little while I fain would linger here;
  Behold! who knows what soul-dividing bars
  Earth's faithful loves may part in other stars?
Nor can love deem the face of death is fair:
A little while I still would linger here.

ELIZABETH AKERS ALLEN (1832-1911)

In a Garret

This realm is sacred to the silent past;
  Within its drowsy shades are treasures rare
Of dust and dreams; the years are long since last
  A stranger's footfall pressed the creaking stair.

This room no housewife's tidy hand disturbs;
  And here, like some strange presence, ever clings
A homesick smell of dry forgotten herbs,—
  A musty odor as of mouldering things.

Here stores of withered roots and leaves repose,
  For fancied virtues prized in days of yore,
Gathered with thoughtful care, mayhap by those
  Whose earthly ills are healed forever more.

Here shy Arachne winds her endless thread,
  And weaves her silken tapestry unseen,
Veiling the rough-hewn timbers overhead,
  And looping gossamer festoons between.

Along the low joists of the sloping roof,
  Moth-eaten garments hang, a gloomy row,
Like tall fantastic ghosts, which stand aloof,
  Holding grim converse with the long ago.

Here lie remembrancers of childish joys,—
  Old fairy-volumes, conned and conned again,
A cradle, and a heap of battered toys,
  Once loved by babes who now are bearded men.

Here, in the summer, at a broken pane,
  The yellow wasps come in, and buzz and build
Among the rafters; wind and snow and rain
  All enter, as the seasons are fulfilled.

This mildewed chest, behind the chimney, holds
  Old letters, stained and nibbled; faintly show
The faded phrases on the tattered folds
  Once kissed, perhaps, or tear-wet—who may know.

I turn a page like one who plans a crime,
  And lo! love's prophecies and sweet regrets,
A tress of chestnut hair, a love-lorn rhyme,
  And fragrant dust that once was violets.

I wonder if the small sleek mouse, that shaped
  His winter nest between these time-stained beams,
Was happier that his bed was lined and draped
  With the bright warp and woof of youthful dreams?

Here where the gray incessant spiders spin,
  Shrouding from view the sunny world outside,
A golden bumblebee has blundered in
  And lost the way to liberty, and died.

So the lost present drops into the past;
  So the warm living heart, that loves the light,
Faints in the unresponsive darkness vast
  Which hides time's buried mysteries from sight.

Why rob these shadows of their sacred trust?
  Let the thick cobwebs hide the day once more;
Leave the dead years to silence and to dust,
  And close again the long unopened door.

MARY ASHLEY TOWNSEND (1832-1901)

Down the Bayou

The cypress swamp around me wraps its spell,
With hushing sounds in moss-hung branches there,
Like congregations rustling down to prayer,
While Solitude, like some unsounded bell,
Hangs full of secrets that it cannot tell,
And leafy litanies on the humid air
Intone themselves, and on the tree-trunks bare
The scarlet lichen writes her rubrics well.
The cypress-knees take on them marvellous shapes
Of pigmy nuns, gnomes, goblins, witches, fays,
The vigorous vine the withered gum-tree drapes,
Across the oozy ground the rabbit plays,
The moccasin to jungle depths escapes,
And through the gloom the wild deer shyly gaze.

JOHN ALBEE (1833-1915)

Landor

Come, Walter Savage Landor, come this way;
Step through the lintel low, with prose or verse,
Tallest of latter men; the early star
And latest setting sun of great compeers;
Through youth, through manhood, and extremest age,
Strong at the root, and at the top, blossoms
Perennial. When culled the fields around

Still calling up the great for wisest talk,
Or singing clear some fresh, melodious stave,
Not sickly-sweet, but like ripe autumn fruit,
Of which not one but all the senses taste,
And leave uncloyed the dainty appetite.
Great English master of poetic art,
In these late times that dandle every muse,
Here mayst thou air all day thine eloquence,
And I a never weary listener,
If thou at eve wilt sing one witty song,
Or chant some line of cadenced, classic hymn.

EDMUND CLARENCE STEDMAN (1833-1908)

Pan in Wall Street

Just where the Treasury's marble front
    Looks over Wall Street's mingled nations;
Where Jews and Gentiles most are wont
    To throng for trade and last quotations;
Where, hour by hour, the rates of gold
    Outrival, in the ears of people,
The quarter-chimes, serenely tolled
    From Trinity's undaunted steeple,—

Even there I heard a strange, wild strain
    Sound high above the modern clamor,
Above the cries of greed and gain,
    The curbstone war, the auction's hammer;
And swift, on Music's misty ways,
    It led, from all this strife for millions,
To ancient, sweet-do-nothing days
    Among the kirtle-robed Sicilians.

And as it stilled the multitude,
    And yet more joyous rose, and shriller,
I saw the minstrel, where he stood
    At ease against a Doric pillar:
One hand a droning organ played,
    The other held a Pan's-pipe (fashioned
Like those of old) to lips that made
    The reeds give out that strain impassioned.

'Twas Pan himself had wandered here
    A-strolling through this sordid city,
And piping to the civic ear
    The prelude of some pastoral ditty!

The demigod had crossed the seas,—
  From haunts of shepherd, nymph, and satyr,
And Syracusan times,—to these
  Far shores and twenty centuries later.

A ragged cap was on his head;
  But—hidden thus—there was no doubting
That, all with crispy locks o'erspread,
  His gnarlëd horns were somewhere sprouting;
His club-feet, cased in rusty shoes,
  Were crossed, as on some frieze you see them,
And trousers, patched of divers hues,
  Concealed his crooked shanks beneath them.

He filled the quivering reeds with sound,
  And o'er his mouth their changes shifted,
And with his goat's-eye looked around
  Where'er the passing current drifted;
And soon, as on Trinacrian hills
  The nymphs and herdsmen ran to hear him,
Even now the tradesmen from their tills,
  With clerks and porters, crowded near him.

The bulls and bears together drew
  From Jauncey Court and New Street Alley,
As erst, if pastorals be true,
  Came beasts from every wooded valley;
The random passers stayed to list,—
  A boxer Ægon, rough and merry,
A Broadway Daphnis, on his tryst
  With Nais at the Brooklyn Ferry.

A one-eyed Cyclops halted long
  In tattered cloak of army pattern,
And Galatea joined the throng,—
  A blowsy, apple-vending slattern;
While old Silenus staggered out
  From some new-fangled lunch-house handy,
And bade the piper, with a shout,
  To strike up Yankee Doodle Dandy!

A newsboy and a peanut-girl
  Like little Fauns began to caper:
His hair was all in tangled curl,
  Her tawny legs were bare and taper;
And still the gathering larger grew,
  And gave its pence and crowded nigher,
While aye the shepherd-minstrel blew
  His pipe, and struck the gamut higher.

O heart of Nature, beating still
  With throbs her vernal passion taught her,—
Even here, as on the vine-clad hill,
  Or by the Arethusan water!
New forms may fold the speech, new lands
  Arise within these ocean-portals,
But Music waves eternal wands,—
  Enchantress of the souls of mortals!

So thought I,—but among us trod
  A man in blue, with legal baton,
And scoffed the vagrant demigod,
  And pushed him from the step I sat on.
Doubting I mused upon the cry,
  "Great Pan is dead!'—and all the people
Went on their ways:—and clear and high
  The quarter sounded from the steeple.

CHARLES HENRY WEBB (1834-1905)

Dum Vivimus Vigilamus

Turn out more ale, turn up the light;
I will not go to bed to-night.
Of all the foes that man should dread
The first and worst one is a bed.
Friends I have had both old and young,
And ale we drank and songs we sung:
Enough you know when this is said,
That, one and all,—they died in bed.
  In bed they died and I'll not go
  Where all my friends have perished so.
  Go you who glad would buried be,
  But not to-night a bed for me.

For me to-night no bed prepare,
But set me out my oaken chair.
And bid no other guests beside
The ghosts that shall around me glide;
In curling smoke-wreaths I shall see
A fair and gentle company.
Though silent all, rare revellers they,
Who leave you not till break of day.
  Go you who would not daylight see,
  But not to-night a bed for me:
  For I've been born and I've been wed—
  All of man's peril comes of bed.

And I'll not seek—whate'er befall—
Him who unbidden comes to all.
A grewsome guest, a lean-jawed wight—
God send he do not come to-night!
But if he do, to claim his own,
He shall not find me lying prone;
But blithely, bravely, sitting up,
And raising high the stirrup-cup.
   Then if you find a pipe unfilled,
    An empty chair, the brown ale spilled;
   Well may you know, though naught be said,
   That I've been borne away to bed.

GEORGE ARNOLD (1834-1865)

Beer

Here,
With my beer
I sit,
While golden moments flit:
Alas!
They pass
Unheeded by:
And, as they fly,
I,
Being dry,
Sit, idly sipping here
My beer.

O, finer far
Than fame, or riches, are
The graceful smoke-wreaths of this free cigar!
   Why
    Should I
   Weep, wail, or sigh?
   What if luck has passed me by?
What if my hopes are dead,—
My pleasures fled?
   Have I not still
    My fill
Of right good cheer,—
Cigars and beer?

   Go, whining youth,
    Forsooth!
Go, weep and wail,
Sigh and grow pale,
   On the old times,
   Weave melancholy rhymes

Whose joys like shadowy ghosts appear,
But leave to me my beer!
  Gold is dross,—
  Love is loss,—
So, if I gulp my sorrows down,
Or see them drown
In foamy draughts of old nut-brown,
Then do I wear the crown,
  Without the cross!

HARRIET McEWEN KIMBALL (1834-1917)

The Guest

Speechless Sorrow sat with me;
I was sighing wearily;
Lamp and fire were out; the rain
Wildly beat the window-pane.
In the dark I heard a knock,
And a hand was on the lock;
One in waiting spake to me,
  Saying sweetly,
"I am come to sup with thee."

All my room was dark and damp:
"Sorrow," said I, "trim the lamp,
Light the fire, and cheer thy face,
Set the guest-chair in its place."
And again I heard the knock;
In the dark I found the lock:—
"Enter, I have turned the key;
  Enter, Stranger,
Who art come to sup with me."

Opening wide the door he came,
But I could not speak his name;
In the guest-chair took his place,
But I could not see his face.
When my cheerful fire was beaming,
When my little lamp was gleaming,
And the feast was spread for three,
  Lo, my MASTER
Was the Guest that supped with me!

JOHN JAMES PIATT (1835-?)

Torch-Light in Autumn

I lift this sumach-bough with crimson flare,
  And, touched with subtle pangs of dreamy pain,
Through the dark wood a torch I seem to bear
  In Autumn's funeral train.

CELIA THAXTER (1835-1894)

The Sandpiper

Across the narrow beach we flit,
  One little sandpiper and I,
And fast I gather, bit by bit,
  The scattered driftwood bleached and dry.
The wild waves reach their hands for it,
  The wild wind raves, the tide runs high,
As up and down the beach we flit,—
  One little sandpiper and I.

Above our heads the sullen clouds
  Scud black and swift across the sky;
Like silent ghosts in misty shrouds
  Stand out the white lighthouses high.
Almost as far as eye can reach
  I see the close-reefed vessels fly,
As fast we flit along the beach,—
  One little sandpiper and I.

I watch him as he skims along,
  Uttering his sweet and mournful cry.
He starts not at my fitful song,
  Or flash of fluttering drapery.
He has no thought of any wrong;
  He scans me with a fearless eye:
Staunch friends are we, well tried and strong,
  The little sandpiper and I.

Comrade, where wilt thou be to-night
  When the loosed storm breaks furiously?
My driftwood fire will burn so bright!
  To what warm shelter canst thou fly?
I do not fear for thee, though wroth
  The tempest rushes through the sky:
For are we not God's children both,
  Thou, little sandpiper, and I?

LOUISE CHANDLER MOULTON (1835-1908)

Hic Jacet

So Love is dead that has been quick so long!
Close, then, his eyes, and bear him to his rest,

With eglantine and myrtle on his breast,
And leave him there, their pleasant scents among;
And chant a sweet and melancholy song
About the charms whereof he was possessed,
And how of all things he was loveliest,
And to compare with aught were him to wrong.
Leave him beneath the still and solemn stars,
That gather and look down from their far place
With their long calm our brief woes to deride,
Until the Sun the Morning's gate unbars
And mocks, in turn, our sorrows with his face;—
And yet, had Love been Love, he had not died.

Were but My Spirit Loosed upon the Air

Were but my spirit loosed upon the air——
    By some High Power who could Life's chains unbind,
    Set free to seek what most it longs to find- -
To no proud Court of Kings would I repair:
I would but climb, once more, a narrow stair,
    When day was wearing late, and dusk was kind;
    And one should greet me to my failings blind,
Content so I but shared his twilight there.

Nay! well I know he waits not as of old—
    I could not find him in the old-time place—
I must pursue him, made by sorrow bold,
    Through worlds unknown, in strange celestial race,
Whose mystic round no traveller has told,
    From star to star, until I see his face.

Love's Resurrection Day

Round among the quiet graves,
    When the sun was low,
Love went grieving,—Love who saves:
    Did the sleepers know?

At his touch the flowers awoke,
    At his tender call
Birds into sweet singing broke,
    And it did befall

From the blooming, bursting sod
    All Love's dead arose,
And went flying up to God
    By a way Love knows.

IRVING BROWNE (1835-1899)

My New World

My prow is tending toward the west,
Old voices growing faint, dear faces dim,
  And all that I have loved the best
Far back upon the waste of memory swim.
  My old world disappears:
  Few hopes and many fears
    Accompany me.

But from the distance fair
A sound of birds, a glimpse of pleasant skies,
  A scent of fragrant air,
  All soothingly arise
In cooing voice, sweet breath, and merry eyes
  Of grandson on my knee.
  And ere my sails be furled,
    Kind Lord, I pray
    Thou let me live a day
  In my new world.

Man's Pillow

A baby lying on his mother's breast
    Draws life from that sweet fount;
        He takes his rest
        And heaves deep sighs;
        With brooding eyes
        Of soft content

She shelters him within that fragrant nest,
    And scarce refrains from crushing him
        With tender violence,
    His rosebud mouth, each rosy limb
        Excite such joy intense;
    Rocked on that gentle billow,
        She sings into his ear
    A song that angels stoop to hear.
    Blest child and mother doubly blest!
        Such his first pillow.

A man outwearied with the world's mad race
    His mother seeks again;
        His furrowed face,
        His tired gray head,
        His heart of lead
        Resigned he yields;

> She covers him in some secluded place,
> And kindly heals the earthy scar
> Of spade with snow and flowers,
> While glow of sun and gleam of star,
> And murmuring rush of showers,
> And wind-obeying willow
> Attend his unbroken sleep;
> In this repose secure and deep,
> Forgotten save by One, he leaves no trace.
> Such his last pillow.

FRANCES LAUGHTON MACE (1836-1899)

Alcyone

I

Among the thousand, thousand spheres that roll,
Wheel within wheel, through never-ending space,
A mighty and interminable race,
Yet held by some invisible control,
And led as to a sure and shining goal,
One star alone, with still, unchanging face,
Looks out from her perpetual dwelling-place,
Of these swift orbs the centre and the soul.
Beyond the moons that beam, the stars that blaze,
Past fields of ether, crimson, violet, rose,
The vast star-garden of eternity,
Behold! it shines with white immaculate rays,
The home of peace, the haven of repose,
The lotus-flower of heaven, Alcyone.

II

It is the place where life's long dream comes true;
On many another swift and radiant star
Gather the flaming hosts of those who war
With powers of darkness; those stray seraphs, too,
Who hasten forth God's ministries to do:
But here no sounds of eager trumpets mar
The subtler spell which calls the soul from far,
Its wasted springs of gladness to renew.
It is the morning land of the Ideal,
Where smiles, transfigured to the raptured sight,
The joy whose flitting semblance now we see;
Where we shall know, as visible and real,
Our life's deep aspiration, old yet new,
In the sky-splendor of Alcyone.

III

What lies beyond we ask not. In that hour
When first our feet that shore of beauty press,
It is enough of heaven, its sweet success,
To find our own. Not yet we crave the dower
Of grander action and sublimer power;
We are content that life's long loneliness
Finds in love's welcoming its rich redress,
And hopes, deep hidden, burst in perfect flower.
Wait for me there, O loved of many days!
Though with warm beams some beckoning planet glows,
Its dawning triumphs keep, to share with me:
For soon, far winging through the starry maze,
Past fields of ether, crimson, violet, rose,
I follow, follow to Alcyone!

WILLIAM WINTER (1836-1917)

From "Arthur"

Thou idol of my constant heart,
    Thou child of perfect love and light,
That sudden from my side didst part,
    And vanish in the sea of night,
Through whatsoever tempests blow
My weary soul with thine would go.

Say, if thy spirit yet have speech,
    What port lies hid within the pall,
What shore death's gloomy billows reach,
    Or if they reach no shore at all!
One word—one little word—to tell
That thou art safe and all is well!

The anchors of my earthly fate,
    As they were cast so must they cling;
And naught is now to do but wait
    The sweet release that time will bring,
When all these mortal moorings break,
For one last voyage I must make.

Say that across the shuddering dark—
    And whisper that the hour is near—
Thy hand will guide my shattered bark

Till mercy's radiant coasts appear,
Where I shall clasp thee to my breast,
And know once more the name of rest.

Heaven's Hour

Can I forget?—no, never, while my soul
Lives to remember that imperial night
When through the spectral church I heard them roll,
Those organ tones of glory, and my sight
Grew dim with tears, while ever new delight
Throbbed in my heart, and through the shadowy dread
The pale ghosts wandered, and a deathly chill
Froze all my being,—the mysterious thrill
That tells the awful presence of the dead!
Yet not the dead, but strayed from heavenly bowers,
Pure souls that live with other lives than ours:
For sure I am that ecstasy of sound
Lured one sweet spirit from his holy ground,
Who dwells in the perpetual land of flowers.

SARAH MORGAN BRYAN PIATT (1836-1919)

The Witch in the Glass

"My mother says I must not pass
Too near that glass;
She is afraid that I will see
A little witch that looks like me,
With a red, red mouth to whisper low
The very thing I should not know!"

"Alack for all your mother's care!
A bird of the air,
A wistful wind, or (I suppose
Sent by some hapless boy) a rose,
With breath too sweet, will whisper low
The very thing you should not know!"

THOMAS BAILEY ALDRICH (1837-1907)

Heredity

A soldier of the Cromwell stamp,
With sword and psalm-book by his side,

At home alike in church and camp:
Austere he lived, and smileless died.

But she, a creature soft and fine—
From Spain, some say, some say from France;
Within her veins leapt blood like wine—
She led her Roundhead lord a dance!

In Grantham church they lie asleep;
Just where, the verger may not know.
Strange that two hundred years should keep
The old ancestral fires aglow!

In me these two have met again;
To each my nature owes a part:
To one, the cool and reasoning brain;
To one, the quick, unreasoning heart.

WILLIAM DEAN HOWELLS (1837-1920)

Sometimes, When after Spirited Debate

Sometimes, when after spirited debate
Of letters or affairs, in thought I go
Smiling unto myself, and all aglow
With some immediate purpose, and elate
As if my little, trivial scheme were great,

And what I would so were already so:
Suddenly I think of her that died, and know,
Whatever friendly or unfriendly fate
Befall me in my hope or in my pride,
It is all nothing but a mockery,
And nothing can be what it used to be,
When I could bid my happy life abide,
And build on earth for perpetuity,
Then, in the deathless days before she died.

JOHN BURROUGHS (1837-1921)

Waiting

Serene, I fold my hands and wait,
  Nor care for wind, or tide, or sea;
I rave no more 'gainst time or fate.
  For, lo! my own shall come to me.

I stay my haste, I make delays,
  For what avails this eager pace?
I stand amid the eternal ways,
  And what is mine shall know my face.

Asleep, awake, by night or day,
  The friends I seek are seeking me;
No wind can drive my bark astray,
  Nor change the tide of destiny.

What matter if I stand alone?
  I wait with joy the coming years;
My heart shall reap where it has sown,
  And garner up its fruit of tears.

The waters know their own and draw
  The brook that springs in yonder height;
So flows the good with equal law
  Unto the soul of pure delight.

The stars come nightly to the sky;
  The tidal wave unto the sea;
Nor time, nor space, nor deep, nor high,
  Can keep my own away from me.

JOHN HAY (1838-1905)

Jim Bludso of the Prairie Belle

Wall, no! I can't tell whar he lives,
  Becase he don't live, you see;
Leastways, he's got out of the habit
  Of livin' like you and me.
Whar have you been for the last three year
  That you haven't heard folks tell
How Jimmy Bludso passed in his checks
  The night of the Prairie Belle?

He weren't no saint,—them engineers
  Is all pretty much alike,—
One wife in Natchez-under-the-Hill
  And another one here, in Pike:
A keerless man in his talk was Jim,
  And an awkward hand in a row,
But he never flunked, and he never lied,—
  I reckon he never knowed how.

And this was all the religion he had,—
  To treat his engine well;
Never be passed on the river;
  To mind the pilot's bell;
And if ever the Prairie Belle took fire,—
  A thousand times he swore
He'd hold her nozzle agin the bank
  Till the last soul got ashore.

All boats has their day on the Mississip,
  And her day come at last,—
The Movastar was a better boat,
  But the Belle she *wouldn't* be passed.
And so she come tearin' along that night—
  The oldest craft on the line—
With a nigger squat on her safety-valve,
  And her furnace crammed, rosin and pine.

The fire bust out as she clared the bar,
  And burnt a hole in the night,
And quick as a flash she turned, and made
  For that willer-bank on the right.
There was runnin' and cursin', but Jim yelled out,
  Over all the infernal roar,
"I'll hold her nozzle agin the bank
  Till the last galoot's ashore."

Through the hot, black breath of the burnin' boat
  Jim Bludso's voice was heard,
And they all had trust in his cussedness,
  And knowed he would keep his word.
And, sure's you're born, they all got off
  Afore the smokestacks fell,—
And Bludso's ghost went up alone
  In the smoke of the Prairie Belle.

He weren't no saint,—but at jedgment
  I'd run my chance with Jim,
'Longside of some pious gentlemen
  That wouldn't shook hands with him.
He seen his duty, a dead-sure thing,—
  And went for it thar and then;
And Christ ain't a going to be too hard
  On a man that died for men.

JAMES RYDER RANDALL (1839-1908)

From "My Maryland"

The despot's heel is on thy shore,
    Maryland!
His torch is at thy temple door,
    Maryland!
Avenge the patriotic gore
That flecked the streets of Baltimore,
And be the battle-queen of yore,
    Maryland, my Maryland!

Hark to an exiled son's appeal,
    Maryland!
My Mother State, to thee I kneel,
    Maryland!
For life and death, for woe and weal,
Thy peerless chivalry reveal,
And gird thy beauteous limbs with steel,
    Maryland, my Maryland!

Thou wilt not cower in the dust,
    Maryland!
Thy beaming sword shall never rust,
    Maryland!
Remember Carroll's sacred trust,
Remember Howard's warlike thrust,
And all thy slumberers with the just,
    Maryland, my Maryland!

Thou wilt not yield the Vandal toll,
    Maryland!
Thou wilt not crook to his control,
    Maryland!
Better the fire upon thee roll,
Better the shot, the blade, the bowl,
Than crucifixion of the soul,
    Maryland, my Maryland!

I hear the distant thunder hum,
    Maryland!
The Old Line's bugle, fife, and drum,
    Maryland!
She is not dead, nor deaf, nor dumb;

Huzza! she spurns the Northern scum!
She breathes! She burns! She'll come!
    She'll come!
        Maryland, my Maryland!

ABRAM JOSEPH RYAN (1839-1888)

The Conquered Banner

Furl that Banner, for 'tis weary;
Round its staff 'tis drooping dreary:
    Furl it, fold it,—it is best;
For there's not a man to wave it,
And there's not a sword to save it,
And there's not one left to lave it
In the blood which heroes gave it,
And its foes now scorn and brave it:
    Furl it, hide it,—let it rest!

Take that Banner down! 'tis tattered;
Broken is its staff and shattered;
And the valiant hosts are scattered,
    Over whom it floated high.
Oh, 'tis hard for us to fold it,
Hard to think there's none to hold it,
Hard that those who once unrolled it
    Now must furl it with a sigh!

Furl that Banner—furl it sadly!
Once ten thousands hailed it gladly,
And ten thousands wildly, madly,
    Swore it should forever wave;
Swore that foeman's sword should never
Hearts like theirs entwined dissever,
Till that flag should float forever
    O'er their freedom or their grave!

Furl it! for the hands that grasped it.
And the hearts that fondly clasped it,
    Cold and dead are lying low;
And that Banner—it is trailing.
While around it sounds the wailing
    Of its people in their woe.

For, though conquered, they adore it.—
Love the cold, dead hands that bore it,
Weep for those who fell before it,

Pardon those who trailed and tore it;
And oh, wildly they deplore it,
    Now to furl and fold it so!

Furl that Banner! True, 'tis gory,
Yet 'tis wreathed around with glory,
And 'twill live in song and story
    Though its folds are in the dust!
For its fame on brightest pages,
Penned by poets and by sages,
Shall go sounding down the ages—
    Furl its folds though now we must.

Furl that Banner, softly, slowly!
Treat it gently—it is holy,
    For it droops above the dead.
Touch it not—unfold it never;
Let it droop there, furled forever.—
    For its people's hopes are fled!

FRANCIS BRET HARTE (1839-1902)

Dickens in Camp

(1812-1870)

Above the pines the moon was slowly drifting,
    The river sang below;
The dim Sierras, far beyond, uplifting
    Their minarets of snow.

The roaring camp-fire, with rude humor, painted
    The ruddy tints of health
On haggard face and form that drooped and fainted
    In the fierce race for wealth;

Till one arose, and from his pack's scant treasure
    A hoarded volume drew,
And cards were dropped from hands of listless leisure,
    To hear the tale anew.

And then, while round them shadows gathered faster,
    And as the firelight fell,
He read aloud the book wherein the Master
    Had writ of "Little Nell."

Perhaps 'twas boyish fancy,—for the reader
    Was youngest of them all,—

But, as he read, from clustering pine and cedar
    A silence seemed to fall;

The fir-trees, gathering closer in the shadows,
    Listened in every spray,
While the whole camp, with "Nell," on English meadows
    Wandered and lost their way.

And so in mountain solitudes—o'ertaken
    As by some spell divine—
Their cares dropped from them like the needles shaken
    From out the gusty pine.

Lost is that camp, and wasted all its fire:
    And he who wrought that spell?—
Ah! towering pine and stately Kentish spire,
    Ye have one tale to tell!

Lost is that camp, but let its fragrant story
    Blend with the breath that thrills
With hop-vines incense all the pensive glory
    That fills the Kentish hills.

And on that grave where English oak and holly
    And laurel wreathes entwine,
Deem it not all a too presumptuous folly—
    This spray of Western pine!

Plain Language from Truthful James
(*Table Mountain,* 1870)

Which I wish to remark,
    And my language is plain,
That for ways that are dark
    And for tricks that are vain,
The heathen Chinee is peculiar:
    Which the same I would rise to explain.

Ah Sin was his name;
    And I shall not deny,
In regard to the same,
    What that name might imply;
But his smile it was pensive and childlike.
    As I frequent remarked to Bill Nye.

It was August the third,
    And quite soft was the skies;
Which it might be inferred

That Ah Sin was likewise;
Yet he played it that day upon William
And me in a way I despise.

Which we had a small game,
And Ah Sin took a hand:
It was Euchre. The same
He did not understand;
But he smiled, as he sat by the table,
With the smile that was childlike and bland.

Yet the cards they were stocked
In a way that I grieve,
And my feelings were shocked
At the state of Nye's sleeve,
Which was stuffed full of aces and bowers,
And the same with intent to deceive.

But the hands that were played
By that heathen Chinee,
And the points that he made,
Were quite frightful to see,—
Till at last he put down a right bower,
Which the same Nye had dealt unto me.

Then I looked up at Nye,
And he gazed upon me;
And he rose with a sigh,
And said, "Can this be?
We are ruined by Chinese cheap labor,"—
And he went for that heathen Chinee.

In the scene that ensued
I did not take a hand,
But the floor it was strewed,
Like the leaves on the strand,
With the cards that Ah Sin had been hiding,
In the game "he did not understand."

In his sleeves, which were long,
He had twenty-four packs,—
Which was coming it strong,
Yet I state but the facts;
And we found on his nails, which were taper,
What is frequent in tapers,—that's wax.

Which is why I remark,
And my language is plain,
That for ways that are dark,

And for tricks that are vain,
The heathen Chinee is peculiar,—
Which the same I am free to maintain.

The Society upon the Stanislaus

I reside at Table Mountain, and my name is Truthful James;
I am not up to small deceit, or any sinful games;
And I'll tell in simple language what I know about the row
That broke up our Society upon the Stanislow.

But first I would remark, that it is not a proper plan
For any scientific gent to whale his fellow-man,
And, if a member don't agree with his peculiar whim,
To lay for that same member for to "put a head" on him.

Now nothing could be finer or more beautiful to see
Than the first six months' proceedings of that same Society,
Till Brown of Calaveras brought a lot of fossil bones
That he found within a tunnel near the tenement of Jones.

Then Brown he read a paper, and he reconstructed there,
From those same bones, an animal that was extremely rare;
And Jones then asked the Chair for a suspension of the rules,
Till he could prove that those same bones was one of his
        lost mules.

Then Brown he smiled a bitter smile, and said he was at
        fault,—
It seemed he had been trespassing on Jones's family vault:
He was a most sarcastic man, this quiet Mr. Brown,
And on several occasions he had cleaned out the town.

Now I hold it is not decent for a scientific gent
To say another is an ass,—at least, to all intent;
Nor should the individual who happens to be meant
Reply by heaving rocks at him, to any great extent.

Then Abner Dean of Angel's raised a point of order—when
A chunk of old red sandstone took him in the abdomen,
And he smiled a kind of sickly smile, and curled up on the
        floor,
And the subsequent proceedings interested him no more.

For, in less time than I write it, every member did engage
In a warfare with the remnants of a palæozoic age;
And the way they heaved those fossils in their anger was
        a sin,
Till the skull of an old mammoth caved the head of Thomp-
son in.

And this is all I have to say of these improper games,
For I live at Table Mountain, and my name is Truthful
    James.;
And I've told in simple language what I know about the row
That broke up our Society upon the Stanislow.

"Jim"

Say there! P'r'aps
Some of you chaps
   Might know Jim Wild?
Well,—no offense:
Thar ain't no sense
   In gittin' riled!

Jim was my chum
   Up on the Bar:
That's why I come
   Down from up yar,
Lookin' for Jim.
Thank ye, sir! *You*
Ain't of that crew,—
   Blest if you are!

Money? Not much:
   That ain't my kind;
I ain't no such.
   Rum? I don't mind,
Seein' it's you.

Well, this yer Jim,—
Did you know him?
Jes' 'bout your size;
Same kind of eyes;—
Well, that is strange:
   Why, it's two year
   Since he came here,
Sick, for a change.

Well, here's to us:
   Eh?
The h—— you say!
   Dead?
That little cuss?
What makes you star',
You over thar?
Can't a man drop
'S glass in yer shop

But you must r'ar?
  It wouldn't take
  D——d much to break
You and your bar.

          Dead!
Poor—little—Jim!
Why, thar was me,
Jones, and Bob Lee,
Harry and Ben,—
No-account men:
Then to take *him!*

Well, thar—Good-by.
No more, sir—I——
          Eh?
What's that you say?
Why, dern it!—sho!—
No? Yes! By Joe!
          Sold!
Sold! Why, you limb,
You ornery,
  Derned, old,
Long-legged Jim!

What the Bullet Sang

O joy of creation
          To be!
O rapture to fly
          And be free!
Be the battle lost or won,
Though its smoke shall hide the sun,
I shall find my love,—the one
          Born for me!
I shall know him where he stands,
          All alone,
With the power in his hands
          Not o'erthrown;
I shall know him by his face,
By his godlike front and grace;
I shall hold him for a space,
          All my own!

It is he—O my love!
          So bold!
It is I—all thy love
          Foretold!
It is I. O love! what bliss!

Dost thou answer to my kiss?
O sweetheart! what is this
    Lieth there so cold?

EDWARD ROWLAND SILL (1841-1887)

The Fool's Prayer

The royal feast was done; the King
  Sought some new sport to banish care,
And to his jester cried: "Sir Fool,
  Kneel now, and make for us a prayer!"

The jester doffed his cap and bells,
  And stood the mocking court before;
They could not see the bitter smile
  Behind the painted grin he wore.

He bowed his head, and bent his knee
  Upon the monarch's silken stool;
His pleading voice arose: "O Lord,
  Be merciful to me, a fool!

"No pity, Lord, could change the heart
  From red with wrong to white as wool:
The rod must heal the sin; but, Lord,
  Be merciful to me, a fool!

"'Tis not by guilt the onward sweep
  Of truth and right, O Lord, we stay;
'Tis by our follies that so long
  We hold the earth from heaven away.

"These clumsy feet, still in the mire,
  Go crushing blossoms without end;
These hard, well-meaning hands we thrust
  Among the heart-strings of a friend.

"The ill-timed truth we might have kept—
  Who knows how sharp it pierced and stung!
The word we had not sense to say—
  Who knows how grandly it had rung!

"Our faults no tenderness should ask,
  The chastening stripes must cleanse them all;
But for our blunders—oh, in shame
  Before the eyes of heaven we fall.

"Earth bears no balsam for mistakes;
  Men crown the knave, and scourge the tool
That did his will; but Thou, O Lord,
  Be merciful to me, a fool!"

The room was hushed; in silence rose
  The King, and sought his gardens cool,
And walked apart, and murmured low,
  "Be merciful to me, a fool!"

JOAQUIN MILLER (1841-1913)

Crossing the Plains

What great yoked brutes with briskets low,
With wrinkled necks like buffalo,
With round, brown, liquid, pleading eyes,
That turned so low and sad to you,
That shone like love's eyes soft with tears,
That seemed to plead, and make replies,
The while they bowed their necks and drew
The creaking load; and looked at you.
Their sable briskets swept the ground,
Their cloven feet kept solemn sound.

Two sullen bullocks led the line,
Their great eyes shining bright like wine;
Two sullen captive kings were they,
That had in time held herds at bay,
And even now they crushed the sod
With stolid sense of majesty,
And stately stepped and stately trod,
As if 'twere something still to be
Kings even in captivity.

Twilight at the Heights

The brave young city by the Balboa seas
Lies compassed about by the hosts of night—
Lies humming, low, like a hive of bees;
And the day lies dead. And its spirit's flight
Is far to the west; while the golden bars
That bound it are broken to a dust of stars.

Come under my oaks, oh, drowsy dusk!
The wolf and the dog; dear incense hour
When Mother Earth hath a smell of musk,

And things of the spirit assert their power—
When candles are set to burn in the west—
Set head and foot to the day at rest.

Dead in the Sierras

His footprints have failed us,
Where berries are red,
And madroños are rankest,—
The hunter is dead!

The grizzly may pass
By his half-open door;
May pass and repass
On his path, as of yore;

The panther may crouch
In the leaves on his limb;
May scream and may scream,—
It is nothing to him.

Prone, bearded, and breasted
Like columns of stone;
And tall as a pine—
As a pine overthrown!

His camp-fires gone,
What else can be done
Than let him sleep on
Till the light of the sun?

Ay, tombless! what of it?
Marble is dust,
Cold and repellent;
And iron is rust.

Columbus

Behind him lay the gray Azores,
Behind the Gates of Hercules;
Before him not the ghost of shores;
Before him only shoreless seas.
The good mate said: "Now must we pray,
For lo! the very stars are gone.
Brave Adm'r'l, speak! What shall I say?"
"Why, say: 'Sail on! sail on! and on!'"

My men grow mutinous day by day;
My men grow ghastly, wan and weak.
The stout mate thought of home; a spray

Of salt wave washed his swarthy cheek.
"What shall I say, brave Adm'r'l, say,
If we sight naught but seas at dawn?"
"Why, you shall say at break of day:
'Sail on! sail on! sail on! and on!'"

They sailed and sailed, as winds might blow,
Until at last the blanched mate said:
"Why, now not even God would know
Should I and all my men fall dead.
These very winds forget their way,
For God from these dread seas is gone.
Now speak, brave Adm'r'l, speak and say——"
He said: "Sail on! sail on! and on!"

They sailed. They sailed. Then spake the mate:
"This mad sea shows his teeth tonight.
He curls his lip, he lies in wait,
He lifts his teeth as if to bite!
Brave Adm'r'l, say but one good word:
What shall we do when hope is gone?"
The words leapt like a leaping sword:
"Sail on! sail on! sail on! and on!"

Then pale and worn, he paced his deck,
And peered through darkness. Ah, that night
Of all dark nights! And then a speck—
A light! A light! At last a light!
It grew, a starlit flag unfurled!
It grew to be Time's burst of dawn.
He gained a world; he gave that world
Its grandest lesson: "On! sail on!"

The Defense of the Alamo

Santa Ana came storming, as a storm might come;
There was rumble of cannon; there was rattle of blade;
There was cavalry, infantry, bugle and drum—
Full seven proud thousand in pomp and parade,
The chivalry, flower of all Mexico;
And a gaunt two hundred in the Alamo!

And thirty lay sick, and some were shot through;
For the siege had been bitter, and bloody, and long.
"Surrender, or die!"—"Men, what will *you* do?"
And Travis, great Travis, drew sword, quick and strong;
Drew a line at his feet. . . . "Will you come? Will you go?
I die with my wounded, in the Alamo."

Then Bowie gasped, "Guide me over that line!"
Then Crockett, one hand to the sick, one hand to his gun,
Crossed with him; then never a word or a sign
Till all, sick or well, all, all, save but one,
One man. Then a woman stopped praying, and slow
Across, to die with the heroes of the Alamo.

Then that one coward fled, in the night, in that night,
When all men silently prayed and thought
Of home; of tomorrow; of God and the right;
Till dawn; then Travis sent his single last cannon-shot,
In answer to insolent Mexico,
From the old bell-tower of the Alamo.

Then came Santa Ana; a crescent of flame:
Then the red *escalade;* then the fight hand to hand:
Such an unequal fight as never had name
Since the Persian hordes butchered that doomed Spartan band.
All day—all day and all night, and the morning? so slow,
Through the battle smoke mantling the Alamo.

Then silence! Such silence! Two thousand lay dead
In a crescent outside! And within? Not a breath
Save the gasp of a woman, with gory, gashed head,
All alone, with her dead there, waiting for death;
And she but a nurse. Yet when shall we know
Another like this of the Alamo?

Shout "Victory, victory, victory ho!"
I say, 'tis not always with the hosts that win;
I say that the victory, high or low,
Is given the hero who grapples with sin,
Or legion or single; just asking to know
When duty fronts death in his Alamo.

KATE PUTNAM OSGOOD (1841—)

Driving Home the Cows

Out of the clover and blue-eyed grass
    He turned them into the river-lane;
One after another he let them pass,
    Then fastened the meadow-bars again.

Under the willows, and over the hill,
    He patiently followed their sober pace;
The merry whistle for once was still,
    And something shadowed the sunny face.

Only a boy! and his father had said
  He never could let his youngest go:
Two already were lying dead
  Under the feet of the trampling foe.

But after the evening work was done,
  And the frogs were loud in the meadow-swamp,
Over his shoulder he slung his gun
  And stealthily followed the foot-path damp.

Across the clover, and through the wheat,
  With resolute heart and purpose grim,
Though cold was the dew on his hurrying feet
  And the blind bat's flitting startled him.

Thrice since then had the lanes been white,
  And the orchards sweet with apple-bloom;
And now, when the cows came back at night,
  The feeble father drove them home.

For news had come to the lonely farm
  That three were lying where two had lain;
And the old man's tremulous, palsied arm
  Could never lean on a son's again.

The summer day grew cool and late.
  He went for the cows when the work was done;
But down the lane, as he opened the gate,
  He saw them coming one by one:

Brindle, Ebony, Speckle, and Bess,
  Shaking their horns in the evening wind;
Cropping the buttercups out of the grass—
  But who was it following close behind?

Loosely swung in the idle air
  The empty sleeve of army blue;
And worn and pale, from the crisping hair,
  Looked out a face that the father knew.

For Southern prisons will sometimes yawn,
  And yield their dead unto life again;
And the day that comes with a cloudy dawn
  In golden glory at last may wane.

The great tears sprang to their meeting eyes;
  For the heart must speak when the lips are dumb:
And under the silent evening skies
  Together they followed the cattle home.

CHARLES EDWARD CARRYL (1841—)

Robinson Crusoe's Story

The night was thick and hazy
    When the "Piccadilly Daisy"
Carried down the crew and captain in the sea;
    And I think the water drowned 'em;
    For they never, never found 'em
And I know they didn't come ashore with me.

Oh! 'twas very sad and lonely
    When I found myself the only
Population on this cultivated shore;
    But I've made a little tavern
    In a rocky little cavern,
And I sit and watch for people at the door.

I spent no time in looking
    For a girl to do my cooking,
As I'm quite a clever hand at making stews;
    But I had that fellow Friday,
    Just to keep the tavern tidy,
And to put a Sunday polish on my shoes.

I have a little garden
    That I'm cultivating lard in,
As the things I eat are rather tough and dry;
    For I live on toasted lizards,
    Prickly pears, and parrot gizzards,
And I'm really very fond of beetle-pie.

The clothes I had were furry,
    And it made me fret and worry
When I found the moths were eating off the hair;
    And I had to scrape and sand 'em,
    And I boiled 'em and I tanned 'em,
Till I got the fine morocco suit I wear.

I sometimes seek diversion
    In a family excursion
With the few domestic animals you see;
    And we take along a carrot
    As refreshment for the parrot,
And a little can of jungleberry tea.

Then we gather as we travel,
    Bits of moss and dirty gravel,
And we chip off little specimens of stone;

And we carry home as prizes
Funny bugs, of handy sizes,
Just to give the day a scientific tone.

If the roads are wet and muddy
We remain at home and study,—
For the Goat is very clever at a sum,—
And the Dog, instead of fighting,
Studies ornamental writing,
While the Cat is taking lessons on the drum.

We retire at eleven,
And we rise again at seven;
And I wish to call attention, as I close,
To the fact that all the scholars
Are correct about their collars,
And particular in turning out their toes.

SIDNEY LANIER (1842-1881)

The Marshes of Glynn

Glooms of the live-oaks, beautiful-braided and woven
With intricate shades of the vines that myriad-cloven
Clamber the forks of the multiform boughs,—
    Emerald twilights,—
    Virginal shy lights,
Wrought of the leaves to allure to the whisper of vows,
When lovers pace timidly down through the green colonnades
Of the dim sweet woods, of the dear dark woods,
  Of the heavenly woods and glades,
That run to the radiant marginal sand-beach within
    The wide sea-marshes of Glynn;—

Beautiful glooms, soft dusks in the noonday fire,—
Wildwood privacies, closets of lone desire,
Chamber from chamber parted with wavering arras of
    leaves,—
Cells for the passionate pleasure of prayer to the soul that
    grieves,
Pure with a sense of the passing of saints through the wood,
Cool for the dutiful weighing of ill with good;—

O braided dusks of the oak and woven shades of the vine,
While the riotous noonday sun of the June-day long did shine
Ye held me fast in your heart and I held you fast in mine;
But now when the moon is no more, and riot is rest,
And the sun is a-wait at the ponderous gate of the West,
And the slant yellow beam down the wood-aisle doth seem
Like a lane into heaven that leads from a dream—

Ay, now, when my soul all day hath drunken the soul of the
  oak,
And my heart is at ease from men, and the wearisome sound
  of the stroke
  Of the scythe of time and the trowel of trade is low,
  And belief overmasters doubt, and I know that I know,
  And my spirit is grown to a lordly great compass within,
That the length and the breadth and the sweep of the marshes
  of Glynn
Will work me no fear like the fear they have wrought me of
  yore
When length was fatigue, and when breadth was but bitter-
  ness sore,
And when terror and shrinking and dreary unnamable pain
Drew over me out of the merciless miles of the plain,—
Oh, now, unafraid, I am fain to face
  The vast sweet visage of space.
To the edge of the wood I am drawn, I am drawn,
Where the gray beach glimmering runs, as a belt of the dawn,
  For a mete and a mark
  To the forest-dark:—
          So:
Affable live-oak, leaning low,—
Thus—with your favor—soft, with a reverent hand,
(Not lightly touching your person, Lord of the land!)
Bending your beauty aside, with a step I stand
On the firm-packed sand,
         Free
By a world of marsh that borders a world of sea.
  Sinuous southward and sinuous northward the shimmering
  band
  Of the sand-beach fastens the fringe of the marsh to the
  folds of the land.
Inward and outward to northward and southward the beach-
  lines linger and curl
As a silver-wrought garment that clings to and follows the
  firm sweet limbs of a girl.
Vanishing, swerving, evermore curving again into sight,
Softly the sand-beach wavers away to a dim gray looping of
  light.
And what if behind me to westward the wall of the woods
  stands high?
The world lies east: how ample, the marsh and the sea and
  the sky!
A league and a league of marsh-grass, waist-high, broad in
  the blade,
Green, and all of a height, and unflecked with a light or a
  shade,

Stretch leisurely off, in a pleasant plain,
To the terminal blue of the main.
Oh, what is abroad in the marsh and the terminal sea?
  Somehow my soul seems suddenly free
From the weighing of fate and the sad discussion of sin,
By the length and the breadth and the sweep of the marshes
  of Glynn.

Ye marshes, how candid and simple and nothing-withholding
  and free
Ye publish yourselves to the sky and offer yourselves to the
  sea!
Tolerant plains, that suffer the sea and the rains and the sun,
Ye spread and span like the catholic man who hath mightily
  won
God out of knowledge and good out of infinite pain
And sight out of blindness and purity out of a stain.

As the marsh-hen secretly builds on the watery sod,
Behold I will build me a nest on the greatness of God:
I will fly in the greatness of God as the marsh-hen flies
In the freedom that fills all the space 'twixt the marsh and
  the skies:
By so many roots as the marsh-grass sends in the sod
I will heartily lay me a-hold on the greatness of God:
Oh, like to the greatness of God is the greatness within
The range of the marshes, the liberal marshes of Glynn.

And the sea lends large, as the marsh: lo, out of his plenty
  the sea
Pours fast: full soon the time of the flood-tide must be:
Look how the grace of the sea doth go.
About and about through the intricate channels that flow
          Here and there,
              Everywhere,
Till his waters have flooded the uttermost creeks and the low-
  lying lanes,
And the marsh is meshed with a million veins,
That like as with rosy and silvery essences flow
  In the rose-and-silver evening glow.
          Farewell, my Lord Sun!
The creeks overflow: a thousand rivulets run
'Twixt the roots of the sod; the blades of the marsh-grass
  stir;
Passeth a hurrying sound of wings that westward whirr;
Passeth, and all is still; and the currents cease to run;
And the sea and the marsh are one.

How still the plains of the waters be!
The tide is in his ecstasy;

SALEM COLLEGE
LIBRARY
Winston-Salem, N. C.

The tide is at his highest height;
    And it is night.
And now from the Vast of the Lord will the waters of sleep
Roll in on the souls of men,
But who will reveal to our waking ken
The forms that swim and the shapes that creep
        Under the waters of sleep?
And I would I could know what swimmeth below when the
    tide comes in
On the length and the breadth of the marvellous marshes of
    Glynn.

Evening Song

    Look off, dear Love, across the sallow sands,
        And mark yon meeting of the sun and sea,
    How long they kiss in sight of all the lands.
        Ah! longer, longer, we!

    Now in the sea's red vintage melts the sun,
        As Egypt's pearl dissolved in rosy wine,
    And Cleopatra night drinks all. 'Tis done,
        Love, lay thine hand in mine.

    Come forth, sweet stars, and comfort heaven's heart;
        Glimmer, ye waves, round else unlighted sands.
    O night! Divorce our sun and sky apart,
        Never our lips, our hands.

Song of the Chattahoochee

    Out of the hills of Habersham,
      Down the valleys of Hall,
I hurry amain to reach the plain,
Run the rapid and leap the fall,
Split at the rock and together again,
Accept my bed, or narrow or wide,
And flee from folly on every side
With a lover's pain to attend the plain
    Far from the hills of Habersham,
    Far from the valleys of Hall.

    All down the hills of Habersham,
    All down the valleys of Hall,
The rushes cried, *Abide, abide,*
The wilful waterweeds held me thrall,
The laving laurel turned my tide,
The ferns and the fondling grass said *Stay,*

The dewberry dipped for to work delay,
And the little reeds sighed, *Abide, abide,*
  Here in the hills of Habersham,
  Here in the valleys of Hall.

High o'er the hills of Habersham,
  Veiling the valleys of Hall,
The hickory told me manifold
Fair tales of shade, the poplar tall
Wrought me her shadowy self to hold,
The chestnut, the oak, the walnut, the pine,
Overleaning, with flickering meaning and sign,
Said, *Pass not, so cold, these manifold*
  Deep shades of the hills of Habersham,
  These glades in the valleys of Hall.

And oft in the hills of Habersham,
  And oft in the valleys of Hall,
The white quartz shone, and the smooth brook-stone
Did bar me of passage with friendly brawl,
And many a luminous jewel lone
—Crystals clear or a-cloud with mist,
Ruby, garnet and amethyst—
Made lures with the lights of streaming stone,
  In the clefts of the hills of Habersham,
  In the beds of the valleys of Hall.

But oh, not the hills of Habersham,
  And oh, not the valleys of Hall,
Avail: I am fain for to water the plain.
Downward the voices of Duty call—
Downward, to toil and be mixed with the main.
The dry fields burn, and the mills are to turn,
And a myriad flowers mortally yearn,
And the lordly main from beyond the plain
  Calls o'er the hills of Habersham,
  Calls through the valleys of Hall.

AMBROSE BIERCE (1842-?)

Another Way

I lay in silence, dead. A woman came
  And laid a rose upon my breast, and said,
"May God be merciful." She spoke my name,
  And added, "It is strange to think him dead.

"He loved me well enough, but 'twas his way
  To speak it lightly." Then, beneath her breath:
"Besides"—I knew what further she would say,

But then a footfall broke my dream of death.
To-day the words are mine. I lay the rose
Upon her breast, and speak her name, and deem
It strange indeed that she is dead. God knows
I had more pleasure in the other dream.

T. A. H.

Yes, he was that, or that, as you prefer,—
Did so and so, though, faith, it wasn't all;
Lived like a fool, cr a philosopher,
And had whatever's needful to a fall.
As rough inflections on a planet merge
In the true bend of the gigantic sphere,
Nor mar the perfect circle of its verge,
So in the survey of his worth the small
Asperities of spirit disappear,
Lost in the grander curves of character.
He lately was hit hard; none knew but I
The strength and terror of that ghastly stroke,—
Not even herself. He uttered not a cry,
But set his teeth and made a revelry;
Drank like a devil,—staining sometimes red
The goblet's edge; diced with his conscience; spread,
Like Sisyphus, a feast for Death, and spoke
His welcome in a tongue so long forgot
That even his ancient guest remembered not
What race had cursed him in it. Thus my friend,
Still conjugating with each failing sense
The verb "to die" in every mood and tense,
Pursued his awful humor to the end.
When, like a stormy dawn, the crimson broke
From his white lips, he smiled and mutely bled,
And, having meanly lived, is grandly dead.

RICHARD WATSON GILDER (1844-1909)

The Celestial Passion

O white and midnight sky! O starry bath!
Wash me in thy pure, heavenly, crystal flood;
Cleanse me, ye stars, from earthly soil and scath;
Let not one taint remain in spirit or blood!
Receive my soul, ye burning, awful deeps;
Touch and baptize me with the mighty power
That in ye thrills, while the dark planet sleeps;
Make me all yours for one blest, secret hour!
O glittering host! O high angelic choir!
Silence each tone that with thy music jars;

Fill me even as an urn with thy white fire
Till all I am is kindred to the stars!
Make me thy child, thou infinite, holy night—
So shall my days be full of heavenly light!

The Song of a Heathen

(Sojourning in Galilee, A. D. 32)

If Jesus Christ is a man,—
    And only a man,—I say
That of all mankind I cleave to him,
    And to him will I cleave alway.

If Jesus Christ is a God,—
    And the only God,—I swear
I will follow Him through heaven and hell,
    The earth, the sea, and the air!

JOHN BOYLE O'REILLY (1844-1890)

A White Rose

The red rose whispers of passion,
    And the white rose breathes of love;
Oh, the red rose is a falcon,
    And the white rose is a dove.

But I send you a cream-white rosebud
    With a flush on its petal tips;
For the love that is purest and sweetest
    Has a kiss of desire on the lips.

JAMES MAURICE THOMPSON (1844-1901)

Written on a Fly-Leaf of Theocritus

Those were good times, in olden days,
    Of which the poet has his dreams,
When gods beset the woodland ways,
    And lay in wait by all the streams.

One could be sure of something then
    Severely simple, simply grand,
Or keenly, subtly sweet, as when
    Venus and Love went hand in hand.

Now I would give (such is my need)
  All the world's store of rhythm and rhyme
To see Pan fluting on a reed
  And with his goat-hoof keeping time!

GEORGE THOMAS LANIGAN (1845-1886)

A Threnody

The Ahkoond of Swat is dead.—*London Papers.*

What, what, what,
What's the news from Swat?
    Sad news,
    Bad news,
Comes by the cable led
Through the Indian Ocean's bed,
Through the Persian Gulf, the Red
Sea and the Med-
Iterranean—he's dead;
The Ahkoond is dead!

For the Ahkoond I mourn,
    Who wouldn't?
He strove to disregard the message stern,
    But he Ahkoodn't.
Dead, dead, dead;
    (Sorrow Swats!)
Swats wha hae wi' Ahkoond bled,
Swats whom he hath often led
Onward to a gory bed,
    Or to victory,
    As the case might be,
        Sorrow Swats!
Tears shed,
    Shed tears like water,
Your great Ahkoond is dead!
    That Swats the matter!

Mourn, city of Swat!
Your great Ahkoond is not,
But lain 'mid worms to rot.
His mortal part alone, his soul was caught
    (Because he was a good Ahkoond)
    Up to the bosom of Mahound.
Though earthy walls his frame surround
(Forever hallowed be the ground!)
And sceptics mock the lowly mound
And say "He's now of no Ahkoond!"

His soul is in the skies,—
The azure skies that bend above his loved
    Metropolis of Swat.
He sees with larger, other eyes,
Athwart all earthly mysteries—
    He knows what's Swat.

Let Swat bury the great Ahkoond
With a noise of mourning and of lamentation!
Let Swat bury the great Ahkoond
    With the noise of the mourning of the
        Swattish nation!
    Fallen is at length
    Its tower of strength,
Its sun is dimmed ere it had nooned;
Dead lies the great Ahkoond,
    The great Ahkoond of Swat
    Is not!

JOHN BANISTER TABB (1845-1909)

Evolution

Out of the dusk a shadow,
    Then, a spark;
Out of the cloud a silence,
    Then, a lark;
Out of the heart a rapture,
    Then, a pain;
Out of the dead, cold ashes,
    Life again.

The Sisters

The waves forever move;
The hills forever rest:
Yet each the heavens approve,
And Love alike hath blessed
A Martha's household care,
A Mary's cloistered prayer.

Anonymous

Anonymous—nor needs a name
To tell the secret whence the flame,
With light, and warmth, and incense, came
A new creation to proclaim.
So was it when, His labor done,
God saw His work, and smiled thereon:
His glory in the picture shone,
But name upon the canvas, none.

Departed

They cannot wholly pass away,
    How far soe'er above;
Nor we, the lingerers, wholly stay
    Apart from those we love:
For spirits in eternity,
    As shadows in the sun,
Reach backward into Time, as we,
    Like lifted clouds, reach on.

WILL CARLETON (1845-1912)

Out of the Old House, Nancy

Out of the old house, Nancy—moved up into the new;
All the hurry and worry is just as good as through.
Only a bounden duty remains for you and I—
And that's to stand on the doorstep here, and bid the old
    house good-by.

What a shell we've lived in, these nineteen or twenty years!
Wonder it hasn't smashed in, and tumbled about our ears;
Wonder it's stuck together, and answered till to-day;
But every individual log was put up here to stay.

Things looked rather new, though, when this old house was
    built;
And things that blossomed you would've made some woman
    wilt;
And every other day, then, as sure as day would break,
My neighbor Ager come this way invitin' me to "shake."

And you, for want of neighbors, was sometimes blue and sad,
For wolves and bears and wildcats was the nearest ones you
    had;
But, lookin' ahead to the clearin', we worked with all our
    might,
Until we was fairly out of the woods, and things was goin'
    right.

Look up there at our new house!—ain't it a thing to see?
Tall and big and handsome, and new as new can be;
All in apple-pie order, especially the shelves,
And never a debt to say but what we own it all ourselves.

Look at our old log-house—how little it now appears!
But it's never gone back on us for nineteen or twenty years;

An' I won't go back on it now, or go to pokin' fun—
There's such a thing as praisin' a thing for the good that it
  has done.

Probably you remember how rich we was that night,
When we was fairly settled, an' had things snug and tight:
We feel as proud as you please, Nancy, over our house that's
  new,
But we felt as proud under this old roof, and a good deal
  prouder, too.

Never a handsomer house was seen beneath the sun:
Kitchen and parlor and bedroom—we had 'em all in one;
And the fat old wooden clock that we bought when we come
  West,
Was tickin' away in the corner there, and doin' its level
  best.

Trees was all around us, a-whisperin' cheering words;
Loud was the squirrel's chatter, and sweet the songs of birds;
And home grew sweeter and brighter—our courage began to
  mount—
And things looked hearty and happy then, and work appeared
  to count.

And here one night it happened, when things was goin' bad,
We fell in a deep old quarrel—the first we ever had;
And when you give out and cried, then I, like a fool, give in,
And then we agreed to rub all out, and start the thing ag'in.

Here it was, you remember, we sat when the day was done,
And you was a-makin' clothing *that wasn't for either one;*
And often a soft word of love, I was soft enough to say,
And the wolves was howlin' in the woods not twenty rods
  away.

Then our first-born baby—a regular little joy,
Though I fretted a little because it wasn't a boy;
Wa'n't she a little flirt, though, with all her pouts and smiles?
Why, settlers come to see that show a half a dozen miles.

Yonder sat the cradle—a homely, home-made thing—
And many a night I rocked it, providin' you would sing;
And many a little squatter brought up with us to stay,—
And so that cradle, for many a year, was never put away.

How they kept a-comin' so cunnin' and fat and small!
How they growed! 'twas a wonder how we found room for
  'em all;

But though the house was crowded, it empty seemed that day
When Jennie lay by the fireplace there, and moaned her life
    away.

An' right in there the preacher, with Bible and hymn-book,
    stood,
" 'Twixt the dead and the living," and "hoped 'twould do us
    good":
And the little whitewood coffin on the table there was set,
And now as I rub my eyes it seems as if I could see it yet.

Then that fit of sickness it brought on you, you know;
Just by a thread you hung, and you e'en-a'-most let go;
And here is the spot I tumbled, an' give the Lord his due,
When the doctor said the fever'd turned, an' he could fetch
    you through.

Yes, a deal has happened to make this old house dear:
Christenin's, funerals, weddin's—what haven't we had here?
Not a log in this buildin' but its memories has got,
And not a nail in this old floor but touches a tender spot.

Out of the old house, Nancy,—moved up into the new;
All the hurry and worry is just as good as through;
But I tell you a thing right here, that I ain't ashamed to say,
There's precious things in this old house we never can take
    away.

Here the old house will stand, but not as it stood before:
Winds will whistle through it, and rains will flood the floor;
And over the hearth, once blazing, the snowdrifts oft will
    pile,
And the old thing will seem to be a-mournin' all the while.

Fare you well, old house! you're naught that can feel or see,
But you seem like a human being—a dear old friend to me;
And we never will have a better home, if *my* opinion stands,
Until we commence a-keepin' house in the house not made
    with hands.

LLOYD MIFFLIN (1846-1921)

The Ship

I lay on Delos of the Cyclades
At evening, on a cape of golden land;
The blind Bard's book was open in my hand,
There where the Cyclops makes the Odyssey's
Calm pages tremble as Odysseus flees.
Then, stately, like a mirage o'er the sand,

A phantom ship across the sunset strand
Rose out of dreams and clave the purple seas;
Straight on that city's bastions did she run—
Whose toppling turrets on their donjons hold
Bells that to mortal ears have never tolled—
Then drifted down the gateways of the sun
With fading pennon and with gonfalon,
And cast her anchors in the pools of gold.

The Doors

As through the Void we went I heard his plumes
Strike on the darkness. It was passing sweet
To hold his hand and feel that thin air beat
Against our pinions as we winged those glooms
Of Ebon, through which Atropos still dooms
Each soul to pass. Then presently our feet
Found footing on a ledge of dark retreat,
And opposite appeared two doors of tombs
Seen by the star upon the angel's head
That made dim twilight; there I caught my breath:
"Why pause we here?" The angel answering said,
"The journey ends. These are the Doors of Death;
Lo, now they open, inward, for the dead."
And then a Voice,—"Who next that entereth?"

The Flight

Upon a cloud among the stars we stood.
The angel raised his hand and looked and said,
"Which world, of all yon starry myriad,
Shall we make wing to?" The still solitude
Became a harp whereon his voice and mood
Made spheral music round his haloed head.
I spake—for then I had not long been dead—
"Let me look round upon the vasts, and brood
A moment on these orbs ere I decide . . .
What is yon lower star that beauteous shines
And with soft splendor now incarnadines
Our wings?—There would I go and there abide."
He smiled as one who some child's thought divines:
"That is the world where yesternight you died."

EDGAR FAWCETT (1847-1904)

To an Oriole

How falls it, oriole, thou hast come to fly
In tropic splendor through the Northern sky?

At some glad moment was it nature's choice
To dower a scrap of sunset with a voice?
Or did some orange tulip, flaked with black,
In some forgotten garden, ages back,
Yearning toward Heaven until its wish was heard,
Desire unspeakably to be a bird?

JAMES JEFFREY ROCHE (1847-1908)

The Skeleton at the Feast

We summoned not the Silent Guest,
  And no man spake his name;
By lips unseen our Cup was pressed,
And mid the merry song and jest,
  The Uninvited came.

Wise were they in the days of old,
  Who gave the Stranger place;
And when the joyous catch was trolled,
And toasts were quaffed and tales were told,
  They looked him in the face.

God save us from the skeleton
  Who sitteth at the feast!
God rest the manly spirit gone,
Who sat beside the Silent One,
  And dreaded him the least!

The Net of Law

The net of law is spread so wide,
No sinner from its sweep may hide.

Its meshes are so fine and strong,
They take in every child of wrong.

O wondrous web of mystery!
Big fish alone escape from thee!

WALTER LEARNED (1847-1915)

To Critics

When I was seventeen I heard
  From each censorious tongue,
"I'd not do that if I were you;
  You see you're rather young."

Now that I number forty years,
  I'm quite as often told
Of this or that I shouldn't do
  Because I'm quite too old.

O carping world! If there's an age
  Where youth and manhood keep
An equal poise, alas! I must
  Have passed it in my sleep.

Growing Old

Sweet sixteen is shy and cold,
Calls me "sir," and thinks me old;
Hears in an embarrassed way
All the compliments I pay;

Finds my homage quite a bore,
Will not smile on me, and more
To her taste she finds the noise
And the chat of callow boys.

Not the lines around my eye,
Deepening as the years go by;
Not white hairs that strew my head,
Nor my less elastic tread;

Cares I find, nor joys I miss,
Make me feel my years like this:—
Sweet sixteen is shy and cold,
Calls me "sir," and thinks me old.

EDWARD KING (1848-1896)

A Woman's Execution

(Paris, 1871)

Sweet-breathed and young,
  The people's daughter,
No nerves unstrung,
  Going to slaughter!

"Good morning, friends,
  You'll love us better,—
Make us amends:
  We've burst your fetter!

"How the sun gleams!
  (Women are snarling):
Give me your beams,
  Liberty's darling!

"Marie's my name;
  Christ's mother bore it.
That badge? No shame:
  Glad that I wore it!"

(Hair to her waist,
  Limbs like a Venus):
Robes are displaced:
  "Soldiers, please screen us!

"He at the front?
  That is my lover:
Stood all the brunt;—
  Now—the fight's over.

"Powder and bread
  Gave out together:
Droll! to be dead
  In this bright weather!

"Jean, boy, we might
  Have married in June!
This the wall? Right!
  Vive la Commune!"

JOEL CHANDLER HARRIS (1848-1908)

De Big Bethel Church

De Big Bethel chu'ch! de Big Bethel chu'ch!
  Done put ole Satun behin' um;
Ef a sinner git loose fum enny udder chu'ch,
  De Big Bethel chu'ch will fin' um!
Hit's good ter be dere, en it's sweet ter be dere,
  Wid de sisterin all aroun' you—
A-shakin' dem shackles er mussy en love
  Wharwid de Lord is boun' you—

Hit's sweet ter be dere en lissen ter de hymes,
  En hear dem mo'ners a-shoutin'—
Dey done reach de place whar der ain't no room
  Fer enny mo' weepin' en doubtin'!

Hit's good ter be dere w'en de sinners all jine
  Wid de brudderin in dere singin',
An' it look like Gaberl gwine ter rack up an' blow
  En set dem heav'm bells ter ringin'!

Oh, de Big Bethel chu'ch! de Big Bethel chu'ch,
  Done put ole Satun behin' um;
Ef a sinner git locse fum enny udder chu'ch,
  De Big Bethel Chu'ch will fin' um!

WILL HENRY THOMPSON (1848—)

The High Tide at Gettysburg

A cloud possessed the hollow field,
The gathering battle's smoky shield;
  Athwart the gloom the lightning flashed,
  And through the cloud some horseman dashed,
And from the heights the thunder pealed.

Then at the brief command of Lee,
Moved out that matchless infantry,
  With Pickett leading grandly down,
  To rush against the roaring crown
Of those dread heights of destiny.

Far heard above the angry guns,
A cry across the tumult runs:
  The voice that rang through Shiloh's woods,
  And Chickamauga's soltitudes:
The fierce South cheering on her sons!

Ah, how the withering tempest blew
Against the front of Pettigrew!
  A Khamsin wind that scorched and singed,
  Like that infernal flame that fringed
The British squares at Waterloo!

A thousand fell where Kemper led;
A thousand died where Garnett bled;
  In blinding flame and strangling smoke,
  The remnant through the batteries broke,
And crossed the works with Armistead.

"Once more in Glory's van with me!"
Virginia cried to Tennessee:
  "We two together, come what may,
  Shall stand upon those works to-day!"
The reddest day in history.

Brave Tennessee! In reckless way
Virginia heard her comrade say:
 "Close round this rent and riddled rag!"
 What time she set her battle-flag
Amid the guns of Doubleday.

But who shall break the guards that wait
Before the awful face of Fate?
 The tattered standards of the South
 Were shrivelled at the cannon's mouth,
And all her hopes were desolate.

In vain the Tennesseean set
His breast against the bayonet;
 In vain Virginia charged and raged,
 A tigress in her wrath uncaged,
Till all the hill was red and wet!

Above the bayonets, mixed and crossed,
Men saw a gray, gigantic ghost
 Receding through the battle-cloud,
 And heard above the tempest loud
The death-cry of a nation lost!

The brave went down! Without disgrace
They leaped to ruin's red embrace;
 They only heard Fame's thunders wake,
 And saw the dazzling sun-burst break
In smiles on Glory's bloody face!

They fell, who lifted up a hand
And bade the sun in heaven to stand;
 They smote and fell, who set the bars
 Against the progress of the stars,
And stayed the march of Motherland!

They stood, who saw the future come
On through the fight's delirium;
 They smote and stood, who held the hope
 Of nations on that slippery slope,
Amid the cheers of Christendom!

God lives! He forged the iron will,
That clutched and held that trembling hill!
 God lives and reigns! He built and lent
 The heights for Freedom's battlement,
Where floats her flag in triumph still!

Fold up the banners! Smelt the guns!
Love rules. Her gentler purpose runs.
  A mighty mother turns in tears,
  The pages of her battle years,
Lamenting all her fallen sons!

JOHN VANCE CHENEY (1848-1922)

The Happiest Heart

Who drives the horses of the sun
Shall lord it but a day;
Better the lowly deed were done,
And kept the humble way.

The rust will find the sword of fame,
The dust will hide the crown;
Ay, none shall nail so high his name
Time will not tear it down.

The happiest heart that ever beat
Was in some quiet breast
That found the common daylight sweet,
And left to Heaven the rest.

EMMA LAZARUS (1849-1887)

Venus of the Louvre

Down the long hall she glistens like a star,
The foam-born mother of Love, transfixed to stone,
Yet none the less immortal, breathing on.
Time's brutal hand hath maimed but could not mar,
When first the enthralled enchantress from afar
Dazzled mine eyes, I saw not her alone,
Serenely poised on her world-worshipped throne,
As when she guided once her dove-drawn car,—
But at her feet a pale, death-stricken Jew,
Her life adorer, sobbed farewell to love.
Here *Heine* wept! Here still he weeps anew,
Nor ever shall his shadow lift or move,
While mourns one ardent heart, one poet-brain,
For vanished Hellas and Hebraic pain.

FRANCIS SALTUS SALTUS (1849-1889)

The Sphinx Speaks

Carved by a mighty race whose vanished hands
Formed empires more destructible than I,
In sultry silence I forever lie,
Wrapped in the shifting garment of the sands.
Below me, Pharaohs's scintillating bands
With clashings of loud cymbals have passed by,
And the eternal reverence of the sky
Falls royally on me and all my lands.
The record of the future broods in me;
I have with worlds of blazing stars been crowned,
But none my subtle mystery hath known
Save one, who made his way through blood and sea,
The Corsican, prophetic and renowned,
To whom I spake, one awful night alone!

EUGENE FIELD (1850-1895)

Wynken, Blynken, and Nod

Wynken, Blynken, and Nod one night
  Sailed off in a wooden shoe,—
Sailed on a river of crystal light
  Into a sea of dew.
"Where are you going, and what do you wish?"
  The old moon asked the three.
"We have come to fish for the herring-fish
  That live in this beautiful sea;
Nets of silver and gold have we,"
        Said Wynken,
        Blynken,
        And Nod.

The old moon laughed and sang a song,
  As they rocked in the wooden shoe;
And the wind that sped them all night long
  Ruffled the waves of dew;
The little stars were the herring-fish
  That lived in the beautiful sea.
"Now cast your nets wherever you wish,—
  Never afeard are we!"
So cried the stars to the fishermen three,
        Wynken,
        Blynken,
        And Nod.

All night long their nets they threw
  To the stars in the twinkling foam,—
Then down from the skies came the wooden shoe,
  Bringing the fishermen home:
'Twas all so pretty a sail, it seemed
  As if it could not be;
And some folk thought 'twas a dream they'd dreamed
  Of sailing that beautiful sea;
But I shall name you the fishermen three:
          Wynken,
          Blynken,
          And Nod.

Wynken and Blynken are two little eyes,
  And Nod is a little head,
And the wooden shoe that sailed the skies
  Is a wee one's trundle-bed;
So shut your eyes while Mother sings
  Of wonderful sights that be,
And you shall see the beautiful things
  As you rock on the misty sea
Where the old shoe rocked the fishermen three,—
          Wynken,
          Blynken,
          And Nod.

Little Boy Blue

The little toy dog is covered with dust,
  But sturdy and staunch he stands;
And the little toy soldier is red with rust,
  And his musket moulds in his hands.
Time was when the little toy dog was new,
  And the soldier was passing fair;
And that was the time when our Little Boy Blue
  Kissed them and put them there.

"Now, don't you go till I come," he said,
  "And don't you make any noise!"
So, toddling off to his trundle-bed,
  He dreamt of the pretty toys;
And, as he was dreaming, an angel song
  Awakened our Little Boy Blue—
Oh! the years are many, the years are long,
  But the little toy friends are true!

Ay, faithful to Little Boy Blue they stand,
  Each in the same old place,
Awaiting the touch of a little hand,
  The smile of a little face;
And they wonder, as waiting the long years through
  In the dust of that little chair,
What has become of our Little Boy Blue,
  Since he kissed them and put them there.

The Lyttel Boy

Some time there ben a lyttel boy
  That wolde not renne and play,
And helpless like that little tyke
  Ben allwais in the way.
"Goe, make you merrie with the rest,"
  His weary moder cried;
But with a frown he catcht her gown
  And hong untill her side.

That boy did love his moder well,
  Which spake him faire I ween;
He loved to stand and hold her hand
  And ken her with his een;
His cosset bleated in the croft,
  His toys unheeded lay,—
He wolde not goe, but, tarrying soe,
  Ben allwais in the way.

Godde loveth children and doth gird
  His throne with soche as these,
And he doth smile in plaisaunce while
  They cluster at his knees;
And some time, when he looked on earth
  And watched the bairns at play,
He kenned with joy a lyttel boy
  Ben allwais in the way.

And then a moder felt her heart
  How that it ben to-torne,
She kissed eche day til she ben gray
  The shoon he use to worn;
No bairn let hold untill her gown
Nor played upon the floore.—
Godde's was the joy; a lyttel boy
  Ben in the way no more!

GEORGE PARSONS LATHROP (1851-1898)

Remembrance

Under the apple bough
    Love, in a dream of leaves,
Dreamed we of love, as now,—
    All that gives beauty or grieves.

Over the sad world then
    Curved like the sky that bough;
I was in heaven then,—
    You are in heaven now.

EDWIN MARKHAM (1852—)

The Man with the Hoe

[Written after seeing Millet's world-famous picture of a
brutalized toiler. Copyright, 1922, by Edwin Markham.
Used by permission.]

God made man in his own image
in the image of God made He him.
                                —Genesis.

Bowed by the weight of centuries he leans
Upon his hoe and gazes on the ground,
The emptiness of ages in his face,
And on his back the burden of the world.
Who made him dead to rapture and despair,
A thing that grieves not and that never hopes,
Stolid and stunned, a brother to the ox?
Who loosened and let down this brutal jaw?
Whose was the hand that slanted back this brow?
Whose breath blew out the light within this brain?

Is this the Thing the Lord God made and gave
To have dominion over sea and land;
To trace the stars and search the heavens for power;
To feel the passion of Eternity?
Is this the Dream He dreamed who shaped the suns
And marked their ways upon the ancient deep?
Down all the caverns of Hell to their last gulf
There is no shape more terrible than this—
More tongued with censure of the world's blind greed—
More filled with signs and portents for the soul—
More packt with danger to the universe.

What gulfs between him and the seraphim!
Slave of the wheel of labor, what to him
Are Plato and the swing of Pleiades?
What the long reaches of the peaks of song,
The rift of dawn, the reddening of the rose?
Through this dread shape the suffering ages look;
Time's tragedy is in that aching stoop;
Through this dread shape humanity betrayed,
Plundered, profaned, and disinherited,
Cries protest to the Judges of the World,
A protest that is also prophecy.

O masters, lords, and rulers in all lands,
Is this the handiwork you give to God,
This monstrous thing distorted and soul-quenched?
How will you ever straighten up this shape;
Touch it again with immortality;
Give back the upward looking and the light;
Rebuild in it the music and the dream;
Make right the immemorial infamies,
Perfidious wrongs, immedicable woes?

O masters, lords, and rulers in all lands,
How will the Future reckon with this Man?
How answer his brute question in that hour
When whirlwinds of rebellion shake all shores?
How will it be with kingdoms and with kings—
With those who shaped him to the thing he is—
When this dumb Terror shall rise to judge the world,
After the silence of the centuries?

Lincoln, the Man of the People

When the Norn Mother saw the Whirlwind Hour
Greatening and darkening as it hurried on,
She left the Heaven of Heroes and came down
To make a man to meet the mortal need.
She took the tried clay of the common road—
Clay warm yet with the genial heat of Earth
Dasht through it all a strain of prophecy;
Tempered the heap with thrill of human tears;
Then mixt a laughter with the serious stuff.

Into the shape she breathed a flame to light
That tender, tragic, ever-changing face;
And laid on him a sense of the Mystic Powers,
Moving—all husht—behind the mortal veil.
Here was a man to hold against the world,
A man to match the mountains and the sea.

The color of the ground was in him, the red earth;
The smack and tang of elemental things:
The rectitude and patience of the cliff;
The good-will of the rain that loves all leaves;
The friendly welcome of the wayside well;
The courage of the bird that dares the sea;
The gladness of the wind that shakes the corn;
The pity of the snow that hides all scars;
The secrecy of streams that make their way
Under the mountain to the rifted rock;
The tolerance and equity of light
That gives as freely to the shrinking flower
As to the great oak flaring at the wind—
To the grave's low hill as to the matterhorn
That shoulders out the sky.

Sprung from the West,
He drank the valorous youth of a new world.
The strength of virgin forests braced his mind,
The hush of spacious prairies stilled his soul.
His words were oaks in acorns; and his thoughts
Were roots that firmly gript the granite truth.
   Up from log cabin to the Capitol,
One fire was on his spirit, one resolve—
To send the keen ax to the root of wrong,
Clearing a free way for the feet of God,
He built the rail-pile as he built the State,
Pouring his splendid strength through every blow:
The eyes of conscience testing every stroke,
To make his deed the measure of a man.
The grip that swung the ax in Illinois
Was on the pen that set a people free.

So came the Captain with the mighty heart;
And when the judgment thunders split the house,
Wrenching the rafters from their ancient rest,
He held the ridgepole up, and spiked again
The rafters of the Home. He held his place—
Held the long purpose like a growing tree—
Held on through blame and faltered not at praise.
And when he fell in whirlwind, he went down
As when a lordly cedar, green with boughs,
Goes down with a great shout upon the hills,
And leaves a lonesome place against the sky.

A Look into the Gulf

I looked one night, and there Semiramis,

With all her morning doves about her head,
Sat rocking on an ancient road of Hell.
Withered and eyeless, chanting to the moon
Snatches of song they sang to her of old
Upon the lighted roofs of Nineveh.
And then her voice rang out with rattling laugh:
"The bugles! they are crying back again—
Bugles that broke the nights of Babylon,
And then went crying on through Nineveh.

.   .   .   .   .   .

Stand back, ye trembling messengers of ill!
Women, let go my hair: I am the Queen,
A whirlwind and a blaze of swords to quell
Insurgent cities. Let the iron tread
Of armies shake the earth. Look, lofty towers:
Assyria goes by upon the wind!"
And so she babbles by the ancient road,
While cities turned to dust upon the Earth
Rise through her whirling brain to live again—
Babbles all night, and when her voice is dead
Her weary lips beat on without a sound.

MAURICE FRANCIS EGAN (1852-1924)

Maurice de Guérin

The old wine filled him, and he saw, with eyes
Anoint of Nature, fauns and dryads fair
Unseen by others; to him maidenhair
And waxen lilacs, and those birds that rise
A-sudden from tall reeds at slight surprise.
Brought charmëd thoughts; and in earth everywhere
He, like sad Jacques, found a music rare
As that of Syrinx to old Grecians wise.
A pagan heart. a Christian soul had he,
He followed Christ, yet for dead Pan he sighed.
Till earth and heaven met within his breast;
As if Theocritus in Sicily
Had come upon the Figure crucified
And lost his gods in deep, Christ-given rest.

HENRY VAN DYKE (1852—)

An Angler's Wish

I

When tulips bloom in Union Square,
And timid breaths of vernal air
    Go wandering down the dusty town,
Like children lost in Vanity Fair;

When every long, unlovely row
Of westward houses stands aglow,
    And leads the eyes towards sunset skies
Beyond the hills where green trees grow,—

Then weary seems the street parade,
And weary books, and weary trade:
    I'm only wishing to go a-fishing;
For this the month of May was made.

II

I guess the pussy-willows now
Are creeping out on every bough
    Along the brook; and robins look
For early worms behind the plough.

The thistle-birds have changed their dun
For yellow coats, to match the sun;
    And in the same array of flame
The dandelion show's begun.

The flocks of young anemones
Are dancing round the budding trees:
    Who can help wishing to go a-fishing
In days as full of joy as these?

III

I think the meadow-lark's clear sound
Leaks upward slowly from the ground,
    While on the wing the blue-birds ring
Their wedding-bells to woods around.

The flirting chewink calls his dear
Behind the bush; and very near,
  Where water flows, where green grass grows,
Song-sparrows gently sing, "Good cheer."

And, best of all, through twilight's calm
The hermit-thrush repeats his psalm.
  How much I'm wishing to go a-fishing
In days so sweet with music's balm!

IV

'Tis not a proud desire of mine;
I ask for nothing superfine;
  No heavy weight, no salmon great,
To break the record—or my line:

Only an idle little stream,
Whose amber waters softly gleam,
  Where I may wade, through woodland shade,
And cast the fly, and loaf, and dream:

Only a trout or two, to dart
From foaming pools, and try my art:
  No more I'm wishing—old-fashioned fishing,
And just a day on Nature's heart.

JAMES WHITCOMB RILEY (1852-1916)

A Life-Lesson

There! little girl, don't cry!
  They have broken your doll, I know
    And your tea-set blue,
    And your play-house, too,
  Are things of the long ago;
    But childish troubles will soon pass by.—
    There! little girl don't cry!

There! little girl, don't cry!
  They have broken your slate, I know;
    And the glad, wild ways
    Of your school-girl days
  Are things of the long ago:
    But life and love will soon come by.—
    There! little girl don't cry!

There! little girl, don't cry!
  They have broken your heart, I know;
    And the rainbow gleams
    Of your youthful dreams
  Are things of the long ago;
    But Heaven holds all for which you sigh.—
      There! little girl, don't cry!

Bereaved

Let me come in where you sit weeping,—ay,
Let me, who have not any child to die,
Weep with you for the little one whose love
    I have known nothing of.

The little arms that slowly, slowly loosed
Their pressure round your neck; the hands you used
To kiss.—Such arms—such hands I never knew.
    May I not weep with you?

Fain would I be of service—say some thing,
Between the tears, that would be comforting,—
But ah! so sadder than yourselves am I,
    Who have no child to die.

A Parting Guest

What delightful hosts are they—
  Life and Love!
Lingeringly I turn away,
  This late hour, yet glad enough
They have not withheld from me
  Their high hospitality.
So, with face lit with delight,
And all gratitude, I stay,
  Yet to press their hands and say,
"Thanks.—So fine a time! Good-night!"

[From the Biographical Edition of the complete works of
  James Whitcomb Riley. Copyright, 1913. Used by
    special permission of the Publishers, The
      Bobbs-Merrill Company.]

ROBERT UNDERWOOD JOHNSON (1853—)

The Wistful Days

What is there wanting in the Spring?
  The air is soft as yesteryear;
  The happy nested green is here,
And half the world is on the wing.
    The morning beckons, and like balm
    Are westward waters blue and calm.
Yet something's wanting in the Spring.

What is it wanting in the Spring?
  O April, lover to us all,
  What is so poignant in thy thrall
When children's merry voices ring?
    What haunts us in the cooing dove
    More subtle than the speech of Love?
What nameless lack or loss of Spring?

Let youth go dally with the Spring,
  Call her the dear, the fair, the young;
  And all her graces ever sung
Let him, once more rehearsing, sing.
    They know, who keep a broken tryst,
    Till something from the Spring be missed
We have not truly known the Spring.

IRWIN RUSSELL (1853-1879)

De Fust Banjo

Go 'way, fiddle! folks is tired o' hearin' you a-squawkin'.
Keep silence fur yo' betters!—don't you heah de banjo
  talkin'?
About de possum's tail she's gwine to lecter—ladies, listen!—
About de ha'r whut isn't dar, an' why de ha'r is missin':

"Dar's gwine to be a' oberflow," said Noah, lookin' solemn—
Fur Noah tuk the "Herald," an' he read de ribber column—
An' so he sot his hands to wuk a-cl'arin' timber-patches,
An' 'lowed he's gwine to build a boat to beat the steamah
  Natchez.

Ol' Noah kep' a-nailin' an' a-chippin' an' a-sawin';
An' all de wicked neighbors kep' a-laughin' an' a-pshawin';
But Noah didn't min' 'em, knowin' whut wuz gwine to happen:
An' forty days an' forty nights de rain it kep' a-drappin'.

Now, Noah had done cotched a lot ob ebry sort o' beas'es—
Ob all de shows a-trabbelin', it beat 'em all to pieces!
He had a Morgan colt an' sebral head o' Jarsey cattle—
An' druv 'em 'board de Ark as soon's he heered de thunder
    rattle.

Den sech anoder fall ob rain!—it come so awful hebby,
De ribber riz immejitly, an' busted troo de lebbee;
De people all wuz drownded out—'cep' Noah an' de critters,
An' men he'd hired to work de boat—an' one to mix de
    bitters.

De Ark she kep' a-sailin' an' a-sailin' *an'* a-sailin';
De lion got his dander up, an' like to bruk de palin';
De sarpints hissed; de painters yelled; tell, whut wid all de
    fussin',
You c'u'dn't hardly heah de mate a-bossin' 'roun' an' cussin'.

Now Ham, de only nigger whut wuz runnin' on de packet,
Got lonesome in de barber-shop, an' c'u'dn't stan' de racket;
An' so, fur to amuse he-se'f, he steamed some wood an' bent
    it,
An' soon he had a banjo made—de fust dat wuz invented.

He wet de ledder, stretched it on; made bridge an' screws an'
    aprin;
An' fitted in a proper neck—'twuz berry long an' tap'rin';
He tuk some tin, an' twisted him a thimble fur to ring it;
An' den de mighty question riz: how wuz he gwine to string
    it?

De 'possum had as fine a tail as dis dat I's a-singin';
De ha'r's so long an' thick an' strong,—des fit fur banjo-
    stringin';
Dat nigger shaved 'em off as short as wash-day-dinner graces;
An' sorted ob 'em by de size, f'om little E's to basses.

He strung her, tuned her, struck a jig,—'twuz "Nebber min'
    de wedder,"—
She soun' like forty-lebben bands a-playin' all togedder;
Some went to pattin'; some to dancin': Noah called de fig-
    gers;
An' Ham he sot an' knocked de tune, de happiest ob niggers!

Now, sence dat time—it's mighty strange—dere's not de
    slightes' showin'
Ob any ha'r at all upon de 'possum's tail a-growin';
An' curi's, too, dat nigger's ways: his people nebber los' 'em—
Fur whar you finds de nigger—dar's de banjo an' de 'possum!

YOUNG EWING ALLISON (1853—)

The Dead Men's Song

Fifteen men on the Dead Man's Chest,
  Yo-ho-ho and a bottle of rum!
Drink and the devil had done for the rest,
  Yo-ho-ho and a bottle of rum!
The mate was fixed by the bo'sun's pike
An' the bo'sun brained with a marlin-spike,
And the cookie's throat was marked belike
It had been clutched by fingers ten.
And there they lay, all good dead men,
Like break o' day in a boozin' ken—
  Yo-ho-ho and a bottle of rum!

Fifteen men of a whole ship's list,
  Yo-ho-ho and a bottle of rum!
Dead and bedamned and their souls gone whist,
  Yo-ho-ho and a bottle of rum!
The skipper lay with his nob in gore
Where the scullion's axe his cheek had shore,
And the scullion he was stabbed times four;
And there they lay, and the soggy skies
Dripped ceaselessly in upstaring eyes,
By murk sunset and by foul sunrise—
  Yo-ho-ho and a bottle of rum!

Fifteen men of 'em stiff and stark,
  Yo-ho-ho and a bottle of rum!
Ten of the crew bore the murder mark,
  Yo-ho-ho and a bottle of rum!
'Twas a cutlass swipe or an ounce of lead,
Or a gaping hole in a battered head,
  And the scuppers' glut of a rotting red.
And there they lay, ay, damn my eyes,
Their lookouts clapped on Paradise,
Their souls gone just the contrawise—
  Yo-ho-ho and a bottle of rum!

Fifteen men of 'em good and true,
  Yo-ho-ho and a bottle of rum!
Every man Jack could 'a' sailed with Old Pew,
  Yo-ho-ho and a bottle of rum!
There was chest on chest of Spanish gold
And a ton of plate in the middle hold,
And the cabin's riot of loot untold—
And there they lay that had took the plum,

With sightless eyes and with lips struck dumb,
And we shared all by rule o' thumb—
  Yo-ho-ho and a bottle of rum!

More was seen through the stern light's screen,
  Yo-ho-ho and a bottle of rum!
Chartings undoubt where a woman had been,
  Yo-ho-ho and a bottle of rum!
A flimsy shift on a bunker cot
With a dirk slit sheer through the bosom spot
And the lace stiff dry in a purplish rot—
Or was she wench or shuddering maid,
She dared the knife and she took the blade—
Faith, there was stuff for a plucky jade!
  Yo-ho-ho and a bottle of rum!

Fifteen men on the Dead Man's Chest,
  Yo-ho-ho and a bottle of rum!
Drink and the devil had done for the rest,
  Yo-ho-ho and a bottle of rum!
We wrapped 'em all in a mainsail tight,
With twice ten turns of a hawser's bight,
And we heaved 'em over and out of sight,
With a yo-heave-ho and a fare-ye-well,
And a sullen plunge in a sullen swell,
Ten fathoms along on the road to hell—
  Yo-ho-ho and a bottle of rum!

EDITH MATILDA THOMAS (1854—)

The Tears of the Poplars

Hath not the dark stream closed above thy head,
With envy of thy light, thou shining one?
Hast thou not, murmuring, made thy dreamless bed
Where blooms the asphodel, far from all sun?
But thou—thou dost obtain oblivious ease,
While here we rock and moan—thy funeral trees.

Have we not flung our tresses on the stream?
Hath not thy friend, the snowy cygnet, grieved,
And ofttimes watched for thy returning beam,
With archèd neck—and ofttimes been deceived?
A thousand years, and yet a thousand more,
Hast thou been mourned upon this reedy shore.

How long, how long since, all the summer day,
Earth heard the heavens sound from pole to pole,
While legion clouds stood forth in bright array;

Yet no rain followed on the thunder's roll!
Beneath that glittering legion shrank the seas,
And fire unseen was borne upon the breeze.

The ground was smouldering fire beneath our tread,
The forest dropped the leaf, and failed all grass.
The souls of stricken men their bodies fled,
And, sighing, flocked the wind.—We heard them pass!
The priest, that scanned the portent of the skies,
Fell reeling back, with pierced and shrivelled eyes.

But ah, he saw not what our sight discerned—
The flying chariot-wheel, with fervid tire—
The steeds that unaccustomed guidance spurned
With fateful hoof and breath that scattered fire—
He saw not thee and thine unmeasured fall,
And Jove, unheeding, in his cloudy hall!

Dragged headlong by those swift immortal horse,
Up to our sire went thy vain cry for aid;
Neither he cast a bound, to check their course,
Nor on the golden rein a hand he laid.
Brother beloved, what foe could so deceive,
Bidding thee dare what scarcely gods achieve?

Alas! that we remember—and forget!
For, if we sometimes gain a brief repose,
Soon are we roused, by sudden fear beset;
Then, through our silver boughs a shudder goes,
Our heads we lift, we search the azure gloom,
As though thou still wert falling to thy doom!

Upon the earth no loves were ever ours;
Man greets us from afar, but comes not near,
Nor even round our dark unwindowed towers
Throng the light birds—so much our grief they fear!
We sigh—we tremble—'tis not to the breeze—
Brother beloved, we are thy funeral trees!

Evoe!

"Many are the wand-bearers, few are the true
bacchanals."

I

Many are the wand-bearers;
  Their windy shouts I hear,
Along the hillside vineyard,
  And where the wine runs clear;

They show the vine-leaf chaplet,
  The ivy-wreathen spear.
But the god, the true Iacchus,
  He does not hold them dear.

II

Many are the wand-bearers,
  And bravely are they clad;
Yes, they have all the tokens
  His early lovers had.
They sing the master passions,
  Themselves unsad, unglad;
And the god, the true Iacchus—
  He knows they are not mad!

III

Many are the wand-bearers;
  The fawn-skin bright they wear;
There are among them mænads,
  That rave with unbound hair.
They toss the harmless firebrand—
  It spends itself in air:
And the god, the true Iacchus,
  He smiles—and does not care.

IV

Many are the wand-bearers.
  And who (ye ask) am I?
One who was born in madness,
  "Evoe!" my first cry—
Who dares, before your spear-points,
  To challenge and defy;
And the god, the true Iacchus,
  So keep me till I die!

V

Many are the wand-bearers.
  I bear with me no sign;
Yet, I was mad, was drunken,
  Ere yet I tasted wine;
Nor bleeding grape can slacken
  The thirst wherewith I pine;
And the god, the true Iacchus
  Hears now this song of mine.

The Quiet Pilgrim

(Isaiah XXXIII, 15)

When on my soul in nakedness
His swift, avertless hand did press,
Then I stood still, nor cried aloud,
Nor murmured low in ashes bowed;
And, since my woe is utterless,
To supreme quiet I am vowed;
Afar from me be moan and tears,—
I shall go softly all my years.

Whenso my quick, light-sandaled feet
Bring me where Joys and Pleasures meet,
I mingle with their throng at will;
They know me not an alien still,
Since neither words nor ways unsweet
Of storëd bitterness I spill;
Youth shuns me not, nor gladness fears,—
For I go softly all my years.

Whenso I come where Griefs convene,
And in my ear their voice is keen,
They know me not, as on I glide,
That with Arch Sorrow I abide.
They haggard are, and drooped of mien,
And round their brows have cypress tied:
Such shows I leave to light Grief's peers,—
I shall go softly all my years.

Yea, softly! heart of hearts unknown,
Silence hath speech that passeth moan,
More piercing-keen than breathëd cries
To such as heed, made sorrow-wise.
But save this voice without a tone,
That runs before me to the skies,
And rings above thy ringing spheres,
Lord, I go softly all my years!

GEORGE EDWARD WOODBERRY (1855—)

At Gibraltar

I

England, I stand on thy imperial ground,
Not all a stranger; as thy bugles blow,
I feel within my blood old battles flow,—

The blood whose ancient founts in thee are found.
Still surging dark against the Christian bound
Wide Islam presses; well its peoples know
Thy heights that watch them wandering below;
I think how Lucknow heard their gathering sound.
I turn, and meet the cruel, turbaned face.
England, 'tis sweet to be so much thy son!
I feel the conqueror in my blood and race;
Last night Trafalgar awed me, and to-day
Gibraltar wakened; hark, thy evening gun
Startles the desert over Africa!

II

Thou art the rock of empire, set mid-seas
Between the East and West, that God has built;
Advance thy Roman borders where thou wilt,
While run thy armies true with his decrees;
Law, justice, liberty,—great gifts are these:
Watch that they spread where English blood is spilt,
Lest, mixed and sullied with his country's guilt,
The soldier's life-stream flow, and Heaven displease!
Two swords there are: one naked, apt to smite,
Thy blade of war; and, battle-storied, one
Rejoices in the sheath, and hides from light.
American I am; would wars were done!
Now westward, look, my country bids good-night,—
Peace to the world from ports without a gun!

ELLA WHEELER WILCOX (1855-1919)

Solitude

Laugh, and the world laughs with you;
    Weep, and you weep alone;
For this brave old earth must borrow its mirth,
    It has trouble enough of its own.
Sing, and the hills will answer;
    Sigh! it is lost on the air:
The echoes bound to a joyful sound,
    But shrink from voicing care.

Rejoice, and men will seek you;
    Grieve, and they turn and go:
They want full measure of all your pleasure,
    But they do not want your woe.
Be glad, and your friends are many;
    Be sad, and you lose them all,—
There are none to decline your nectared wine,
    But alone you must drink life's gall.

Feast, and your halls are crowded;
  Fast, and the world goes by.
Succeed and give, and it helps you live,
  But no man can help you die.
There is room in the halls of pleasure
  For a long and lordly train:
But one by one we must all file on
  Through the narrow aisles of pain.

HENRY CUYLER BUNNER (1855-1896)

Behold the Deeds!

(Being the plaint of Adolphe Culpepper Ferguson, Salesman
of Fancy Notions, held in durance of his Landlady
for a "failure to connect" on a Saturday night.)

I would that all men my case would know,
  How grievously I suffer for no sin:
I, Adolphe Culpepper Ferguson, for lo!
  I of my landlady am lockèd in
For being short on this sad Saturday,
Nor having shekels of silver wherewith to pay:
She turned and is departed with my key;
Wherefore, not even as other boarders free,
  I sing (as prisoners to their dungeon-stones
When for ten days they expiate a spree):
  Behold the deeds that are done of Mrs. Jones!

One night and one day have I wept my woe;
  Nor wot I, when the morrow doth begin
If I shall have to write to Briggs & Co.,
  To pray them to advance the requisite tin
For ransom of their salesman, that he may
Go forth as other boarders go alway—
As those I hear now flocking from their tea,
Led by the daughter of my landlady
  Piano-ward. This day, for all my moans,
Dry-bread and water have been servèd me.
  Behold the deeds that are done of Mrs. Jones!

Miss Amabel Jones is musical, and so
  The heart of the young he-boarder doth win,
Playing "The Maiden's Prayer" *adagio*—
  That fetcheth him, as fetcheth the "bunko skin"
The innocent rustic. For my part, I pray
That Badarjewska maid may wait for aye
Ere sits she with a lover, as did we

Once sit together, Amabel! Can it be
  That all that arduous wooing not atones
For Saturday's shortness of trade dollars three?
  Behold the deeds that are done of Mrs. Jones!

Yea! She forgets that arm that was wont to go
  Around her waist. She wears a buckle whose pin
Galleth the crook of her young man's elbow.
  I forget not, for I that youth have been!
Smith was aforetime the Lothario gay.
Yet once, I mind me, Smith was forced to stay
Close in his room. Not calm as I was he;
But his noise brought no pleasurance, verily.
  Small ease he got of playing on the bones
Or hammering on the stove-pipe, that I see.
  Behold the deeds that are done of Mrs. Jones!

Thou, for whose fear the figurative crow
  I eat, accursed be thou and all thy kind!
Thee I will show up—yea, up I will show
  Thy too-thick buckwheats and thy tea too thin.
Ay! here I dare thee, ready for the fray:
Thou dost *not* "keep a first-class house," I say!
It does not with the advertisements agree.
Thou lodgest a Briton with a puggaree,
  And thou hast harbored Jacobses and Cohns,
Also a Mulligan. Thus denounce I thee!
  Behold the deeds that are done of Mrs. Jones!

Envoy

Boarders! the worst I have not told to ye:
She hath stolen my trousers, that I may not flee
  Privily by the window. Hence these groans.
There is no fleeing in a *robe de nuit*.
  Behold the deeds that are done of Mrs. Jones!

A Pitcher of Mignonette

A pitcher of mignonette
  In a tenement's highest casement,—
Queer sort of flower-pot—yet
That pitcher of mignonette
Is a garden in heaven set.
  To the little sick child in the basement—
The pitcher of mignonette,
  In a tenement's highest casement.

LIZETTE WOODWORTH REESE (1856—)

Tears

When I consider life and its few years—
A wisp of fog between us and the sun;
A call to battle, and the battle done
Ere the last echo dies within our ears;
A rose choked in the grass; an hour of fears;
The gusts that past a darkening shore do beat;
The burst of music down an unlistening street,—
I wonder at the idleness of tears.
Ye old, old dead, and ye of yesternight,
Chieftains, and bards, and keepers of the sheep,
By every cup of sorrow that you had,
Loose me from tears, and make me see aright
How each hath back what once he stayed to weep:
Homer his sight, David his little lad!

Immortality

Battles nor songs can from oblivion save,
  But Fame upon a white deed loves to build:
From out that cup of water Sidney gave,
  Not one drop has been spilled.

Telling the Bees

Bathsheba came out to the sun,
Out to our wallèd cherry-trees;
The tears adown her cheek did run,
Bathsheba standing in the sun,
Telling the bees.

My mother had that moment died;
Unknowing, sped I to the trees,
And plucked Bathsheba's hand aside;
Then caught the name that there she cried
Telling the bees.

Her look I never can forget,
I that held sobbing to her knees;
The cherry-boughs above us met;
I think I see Bathsheba yet
Telling the bees.

HARRY THURSTON PECK (1856-1914)

Heliotrope

Amid the chapel's chequered gloom
  She laughed with Dora and Flora,
And chattered in the lecture-room,—
    That saucy little sophomora!
      Yet while, as in her other schools,
        She was a privileged transgressor,
      She never broke the simple rules
        Of one particular professor.

But when he spoke of varied lore,
  Paroxytones and modes potential,
She listened with a face that wore
  A look half fond, half reverential.
    To her that earnest voice was sweet,
      And though her love had no confessor,
    Her girlish heart lay at the feet
      Of that particular professor.

And he had learned, among his books
  That held the lore of ages olden,
To watch those ever changing looks,
  The wistful eyes, the tresses golden,
    That stirred his pulse with passion's pain
      And thrilled his soul with soft desire,
    And bade fond youth return again
      Crowned with his coronet of fire.

Her sunny smile, her winsome ways,
  Were more to him than all his knowledge,
And she preferred his words of praise
  To all the honors of the college.
    Yet "What am foolish I to him?"
      She whispered to her heart's confessor.
    "She thinks me old and gray and grim,"
      In silence pondered the professor.

Yet once when Christmas bells were rung
  Above ten thousand solemn churches,
And swelling anthems grandly sung
  Pealed through the dim cathedral arches,—
    Ere home returning, filled with hope,
      Softly she stole by gate and gable,
    And a sweet spray of heliotrope
      Left on his littered study-table.

Nor came she more from day to day
  Like sunshine through the shadows rifting:
Above her grave, far, far away,
  The ever silent snows were drifting;
    And those who mourned her winsome face
    Found in its stead a swift successor
    And loved another in her place—
    All, save the silent old professor.

But, in the tender twilight gray,
  Shut from the sight of carping critic,
His lonely thoughts would often stray
  From Vedic verse and tongues Semitic,
    Bidding the ghost of vanished hope
    Mock with its past the sad possessor
    Of the dead spray of heliotrope
    That once she gave the old professor.

ALICE BROWN (1857—)

Cloistered

Seal thou the window! Yea, shut out the light
And bar my door to all the airs of spring.
Yet in my cell, concealed from curious sight,
Here will I sit and sing.

Deaf, blind, and wilt Thou have me dumb, also,
Telling in silence these sad beads of days?
So let it be: though no sweet numbers flow,
My breath shall be Thy praise.

Yea, though Thou slay the life wherein men see
The upward-mounting flame, the failing spark,
My heart of love, that heart Thou gavest me,
Shall beat on in the dark.

The West-Country Lover

Then, lady, at last thou art sick of my sighing?
Good-bye!
So long as I sue, thou wilt still be denying?
Good-bye!
Ah, well! shall I vow then to serve thee forever,
And swear no unkindness our kinship can sever?
Nay, nay, dear my lass! here's an end of endeavor.
Good-bye!

Yet let no sweet ruth for my misery grieve thee.
Good-bye!
The man who has loved knows as well how to leave thee.
Good-bye!
The gorse is enkindled, there's bloom on the heather,
And love is my joy, and so too is fair weather;
I still ride abroad, though we ride not together.
Good-bye!

My horse is my mate; let the wind be my master.
Good-bye!
Though Care may pursue, yet my hound follows faster.
Good-bye!
The red deer's a-tremble in coverts unbroken.
He hears the hoof-thunder; he scents the death-token.
Shall I mope at home, under vows never spoken?
Good-bye!

The brown earth's my book, and I ride forth to read it.
Good-bye!
The stream runneth fast, but my will shall outspeed it.
Good-bye!
I loved thee, dear lass, but I hate the hag Sorrow,
As sun follows rain, and to-night has its morrow,
So I'll taste of joy, though I steal, beg, or borrow!
Good-bye!

BEN KING (1857-1894)

If I Should Die Tonight

If I should die tonight
And you should come to my cold corpse and say,
Weeping and heartsick o'er my lifeless clay—
If I should die tonight
And you should come in deepest grief and woe
And say, "Here's that ten dollars that I owe"—
I might arise in my large white cravat
And say, "What's that?"
If I should die tonight
And you should come to my cold corpse and kneel,
Clasping my bier to show the grief you feel—
I say, if I should die tonight
And you should come to me, and there and then
Just even hint 'bout payin' me that ten,
I might arise the while:
But I'd drop dead again.

WILLIAM LINDSEY (1858-1922)

En Garde, Messieurs

En garde, Messieurs, too long have I endured,
Too long with patience borne the world's rebuff;
Now he who shoulders me shall find me rough;
The weakness of an easy soul is cured.

I've shouted, leathern-lunged, when fame or gold
Were won by others, turned to aid my friend;—
Dull-pated ever,—but such follies end;
Only a fool's content, and in the cold.

My doublet is in tatters, and my purse
Waves in the wind, light as my lady's fan;
Only my sword is bright; with it I plan
To win success, or put my sword to nurse.

I wait no longer for the primal blow;
Henceforth my stroke is first, I give offense;
I claim no more an over-dainty sense,
I brook no blocking where I plan to go.

En garde, Messieurs! and if my hand is hard,
Remember I've been buffeted at will;
I am a whit impatient, and 'tis ill
To cross a hungry dog, Messieurs, en garde.

HORACE L. TRAUBEL (1858-1919)

I Served in a Great Cause

I served in a great cause:
Long had I doubted the call I heard, wantoning the seasons
      dead;
The opportune days were deserts, the sunlight fell on a
      waste,
But the dawn brought me face to face with itself, with the
      opening flowers:
I looked upon my sea casting its wrecks down the shore in the
      storm,
The wrecks, my useless volitions, disordered, missent, ill-pro-
      tected, to the deep,
The resurrected programme of self veined red with the blood
      of my birth,

The futile hours past, the distrusted images recalled,
In tumult of desire, in quietude of achievement, in effacement
    of unbelief.

I served the great cause, the great cause served me;
There were never any debts between us, the compact was
    without obligation;
I answered its cry, it answered my cry;
The seed in the ground hungered for light, the light pierced
    the earth with unerring love—
We met, we ran together, appointed mates.

I served not as one who follows or one who leads;
I served not in abasement, on my knees, with my head in the
    dust;
I served proudly, accepted, accepting,
The cloudland phantoms never misting the prospect,
The sunshine sirens never dazing the day with their splendor,
Ever in my heart crowding ancient and unborn dreams,
Cresting the hills and making the valleys fertile.

I served in a great cause:
I served without heroism, without virtue, with no promises
    of success, with no near destination of treasure;
I was on the march, I contained that which persevered me
    to ends unseen, no footsore night relaxed my pace;
There was only the press of invisible hands, only gray-brown
    eyes of invitation,
Only my franchised heart to fuel the fires to suns.

HELEN GRAY CONE (1859—)

A Chant of Love for England

A song of hate is a song of Hell;
Some there be that sing it well.
Let them sing it loud and long,
We lift our hearts in a loftier song:
We lift our hearts to heaven above,
Singing the glory of her we love,—
    England!

Glory of thought and glory of deed,
Glory of Hampden and Runnymede;
Glory of ships that sought far goals,
Glory of swords and glory of souls!
Glory of songs, mounting as birds,
Glory immortal of magical words;
Glory of Milton, glory of Nelson,

Tragical glory of Gordon and Scott;
Glory of Shelley, glory of Sidney,
Glory transcendant that perishes not,—
Her's is the story, her's the glory,
  England!

Shatter her beauteous breast ye may,
The spirit of England none can slay!
Dash the bomb on the dome of St. Paul's;
Deem ye the name of the Admiral falls?
Pry ye the stone from the chancel floor,—
Dream ye that Shakespeare lives no more?
Where is the giant shot that kills
Wordsworth walking the old green hills?
Trample the red rose on the ground,—
Keats is Beauty while earth spins round!
Bind her, grind her, burn her with fire,
Cast her ashes into the sea,—
She shall escape, she shall aspire,
She shall arise to make men free:
She shall arise in a sacred scorn,
Lighting the lives that are yet unborn;
Spirit supernal, Splendour eternal,
  England!

FRANK DEMPSTER SHERMAN (1860-1916)

To a Rose

Go, Rose, and in her golden hair
 You shall forget the garden soon;
The sunshine is a captive there
 And crowns her with a constant noon.
And when your spicy odor goes,
 And fades the beauty of your bloom,
Think what a lovely hand, O Rose,
 Shall place your body in the tomb!

CLINTON SCOLLARD (1860—)

As I Came Down from Lebanon

As I came down from Lebanon,
Came winding, wandering slowly down
Through mountain passes bleak and brown,
The cloudless day was well-nigh done.
The city, like an opal set

In emerald, showed each minaret
Afire with radiant beams of sun,
And glistened, orange, fig, and lime,
Where song-birds made melodious chime,
As I came down from Lebanon.

As I came down from Lebanon,
Like lava in the dying glow,
Through olive orchards far below
I saw the murmuring river run;
And 'neath the wall upon the sand
Swart sheiks from distant Samarcand,
With precious spices they had won,
Lay long and languidly in wait
Till they might pass the guarded gate,
As I came down from Lebanon.

As I came down from Lebanon,
I saw strange men from lands afar,
In mosque and square and gay bazaar,
The Magi that the Moslem shun,
And Grave Effendi from Stamboul,
Who sherbet sipped in corners cool;
And, from the balconies o'errun
With roses, gleamed the eyes of those
Who dwell in still seraglios,
As I came down from Lebanon.

As I came down from Lebanon,
The flaming flower of daytime died,
And Night, arrayed as is a bride
Of some great king, in garments spun
Of purple and the finest gold,
Outbloomed in glories manifold,
Until the moon, above the dun
And darkening desert, void of shade,
Shone like a keen Damascus blade,
As I came down from Lebanon.

RICHARD BURTON (1861—)

The City of the Dead

They do neither plight nor wed
In the city of the dead,
In the city where they sleep away the hours;
But they lie, while o'er them range
Winter blight and Summer change,
And a hundred happy whisperings of flowers;

No, they neither wed nor plight,
And the day is like the night,
For their vision is of other kind than ours.

They do neither sing nor sigh
In that burg of by and by,
Where the streets have grasses growing cool and long;
But they rest within their bed,
Leaving all their thoughts unsaid,
Deeming silence better far than sob or song.
No, they neither sigh nor sing,
Though the robin be a-wing,
Though the leaves of Autumn march a million strong.

There is only rest and peace
In the City of Surcease
From the failings and the wailings 'neath the sun,
And the wings of the swift years
Beat but gently o'er their biers,
Making music to the sleepers every one.
There is only peace and rest;
But to them it seemeth best,
For they lie at peace and know that life is done.

LOUISE IMOGEN GUINEY (1861-1920)

Tryste Noël

The Ox he openeth wide the Doore,
    And from the Snowe he calls her inne,
And he hath seen her smile therefore,
    Our Ladye without Sinne.
        Now soone from Sleep
        A Starre shall leap,
And soone arrive both King and Hinde:
            Amen, Amen,
But, the place co'd I but finde!

The Ox hath hushed his voyce and bent
    Trewe eyes of Pity ore the Mow,
And on his lovelie Neck, forspent,
    The Blessed lays her Browe.
        Around her feet
        Full Warme and Sweete
His bowerie Breath doth meeklie dwell:
            Amen, Amen,
But sore am I with Vaine Travèl!

The Ox is host in Judah stall
    And Host of more than onelie one,
For close she gathereth withal

Our Lorde her littel Sonne.
Glad Hinde and King
Their Gyfte may bring,
But wo'd tonight my Teares were There,
                Amen, Amen:
Between her Bosom and her hayre!

Of Joan's Youth

I would unto my fair restore
A simple thing:
The flushing cheek she had before!
Out-velveting
No more, no more,
On our sad shore,
The carmine grape, the moth's auroral wing.

Ah, say how winds in flooding grass
Unmoor the rose;
Or guileful ways the salmon pass
To sea, disclose;
For so, alas,
With Love, alas,
With fatal, fatal Love a girlhood goes.

ROBERT CAMERON ROGERS (1862-1912)

The Rosary

The hours I spent with thee, dear heart,
    Are as a string of pearls to me;
I count them over, every one apart,
                My rosary.
Each hour a pearl, each pearl a prayer,
    To still a heart in absence wrung;
I tell each bead unto the end and there
                A cross is hung.
Oh memories that bless—and burn!
    Oh barren gain—and bitter loss!
I kiss each bead, and strive at last to learn
                To kiss the cross,
                Sweetheart,
                To kiss the cross.

HENRY HOLCOMB BENNETT (1863—)

The Flag Goes By

Hats off!
Along the street there comes

A blare of bugles, a ruffle of drums,
A flash of color beneath the sky:
Hats off!
The flag is passing by!

Blue and crimson and white it shines,
Over the steel-tipped, ordered lines.
Hats off!
The colors before us fly;
But more than the flag is passing by.

Sea-fights and land-fights, grim and great,
Fought to make and to save the State:
Weary marches and sinking ships;
Cheers of victory on dying lips;

Days of plenty and years of peace;
March of a strong land's swift increase;
Equal justice, right and law,
Stately honor and reverend awe;

Sign of a nation, great and strong
To ward her people from foreign wrong:
Pride and glory and honor,—all
Live in the colors to stand or fall.

Hats off!
Along the street there comes
A blare of bugles, a ruffle of drums;
And loyal hearts are beating high:
Hats off!
The flag is passing by!

OLIVER HERFORD (1863—)

Child's Natural History

GEESE

Ev-er-y child who has the use
Of his sen-ses knows a goose.
Sees them un-der-neath the tree
Gath-er round the goose-girl's knee,
While she reads them by the hour
From the works of Scho-pen-hau-er.
How pa-tient-ly the geese at-tend!
But do they re-al-ly com-pre-hend
What Scho-pen-hau-er's driv-ing at?

Oh, not at all; but what of that?
Nei-ther do I; nei-ther does she;
And, for that mat-ter, nor does he.

THE MON-GOOS

This, children, is the famed Mon-goos.
He has an ap-pe-tite ab-struse:
Strange to re-late, this crea-ture takes
A cu-ri-ous joy in eat-ing snakes—
All kinds—though, it must be con-fessed
He likes the poi-son-ous ones the best.
From him we learn how ve-ry small
A thing can bring a-bout a Fall.
O Mon-goos, where were you that day,
When Mistress Eve was led a-stray?
If you'd but seen the ser-pent first,
Our parents would not have been cursed,
And so there would be no ex-cuse
For MILTON, but for you—Mon-goos!

GEORGE SANTAYANA (1863—)

"As in the Midst of Battle"

As in the midst of battle there is room
    For thoughts of love, and in foul sin for mirth;
    As gossips whisper of a trinket's worth
Spied by the death-bed's flickering candle-gloom;
As in the crevices of Cæsar's tomb
    The sweet herbs flourish on a little earth:
    So in this great disaster of our birth
We can be happy, and forget our doom.
For morning, with a ray of tenderest joy
    Gilding the iron heaven, hides the truth,
And evening gently woos us to employ
    Our grief in idle catches. Such is youth;
Till from that Summer's trance we wake, to find
Despair before us, vanity behind.

"What Riches Have You?"

What riches have you that you deem me poor,
Or what large comfort that you call me sad?
Tell me what makes you so exceeding glad:
Is your earth happy or your heaven sure?
I hope for heaven, since the stars endure

And bring such tidings as our fathers had.
I know no deeper doubt to make me mad,
I need no brighter love to keep me pure.
To me the faiths of old are daily bread;
I bless their hope, I bless their will to save,
And my deep heart still meaneth what they said.
It makes me happy that the soul is brave,
And, being so much kinsman to the dead,
I walk contented to the peopled grave.

ROBERT LOVEMAN (1864-1923)

April Rain

It is not raining rain for me,
    It's raining daffodils;
In every dimpled drop I see
    Wild flowers on the hills.

The clouds of gray engulf the day
    And overwhelm the town;
It is not raining rain to me,
    It's raining roses down.

It is not raining rain to me,
    But fields of clover bloom,
Where any buccaneering bee
    Can find a bed and room.

A health unto the happy,
    A fig for him who frets!
It is not raining rain to me,
    It's raining violets.

RICHARD HOVEY (1864-1900)
AND BLISS CARMAN (1861—)

The Wander-Lovers

Down the world with Marna!
That's the life for me!
Wandering with the wandering wind,
Vagabond and unconfined!
Roving with the roving rain
Its unboundaried domain!
Kith and kin of wander-kind,
Children of the sea!

Petrels of the sea-drift!
Swallows of the lea!
Arabs of the whole wide girth
Of the wind-encircled earth!
In all climes we pitch our tents,
Cronies of the elements,
With the secret lords of birth
Intimate and free.

All the seaboard knows us
From Fundy to the Keys;
Every bend and every creek
Of abundant Chesapeake;
Ardise hills and Newport coves
And the far-off orange groves,
Where Floridian oceans break,
Tropic tiger seas.

Down the world with Marna,
Tarrying there and here!
Just as much at home in Spain
As in Tangier or Touraine!
Shakespeare's Avon knows us well,
And the crags of Neufchâtel;
And the ancient Nile is fain
Of our coming near.

Down the world with Marna,
Daughter of the air!
Marna of the subtle grace,
And the vision in her face!
Moving in the measures trod
By the angels before God!
With her sky-blue eyes amaze
And her sea-blue hair!

Marna with the trees' life
In her veins a-stir!
Marna of the aspen heart
Where the sudden quivers start!
Quick-responsive, subtle child,
Artless as an artless child,
Spite of all her reach of art!
Oh, to roam with her!

Marna with the wind's will,
Daughter of the sea!
Marna of the quick disdain,
Starting at the dream of stain!
At a smile with love aglow,

At a frown a statued woe,
Standing pinnacled in pain
Till a kiss sets free!

Down the world with Marna,
Daughter of the fire!
Marna of the deathless hope,
Still alert to win new scope
Where the wings of life may spread
For a flight unhazarded!
Dreaming of the speech to cope
With the heart's desire!

Marna of the far quest
After the divine!
Striving ever for some goal
Past the blunder-god's control!
Dreaming of potential years
When no day shall dawn in fears!
That's the Marna of my soul,
Wander-bride of mine!

Envoy

From "More Songs from Vagabondia"

Whose furthest footstep never strayed
Beyond the village of his birth
Is but a lodger for the night
In this old wayside inn of earth.

To-morrow he shall take his pack,
And set out for the ways beyond
On the old trail from star to star,
An alien and a vagabond.

The Sea Gipsy

I am fevered with the sunset,
I am fretful with the bay,
For the wander-thirst is on me
And my soul is in Cathay.

There's a schooner in the offing,
With her topsails shot with fire,
And my heart has gone aboard her
For the Islands of Desire.

I must forth again to-morrow!
With the sunset I must be

Hull down on the trail of rapture
In the wonder of the Sea.

Love in the Winds

When I am standing on a mountain crest,
Or hold the tiller in the dashing spray,
My love of you leaps foaming in my breast,
Shouts with the winds and sweeps to their foray;
My heart bounds with the horses of the sea,
And plunges in the wild ride of the night,
Flaunts in the teeth of tempest the large glee
That rides out Fate and welcomes gods to fight.
Ho, love, I laugh aloud for love of you,
Glad that our love is fellow to rough weather,—
No fretful orchid hothoused from the dew,
But hale and hardy as the highland heather,
Rejoicing in the wind that stings and thrills,
Comrade of ocean, playmate of the hills.

ROBERT W. CHAMBERS (1865—)

The Recruit

Sez Corporal Madden to Private McFadden:
    "Bedad, yer a bad 'un!
    Now turn out yer toes!
    Yer belt is unhookit,
    Yer cap is on crookit,
    Ye may not be dhrunk,
    But, be jabbers, ye look it!
        Wan—two!—
        Wan—two!—
Ye monkey-faced divil, I'll jolly ye through!
        Wan—two!—
        Time! Mark!
Ye march like the aigle in Cintheral Parrk!"

Sez Corporal Madden to Private McFadden:
    "A saint it ud sadden
    To dhrill such a mug!
    Eyes front!—ye baboon, ye!—
    Chin up!—ye gossoon, ye!
    Ye've jaws like a goat—
    Halt! ye leather-lipped loon, ye!
        Wan—two!
        Wan—two!

Ye whiskered orang-outang, I'll fix you!
      Wan—two!—
      Time! Mark!
Ye've eyes like a bat!—can ye see in the dark?"

Sez Corporal Madden to Private McFadden:
      "Yer figger wants padd'n—
      Sure, man, ye've no shape!
      Behind ye yer shoulders
      Stick out like two bowlders;
      Yer shins is as thin
      As a pair of pen-holders!
         Wan—two!
         Wan—two!
Yer belly belongs on yer back, ye Jew!
      Wan—two!—
      Time! Mark!
I'm dhry as a dog—I can't shpake but I bark!"

Sez Corporal Madden to Private McFadden:
      "Me heart it ud gladden
      To blacken yer eye.
      Ye're gettin' too bold, ye
      Compel me to scold ye,—
      'Tis halt! that I say,—
      Will ye heed what I told ye?
         Wan—two!
         Wan—two!
Be jabers, I'm dhryer than Brian Boru!
      Wan—two!—
      Time! Mark!
What's wur-ruk for chickens is sport for the lark!"

Sez Corporal Madden to Private McFadden:
      "I'll not stay a gadd'n
      Wid dagoes like you!
      I'll travel no farther,
      I'm dyin' for—wather;—
      Come on, if ye like,—
      Can ye loan me a quather?
         Ya-as, you,
         What,—two?
And ye'll pay the potheen? Ye're a daisy! Whurroo!
         You'll do!
      Whist! Mark!
The Rigiment's flatthered to own ye, me spark!"

MADISON CAWEIN (1865-1914)

The Rain-Crow

Can freckled August,—drowsing warm and blonde
  Beside a wheat-shock in the white-topped mead,
In her hot hair the oxeyed daisies wound,—
  O bird of rain, lend aught but sleepy heed
  To Thee? when no plumed weed, no feather'd seed
Blows by her; and no ripple breaks the pond,
  That gleams like flint between its rim of grasses,
  Through which the dragonfly forever passes
    Like splintered diamond.

Drouth weights the trees, and from the farmhouse eaves
  The locust, pulse-beat of the summer day,
Throbs; and the lane, that shambles under leaves
  Limp with the heat—a league of rutty way—
  Is lost in dust; and sultry scents of hay
Breathe from the panting meadows heaped with sheaves.
  Now, now, O bird, what hint is there of rain,
  In thirsty heaven or on burning plain,
    That thy keen eye perceives?

But thou art right. Thou prophesiest true.
  For hardly hast thou ceased thy forecasting,
When, up the western fierceness of scorched blue,
  Great water-carrier winds their buckets bring
  Brimming with freshness. How their dippers ring
And flash and rumble! lavishing dark dew
  On corn and forestland, that, streaming wet,
  Their hilly backs against the downpour set,
    Like giants vague in view.

The butterfly, safe under leaf and flower,
  Has found a roof, knowing how true thou art;
The bumble-bee, within the last half-hour,
  Has ceased to hug the honey to its heart;
  While in the barnyard, under shed and cart.
Brood-hens have housed.—But I, who scorned thy power,
  Barometer of the birds.—like August there,—
  Beneath a beech, dripping from foot to hair,
    Like some drenched truant, cower.

Here Is the Place Where Loveliness Keeps House

Here is the place where Loveliness keeps house,
Between the river and the wooded hills,
Within a valley where the Springtime spills

Her firstling wind-flowers under blossoming boughs:
Where Summer sits braiding her warm, white brows
With bramble-roses; and where Autumn fills
Her lap with asters; and old Winter frills
With crimson haw and hip his snowy blouse.
Here you may meet with Beauty. Here she sits
Gazing upon the moon, or all the day
Tuning a wood-thrush flute, remote, unseen:
Or when the storm is out, 'tis she who flits
From rock to rock, a form of flying spray,
Shouting, beneath the leaves' tumultuous green.

ANNE REEVE ALDRICH (1866-1892)

Recollection

How can it be that I forget
　　The way he phrased my doom,
When I recall the arabesques
　　That carpeted the room?

How can it be that I forget
　　His look and mien that hour,
When I recall I wore a rose,
　　And still can smell the flower?

How can it be that I forget
　　Those words that were the last,
When I recall the tune a man
　　Was whistling as he passed?

These things are what we keep from life's
　　Supremest joy or pain;
For Memory locks her chaff in bins
　　And throws away the grain.

A Little Parable

I made the cross myself whose weight
　　Was later laid on me.
This thought is torture as I toil
　　Up life's steep Calvary.

To think mine own hands drove the nails!
　　I sang a merry song,
And chose the heaviest wood I had
　　To build it firm and strong.

If I had guessed—if I had dreamed
Its weight was meant for me,
I should have made a lighter cross
To bear up Calvary!

GELETT BURGESS (1866—)

The Purple Cow

Reflections on a Mythic Beast,
Who's Quite Remarkable, at Least.

I never saw a Purple Cow;
I never Hope to See One;
But I can Tell you, Anyhow,
I'd rather See than Be One.

DORA READ GOODALE (1866—)

The Judgment

Thou hast done evil
And given place to the devil;
Yet so cunningly thou concealest
The thing which thou feelest,
That no eye espieth it,
Satan himself denieth it.
Go where it chooseth thee,
There is none that accuseth thee;
Neither foe nor lover
Will the wrong uncover;
The world's breath raiseth thee,
And thy own past praiseth thee.
Yet know thou this:
At quick of thy being
Is an eye all-seeing,
The snake's wit evadeth not,
The charmed lip persuadeth not;
So thoroughly it despiseth
The thing thy hand prizeth,
Though the sun were thy clothing,
It should count thee for nothing.
Thine own eye divineth thee,
Thine own soul arraigneth thee;
God himself cannot shrive thee
Till that judge forgive thee.

ARTHUR COLTON (1868—)

To Faustine

Sometime, it may be, you and I
In some deserted yard will lie
Where Memory fades away;
Caring no more for Love his dreams,
Busy with new and alien themes,
The saints and sages say.

But let our graves be side by side,
So idlers may at evening tide
Pause there a moment's space:
"Ah, they were lovers who lie here;
Else why these low graves laid so near,
In this forgotten place?"

EDGAR LEE MASTERS (1868—)

From "The New Spoon River"

MORGAN OAKLEY

There is a time for vine leaves in the hair,
And a time for thorns on the brow,
Even as life is both ecstasy and agony,
And as Nature grows both leaves and thorns.
In youth I knew love and victory;
In age loneliness and pain.
But life is to be lived neither as leaves,
Nor as thorns, but through both.
I came to the wisdom of barren boughs,
And the desolation of unleaved thorns,
Which remembered the leaves!

BERTRAND HUME

To recall and revision blue skies;
To imagine the summer's clouds;
To remember mountains and wooded slopes,
And the blue of October water;
To face the shark gray spray of the sea;
To listen in dreams to voices singing,
Voices departed, but never forgotten;
To feel the kisses of vanished lips,
And see the eyes of rapture,
And hear the whispers of sacred midnights. . . .

To live over the richness of life,
Never fully lived;
To see it all, as from a window that looks
Upon a garden of flowers and distant hills,
From which your broken body is barred. . . .
O life! O unutterable beauty,
To leave you, knowing that you were never loved enough,
Wishing to live you all over
With all the soul's wise will!

HOWARD LAMSON

Ice cannot shiver in the cold,
Nor stones shrink from the lapping flame.
Eyes that are sealed, no more have tears;
Ears that are stopped hear nothing ill;
Hearts turned to silt are strange to pain;
Tongues that are dumb report no loss;
Hands stiffened, well may idle be;
No sigh is from a breathless breast.
Beauty may fade, but closed eyes see not;
Sorrow may wail, but stopped ears hear not;
Work is, but folded hands need work not;
Nothing to say is for dumb tongues.
The rolling earth rolls on and on
With trees and stones and winding streams—
My dream is what the hill-side dreams!

CLEANTHUS TRILLING

The urge of the seed: the germ.
The urge of the germ: the stalk.
The urge of the stalk: leaves.
The urge of leaves: the blossom.

The urge of the blossom: to scatter pollen.
The urge of the pollen: the imagined dream of life
The urge of life: longing for to-morrow.
The urge of to-morrow: Pain.
The urge of Pain: God.

HENRY DITCH

As a boy old bachelors and old maids
Were pointed out to me as hearts of ideal devotion.
Consecrated to the memory of a lost love,
Or a departed love.
It was not that, as I learned for myself,
That kept their souls from marriage:
If the sun of March brings April breezes,
And tempts the blossoms forth

To the numbing fingers of sudden frost,
And the flail of bitter snow,
The soul of the tree sinks down exhausted,
And cannot bud again.
And that is love forced back by fear,
And robbed of its power to try again
In life's precarious garden!

LOUISE HEDEEN

Carve me a cherub! All of me head and wings,
Resting on shoulderless arms that enclosed me.
What was the heart of me? Always the head of me!
What were my longings but restless wings,
Stretched ever for flight in the wonder of waiting,
The far heard cry of a mate, or an April caprice?
Once in the midst of a spring that I searched for,
Spring that I found at the last, in a moment
Off I flew, leaving the blossoms, the vision:
Leaves of the sky between leaves of the lilac;
Skies in my wings' soft hollows, that nestled
With kisses of eyes closed down in passion.
Up then I soared searching the lips of that sky.
I broke my wing with a clinging tendril and fell,
To a covert of grass and roots, where I brooded,
A beauty forsaken, nursing an endless pain!

WILLIAM VAUGHN MOODY (1869-1910)

From "Song-Flower and Poppy"

IN NEW YORK

He plays the deuce with my writing time,
For the penny my sixth-floor neighbor throws;
He finds me proud of my pondered rhyme,
And he leaves me—well, God knows
It takes the shine from a tunester's line
When a little mate of the deathless Nine
Pipes up under your nose!

For listen, there is his voice again,
Wistful and clear and piercing sweet.
Where did the boy find such a strain
To make a dead heart beat?
And how in the name of care can he bear
To jet such a fountain into the air
In this gray gulch of a street?

Tuscan slopes or the Piedmontese?
Umbria under the Apennine?
South where the terraced lemon-trees

Round rich Sorrento shine?
Venice moon on the smooth lagoon?—
Where have I heard that aching tune,
That boyish throat divine?

.   .   .   .

O hark! How it blooms in the falling dark,
That flower of mystical yearning song:
Sad as a hermit-thrush, as a lark
Uplifted, glad, and strong.
Heart, we have chosen the better part!
Save sacred love and sacred art,
Nothing is good for long.

AT ASSISI

Before St. Francis' burg I wait,
Frozen in spirit, faint with dread;
His presence stands within the gate,
Mild splendor rings his head.
Gently he seems to welcome me:
Know he not I am quick, and he
Is dead, and priest of the dead?

I turn away from the gray church pile;
I dare not enter, thus undone:
Here in the roadside grass awhile
I will lie and watch for the sun.
Too purged of earth's good glee and strife,
Too drained of the honeyed lusts of life
Was the peace these old saints won!

And lo! how the laughing earth says no.
To the fear that mastered me;
To the blood that aches and clamors so
How it whispers "Verily."
Here by my side, marvellous-dyed,
Bold stray-away from the courts of pride,
A poppy-bell flaunts free.

St. Francis sleeps upon his hill,
And a poppy-flower laughs down his creed;
Triumphant light her petals spill,
His shrines are dim indeed.
Men build and plan, but the soul of man,
Coming with haughty eyes to scan,
Feels richer, wilder need.

How long, old builder Time, wilt bide
Till, at thy thrilling word,
Life's crimson pride shall have to bride

The spirit's white accord,
Within that gate of good estate
Which thou must build us soon or late,
Hoar workman of the Lord?

Heart's Wild-Flower

To-night her lids shall lift again, slow, soft, with vague
    desire,
And lay about my breast and brain their hush of spirit fire,
And I shall take the sweet of pain as the laborer his hire.
And though no word shall e'er be said to ease the ghostly
    sting,
And though our hearts, unhoused, unfed, must still go wan-
    dering,
My sign is set upon her head while stars do meet and sing.

Not such a sign as women wear who make their forehead
    tame
With life's long tolerance, and bear love's sweetest, humblest
    name,
Nor such as passion eateth bare with its crown of tears and
    flame.

Nor such a sign as happy friend sets on his friend's dear
    brow
When meadow-pipings break and bend to a key of autumn
    woe,
And the woodland says playtime's at end, best unclasp hands
    and go.

But where she strays, through blight or blooth, one fadeless
    flower she wears,
A little gift God gave my youth,—whose petals dim were
    fears,
Awes, adorations, songs of ruth, hesitancies, and tears.

O heart of mine, with all the powers of white beatitude,
What are the dearest of God's dowers to the children of
    his blood?
How blow the shy, shy wilding flowers in the hollows of his
    wood?

EDWIN ARLINGTON ROBINSON (1869—)

Luke Havergal

Go to the western gate, Luke Havergal,—
There where the vines cling crimson on the wall,—

And in the twilight wait for what will come.
The wind will moan, the leaves will whisper some,—
Whisper of her, and strike you as they fall;
But go, and if you trust her she will call.
Go to the western gate, Luke Havergal—
Luke Havergal.

No, there is not a dawn in eastern skies
To rift the fiery night that's in your eyes;
But there, where western glooms are gathering,
The dark will end the dark, if anything:
God slays Himself with every leaf that flies,
And hell is more than half of paradise.
No, there is not a dawn in eastern skies—
In eastern skies.

Out of a grave I come to tell you this,—
Out of a grave I come to quench the kiss
That flames upon your forehead with a glow
That binds you to the way that you must go.
Yes, there is yet one way to where she is,—
Bitter, but one that faith can never miss.
Out of a grave I come to tell you this—
To tell you this.

There is the western gate, Luke Havergal,
There are the crimson leaves upon the wall.
Go,—for the winds are tearing them away,—
Nor think to riddle the dead words they say,
Nor any more to feel them as they fall;
But go! and if you trust her she will call.
There is the western gate, Luke Havergal—
Luke Havergal.

[From "The Children of the Night"; copyright, 1896, 1897,
   by Edwin Arlington Robinson; published by Charles
   Scribner's Sons. By permission of the publishers.]

Miniver Cheevy

Miniver Cheevy, child of scorn,
   Grew lean while he assailed the seasons;
He wept that he was ever born,
   And he had reasons.

Miniver loved the days of old
   When swords were bright and steeds were prancing;
The vision of a warrior bold
   Would set him dancing.

Miniver sighed for what was not,
  And dreamed, and rested from his labors;
He dreamed of Thebes and Camelot,
  And Priam's neighbors.

Miniver mourned the ripe renown
  That made so many a name so fragrant;
He mourned Romance, now on the town,
  And Art a vagrant.

Miniver loved the Medici,
  Albeit he had never seen one;
He would have sinned incessantly
  Could he have been one.

Miniver cursed the commonplace,
  And eyed a khaki suit with loathing;
He missed the medieval grace
  Of iron clothing.

Miniver scorned the gold he sought,
  But sore annoyed was he without it;
Miniver thought, and thought, and thought,
  And thought about it.

Miniver Cheevy, born too late,
  Scratched his head and kept on thinking;
Miniver coughed, and called it fate,
  And kept on drinking.

[From "The Town Down the River"; copyright, 1910, by
Charles Scribner's Sons. By permission of the publishers.]

The Master

[Supposed to have been written not long
after the Civil War]

A flying word from here and there
Had sown the name at which we sneered,
But soon the name was everywhere,
To be reviled and then revered:
A presence to be loved and feared,
We cannot hide it, or deny
That we, the gentlemen who jeered,
May be forgotten by and by.

He came when days were perilous
And hearts of men were sore beguiled;

And having made his note of us,
He pondered and was reconciled.
Was ever master yet so mild
As he, and so untamable?
We doubted, even when he smiled,
Not knowing what he knew so well.

He knew that undeceiving fate
Would shame us whom he served unsought;
He knew that he must wince and wait—
The jest of those for whom he fought;
He knew devoutly what he thought
Of us and of our ridicule;
He knew that we must all be taught
Like little children in a school.

We gave a glamor to the task
That he encountered and saw through,
But little of us did he ask,
And little did we ever do.
And what appears if we review
The season when we railed and chaffed?
It is the face of one who knew
That we were learning while we laughed.

The face that in our vision feels
Again the venom that we flung,
Transfigured to the world reveals
The vigilance to which we clung.
Shrewd, hallowed, harassed, and among
The mysteries that are untold,
The face we see was never young
Nor could it ever have been old.

For he, to whom we had applied
Our shopman's test of age and worth,
Was elemental when he died,
As he was ancient at his birth:
The saddest among kings of earth,
Bowed with a galling crown, this man
Met rancor with a cryptic mirth,
Laconic—and Olympian.

The love, the grandeur, and the fame,
Are bounded by the world alone;
The calm, the smoldering, and the flame
Of awful patience were his own:
With him they are forever flown
Past all our fond self-shadowings,
Wherewith we cumber the Unknown
As with inept, Icarian wings.

For we were not as other men:
'Twas ours to soar and his to see.
But we are coming down again,
And we shall come down pleasantly;
Nor shall we longer disagree
On what it is to be sublime,
But flourish in our perigee
And have one Titan at a time.

[From "The Town Down the River"; copyright, 1910, by
Charles Scribner's Sons. By permission of the publishers.]

GEORGE STERLING (1869—)

The Black Vulture

Aloof upon the day's immeasured dome,
He holds unshared the silence of the sky.
Far down his bleak, relentless eyes descry
The eagle's empire and the falcon's home—
Far down, the galleons of sunset roam;
His hazards on the sea of morning lie;
Serene, he hears the broken tempest sigh
Where cold sierras gleam like scattered foam.
And least of all he holds the human swarm—
Unwitting now that envious men prepare
To make their dream and its fulfillment one
When, poised above the caldrons of the storm,
Their hearts, contemptuous of death, shall dare
His roads between the thunder and the sun.

A Legend of the Dove

Soft from the linden's bough,
Unmoved against the tranquil afternoon,
Eve's dove laments her now:
"Ah, gone! long gone! Shall I not find thee soon?"

That yearning in his voice
Told not to Paradise a sorrow's tale:
As other birds rejoice
He sang, a brother to the nightingale.

By twilight on her breast
He saw the flower asleep, the star awake,
And calling her from rest,
Made all the dawn melodious for her sake.

And then the Tempter's breath,
The sword of exile and the mortal chain——

The heritage of death,
That gave her heart to dust, his own to pain. . . .

In Eden desolate,
The seraph heard his lonely music swoon,
   As now, reiterate:
"Ah, gone! long gone! Shall I not find thee soon?"

Omnia Exeunt in Mysterium

The stranger in the gates—lo! that am I,
And what my land of birth, I do not know,
Nor yet the hidden land to which I go.
One may be lord of many, ere he die,
But know himself he shall not, nor his woe,
Nor to what sea the tears of wisdom flow,
Nor why one star is taken from the sky.

An urging is upon him evermore,
And though he bide, his soul is wanderer,
Scanning the shadows with a sense of haste——
Where fade the tracks of all who went before:
A dim and solitary traveller
On ways that end in evening and in waste.

STEPHEN CRANE (1870-1900)

Why?

Behold, the grave of a wicked man,
And near it, a stern spirit.
There came a drooping maid with violets,
But the spirit grasped her arm.
"No flowers for him," he said.
The maid wept:
"Ah, I loved him."
But the spirit, grim and frowning:
"No flowers for him."

Now, this is it—
If the spirit was just,
Why did the maid weep?

Content

A youth in apparel that glittered
Went to walk in a grim forest.
There he met an assassin
Attired all in garb of old days;
He, scowling through the thickets,
And dagger poised quivering,

Rushed upon the youth.
"Sir," said this latter,
"I am encnanted, believe me.
To die thus,
In this mediæval fashion,
According to the best legends;
Ah, what joy!"
Then took he the wound, smiling,
And died, content.

Ancestry

Once I saw mountains angry,
And ranged in battle-front.
Against them stood a little man;
Ay, he was no bigger than my finger.
I laughed, and spoke to one near me,
"Will he prevail?"
"Surely," replied this other;
"His grandfathers beat them many times."
Then did I see much virtue in grandfathers,—
At least, for the little man
Who stood against the mountains.

T. A. DALY (1871—)

Mia Carlotta

Giuseppe, da barber, ees greata for "mash,"
He gotta da bigga, da blacka mustache,
Good clo'es an' good styla an' playnta good cash.

W'enevra Giuseppe ees walk on da street,
Da peopla dey talka, "How nobby! how neat!
How softa da handa, how smalla da feet."

He raisa hees hat an' he shaka hees curls,
An' smila weeth teetha so shiny like pearls;
O! many da heart of da seelly young girls
He gotta.
Yes, playnta he gotta—
But notta
Carlotta!

Giuseppe, da barber, he maka da eye,
An' lika de steam engine puffa an' sigh,
For catcha Carlotta w'en she ees go by.

Carlotta she walka weeth nose in da air,
An' look through Giuseppe weeth far-away stare,
As eef she no see dere ees som'body dere.

Giuseppe, da barber, he gotta da cash,
He gotta da clo'es an' da bigga mustache,
He gotta da seelly young girls for da "mash,"
                    But notta—
            You bat my life, notta—
                    Carlotta.
                    I gotta!

The Mother

She was so frail, my little one,
    She had not yet begun to stir
Her tiny limbs; from sun to sun,
    This breast, these arms maternal were
    The bounded universe for her.

But now far spaces feel her might,
    And sad, sweet thoughts of her arise
With every sun; she stirs the night
    With sighing winds, and from the skies
    She looks at me with starry eyes.

EDWIN FORD PIPER (1871—)

Sweetgrass Range

Come sell your pony, cowboy—
    Sell your pony to me;
Braided bridle and your puncher saddle,
    And spend your money free.

"If I should sell my pony,
    And ride the range no more,
Nail up my hat and my silver spurs
    Above my shanty door;

"And let my door stand open wide
    To the snow and the rain and sun;
And bury me under the green sweetgrass
    Where you hear the river run."

As I came down the sweetgrass range
    And by the cabin door,
I heard a singing in the early dusk
    Along the river shore;

I heard a singing to the early stars,
    And the tune of a pony's feet.
The joy of the riding singer
    I never shall forget.

PAUL LAURENCE DUNBAR (1872-1906)

Discovered

Seen you down at chu'ch las' night,
   Nevah min', Miss Lucy.
What I mean? Oh, dat's all right,
   Nevah min', Miss Lucy.
You was sma't ez sma't could be,
But you couldn't hide f'om me.
Ain't I got two eyes to see!
   Nevah min', Miss Lucy.

Guess you thought you's awful keen;
   Nevah min', Miss Lucy.
Evahthing you done, I seen;
   Nevah min', Miss Lucy.
Seen him tek yo' ahm jes' so,
When he got outside de do'—
Oh, I know dat man's yo' beau!
   Nevah min', Miss Lucy.

Say now, honey, wha'd he say?—
   Nevah min', Miss Lucy.
Keep yo' secrets—dat's yo' way—
   Nevah min', Miss Lucy.
Won't tell me an' I'm yo' pal!
I'm gwine tell his othah gal,—
Know huh, too, huh name is Sal.
   Nevah min', Miss Lucy.

Compensation

Because I had loved so deeply,
   Because I had loved so long,
God in His great compassion
   Gave me the gift of song.

Because I have loved so vainly,
   And sung with such faltering breath,
The Master, in infinite mercy,
   Offers the boon of Death.

FRANCIS SHAW (1872—)

Who Loves the Rain

Who loves the rain,
And loves his home,

And looks on life with quiet eyes,
  Him will I follow through the storm;
  And at his hearth-fire keep me warm;
Nor hell nor heaven shall that soul surprise,
  Who loves the rain,
    And loves his home,
And looks on life with quiet eyes.

JOHN COWPER POWYS (1872—)

Candle Light

Hush, true Love, as we sit and think
And talk to shadows and watch the coals
Redden up from beyond the brink
Of the common reach of our souls.

Do you not catch a cry in the air?
No! That is the wind in the chimney calling!
That is a curtain fluttering there!
That is a dead branch falling!

Burning wood when candles are lit
Has a bitter-sweet breath that can carry far;
That can carry two lovers from where they sit
To the edge of the sea and over it
Where the unknown islands are.

Burning wood has a wizard spell
Full of old sad stories and long-dead things;
Like myrrh and cassia is that smell,
From the sepulchres of kings.

And whenever lovers like you and me
Sit together of a winter's night,
There's a cry on the wind, there's a cry on the sea
There's a tongue in the candlelight.

And a great host gathers out of the dark
From wild far places, from sunk sea-walls,
From fallen roofs where hyenas bark
From ruined tents and kraals.

It gathers toward us while you and I
Talk to old shadows and sit and stare,
And let time and space and the world go by
Like smoke upon the air.

And as we gaze at the reddening coals
Lost in that amorous host are we;
That vast procession of lovers' souls
Drowns our identity.

GUY WETMORE CARRYL (1873-1904)

The Sycophantic Fox and the Gullible Raven

A raven sat upon a tree,
    And not a word he spoke, for
His beak contained a piece of Brie,
    Or, maybe, it was Roquefort.
        We'll make it any kind you please—
        At all events it was a cheese.

Beneath the tree's umbrageous limb
    A hungry fox sat smiling;
He saw the raven watching him,
    And spoke in words beguiling:
        "J'admire," said he, *"ton beau plumage,"*
        (The which was simply persiflage.)

Two things there are, no doubt you know,
    To which a fox is used:
A rooster that is bound to crow,
    A crow that's bound to roost;
        And whichsoever he espies
        He tells the most unblushing lies.

"Sweet fowl," he said, "I understand
    You're more than merely natty,
I hear you sing to beat the band
    And Adelina Patti.
        Pray render with your liquid tongue
        A bit from 'Götterdämmerung.' "

This subtle speech was aimed to please
    The crow, and it succeeded;
He thought no bird in all the trees
    Could sing as well as he did.
        In flattery completely doused,
        He gave the "Jewel Song" from "Faust."

But gravitation's law, of course,
    As Isaac Newton showed it,
Exerted on the cheese its force,
    And elsewhere soon bestowed it.
        In fact, there is no need to tell
        What happened when to earth it fell.

I blush to add that when the bird
      Took in the situation
He said one brief, emphatic word,
      Unfit for publication.
            The fox was greatly startled, but
            He only sighed and answered "Tut."

THE MORAL is: A fox is bound
      To be a shameless sinner.
And also: When the cheese comes round
      You know it's after dinner.
            But (what is only known to few)
            The fox is after dinner, too.

ARTHUR STRINGER (1874—)

You Bid Me to Sleep

You bid me to sleep,—
But why, O Daughter of Beauty,
Was beauty thus born in the world?
Since out of these shadowy eyes
The wonder shall pass!
And out of this surging and passionate breast
The dream shall depart!
And out of these delicate rivers of warmth
The fire shall wither and fail!

And youth like a bird from your body shall fly!
And Time like a fang on your flesh shall feed!
And this perilous bosom that pulses with love
Shall go down to the dust from which it arose,—
Yet Daughter of Beauty, close,
Close to its sumptuous warmth
You hold my sorrowing head,
And smile with shadowy eyes,
And bid me to sleep again!

JOSEPHINE PRESTON PEABODY (1874—)

The Singing Man

He sang above the vineyards of the world.
      And after him the vines with woven hands
Clambered and clung, and everywhere unfurled
      Triumphing green above the barren lands;

Till high as gardens grow, he climbed, he stood,
  Sun-crowned with life and strength, and singing toil,
And looked upon his work; and it was good;
  The corn, the wine, the oil.

He sang above the noon. The topmost cleft
  That grudged him footing on the mountain scars
He planted and despaired not; till he left
  His vines soft breathing to the host of stars.
He wrought, he tilled; and even as he sang,
  The creatures of his planting laughed to scorn
The ancient threat of deserts where there sprang
  The wine, the oil, the corn!

He sang not for abundance.—Over-lords
  Took of his tilth. Yet was there still to reap,
The portion of his labor; dear rewards
  Of sunlit day, and bread, and human sleep.
He sang for strength; for glory of the light.
  He dreamed above the furrows, "They are mine!"
When all he wrought stood fair before his sight
  With corn, and oil, and wine.

ANNA HEMPSTEAD BRANCH

Grieve Not, Ladies

Oh, grieve not, Ladies, if at night
  Ye wake to feel your beauty going.
It was a web of frail delight,
  Inconstant as an April snowing.

In other eyes, in other lands,
  In deep fair pools, new beauty lingers,
But like spent water in your hands
  It runs from your reluctant fingers.

Ye shall not keep the singing lark
  That owes to earlier skies its duty.
Weep not to hear along the dark
  The sound of your departing beauty.

The fine and anguished ear of night
  Is tuned to hear the smallest sorrow.
Oh, wait until the morning light!
  It may not seem so gone to-morrow!

But honey-pale and rosy-red!
  Brief lights that made a little shining!
Beautiful looks about us shed——
  They leave us to the old repining.

Think not the watchful dim despair
  Has come to you, the first, sweet-hearted!
For oh, the gold in Helen's hair!
  And how she cried when that departed!

Perhaps that one that took the most,
  The swiftest borrower, wildest spender,
May count, as we do not, the cost——
  And grow to us more true and tender.

Happy are we if in his eyes
  We see no shadow of forgetting.
Nay—if our star sinks in those skies
  We shall not wholly see its setting.

Then let us laugh as do the brooks
  That such immortal youth is ours,
If memory keeps for them our looks
  As fresh as are the spring-time flowers.

Oh, grieve not, ladies, if at night
  Ye wake to feel the cold December!
Rather recall the early light
  And in your loved one's arms, remember.

The Monk in the Kitchen

I

Order is a lovely thing;
On disarray it lays its wing,
Teaching simplicity to sing.
It has a meek and lowly grace,
Quiet as a nun's face.
Lo—I will have thee in this place!
Tranquil well of deep delight,
All things that shine through thee appear
As stones through water, sweetly clear.
Thou clarity,
That with angelic charity
Revealest beauty where thou art,
Spread thyself like a clean pool.
Then all the things that in thee are,

Shall seem more spiritual and fair,
Reflection from serener air——
Sunken shapes of many a star
In the high heavens set afar.

II

Ye stolid, homely, visible things,
Above you all brood glorious wings
Of your deep entities, set high,
Like slow moons in a hidden sky.
But you, their likenesses, are spent
Upon another element.
Truly ye are but seemings—
The shadowy cast-off gleamings
Of bright solidities. Ye seem
Soft as water, vague as dream;
Image, cast in a shifting stream.

III

What are ye?
I know not.
Brazen pan and iron pot,
Yellow brick and gray flag-stone
That my feet have trod upon—
Ye seem to me
Vessels of bright mystery.
For ye do bear a shape, and so
Though ye were made by man, I know
An inner Spirit also made,
And ye his breathings have obeyed.

IV

Shape, the strong and awful Spirit,
Laid his ancient hand on you.
He waste chaos doth inherit;
He can alter and subdue.
Verily, he doth lift up
Matter, like a sacred cup.
Into deep substance he reached, and lo
Where ye were not, ye were; and so
Out of useless nothing, ye
Groaned and laughed and came to be.
And I use you, as I can,
Wonderful uses, made for man,
Iron pot and brazen pan.

V

What are ye?
I know not;
Nor what I really do
When I move and govern you.
There is no small work unto God.
He requires of us greatness;
Of his least creature
A high angelic nature,
Stature superb and bright completeness.
He sets to us no humble duty.
Each act that he would have us do
Is haloed round with strangest beauty;
Terrific deeds and cosmic tasks
Of his plainest child he asks.
When I polish the brazen pan
I hear a creature laugh afar
In the gardens of a star,

And from his burning presence run
Flaming wheels of many a sun.
Whoever makes a thing more bright,
He is an angel of all light.
When I cleanse this earthen floor
My spirit leaps to see
Bright garments trailing over it,
A cleanness made by me.
Purger of all men's thoughts and ways,
With labor do I sound Thy praise,
My work is done for Thee.
Whoever makes a thing more bright,
He is an angel of all light.
Therefore let me spread abroad
The beautiful cleanness of my God.

VI

One time in the cool of dawn
Angels came and worked with me.
The air was soft with many a wing.
They laughed amid my solitude
And cast bright looks on everything.
Sweetly of me did they ask
That they might do my common task.
And all were beautiful—but one
With garments whiter than the sun
Had such a face
Of deep, remembered grace:
That when I saw I cried—"Thou art

The great Blood-Brother of my heart.
Where have I seen thee?"—And he said,
"When we are dancing round God's throne,
How often thou art there.
Beauties from thy hands have flown
Like white doves wheeling in mid air.
Nay—thy soul remembers not?
Work on, and cleanse thy iron pot."

VII

What are we? I know not.

AMY LOWELL (1874-1925)

Anticipation

I have been temperate always,
But I am like to be very drunk
With your coming.
There have been times
I feared to walk down the street
Lest I should reel with the wine of you,
And jerk against my neighbors
As they go by.
I am parched now, and my tongue is horrible in my mouth,
But my brain is noisy
With the clash and gurgle of filling wine-cups.

A Gift

See! I give myself to you, Beloved!
My words are little jars
For you to take and put upon a shelf.
Their shapes are quaint and beautiful,
And they have many pleasant colors and lustres
To recommend them.
Also the scent from them fills the room
With sweetness of flowers and crushed grasses.

When I shall have given you the last one
You will have the whole of me,
But I shall be dead.

THEODOSIA GARRISON (1874—)

Stains

The three ghosts on the lonesome road
Spake each to one another,

"Whence came that stain about your mouth
    No lifted hand may cover?"
"From eating of forbidden fruit,
    Brother, my brother."

The three ghosts on the sunless road
    Spake each to one another,
"Whence came that red burn on your foot
    No dust nor ash may cover?"
"I stamped a neighbor's hearth-flame out,
    Brother, my brother."

The three ghosts on the windless road
    Spake each to one another,
"Whence came that blood upon your hand
    No other hand may cover?"
"From breaking of a woman's heart,
    Brother, my brother."

"Yet on the earth clean men we walked,
    Glutton and Thief and Lover;
White flesh and fair it hid our stains
    That no man might discover."
"Naked the soul goes up to God,
    Brother, my brother."

ROBERT W. SERVICE (1874—)

The Song of the Soldier-Born

Give me the scorn of the stars and a peak defiant;
Wail of the pines and a wind with the shout of a giant;
Night and a trail unknown and a heart reliant.

Give me to live and love in the old, bold fashion;
A soldier's billet at night and a soldier's ration:
A heart that leaps to the fight with a soldier's passion.

For I hold as a simple faith there's no denying:
The trade of a soldier's the only trade worth plying;
The death of a soldier's the only death worth dying.

So let me go and leave your safety behind me;
Go to the spaces of hazard where nothing shall bind me;
Go till the word is War—and then you will find me.

Then you will call me and claim me because you will need me;
Cheer me and gird me and into the battle-wrath speed me. . . .
And when it's over, spurn me and no longer heed me.

For guile and a purse gold-greased are the arms you carry;
With deeds of paper you fight and with pens you parry;
You call on the hounds of the law your foes to harry.

You with your "Art for its own sake," posing and prinking;
You with your "Live and be merry," eating and drinking;
You with your "Peace at all hazard," from bright blood
  shrinking.

Fools! I will tell you now: though the red rain patters,
And a million of men go down, it's little it matters. . . .
There's the Flag unflung to the stars, though it streams in
  tatters.

There's a glory gold never can buy to yearn and to cry for;
There's a hope that's as old as the sky to suffer and sigh
  for;
There's a faith that out-dazzles the sun to martyr and die
  for.

Ah no! it's my dream that War will never be ended;
That men will perish like men, and valor be splendid;
That the Flag by the sword will be served, and honor de-
  fended.

That the tale of my fights will never be ancient story;
That though my eye may be dim and my beard be hoary,
I'll die as a soldier dies on the Field of Glory.

So give me a strong right arm for a wrong's swift righting;
Stave of a song on my lips as my sword is smiting;
Death in my boots may-be, but fighting, fighting.

[From "Rhymes of a Red Cross Man," by Robert W. Service,
    author of "Spell of the Yukon and Other Verses,"
      "Ballads of a Cheechako" and "Ballads of a
        Bohemian," published by Barse &
            Hopkins, New York.]

ROSE O'NEILL (1874—)

Love-Ending

Go, go,
Complete the overthrow!
Low lutes that were so loud!
Proud eyes for weeping!
(O, poor that were so proud!)
Tall grain for good reaping—

Slain kings for sound sleeping!
Cold hearts no hearth shall warm!
Long roads for rueing!
　　How to perform
　　This wonder of undoing!

Beat down
The alabaster town!
With what downfall!
Of amethystine hall!
Shatter the towers,
The feasts of fruit and flowers,
The crystal cups and all—
Tear the silver sleeve
And break the golden bell!
　　How to achieve
　　This pale feat of farewell!

Part, part,
Loose the prisoned heart!
The velvet vassal flies—
To the wind he goes!
But no, he turns and lies
Against me like a rose,
With his slaying eyes!
Intercept the sun
That I may not see!
　　How to be done
　　With this Gethsemane!

Wait, wait,
Rend the delicate,
The woven strands with care:
With care divide
The intertwinèd hair,
And side from side
Withdraw the fair from fair!
Make far the fair and fain!
Fold back the stubborn arm!
　　How to attain
　　This irretrievable harm!

Undo
The arms that tether you!
Unclasp the impearlèd belt
Softly not to wound;
Let the girdle melt,
Parting, half unfelt
Where once the lover swooned.

Still, the fingers hold;
The moony cincture tying!
> *How to be bold*
> *With this excess of dying!*

Be still;
Yield th' embracing will!
Close the fluted ears
On flutes that cease to speak.
Never any more
Spill the honied tears
Down the kissèd cheek!
Come out and close the door,
Nor listen at the key.
> *How to restore*
> *The plucked fruit to the tree!*

Then, then,
Turn back and part again!
Console the ruined love!
The crownèd creature falls
With his illustrious walls.
How fares my dove?
See who leans and calls!
Look once more. And so—
Close from further knowing.
> *How, now, to go*
> *With this redeemless going!*

There, there,
Leave the folden Care!
Let the heapèd heaven—
The princely prostrate lie.
Last—the Look be riven!
Then go carefully,
Lest he stir and sigh.
So, with subtle stride
The dead are left with speed.
> *How now to hide*
> *The consummated deed!*

Faun-Taken

Who was it then that lately took me in the wood?
And was it I that lay twice seven nights on leaves,
With musky hair against my side!
That cruel hair that kept me kindly from the cold!
Gold, gold!
Of yellow eyes that glance and hide!
Am I the maddened one that goes—and grieves
For lack of laughter laughing till I died?

Oh, drouth of grapey laughter, dearth and drouth!
Twice seven days are but a blurring ring
That circles round the corner of a mouth!
Oh, wide, wide mouths that bellow so, or fling
That fluting up to birds like spurted wine!
But, ah, no more, those sounds without a name—
No more that ambiguous grace of god and ape,
Where strange feet dance upon the dripping grape—
Those feet one must not see—that wounded mine!

Let me but once look back again and pass.
Once only see him again—and groan and go—
The lips that laugh in the grass—
That kiss in a way one must not know!
The lips that cling the mouths of pipes and suck
The roots of frightened flowers too pale to pluck;
The curls that vine o'er what one must not see—
Those horney hiders that so gorèd me!
Then, run and run—again to the hearths, the roofs!
But close behind,—the pipes, the pipes,—the hoofs!

ZONA GALE (1874—)

The Sky-Goer

He understood what it is that we are trying to work out.
He was very old, and from the secret swing of planets
To the secret decencies in human hearts, he understood.
I used to watch him watering his lawn, scattering the food
     for the woodpecker,
Sweeping the crossing before his house. It was not that there
     was light
About him, visible to the eye, as in the old paintings.
Rather, an influence came from him in little breaths.
When we were with him we became other.
He saw us all as if we were that which we dreamed our-
     selves.
He saw the town already clothed on for its To-morrow,
He saw the world, beating like a heart, beating like a heart.
"How may I, too, know?" I wanted to cry to him. Instead
I only said: "And how is it with you?" But he answered
Both questions by the look in his eyes. For he had come to
     quietness.
He had come to the place where sun and moon meet
And where the spaces of the heavens open their doors.
He was understanding and love and the silence.
He was the voice of these, as he fed the woodpecker.

North Star

His boy had stolen some money from a booth
At the County Fair. I found the father in his kitchen.
For years he had driven a dray and the heavy lifting
Had worn him down. So through his evenings
He slept by the kitchen stove as I found him.
The mother was crying and ironing.
I thought about the mother,
For she brought me a photograph
Taken at a street fair on her wedding day.
She was so trim and white and he so neat and alert.
In the picture with their friends about them—
I saw that she wanted me to know their dignity from the first.
But afterward I thought more about the father.
For as he came with me to the door
I could not forbear to say how bright and near the stars
     seemed.
Then he leaned and peered from beneath his low roof
And he said:
"There used to be a star called the Nord Star."

FREDERIC RIDGELY TORRENCE (1875—)

The Singers in a Cloud

Overhead at sunset all heard the choir.
Nothing could be seen except jewelled gray
Raining beauty earthward, flooding with desire
All things that listened there in the broken day;
Songs from freer breathers, their unprisoned fire
Out of cloudy fountains, flying and hurled,
Fell and warmed the world.

Sudden came a wind and birds were laid bare,
Only music warmed them round their brown breasts.
They had sent the splendors pouring through the air,
Love was their heat and home far above their nests.
Light went softly out and left their voices there:
Starward passed forever all that great cry,
Burning, round the sky.

On the earth the battles war against light,
Heavy lies the harrow, bitter the field.
Beauty, like a river running through the night,

Streams past the stricken ones whom it would have healed,
But the darkened faces turn away from sight.
Blind, bewildered nations sow, reap and fall,
Shadows gather all.

Far above the birdsong bright shines the gold.
Through the starry orchards earth's paths are hung;
As she moves among them glowing fruits unfold,
So that the heavens there reawaken young.
Overhead is beauty, healing for the old.
Overhead is morning, nothing but youth,
Only lovely youth.

Evensong

Beauty calls and gives no warning,
Shadows rise and wander on the day.
In the twilight, in the quiet evening,
We shall rise and smile and go away.
Over the flaming leaves
Freezes the sky.
It is the season grieves,
Not you, not I.
All our spring-times, all our summers,
We have kept the longing warm within.
Now we leave the after-comers
To attain the dreams we did not win.
Oh, we have wakened, Sweet, and had our birth,
And that's the end of earth;
And we have toiled and smiled and kept the light,
And that's the end of night.

PERCY MACKAYE (1875—)

The Automobile

Fluid the world flowed under us: the hills
    Billow on billow of umbrageous green
    Heaved us, aghast, to fresh horizons, seen
One rapturous instant, blind with flash of rills
And silver-rising storms and dewy stills
    Of dripping boulders, till the dim ravine
    Drowned us again in leafage, whose serene
Coverts grew loud with our tumultuous wills.

Then all of Nature's old amazement seemed
    Sudden to ask us: "Is this also man?
    This plunging, volant, land-amphibian

What Plato mused and Paracelsus dreamed?
  Reply!" And piercing us with ancient scan,
The shrill, primeval hawk gazed down—and screamed.

France

Half artist and half anchorite,
  Part siren and part Socrates,
Her face—alluring and yet recondite—
  Smiled through her salons and academies.

Lightly she wore her double mask,
  Till sudden, at war's kindling spark,
Her inmost self, in shining mail and casque,
  Blazed to the world her single soul—
                              Jeanne d'Arc!

WILLA SIBERT CATHER (1875—)

The Palatine

IN THE "DARK AGES"

"Have you been with the King to Rome,
  Brother, big brother?"
"I've been there and I've come home,
  Back to your play, little brother."

"Oh, how high is Cæsar's house,
  Brother, big brother?"
"Goats about the doorways browse;
Night-hawks nest in the burnt roof-tree.
Home of the wild bird and home of the bee,
A thousand chambers of marble lie
Wide to the sun and the wind and the sky.
Poppies we find amongst our wheat
Grow on Cæsar's banquet seat.
Cattle crop and neat-herds drowse
On the floors of Cæsar's house."

"But what has become of Cæsar's gold,
  Brother, big brother?"
"The times are bad and the world is old——
Who knows the where of the Cæsar's gold?
Night comes black o'er the Cæsar's hill;
The wells are deep and the tales are ill;
Fireflies gleam in the damp and mold——
All that is left of the Cæsar's gold.
  Back to your play, little brother."

"What has become of the Cæsar's men,
    Brother, big brother?"
"Dogs in the kennel and wolf in the den
Howl for the fate of the Cæsar's men,
Slain in Asia, slain in Gaul,
By Dacian border and Persian wall.
Rhineland orchard and Danube fen
Fatten their roots on Cæsar's men."

"Why is the world so sad and wide,
    Brother, big brother?"
"Saxon boys by their fields that bide
Need not know if the world is wide.
Climb no mountain but Shere-end hill,
Cross no water but goes to mill.
Ox in the stable and cow in the byre,
Smell of the wood-smoke and sleep by the fire;
Sun-up in seed-time—a likely lad
Hurts not his head that the world is sad.
    Back to your play, little brother."

ROBERT FROST (1875—)

After Apple-Picking

My long two-pointed ladder's sticking through a tree
Toward heaven still,
And there's a barrel that I didn't fill
Beside it, and there may be two or three
Apples I didn't pick upon some bough.
But I am done with apple-picking now.
Essence of winter sleep is on the night,
The scent of apples: I am drowsing off.
I cannot rub the strangeness from my sight
I got from looking through a pane of glass
I skimmed this morning from the drinking trough
And held against the world of hoary grass.
It melted, and I let it fall and break.
But I was well
Upon my way to sleep before it fell,
And I could tell
What form my dreaming was about to take.
Magnified apples appear and disappear,
Stem end and blossom end,
And every fleck of russet showing clear.
My instep arch not only keeps the ache,
It keeps the pressure of a ladder-round.
I feel the ladder sway as the boughs bend.

And I keep hearing from the cellar bin
The rumbling sound
Of load on load of apples coming in.
For I have had too much
Of apple-picking: I am overtired
Of the great harvest I myself desired.
There were ten thousand thousand fruit to touch,
Cherish in hand, lift down, and not let fall.
For all
That struck the earth,
No matter if not bruised or spiked with stubble,
Went surely to the cider-apple heap
As of no worth.
One can see what will trouble
This sleep of mine, whatever sleep it is.
Were he not gone,
The woodchuck could say whether it's like his
Long sleep, as I describe its coming on,
Or just some human sleep.

The Road Not Taken

Two roads diverged in a yellow wood,
And sorry I could not travel both
And be one traveller, long I stood
And looked down one as far as I could
To where it bent in the undergrowth;

Then took the other, as just as fair,
And having perhaps the better claim,
Because it was grassy and wanted wear;
Though as for that the passing there
Had worn them really about the same.

And both that morning equally lay
In leaves no step had trodden black.
Oh, I kept the first for another day!
Yet knowing how one way leads on to way,
I doubted if I should ever come back.

I shall be telling this with a sigh
Somewhere ages and ages hence:
Two roads diverged in a wood, and I——
I took the one less travelled by,
And that has made all the difference.

Birches

When I see birches bend to left and right
Across the lines of straighter, darker trees,

I like to think some boy's been swinging them.
But swinging doesn't bend them down to stay.
Ice-storms do that. Often you must have seen them
Loaded with ice a sunny winter morning
After a rain. They click upon themselves
As the breeze rises, and turn many-colored
As the stir cracks and crazes their enamel.
Soon the sun's warmth makes them shed crystal shells,
Shattering and avalanching on the snow-crust——
Such heaps of broken glass to sweep away
You'd think the inner dome of heaven had fallen.

They are dragged to the withered bracken by the load,
And they seem not to break; though once they are bowed
So low for long, they never right themselves:
You may see their trunks arching in the woods
Years afterward, trailing their leaves on the ground
Like girls on hands and knees that throw their hair
Before them over their heads to dry in the sun.
But I was going to say when Truth broke in
With all her matter-of-fact about the ice-storm
(Now am I free to be poetical?)
I should prefer to have some boy bend them
As he went out and in to fetch the cows——
Some boy too far from town to learn baseball,
Whose only play was what he found himself,
Summer and winter, and could play alone.
One by one he subdued his father's trees
By riding them down over and over again
Until he took the stiffness out of them,
And not one but hung limp, not one was left

For him to conquer. He learned all there was
To learn about not launching out too soon
And so not carrying the tree away
Clear to the ground. He always kept his poise
To the top branches, climbing carefully
With the same pains you use to fill a cup
Up to the brim, and even above the brim.
Then he flung outward, feet first, with a swish,
Kicking his way down through the air to the ground.
So was I once myself a swinger of birches.
And so I dream of going back to be.
It's when I'm weary of considerations,
And life is too much like a pathless wood
Where your face burns and tickles with the cobwebs
Broken across it, and one eye is weeping
From a twig's having lashed across it open.
I'd like to get away from earth awhile
And then come back to it and begin over.

May no fate wilfully misunderstand me
And half grant what I wish and snatch me away
Not to return. Earth's the right place to love:
I don't know where it's likely to go better.
I'd like to go by climbing a birch tree,
And climb black branches up a snow-white trunk,
Toward heaven, till the tree could bear no more,
But dipped its top and set me down again.
That would be good both going and coming back.
One could do worse than be a swinger of birches.

ELEANOR ROGERS COX (1875—)

To a Portrait of Whistler in the Brooklyn Art Museum

What waspish whim of Fate
    Was this that bade you here
Hold dim, unhonored state,
    No single courtier near?

Is there, of all who pass,
    No choice, discerning few
To poise the ribboned glass
    And gaze enwrapt on you?

Sword-soul that from its sheath
    Laughed leaping to the fray,
How calmly underneath
    Goes Brooklyn on her way!

Quite heedless of that smile—
    Half-devil and half-god,
Your quite unequalled style,
    The airy heights you trod.

Ah, could you from earth's breast
    Come back to take the air,
What matter here for jest
    Most exquisite and rare!

But since you may not come,
    Since silence holds you fast,
Since all your quips are dumb
    And all your laughter past—

I give you mine instead,
    And something with it too
That Brooklyn leaves unsaid—
    The world's fine homage due.

Ah, Prince, you smile again—
"My faith, the court is small!"
I know, dear James—but then
It's I or none at all!

LOUISE DRISCOLL (1875—)

Marigolds

Do you like marigolds?
If you do
Then my garden is
Gay for you!

I've been cutting their
Fragrant stalks
Where they lean on
The garden walks.

The head's too heavy for
The brittle stem,
A careless touch and
You've broken them.

Each one shines like a
Separate star
Set in some heaven where
Gardens are.

My hands smell of the
Herblike scent,
Telling what garden
Way I went.

Pungent, vivid and
Strong, they stay
Long after Summer has
Gone away.

Do you like marigolds?
Here's a pledge
To meet the frost with
A golden edge—

To go as far as
A weak thing may
Linking tomorrow with
Yesterday!

Harbury

All the men of Harbury go down to the sea in ships,
The wind upon their faces, the salt upon their lips.

The little boys of Harbury when they are laid to sleep,
Dream of masts and cabins and the wonders of the deep.

The women-folk of Harbury have eyes like the sea,
Wide with watching wonder, deep with mystery.

I met a woman: "Beyond the bar," she said,
"Beyond the shallow water where the green lines spread,

"Out beyond the sand-bar and the white spray,
My three sons wait for the Judgment Day."

I saw an old man who goes to sea no more,
Watch from morn to evening down on the shore.

"The sea's a hard mistress," the old man said;
"The sea is always hungry and never full fed.

"The sea had my father and took my son from me—
Sometimes I think I see them, walking on the sea!

"I'd like to be in Harbury on the Judgment Day,
When the word is spoken and the sea is wiped away.

"And all the drowned fisher boys, with seaweed in their hair,
Rise and walk to Harbury to greet the women there.

"I'd like to be in Harbury to see the souls arise,
Son and mother hand in hand, lovers with glad eyes.

"I think there would be many who would turn and look with
    me,
Hoping for another glimpse of the cruel sea!

"They tell me that in Paradise the fields are green and still,
With pleasant flowers everywhere that all may take who will,

"And four great rivers flowing from out the Throne of God
That no one ever drowns in and souls may cross dry-shod.

"I think among those wonders there will be men like me,
Who miss the old salt danger of the singing sea.

"For in my heart, like some old shell, inland, safe and dry,
Anyone who harks will still hear the sea cry."

GRACE FALLOW NORTON (1876—)

O Sleep

Take me upon thy breast,
   O river of rest.
Draw me down to thy side,
   Slow-moving tide.
Carry out beyond reach
   Of song or of speech
This body and soul forespent.
   To thy still continent,
Where silence hath his home,
   Where I would come,
Bear me now in thy deep
   Bosom, Sleep,
     O Sleep.

ARTHUR UPSON (1877-1908)

From "The City"

AGAMEDE'S SONG

Grow, grow, thou little tree,
His body at the roots of thee;
Since last year's loveliness in death
The living beauty nourisheth.

Bloom, bloom, thou little tree,
Thy roots around the heart of me;
Thou can'st not blow too white and fair
From all the sweetness hidden there.

Die, die, thou little tree,
And be as all sweet things must be;
Deep where thy petals drift, I, too,
Would rest the changing seasons through.

Ex Libris

In an old book at even as I read
  Fast fading words adown my shadowy page,
  I crossed a tale of how, in other age,
At Arqua, with his books around him, sped
The word to Petrarch; and with noble head
  Bowed gently o'er his volume, that sweet sage
  To silence paid his willing seigniorage.
And they who found him, whispered, "He is dead!"

Thus timely from old comradeships would I
  To silence also rise. Let there be night,
Stillness, and only those staid watchers by,
  And no light shine save my low study light—
Lest of his kind intent some human cry
  Interpret not the messenger aright.

CHARLES HANSON TOWNE (1877—)

Baboon

At eight o'clock in the evening,
  And at two in the afternoon,
The monster curtains open,
  The fiddles creak and croon,
And then I bow to the people,
  A lumbering baboon.

I wonder why I do it?
  Why do the humans stare
From even rows of shadow
  Behind the footlights' glare?
Why do I go through my weary tricks
  On a table and a chair?

They laugh and clap and giggle,
  They never seem to tire,
For I am quite amusing
  As I dance upon a wire,
Or leap, at my master's signal,
  Through golden hoops of fire.

I cannot smile, like the people,
  I cannot speak at all;
I pirouette insanely
  In the foolish carnival;
Yet could I laugh, O I would laugh
  When the velvet curtains fall!

For I wonder why those people
  Sit in such even rows,
And smile at my useless knowledge,
  Laugh at my mincing toes,
And dream that they have wisdom!—
  How little a human knows!

And why do they always gather
  In houses bright and hot,
When they might be out in the open
  In a place I've never forgot?
Why do they hive in a shell like this,
  And bid me share their lot?

And why is my life a schedule,
  Run by rote and rule?
I was not meant for theatres,
  I was not made for school;
I was not meant to caper here,
  A thing of ridicule!

I was not meant to be the slave
  Of a man in a shiny suit,
To bring the golden dollars in,
  To stand up and salute;
The good God put me in the world
  To be a happy brute!

But at eight o'clock each evening,
  And at two in the afternoon,
The monster curtains open,
  The fiddles creak and croon;
And I bow to the senseless people—
  A sensible baboon!

Of One Self-Slain

When he went blundering back to God,
  His songs half written, his work half done,
Who knows what paths his bruised feet trod,
  What hills of peace or pain he won?

I hope God smiled, and took his hand,
  And said, "Poor truant, passionate fool!
Life's book is hard to understand—
  Why couldst thou not remain at school?"

ADELAIDE CRAPSEY (1878-1914)

Dirge

Never the nightingale,
  Oh, my dear,
Never again the lark
  Thou wilt hear;

Though dusk and the morning still
Tap at thy window-sill,
Though ever love call and call
Thou wilt not hear at all,
   My dear, my dear.

The Lonely Death

In the cold I will rise, I will bathe
In waters of ice; myself
Will shiver and shrive myself,
Alone in the dawn, and anoint
Forehead and feet and hands;
I will shutter the windows from light,
I will place in their sockets the four
Tall candles and set them a-flame
In the grey of the dawn; and myself
Will lay myself straight in my bed,
And draw the sheet under my chin.

DON MARQUIS (1878—)

The Name

It shifts and shifts from form to form,
  It drifts and darkles, glooms and glows,
It is the passion of the storm,
  The poignance of the rose;
Through changing shapes, through devious ways,
  By noon or night, through cloud or flame,
My heart hath followed all my days
  Something I cannot name.

In sunlight on some woman's hair,
  Or starlight in some woman's eyne—
Or in low laughter smothered where
  Her red lips wedded mine—
My heart has known, and thrilled to know,
  This unnamed presence that it sought;
And when thy heart hath found it so,
  "Love is the name," I thought.

Sometimes when sudden afterglows
  In futile glory storm the skies
Within their transient gold and rose
  The secret stirs and dies;
Or when the trembling Morn walks o'er
  The troubled seas with feet of flame
My awed heart whispers, *"Ask no more,*
  For Beauty is the name!"

Or dreaming in old chapels where
    The dim aisles pulse with murmurings
That part are music, part are prayer—
    (Or rush of hidden wings)—
I often lift a startled head
    To some saint's carven countenance,
Half fancying that the lips have said,
    "All names mean God perchance."

Those That Come Back

I, too, have heard strange whispers, seen
A stealthy mist rise from the Summer's green,
And felt, even in the loud and candid noon,
A central silence and chill secrecy
Laid close against the human heat of me;
But never under sun nor moon,
Nor through the choked, ambiguous utterance of the rain,
Has any presence made his meaning plain . . .
Perhaps these ghosts are helpless ghosts and weak,
Or when they see us, grow too sad to speak.

The Tom-Cat

At midnight in the alley
    A Tom-cat comes to wail,
And he chants the hate of a million years
    As he swings his snaky tail.

Malevolent, bony, brindled,
    Tiger and devil and bard,
His eyes are coals from the middle of Hell
    And his heart is black and hard.

He twists and crouches and capers
    And bares his curved sharp claws,
And he sings to the stars of the jungle nights
    Ere cities were, or laws.

Beast from a world primeval,
    He and his leaping clan,
When the blotched red moon leers over the roofs,
    Give voice to their scorn of man.

He will lie on a rug to-morrow
    And lick his silky fur,
And veil the brute in his yellow eyes
    And play he's tame, and purr.

But at midnight in the alley
 He will crouch again and wail,
And beat the time for his demon's song
 With the swing of his demon's tail.

The Spinks

Dear Mrs. Spink has had so very many
Doctors! . . . a fact of which her lord seems proud.
I've heard him urging in a jolly crowd:
"Tell them about that last big tumor, Jenny!"
And Jenny lisps and tells, nor spares us any
Details . . . She tells us All! And we sit bowed
And listen while Spink murmurs half aloud:
"Her stomach has cost me a pretty penny!"

And after dinner, with the coffee cup,
The Spinks perform a friendly fireside clinic
And she glows as her husband cuts her up,
And his the zest of any surgeon-cynic . . .
I never knew before, I sometimes think,
A woman half so well as Mrs. Spink.

A Gentleman of Fifty Soliloquizes

Should chance strike out of me some human heat
 Leap not at that and think to grasp my soul!
I flee new bonds. My self must still retreat
 Down devious ways to keep me free and whole.

Give me your mind, and I will give you mine.
 Then should it change no heart will bleed or burn.
Give me your wits. I want no heart of thine.
 You'll ask too much of life-blood in return.

There was a golden lad in years long gone . . .
 We twain together left the ways of men
And roamed the starry heights, the fields of dawn,
 In youth and gladness. This comes not again.

Give me your mirth. It bores me when you weep.
My loves you cannot touch. They're buried deep.

CARL SANDBURG (1878—)

Chicago

Hog Butcher for the World,
Tool Maker, Stacker of Wheat,

Player with Railroads and the Nation's Freight Handler;
Stormy, husky, brawling,
City of the Big Shoulders:
They tell me you are wicked and I believe them, for I have
    seen your painted women under the gas lamps luring the
    farm boys.
And they tell me you are crooked and I answer: Yes, it is
    true I have seen the gunman kill and go free to kill again.
And they tell me you are brutal and my reply is: On the faces
    of women and children I have seen the marks of wanton
    hunger.
And having answered so I turn once more to those who sneer
    at this my city, and I give them back the sneer and say
    to them:
Come and show me another city with lifted head singing so
    proud to be alive and coarse and strong and cunning.
Flinging magnetic curses amid the toil of piling job on job,
    here is a tall bold slugger set vivid against the little soft
    cities;
Fierce as a dog with tongue lapping for action, cunning as a
    savage pitted against the wilderness,
        Bareheaded,
        Shoveling,
        Wrecking,
        Planning,
        Building, breaking, rebuilding,
Under the smoke, dust all over his mouth, laughing with white
    teeth,
Under the terrible burden of destiny laughing at a young
    man laughs,
Laughing even as an ignorant fighter laughs who has never
    lost a battle,
Bragging and laughing that under his wrist is the pulse, and
    under his ribs the heart of the people,
                    Laughing!
Laughing the stormy, husky, brawling laughter of Youth, half-
    naked, sweating, proud to be Hog Butcher, Tool Maker,
    Stacker of Wheat, Player with Railroads and Freight
    Handler to the Nation.

At a Window

Give me hunger,
O you gods that sit and give
The world its orders.
Give me hunger, pain and want,
Shut me out with shame and failure
From your doors of gold and fame,
Give me your shabbiest, weariest hunger!

But leave me a little love,
A voice to speak to me in the day end,
A hand to touch me in the dark room
Breaking the long loneliness.

In the dusk of day-shapes
Blurring the sunset,
One little wandering, western star
Thrust out from the changing shores of shadow
Let me go to the window,
Watch there the day-shapes of dusk
And wait and kno<u>w</u> the coming
Of a little love.

Joy

Let Joy keep you.
Reach out your hands
And take it when it runs by,
As the Apache dancer
Clutches his woman.
I have seen them
Live long and laugh loud,
Sent on singing, singing,
Smashed to the heart
Under the ribs
With a terrible love.
Joy always,
Joy everywhere——
Let joy kill you!
Keep away from little deaths.

ELSA BARKER

The Frozen Grail

(To Peary and his men, before the last expedition)

Why sing the legends of the Holy Grail,
The dead crusaders of the Sepulchre,
While these men live? Are the great bards all dumb?
Here is a vision to shake the blood of Song,
And make Fame's watchman tremble at his post.

What shall prevail against the spirit of man,
When cold, the lean and snarling wolf of hunger,
The threatening spear of ice-mailed Solitude,
Silence, and space, and ghostly-footed fear

Prevail not? Dante, in his frozen hell
Shivering, endured no bleakness like the void
These men have warmed with their own flaming will,
And peopled with their dreams. The wind from fierce
Arcturus in their faces, at their backs
The whip of the world's doubt, and in their souls
Courage to die—if death shall be the price
Of that cold cup that will assuage their thirst;
They climb and fall and stagger toward the goal.
They lay themselves the road whereby they travel,
And sue God for a franchise. Does He watch
Behind the lattice of the boreal lights?
In that grail chapel of their stern-vowed quest,
Ninety of God's long paces towards the North,
Will they behold the splendor of His face?
To conquer the world must man renounce the world?
These have renounced it. Had ye only faith
Ye might move mountains, said the Nazarene.
Why, these have faith to move the zones of man
Out to the point where All and Nothing meet.
They catch the bit of death between their teeth,
In one wild dash to trample the unknown
And leap the gates of Knowledge. They have dared
Even to defy the sentinel that guards
The doors of the forbidden—dared to hurl
Their breathing bodies after the Ideal,
That like the heavenly kingdom must be taken
Only by violence. The star that leads
The leader of this quest has held the world
True to its orbit for a million years.

And shall he fail? They never fail who light
Their lamp of faith on the unwavering flame
Burnt for the altar service of the Race
Since the beginning. He shall find the strange—
The white immaculate Virgin of the North,
Whose steady gaze no mortal ever dared,
Whose icy hand no human ever grasped.
In the dread silence and the solitude
She waits and listens through the centuries
For one indomitable, destined soul,
Born to endure the glory of her eyes,
And lift his warm lips to the frozen Grail.

MARGARET WIDDEMER

Remembrance: Greek Folk-Song

Not unto the forest—not unto the forest, O my lover!
Why do you lead me to the forest?

Joy is where the temples are, lines of dancers swinging far,
    Drums and lyres and viols in the town
        (It is dark in the forest)
And the flapping leaves will blind me and the clinging vines
      will bind me
    And the thorny rose boughs tear my saffron gown—
      And I fear the forest.

Not unto the forest—not unto the forest, O my lover!
There was one once who led me to the forest:
Hand in hand we wandered mute, where was neither lyre nor
      flute,
    Little stars were bright against the dusk
      (There was wind in the forest)
And the thicket of wild rose breathed across our lips locked
      close
    Dizzy perfumings of spikenard and musk . . .
      I am tired of the forest.

Not unto the forest—not unto the forest, O my lover!
Take me from the silence of the forest!
I will love you by the light and the beat of drums at night
    And echoing of laughter in my ears,
      But here in the forest
I am still, remembering a forgotten, useless thing,
    And my eyelids are locked down for fear of tears—
      There is memory in the forest.

The Factories

I have shut my little sister in from life and light
(For a rose, for a ribbon, for a wreath across my hair),
I have made her restless feet still until the night,
Locked from sweets of summer and from wild spring air;
I who ranged the meadowlands, free from sun to sun,
Free to sing and pull the buds and watch the far wings fly,
I have bound my sister till her playing-time was done—
Oh, my little sister, was it I? Was it I?

I have robbed my sister of her day of maidenhood
(For a robe, for a feather, for a trinket's restless spark),
Shut from love till dusk shall fall, how shall she know good,
How shall she go scatheless through the sinlit dark?
I who could be innocent, I who could be gay,
I who could have love and mirth before the light went by,
I have put my sister in her mating-time away—
Sister, my young sister, was it I? Was it I?

I have robbed my sister of the lips against her breast
(For a coin, for the weaving of my children's lace and lawn).
Feet that pace beside the loom, hands that cannot rest—
How can she know motherhood, whose strength is gone?
I who took no heed of her, starved and labor-worn,
I against whose placid heart my sleepy gold-heads lie,
Round my path they cry to me, little souls unborn—
God of life! Creator! It was I! It was I!

ALICE BLAINE DAMROSCH

Swimming by Night

It is night-time; all the waters round me
Grow electric, tenser, in the starlight.
See, the Milky Way is full of splendor.
Over there the white star and the red star
Beckon from their pinnacles of silence.
All the larger waves are tipped with glory,
And the little ripples pause and whisper,
As they touch my cheek with ghostly fingers.
I will swim till I can swim no longer.
I will spurn the shore that blots the starlight
From my vision, I will shake it from me,
Strike out boldly into open waters.
I know sometime that my strength will falter,
That I must turn shoreward, leave my star-search,
Give in to the sweet, soft, acquiescent
Land breeze, redolent with sleeping hay-fields.
How I hate it, I would fill my nostrils
With the sharper, freer breath of heaven,
Raising up my head once in so often
From the waters for great drafts of glory.
In me is the strength of gods; I battle
With the waves and buffet them for pleasure,
I will beat them, break them in my passing,
Feel them close again behind my shoulder;
Every muscle has its strength for service,
Now I summon all to do my pleasure,
Bid them bear me out into the darkness.
Far off where the startled night bird circles,
Half awakened by my silent coming,
Frightened by my dim arm rising, falling,
I will go, yes, there and even farther.
I will seek the source of the creation,
Swim with mighty strokes to the horizon,
Where the drowned stars and the stars in heaven
Meet and mingle in new constellations;

I will reach them, dare to touch them even,
Cleansed and purified by many waters,
Even I may breathe upon their splendor.
It is written that the night must vanish,
But this hour is mine, I will not yield it,
I defy the dawn to take it from me. . . .
Oh, to live and battle thus forever!

NICHOLAS VACHEL LINDSAY (1879—)

From "The Congo"

Fat black bucks in a wine-barrel room,
Barrel-house kings, with feet unstable,
Sagged and reeled and pounded on the table,   [A deep
Pounded on the table,   rolling bass.]
Beat an empty barrel with the handle of a broom,
Hard as they were able,
Boom, boom, *boom*,
With a silk umbrella and the handle of a broom,
Boomlay, boomlay, boomlay, *boom*.
Then I had religion, *then* I had a vision.
I could not turn from their revel in derision.
Then I saw the Congo, creeping through the black,   [More
Cutting through the jungle with a golden track.   deliberate.
Then along that riverbank   Solemnly chanted.]
A thousand miles
Tattooed cannibals danced in files;
Then I heard the boom of the blood-lust song
And a thigh-bone beating on a tin-pan gong. [A rapidly piling
And *"Blood!"* screamed the whistles and the fifes   climax
of the warriors;   of speed and racket.]
"Blood!" screamed the skull-faced, lean witch-doctors;
"Whirl ye the deadly voo-doo rattle,
Harry the uplands,
Steal all the cattle,
Rattle-rattle, rattle-rattle,
Bing!
Boomlay, boomlay, boomlay, *boom!"*
A roaring, epic, rag-time tune   [With a philosophic pause.]
From the mouth of the Congo
To the Mountains of the Moon.
Death is an Elephant,
Torch-eyed and horrible,   [Shrilly and with a
Foam-flanked and terrible.   heavily accented metre.]
Boom, steal the pygmies,
Boom, kill the Arabs,
Boom, kill the white men,

Hoo, Hoo, Hoo.   [Like the wind
Listen to the yell of Leopold's ghost   in the chimney.]
   Burning in Hell for his hand-maimed host.
   Hear how the demons chuckle and yell
   Cutting his hands off, down in Hell.
   Listen to the creepy proclamation,
   Blown through the lairs of the forest-nation,
   Blown past the white-ants' hill of clay,
   Blown past the marsh where the butterflies play:—
   "Be careful what you do,
Or Mumbo-Jumbo, God of the Congo,   [All the
And all of the other   sounds very golden.
Gods of the Congo,   Heavy accents very
Mumbo-Jumbo will hoo-doo you,   heavy. Light accents
Mumbo-Jumbo will hoo-doo you,   very light. Last line
Mumbo-Jumbo will hoo-doo you."   whispered.]

General William Booth Enters into Heaven

(*To be sung to tune of The Blood of the Lamb with indicated instruments.*)

Booth led boldly with his big bass drum,
   Are you washed in the blood of the Lamb?
The saints smiled gravely, and they said, "He's
   come."
   Are you washed in the blood of the Lamb?   [Bass drum]
Walking lepers followed, rank on rank,
Lurching bravos from the ditches dank,
Drabs from the alleyways and drug-fiends pale—
Minds still passion ridden, soul-powers frail!
Vermin-eaten saints with mouldy breath
Unwashed legions with the ways of death——
   Are you washed in the blood of the Lamb?

Every slum had sent its half-a-score
The round world over—Booth had groaned for
   more.
Every banner that the wide world flies
Bloomed with glory and transcendent dyes.
Big-voiced lasses made their banjos bang!   [Banjos]
Tranced, fanatical, they shrieked and sang,
   Are you washed in the blood of the Lamb?
Hallelujah! It was queer to see
Bull-necked convicts with that land make free!
Loons with bazoos blowing blare, blare, blare——
On, on, upward through the golden air.
   Are you washed in the blood of the Lamb?

Booth died blind, and still by faith he trod,
Eyes still dazzled by the ways of God.
Booth led boldly and he looked the chief: [Bass drums
Eagle countenance in sharp relief,   slower and
Beard a-flying, air of high command   softer]
Unabated in that holy land.
Jesus came from out the Court-House door,
Stretched his hands above the passing poor.
Booth saw not, but led his queer ones there   [Flutes]
Round and round the mighty Court-House Square.
Yet in an instant all that blear review
Marched on spotless, clad in raiment new.
The lame were straightened, withered limbs un-
     curled,
And blind eyes opened on a new sweet world.

Drabs and vixens in a flash made whole!
Gone was the weasel-head, the snout, the jowl;   [Bass drums
Sages and sybils now, and athletes clean,   louder and
Rulers of empires, and of forests green!   faster]
The hosts were sandalled and their wings were
     fire——
     Are you washed in the blood of the Lamb?
But their noise played havoc with the angel-choir. [Grand
     Are you washed in the blood of the Lamb?   chorus
Oh, shout Salvation! it was good to see   tambourines
Kings and princes by the Lamb set free.   ——all
The banjos rattled and the tambourines   instruments
Jing-jing-jangled in the hands of Queens!   in full
                                                     blast]

And when Booth halted by the curb for prayer,
He saw his Master through the flag-filled air.

Christ came gently with a robe and crown
For Booth the Soldier while the throng knelt   [Reverently
     down.   Sung—no
He saw King Jesus—they were face to face,   instruments]
And he knelt a-weeping in that holy place.
     Are you washed in the blood of the Lamb?

The Eagle That Is Forgotten
(John P. Altgeld, 1847-1902)

Sleep softly . . . eagle forgotten . . . under the stone.
Time has its way with you there, and the clay has its own.
"We have buried him now," thought your foes, and in secret
     rejoiced.
They made a brave show of their mourning, their hatred
     unvoiced.

They had snarled at you, barked at you, foamed at you, day
    after day,
Now you were ended. They praised you . . . and laid you
    away.
The others, that mourned you in silence and terror and truth,
The widow bereft of her crust, and the boy without youth,
The mocked and the scorned and the wounded, the lame and
    the poor,
That should have remembered forever, . . . remember no
    more.
Where are those lovers of yours, on what name do they call,
The lost, that in armies wept over your funeral pall?
They call on the names of a hundred high-valiant ones,
A hundred white eagles have risen, the sons of your sons.
The zeal in their wings is a zeal that your dreaming began,
The valor that wore out your soul in the service of man.
Sleep softly . . . eagle forgotten . . . under the stone.
Time has its way with you there, and the clay has its own.
Sleep on, O brave-hearted, O wise man that kindled the
    flame—
To live in mankind is far more than to live in a name,
To live in mankind, far, far more than to live in a name!—

The Flower of Mending

(To Eudora, after I had had certain dire
adventures)

When Dragon-fly would fix his wings,
When Snail would patch his house,
When moths have marred the overcoat
Of tender Mister Mouse,

The pretty creatures go with haste
To the sunlit blue-grass hills
Where the Flower of Mending yields the wax
And webs to help their ills.

The hour the coats are waxed and webbed
They fall into a dream,
And when they wake the ragged robes
Are joined without a seam.

My heart is but a dragon-fly,
My heart is but a mouse,
My heart is but a haughty snail
On a little stony house.

Your hand was honey-comb to heal,
Your voice a web to bind:
You were a Mending Flower to me
To cure my heart and mind.

LOUIS V. LEDOUX (1880—)

From "The Story of Eleusis"

HYMN TO DEMETER

Weave the dance, and raise again the sacred chorus;
  Wreathe the garlands of the spring about the hair;
Now once more the meadows' burst in bloom before us,
  Crying swallows dart and glitter through the air.
Glints the plowshare in the brown and fragrant furrow;
  Pigeons coo in shady coverts as they pair;
Come the furtive mountain folk from cave and burrow,
  Lean, and blinking at the sunlight's sudden glare.

Bright through midmost heaven moves the lesser Lion;
  Hide the Hyades in ocean caverns hoar;
Past the shoulders of the sunset flames Orion,
  Following the sisters seaward evermore,
Gleams the east at evening, lit by low Arcturus;
  Out to subtle-scented dawns beside the shore,
Yet a little and the Pleiades will lure us:
  Weave the dance and raise the chorus as of yore.
Far to eastward up the fabled gulf of Issus,
  Northward, southward, westward, now the trader goes,
Passing headlands clustered yellow with narcissus,
  Bright with hyacinth, with poppy, and with rose,
Shines the sea and falls the billow as undaunted,
  Past the rising of the stars that no man knows,
Sails he onward through the islands siren-haunted,
  Till the clashing gates of rock before him close.

Kindly Mother of the beasts and birds and flowers,
  Gracious bringer of the barley and the grain,
Earth awakened feels thy sunlight and thy showers;
  Great Demeter! Let us call thee not in vain:
Lead us safely from the seed-time to the threshing,
  Past the harvest and the vineyard's purple stain;
Let us see thy corn-pale hair the sunlight meshing,
  When the sounding flails of autumn swing again.

JOHN G. NEIHARDT (1881—)

April Theology

Oh, to be breathing and hearing and feeling and seeing!
Oh, the ineffably glorious privilege of being!
All of the World's lovely girlhood, unfleshed and made spirit,
Broods out in the sunlight this morning—I see it, I hear it!

So read me no text, O my Brothers, and preach me no creeds;
I am busy beholding the glory of God in His deeds!
See! Everywhere buds coming out, blossoms flaming, bees
          humming!
Glad athletic Growers up-reaching, things striving, becoming!

Oh, I know in my heart, in the sun-quickened, blossoming
          soul of me,
This something called self is a part, but the World is the
          whole of me!
I am one with these growers, these singers, these earnest
          becomers—
Co-heirs of the summer to be and past æons of summers!

I kneel not nor grovel; no prayer with my lips shall I fashion.
Close-knit in the fabric of things, fused with one common
          passion—
To go on and become something greater—we Growers are
          one;
None more in the World than a bird and none less than the
          sun;
But all woven into the glad indivisible Scheme,
God fashioning out in the Finite a part of His Dream!

Out here where the world-love is flowing, unfettered, unpriced,
I feel all the depth of the man-soul and girl-heart of Christ!
'Mid this rict of pink and white flame in this miracle weather,
Soul to soul, merged in one, God and I dream the vast
          Dream together.
We are one in the doing of things that are done and to be:
I am part of my God as a raindrop is part of the Sea!

What! House me my God! Take me in where no blossoms
          are blowing?
No riot of green and no sky, and no bird-song, no growing?
Parcel out what is already mine, like a vender of staples?
*See! Yonder my God burns revealed in the sap-drunken
          maples!*

WITTER BYNNER (1881—)

From "The New World"

Grieve not for the invisible transported brow
On which like leaves the dark hair grew,
Nor for those lips of laughter that are now
Laughing in sun and dew,
Nor for those limbs that, fallen low
And seeming faint and slow,
Shall alter and renew
Their shape and hue
Like birches white before the moon
Or the wild cherry-bough
In spring or the round sea
And shall pursue
More ways of swiftness than the swallow dips
Among and find more winds than ever blew
The straining sails of unimpeded ships!
Mourn not! . . . Yield only happy tears
To deeper beauty than appears!

The Mystic

By seven vineyards on one hill
We walked. The native wine
In clusters grew beside us two,
For your lips and for mine,

When "Hark!" you said—"Was that a bell
In a bubbling spring we heard?"
But I was wise and closed my eyes
And listened to a bird;

For as summer leaves are bent and shake
With singers passing through,
So moves in me continually
The wingèd breath of you.

You tasted from a single vine
And took from that your fill—
But I inclined to every kind,
All seven on one hill.

PADRAIC COLUM (1881—)

The Sea Bird to the Wave

On and on,
O white brother!

Thunder does not daunt thee!
How thou movest!
By thine impulse—
With no wing!
Fairest thing
The wide sea shows me!
On and on
O white brother!
Art thou gone!

River-Mates

I'll be an otter, and I'll let you swim
A mate beside me; we will venture down
A deep, dark river, when the sky above
Is shut of the sun; spoilers are we,
Thick-coated; no dog's tooth can bite at our veins,
With eyes and ears of poachers; deep earthed ones
Turned hunters; let him slip past
The little vole; my teeth are on an edge
For the King-fish of the River!

I hold him up,
The glittering salmon that smells of the sea;
I hold him high and whistle!
    Now we go
Back to our earths; we will tear and eat
Sea-smelling salmon; you will tell the cubs
I am the Booty-bringer, I am the Lord
Of the River; the deep, dark, full and flowing River!

FRANKLIN P. ADAMS (1881—)

The Rich Man

The rich man has his motor-car,
  His country and his town estate.
He smokes a fifty-cent cigar
  And jeers at Fate.

He frivols through the livelong day,
  He knows not Poverty, her pinch.
His lot seems light, his heart seems gay;
  He has a cinch.

Yet though my lamp burns low and dim,
  Though I must slave for livelihood—
Think you that I would change with him?
  You bet I would!

HERMANN HAGEDORN (1882—)

Departure

My true love from her pillow rose
    And wandered down the summer lane.
She left her house to the wind's carouse,
    And her chamber wide to the rain.

She did not stop to don her coat,
    She did not stop to smooth her bed—
But out she went in glad content
    There where the bright path led.

She did not feel the beating storm,
    But fled like a sunbeam, white and frail,
To the sea, to the air, somewhere, somewhere—
    I have not found her trail.

THOMAS S. JONES, JR. (1882—)

Sometimes

Across the fields of yesterday
    He sometimes comes to me,
A little lad just back from play—
    The lad I used to be.

And yet he smiles so wistfully
    Once he has crept within,
I wonder if he hopes to see
    The man I might have been.

From the Hills

For you the white-wracked waste—yet not for me—
    The roar of tempests and the storm-god's song,
All that is sad and strange and sweet at sea,
    All that is fierce and strong.

I too have tasted of the salt-sea wine
    And heard a-riot the wild winds at play;
The heart's full beat, the joyous anodyne
    Of salt-sea spray.

This, this at last—a quiet intervale,
    Kissed by soft lights and gladdened by the sun;
You, of the curling surf, the blast, the gale—
    I, of oblivion.

JAMES OPPENHEIM (1882—)

A Handful of Dust

I stooped to the silent earth and lifted a handful of her dust.
Was it a handful of humanity I held?
Was it the crumbled and blown beauty of a woman or a babe?
For over the hills of earth blows the dust of the withered
    generations;
And not a water-drop in the sea but was once a blood-drop
    or a tear,
And not an atom of sap in leaf or bud but was once the love-
    sap in a human being;
And not a lump of soil but was once the rosy curve of lip
    or breast or cheek.
Handful of dust, you stagger me;
I did not dream the world was so full of the dead,
And the air I breathe so rich with the bewildering past.
Kiss of what girls is on the wind?
Whisper of what lips is in the cup of my hand?
Cry of what deaths is in the break of the wave tossed by the
    sea?
I am enfolded in an air of rushing wings;
I am engulfed in clouds of love-lives gone.
Who leans yonder? Helen of Greece?
Who walks with me? Isolde?
The trees are shaking down the blossoms from Juliet's breast,
And the bee drinks honey from the lips of David.

Come, girl, my comrade;
Stand close, sun-tanned one, with your bright eyes lifted.
Behold this dust!
This is you: this of the earth under our feet is you.
Raised by what miracle? Shaped by what magic?
Breathed into by what god?

And a hundred years hence one like myself may come,
And stoop, and take a handful of the yielding earth,
And never dream that in his palm
Lies she that laughed and ran and lived beside this sea
On an afternoon a hundred years before.

Listen to the dust in this hand.
Who is trying to speak to us?

The Lonely Child

Do you think, my boy, when I put my arms around you
To still your fears,

That it is I who conquer the dark and the lonely night?
My arms seem to wrap love about you,
As your little heart fluttering at my breast
Throbs love through me. . . .

But, dear one, it is not your father:
Other arms are about you, drawing you near,
And drawing the Earth near, and the Night near,
And your father near. . . .

Some day you shall lie alone at nights,
As now your father lies;
And in those arms, as a leaf fallen on a tranquil stream,
Drift into dreams and healing sleep.

The Runner in the Skies

Who is the runner in the skies
With her blowing scarf of stars,
And our earth and sun hovering like bees about her blossom-
    ing heart!
Her feet are on the winds where space is deep;
Her eyes are nebulous and veiled;
She hurries through the night to a far lover.

BERTON BRALEY (1882—)

To a Photographer

I have known love and hate and work and fight;
    I have lived largely, I have dreamed and planned,
    And Time, the Sculptor, with a master hand
Has graven on my face for all men's sight
Deep lines of joy and sorrow, growth and blight
    Of labor and of service and command
    —And now you show me this, this waxen, bland
And placid face, unlined, unwrinkled, white.

This is not I—this fatuous thing you show,
    Retouched and smoothed and prettified to please,
Put back the wrinkles and the lines I know;
    I have spent blood and tears achieving these,
Out of the pain, the struggle and the wrack
These are my scars of battle—put them back!

ALFRED KREYMBORG (1883—)

Old Manuscript

The sky
is that beautiful old parchment
in which the sun
and the moon
keep their diary.
To read it all,
one must be a linguist
more learned than Father Wisdom;
and a visionary
more clairvoyant than Mother Dream.
But to feel it,
one must be an apostle:
one who is more than intimate
in having been, always,
the only confidant—
like the earth
or the sea.

HARRY KEMP (1883—)

Prithee, Strive Not

Prithee, strive not to remember
  Ancient love burnt out and dead;
Blow not on the blackened ember,—
  Ash will ne'er again give red.

Lift the latch—another lover
  Waits upon thy kiss without:
All the old things have gone over
  That the heart went mad about.

The Conquerors

I saw the Conquerors riding by
  With trampling feet of horse and men:
Empire on empire like the tide
  Flooded the world and ebbed again;

A thousand banners caught the sun,
  And cities smoked along the plain,
And laden down with silk and gold
  And heaped-up pillage groaned the wain.

I saw the Conquerors riding by,
  Splashing through loathsome floods of war—
The Crescent leaning o'er its hosts,
  And the barbaric scimitar,—

And continents of moving spears,
  And storms of arrows in the sky,
And all the instruments sought out
  By cunning men that men may die!

I saw the Conquerors riding by
  With cruel lips and faces wan:
Musing on kingdoms sacked and burned
  There rode the Mongol Genghis Khan;

And Alexander, like a god,
  Who sought to weld the world in one;
And Cæsar with his laurel wreath;
  And like a thing from Hell the Hun;

And leading, like a star the van,
  Heedless of upstretched arm and groan,
Inscrutable Napoleon went
  Dreaming of empire, and alone . . .

Then all they perished from the earth
  As fleeting shadows from a glass,
And, conquering down the centuries,
  Came Christ, the Swordless, on an ass!

MAX EASTMAN (1883—)

To a Tawny Thrush

Pine spirit!
Breath and voice of a wild glade!
In the wild forest near it,
In the cool hemlock or the leafy limb,
Whereunder
Thou didst run and wander
Thro' the sun and shade,
An elvish echo and a shadow dim,
There in the twilight thou dost lift thy song,
And give the stilly woods a silver tongue.
Out of what liquid is thy laughing made
A sister of the water thou dost seem,
The quivering cataract thou singest near,
Whose glistening stream,
Unto the listening ear,

Thou dost outrun with thy cascade
Of music beautiful and swift and clear—
A joy unto the mournful forest given!
As when afar

A travelling star
Across our midnight races,
A moving gleam that quickly ceases,
Lost in the blue black abyss of heaven,
So doth thy light and silver singing
Start and thrill
The silence round thy piney hill,
Unto the sober hour a jewel bringing—
A mystery—a strain of rhythm fleeing—
A vagrant echo winging
Back to the unuttered theme of being!

At the Aquarium

Serene the silver fishes glide,
Stern-lipped, and pale, and wonder-eyed!
As through the agèd deeps of ocean,
They glide with wan and wavy motion!
They have no pathway where they go,
They flow like water to and fro.
They watch with never winking eyes,
They watch with staring, cold surprise,
The level people in the air,
The people peering, peering there,
Who wander also to and fro,
And know not why or where they go,
Yet have a wonder in their eyes,
Sometimes a pale and cold surprise.

MARGUERITE WILKINSON (1883—)

Before Dawn in the Woods

Upon our eyelids, dear, the dew will lie,
    And on the roughened meshes of our hair,
While little feet make bold to scurry by
    And half-notes shrilly cut the quickened air.

Our clean, hard bodies, on the clean, hard ground
    Will vaguely feel that they are full of power,
And they will stir, and stretch, and look around,
    Loving the early, chill, half-lighted hour.

Loving the voices in the shadowed trees,
  Loving the feet that stir the blossoming grass—
Oh, always we have known such things as these,
  And knowing, can we love and let them pass?

FRANCIS HACKETT (1883—)

The Dead Aviator

So endlessly the gray-lipped sea
Kept me within his eye,
And lean he licked his hollow flanks
And followed up the sky.

I was the lark whose song was heard
When I was lost to sight,
I was the golden arrow loosed
To pierce the heart of night.

I fled the little earth, I climbed
Above the rising sun,
I met the morning in a blaze
Before my hour was gone.

I ran beyond the rim of space,
Its veins I flung aside,
Laughter was mine and mine was youth
And all my own was pride.

From end to end I knew the way,
I had no doubt nor fear,
The minutes were a forfeit paid
To fetch the landfall near.

But all at once my heart I held,
My carol frozen died—
A white cloud laid her cheek to mine
And wove me to her side.

Her icy fingers clasped my flesh,
Her hair dropped in my face,
And up we fell and down we rose
And twisted into space.

Laughter was mine, and mine was youth,
I pressed the edge of life,
I kissed the sun and raced the wind,
I found immortal strife.

Out of myself I spent myself,
I lost the mortal share,
My grave is in the ashen plain,
My spirit in the air.

Good-by, sweet pride of man that flew,
Sweet pain of man that bled,
I was the lark that spilled his heart,
The golden arrow sped.

So endlessly the gray-lipped sea
Kept me within his eye,
And lean he licked his hollow flanks
And followed up the sky.

ARTHUR DAVISON FICKE (1883.—)

To an Old Friend

You have determined all that life should be;
I think it still an infinite mystery:—
Therefore we disagree.

Go, friend, and trouble not our happy past
With memory of the parting here at last
Amid confusions vast.

Go—and remember me as one astray,
If so you will. Aye, if you chose it, pray
For my misguided way.

Perhaps,—who knows?—from deeps I must explore
I shall look back regretful to the shore
Where we two walked before.

Or else, perhaps, across a troubled sea
My reckless sail shall push inflexibly
Till the west swallows me.

Then warnings of my doom your children tell.—
Say that your friend, whose life was launched so well,
Went to eternal hell.

Or will you be more honest?—will you say
That in the closing of a stormy day
Your friend once sailed away—

And that 'mid foam that deafened all replies
He passed beyond the vision of your eyes
    To luminous western skies?

From "Sonnets of a Portrait-Painter"

I am in love with high far-seeing places
That look on plains half-sunlight and half-storm,—
In love with hours when from the circling faces
Veils pass, and laughing fellowship glows warm.
You who look on me with grave eyes where rapture
And April love of living burn confessed,—
The gods are good! The world lies free to capture!
Life has no walls. O take me to your breast!
Take me,—be with me for a moment's span!—
I am in love with all unveilèd faces.
I seek the wonder at the heart of man;
I would go up to the far-seeing places.
While youth is ours, turn toward me for a space
The marvel of your rapture-lighted face!

The Three Sisters

Gone are the three, those sisters rare
    With wonder-lips and eyes ashine.
One was wise and one was fair,
    And one was mine.

Ye mourners, weave for the sleeping hair
    Of only two, your ivy vine.
For one was wise and one was fair,
    But one was mine.

GEORGE SYLVESTER VIERECK (1884—)

The Candle and the Flame

Thy hands are like cool herbs that bring
    Balm to men's hearts, upon them laid;
    Thy lovely petalled lips are made
As any blossom of the spring.
But in thine eyes there is a thing,
    O Love, that makes me half afraid.

For these are old, old eyes. . . . They gleam
Between the waking and the dream
    With antique wisdom, like a bright

Lamp strangled by the temple's veil
   That beckons to the acolyte
Who prays with trembling lips and pale
   Through the long watches of the night.

They are as old as life. They were
   When proud Gomorrah reared its head
A new-born city. They were there
   When in the places of the dead
Men swathed the body of the Lord.
   They visioned Pa-wak raise the wall
   Of China. They saw Carthage fall
And marked the grim Hun lead his horde.

There is no secret anywhere
   Nor any joy or shame that lies
   Not writ somehow in those child-eyes
   Of thine, O Love, in some strange wise.
Thou art the lad Endymion,
   And that great queen with spice and myrrh
From Araby, whom Solomon
   Delighted, and the lust of her.

The legions marching from the sea
With Cæsar's cohorts sang of thee,
   How thy fair head meant more to him
Than all the land of Italy.
Yea, in the old days thou wast she
   Who lured Mark Antony from home
To death and Egypt, seeing he
   Lost love when he lost Rome.

Thou saw'st old Tubal strike the lyre,
   Yea, first for thee the poet hurled
Defiance at the starry choir!
Thou art the romance and the fire,
   Thou art the pageance and the strife,
The clamour, mounting high and higher,
   From all the lovers in the world
   To all the lords of love and life.

     . . . . .
Perhaps the passions of mankind
   Are but the torches mystical
Lit by some spirit-hand to find
The dwelling of the Master-mind
   That knows the secret of it all,
In the great darkness and the wind.

We are the Candle, Love the Flame,
  Each little life-light flickers out,
Love bides, immortally the same:
When of life's fever we shall tire
He will desert us and the fire
  Rekindle new in prince and lout.

Twin-born of knowledge and of lust,
  He was before us, he shall be
  Indifferent still of thee and me,
When shattered is life's golden cup,
When thy young limbs are shrivelled up,
And when my heart is turned to dust.

Nay, sweet, smile not to know at last
  That thou and I, or knave or fool,
  Are but the involitient tool
Of some world-purpose, vague and vast.
No bar to passion's fury set,
  With monstrous poppies spice the wine,
  For only drunk are we divine,
And only mad shall we forget!

SARA TEASDALE (1884—)

The Flight

Look back with longing eyes and know that I will follow,
Lift me up in your love as a light wind lifts a swallow,
Let our flight be far in sun or windy rain—
But what if I heard my first love calling me again?

Hold me on your heart as the brave sea holds the foam,
Take me far away to the hills that hide your home;
Peace shall thatch the roof and love shall latch the door—
But what if I heard my first love calling me once more?

Debt

What do I owe to you
  Who loved me deep and long?
You never gave my spirit wings
  Or gave my heart a song.

But oh, to him I loved
  Who loved me not at all,
I owe the little open gate
  That led through heaven's wall.

Four Winds

"Four winds blowing through the sky,
You have seen poor maidens die,
Tell me then what I shall do
That my lover may be true."
Said the wind from out the south,
"Lay no kiss upon his mouth,"
And the wind from out the west,
"Wound the heart within his breast,"
And the wind from out the east,
"Send him empty from the feast,"
And the wind from out the north,
"In the tempest thrust him forth;
When thou art more cruel than he,
Then will love be kind to thee."

The Answer

When I go back to earth
And all my joyous body
Puts off the red and white
That once had been so proud,
If men should pass above
With false and feeble pity,
My dust will find a voice
To answer them aloud:

"Be still, I am content,
Take back your poor compassion!—
Joy was a flame in me
Too steady to destroy.
Lithe as a bending reed
Loving the storm that sways her—
I found more joy in sorrow
Than you could find in joy."

CHARLES L. O'DONNELL, C.S.C. (1884—)

Forgiveness

Now God be thanked that roads are long and wide,
    And four far havens in the scattered sky:
    It would be hard to meet and pass you by.

And God be praised there is an end of pride,
    And pity only has a word to say,
    While memory grows dim as time grows gray.

For, God His word, I gave my best to you,
All that I had, the finer and the sweet,
To make—a path for your unquiet feet.

Their track is on the life they trampled through;
Such evil steps to leave such hallowing.
Now God be with them in their wandering.

The Poet's Bread

Morn offers him her flasked light
That he may slake his thirst of soul
And for his hungry heart will Night
Her wonder-cloth of stars outroll.

However fortune goes or comes
He has his daily certain bread,
Taking the heaven's starry crumbs,
And with a crust of sunset fed.

EUNICE TIETJENS (1884—)

Completion

My heart has fed today.
My heart, like hind at play,
Has grazed in fields of love, and washed in streams
Of quick, imperishable dreams.

In moth-white beauty shimmering,
Lovely as birches in the moon glimmering,
From coigns of sleep my eyes
Saw dawn and love arise.

And like a bird at rest,
Steady in a swinging nest,
My heart at peace lay gloriously
While wings of ecstasy
Beat round me and above.

I am fulfilled of love.

Parting after a Quarrel

You looked at me with eyes grown bright with pain
Like some trapped thing's. And then you moved your head
Slowly from side to side, as though the strain
Ached in your throat with anger and with dread.

And then you turned and left me, and I stood
With a queer sense of deadness over me,
And only wondered dully that you could
Fasten your trench-coat up so carefully

Till you were gone. Then all the air was thick
With my last words that seemed to leap and quiver.
And in my heart I heard the little click
Of a door that closes—quietly, forever.

EZRA POUND (1885—)

Δ'ΩΙΑΡ

Be in me as the eternal moods
          of the bleak wind, and not
As transient things are—
          gaiety of flowers.
Have me in the strong loneliness
          of sunless cliffs
And of grey waters.
          Let the gods speak softly of us
In days hereafter,
          The shadowy flowers of Orcus
Remember Thee.

Ortus

How have I labored?
How have I not labored
To bring her soul to birth,
To give these elements a name and a centre!

She is beautiful as the sunlight, and as fluid.
She has no name, and no place.
How have I labored to bring her soul into separation;
To give her a name and her being!
Surely you are bound and entwined,
You are mingled with the elements unborn;
I have loved a stream and a shadow.

I beseech you enter your life.
I beseech you learn to say "I"
When I question you:
For you are no part, but a whole;
No portion, but a being.

Piccadilly

Beautiful, tragical faces—
Ye that were whole, and are so sunken;

And, O ye vile, ye that might have been loved,
That are so sodden and drunken,
      Who hath forgotten you?

O wistful, fragile faces, few out of many!

The crass, the coarse, the brazen,
God knows I cannot pity them, perhaps, as I should do;
But oh, ye delicate, wistful faces,
      Who hath forgotten you?

Ballad of the Goodly Fere

Simon Zelotes speaketh it somewhile after the
      Crucifixion.

Ha' we lost the goodliest fere o' all
  For the priests and the gallows tree?
Aye lover he was of brawny men,
  O' ships and the open sea.

When they came wi' a host to take Our Man
  His smile was good to see.
"First let these go!" quo' our goodly Fere,
  "Or I'll see ye damned," says he.

Aye he sent us out through the crossed high spears
  And the scorn of his laugh rang free,
"Why took ye not me when I walked about
  Alone in the town?" says he.

Oh, we drank his "Hale" in the good red wine
  When we last made company.
No capon priest was the goodly Fere,
  But a man o' men was he.

I ha' seen him drive a hundred men
  Wi' a bundle o' cords swung free.
That they took the high and holy house
  For their pawn and treasury.

They'll no' get him a' in a book, I think,
  Though they write it cunningly;
No mouse of the scrolls was the goodly Fere
  But aye loved the open sea.

If they think they ha' snared our goodly Fere
  They are fools to the last degree.
"I'll go to the feast," quo' our goodly Fere,
  "Though I go to the gallows tree."

"Ye ha' seen me heal the lame and blind,
  And wake the dead," says he.
"Ye shall see one thing to master all:
  'Tis how a brave man dies on the tree."

A son of God was the goodly Fere
  That bade his brothers be.
I ha' seen him cow a thousand men.
  I have seen him upon the tree.

He cried no cry when they drave the nails
  And the blood gushed hot and free.
The hounds of the crimson sky gave tongue,
  But never a cry cried he.

I ha' seen him cow a thousand men
  On the hills o' Galilee.
They whined as he walked out calm between,
  Wi' his eyes like the gray o' the sea.

Like the sea that brooks no voyaging,
  With the winds unleashed and free,
Like the sea that he cowed at Geneseret
  Wi' tweg words spoke suddenly.

A master of men was the goodly Fere,
  A mate of the wind and sea.
If they think they ha' slain our goodly Fere
  They are fools eternally.

I ha' seen him eat o' the honey-comb
Sin' they nailed him to the tree.

LOUIS UNTERMEYER (1885—)

Landscapes

The rain was over, and the brilliant air
    Made every little blade of grass appear
    Vivid and startling—everything was there
With sharpened outlines, eloquently clear,
As though one saw it in a crystal sphere.
The rusty sumac with its struggling spires;
The golden-rod with all its million fires;
(A million torches swinging in the wind)

A single poplar, marvellously thinned,
Half like a naked boy, half like a sword;
Clouds, like the naughty banners of the Lord;
A group of pansies with their shrewish faces,
Little old ladies cackling over laces;
The quaint, unhurried road that curved so well;
The prim petunias with their rich, rank smell;
The lettuce-birds, the creepers in the field—
How bountifully were they all revealed!
How arrogantly each one seemed to thrive—
So frank and strong, so radiantly alive!

And over all the morning-minded earth
There seemed to spread a sharp and kindling mirth,
Piercing the stubborn stones until I saw
The toad face heaven without shame or awe,
The ant confront the stars, and every weed
Grow proud as though it bore a royal seed;
While all the things that die and decompose
Sent forth their bloom as richly as the rose. . . .
Oh, what a liberal power that made them thrive
And keep the very dirt that died, alive.

And now I saw the slender willow-tree
No longer calm or drooping listlessly,
Letting its languid branches sway and fall
As though it danced in some sad ritual;
But rather like a young, athletic girl,
Fearless and gay, her hair all out of curl,
And flying in the wind—her head thrown back,
Her arms flung up, her garments flowing slack,
And all her rushing spirits running over. . . .
What made a sober tree seem such a rover—
Or made the staid and stalwart apple-trees,
That stood for years knee-deep in velvet peace,
Turn all their fruit to little worlds of flame,
And burn the trembling orchard there below.
What lit the heart of every golden-glow—
Oh, why was nothing weary, dull or tame?
Beauty it was, and keen, compassionate mirth
That drives the vast and energetic earth.

And, with abrupt and visionary eyes,
I saw the huddled tenements arise.
Here where the merry clover danced and shone
Sprang agonies of iron and of stone;
There, where green Silence laughed or stood enthralled,
Cheap music blared and evil alleys sprawled.
The roaring avenues, the shrieking mills;

Brothels and prisons on those kindly hills—
The menace of these things swept over me;
A threatening, unconquerable sea. . . .

A stirring landscape and a generous earth!
Freshening courage and benevolent mirth—
And then the city, like a hideous sore. . . .
Good God, and what is all this beauty for?

Caliban in the Coal Mines

God, we don't like to complain,
  We know that the mine is no lark—
But—there's the pools from the rain;
  But—there's the cold and the dark.

God, you don't know what it is—
  You, in Your well-lighted sky,
Watching the meteors whiz;
  Warm, with the sun always by.

God, if You had but the moon
  Stuck in Your cap for a lamp,
Even You'd tire of it soon,
  Down in the dark and the damp.

Nothing but blackness above,
  And nothing that moves but the cars—
God, if You wish for our love,
  Fling us a handful of stars!

SEAMUS O'SHEEL (1886—)

"They Went Forth to Battle but They Always Fell"

They went forth to battle but they always fell;
  Their eyes were fixed above the sullen shields;
Nobly they fought and bravely, but not well,
And sank heart-wounded by a subtle spell.
  They knew not fear that to the foeman yields,
  They were not weak, as one who vainly wields
A futile weapon; yet the sad scrolls tell
How on the hard-fought field they always fell.

It was a secret music that they heard,
  A sad sweet plea for pity and for peace;
And that which pierced the heart was but a word,
Though the white breast was red-lipped where the sword
  Pressed a fierce cruel kiss, to put surcease
  On its hot thirst, but drank a hot increase.

Ah, they by some strange troubling doubt were stirred,
And died for hearing what no foeman heard.

They went forth to battle but they always fell:
　　Their might was not the might of lifted spears;
Over the battle-clamor came a spell
Of troubling music, and they fought not well.
　　Their wreaths are willows and their tribute, tears;
　　Their names are old sad stories in men's ears;
Yet they will scatter the red hordes of Hell,
Who went to battle forth and always fell.

JEAN STARR UNTERMEYER (1886—)

Sinfonia Domestica

When the white wave of a glory that is hardly I
　　Breaks through my mind and washes it clean,
I know at last the meaning of my ecstasy,
　　And know at last my wish and what it can mean.

To have sped out of life that night—to have vanished
　　Not as a vision, but as something touched, yet grown
Radiant as the moonlight, circling my naked shoulder;
　　Wrapped in a dream of beauty, longed for, but never
　　　known.

For how with our daily converse, even the sweet sharing
　　Of thoughts, of food, of home, of common life,
How shall I be that glory, that last desire
　　For which men struggle?　Is Romance in a wife?

Must I bend a heart that is bowed to breaking
　　With a frustration, inevitable and slow,
And bank my flame to a low hearth fire, believing
　　You'll come for warmth and life to its tempered glow?

Shall I mould my hope anew, to one of service,
　　And tell my uneasy soul "Behold, this is good."
And meet you (if we do meet), even at Heaven's threshold,
　　With ewer and basin, with clothing and with food?

WILLIAM ROSE BENÉT (1886—)

The Falconer of God

I flung my soul to the air like a falcon flying.
I said, "Wait on, wait on, while I ride below!
　　I shall start a heron soon
　　In the marsh beneath the moon—

A strange white heron rising with silver on its wings,
    Rising and crying
    Wordless, wondrous things;
    The secret of the stars, of the world's heart-strings
    The answer to their woe.
Then stoop thou upon him, and grip and hold him so."

My wild soul waited on as falcons hover.
I beat the reedy fens as I trampled past.
    I heard the mournful loon
    In the marsh beneath the moon.
And then, with feathery thunder, the bird of my desire
    Broke from the cover
    Flashing silver fire.
    High up among the stars I saw his pinions spire.
    The pale clouds gazed aghast
As my falcon stooped upon him, and gript and held him fast.

My soul dropped through the air—with heavenly plunder?—
Gripping the dazzling bird my dreaming knew?
    Nay! but a piteous freight,
    A dark and heavy weight
Despoiled of silver plumage, its voice forever stilled,—
    All of the wonder
    Gone that ever filled
    Its guise with glory. O bird that I have killed,
    How brilliantly you flew
Across my rapturous vision when first I dreamed of you!

Yet I fling my soul on high with new endeavor,
And I ride the world below with a joyful mind.
    I shall start a heron soon
    In the marsh beneath the moon—
A wondrous silver heron its inner darkness fledges!
    I beat forever
    The fens and the sedges.
    The pledge is still the same—for all disastrous pledges,
    All hopes resigned!
My soul still flies above me for the quarry it shall find!

ZOË AKINS (1886—)

This Is My Hour

In rain and twilight mist the city street,
    Hushed and half-hidden, might this instant be
    A dark canal beneath our balcony,
Like one in Venice, Sweet.

The street-lights blossom, star-wise, one by one;
　A lofty tower the shadows have not hid
　　Stands out—part column and part pyramid—
Holy to look upon.

The dusk grows deeper, and on silver wings
　The twilight flutters like a weary gull
　　Toward some sea-island, lost and beautiful
Where a sea-syren sings.

"This is my hour," you breathe with quiet lips;
　And filled with beauty, dreaming and devout,
　　We sit in silence, while our thoughts go out—
Like treasure-seeking ships.

One Woman

Since I heard them speak of her great shame
　I looked upon her face with curious eyes,
　　But pity in my heart became surprise,—
Finding not any havoc there, nor flame;
Only a little smile that went and came,
　As if she knew a mirth too great and wise
　　And far too proud to serve the world with lies,
Disdaining as she did its praise or blame.

She who had passed through sin, as through a door,
　Stayed not upon the steps to wail and beat
Against a portal closed for evermore;
　But smiled, and went her way with tireless feet,
　　When night had passed and the long day begun;—
So Hagar faced the desert with her son.

The Wanderer

The ships are lying in the bay,
　The gulls are swinging round their spars;
My soul as eagerly as they
　Desires the margin of the stars.

So much do I love wandering,
　So much I love the sea and sky,
That it will be a piteous thing
　In one small grave to lie.

"H. D." (pseud. of Hilda Doolittle, Mrs. Richard Aldington)
(1886—)

Priapus

KEEPER OF THE ORCHARDS

I saw the first pear
As it fell.
The honey-seeking golden-branded,
The yellow swarm
Was not more fleet than I,
(Spare us from loveliness!)
And I fell prostrate,
Crying,
"Thou hast flayed us with thy blossoms;
Spare us the beauty
Of fruit-trees!"
The honey-seeking
Paused not,
The air thundered with their song,
And I alone was prostrate.

O rough-hewn
God of the orchard,
I bring thee an offering:
Do you, alone unbeautiful
(Son of the god),
Spare us from loveliness.
The fallen hazel-nuts,
Stripped late of their green sheaths,
The grapes, red-purple,
Their berries
Dripping with wine,
Pomegranates already broken,
And shrunken figs,
And quinces untouched,
I bring thee as offering.

JOYCE KILMER (1886-1918)

Trees

I think that I shall never see
A poem lovely as a tree.

A tree whose hungry mouth is prest
Against the sweet earth's flowing breast;

A tree that looks at God all day,
And lifts her leafy arms to pray;

A tree that may in summer wear
A nest of robins in her hair;

Upon whose bosom snow has lain;
Who intimately lives with rain.

Poems are made by fools like me,
But only God can make a tree.

Ballade of My Lady's Beauty

Squire Adam had two wives, they say,
  Two wives had he, for his delight,
He kissed and clypt them all the day
    And clypt and kissed them all the night.
  Now Eve like ocean foam was white
And Lilith roses dipped in wine,
  But though they were a goodly sight
No lady is so fair as mine.

To Venus some folk tribute pay
  And Queen of Beauty she is hight,
And Sainte Marie the world doth sway
    In cerule napery bedight.
  My wonderment these twain invite,
Their comeliness it is divine,
  And yet I say in their despite,
No lady is so fair as mine.

Dame Helen caused a grievous fray,
  For love of her brave men did fight,
The eyes of her made sages fey
    And put their hearts in woful plight.
  To her no rhymes will I indite,
For her no garlands will I twine,
  Though she be made of flowers and light
No lady is so fair as mine.

L'Envoi

Prince Eros, Lord of lovely might
  Who on Olympus dost recline,
Do I not tell the truth aright?
  No lady is so fair as mine.

Old Poets

(For Robert Cortes Holliday)

If I should live in a forest
  And sleep underneath a tree,
No grove of impudent saplings
  Would make a home for me.

I'd go where the old oaks gather,
  Serene and good and strong,
And they would not sigh and tremble
  And vex me with a song.

The pleasantest sort of poet
  Is the poet who's old and wise,
With an old white beard and wrinkles
  About his kind old eyes.

For these young flippertigibbets
  A-rhyming their hours away,
They won't be still like honest men
  And listen to what you say.

The young poet screams forever
  About his sex and soul;
But the old man listens, and smokes his pipe,
  And polishes its bowl.

There should be a club for poets
  Who have come to seventy year.
They should sit in a great hall drinking
  Red wine and golden beer.

They would shuffle in of an evening,
  Each one to his cushioned seat,
And there would be mellow talking
  And silence rich and sweet.

There is no peace to be taken
  With poets who are young,
For they worry about the wars to be fought
  And the songs that must be sung.

But the old man knows that he's in his chair
  And that God's on His throne in the sky.
So he sits by the fire in comfort
  And he lets the world spin by.

Wealth

(For Aline)

From what old ballad, or from what rich frame
    Did you descend to glorify the earth?
Was it from Chaucer's singing book you came?
    Or did Watteau's small brushes give you birth?

Nothing so exquisite as that slight hand
    Could Raphael or Leonardo trace.
Nor could the poets know in Fairyland
    The changing wonder of your lyric face.

I would possess a host of lovely things,
    But I am poor and such joys may not be.
So God who lifts the poor and humbles kings
    Sent loveliness itself to dwell with me.

Dave Lilly

There's a brook on the side of Greylock that used to be full
    of trout,
But there's nothing there now but minnows; they say it is
    all fished out.
I fished there many a Summer day some twenty years ago,
And I never quit without getting a mess of a dozen or so.

There was a man, Dave Lilly, who lived on the North Adams
    road,
And he spent all his time fishing, while his neighbors reaped
    and sowed.
He was the luckiest fisherman in the Berkshire hills, I think.
And when he didn't go fishing he'd sit in the tavern and
    drink.

Well, Dave is dead and buried, and nobody cares very much;
They have no use in Greylock for drunkards and loafers
    and such.
But I always liked Dave Lilly, he was pleasant as you could
    wish;
He was shiftless and good-for-nothing, but he certainly could
    fish.

The other night I was walking up the hill from Williamstown
And I came to the brook I mentioned, and I stopped on the
    bridge and sat down.

I looked at the blackened water with its little flecks of white
And I heard it ripple and whisper in the still of the Summer
    night.

And after I'd been there a minute it seemed to me I could feel
The presence of someone near me, and I heard the hum of
    a reel.
And the water was churned and broken, and something was
    brought to land
By a twist and flirt of a shadowy rod in a deft and shadowy
    hand.

I scrambled down to the brookside and hunted all about;
There wasn't a sign of a fisherman; there wasn't a sign of
    a trout.
But I heard somebody chuckle behind the hollow oak
And I got a whiff of tobacco like Lilly used to smoke.

It's fifteen years, they tell me, since anyone fished that brook;
And there's nothing in it but minnows that nibble the bait
    off your hook.
But before the sun has risen and after the moon has set
I know that it's full of ghostly trout for Lilly's ghost to get.

I guess I'll go to the tavern and get a bottle of rye
And leave it down by the hollow oak, where Lilly's ghost
    went by.
I meant to go up on the hillside and try to find his grave
And put some flowers on it—but this will be better for Dave.

JOHN HALL WHEELOCK (1886—)

Pitiless Beauty

Beauty will not let me rest
    Either night nor day,
Like a voice within my breast
    Calling me away.

When the morning, sad and vast,
    Rises through the stars,
I am summoned forth again
    To the endless wars;

Evening, with her myriad eyes,
    Will not let me sleep,
Sick for Beauty on my bed
    The long hours creep.

O Beauty, cruel and stupendous!
Hounded, out of breath,
I fly you through the gloom tremendous
Down the slopes of Death.

From "The Divine Fantasy"

All afternoon the passion of heaven spent
On earth its fiery fury in blind, bright
Lightnings of dread and laughters of delight
Down shuddering deeps of shaken thunder, where
The delirious longing loosed its sorrowing hair
Of wind and shower and overshadowing cloud
Across the belovèd face, in darkness bowed
Or glimmering light revealed; and cried aloud
For anger of utter ecstasy; and shed
The wild love of the rushing rain that sped
To the thrilled heart, consenting, of the dim
And rapturous earth, that lifted up to him
Drowsed lips of thirsty flowers: and the cup
Of every flower for joy was lifted up,
And drank, and swayed! So, wearied out at length,
Flagged the bright pulses, and the ebbing strength,
With muttering of remembered thunders, passed
Down the large shores of evening; till at last
The exhausted heaven of twilight from afar
Shone washed of all her sorrows; and a star
Brooded above the fading storm, and saw
The winnowed reaches deepening into awe
Of gradual darkness, and the fields that lay
All drenched and wearied out at dusk of day
And the worn end of things; while far away
The receding fury moaned.

JOHN GOULD FLETCHER (1886—)

Vision

You who flutter and quiver
An instant
Just beyond my apprehension;
Lady,
I will find the white orchid for you,
If you will but give me
One smile between those wayward drifts of hair.

I will break the wild berries that loop themselves over the
    marsh-pool,
For your sake,

And the long green canes that swish against each other,
I will break, to set in your hands.
For there is no wonder like to you,
You who flutter and quiver
An instant
Just beyond my apprehension.

From "Irradiations"

As I wandered over the city through the night,
I saw many strange things:
But I have forgotten all
Except one painted face.
Gaudy, shameless night-orchid,
Heavy, flushed, sticky with narcotic perfume,
There was something in you which made me prefer you
Above all the feeble forget-me-nots of the world.
You were neither burnt out nor pallid,
There was plain, coarse, vulgar meaning in every line of you,
And no make-believe:
You were at least alive,
When all the rest were but puppets of the night.

VINCENT STARRETT (1886—)

Villon Strolls at Midnight

"There is an eerie music, Tabary,
In the malevolence of the wind to-night.
Think you the spirits of the damned make flight
O' midnights? Gad, a wench I used to see
Heard all the ghosts of history ride past
Her window on a shrieking gale like this. . . .
Look! Where the moonlight and the shadows kiss!
Saw you aught move? . . . Poor jade, she died unmassed.

"See where the gibbet riseth, gaunt and slim. . . .
(Curse me! The wind hath thrust my entrails through.)
It beareth fruit to-night. . . . Not me, nor you! . . .
Hark to the clatter of the bones of him.
They rattle like . . . Ah, do you catch your breath? . . .
Like castanets, clapped in the hands of Death!"

Dancer

Talcumed into a ghost, she slowly sways
To the wild music of an Eastern dance,
Weaving from light to shadow; and her glance
Holds the blue innocence of sweet amaze.

This is a lissome thing that bends its gaze
Into my gilded box . . . and is it chance
That I am in the line of her advance?
'Tis a seductive theme the viol plays!

Something of fury hurries through my veins. . . .
If she would only cover up her knees!
Is there none here to stop those panic strains?
Fiddles of madness . . . flagrant ecstasies . . .
Let the earth crumble! Slay the Pope of Rome!
Unsheathe your eyes again, Girl. Drive them home!

ORRICK JOHNS (1887—)

Wild Plum

They are unholy who are born
    To love wild plum at night,
Who once have passed it on a road,
    Glimmering and white.

It is as though the darkness had
    Speech of silver words,
Or as though a cloud of stars
    Perched like ghostly birds.

They are unpitied from their birth
    And homeless in men's sight,
Who love better than the earth,
    Wild plum at night.

Dilemma

What though the moon should come
    With a blinding glow,
And the stars have a game
    On the wood's edge . . .
A man would have to still
    Cut and weed and sow,
And lay a white line
    When he plants a hedge.

What though God
    With a great sound of rain
Came to talk of violets
    And things people do . . .
I would have to labour
    And dig with my brain
Still to get a truth
    Out of all words new.

ALAN SEEGER (1888-1916)

"I Have a Rendezvous with Death"

I have a rendezvous with Death
At some disputed barricade,
When Spring comes back with rustling shade
And apple-blossoms fill the air—
I have a rendezvous with Death
When Spring brings back blue days and fair.

It may be he shall take my hand
And lead me into his dark land
And close my eyes and quench my breath—
It may be I shall pass him still.
I have a rendezvous with Death
On some scarred slope of battered hill,
When Spring comes round again this year
And the first meadow-flowers appear.

God knows 'twere better to be deep
Pillowed in silk and scented down,
Where Love throbs out in blissful sleep,
Pulse nigh to pulse, and breath to breath,
Where hushed awakenings are dear. . . .
But I've a rendezvous with Death
At midnight in some flaming town,
When Spring trips north again this year,
And I to my pledged word am true,
I shall not fail that rendezvous.

THOMAS STEARNS ELIOT (1888—

The Love Song of J. Alfred Prufrock

S'io credesse che mia risposta fosse
A persona che mai tornasse el mondo,
Questa fiamma staria senza piu scosse.
Ma perciocche giammai di questo fondo
Non torno vivo alcun, s' i'odo il vero
Senza tema d'infamia ti rispondo.

Let us go, then, you and I,
When the evening is spread out against the sky
Like a patient etherized upon a table;

Let us go, through certain half-deserted streets,
The muttering retreats
Of restless nights in one-night cheap hotels
And sawdust restaurants with oyster-shells:
Streets that follow like a tedious argument
Of insidious intent
To lead you to an overwhelming question. . . .
Oh, do not ask, "What is it?"
Let us go and make our visit.

In the room the women come and go,
Talking of Michelangelo.

The yellow fog that rubs its back upon the window-panes,
The yellow smoke that rubs its muzzle on the window-panes,
Licked its tongue into the corners of the evening,
Lingered upon the pools that stand in drains,
Let fall upon its back the soot that falls from chimneys,
Slipped by the terrace, made a sudden leap,
And seeing that it was a soft October night,
Curled once about the house, and fell asleep.

And indeed there will be time
For the yellow smoke that slides along the street,
Rubbing its back upon the window-panes;
There will be time, there will be time
To prepare a face to meet the faces that you meet;
There will be time to murder and create,
And time for all the works and days of hands
That lift and drop a question on your plate;
Time for you and time for me,
And time yet for a hundred indecisions,
And for a hundred visions and revisions,
Before the taking of a toast and tea.

In the room the women come and go,
Talking of Michelangelo.

And indeed there will be time
To wonder, "Do I dare?" and, "Do I dare?"
Time to turn back and descend the stair,
With a bald spot in the middle of my hair—
(They will say: 'How his hair is growing thin!")
My morning coat, my collar mounting firmly to the chin,
My necktie rich and modest, but asserted by a simple pin—
(They will say: "But how his arms and legs are thin!")
Do I dare
Disturb the universe?
In a minute there is time
For decisions and revisions which a minute will reverse.

For I have known them all already, known them all:
Have known the evenings, mornings, afternoons,
I have measured out my life with coffee spoons;
I know the voices dying with a dying fall
Beneath the music from a farther room,
    So how should I presume?

And I have known the eyes already, known them all—
The eyes that fix you in a formulated phrase,
And when I am formulated, sprawling on a pin,
When I am pinned and wriggling on the wall,
Then how should I begin
To spit out all the butt-ends of my days and ways?
And how should I presume?

And I have known the arms already, known them all—
Arms that are bracketed and white and bare
(But in the lamplight, downed with light brown hair!)
Is it perfume from a dress
That makes me so digress?
Arms that lie along a table, or wrap about a shawl.
    And should I then presume?
    And how should I begin?

       .   .   .   .
Shall I say, I have gone at dusk through narrow streets
And watched the smoke that rises from the pipes
Of lonely men in shirt-sleeves, leaning out of windows? . . .

I should have been a pair of ragged claws
Scuttling across the floors of silent seas.

       .   .   .   .
And the afternoon, the evening, sleeps so peacefully!
Smoothed by long fingers,
Asleep . . . tired . . . or it malingers,
Stretched on the floor, here beside you and me.
Should I, after tea and cakes and ices,
Have the strength to force the moment to its crisis?
But though I have wept and fasted, wept and prayed,
Though I have seen my head (grown slightly bald) brought
    in upon a platter,
I am no prophet—and here's no great matter;
I have seen the moment of my greatness flicker,
And I have seen the eternal Footman hold my coat, and
    snicker,
And in short, I was afraid.

And would it have been worth it, after all,
After the cups, the marmalade, the tea,
Among the porcelain, among some talk of you and me,
Would it have been worth while,
To have bitten off the matter with a smile,

To have squeezed the universe into a ball,
To roll it toward some overwhelming question,
To say: "I am Lazarus, come from the dead,
Come back to tell you all, I shall tell you all"—
If one, settling a pillow by her head,
    Should say: "That is not what I meant at all;
    That is not it, at all."

And would it have been worth it, after all,
Would it have been worth while,
After the sunsets and the dooryards and the sprinkled streets,
After the novels, after the teacups, after the skirts that trail
        along the floor—
And this, and so much more?—
It is impossible to say just what I mean!
But as if a magic lantern threw the nerves in patterns on a
        screen:
Would it have been worth while
If one, settling a pillow or throwing off a shawl,
And turning toward the window, should say:
    "That is not it at all,
    That is not what I meant, at all."

            .   .   .   .

No! I am not Prince Hamlet, nor was meant to be;
Am not attendant lord, one that will do
To swell a progress, start a scene or two,
Advise the prince; no doubt, an easy tool,
Deferential, glad to be of use,
Politic, cautious, and meticulous;
Full of high sentence, but a bit obtuse;
At times, indeed, almost ridiculous—
Almost, at times, the Fool.

I grow old . . . I grow old . . .
I shall wear the bottoms of my trousers rolled.

Shall I part my hair behind? Do I dare to eat a peach?
I shall wear white flannel trousers and walk upon the beach.
I have heard the mermaids singing, each to each.

I do not think that they will sing to me.

I have seen them riding seaward on the waves
Combing the white hair of the waves blown back
When the wind blows the water white and black.

We have lingered in the chambers of the sea
By sea-girls wreathed with seaweed red and brown
Till human voices wake us, and we drown.

ALINE KILMER (1888—)

Sanctuary

God has builded a house with a low lintel
And in it He has put all manner of things.
Follow the clue through the mazes that lead to His door:
Look in, look in! see what is there for our finding.
Peace is there like a pearl, and rest and the end of seeking.
Light is there and refreshment and quiet joy.
There we shall find for our use wide beautiful wings,
Ecstasy, solitude, space: or for those who have been too lonely
The love of friends, the warmth of a homely fire.
O never grieve again for the piteous ending
Of loveliness that could not be made to last.
There all bright passing beauty is held forever,
Free from the sense of tears, to be loved without regret.
There we shall find at their source music and love and laughter,
Color and subtle fragrance and soft incredible textures.
Be sure we shall find what our weary hearts desire:
If we are tired of light there shall be velvet darkness
Falling across long fields, with stars, and a low voice calling,
Calling at last the word we thought would never be spoken.
But we, being hard and foolish and proud and mortal,
Are slow to bend and enter that humble portal.

One Shall Be Taken and the Other Left

There is no Rachel any more
    And so it does not really matter.
        Leah alone is left, and she
        Goes her own way inscrutably.

    Soft-eyed she goes, content to scatter
Fine sand along a barren shore
Where there was sand enough before:
    Or from a well that has no water

        Raising a futile pitcher up,
        Lifts to her lips an empty cup.
    Now she is Laban's only daughter:
There is no Rachel any more.

To Sappho, About Her Apple

The highest apple swinging in the treetop
Fell in my two hands, eagerly uplifted.

For though I knew its height was half its fairness,
    Still I would have it.

Now I am wise with centuries of wisdom.
I lift my voice to give your ashes comfort:
Sappho, the tempting fruit that hung abov⁻ vou
    Was hard and bitter.

"The Heart Knoweth Its Own Bitterness"

The heart knoweth? If this be true indeed
    Then the thing that I bear in my bosom is not a heart;
For it knows no more than a hollow, whispering reed
    That answers to every wind.
    I am sick of the thing! I think we had better part.

My heart will come to any piper's calling,
    A fool in motley that dances for any king;
But my body knows, and its tears unbidden falling
    Say that my heart has sinned.
    You would have my heart? You may. I am sick of the
        thing.

Light Lover

Why don't you go back to the sea, my dear?
    I am not one who would hold you;
The sea is the woman you really love,
    So let hers be the arms that fold you.
Your bright blue eyes are a sailor's eyes,
    Your hungry heart is a sailor's too.
And I know each port that you pass through
Will give one lass both bonny and wise
Who has learned light love from a sailor's eyes.
If you ever go back to the sea, my dear,
    I shall miss you—yes, can you doubt it?
But women have lived through worse than that,
    So why should we worry about it?
Take your restless heart to the restless sea,
    Your light, light love to a lighter lass,
Who will smile when you come and smile when you pass.
Here you can only trouble me.
Oh, I think you had better go back to sea!

LEW SARETT (1888—)

Leave Me to My Own

Oh, leave me to my own;
Unglorified—perchance unknown,
    One of a nameless band

Of gipsy cloud and silent butte and fir.
Oh, let me stand
Against the whipping wind, in the lavender
Of dusk, like a mighty limber-pine
At timber-line—
Unyielding, stiff,
Unbent of head
Among the ageless dead—
One with the mountain's cliff
And the imperturbable stone.
And when the winter gales intone
Among my boughs a dread
And melancholy sweep
Of song, and some mysterious hand
Brushes my heart
In a mournful melody, weep
No tear for me, nor moan—
Pray, stand apart
From me, and leave me to my own;
For in the high blue valleys of this land,
When the afterglow
Lingers among the glaciers, I shall know
Again the calm
Of dusk, the dewy balm
Of sleep, release
From pain—and utter peace.

Oh, leave me to the wild companionship
Of firs that toss
In the windy night and drip
Their wild wet rains upon the moss;
To the columbine
That strives to slip
Shyly among my roots and tip
Its sparkling wine
Upon my grassy shrine;
To the brotherhood
Of bending skies bestrown
With stars above the soundless solitude—
Of waterfalls that fling upon the night
A stony broken music from their height—
Oh, leave me to my own.

CONRAD AIKEN (1889—)

Music I Heard

Music I heard with you was more than music,
And bread I broke with you was more than bread.

Now I am without you, all is desolate,
All that was once so beautiful is dead.

Your hands once touched this table and this silver,
And I have seen your fingers hold this glass.
These things do not remember you, beloved:
And yet your touch upon them will not pass.

For it was in my heart you moved among them,
And blessed them with your hands and with your eyes.
And in my heart, they will remember always:
They knew you once, O beautiful and wise!

CHRISTOPHER MORLEY (1890—)

To a Post-Office Inkwell

How many humble hearts have dipped
In you, and scrawled their manuscript!
How shared their secrets, told their cares,
Their curious and quaint affairs!
Your poor of ink, your scratchy pen,
Have moved the lives of unborn men,
And watched young people, breathing hard,
Put Heaven on a postal card.

SAMUEL HOFFENSTEIN (1890—)

To Claire

I

You are too fair to get for nothing;—
I pay, and still am in arrears;
Gold could not buy you—no, nor glory:
Only tears.

The heart must break before your altar
After the doves and fruit are laid—
You, the shrine of whose love and beauty
Stands in shade.

The wreath in your hair was bought with my sorrow;
'Twas I that paid for it, leaf by leaf;—
Youth could not buy you—no, nor dreaming:
Only grief.

II

You called them not by name, nor saw the way,
But heard the dim persuasion of your soul,
And followed love and beauty all your day,
And reached in darkness many an easy goal,
And spent your heart upon them.   Then the years
Brought grief and wisdom and a clearer sight:

You gathered up your residue of tears,
And saw, at last, the summit in the light,
And climbed, and found your place.   But there is one,
Who, for your seeking, shall not rest again;
Who shall restore an unremembered sun,
And follow your lost footsteps in his brain,
And find this strange companion on his quest:
Love, with eternal Sorrow at her breast.

EDNA ST. VINCENT MILLAY (1892—)

Afternoon on a Hill

I will be the gladdest thing
    Under the sun!
I will touch a hundred flowers
    And not pick one.

I will look at cliffs and clouds
    With quiet eyes,
Watch the wind bow down the grass
    And the grass rise.

And when lights begin to show
    Up from the town,
I will mark which must be mine,
    And then start down!

Elaine

Oh, come again to Astolat!
    I will not ask you to be kind.
And you may go when you will go,
    And I will stay behind.

I will not say how dear you are,
    Or ask you if you hold me dear,

Or trouble you with things for you
   The way ı did last year.

So still the orchard, Lancelot,
   So very still the lake shall be,
You could not guess—though you should guess—
   What is become of me.

So wide shall be the garden walk,
   The garden seat so very wide,
You needs must think—if you should think—
   The lily maid had died.

Save that, a little way away,
   I'd watch you for a little while,
To see you speak, the way you speak,
   And smile,—if you should smile.

Lament

Listen, children:
Your father is dead.
From his old coats
I'll make you little jackets;
I'll make you little trousers
From his old pants.
There'll be in his pockets
Things he used to put there,
Keys and pennies
Covered with tobacco;
Dan shall have the pennies
To save in his bank;
Anne shall have the keys
To make a pretty noise with.
Life must go on,
And the dead be forgotten;
Life must go on,
Tho good men die;
Anne, eat your breakfast;
Dan, take your medicine;
Life must go on;
I forget just why.

MAXWELL BODENHEIM (1892—)

The Old Jew

No fawn-tinged hospital pajamas could cheat him of his
   Austerity,

Which tamed even the doctors with its pure fire.
They examined him; made him bow to them:
Massive altars were they, at whose swollen feet grovelled a
  worshipper.
Then they laughed, half in scorn of him; and then there came
  a miracle.
The little man was above them in a bound.
His austerity, like an irresistible sledge-hammer, drove them
  lower and lower.
They dwindled while he soared.

Advice to a Buttercup

Undistinguished buttercup,
Lost among myriads of others,
To the red ant eyeing you
You are giant stillness.
He pauses on the boulder of a clod,
Baffled by your nearness to the sky,
But to the black loam at your feet
You are the atom of a pent-up dream.
Undistinguished buttercup,
Take your little breath of contemplation,
Undisturbed by haughty tricks of space.

To a Friend

Your head is steel cut into drooping lines
That make a mask satirically meek:
Your face is like a tired devil weak
From drinking many valued and unsought wines.
The sullen skepticism of your eyes
Forever trying to transcend itself,
Is often entered by a wistful elf
Who sits naively unperturbed and wise.

And this same remnant, with its youthful wiles
Held curiously apart from blasphemies,
Twirls starlight shivers out upon your sneers
And changes them to little, startled smiles.
And all your insolence drops to its knees
Before the half-won grandeur of past years.

JULIA COOLEY (1893—)

Vide Astra

Say not so briefly that the stars to-night
Are fair, as if to name them flocks of light,

Those hosted stars that all unheeded ride,
Unloved, unsought and unidentified.
Though they be severed similarities,
Say not they glint with sameness through the trees
And flash alike before your sightless eyes.
Say rather that you see blue Vega rise
To cap the topmost wave of heaven with fire,
Where flies, bright with her sapphire song, the Lyre!
Say that Arcturus gleams with torrid red,
And casts the image of his burning head,
His giant, million-sunned intensity
Into our minimizing earthly sea,
As one red spark upon the smitten wave!
Say that the Crown, whose perfectness you crave,
That mystic, radiant, half-unfinished Crown,
Whose candles the deep seas of Heaven cannot drown,
Shines like a nightly promise to your soul.
Say that over the horizon's bowl
Most lightly twinkles Bernice's hair,
In ecstasy of beauty,—maddening-fair.
Say that the Lynx glows watchfully and near,
With burnished eyes, striking your heart with fear.
Then turn, and fear no more! The White Swan brings
Tranquillity, flying with peaceful wings,
Serenely, with the starred world, to the west.
Say that bright Scorpius flashes without rest
In the warm South, while scorched Antares burns
Upon its heart, and near skies, as it turns,
Are bubbling with the heat! Say that you see
Great Pegasus plunge upward recklessly,
From the abandoned East, and that near by
Andromeda stands tall in the mid-sky,
While Perseus arches guarding at her side.
Then look once more, while the deep heavens glide.
The North holds clusters other than the Bear,
For there flames Cassiopeia in her floating chair.

Say not, in loveless haste, the stars to-night
Are fair. Blind joying! Know each leaping light!
Behold each star, embarked in sundered flight.
Name every flame! Rejoice the soul of sight!

MAURICE A. HANLINE (1895—)

A Song of Pierrot

The cloak of laughter I have worn
    Has only served to hide the smart.
The bells and bladder I have born
    Could make no echo in my heart.

And all the places where I go
    Are sweet with memories of you yet.
The laughing footsteps of Pierrot
    Are always searching for Pierrette.

Upon my face a painted smile,
    Upon my lips a scarlet stain,
Before my feet an endless mile
    That I must dance despite the pain.
Along the road red poppies grow.
    Perhaps your scarlet lips have set
Upon their petals for Pierrot
    A tithe of kisses, dear Pierrette.

The lips I knew have left their scars,
    Each rose beneath had hid a thorn.
Your love was lost beneath the stars.
    I could not wait until the morn.
The night was lonely, love, and so
    I sought the roses to forget,
But they have withered and Pierrot
    Longs for the kisses of Pierrette.

If in your place you hear my song,
    Hear too, beneath, the strain of tears.
I dance before the grinning throng
    Their mocking laughter fills my ears.
My giddy steps are all they know,
    They do not see my eyes are wet.
I am a tired, lost Pierrot.
    Where are you hiding, my Pierrette?

L'ENVOI

Ah, princess, I shall never know.
    You smile and smile and say, "Forget."
The tears and laughter of Pierrot
    Are but the playthings of Pierrette.

MARY CAROLYN DAVIES

Cloistered

To-night the little nun-girl died.
    Her hands were laid
Across her breast; the last sun tried
    To kiss her quiet braid;
And where the little river cried,
    Her grave was made.

The little nun-girl's soul, in awe,
  Went silently
To where her brother Christ she saw
  Under the Living Tree;
He sighed, and his face seemed to draw
  Her tears, to see.
He laid his hands on her hands mild,
  And gravely blessed;

"Blind, they that kept you so," he smiled,
  With tears unguessed.
"Saw they not Mary held a child
  Upon her breast?"

The Day Before April

The day before April
  Alone, alone,
I walked in the woods
  And I sat on a stone.

I sat on a broad stone
  And sang to the birds.
The tune was God's making
  But I made the words.

ELINOR WYLIE

Peregrine

Liar and bragger,
  He had no friend
Except a dagger
  And a candle-end;
The one he read by;
  The one scared cravens;
And he was fed by
  The Prophet's ravens.
Such haughty creatures
  Avoid the human;
They fondle nature's
  Breast, not woman—
A she-wolf's puppies—
  A wild-cat's pussy-fur:
Their stirrup-cup is
  The pride of Lucifer.
A stick he carried,
  Slept in a lean-to;

He'd never married,
  And he didn't mean to.
He'd tried religion
  And found it pleasant;
He relished a pigeon
  Stewed with a pheasant
In an iron kettle;
  He built stone ovens.
He'd never settle
  In any province.
He made pantries
  Of Vaux and Arden
And the village gentry's
  Kitchen-garden.
Fruits within yards
  Were his staples;
He drank whole vineyards
  From Rome to Naples,
Then went to Brittany
  For the cider.
He could sit any
  Horse, a rider
Outstripping Cheiron's
  Canter and gallop.
Pau's environs,
  The pubs of Salop,
Wells and Bath inns
  Shared his pleasure
With taverns of Athens;
  The Sultan's treasure
He'd seen in Turkey;
  He'd known London
Bright and murky.
  His bones were sunned on
Paris benches
  Beset by sparrows;
Roman trenches,
  Cave-men's barrows,
He liked impartial;
  He liked an Abbey.
His step was martial;
  Spent and shabby
He wasn't broken;
  A dozen lingoes
He must have spoken.
  As a king goes
He went, not minding
  That he lived seeking
And never finding.

He'd visit Peking
And then be gone soon
  To the far Canaries;
He'd cross a monsoon
  To chase vagaries.
He loved a city
  And a street's alarums;
Parks were pretty
  And so were bar-rooms.
He loved fiddles;
  He talked with rustics;
Life was riddles
  And queer acrostics.
His sins were serried,
  His virtues garish;
His corpse was buried
  In a country parish.
Before he went hence—
  God knows where—
He spoke this sentence
  With a princely air:
"The noose draws tighter;
  This is the end;
I'm a good fighter,
  But a bad friend:
I've played the traitor
  Over and over;
I'm a good hater,
  But a bad lover."

Let No Charitable Hope

Now let no charitable hope
  Confuse my mind with images
Of eagle and of antelope:
  I am in nature none of these.

ADA FOSTER MURRAY

Her Dwelling Place

Amid the fairest things that grow
  My lady hath her dwelling place;
Where runnels flow, and frail buds blow
  As shy and pallid as her face.

The wild, bright creatures of the wood
  About her fearless flit and spring;

To light her dusky solitude
  Comes April's earliest offering.

The calm Night from her urn of rest
  Pours downward an unbroken stream;
All day upon her mother's breast
  My lady lieth in a dream.

Love could not chill her low, soft bed
  With any sad memorial stone;
He put a red rose at her head—
  A flame as fragrant as his own.

The Shadowed Star

The rosy lamp, the leaping flame,
The friendly pauses in the game—
  I had not felt your breath for years,

Nor heard in dreams the sweet old name;
Why was it, dearest, that you came
  To thrill my heart with sudden tears?

Through whirling systems, alien, vast,
My flesh and soul, it seems, have passed,
  And you have circled far, so far;

What harmony of interchange
Has brought my planet in your range,
  What shadow trembles through your star?

The One Who Stayed

I met a woman old and grey
And sought to cheer her lonely way.

A girl flashed by us, all aglow;
"Your child?" I said; she answered, "No,

"I have but one, and she is dead;
Yet seven others live," she said;

"Live, but we live so far apart
I hold them only in my heart;

"But one who has no dwelling-place
In earthly time or earthly space,

"She nestles in my arms at night,
She greets me when the morn is bright;

"Her winsome smile, her baby ways
Make glad my bleak November days."

She looked across the waters grey,
Then pressed my hand and turned away.

When You Came

There were blossoms all unblown,
    They had known the rain so much;
There were angels in the stone
    Waiting for the master's touch;
Sweetest songs were still unsung,
Tenderest chords were left unstrung,
    When you came.

Summer sinks beneath the snow,
Pale grows every morning's glow;
Yet the wonder does not die
Of the dawn that flushed the sky
    When you came.

MORRIS ABEL BEER

Old Garrets

Whenever I see old garrets I think of mice and cheese,
    And slender, wistful poets who dream by candle-light,
I think of winds that shiver and wailing leafless trees,
    And winding, wooden stairways that creak in hush of
    night.
I see dim, wrinkled parchments, a dusty quill or two,
    A narrow, paneless window that frames a sparkling sky,
Stained walls and broken ceilings the rain has eaten through,
    A dried-up china ink-pot,—a shelf with books piled high.
Within those dingy garrets in yellow candle-glow,
    What fadeless visions blossomed, what deathless dreams
    had birth,
What flaming songs leapt starward from poets' roofs be-
    low,
    When city streets lay sleeping and night had stilled the
    earth!
Now a house that is rich and modern is a pleasant dwell-
    ing place,

But a poet should live in a garret where the witching
  moonlight streams,
Alone with the whispering stars and apart from the world's
  mad race,
Reigning in indolent ease, a king in his palace of dreams!

The Puddle

The lady with the broom beheld dismayed
  A puddle that the rain had left behind;
"More work for me, to clean the pavement now,—
  But little rest I find."

And so with weariness she plied her broom,—
  The ugly pool soon vanished with the day;
But the poet from his window watched her sweep
  The evening star away!

OLIVE TILFORD DARGAN

From "The Cycle's Rim"

Deep lies thy body, jewel of the sea,
Locked down with wave on wave. Pearl-drift among
The coral towers, and yet not thee, not thee!
So lightly didst thou mount, blue rung o'er rung,
The lustered ladder rippling from that land
Of strangely boughed and wooing wilderness.
Province of dream unwaning, dream yet banned
From sleepers in the sun; but thou, as presses
The lark that feels his song, sped to thy sky.
O unrepressed! If thou wouldst choose be gone,
What sea-charm then could stay thee, bid thee lie
Too deep for cock-crow earth or heaven's dawn?
Yet must I chant these broken, mortal staves,
And lay my leaf of laurel on the waves.

      .   .   .

My prayers are thee! But, Dear, what means this thing?
That we do walk together as a wind,
Heedless of garden gates where sigh and cling
The little roses that once sought to bind
Our hearts to time; making no pause beside
Blue, curling waters where our thoughts like doves
Drifted to wild-leaf nest; smiling where cried
The tragic marshes with strange shadow loves
That bound us from the sun. The maples burn
Their April wicks of passion; willows yet

Light their slim candles at the dawn's fire-urn;
But here is glow that no Spring ever lit;
Nor hills of vision where we fainting fell
May hold us now, so pale their miracle.

.   .   .   .

No longer backward, treading a lost dream,
But where the Future lifts her morning stole;
Past nations that embracing know one name,
Past faces like the flowers of one soul,
God's soul, humanity. Bells never choired
From time's old sweetness with the sweet of these
Making clear song of all that dim aspired
In our old struggles, barren ecstasies,
Tears and despairs. O lordliest Love, that keepst
Eternal pact with Life, naught can discrown
Thee of one bud of flame howe'er thou weepst;
For though these bodies dear are beaten down,
As ocean triumphs by her broken waves,
Thy tidal breath breaks warm above thy graves.

.   .   .   .

Beloved, if I keep my spirit fed,
Hear not the rustling world, forget her bays,
Naught caring if I go unlaurelled
In eyes of fortune, so I fill my days
With thoughts that bud and bloom for heavenly wear,
Sending my soul to seek thy country out,
Spending still hours in wondering of thee there,
And making vision sweet of every doubt,
Wilt thou not come some perfect eve to touch,
As might a god, with visitant fair feet,
The meadows where I wait, nor scorn too much
The habits of my earth, but even let
Thy hand be first upon a daisy nigh,
And stand with me to watch the swallows fly?

EDWIN JUSTUS MAYER (1896—)

The Poet Dreams of the Wings of Death

O Sea of Dust, I stand upon your shore,
And hear the heavy waves forevermore
Reverberate, and cast their dark foam up
Into the sky, and soil that golden cup:
I stand upon your shore, and think and ponder
Till Desolation takes the part of Wonder,

Seeing how sad the life we lead must be,
O sad, prevailing and omnipotent Sea!
Dust in our mouths through all eternity.

But I have wings, you shall not hold me down;
But I have wings, you shall not make me drown;
But I have wings, and I shall fly from you!
Even now I leave you, and I climb the blue
And brightening skies, as angels might have done
In the far times before the moon and sun;
And mounted ever higher, ever higher,
Lighting the blossoms in the lanes of morn
And paths of night, until they reached their bourne,
And smiled, and rested; and laid aside their fire;
Their impulse and their genius; but retained
The sweetness of them, as when day has rained
And thundered, birds that sang through all, fall still,
Hearing the rainbow music sounding above the hill.

STEPHEN VINCENT BENÉT (1898—)

From "Death-Chant of the Centaurs"

Close his eyes with the coins; bind his chin with the shroud;
Carry this clay along, in the time of the westing cloud;
Lay you the cakes beside, for the three-mouthed dog of Hell;
Slain on the grass in fight, surely his end is well.
Love was the wind he sought, ignorant when it went;
Now he has clasped it close, silent and eloquent;
Slow as the stream and strong, answering knee to knee,
Carry this clay along—it is more wise than we.

JESSIE RITTENHOUSE

Debt

My debt to you, Belovèd,
    Is one I cannot pay
In any coin of any realm
    On any reckoning day;

For where is he shall figure
    The debt, when all is said,
To one who makes you dream again
    When all the dreams are dead?

Or where is the appraiser
Who shall the claim compute
Of one who makes you sing again
When all the songs were mute?

The Radiant Loss

Oh, I have lived to be so glad
You failed me long ago,
So glad you cast away the love
That I had lavished so,
So glad that you were dull and blind,
So glad you did not know!

For in a way I had not dreamed
I built my life anew,
And all the structure of my days
Into a wonder grew;
And, oh, you left me free to love
A greater one than you.

LOLA RIDGE

From "The Ghetto"

Lights go out
And the stark trunks of the factories
Melt into the drawn darkness,
Sheathing like a seamless garment.
And mothers take home their babies,
Waxen and delicately curled,
Like little potted flowers closed under the stars. . . .

Lights go out . . .
And colors rush together,
Fusing and floating away.
Pale worn gold like the settings of old jewels . . .
Mauve, exquisite, tremulous, and luminous purples,
And burning spires in aureoles of light
Like shimmering auras.

They are covering up the pushcarts . . .
Now all have gone save an old man with mirrors—
Little oval mirrors like tiny pools.
He shuffles up a darkened street
And the moon burnishes his mirrors till they shine like phos-
    phorus. . . .
The moon like a skull,
Staring out of eyeless sockets at the old men trundling home
    the pushcarts.

ROBERT MUNGER

The Derelict

Thou grim, unburied corpse of wind and sea!
The lonely mid-most ocean's livid face
Shudders to feel, as on you drift apace,
How much o'erpassed, how multiplied by thee
Is its own loneliness; no depth could be
Too deep for your last sepulchre, a place
To hide forever all the ghostly trace
Of your mute witnessing of agony.
And when the moonless midnight holds you fast
And sea and utter gloom mingle and glide
Into each other's arms, her bosom vast,
Swelling to meet the darkness like a bride,
Almost might God himself start back aghast
At that black water lapping at your side.

HANIEL LONG

Song

Poppies paramour the girls;
  Lilies put the boys to bed;
Death is nothing else than this
  After everything is said.

They are safe and shall not fade,
  After everything is done,
Past the solace of the shade
  Or the rescue of the sun.

His Deaths

He bore the brunt of it so long
And carried it off with wine and song,
The neighbours paused and raised an eye
At hearing he had learned to die.

'Twas on a Friday that he died,
But Easter day his neighbours spied
His usual figure on the streets,
And one and all were white as sheets.

I died, said he, on Good Friday,
But someone rolled the stone away,

And I come back to you alive
To die tonight at half past five.

Monday at Babylon I fall,
And Tuesday on the Chinese Wall,
Wednesday I die on the Thracian plain,
And Thursday evening at Compiegne·

Saturday, Sunday, Monday too,
I die and come to life anew;
Neighbours like Thomas look and touch,
Amazed that I can live so much.

WALTER ADOLPHE ROBERTS

Villanelle of the Living Pan

Pan is not dead, but sleeping in the brake,
 Hard by the blue of some Ægean shore.
Ah, flute to him, Beloved, he will wake.

Vine leaves have drifted o'er him, flake by flake,
 And with dry laurel he is covered o'er.
Pan is not dead, but sleeping in the brake.

The music that his own cicadas make
 Comes to him faintly, like forgotten lore.
Ah, flute to him, Beloved, he will wake.

Let not the enemies of Beauty take
 Unction of soul that he can rise no more.
Pan is not dead, but sleeping in the brake,

Dreaming of one that for the goat god's sake
 Shall pipe old tunes and worship as of yore.
Ah, flute to him, Beloved, he will wake.

So once again the Attic coast shall shake
 With a cry greater than it heard before:
"Pan is not dead, but sleeping in the brake!"
Ah, flute to him, Beloved, he will wake.

JOHN FARRAR (1896—)

When Amaryllis Bowls

My Amaryllis was not made
Like ordinary souls!
The Milky Way's her bowling green,
She uses moons for bowls.

She swings them down the starry sward
Till all of Heaven wakes.
Oh! Truly she's no common girl—
She wins eternal stakes!

Magic

Turn apple blooms to silver,
Turn buttercups to gold?
That's a very common gift,
Age on ages old;

But when my Amaryllis smiles,
A half a second after,
Her Midas touch transmutes the world
From grumpiness to laughter!

THE END

INDEX OF FIRST LINES

A

D

E

F

G

H

I

P

R

S

T

Y

INDEX OF TITLES

389

INDEX OF AUTHORS